D1154110

The Civil War Soldier

The Civil War Soldier

A Historical Reader

EDITED BY

Michael Barton and Larry M. Logue

New York University Press

NEW YORK AND LONDON

NEW YORK UNIVERSITY PRESS
New York and London

Library of Congress Cataloging-in-Publication Data
The Civil War soldier : a historical reader / edited by Michael Barton
and Larry M. Logue.
p. cm.
Includes bibliographical references and index.
ISBN 0-8147-9879-9 (acid-free paper)—ISBN 0-8147-9880-2 (pbk. :
acid-free paper)
1. United States. Army—History—Civil War, 1861–1865. 2. Confederate
States of America. Army—History. 3. Soldiers—United
States—History—19th century. 4. Soldiers—Confederate States of
America—History. 5. United States. Army—Military life—History—19th
century. 6. Confederate States of America. Army—Military life. 7.
United States—History—Civil War, 1861–1865—Social aspects. I.
Barton, Michael. II. Logue, Larry M., 1947–
E607 .C58 2002
973.7'83—dc21   2002003874

To the historians of soldiering

Contents

Acknowledgments   *xi*

Introduction: The Soldiers and the Scholars   I
    Michael Barton and Larry M. Logue

PART I Who Soldiers Were   7

1 What Manner of Men   9
    Bell Irvin Wiley

2 Have Social Historians Lost the Civil War?
  Some Preliminary Demographic Speculations   33
    Maris A. Vinovskis

3 Who Joined the Confederate Army?
  Soldiers, Civilians, and Communities in Mississippi   44
    Larry M. Logue

4 Yankee Recruits, Conscripts, and Illegal Evaders   57
    James W. Geary

5 To "Don the Breeches, and Slay Them with a Will!"
  A Host of Women Soldiers   69
    Elizabeth D. Leonard

PART II How Soldiers Lived   83

6 On the March   85
    Carlton McCarthy

7 The Life of the Common Soldier in the Union Army,
  1861–1865   92
    Fred A. Shannon

 8   From Finery to Tatters   108
     Bell Irvin Wiley

 9   Fun, Frolics, and Firewater   122
     James I. Robertson, Jr.

PART III How Soldiers Fought   141

10   The Negro as a Soldier   143
     Thomas Wentworth Higginson

11   Heroes and Cowards   155
     Bell Irvin Wiley

12   The Confederate as a Fighting Man   176
     David Donald

13   The Rebels Are Barbarians   190
     Grady McWhiney and Perry D. Jamieson

14   The Infantry Firefight   199
     Paddy Griffith

15   Leaving Their Mark on the Battlefield   228
     Joseph T. Glatthaar

16   The Nature of Battle   260
     Earl J. Hess

PART IV How Soldiers Felt   281

17   Trials of Soul   283
     Bell Irvin Wiley

18   A Study of Morale in Civil War Soldiers   312
     Pete Maslowski

19   Christian Soldiers
     The Meaning of Revivalism in the Confederate
     Army   327
     Drew Gilpin Faust

20   From Volunteer to Soldier
     The Psychology of Service   354
       Reid Mitchell

21   Emotional Responses to Combat   386
       Joseph Allan Frank and George A. Reaves

22   "Dangled over Hell"
     The Trauma of the Civil War   396
       Eric T. Dean, Jr.

PART V What Soldiers Believed   423

23   The Values of Civil War Soldiers   425
       Michael Barton

24   Embattled Courage   436
       Gerald F. Linderman

25   On the Altar of My Country   456
       James M. McPherson

26   Holding On   472
       Earl J. Hess

27   The Civil War Soldier and the Art of Dying   485
       Drew Gilpin Faust

     Index   513

     About the Editors   516

Acknowledgments

We are grateful to Niko Pfund for agreeing that our proposal for this anthology was a good idea, to Susan Livingston for compiling and editing material, and to Eric Zinner, Despina Papazoglou Gimbel, and Emily Park of New York University Press for shepherding everything to completion. We appreciate also the permission to reprint that was granted by the authors, publishers, and copyright holders of this Civil War research.

Introduction
The Soldiers and the Scholars

Michael Barton and Larry M. Logue

On the afternoon of April 12, 2000, South Carolina's state senators were debating what to do about the Confederate flag flying on top of the state capitol dome. They were intense but courteous in their dispute. Democrats did not accuse Republicans of being callous for wanting to fly an emblem that could be offensive, and Republicans did not call Democrats traitors for wanting to haul down a symbol of southern "heritage." Pro-flag, white senators spoke of their "love" for their African American foes on the floor, while anti-flag, black senators assured their white opponents that they did not consider them racists. But their recognition of the importance of civility showed indirectly how divisive their disagreement was. Even though, as one Charleston senator said, April 12 happened to be, for his city, the anniversary of "the beginning and the end" of the war between the states, these legislators were showing that the conflict survived in them and their constituents. "There is more here than the flag," said another senator.

What helped them settle their dispute was their remembering the soldiers who rallied 'round the flag. "His blood runs warm for the memory of those soldiers," said one senator, praising a colleague willing to compromise. "You been at that cemetery with me, sweating in the heat in May, on Confederate Memorial Day," he declared. In praise of his own forebears, he even quoted a northern warrior, Colonel Joshua Chamberlain, who said that southerners "fought as they were taught, true to such ideals as they saw." The senator continued, "None of us want revenge, none of us want hate. We want an avenue that can somehow bring our people together. . . . Like General Lee at Appomattox, we need to get terms."

Ultimately, the senators found their avenue and came to terms: They voted the flag be removed from the capitol dome—and placed in a nearby memorial plaza, a more visible and public site for remembering soldiers.

This event and its machinations, although revealingly southern, are also American in their significance, for northern legislatures would likewise rise to defend, if not debate, their own Civil War memorials. The statue of the Union soldier in the town square of New Bloomfield, Pennsylvania, would be protected as proudly as the Confederate monument in the center of Oxford, Mississippi. Americans may forget the causes and details of their most destructive war, but they remember the figures of the soldiers who fought it, the men whose battlefield experiences are the occasion for this volume.

Since 1980 a good many provocative books and articles have been written about the lives of Civil War soldiers—indeed, this might be called the liveliest topic in middle period historiography. During the same period, some useful review essays and synthetic studies have been formulated about that body of work. What would be practical to have now, we think, is a compact sampler of this recent scholarship, and thus we present this anthology. To be sure, there is still value in the earliest books written about soldier life, so we have included portions of a few studies published in the decade or two after the war ended. Readers will also find here selections from the half-century-old writings of the late Bell Irvin Wiley, included because his scholarship on Civil War soldiers has been the paradigm for us all, whether we support or amend it.

We have organized everything under simple and concrete headings: Who the soldiers were, how they lived, how they fought, how they felt, and what they believed. The academic articles and book chapters we have excerpted here represent, we think, some of the most popular and satisfying historical writing recently offered to the public. Certainly this writing has helped stimulate the American people's uncommon interest in the common soldier of the Civil War.

This anthology offers a glimpse of changes over time in the questions historians have asked about soldiers' experience, and reveals themes and contrasts in the answers they have found. Without stepping on the headnotes that follow or reiterating review articles, let us preview some key features of the scholarship on Civil War soldiers.[1]

Some reviewers contend that a consensus has emerged on many issues, but we are more impressed with the number of serious disputes that remain to be resolved. For example, some historians contend that Confederate soldiers represented a distinctive military tradition, while others maintain that they did not. Some historians claim that both North and South were fighting to defend their distinctive values, while others say they fought for their comrades instead, just as did soldiers in World War II. Were troops embittered and their personalities transformed by the war, or did they accept the experience and come to honor it? Historians disagree on the answer. This and other questions beg to be settled.

In our own research we have been deeply interested in one overarching question: What were the essential social, cultural, and even psychological differences between Union and Confederate soldiers? Some historians find that the soldiers were more similar than diverse, or that their main difference was their disagreement over a common value-liberty. We grant the northern and southern soldiers' similarities, but we have paid particular attention to the trait of self-control, seeing that as one of the significant differences between North and South. Without doubt, the question of sectional differences will continue to vex and stimulate Civil War historians.

Methodology has also proven controversial in studies of soldiering. When they examine armies, historians face a fundamental question: How should we generalize about large populations that lived in the past? Civil War historiography has never been a showplace for social science approaches to history, yet, when we ask whether the southern population and army were different from northerners, we are asking a question that is implicitly quantitative. Some historians have criticized the use of content analysis, a technique for tabulating the linguistic evidence of Civil War documents, yet others, without calling their work content analysis, explicitly quantify soldiers' values.[2] We recommend that readers of this anthology pay close attention to the authors' methods for approaching their evidence and to the interpretations they make.

Finally, we, and others, have questions about Bell Irvin Wiley's scholarship. The academic work on Civil War soldiers chiefly begins with, and in many ways still rests upon, his writings. But while praising his industry in the archives, his detail-filled prose, and his humane sensibility, now his successors find some of his main conclusions fallible. It seems to us that some of his judgments were prompted by the social and political conditions under which he wrote. For example, Wiley emphasized the similarity between northern and southern soldiers and their lack of divisive ideology. Perhaps that position, with its overtone of national unity, should have been expected in the middle of World War II, when *Johnny Reb* was published (1943); and in the middle of the Cold War, when *Billy Yank* was released (1952).

Such social and political conditions could also help explain why Wiley was unfailingly moderate in his treatment of the men, balancing evidence of soldiers' vices with indications of their virtues. His generous depictions of the troops on both sides would not have been offensive to any section of the nation. The trouble is that Wiley's understandable inclination seems to have kept him from fixing on the soldiers' values, which, according to James M. McPherson's close study of their personal documents, "almost leap from many pages."[3] Even after we try to place Wiley's histories in their own historical context, the troubling question remains: How could the old master of Civil War soldier studies have denied what today's scholarship finds so apparent? Wiley, for example, asserted that it would be impossible to tell a Union soldier's diary or letter from a Confederate soldier's diary or letter on the basis of content alone, yet sociolinguistic research has indicated otherwise.[4] No one questions Wiley's engrossing portrayal of soldiers' daily lives and labors, but historians' recent probings of soldiers' attitudes and behavior signal a new departure in scholarship.

If this brief introduction accentuates some of the pressing scholarly problems still to be solved, it does not mean to imply that historiography has failed us. In fact, historians' progress toward understanding Civil War soldiers makes this volume timely, possible, and necessary. One could even say that the high quality of the questions remaining, or just now appearing, shows how continuously wonderful the subject can be.

NOTES

1. Reviews of the recent literature on Civil War soldiers include Marvin R. Cain, "A 'Face of Battle' Needed: An Assessment of Motives and Men in Civil War Historiography," *Civil War History*, 27 (1982), 5–27; Conrad C. Crane, "Mad Elephants, Slow Deer, and Baseball on the Brain: The Writings and

Character of Civil War Soldiers," *Mid-America: An Historical Review*, 68 (1986), 121–40; Daniel E. Sutherland, "Getting the 'Real War' into the Books," *Virginia Magazine of History and Biography*, 98 (April 1990), 193–220; Gary W. Gallagher, "Home Front and Battlefield: Some Recent Literature Relating to Virginia and the Confederacy," *Virginia Magazine of History and Biography*, 98 (April 1990), 135–68; Joseph T. Glatthaar, "The 'New' Civil War History: An Overview," *Pennsylvania Magazine of History and Biography*, 115 (July 1991), 339–69; William Garrett Piston, "Enlisted Soldiers," in Steven E. Woodworth, ed., *The American Civil War: A Handbook of Literature and Research* (Westport, CT: Greenwood, 1996), 454–65; Reid Mitchell, " 'Not the General but the Soldier': The Study of Civil War Soldiers," in James M. McPherson and William J. Cooper, Jr., eds., *Writing the Civil War: The Quest to Understand* (Columbia, SC: University of South Carolina Press, 1998), 81–95; Joseph Glatthaar, "Battlefield Tactics," in McPherson and Cooper, eds., *Writing the Civil War: The Quest to Understand*, 60–80; Mark Grimsley, "In Not So Dubious Battle: The Motivations of American Civil War Soldiers," *Journal of Military History*, 62 (January 1998), 175–88; and Joseph Glatthaar, "The Common Soldier of the Civil War," in John Y. Simon and Michael E. Stevens, eds., *New Perspectives on the Civil War: Myths and Realities of the National Conflict* (Madison, WI: Madison House, 1998), 119–44. See also Earl J. Hess's introduction to the second edition of *Liberty, Virtue, and Progress; Northerners and Their War for the Union* (New York: Fordham University Press, 1997), xv–xviii, for his reflections on the scholarship since the publication of his first edition. An anthology of Bell Irvin Wiley's scholarship has recently been published: Hill Jordan, James I. Robertson, Jr., and J. H. Segars, eds., *The Bell Irvin Wiley Reader* (Baton Rouge: Louisiana University Press, 2001).

2. For criticisms of content analysis, see Glatthaar, " 'New' Civil War History," 355; and Mitchell, "Not the General,' " 84, 88–89; for an example of quantification without content analysis *per se*, see James M. McPherson, *For Cause and Comrades: Why Men Fought in the Civil War* (New York: Oxford University Press, 1997), 114.

3. McPherson, *For Cause and Comrades*, 91.

4. Michael Barton, *Goodmen: The Character of Civil War Soldiers* (University Park: Pennsylvania State University Press, 1981), chap. 4, esp. 54–55.

Part I

Who Soldiers Were

Chapter 1

What Manner of Men

Bell Irvin Wiley

Bell Irvin Wiley was not the first historian to portray life in the Civil War armies, but his Life of Johnny Reb *(1943) and* Life of Billy Yank *(1952) were far more extensive than earlier efforts, and they became benchmarks for studies of army experience. Wiley, who spent most of his career at Emory University, combed through letters, diaries, muster rolls, and official records in compiling his accounts. The two books are divided into what Wiley saw as the essential features of soldier life — behavior and misbehavior in camp, coping with inadequate food and supplies, the ebb and flow of morale, and the experience of battle, for example. In this selection, the final chapter of* The Life of Johnny Reb, *Wiley describes the variety of characteristics and personality types that made up the Confederate army.*

The men who marched under the Stars and Bars were impressively diverse in character. The full range of their variation can never be known, however, because one of the most fruitful sources of information—the original muster and descriptive rolls—is so incomplete. For some companies such rolls were not even prepared; for many, only a part of the required data was given; and for hundreds of others the records were lost or destroyed. But from rolls that are extant, from comments of travelers, from court-martial proceedings, memoirs, diaries and personal letters, a general idea of the South's soldiery may be obtained.

Scattered through the camps of the Confederacy were men of widely

varied birth and race. The great majority of the rank and file were
Southern-born, of course, but the non-native element was large enough
to figure prominently in the general pattern. A considerable proportion
came from the country north of Mason and Dixon's line. A random
sampling of 42 descriptive rolls covering 21 regiments from six Confederate states yields the names of 86 privates born in eleven northern
states.[1] Of these, 37 were natives of New York, 10 of Illinois, 9 of
Pennsylvania, 7 each of Indiana, Massachusetts and Ohio, and the rest
came from Connecticut, Maine, New Jersey, Vermont and Michigan. An
estimate of the total number of Yankee-born men who served the cause
of the South could be no more than a guess, but the figure must have
run into the thousands.

The foreign-born element in Southern ranks was also large enough to
demand attention. A number of companies were made up entirely of
foreigners, and several regiments were composed largely of this class.[2] In
some Louisiana camps orders on the drill ground were given in French
to polyglot organizations containing Irish as well as Latins; and one of
the most amazing incidents of the war was the objection raised by a
lusty son of Erin to a dictum requiring officers to give their commands
in English instead of in French—"I don't know what Oi'll do," he said
to his lieutenant. "You want us to drill in English and the devil a wurd
I know but French."[3] . . .

Louisiana, whose population in 1860 was more than one-tenth foreign, contributed more non-natives to the Southern cause than any other
state. Some regiments recruited from New Orleans were made up largely
of Irishmen, others of Germans, and still others combined these two
groups with a miscellany from every part of the globe. Company I of the
Tenth Louisiana—which Professor Lonn calls "the Cosmopolitan
Regiment"—was composed of men from no less than fifteen countries;
and in the First Louisiana Regiment thirty-seven nationalities were represented.[4]

Texas was next in the number of foreigners supplied for Confederate
service. Several infantry and cavalry companies from Comal, Gillespie,
Fayette and Colorado Counties were German. Some of the Texas Germans were notoriously unsympathetic toward the Southern cause, but
many served faithfully and gallantly. From the Lone Star State likewise
came companies made up largely of Irish, Mexicans and Poles. And here,
as in Louisiana, many of the organizations were composed of a mixture
of nationalities.[5] . . .

Most of the foreigners who fought for the South were infantrymen, though there were considerable numbers in all branches of the service. Of the various nationalities represented, the Irish were most numerous. Frequently they were rough, quarrelsome, plunderous and impervious to discipline, but for the most part they were blessed with a redeeming good humor. They adapted themselves well to the hardships of camp life, and they enjoyed an excellent reputation as fighters. Next to the Irish in number were the Germans. Their love for music enlivened the atmosphere of many encampments, and when convinced of the rightness of the Confederate cause, as they doubtless were in a majority of cases, they acquitted themselves creditably on the firing line. The British, the French, the Poles, the Canadians, the Dutch, the Austrians and the many other nationalities represented in Southern ranks all made their distinctive contributions to the Lost Cause. The total number of foreigners enrolled in the Confederate Army unfortunately must remain unknown, but there can be no doubt that the figure ran well up into the tens of thousands.[6] To this host of immigrants who wore the gray, particularly to those thousands who yielded up their lives in the service, the South owes an incalculable debt of gratitude and honor.

Another of the diverse groups in the Confederate Army was the Indian. Shortly after the formation of the Secession Government Albert Pike was sent to the trans-Mississippi country to make treaties with the various tribes residing in the red man's territory. The emissary's efforts, notably successful, prepared the way for actual recruiting. In November 1861 the Department of Indian Territory was established with Pike as commanding officer. It was Pike's intention to use Indian soldiers largely for defense of their home area, but his plan was overruled by other considerations.

When General Van Dorn began his campaign for the relief of Missouri in early 1862, four regiments and two battalions had been formed from among the trans-Mississippi red men and half-breeds. Later a fifth regiment and several battalions were created. In the latter part of 1864 the Indian troops were organized into three brigades. These were: The First Brigade, composed of Cherokees, Chickasaws and Osages, commanded by Chief Stand Watie, a valiant officer of whom General S. B. Maxey said, "I wish I had as much energy in some of my white commanders as he displays"; the Second Brigade, made up of Choctaws, led by Tandy Walker; and the Third Brigade, of Creeks and Seminoles, headed by D. N. McIntosh.[7] . . .

The only major encounter in which western Indians took part on a large scale was the Battle of Pea Ridge in early March 1862. As the vanguard of Pike's command came up to join Van Dorn on the eve of this fight, the red men presented a picturesque spectacle. Speaking primarily of the Cherokees, a member of the First Missouri Brigade said:

"They came trotting by our camp on their little Indian ponies, yelling forth their wild whoop . . . Their faces were painted, and their long straight hair, tied in a queue, hung down behind. Their dress was chiefly in the Indian costume—buckskin hunting shirts, dyed of almost every color, leggings, and moccasins of the same material, with little bells, rattles, ear-rings, and similar paraphernalia. Many of them were bareheaded and about half carried only bows and arrows, tomahawks, and war-clubs. . . . They were . . . straight, active, and sinewy in their persons and movements—fine looking specimens of the red man."[8] . . .

Following the Battle of Pea Ridge, activities of the red men were limited largely to raiding and scouting. In September 1862 a force led by D. H Cooper engaged a group of Federal Indians commanded by William A. Phillips. The Confederates were victorious, but both sides acquitted themselves with credit. . . .

The Cherokees and Seminoles were never unanimous in their support of the South, and as Confederates suffered reverses large numbers went over to the Federals. The Cherokees were particularly susceptible to discouragement and defection. On two occasions groups belonging to the command of Colonel John Drew abandoned Confederate ranks under duress and went over to the Yankees en masse; the opinion was widely prevalent in the South that John Ross, principal chief of this nation, conspired with the Yankees for his capture. But many of the Cherokees remained loyal to the Confederacy throughout the war, and their troops were among the best of the Indian fighters. The Choctaws and the Chickasaws were overwhelmingly faithful to the Southern cause.[9]

The Indian soldiers of the Confederacy were victims of shabby treatment by their white superiors. General Pike strove assiduously to secure a square deal for them, but he was far removed from Richmond, and opposed by leaders like Van Dorn, Hindman and Holmes, who were concerned primarily with the protection of white areas and who apparently cared little for the welfare of the red men. Pay, food, clothing and weapons intended for the Indians were diverted by these commanders to other troops. Corruption and fraud were rife in the filling of contracts, and in other phases of government service. A general reorganization of late 1864 resulted in some improvement, but the change came too late to be of much benefit. . . .

The visitor to Southern camps in the first year of the war might expect always to encounter a large number of Negroes. These, to be sure, were not soldiers, but their relation to the fighting force was so vital and so intimate as to merit consideration as a part of the army. Conspicuous among the Negroes attached to military personnel were the body servants. When members of slaveholding families enlisted in 1861 it was quite common for them to take along black members of the household to serve them in camp. Some of the wealthier volunteers had more than one servant, but the usual practice was for a single slave to minister to his own master or to a mess of from four to eight men; in the latter case all members "chipped in" to bear the cost of his maintenance. Non-slaveholders sometimes hired Negroes to act as body servants. The duties of these Negroes consisted mainly of cooking, washing, and of cleaning quarters. Those attached to cavalry companies were required to look after their masters' horses. Many became adept at foraging—a term frequently used in the army to dignify the practice known among civilians as stealing—to supplement the usual leanness of rations issued by commissaries.[10]

During battles the body servant usually remained in the rear out of reach of Federal shells. But a few became so thoroughly imbued with the martial spirit as to grab up muskets during battle and take pot shots at the enemy. There are several instances on record of servants thus engaged killing and capturing Federals. On at least one occasion Confederate domestics made prisoners of Negroes serving Yankee officers. When fighting abated, the colored aide usually loaded himself with canteens and haversacks and went in search of his master. If the latter was wounded, the servant carried him to shelter and sought medical assistance; if he was killed, the domestic made arrangements for his burial or escorted the body home. The relation between master and body servant was usually marked by genuine affection. Frequently intimate association extended back to childhood days. When Confederate masters were ill, they were nursed by their black companions, and when the latter were stricken, they sometimes were attended by their owners with the tenderest solicitude. There were some instances of unfaithfulness and of cruel treatment, but the circumstances of the soldier-servant relationship made these much less frequent in the army than on the plantation.

The life of the body servant was generally not a hard one. He seldom lacked for food, and he usually recouped his wardrobe in the wake of each battle from Yankee sources. He had opportunities to earn money by doing odd jobs for his master's comrades, and the stake thus acquired could be increased or diminished by sessions with fellow servants at dice or cards. Occasional visits home for provisions made it possible for him to play the hero among less fortunate inmates of the slave quarters. In camp his ready laugh—whether inspired by genuine amusement or by a keen sense of appropriateness—was a valuable stimulant to soldier morale, as was his proficiency with song and guitar.[11]

It was with real regret, therefore, that most private soldiers dispensed with the service of their colored associates during the second and third years of conflict. But the increasing scarcity of provisions in the army and the greater need of their labor by civilians made it necessary for the Negroes to be sent home. Those who remained in camp after 1863 were largely the servants of commissioned officers or were employed by the government as musicians, cooks, nurses, hostlers and wagon-drivers.[12]

The largest group of Negroes connected with military affairs were those employed for the construction of fortifications. Early in the war great numbers were hired to throw up works in seacoast and river areas and in other strategic portions of the Confederacy. The intrenchments used in resisting McClellan's peninsula movement were largely the work of Virginia slaves. At first planters responded generously to government calls for laborers, but in the second year of the war impressment sometimes had to be used, and in 1864 levies became the general rule. In February 1864 a Confederate law was passed authorizing the Secretary of War to conscript 20,000 Negroes for military labor. This was only partially due to dwindling patriotism of slaveowners, as many planters felt that their Negroes were neglected and abused while in government employ. The controversy between state and national authorities as to the constitutionality of impressment also colored the picture. Opposition to compulsion eventually reached such proportions as to hinder greatly the program of defense. . . .

Negroes served as soldiers in both the Revolution and the War of 1812, and when the Confederacy was created there was a disposition in some quarters to take free men of color into Southern armies. A regiment was organized in New Orleans, but it was not accepted for Confederate service. In 1863 a proposal to arm slaves was launched by the press, but after a brief discussion the subject was dropped. In January 1864 General Patrick Cleburne revived the question by advocating to a group of fellow officers the enlistment of a large force of slaves and offering them freedom as a reward for faithful service. When Cleburne's action came to the notice of President Davis he ordered suppression of the whole matter. But as the gloom of defeat settled down over the South, sentiment favoring the enlistment of Negroes increased. In November 1864 Davis intimated a willingness to consider a limited use of blacks in the ranks. Finally in March 1865 Congress passed a law authorizing the President to call for as many as 300,000 slaves to serve as soldiers. No assurance of freedom was given. In the month that followed a few companies were organized. Colored recruits attired in resplendent uniforms paraded the streets of Richmond only to be splattered with mud thrown by contemptuous white urchins.[13] The ironic spectacle of Negroes fighting for the cause of Southern independence and the perpetuation of their own bondage was prevented from materializing by Lee's capitulation. Slaves rendered tremendously valuable service to the South by their labor on farms, in factories and on fortifications. There were many Confederate leaders who thought they would also give faithful assistance on the field of battle. But the alacrity with which the great majority seized freedom when it was brought to their reach by Federals gives rise to serious doubt of their fighting long for the Confederacy on any condition save that of general emancipation.[14]

Soldiers who marched in Rebel ranks belonged to a wide variety of occupations and professions. This is brought out by examination of the company rolls. One hundred and seven of these representing 7 states, 28 regiments and 9,000 private soldiers, well distributed as to locality, revealed over 100 occupational classifications. Over half of the enlistees— 5,600 out of 9,000—listed themselves as farmers.[15] Other well-represented groups in the order of their numerical strength were: students, 474; laborers, 472; clerks, 321; mechanics, 318; carpenters, 222; merchants, 138; and blacksmiths, 116. . . .

The ages of those who wore the gray were no less diverse than their vocations. Descriptive rolls usually gave the ages of recruits at the time of their induction, and a sample taken from these records, consisting of 11,000 infantry privates most of whom enlisted in 1861–1862, and representing 11 states, 94 regiments, and 141 companies, revealed a personnel varying from mere boys to old men.[16] One recruit on the list was a lad of 13, 3 were 14 years of age, 31 were 15, 200 were 16, and 366 were 17. Boys under 18 years constituted approximately one-twentieth of the 11,000 cases examined. With the 18-year-olds the figure jumped sharply to 971, the highest of all the age groups, and within the limits of 18–25 over one-third of the total cases were included. A decline set in with 23-year-olds, but each age was well represented on through the 20's, and the number of cases included within the 18–29 range was approximately four-fifths of the total. Men in their 30's comprised approximately one-sixth of the aggregate and those in the 40's, one-twenty-fifth. Eighty-six of the 11,000 fell in the 50–59 group, 12 were 60–69, 1 was 70, and the oldest was 73. . . .

Some of the oldsters of the Confederate Army rendered distinguished service. Private George Taylor of the Sixtieth Virginia Infantry, whose three-score years earned for him the sobriquet of father of the regiment, was cited for gallantry at Frayser's Farm. A Mississippian of advanced age named John Thompson, who enlisted as a private when the war began, fought so valorously at Belmont and at Shiloh as to win a commission. After his death at Chickamauga General Patton Anderson paid him high tribute in an official report as a man and as a soldier.[17] But in all probability most men of fifty years or more who had to march in the ranks were more of a burden than a benefit to the cause which they so patriotically espoused. Exposure, inadequate nourishment, and the strain of campaigning combined with ripe age to acquaint them better with hospital and wagon train than with the field of action. The fate of elderly Rebs is well exemplified by the case of a private, E. Pollard, of the Fifth North Carolina Regiment. This soldier, whose seventy-three years entitle him perhaps to the distinction of being the oldest man regularly enlisted in Confederate service, was taken into the army as a substitute in July 1862. In September 1862 a surgeon who examined him reported that he had been unfit for duty three-fourths of the time since his enlistment. Shortly thereafter he was given a discharge for being "incapable of performing the duties of a soldier on account of Rheumatism and old age."[18]

The boy soldiers made a good record. There were a number of instances of teen-age Rebs receiving mention for bravery in official reports and orders. Following an engagement in early May 1862, General Beauregard said in a general order:

"The Commander of the Forces desires to call the especial attention of the Army to the behavior of Private John Mather Sloan of the 9th Texas Vols., a lad of only 13 years of age who having lost a leg in the affair . . . near Farmington exclaimed 'I have but one regret I shall not soon be able to get at the enemy.' "

The general stated his intention at some future time of publicly decorating the hero with a badge of merit. If this occasion materialized, how the heart of Private Sloan must have thrilled to be thus honored by the "Grand Creole."[19] . . .

Some of the youngsters seen about Southern campfires were buglers and drummer boys who had regularly enlisted. Others were unattached waifs adopted by the troops as mascots.[20] A most interesting group having semiofficial capacity were the drillmasters borrowed temporarily from the cadet corps of Southern military schools to assist in the instruction of raw recruits. Most of these boys were quite young but they called out their orders with impressive manliness.

A North Carolina historian, writing of the Hillsboro Military Academy contingent, said:

"It was certainly a novel sight to see the little cadets from thirteen years old and upwards, each tramping his squad of grown and sometimes grizzled men, over the parade ground and to witness the grim seriousness with which the future veterans took their military subjection to their juniors in years."[21]

The work of these youthful instructors and of their co-workers from the Virginia Military Institute and from a number of other campuses was invaluable.[22] . . .

Under a program sanctioned by government authorities late in the war, students of various Southern institutions were organized into companies and held for reserve purposes[23] The crowning achievement of college boys on the field of battle was that of Virginia Military Institute cadets in the affair at New Market, May 15, 1864. When General Breckenridge engaged the Federal forces led by Sigel, his command consisted in part of a battalion of over two hundred boys from the Virginia college under one of their professors. As the fight progressed the cadets marched steadily forward under heavy fire to a position beyond the town. There they were called on to join with a Virginia regiment to take a battery that was inflicting serious damage on the Rebel lines. In the

advance that ensued the college youths, because of their greater endurance and ardor, outdistanced their veteran comrades, and as a consequence they had to stand in a rain of bullets until the older men could
come up for the final dash. But they held their formation and when the
order came to charge at double quick they rushed gallantly forward. The
guns were soon captured, and when a cadet mounted one of the captured
pieces and waved the Institute flag there was a wild yell of triumph. In
this notable victory at New Market, the boys won for themselves and
their school an undying glory, but at great cost. When the casualties of
battle were counted, it was found that the toll of dead and wounded
included fifty-four cadets, eight of whom were killed.[24]

Considerable argument has been exchanged as to the age and identity
of the most youthful person to serve as a full-fledged Confederate soldier. In 1901 a Floridian wrote the editor of the *Confederate Veteran*
stating that when he surrendered in April 1865 he lacked one month of
being fifteen years old, and that his service dated back to 1861. If this
man's claim be true, he would appear to have undisputed title to the
distinction of being the youngest Rebel.[25] . . .

Variation in education and culture . . . characterized army personnel.
. . . Here and there among the rank and file were to be found men well
versed in the classics and in other branches of learning. Robert Stiles
told of a comrade who kept a diary in modern Greek.[26] Other reliable
sources reveal instances of private soldiers poring over Latin readers and
Greek grammars, or reading the writings of the literary masters.[27] A
South Carolinian wrote his mother that he had been reading Macaulay's
history but that he had been unable to get to the fifth volume. "I wish
to survive this war," he said, "if only to have that pleasure."[28]

The number of well-educated privates scattered through the ranks
was larger in 1861 than at any later time because, as a general rule,
unusual abilities won promotion in a fairly short time, and recruits of
this type were not frequently available as replacements. But in certain
choice organizations made up largely of men of means and culture this
was not the case. . . .

Cavalry and artillery units seem to have held special attraction for
scions of first families. In instances where large numbers of exceptional
men belonged to the same company, only a few could hope to win
commissions within the organization, and many frowned upon the idea
of leaving their congenial associates to seek offices elsewhere. In other
words the opinion prevailed in these select circles that it was better to be

a private in the Richmond Howitzer Battalion or in Hampton's Legion than a lieutenant in most other groups. This sentiment, coupled with the difficulty of getting transfers, explains to a considerable extent the continued presence in the ranks throughout the war of many men of good education and of high social standing.

But the number of these men, like other pleasanter concepts of Southern history, has been exaggerated. The error may be attributed in part to writers of the moonlight-and-magnolia school who saw in the old South a society richly endowed with wealthy landowners who devoted their leisure to the classics. But a more immediate basis for the misconception is to be found perhaps in the greater articulateness of the men composing the choice companies. As a general rule the most interesting and the most widely read of regimental histories and personal memoirs were written by members of the Rockbridge Artillery, of the Richmond Howitzers, and of other exceptional organizations. These books naturally emphasized the cultural and social attainment of the authors' particular groups.[29] There was a tendency for readers to infer that the companies thus described were representative of the army as a whole. Veterans of more ordinary groups either remained silent or wrote volumes of less charm and of a more limited circulation. The result was distortion in favor of the select few.

At the opposite end of the scale were the illiterate, and their number was considerable. When Company A of the Eleventh North Carolina Infantry was mustered into service 27 men of the 100 enrolled had to make their marks when called on to sign the descriptive roll. In another Tar Heel company 36 out of 72 privates signed with an X; in a third, 30 out of 80, in a fourth 54 out of 100; and the average for 14 companies of thirteen different regiments was 40 out of 100. The ratio of illiteracy in these units was undoubtedly higher than in the general run of Confederate organizations, but the great majority of companies throughout the army had anywhere from one to a score of members who could not write their names.

Soldier correspondence and other firsthand evidence indicates that most of the Rebel rank and file lay between the two educational extremes. They were neither learned nor illiterate, though it must be admitted that those who were barely literate were much more numerous than those of fair education. Their schooling, like their culture, reflected in a general way the yeoman society to which most of them belonged.[30]

The thought patterns of common soldiers were interesting and varied.

Prejudices were numerous and strong. Antipathies of the poor toward the rich and of the well-born toward the underprivileged were not so much in evidence as other aversions, but caste consciousness was present to a limited extent, and class friction occasionally provided the spark for disturbances in camp. Yeomen resented the special status enjoyed by planters under the fifteen and twenty-Negro law. A North Carolinian wrote his wife in the fall of 1864 that she might expect him home soon because "all of the gentel men has got out of it [the war] and i don't intend to put my Life betwen them and their propty."[31] . . .

Sensitiveness to class seems to have been voiced more frequently by the rich than by the poor. George Cary Eggleston recalled an instance in a Virginia company where a young private of superior social standing forced a public apology from a lieutenant of ordinary background who had dared to put him on double duty for missing roll call. A Georgian refused in 1861 to obey an order on the ground that the officer issuing the command was no gentleman. Corporal John Hutchins on being called to task for a minor infraction said to his superior, "God damn you, I own niggers up the country," and when private John Shanks was ordered from the drill field to the guardhouse for inebriation he blurted out to his captain, "I will not do it. I was a gentleman before I joined your damned company and by God you want to make a damned slave of me."[32] . . .

The more frequent manifestations of class prejudice on the part of aristocrats were not due solely to greater touchiness on the subject; another factor was the greater impunity with which they could express their sentiment. An Englishman who served in the Confederate Army told of an officer—unpopular because of his assumption of airs—slapping a soldier with a sword during drill. The recipient of the blow threw down his rifle, stepped from the ranks and stabbed the officer to death with his Bowie knife. The company "looked on and applauded; the culprit quietly wiped his knife, resumed his place in the ranks, and dress parade proceeded as if nothing had happened!" Incidents such as this were reckoned as affairs of honor, according to the Englishman, and courts-martial took no cognizance of them.[33] This statement is probably exaggerated, but it derives partial substantiation, at least, from the complaint of a prominent military judge to President Davis that "to convict a soldier of any offense, who has social position, friends, and influence is but a mockery of form."[34]

Flare-ups of prejudice were less frequent as the war progressed. The tightening of discipline required increasing submissiveness of insubordinate aristocrats; common exposure of rich and poor to the dangers of battle and the hardships of camp enhanced mutual respect, and in some cases produced intimate friendships between men of social extremes. A glimpse of the metamorphosis is afforded by the statement of a Low Country youth who served in Hampton's Legion:

> "It would have seemed strange to me once in my ignorance of the world to have found literary taste among mechanics and tradesmen; and yet I have found instances in my own company . . . of admirable taste and large reading."[35]

Prejudice of rural troops toward those from the city was evidenced by the banding of such sobriquets as "parlor soldiers" and "kid glove boys."[36] Metropolitan dandies retorted by ridiculing farm youths for their rusticity. Provincialism likewise found expression in the nicknames applied by soldiers of one state to those of another. Virginians were called the "Buttermilk Brigade"; South Carolinians, "Sand Lappers"; Alabamians, "Yellow Hammers"; Georgians "Goober Grabbers"; and Louisianians, "Tigers."

Local attachment was so strong that Confederate authorities were forced to keep troops of the same state brigaded together, even when military expediency called for their separation. Concession to particularism was carried to the extreme of providing separate hospitals for the sick and wounded of each state. Difficulties between soldiers of different localities were frequent. Mississippians who were put in the same brigade with Florida troops for the Perryville fight accused their unwelcome associates of shooting at them instead of at the Yankees; when subsequently this hybrid organization passed a Mississippi division on parade, men of the latter yelled out the greeting, "Come on out of that Brigade— we won't fire on you."[37]

Troops of the various states were very jealous of their reputation in battle, and woe to that officer or newspaper representative who seemed in his report to favor Tennesseans at the expense of Texans or to give less than a full measure of glory to each of the units composing the Confederacy.[38] One of the factors which caused so much opposition to consolidation of skeleton regiments was dread of the loss of state identity.[39]

The tendency was widespread for soldiers composing one army to disparage those of another. Rebs who followed Bragg and Joe Johnston

referred to those of Lee's command as "Jeff Davis pets"; and they attributed victories on the Virginia front to the fact that Yankees in that
locality did not fight so hard as those opposed to Western commands.
Lee's men in turn berated the fighting qualities of the Army of Tennessee.[40] Shortly after Pemberton's capitulation an Alabamian serving with
Lee wrote in disgust of "the imbecility of officers and the cowardice of
our men at Vixburg." The surrender of that city was, in his opinion,
"the most disgraceful affair in the history of our country," and his chief
consolation was that he was not involved in the shame. "If I live to be a
hundred year's old," he said, "I shall always be proud to know that I
once belonged to the Army of N. Va."[41] . . .

One of the aversions most frequently expressed was that of infantrymen for cavalrymen. The term "buttermilk cavalry" had almost universal use among walking Rebs as a derogatory sobriquet. The connotation
was apparently twofold: softness and thievery—foot soldiers envisaged
equestrians lolling about on their mounts begging or stealing buttermilk
and other delicacies while they themselves toiled along for endless miles
on half rations. An Alabamian expressed a widespread sentiment when
he said that every cavalryman ought to have a board tied on his back
and the word "thief" written thereon so that good people might be on
guard against their depredations. But this branch of the service was more
usually condemned for uselessness and cowardice.[42] Whenever a cavalry
unit rode by a group of infantrymen, the latter would almost invariably
turn loose a flood of invective and derision.[43] One hard-bitten marcher
said that the mounted service steered so clear of dangerous combat as
practically to constitute a life insurance company.[44] . . .

Antipathy of cavalry toward infantry was inconsiderable, though the
former did apply to the latter the uncomplimentary term of "web feet,"
and there was some resentment of the scorn which the foot soldiers
expressed for their conduct as fighters. As a general rule, however, equestrians shrugged their shoulders good-naturedly at revilings and congratulated themselves on their good fortune at being able to do their campaigning on horseback. Typical of many was the attitude expressed by a
Lone Star cavalryman who wrote when he heard of the commissioning
of an infantry acquaintance: "I wood rather be corporal in company F
of the Texas Rangers than to be first Lieu in a flat foot company."[45]

There was a pervasive feeling among volunteers that conscripts were
second-rate soldiers, and manifestations of this attitude tended undoubt-

edly to injure the service. When recruits were inducted under the draft legislation they were already in a bad frame of mind because of the stigma attached to compulsion; the scornful glances and the contemptuous remarks which greeted them in camp were ill-adapted to the making of fighters.[46]

Many conscripts, particularly those brought in by the laws of 1862, were good soldier material, and had they been accorded a wholesome reception by volunteers, the majority of them might have fitted congenially and usefully into the military organization. Some developed into first-class troops in spite of the antipathy which encompassed them. After Fredericksburg General James H. Lane reported that conscripts recently added to his brigade conducted themselves creditably, and General A. P. Hill made the significant observation that in this affair they showed an earnest desire to win the respect of their veteran comrades. Major John Harris who commanded a Tennessee brigade at Murfreesboro paid high tribute to the performance of conscripts who served under him in that battle.[47]

But the great majority of testimony, both of officers and of privates, bristled with such uncomplimentary epithets as cowards, skulkers, shammers, useless and worthless. One colonel declared that he would rather have his regiment reduced to a battalion and his rank to that of a major than to replenish his organization with men forced into service.[48] There was undoubtedly a factual justification for much of the criticism, but few veterans realized that their own unfriendliness contributed markedly to the unhappy situation of which they complained.

The contempt for conscripts was mild in comparison to that provoked by militia and reserves. Kate Cumming told of hearing a soldier mimicking "Joe Brown's Pets," as Georgia militiamen were called, from the top of a boxcar in Marietta. This Reb told piteously of his treatment; how he had been in the service for two whole weeks and as yet had not received a furlough; and how he and other brave reservists were nobly defending the rear of Bragg's army.[49]

An Alabamian reported that when a militia unit was assigned to guard duty in the vicinity of the camp, soldiers of his regiment would go out, take away the guards' guns and compel them to sit for long periods on logs.[50] As for fighting, few full-fledged Rebs expected that of "Bobtail militia." "They had just as well stay . . . [home]," wrote one of Joe Johnston's veterans in 1864; "they aint worth a low country cow tick."[51]

And when one of Lee's men heard that state troops had participated in the defense of Petersburg late in the war he exclaimed: "The militia fought! Long be it remembered."[52]

Another object of great contempt was the staff officer. When Rebs saw young aides dashing about in fine uniforms carrying messages and performing other duties with airs bespeaking a sense of unusual importance, they were annoyed. The feeling that such officers used family influence to get soft positions caused them to be designated by some as yellow sheep-killing dogs, which term was soon shortened to "yaller dogs." When one of these officers rode by, Rebs would begin whistling and whooping as if they were calling hounds.[53] As Hood's army was falling back from Nashville after severe fighting in December 1864, a staff officer who came up ostentatiously to a mud-splattered infantryman and ordered him to halt and face the foe received the significant reply: "You go to hell. I've been there."[54]

In the canine category also were placed those ordinary soldiers who because of pretended ailments hung back with the wagon train on the march or during battle. The epithet applied to these shammers was wagon-dogs, and when Terry's Texas Rangers rode by them they raised a song, written allegedly by a cavalryman; it ran like this:

> Come all you wagon dogs, rejoice—
> I wil sing you a song,
> If you'll join in the chorus—bow wow wow;
> When we go to leave this world,
> We will go above with sheets unfurled—
> bow wow wow.[55]

Court-martial proceedings indicate that prejudices of nationality sometimes figured in disturbances among enlisted men. Private Henry Brandes of Hampton's Legion received a prison sentence for calling a sentinel an "Irish son of a bitch," and another South Carolinian was punished for denouncing a corporal of the guard as a "blind Dutch son of a bitch."[56] Mississippi regiments stationed at Iuka early in the war were opposed to the induction of Irish levee-builders into their organizations, and when officers forced acceptance of the foreign recruits a free-for-all fight ensued.[57]

Certain random types that appeared in Rebel ranks require special notice. Almost every regiment had a braggart who regaled his comrades at every opportunity with tales of his magnificent doings from early childhood down to the present. His accounts were sometimes listened to because of lack of other diversion, but again he would be taunted into silence. Closely akin to the boaster was the self-seeker—the man who in private life had perhaps made a splash as a petty politician, and who in the army became hell-bent for promotion. This type, too, was the butt of many scornful remarks. The dandy was also in evidence. He sported foppishly cut coats and fancy boots, combed his long hair back over his ears, pinned up one side of his hat, donned a feather and imagined himself a cavalier.

Occasionally there was a snob, such as a youngster from Natchez who refused to join one company because it was composed of commoners, and who, when he finally joined another, looked down his nose at most of his associates. "We are two distinct parties," he said on one occasion, "the Aristocrats and the democrats," and he professed nothing but disdain for the latter. He took offense at his colonel for "putting on airs," ceased saluting him, and swore to call him to task after the war for failure to proffer the recognition due one of his high social standing. His attitude was identical with that of another snob who wrote:

> "It is galling for a gentleman to be absolutely and entirely subject to the orders of men who in private life were so far his inferiors, & who when they met him felt rather like taking off their hats to him than giving him law & gospel."[58]

Now and then a brute was found whose soul was so hardened as to make him seemingly impervious to ordinary human emotions. Such a character was a Tennessean who sang in battle from sheer joy of slaughtering, and who would yell out with utmost indifference, "Good-by, Jim," or "Good-by, Sam" as comrades fell one by one at his side; likewise the Louisianian who ran his bayonet through a pig on the march, tossed the gun across his shoulder as if nothing had happened, and bore the squealing animal aloft while it died a slow and painful death.[59]

Another type was the arch-plunderer, a good example of which was Sam Nunnally of the Twenty-first Virginia. Periodically Sam would disappear from camp for interims varying from one to three days. At the end of these absences he would return as mysteriously as he had vanished, but invariably with a plausible excuse and a load of spoils. He was particularly adept at playing wounded after a fight to rifle the pockets of the dead. After one night of such lurid activity he came sneaking into camp with three watches, several knives, some money and various other articles. On another occasion, a foraging excursion among the living yielded not only a large supply of food and other provisions, but a horse for transporting the thief and his prizes.[60]

Almost every regiment had a prankster who was quick to make fun at the expense of the unwary. If a hirsute comrade wished to borrow a razor, he would refuse him positively, but at the same time he would slyly offer his tonsorial services. If the proffer was accepted, the self-appointed barber would shave one half the customer's face with great care, then pocket his razor and take to flight in a roar of laughter.[61] Usually there was a greenhorn for every such mischief-maker—the mentality of a few Rebs ran so low, indeed, as to require their discharge from the service—and the lot of these dullards was as cruel as it was amusing.[62] One such creature was honored with sham election to the post of fifth lieutenant. After the balloting he inquired with all seriousness into the nature of his duties. His electors professed ignorance on the score, and sent him to the lieutenant. This officer, sensing the hoax immediately, replied without hesitation: "His duties are to carry water and catch fleas out of the soldiers' beds." The unsophisticate proceeded to conform in good faith to these instructions until someone convinced him that the whole thing was a joke.[63]

In another instance a recruit of very short stature was brought into camp. Some of his comrades, adjudging him too small to carry a musket, assumed the role of doctors, stripped him, tapped his chest, went through various other motions of a medical examination, and wrote out with charcoal on a scrap of newspaper a certificate of physical disability. The examinee, according to instructions, presented this to his colonel, who laughed and forwarded the case to the brigade surgeon. As a consequence of the joke the recruit received a long furlough.[64]

Eccentrics of various sorts were scattered among the rank and file. An old country gentleman who enlisted in the Twenty-first Virginia took an umbrella to camp, and in sun or rain, on the march and in the field, he insisted on seeking shelter beneath this canopy. His comrades jibed him freely, but to no avail; the parasol remained a constant companion for the duration of his service.[65]

Some of the troops who hailed from the West were very rough in appearance. A Louisianian who in 1863 watched a group of 400 Texans ride by his plantation reported that they bore no resemblance to soldiers. "If the Confederacy has no better soldiers than those we are in A bad roe for stumps," he said; "they looke more like Baboons mounted on gotes than anything else."[66]

Rough-looking likewise were the Mississippi flatboatmen and wharf hands from the waterfronts of Memphis, New Orleans, Mobile and other cities of the Confederateracy[67] Among these, as well as among other groups of formidable mien, there were many individuals whose chief crudities were those of external appearance. But it cannot be denied that the Southern Army had its share of rogues and desperadoes. In Mississippi, Governor Pettus pardoned a number of convicts on condition that they would join the army.[68] From among Federals in Southern military prisons several companies of troops were recruited, and these "galvanized Yankees," as they were called, were generally a tough lot[69] But cutthroats, robbers and knaves were by no means found only among those who came from behind prison walls. Inspection reports and court-martial proceedings cite numerous instances of brigandage and criminality among recruits drawn from the country at large. Some of the irregular cavalry units operating in border districts appear to have been composed largely of thugs.

Another type encountered with regrettable frequency was the loafer. Rebs of this species imposed on their messmates by seeking the lighter duties of cooking, bringing water and cutting wood. They evaded the hardships of campaigning by malingering. When the order came to march they would rush to the surgeon with some complaint calculated to secure assignment to "Company Q," as the sick list was called, so that they might ride the wagon train and be near the food supply. Some of them succeeded in being sent to infirmaries, and loafers once thus ensconced developed one chronic malady after another—though never quite sick enough to miss a meal—until their attachment to the hospital became more or less permanent. Those who thus evaded duty bore the opprobrious designation of "hospital rats," but they were so degenerate as to be utterly beyond shame.[70]

In happy contrast to these faithless wretches were a group who because of their selflessness and their exceptional devotion to duty were worthy to be called patriots. They consistently bore the hardships of camp without complaint; they insisted on taking their place in line of battle even when they were unwell and when their feet were without the protection of shoes; they were always present at roll call; they refused to seek promotion, and they manifested a cheerful spirit in defeat as well as in victory.

But all these were exceptional types. The average Rebel private belonged to no special category. He was in most respects an ordinary person. He came from a middle-class rural society, made up largely of non-slaveholders, and he exemplified both the defects and the virtues of that background. He was lacking in polish, in perspective and in tolerance, but he was respectable, sturdy and independent.

He was comparatively young, and more than likely unmarried. He went to war with a lightheartedness born of detachment and of faith in a swift victory. His morale wavered with the realization that the conflict was to be long and hard. He was nostalgic and war-weary. He felt the blighting hand of sickness, and it was then that his spirit sank to its lowest ebb. His craving for diversion caused him to turn to gambling and he indulged himself now and then in a bit of swearing. But his tendency to give way to such irregularities was likely to be curbed by his deep-seated conventionality or by religious revivals.

He complained of the shortcomings of officers, the scantiness of clothing, the inadequacy of rations, the multiplicity of pests and numerous other trials that beset him, but there was little depth to his complaints, and his cheerfulness outweighed his dejection. Adaptability and good-nature, in fact, were among his most characteristic qualities. He was a gregarious creature, and his attachment to close associates was genuine.

He had a streak of individuality and of irresponsibility that made him a trial to officers during periods of inactivity. But on the battlefield he rose to supreme heights of soldierhood. He was not immune to panic, nor even to cowardice, but few if any soldiers have had more than he of *élan,* of determination, of perseverance, and of the sheer courage which it takes to stand in the face of withering fire.

He was far from perfect, but his achievement against great odds in scores of desperate battles through four years of war is an irrefutable evidence of his prowess and an eternal monument to his greatness as a fighting man.

NOTES

From Bell Irvin Wiley, *The Life of Johnny Reb: The Common Soldier of the Confederacy* (Baton Rouge: Louisiana State University Press, 1978), 322–47. Reprinted by permission.

1. The Southern states represented by these rolls were Alabama, Arkansas, Louisiana, Mississippi, Georgia and Texas. The rolls referred to here and in subsequent connections are largely from the files of the War Records Division of the National Archives, though some are from collections in archives of Southern states and in private depositories.

2. Ella Lonn, *Foreigners in the Confederacy* (Chapel Hill, 1940), 93–131, 200–240. Professor Lonn's scholarly work, to which I am much indebted, is based primarily on descriptive rolls.

3. Southern Historical Society *Papers, XXXI* (1903), 105–106.

4. Lonn, *Foreigners in the Confederacy*, 109, 210.

5. *Ibid.*, 124–128.

6. *Ibid.*, 220.

7. Annie Heloise Abel, *The American Indian as Participant in the American Civil War* (Cleveland, 1919), 25, 155, 326–330; William M. Robinson, Jr., *Justice in Grey?* Cambridge, 1940), 352.

8. Ephraim Anderson, *Memoirs* (St. Louis, 1868), 159–160.

9. Robinson, *op. cit.*, 351–352.

10. Bell Irvin Wiley, *Southern Negroes 1861–1865,* (New Haven, 1938)

11. *Ibid.*, 136–144.

12. *Ibid.*, 110–113, 134.

13. *Ibid.*, 146–160.

14. There were innumerable examples of faithfulness under duress, and of rejections of freedom when offered. But instances of loyalty in invaded areas were restricted largely to old Negroes, and to house servants whose attachment to masters had been strengthened by intimate association, and who, because of their favored position, had much to lose by emancipation. Field hands, who constituted the great majority of servants, generally abandoned their masters when the coming of the Federals guaranteed immunity from punishment. *Ibid.*, 3–23, 63–84.

15. Only 11 of the 9,000 were listed as planters. It is likely, therefore, that compilers of rolls did not always distinguish between small and large agricultural operatives, and that some planters are included among those classed as farmers.

16. Cavalry companies were not included because of the meager descriptive rolls for this branch of the service.

17. *War of the Rebellion: Official Records of the Union and Confederate Armies* (Washington, D.C., 1880–1901), series 1, XI, part 2, 851–852, XXX, part 2, 319–320.

18. Descriptive Roll, Co. D, Fifth North Carolina Regiment; Descriptive Book, Fifth North Carolina Regiment; and Personal File of E. Pollard. All of these items are in the National Archives. The doctor who filled out Pollard's certificate of disability put his age down as sixty-two, but the Descriptive Roll and the Descriptive Book give the age as seventy-three. These latter should be

more reliable than the former. William M. Dame of the Richmond Howitzer Battalion testified that war he knew personally of six men over sixty years of age who served in the ranks throughout the war. William M. Dame, *From the Rapidan to Richmond* (Baltimore, 1920), 2–3.

19. Records of the First Kentucky Brigade, Confederate Archives, chapter II, volume 305, p. 35, manuscript, National Archives.

20. *Confederate Veteran*, II, (1894), 12–13.

21. Walter Clark, editor, *North Carolina Regiments, 1861–1865* (Raleigh and Goldsboro, 1901), V, 637–638. One of the thirteen-year-old Hillsboro boys named William Cain was rated as the best drillmaster in Confederate service by the lieutenant colonel of the Twenty-fifth North Carolina Regiment. Written statement of H. C. Dearing, dated November 13, 1861, manuscript in John L. Bailey Collection, University of North Carolina. Originally drillmasters were engaged under informal arrangements by the states. In 1862 Congress authorized the President to employ them for pay at rates to be fixed by the Secretary of War. James M. Matthews, Statues at Large of the Permanent Government (Richmond, 1862–1864), First Session, chapter 46.

22. Douglas S. Freeman, *R. E. Lee* (New York, 1934), I, 493–494.

23. *O. R.*, series 1, XLI, part 4, 1041–1042.

24. *Battles and Leaders of the Civil War.* (New York, 1887–1888), IV, 483–485. The cadets engaged numbered 260, 35 of whom composed a battery section. The entire corps participated, save about 30 left behind to guard the college buildings. Philip Alexander Bruce, Brave Deeds of Confederate Soldiers (Philadelphia, 1916), 260.

25. *Confederate Veteran*, IX (1901), 352.

26. Robert Stiles, *Four Years Under Marse Robert* (New York, 1903), 49.

27. Henry L. Graves to his mother, Oct. 3, 1862, typescript, Georgia Archives; W. H. Stephenson and Edwin A. Davis, editors, "The Civil War Diary of Willie Micajah Barrow," *Louisiana Historical Quarterly*, 17 (1934), 436–451, 712–730.

28. Charles W. Hutson to his mother, July 13, 1861, typescript, University of North Carolina.

29. E. A. Moore, *The Story of a Cannoneer under Stonewall Jackson* (New York, 1907); Dame, *op. cit.*; Randolph M. McKim, "Glimpses of the Confederate Army," F. T. Miller, editor, *Photographic History of the Civil War* (New York, 1911), VIII; Stiles, *op. cit.*; Carlton McCarthy, *Detailed Minutiae of Soldier Life in the Army of Northern Virginia 1861–1865* (Richmond, 1882).

30. For enlightening information as to the prevalency and character of yeomen in the ante-bellum rural population see Blanche Henry Clark, *The Tennessee Yeoman, 1840–1860* (Nashville, 1942), Herbert Weaver, "Agricultural Population of Mississippi" (unpublished dissertation, 1941), and other studies of middle-class Southern farmers sponsored by Prof. Frank L. Owsley at Vanderbilt

University; also Frank L. and Harriet C. Owsley, "The Economic Basis of Society in the Late Ante-Bellum South," *Journal of Southern History*, VI (1940), 25–45.
    31. Wade H. Hubbard to his wife, Oct. 16, 1864, manuscript, Duke University.
    32. George Cary Eggleston, *A Rebel's Recollections* (N.Y., 1887), 35–36; General Orders, Department of South Carolina, Georgia, and Florida, Confederate Archives, chapter II, volume 40, p. 298–299; volume 43, p. 341–349; General and Special Orders, Division of Virginia Volunteers, ibid., chapter VIII, volume 239, p. 68–69.
    33. *Battle-fields of the South* (London, 1863), I, 17–19.
    34. O.R., series 4, III, 709.
    35. Charles W. Hutson to his family, Sept. 14, 1862.
    36. R. W. Waldrop to his father, July 23, 1861, manuscript, University of North Carolina.
    37. Robert M. Gill to his wife, Aug. 22, and Nov. 27, 1862, manuscript in author's possession.
    38. Eleanor D. Pace, editor, "The Diary and Letters of William P. Rogers, 1846–1862," *Southwestern Historical Quarterly*, XXXII (1929), 293–295; New Orleans Daily Crescent, Jan. 14, 1862.
    39. See O.R., series 4, I, 180; III, 48–49.
    40. Peter McDavid to his sister, Oct. 7, 1863, manuscript, Duke University; Dubose Eggleston to Annie Rouhlac, Sept. 27, 1863, manuscript, University of North Carolina.
    41. Unidentified soldier of Eleventh Alabama Regiment (signature torn off) to Miss Annie Rouhlac, Aug. 7, 1863, manuscript, University of North Carolina.
    42. James A. Hall to Joe Hall, April 18, 1864, manuscript, Alabama Archives.
    43. Henry Slade of Longstreet's Corps wrote to his brother, July 26, 1863: "The cavalry is about *played out* in this Army. They are hollered at and made the laughing stock of the whole Army." Manuscript, Duke University.
    44. Robert M. Gill to his wife, Feb. 2, 1864.
    45. J. W. Rabb to his mother, June 29, 1862, manuscript, University of Texas.
    46. Eggleston, *op. cit.*, 49–51; O. R., series 1, XVIII, 772.
    47. O. R., series 1, XX, part 1, 741; XXI, 647–648, 656.
    48. Pace, *op. cit.*, 294; J. F. J. Caldwell, *History of Gregg's and McGowan's Brigade* (Philadelphia, 1866), 124; Eggleston, *op. cit.*, 49–51; T. C. Deleon, *Four Years in Rebel Capitals* (Mobile, 1890), 185; John Crittenden to his wife, April 13, 1863, typescript, University of Texas; David Thompson to his sister, Jan. 19, 1863, manuscript among Frank Nash Papers, University of North Carolina.
    49. Kate Cumming, *A Journal of Hospital Life in the Confederate Army of Tennessee* (Louisville and New Orleans, 1866), 104.

50. John Crittenden to his wife, no date, no place.

51. C. M. Hardy to his sister, Sept. 18, 1864, typescript, Georgia Archives.

52. Diary of James J. Kirkpatrick, entry of June 10, 1864, manuscript, University of Texas.

53. Sam R. Watkins *"Co Aytch," Maury Grays, Firs Tennessee Regiment, or a Side Show of the Big Show* (Chattanooga, 1900), 39.

54. William J. McMurray, *History of the Twentieth Tennessee Regiment* (Nashville, 1904), 349–350.

55. W. A. Fletcher, *Rebel Private Front and Rear* (Beaumont, Texas, 1908), 99–100.

56. General Orders, Department of South Carolina, Georgia and Florida, Confederate Archives, chapter II, volume 42, p. 94; volume 43, p. 508.

57. Reminiscences of J. M. Montgomery, manuscript in possession of Mrs. B. B. Payne, Greenville, Mississippi.

58. Theodore Mandeville to various members of his family, April 15, Aug. 31, 1861, and March 17, 1862, manuscripts, Louisiana State University; diary of Harry St. John Dixon, entry of May 18, 1863, manuscript, University of North Carolina.

59. Reminiscences of John N. Johnson, 103, typescript, Tennessee State Library; Richard Lewis, *Camp Life of a Confederate Boy* (Charleston, 1883), 11–13.

60. J. O. Casler, *Four Years in the Stonewall Brigade* (Guthrie, Oklahoma 1893), 294–295, 316.

61. Southern Historical Society *Papers*, I (1876), 81.

62. For instances of discharge for mental deficiency see Court-Martial Record, Confederate Archives, chapter I, volumes 194–200 *passim*.

63. David E. Johnston, *The Story of a Confederate Boy* (Portland, Oregon, 1914), 34–35.

64. Charles T. Loehr, *History of the Old First Virginia* (Richmond, 1884), 31.

65. John H. Worsham, *One of Jackson's Foot Cavalry* (New York, 1912), 75–76.

66. Robert A. Newell to Sarah Newell, March 1863, manuscript, Louisiana State University.

67. Richmond *Daily Dispatch*, April 29, 1862.

68. Robinson, *op. cit.*, 97. Pettus sent twenty-five of the toughest criminals to an Alabama penitentiary.

69. Journal of William P. Chambers, *P.M.H.S.*, Centenary Series, V, 350; McMurray, *op. cit.*, 148; U. R. Brooks, editor, *Stories of the Confederacy* (Columbia, S.C., 1912), 313–322.

70. Mobile *Advertiser and Register*, Sept. 11, 1862; Robert M. Gill to his wife, July 4, 1862; Theodore Gerrish and John S. Hutchinson, *The Blue and the Gray* (Bangor, Maine, 1884), 130; *O.R.*, series 1, XLII, part 1, 903.

Chapter 2

Have Social Historians Lost the Civil War?
Some Preliminary Demographic Speculations

Maris A. Vinovskis

Another way of comparing soldiers and noncombatants is to begin with the entire population of a geographic area. Age, occupation, and other characteristics of potential soldiers can be found in the U.S. census, and those who joined the army can be identified in military records. A problem arises, however, when we try to pinpoint the key differences between soldiers and civilians: if men with white-collar positions, for example, were less likely to enlist, was it because of their occupation or because they were older and more likely to have both a white-collar job and a disinclination to join the army? To answer this question, the historian needs to hold other characteristics constant ("control" for them) while examining age, occupation, place of birth, and so on. In the case of the Union army, some historians have done this "controlling" via elaborate tables, but Maris A. Vinovskis of the University of Michigan uses procedures that more concisely sort out soldiers' and civilians' differences. This selection from a 1989 article summarizes Vinovskis's comparisons for men from Newburyport, Massachusetts.

A sizable proportion of military-age white males fought in the Civil War, and many of them died, suffered wounds, or deserted. But did the Civil War affect everyone equally, or were there large differences in the experiences of participants from different ethnic and socioeconomic backgrounds? If it was a "poor man's" fight, for example, as many contemporaries complained, then the human costs of the war would have been disproportionately borne by those in lower-class occupations.

Since there are no detailed national statistics on the characteristics of those who fought and died in the Civil War, it is convenient to pursue those questions on the local level, where participants' characteristics can be determined.[1] Although no city is representative or typical of the North as a whole, Newburyport, Massachusetts, provides a useful setting for such an investigation. In 1860 Newburyport was a small maritime community of thirteen thousand individuals with an ethnically diverse population (almost entirely white but about one-fifth foreign born). The construction of five steam-powered cotton mills had revitalized the city economically in the 1840s and early 1850s, but it suffered hard times after the panic of 1857. During the Civil War itself the city recovered as the demand for its goods and services increased.[2]

One of the major reasons for selecting Newburyport is the availability of excellent military records describing the role of its citizens in the Civil War. Although the city, like most other communities, did not keep complete and detailed records on the townspeople who contributed to the war effort, George W. Creasey, a Civil War veteran himself, devoted nearly three and a half decades of his life to meticulously tracing and recording the Civil War experiences of Newburyport soldiers. He consulted military records in Boston and Washington, D.C., and interviewed many survivors of the war. Although some errors may exist in his work, his compilation provides a more complete and comprehensive record than could be assembled today by someone relying only on surviving written documents.[3]

As part of a larger study of Newburyport during the Civil War, the data compiled by Creasey from military records were linked to demographic and socioeconomic information in the federal manuscript census of 1860. In addition, high school attendance records were linked to the two data sets. Although the results reported here are only a preliminary assessment of the impact of the Civil War on Newburyport residents, they provide a more detailed analysis of participation in the Union forces than heretofore available and suggest the information that can be gleaned from community studies.

Compared with Northerners in general, Newburyport residents were more likely to enroll in the army or navy. The 1,337 different servicemen credited to the city represent 45 percent of the total number of males aged 13 to 43 listed in the 1860 Newburyport census, whereas throughout the North an estimated 35 percent of men of that age-group enrolled.[4] To gather background information on the servicemen from Newburyport, a subset of all of the soldiers and sailors who could be identified in the 1860 federal census for that city was created. The number of soldiers and sailors from Newburyport who could be linked to the 1860 census, however, was only 728—about 55 percent of individuals credited to the city throughout the war and 48 percent of those listed in Creasey's compilation. Although there may be some biases introduced by using the linked set of military and census data, overall this sample provides a fairly accurate picture of the characteristics of males from Newburyport who served in the war.[5]

The ages of Newburyport males serving in the Civil War ranged from 11 to 63 years in 1860. Most were in their late teens or twenties. Only one boy aged 11 in 1860 enrolled later and very few aged 50 and above ever enrolled. This analysis focuses on those aged 12 to 49 in 1860 (that category includes 98 percent of all soldiers or sailors identified in the manuscript census). Information on the military experiences of Newburyport servicemen comes from Creasey. The census provides data on age, ethnicity, occupation, wealth, and enrollment in school. School records report high school attendance.

In the only other study of those who joined or did not join the Union forces, W. J. Rorabaugh used cross tabulation to analyze his Concord, Massachusetts, data. Using that technique, Rorabaugh calculated the percentage of males enlisting by some other variable, such as their property ownership or occupation. That approach does not allow the analyst to make reasonable inferences about the relative importance of each of the independent variables (for example, property ownership or occupation) in predicting whether or not someone enlisted—especially when tests of the strength of those relationships are not calculated.[6] This study improves on Rorabaugh's statistical analysis by employing multiple classification analysis (MCA), which permits assessment of the relationship between each independent variable and whether or not someone from Newburyport enlisted. Thus, it is possible to determine not only the relationship between enlisting and ethnicity, separate from the effects of the other variables, but also the relative ability of the different variables to predict the likelihood of an individual's enlisting.[7]

Since many of the young teenagers who reached military age during the war had not yet entered the labor force or accumulated any personal property in 1860, the sample was separated into two groups. For individuals aged 12 to 17 the occupations and wealth of their parents were used as the indicator; for those aged 18 to 49 their own occupations and wealth were used. To minimize any distortions introduced by using different criteria for the two subgroups, separate multiple classification analyses were run on each group. The two groups were analyzed for the influence of six variables on the enlistment of Newburyport men: age, ethnicity, occupation, wealth, school attendance, and educational attainment.[8]

As expected, age was the best predictor of whether or not someone enlisted in the armed forces. About one-half of those aged 16 to 17 in 1860 fought in the Civil War, as did nearly four-tenths of those aged 18 to 24. Only one-sixth of men in their thirties in 1860 joined the Union forces, and only one-twentieth of those in their forties.[9]

There is considerable controversy over the participation rate of foreign-born men in the Union army. Many scholars claim that foreign-born soldiers predominated in Northern units, but more recent work suggests that foreign-born men were represented at a rate equal to, or less than, that of native-born men. In Newburyport the foreign-born were much less likely to enlist in the Union forces than the native-born. Aliens who had not taken out naturalization papers were not liable to the military draft, and many foreigners in the North were hostile to the entire war effort—especially those who perceived it as an unnecessary crusade to free slaves. Somewhat surprisingly, second-generation Americans were even more likely to serve than children of native parents. Perhaps second-generation youth, who were liable to the draft, wanted to display and prove their attachment to the United States despite any misgivings their parents may have had about the war. Alternatively or in addition, second-generation Americans may have been less able to avoid military service by hiring substitutes or paying the three-hundred-dollar commutation fees. Ethnicity was the second best predictor of participation in the Civil War.[10]

Many contemporaries portrayed the Civil War as a "poor man's" fight since the well-to-do could afford to hire substitutes or pay commutation fees.[11] Therefore, one might expect that in Newburyport unskilled workers or their children would have enlisted in disproportional numbers. Yet the results of the MCAs reveal that among those in the 12 to 17 age-group the sons of fathers employed at high white-collar or skilled jobs joined at much higher rates than the sons of unskilled workers. Among adults, the skilled workers were also more likely to enlist than the unskilled workers, but in that age-group the few individuals in high white-collar occupations were particularly adverse to serving and enrolled at a very low rate (although most of that differential disappears once we control for the effects of the other independent variables).

With regard to wealth, the expected pattern of greater wealth predicting lower enrollment is confirmed but with a surprising similarity in the two rates. The rate of enrollment for youths with parents having less than one hundred dollars total wealth was 29 percent, and the rate for those with the wealthiest parents was 24 percent. Adult males whose total wealth was one thousand dollars or more were less likely to enlist than those with less wealth. Therefore, although there were differences in the rates of enrollment by occupation and wealth, those differences are not large enough to justify describing the war as a "poor man's" fight. [12]

The effect of education on enlistment can be gauged by asking two questions: Did attendance at school deter enlistment? How did the level of education attained affect enlistment? Since most children in nineteenth-century Newburyport completed their education well before they were likely to enlist, few would have declined to join in order to complete their schooling.[13] Those who indicated in the census of 1860 that they were still enrolled in school (either common school, high school, or college) were less likely to enlist than those who had already entered the labor force—even after one controls for the effects of other factors such as the age of the child. Current enrollment in school was the weakest predictor of military participation.

A better indicator of the influence of education on enlistment was high school training. That measure of education was the third best predictor of enlistment. A great swell of patriotic fervor swept through the Newburyport high schools after the war began, yet former high school students were less likely to enroll than those who had not attended any high school. One out of every five former high school students enrolled, but almost one out of every three who never attended high school enrolled.[14]

Thus far we have examined some factors that might predict which Newburyport residents would participate in the Civil War. We now turn to a consideration of the effects of that experience on the participants. Four important measures of the impact of military service are the likelihood of dying, being wounded, being discharged as disabled, or deserting. Many of the studies of the effects of twentieth-century wars on the life course of individuals focus on experiences such as marriage, education, or job mobility without adequate attention to those more direct outcomes of participation in a war.

Of the Newburyport servicemen identified in the manuscript census and aged 12 to 49 in 1860, 13 percent died of wounds or disease during the Civil War. That percentage is somewhat lower than the aggregate estimate that 17 percent of all white Union soldiers and sailors died in the Civil War. To a large degree the lower mortality rate for Newburyport reflects the high proportion of Newburyport men who served in the navy, since the navy suffered fewer losses than the army.

Approximately 16 percent of Newburyport soldiers and sailors were wounded but survived. Altogether, 29 percent of the town's servicemen were either wounded or killed during the Civil War. Only 2 percent of those in the military who could be identified in the federal manuscript census deserted, but as indicated earlier, a much higher proportion of those who could not be identified deserted. Adding the small number who deserted, 31 percent of all Newburyport soldiers in the sample either died, were wounded, or deserted. Thus one out of every eight servicemen from Newburyport who fought for the Union died, and one out of every five who survived the war was either wounded or had deserted.

Many Newburyport soldiers and sailors, including some of the wounded, were discharged from the armed forces as disabled. Almost one out of every five servicemen was discharged due to a disability.[15] Altogether at least 42 percent of those who fought in the Civil War from Newburyport were killed, wounded, deserted, or discharged as disabled. Thus, the immediate adverse effects of the war on many participants' life courses are evident.

Newburyport soldiers' and sailors' chances of being killed or wounded during the Civil War varied, depending on their ages and socioeconomic statuses.[16] As before, the sample was subdivided into those aged 12 to 17 in 1860 and those aged 18 to 49 in 1860 so that young teenagers without occupation or personal wealth could be assigned to appropriate social and economic categories. Each group was analyzed to determine the extent to which age, ethnicity, occupation, wealth, and service experiences can predict casualty outcomes, but space limits us to only a brief discussion of the results.

Servicemen aged 12 to 14 in 1860 were less likely to be killed or wounded than those aged 15 to 17. The obvious explanation for the differential is that many of them became old enough to join only late in the war and therefore served shorter times. Among soldiers and sailors aged 18 to 49 in 1860, the youngest and the oldest were the most likely to be killed or wounded.[17] Although age is the strongest predictor of enlistment in the Civil War, it is the weakest predictor of whether or not a serviceman died or was wounded.

Foreign-born and second-generation soldiers and sailors were more likely to die or to be wounded than servicemen with native parents. Perhaps foreign-born soldiers were more susceptible to diseases since they tended to be less affluent than their native-born comrades. Although foreign-born youths and adults were the least likely to enlist in the Union forces, they were much more likely to be casualties than native-born troops of either age-group.

Servicemen from disadvantaged backgrounds were more likely to be killed or wounded during the Civil War than servicemen with higher-ranking jobs or greater wealth. The generally inverse relationship between socioeconomic status and the probability of dying or being wounded, even when the effects of the other independent variables are controlled for, raises intriguing questions. Was the health of Newbury-port's lower-status citizens generally poorer at enlistment, leaving them more susceptible to diseases? Or were they assigned to units that were given particularly dangerous missions?

The last factor to be considered is the particular branch of service that a Newburyport enlistee joined. This variable was subdivided into three categories—the experience of army privates, of army officers, and of those who enlisted in the navy. Among the younger enlistees, army officers were more likely to be killed or wounded than army privates or those who joined the navy. Among servicemen aged 18 to 49 in 1860, however, army officers were less likely to be wounded or to die than army privates or those in the navy. Overall, this variable was the best predictor of whether or not a serviceman was killed or wounded in the Civil War.

Our examination of Newburyport servicemen indicates widespread participation in the war effort among males aged 13 to 49 in 1860. Although there were some occupational and wealth differences in the rates of enlistment, Union soldiers and sailors were not disproportionately recruited from the lower socioeconomic groups in Newburyport. Second-generation Americans were the most likely to enlist, and the foreign-born were the least likely. Despite the strong support for the war in the secondary schools, those Newburyport youths who received more education were less likely to enlist—even though most of them had already completed their education. However, among adult males Newburyport illiterates were underrepresented in the Union forces.

If the likelihood of a Newburyport resident's participating in the Civil War differed only moderately, depending on his occupation, wealth, or level of education, the likelihood of his being killed or wounded differed considerably depending on those variables. Servicemen from the lower socioeconomic segments of Newburyport society were much more likely to be killed or wounded than those from the more privileged segments. In addition, the foreign-born servicemen experienced particularly high rates of casualties even though they had been less willing to enlist initially. The relative casualty rates among privates and officers in the army were mixed for the two age-groups, but in both groups those in the navy were much less likely to be killed or wounded.

NOTES

From Maris A. Vinovskis, "Have Social Historians Lost the Civil War? Some Preliminary Demographic Speculations," *Journal of American History* 76 (June 1989): 43–50. Reprinted by permission.

1. Few scholars have studied the characteristics of those who fought in the Civil War, but a few historians have analyzed the backgrounds of soldiers in small units. Earl J. Hess. "The 12th Missouri Infantry: A Socio-Military Profile of a Union Regiment," *Missouri Historical Review*, 76 (Oct. 1981), 53–77; David F. Riggs, "Sailors of the U.S.S. *Cairo*: Anatomy of a Gunboat Crew." *Civil War History*, 28 (Sept. 1982), 266–73. On soldiers from a small, western Massachusetts community, see Emily J. Harris, "Sons and Soldiers: Deerfield, Massachusetts and the Civil War," *Civil War History*, 30 (June 1984), 157–71. The only comparison of those who enlisted with those who did not is W. J. Rorabaugh, "Who Fought for the North in the Civil War? Concord, Massachusetts, Enlistments," *Journal of American History*, 73 (Dec. 1986), 695–701.

2. An additional advantage of using Newburyport is the availability of useful monographs about it. See, for example, Benjamin W. Labaree, *Patriots and Partisans: The Merchants of Newburyport, 1764–1815* (Cambridge, Mass., 1962); Susan Grigg. *The Dependent Poor of Newburyport: Studies in Social History, 1800–1830* (Ann Arbor, 1984); and Stephen Thernstrom, *Poverty and Progress: Social Mobility in a Nineteenth Century City* (Cambridge, Mass., 1964); E. Vale Smith, *History of Newburyport from the Earliest Settlement of*

the Country to the Present Time (Newburyport, 1854); John J. Currier, *The History of Newburyport, Massachusetts, 1764–1905* (2 vols., Newburyport, 1906–1909).

3. George W. Creasey, *The City of Newburyport in the Civil War*, from 1861 to 1865 (Boston, 1903). Creasey found that many servicemen's records were inaccurate and had to be corrected from other sources. Indeed, the reliance on any single set of data can be problematic due to reporting errors; therefore, studies drawing on several sources of information are more reliable. Creasey gathered information on everyone in the military whose enlistment was credited to the city of Newburyport or who was a resident of that community but enrolled in another area. In addition, he included the military activities of some former Newburyport citizens who had moved elsewhere before the Civil War. He found information on 1562 soldiers and sailors—225 of whom were credited to other communities.

4. The percentage estimates for Newburyport and the North are based on the total number of servicemen divided by the number of white male residents aged 13 to 43. Since some of the servicemen were under age 13 or above age 43 in 1860, the estimates are slightly higher than the figures would be if we used only the enlistees aged 13 to 43 in 1860. Unfortunately, we do not have complete and comprehensive national information on the ages of enlistees in the Union army and navy.

5. There are several possible explanations for the difficulty in linking enlistees with Newburyport residents enumerated in the federal manuscript census of 1860. First, perhaps a few individuals could not be matched because of inadequate or incorrect information. More likely, some 1860 residents of Newburyport moved elsewhere during the war and some enlistees migrated to Newburyport after the census was taken. Given the high population turnover of antebellum cities, it is difficult to match residents in any community with individuals described in records generated two to five years later—particularly males in their twenties, who were especially mobile. Some soldiers and sailors credited to Newburyport may have lived elsewhere in 1860 but decided to enlist there because of the relatively generous municipal bounties that Newburyport offered to avoid resorting to the draft. In a comparable study of enlistments from Concord, Massachusetts, W. J. Rorabaugh matched 47.8% of those of the military list for that community with the manuscript census data for 1860. Rorabaugh, "Who Fought for the North in the Civil War?" 697.

It is not clear what biases may result from the failure to find many Newburyport soldiers and sailors in the federal manuscript census of 1860. I have used information from Creasey on the age, nativity, and rank at first muster of all soldiers and sailors in a multiple classification analysis (MCA) of individuals who were linked compared with those who were not. It reveals that those aged 19 and under in 1860 were more apt to be found in the 1860 census than men in their early twenties, individuals in the army (especially noncommissioned officers) were more apt to be found than those in the navy, and the native-born were more apt to be found in than the foreign-born. On most indicators of what happened to someone during the war (such as being wounded or killed), there was little difference between the matched and unmatched records. On the issue of desertion, however, there was a significant difference. Only 2% of those linked, but 13% of those not linked, deserted.

6. Rorabaugh, "Who Fought for the North in the Civil War?"

7. Due to limitations of space, the MCA results reported in this essay will not be reproduced in detail. A more comprehensive analysis of the Newburyport soldiers in the Civil War will be published elsewhere later. Anyone interested in the specific tables referred to in this paper should consult the longer, preliminary version of this essay available from the author. For a clear and lucid introduction to the use of MCA, see Frank Andrew, N. J. Morgan, John A. Sonquist, and Laura Klem, *Multiple Classification Analysis* (Ann Arbor, 1973).

8. The division of Newburyport males into two subgroups aged 12 to 17 and 18 to 49 is based on an analysis of the pattern of school attendance in the town on the eve of the Civil War. See Maris A. Vinovskis, "Patterns of High School Attendance in Newburyport, Massachusetts, in 1860," paper presented at the American Historical Association Meeting, New York City, Dec. 1985 (in Vinovski's possession).

9. Rorabaugh found a similar pattern in Concord: 35% of those aged 16 to 20 in 1860 enlisted, 22% of those aged 21 to 29, 13% of those aged 30 to 39, and 8% of those aged 40 to 49. Rorabaugh, "Who Fought for the North in the Civil War?" 696.

10. The most detailed study of foreigners in the Union forces emphasizes the disproportionately high rate of enlistment by the foreign-born. Ella Lonn, *Foreigners in the Union Army and Navy* (Baton Rouge, 1951). For recent questions about that interpretation, see James M. McPherson, *Ordeal by Fire: The Civil War and Reconstruction* (New York, 1982), 358–59. Rorabaugh also found that the Irish were less likely to enlist than the native-born population. Rorabaugh, "Who Fought for the North in the Civil War?" 697. Unfortunately, he did not distinguish between the participation of second-generation Americans and that of young men with native-born parents. Since very few men from either Newburyport or Massachusetts were drafted, it is unlikely that large numbers of second-generation Americans there who lacked funds to hire substitutes or pay commutation fees were drafted. The draft, however, may have induced such individuals to "volunteer" (and thus secure generous bounties) since otherwise they were likely to be drafted. Creasey, *City of Newburyport in the Civil War*, 124–25, 135–36.

11. Eugene C. Murdock, *One Million Men: The Civil War Draft in the North* (Madison, 1971), 178–217.

12. Rorabaugh, looking only at the native-born population, found that the propertyless were much more likely to enlist than the propertied. Enlistees were also underrepresented among the mercantile and professional elite, but over-represented among propertied small shopkeepers, clerks, and skilled workers in their twenties and skilled workers in their thirties. He speculates that "a combination of economic and social malaise" on the eve of the Civil War may explain the socioeconomic differentiation he found in enrollments. Rorabaugh, "Who Fought for the North in the Civil War?" 699. Although Rorabaugh's suggestions are intriguing, they are limited by the small cell sizes in his analysis and his inability to adequately control for the effects of other potentially important variables. Nevertheless, his call for more attention to the socioeconomic differentials in enlistment as well as his attempt to relate them to larger developments in antebellum society are to be commended.

13. Vinovskis, "Patterns of High School Attendance in Newburyport."

14. We have no measure of the years of schooling received by adult males. However, the federal manuscript census of 1860 did indicate the literacy of adults. Many nineteenth-century commentators and twentieth-century historians assumed that illiterates were disproportionately likely to serve in the Union forces. The results of the MCA on males ages 20–49 in 1860 present a different picture. In Newburyport 19% of literate men enlisted, but 6% of the illiterate did. Even after the effects of age, ethnicity, occupation, and wealth are controlled for, illiterates were still less likely to enlist—although the differential between the two groups was considerably narrowed. Overall, an adult male's literacy was the weakest predictor of his participating in the Civil War.

15. Since Creasey did not always indicate whether or not someone discharged for wounds was disabled, the actual percentage of discharged servicemen who were disabled was probably higher than the 20% figure.

16. Separate MCAs were run on whether or not someone was killed, was wounded, or deserted and whether or not someone was killed, was wounded, was disabled, or deserted. The results of the latter two analyses were generally similar to the one based on whether or not a serviceman was killed or wounded (although the percentage of servicemen affected was higher).

17. Future investigations will calculate the likelihood of being killed or wounded, taking into consideration the total months enrolled in the armed forces.

Chapter 3

Who Joined the Confederate Army?
Soldiers, Civilians, and Communities in Mississippi

Larry M. Logue

Historians have also compared Confederate soldiers with southerners who did not join the army. Their findings show some differences from the Union army — wealthier men, especially slaveholders, show some evidence of higher enlistment rates — but the same problem of "sorting out" confronts southern studies, and few early studies went beyond communities or groups of counties. Larry M. Logue of Mississippi College addresses these issues by using a procedure that highlights key differences while controlling for others, and by using a sample of military-age males from throughout Mississippi. This selection from a 1993 article summarizes his findings.

There is no shortage of testimony explaining southerners' decision to join the Confederate army. Civil War soldiers were as voluble about their reasons for enlisting as they were about their wartime experiences, and historians have found central themes in soldiers' reasons for going to war. Soldiers on both sides often simply echoed their leaders' justifications for the war, but beneath Confederate soldiers' political rhetoric lay a deeper, more personal concern for their society's racial equilibrium: the fear of life with the bottom rail on top echoes through southerners' explanations of why they were in the army.[1]

This motivation for southerners' enlistment is a considerable aid in understanding their later experiences. The fear of racial chaos turned against the Confederacy as it became clear that the government could not preserve white supremacy; massive desertion was one tangible result.[2] The double-edged nature of racist fears also helps us to understand what some historians see as the South's failure of will during the war: southern whites' commitment to some form of white supremacy may have remained unshaken even as they withdrew support from the government they had trusted with the preservation of slavery.[3]

Soldiers' stated reasons for going to war are therefore instructive, but there is still more that we can learn from the act of joining the Confederate army. It is impossible to ignore, for example, the importance of sheer numbers as a measure of the Confederacy's commitment to the war. To be sure, there is disagreement about the total number of men who joined the Confederate army and about the number of casualties, but even the low estimates demonstrate an impressive initial devotion to the cause. The majority of southern military-age males joined the army, a much larger proportion than served in the North, and more than a quarter-million died, or one in five of the South's entire military-age population.[4] These figures say nothing about why southerners fought, but the enlistment rates clearly show broad early support, and the casualty figures suggest a considerable willingness to sacrifice for the Confederacy. . . .

This essay focuses on enlistments throughout a southern state, using enlistees' testimony as well as the characteristics of potential soldiers to shed more light on the nature of local circumstance and on the reasons some individuals fought and others did not. Mississippi's characteristics and wartime experience make it an especially promising subject, since it embodied many of the forces that generated both support for and disaffection from the South's cause.

Support for secession was overwhelming in Mississippi, and it was the second state to leave the Union. Yet there was also a substantial undercurrent of anti-Confederate sentiment, visible in the northeastern "disloyal country" early in the war and later among bands of deserters in some of the state's south-central counties.[5] Mississippi also underwent nearly the full variety of wartime experience: some areas sustained lengthy Union occupation, others saw major battles, and still others encountered few Union soldiers before 1865.

Moreover, when they referred to their reasons for enlisting, Mississippi soldiers voiced fears similar to those described above. Few soldiers were as forthright about their racial motivations as was Will Crutcher, a planter's son in his early twenties who joined the army with one of his father's slaves as a servant. Crutcher warned that "the time for action on the part of our entire race is *swiftly passing*, and unless they all awake and get up on their feet like men, they may be compelled to forever crawl upon the ground like worms."[6] But even soldiers who were less explicit about their motivations usually shared Crutcher's conviction that society is necessarily ordered; they also shared his certainty that Union invaders meant to reverse the southern order, with former masters forced to exist somewhere beneath northerners and one-time slaves. The usual reference to this threatened topsy-turvy society was "subjugation." Newspapers warned of "subjugation, confiscation, and emancipation"; sendoff ceremonies for Confederate troops pointed to the "fanatical mercenaries who are now attempting to subjugate us to a worse than Russian despotism"; and the enlistees themselves were convinced that the Union's "cry is still for blood-conquest: Subjugation," even if it "cost[s] the Federal government more to subjugate us than it has cost up to this time."[7] Insofar as the tides of political support, the fortunes of war, and the perceived threat of racial chaos influenced enlistment, Mississippi is an ideal place for investigating the decision to join the Confederate army.

The obvious problems of scale involved in investigating enlistments in an entire state have been addressed here by sampling. The individuals studied here are 1,010 Mississippi males who were between thirteen and forty-five in 1860 (in the war's later years seventeen to forty-nine would be considered eligible military age). The men were chosen at random from the schedules of the 1860 census; they are obviously a tiny fraction of the roughly ninety thousand eligible males in Mississippi, but they are enough to be reasonably representative of the state's military-age population.[8] The principles of sampling indicate that if a hundred more samples of this size were taken, ninety-five would have characteristics that would closely approximate those of the sample used here.

The next step was to trace these 1,010 men in the records of Confederate soldiers collected by the War Department early in this century.[9] These files are a state-by-state compilation of every extant reference to Civil War soldiers in any military record; for Confederate soldiers, the records include all descriptive information that was available from regular army units, home-defense companies, and other military units that left wartime information. The records for Mississippi were searched for each individual in the sample, and he was thus identified as either a soldier or a non-soldier.[10] This process obviously risked misclassifying men who served in units from other states, but a sampling of records from neighboring states suggested that such cases were infrequent.[11]

No matter how reliable the sample, however, census data explicitly tell us nothing about motivations for enlistment. The data can indicate whether soldiers were richer or poorer than noncombatants, for example, but considerations other than economic or occupational classes may have actually influenced the decision to enlist. The soldiers' own testimony is the best evidence of such other influences, and it serves here to shape the investigation of census data.

The method is simple, as long as the questions asked are appropriate both to the testimony and to the census data.[12] Knowledge gained from soldiers' stated motives for enlisting can be the basis for predicting the characteristics of the men who left no records other than the census and, perhaps, their entry into the Confederate army. That is, if fears for white supremacy impelled men to enlist, we should see, first, a high rate of enlistment throughout the Mississippi sample, because the testimony discussed above conveys a shared stake in a racially ordered society.

It is also reasonable to expect, at the same time, an even greater likelihood of enlistment among those with a more tangible stake in white supremacy—those who owned slaves (or whose fathers owned them, in the case of dependent sons), or those who lived in communities where slaves were a large proportion of the population. If the census data confirm the predictions, then we can assert with greater confidence that fears of a topsy-turvy society brought men into the Confederate army, with all that this motivation implies for the nation's fate. If, on the other hand, slave owners were less likely to enlist, for example, or if areas within Mississippi had widely varying enlistment rates, the question of enlistees' motivation will be more difficult to answer. No one has yet claimed that racist fears motivated the entire southern population, but unexpected findings from the census data could underscore the limits of such fears among southerners.

The enlistment rate was indeed high in the Mississippi sample. Sixty-five percent of the 1,010 individuals joined the Confederate army, a remarkable response among a sample that includes 13-year-old boys and 45-year-old men. Enlistments were, of course, more frequent among men in their late teens and early twenties. Seventy-three percent of young men aged 18 to 24 joined Mississippi units; by contrast, only forty percent of men the same ages in Newburyport, Massachusetts, joined the Union army.[13] Because the sequence of each soldier's enlistments and transfers is more difficult to establish than is the fact of his joining the army, reliable dates of enlistment are available for slightly fewer than half of the soldiers in the sample. Of these, 57 percent enlisted in 1861, when Mississippians were "in a fever to get to the field"; another one-third joined in 1862, the year the Confederacy adopted its military draft, leaving eleven percent to join in the war's final years.[14] There is evidence of a sense of alarm in this enlistment-timing: by contrast, in Ashe County, North Carolina, the majority of enlistments occurred in 1862, under the threat of conscription.[15] . . .

We cannot be sure that occupation, the value of real estate holdings, the number of co-residing relatives, the proportion of slaves in the country, or being a dependent son had any effect on enlistment. . . . On the other hand, age itself remains an important predictor of enlistment, as does birthplace: only half of those born outside the slave states, with all other characteristics equal, were likely to join the Confederate army. The remaining significant variables present a contradictory picture. With all else held constant, personal wealth, much of which consisted of slaves, was positively related to enlistment: only 56 of 100 men without any personal property were likely to enlist, but 71 of 100 who owned $11,000 in personal property would join the army. Our expectation is thus far confirmed: enlistments were relatively constant across occupations, landholding, and family size, but they rose as the personal stake in white supremacy increased.

But one other influence on enlistment confounds our prediction. Men living in the river counties, regardless of their investment in slaves or any other observable characteristic, were less likely to join the army than were those living elsewhere in Mississippi. The odds of a riverfront resident enlisting were only about fifty-fifty, whereas the odds of enlistment for an individual living elsewhere were over two to one. The river counties . . . rested more squarely on slavery than did the remainder of Mississippi; all ten river counties (an eleventh county has no census returns) contained more slaves than whites, and in one county slaves were more than ninety percent of the population. Yet rich or poor, farmers or nonfarmers, household heads or dependent sons, riverfront residents showed only about the same willingness to fight for the Confederacy as did men born outside the slave states. Do shared racial fears finally fail to explain enlistment in the Confederate army?

The 1860 census can give us little further help, but other sources can shed some light on circumstances in the river counties. We might begin by modifying our expectations regarding the residents of river counties. It is perfectly plausible that people in the strongholds of slavery had the same devotion to their society as did those living elsewhere, but that they responded differently when it was endangered. Edmund and Louisa Henry, for example, owned a plantation along the Mississippi during the war. They feared the worst as the Union began its campaign for the river: early in 1862, Louisa expected that the enemy "may spare *our* lives, but as to our *property*, God only knows, for I think that the Yankees are utterly devoid of honor and humanity." Fighting, however, seemed impossible: the Henrys had no overseer, "and [Edmund's] presence is absolutely necessary on the place." A neighbor had likewise drawn straws with his overseer to determine who would enlist, and the owner stayed at home. Yet the Henrys supported the war effort: Edmund, who was a physician, treated wounded soldiers, and Louisa made bandages for them.[16]

These planters' reluctance to enlist early in the war was not atypical. Enlistment dates, it should be repeated, must be used with caution because of the large number of uncertain cases, but the dates can be suggestive. The dates indicate that residents of river counties were significantly less likely to enlist in 1861 than were military-age males elsewhere in Mississippi, suggesting a desire on the part of riverfront residents to stand watch over their communities. Military-age males who lived on or in the shadow of the great plantations may thus have sought to defend the racial order by staying at home to guard their holdings against the danger, real or imagined, of slave uprisings and Union invasion.

But it is not clear that large numbers of river-county residents did indeed stay home as guardians of their society. Since their enlistment rates were lower in 1861, we would expect any enumeration made in that year to have found an especially large number of river-county residents still at home. Several counties did such enumerations in late 1861, and three of the lists are extant.[17] The lists are rolls of males eighteen to fifty who were not yet in the army in October and November of the war's first year; one of these military censuses is from Bolivar County, on the Mississippi River, and the others are from Simpson and Winston counties, both of which are in central Mississippi and neither of which had a large population of slaves or produced much cotton.[18] There should have been considerably more military-age males remaining in Bolivar County, but the reverse is true. Of the three counties, Bolivar actually had the smallest proportion of military-age males still at home: the male population from 18 to 50 was 47 percent of what it had been in 1860, versus 59 percent in Winston County and 49 percent in Simpson County.

Three counties are limited evidence indeed, but two more counties that surveyed their military-age population later in the war provide similar results.[19] De Soto County is the northernmost river county in Mississippi, and Attala County lies near the center of the state. Each county had a population of about nine thousand whites in 1860, but their similarities ended there. De Soto County included nearly fourteen thousand slaves and produced over forty thousand bales of cotton in 1869, whereas Attala County had just over five thousand slaves and produced fewer than fifteen thousand bales. Each county took a military census in 1864, when most of the men who would join the Confederate army had already done so: as the enlistment dates discussed above suggest, conscription had produced diminishing returns since 1862, and the Confederacy's worsening military prospects were scant incentive for joining. Only 367 military-age men were left in De Soto County and 407 remained in Attala, out of eligible populations of approximately 2,700 and 2,300 in 1860; approximately 50 men in each county had been exempted from service through the various occupational provisions of the draft. Once again, the river county had the lower proportion of eligible men still at home, 11.6 percent versus 14.6 percent in the central-Mississippi county. The difference between the counties was similar for young and older men alike.

What can we make of these county military censuses? They tell us nothing directly about the decisions of individuals in and outside of the river counties, but they do show that it was unlikely that males in the river counties stayed at home rather than joining the army. Again, since proportionally fewer men enlisted in the river counties, we would expect proportionally more to have been present when local officials tabulated their county's potential soldiers. Instead, the evidence available shows fewer river-county men at home in 1861 and in 1864. The relatively small numbers who enlisted and the similarly small number who still resided in river counties point to a relatively large number who moved elsewhere rather than join the army, putting them among the substantial body of emigrants whose services were lost to the Confederacy.

Historians have often focused on emigrants who were refugees—fleeing from Union invasion toward Confederate strongholds or heading toward the Union lines driven by Confederate oppression—or those who were draft evaders.[20] The behavior of riverfront residents, on the other hand, hints at a different kind of migration. The county military censuses indicate that military-age men were leaving river counties long before Union gunboats appeared on the Mississippi and well before the Confederacy adopted conscription. Indeed, it is likely that the river had an influence of its own on out-migration, in that it provided both motivation and means for leaving the Confederacy.

The Mississippi was the "great thoroughfare" to those who lived along its banks, a lifeline but also an obvious invasion route.[21] Even before the Union's 1862 offensives, it was common knowledge that the river would be a centerpiece of the North's strategy, Confederate fortifications notwithstanding. In September of 1861, James George wrote to his wife that "an attempt will . . . probably be made to invade us by way of the Mississippi."[22] When the invasion began in earnest, riverfront residents felt still more vulnerable. Evangeline Crutcher reported that "[Vicksburg] is fermenting again, about the advance of the Federals down the Tennessee river. . . . Some of the old ladies think that they are going to eat us up right away, but I defy the Yankees to scare me." Crutcher declared that "everybody is going to war right off, and three companies are being raised," but the military censuses suggest that a second surge of enlistments was not the only result of the northern threat.[23] Crutcher did not report an exodus from Vicksburg at this time, but out-migrants were a concern elsewhere along the river. At about the same time as Crutcher was writing to her husband, newspapers in New Orleans were denouncing men who had "packed their bags and gone kiting," and one editor called for martial law to prevent out-migration.[24] The Mississippi brought the war's dangers to the doorsteps of those who lived along it, and . . . the military censuses suggest that packing one's bags was a common reaction.

Racial alarm remains a useful explanation for enlistment, but this essay indicates that the explanation should be qualified: put simply, it depends on where one looks. Just as we would expect, if a personal stake in a racially ordered society motivated enlistment, Mississippians born in slave states or with an investment in slaves were especially likely to join the army. These indications of a personal stake in white supremacy cut across occupations and across many communities, but there was one area in Mississippi whose circumstances overrode the importance of slavery.[25] With all else equal, a river-county resident who owned (or whose father owned) $11,000 in personal property was no more likely to enlist than was an individual living elsewhere who owned no personal property whatever. The available evidence suggests that military-age males on the riverfront began leaving their counties, and possibly the Confederacy, early in the war.

These findings have two implications for our understanding of the Confederacy's fate. First, the enlistment rates from Mississippi's interior accord with soldiers' testimony: whites saw the war as an attack on their position of privilege and authority, and they feared being made subjects of, rather than masters of, a racial hierarchy. The greater their investment in the present form of hierarchy, the more likely they were to fight for its preservation. This finding underscores what is known about developments later in the war. The initial allegiance in the hinterland, that is, was conditional: fighting for the Confederacy was fighting against "subjugation" only so long as the Confederacy appeared able to protect white supremacy. When the Confederacy could no longer do so, southerners withdrew their allegiance and resolved to defend white supremacy as best they could.

But decision-making appears to have worked differently in the river counties of Mississippi. The Confederacy evidently inspired less confidence among river-county residents, no matter what their background or stake in slavery; enlistment data and military censuses suggest that riverfront residents' reluctance to join the army began early in the war. Insofar as they emigrated before the war turned decisively against the South, the behavior of river-county residents works against the failure-of-will theory of Confederate defeat. If the riverfront's vulnerability impelled residents to leave the South early in the war, the Confederacy's strength would have been diminished long before there was any widespread loss of morale; even if residents simply moved to safety elsewhere in the South, their ability to contribute to the Confederacy was disrupted at best and eliminated at worst.

There were undoubtedly other areas in the Deep South where vulnerability was as important in deciding one's attitude toward the Confederacy as was preserving the racial order. Coastlines and other areas along navigable rivers may well have resembled river counties in Mississippi in their low rates of enlistment and higher rates of out-migration.[26] If so, the Confederacy faced one more problem in addition to its well-known handicaps of smaller population, lack of industries, and Unionist opposition. The Confederacy could ill afford to do without the allegiance of any part of its population, and the findings here suggest that Unionism was not the only source of disaffection from the Confederate cause.

This essay supports the view that southerners saw the coming of war in highly personal terms, but it reveals variation in what the personal terms were. In Mississippi's interior, the dominant response to the threat of "subjugation, confiscation, and emancipation" was to take up arms. Along the river, the thoroughfare that made invasion more tangible and immediate, there was less apparent faith in armed resistance, and a common response was out-migration. Knowing these reactions, we can predict patterns in enlistments elsewhere; when we know more about enlistments in other states as well as in Mississippi, we will be better able to assess individual southerners' wartime decision making and will better understand the Confederacy's fate.

NOTES

From Larry M. Logue, "Who Joined the Confederate Army? Soldiers, Civilians, and Communities in Mississippi," *Journal of Social History* 26 (spring 1993): 611–23. Reprinted by permission.

1. Reid Mitchell, *Civil War Soldiers* (New York, 1988), 6; James I. Robertson, Jr., *Soldiers Blue and Gray* (Columbia, S.C., 1988), 3–11.

2. Mitchell, *Civil War Soldiers*, 168–71; Robert C. Kenzer, *Kinship and Neighborhood in a Southern Community: Orange County, North Carolina, 1849–1881* (Knoxville, Tenn., 1987), 81–82, points out that most deserters had enlisted early in the war, when expectations would have been high for the Confederacy's ability to preserve southern society.

3. Kenneth M. Stampp, *The Imperiled Union: Essays on the Background of the Civil War* (New York, 1980), chap. 8; Richard E. Beringer, Herman Hattaway, Archer Jones, and William N. Still, Jr., *Why the South Lost the Civil War* (Athens, Ga., 1986), chaps. 16–17.

4. For a recent effort to reconcile estimates of the number of Civil War soldiers, see James M. McPherson, *Battle Cry of Freedom: The Civil War Era* (New York, 1988), 306–307. On the eligible population and the implications of the number of enlistments and casualties, see Maris A. Vinovskis, "Have Social

Historians Lost the Civil War? Some Preliminary Demographic Speculations," *Journal of American History* 76 (1989): 34–58; Beringer et al., *Why the South Lost*, 11.

5. On the "disloyal country," see John K. Bettersworth, *Confederate Mississippi: The People and Politics of a Cotton State in Wartime* (Baton Rouge, 1943), chap. 11. On later unrest, see Rudy H. Leverett, *Legend of the Free State of Jones* (Jackson, Miss., 1984).

6. William Crutcher to Evangeline Crutcher, April 10, 1862, Crutcher-Shannon Papers, Box 5, Folder 53, Mississippi Department of Archives and History (hereafter cited as MDAH).

7. Canton [Miss.] *American Citizen*, March 15, 1862; Works Progress Administration for Mississippi, Source Material for Mississippi History (82 vols., 1936–38), XXX (Jones County), Assignment No. 18, 140; James Z. George to Elizabeth George, Oct. 10, 1861, James Z. George Papers, Folder 1, MDAH; Joseph M. Jayne, Sr. to Joseph M. Jayne, Jr., June 6, 1862, Lowry-Jayne Family Papers, Box 1, Folder 1, MDAH.

8. Designing and constructing a sample that is to be representative of a large population requires several steps. Determining the number of cases needed demands some knowledge of the population's variability. A preliminary sample of 400 randomly chosen Mississippi males aged 13 to 45 showed that real estate (actually the logarithm of real estate, to control excessive variability) had the largest variation among the census characteristics of interest here, and thus would require the largest sample to achieve reliable results. Real estate was then used in standard formulas for sample size, selecting a 95 percent confidence level and a 5 percent standard error; this produced a required sample size of 1,010 cases. Military-age males were then selected by taking random lines from the 1860 census schedules. Since the other variables would not have required this large a sample, each is well within the confidence and standard error limits specified above. This essay, of course, uses the variables *jointly* rather than singly, and each subdivision of cases, such as when those born outside the slave states are classified by where they lived in 1860, reduces the effective sample size. There are no clear rules for balancing the time constraints of data-gathering against this "small-cell" problem involved in multivariate analysis; the most practical strategy is to minimize the number of variables. This has been done here, especially with occupation and geographic areas, which are discussed below.

9. Compiled Service Records of Confederate Soldiers Who Served in Organizations from the State of Mississippi, Microcopy No. 269, National Archives.

10. This identification is not a foolproof process: the surviving Confederate records are variable in their detail, and some are without the soldier's age or other important information. Deciding on a match between an individual from

the census and one in the military records in such cases is a judgment call based primarily on exact name agreement.

11. The same conclusion is reached in William Harris, *Plain Folk and Gentry in a Slave Society: White Liberty and Black Slavery in Georgia's Hinterlands* (Middletown, Conn., 1985), 198.

12. See Adrian Wilson, "Inferring Attitudes from Behavior," *Historical Methods* 14 (1981): 143–44.

13. Vinovskis, "Social Historians," 46.

14. Governor John J. Pettus, quoted in Bell Irvin Wiley, *The Life of Johnny Reb: The Common Soldier of the Confederacy* (Indianapolis, 1943), 123.

15. Martin Crawford, "Confederate Volunteering and Enlistment in Ashe County, North Carolina, 1861–1862," *Civil War History* 37 (1991): 41, 43.

16. Louisa Henry to Louisa Clark Boddie, April 28, 1862, Boddie Family Papers, Folder 1, MDAH (emphasis in original). Edmund Henry did join a home-defense company in 1863; the neighbor, Byron Willard, did not enlist.

17. (Bolivar County) Military List, 1861; Military Roll of Simpson County; Military Roll of Winston County (Record Group 9, Vol. 50), MDAH.

18. Slaves made up 87 percent of Bolivar County's population and the county's planters raised more than 33,000 bales of cotton in 1860; slaves were 38 and 43 percent of Simpson's and Winston's population, and these counties produced fewer than 5,000 and 10,000 bales of cotton.

19. Report of Persons Liable to Military Duty in [Attala County]; Report of Persons Liable to Military Duty in De Soto County (Record Group 9, Vol. 50), MDAH.

20. Steven V. Ash, "Poor Whites in the Occupied South, 1861–1865," *Journal of Southern History* 57 (1991): 39–62; Mary Elizabeth Massey, *Refugee Life in the Confederacy* (Baton Rouge, 1964); Daniel E. Sutherland, "Looking for a Home: Louisiana Emigrants during the Civil War and Reconstruction," *Louisiana History* 21 (1980): 341–59; Albert B. Moore, *Conscription and Conflict in the Confederacy* (New York, 1924), 47–48, 61.

21. Louisa Henry to Louisa Clark Boddie, April 28, 1862, Boddie Family Papers, Folder 1, MDAH.

22. James Z. George to Elizabeth George, Sept. 16, 1861, James Z. George Papers, Folder 1, MDAH.

23. Evangeline Crutcher to William Crutcher, Feb. 9, 1862, Crutcher-Shannon Papers, Box 5, Folder 53, MDAH.

24. Quoted in Massey, *Refugee Life*, 21. The Confederacy's efforts to regulate out-migration through the Provost Guard are described in Kenneth Radley, *Rebel Watchdog: The Confederate States Army Provost Guard* (Baton Rouge, 1989), chap. 7.

25. It should be noted that the results here do not mean that there were no county-to-county or neighborhood-by-neighborhood differences in enlistment in

Mississippi, but rather that there were no enlistment patterns across counties except for the river-county pattern discussed above; enlistments by neighborhoods within counties are beyond the scope of this essay.

26. There are too few Gulf-Coast residents in the Mississippi sample to allow a separate analysis. However, if residents of coastal countries are added to river-county residents . . . the difference in enlistments compared to the rest of the state becomes more pronounced; this suggests that the response to the war was indeed similar in the river counties and coast.

Chapter 4

Yankee Recruits, Conscripts, and Illegal Evaders

James W. Geary

Americans had resorted to various forms of state and local conscription before, but the Civil War saw the first national drafts. The Confederacy adopted a draft in April 1862, and the North followed suit in March 1863. Both sides provided legal means for men to avoid serving: the South exempted individuals in certain occupations, the Union excused men who were the sole support of their families as well as those who paid a $300 "commutation" fee, and both sides allowed men to hire a substitute to serve in their place. Records kept by conscription officials are useful for evaluating the often-repeated claim that this was a "rich man's war and a poor man's fight," as well as for understanding the composition of the armies. In this selection from We Need Men, *his 1991 study of Union conscription, James W. Geary, emeritus professor at Kent State University, profiles draftees and exempted men.*

Historians usually agree on why Northern men volunteered for the army. Community pride, patriotism, a desire to participate in preserving the Union and to prove one's manhood on the battlefield rank among the dominant reasons that motivated men in the early part of the war. High bounties were a primary influence for many of those who waited until later to enlist.[1] Little is known, however, about why so many men waited to be drafted. High wages at home dissuaded some men from enlisting. A reluctance to go to war combined with the visual effects of disabled veterans returning home was another deterrent. Other men had little reason to fear the draft because of the availability of commutation and substitution. "Hear well," wrote James Bamon in a rather nonchalant letter to a friend, "I am drafted into the survice [sic] of the united [sic] States. I am gointo [sic] put a man in for one year" for a thousand dollars.[2]

Data have been analyzed from the "Descriptive Books" and their equivalents in the Records of the Provost Marshal General's Bureau at the National Archives in an effort to better understand how federal conscription affected Northern men. As in any historical study, the availability of extant and useful source material is a major consideration. In Record Group 110, unfortunately, not all district records are complete. Of the six draft districts in Michigan, for example, only the second and third districts contain relatively thorough information. Of the 435 men who paid commutation in Delaware under the 1863 call, usable information is available on only 4 of them. Consequently, this group was deleted entirely rather than inflating the category of unknowns. The first-district records for Rhode Island contain information on conscripts, which is included, but no data are provided on those who paid commutation or furnished a substitute.[3]

Within the limitations of extant material, localities are included that not only reflect geographical diversity but also urban-rural and political differences. In addition to Delaware, Michigan, and Rhode Island, there are sources from the states of Iowa, Kansas, New Hampshire, and the thirtieth district of New York.[4] Not all of these areas were liable to all four federal draft. . . . The placement of individuals into occupational clusters relies mainly on the classifications developed by Theodore Hershberg and Robert Dockhorn for 1860 American society.[5]

The occupations of these men represented a broad spectrum encompassing more than 450 separate vocational pursuits. On a purely alphabetical scale, they ranged from accountants to wood sellers. Between these extremes, attorneys and pail makers shared the dubious status of being held to service with shoemakers and sleigh makers, druggists and wheelwrights, boat pilots and tinkers, sextons and saloon keepers, laborers and publishers, railroaders and balloonists, necromancers and physicians, jewelers and stonecutters, bird fanciers and veterinary surgeons.[6] . . .

Drafted Union men who were not fortunate enough to receive an exemption were held to service and had ten days in which to pay commutation, find a substitute, or enter the army. A survey of the 14,336 drafted men who faced these choices and how they compared to other men across their occupational group requires a different approach to the data . . .

Unskilled workers were, within their group, the least likely to escape conscription, but a surprising 11.6 percent of professionals experienced difficulty, as did 30.7 percent of the farmers and 17.8 percent of the skilled workers. With 5.5 percent, members of the commercial classes enjoyed the greatest advantage for escaping personal service. Professional men and skilled workers, with 58.7 percent, hired substitutes in the same proportion, while those in the white-collar occupations led all groups with 66.5 percent. Unskilled workers and farmers with 41.3 and 44.2 percent, respectively, furnished the fewest; nevertheless, over two-fifths of them found replacements. With a range of 23.5 to 29.7 percent, approximately one-fourth of all drafted men managed to pay commutation regardless of their status. This suggests that widespread access to the three-hundred-dollar exemption fee was available to all groups. To a lesser extent, a similar pattern emerges in the hiring of substitutes. . . .

Unskilled workers, with 34.8 percent, were the most likely to be conscripted within their occupational category. This figure can be misleading, however, because only 1,827 of the 14,336 men held to service were from this group. This represents only 12.7 percent of the total pool and is lower than their proportion in the Union army and in the Northern male population at large. . . . Considering that skilled workers comprised a quarter of these same populations and that only 2,361 were held, the proportion drafted from their group also was significantly lower, with 16.5 percent. Conversely, 7,218 farmers made up more than half of the men held. At 50.4 percent, a farmer's chance of being liable to the draft was higher. . . .

A higher proportion of farmers entered the army than their numbers warranted. They also made up almost 63 percent of the conscript pool. Another 18.1 percent of the pool consisted of unskilled workers, but since they represented 16.7 percent of the population and approximately 15 percent of all Union troops, the draft did not fall disproportionately on this group to a significant extent. . . . Men in the commercial and professional classes, and skilled workers, were less likely to enter the army. When held to service they were more likely than not to pay three hundred dollars or provide a substitute. . . .

Conscription fell heaviest on farmers and to a much lesser extent on unskilled workers. Also, farmers received only 33.7 percent of the exemptions for humanitarian causes. . . . Only 10.3 percent of farmers were excused for being aliens, which indicates that most farmers were native-born. They fared much better in obtaining exemptions for physical disability, and of the 4,853 men in this sample, farmers received 41 percent of them. Unskilled workers received a higher proportion of exemptions for hardship and for alien status than their numbers warranted, but they were released less often for physical disability.

The greatest beneficiaries of the hardship and alien exemptions were skilled and unskilled workers and members of the white-collar classes. Skilled workers also claimed almost one-fourth of all disability exemptions. This percentage paralleled their proportional representation both in the general population and in the army. In the area of medical exemptions, the white-collar and commercial classes (14.9 percent) fared best of all whether compared to their proportional representation in the Union army or the general population. They received more disability exemptions than their numbers warranted.

The age of Union soldiers ranged from 12 to 70, with 98 percent of the concentration falling between 18 and 45. Compared to the average Union soldier, drafted men tended to be older. This trend is not surprising, since the age of liability was limited to a span of 20-to-45 years of age. The median age for all Union soldiers was 23.5, but it increased significantly to 29.4 years for those held to service.[7] Drafted men who paid commutation tended to be the youngest, with a median of 28.7. Over half of them (56.5 percent) were under 30 years old. Those who furnished substitutes had a median age of 29.5, and less than half (45.6 percent) were under 30. Conscripts comprised the oldest class with a median age of 30.1. Less than half of them (46.6 percent) also were under 30.

Conscription tended to force older men into the army or at least required them to furnish a substitute or pay commutation. The system was less successful in encouraging the foreign-born either to serve or to provide some form of alternate service. They comprised approximately one-fourth of the army but provided only 16.8 percent of the conscripts and 12.4 percent of the substitutes. Only 9.4 percent contributed to the commutation fund. In the aggregate, the 1,830 foreign-born represented 12.7 percent of the men held. With 865, those born in Germany were the largest contingent, followed by Ireland with 360 and England with 226 men. Among the other countries represented were Austria, Belgium, France, Holland, Switzerland, and Russia.

The absence of widespread liability to the actual draft among the foreign-born can be attributed mainly to the policy that exempted aliens who had neither voted nor declared their intention to become United States citizens. Those who had inadvertently violated this policy, thereby forfeiting their special exemption status, sometimes chose another path of evasion.

The American military tradition is multidimensional, but where the threat of compulsory service exists or where the conflict has been a divisive one, men of military age (and in some cases their families) have responded predictably. For a variety of reasons, many volunteered. As others faced the prospect of being called into service, some grudgingly went, whereas others relied on a variety of legal deferments to escape or to postpone service in an unpopular war. Those who could not qualify for a special exemption, or for reasons of conscience, sometimes skedaddled.

In the American Revolution, 50,000 to 100,000 Loyalists and their families are estimated to have left the colonies rather than side with their neighbors in the fight against the British Crown.[8] They were motivated to leave mainly for ideological reasons. Although they did not have to face the specter of national conscription, they would have been expected to contribute to their local militias in one form or another had they remained in their communities.

Protest against a conscription system or a particular conflict in the twentieth century has assumed numerous forms but generally has involved a decision not to register for the draft or to leave for another country. Despite the improved efficiency of drafting, conflicting figures nevertheless make it difficult to gauge the extent to which these activities have occurred in modern times. In part this is due to various provisions for liberal deferments, particularly for married men, students, and those in certain occupations. The availability of these deferments, as well as allowances for conscientious objectors, helped mitigate hard personal choices concerning the draft.[9] In any case, the best estimate of draft evasion in World War I appears to be 12 percent. For later conflicts, the figures are even more elusive. In World War II, estimates range from 500,000 delinquents, or approximately 5 percent of the 10 million inductees, to a low of 0.5 percent. For the Vietnam War, one student suggests a figure of 100,000 deserters and evaders but excludes those men who received questionable deferments or who failed to register.

Also, this calculation is very conservative given the delinquency rate of over 20 percent early in the Vietnam War.[10]

Illegal evasion also occurred in the North during the Civil War. There were 161,244 men who, in the words of Robert Sterling, chose "the other less honorable avenues of escape." By later standards this is a precise figure, but it applies only to the two-year period of federal conscription. In addition to this group, an estimated 40,000 to 50,000 other Union men evidently "skedaddled" in 1861 and 1862 rather than face their respective state drafts.[11] These 161,244 men represented 20.8 percent of the names drawn under the four federal calls, or 12.8 percent of the number of troops that are estimated to have been raised between 1863 and 1865.

The Union men who failed to appear for the federal draft have been discussed in a thought-provoking study. Peter Levine believes that the draft discriminated against the "unpropertied," and he is critical of historians for ignoring illegal draft evasion because of their "preoccupation with commutation as a measure of the impact of conscription on particular kinds of people." Instead of basing interpretations on economic determinism, Levine, referring to earlier findings of Richard D. Brown and Eric Foner, contends that the draft not only "outlined class distinctions in terms of property, but also . . . in terms of culture and values." Although illegal draft evasion occurred in all types of constituencies later in the war, areas that experienced the highest incidence of this activity tended to be Democratic, Catholic, and foreign-born. Levine's belief is in accord with Robert Sterling's tentative conclusion that overt draft resistance emerged among populations that were predominantly Democratic, foreign-born, Catholic, and poor. Levine admits that his findings too are speculative because of "the need to identify more precisely the people who became illegal draft evaders."[12]

Levine's conclusions raise some interesting questions and issues that deserve further consideration. Foremost among these is the absence of extensive data, which may very well limit, if not preclude, further studies on the characteristics of Civil War men who failed to appear. This dearth of information is understandable since drafting officials in most instances recorded only a man's name, and not other vital data, if a man did not report. Thus, a researcher examining the presumed social status of illegal evaders through an occupational analysis would encounter difficulty because of incomplete or nonexistent source material. Also, to increase the validity of a study on illegal evasion, the researcher should select an area that will permit comparison with those men who chose to escape the draft through commutation or substitution. However, only seven states, primarily in the East and New England, were subject to all four drafts, and the data for most of these areas are scanty.[13] . . .

One of the greatest difficulties in dealing with illegal evasion is identifying exactly who chose not to appear before the examining board. Not all of these men deliberately failed to report. . . . The enrollment process was at times sporadic and was not subject to systematic verification. As such, men were ordered to report who had died, who had moved, or who already had entered the army. In the first draft sailors posed a special problem, since they were not exempt from the draft until February 1864. Some were ordered to report but could not appear because they were in active service with the Union navy.[14]

The only relatively complete information uncovered on the failure to report in the seven geographical areas examined here comes from the thirtieth district of New York. Unfortunately, it is limited solely to the last draft call, which was conducted in this district from March 17 to April 6, 1865. The area under discussion encompassed Erie County, New York, which includes Buffalo and is adjacent to the Canadian border. Its proximity to Canada is important because the city was a haven for draft dodgers during the Civil War. Widespread crimping occurred as unscrupulous agents crossed into Fort Erie, drugged British soldiers, and put the sedated men into the Union army. The vast extent of this activity contributed greatly to the strained relations between the United States and Great Britain.[15] Politically, the district was heavily Democratic, and for both the Thirty-eighth and Thirty-ninth Congresses, a Democratic representative was elected. In the 1864 presidential election, only 49.4 percent of the votes cast in Buffalo went to Abraham Lincoln, which was below the national average of 53 percent.[16] Although the thirtieth district is not the ideal sample for drawing firm conclusions about the typical person who failed to report, it does reveal some information on Northern delinquents. . . .

Of those men classified as draft evaders in the thirtieth district, 44.3 percent were unskilled workers. A significant proportion of men in the skilled and white-collar classes were also among the skedaddlers. Class lines, however, are not necessarily that clear. Compared to the occupational distribution of Union troops, proportionally more skilled and unskilled workers furnished substitutes or were conscripted in this draft. Furthermore, 1,708 men were drawn in this district, and the 497 evaders represented 29.1 percent of this total. The high number of men who failed to report is curious, since there was a reasonable expectation that the war would be over soon. With a median age of 31.3 years, these 497 delinquents were older than the average man who was held to service. Even more significant, over two-thirds of them, 68 percent, were foreign-born. Of the 341 foreign delinquents in this category, 193 were German, and another 93 were Irish. This finding helps to confirm Levine's suspicion that the foreign-born comprised many of the "illegal evaders."[17]

Until more is known about these evaders, the rest of Levine's tentative conclusions remain open to debate. Delinquency was not a phenomenon peculiar to the Civil War; it has appeared in one form or another whenever compulsory service has been instituted in America. For some wars, the incidence of draft evasion is comparable to that of the Civil War North. When factors such as institutionalized deferments, exemptions, and the failure to register are taken into account, these Union draft evaders may have composed less of a problem.[18] Another important variable is the fact that no residency requirement existed for Union volunteers. Those who enlisted were credited to the localities that recruited them, not to the ones in which they lived. When a man enlisted without notifying the authorities in his home district, he would be listed as a delinquent if his name was drawn in the draft.

Within this broader perspective, further postulations can be made about who Union illegal evaders were. Aside from those who were not notified by virtue of already being in service or for other reasons, some men may have been influenced to flee by ideological considerations. Certainly family ties and strong commitments to a belief persuaded a few men not to fight in the Union army, especially if they lived in the border states. As McPherson and Wiley have shown, the foreign-born were underrepresented in the Union army. Many of them felt no great affinity or patriotic call for fighting in a foreign army for a foreign cause, and this attitude certainly did not change with the advent of federal conscription. Other would-be soldiers undoubtedly refused to lay their lives on the line to eliminate slavery. However, illegal evasion occurred in the North before emancipation became an issue. No doubt, too, there existed other reasons that transcend all civilizations and wars. In September 1861, one Iowa citizen in a letter to a friend revealed that he felt both of them were really *runts* who were physically incapable of serving; but, just in case they were taken in the state draft, they should be ready to move to Canada. He told of a mutual acquaintance who had been notified to report and who was preparing to leave "*instanter* for parts unknown."[19] As reflected in this letter, some men were cowards, and cultural and ideological considerations notwithstanding, they would not serve under any circumstances.

Despite the limited evidence on illegal evaders in the North, Levine adds to the knowledge on Civil War conscription. His work marks the first scholarly effort to consider those who failed to report, and to view the draft in the context of reactions to the currents of modernization that were occurring throughout the Civil War North. As cultures, values, and attitudes were undergoing change, citizens were faced with "conflicting claims of allegiance between familiar, local-community ties and the demands of an intruding national authority."[20] Within this context, and in spite of certain reservations with the applicability of the modernization thesis for mid-nineteenth-century studies, he has done more than merely taken an abstraction and given it reality.[21] His supposition of a relationship between illegal draft evaders and modernization, however, may be more appropriate for the drafting system that emerged in World War I, during the more modern "*Nation-State*" phase of American military history, than for the Civil War North.[22]

Until further evidence on illegal evaders becomes available, historians must rely on variables such as commutation and substitution for assessing how the draft affected Union males. Men in all occupational settings took advantage of these privileges, and the extant evidence indicates that the draft fell most disproportionately on farmers when compared to their representation in the Union army and the total male population. Nevertheless, the draft was not that burdensome on most farmers, given that only 46,347 Union men became conscripts. Why then was there so much antagonism toward conscription? This question can only be answered by examining the draft within a larger context of Northern attitudes and perceptions toward Provost Marshal General James B. Fry, his bureau, and other factors that emerged in the last two years of the war.

NOTES

From James W. Geary, *We Need Men: The Union Draft in the Civil War* (Dekalb: Northern Illinois University Press, 1991), 92–102. Reprinted by permission.

1. On the importance of bounties as a motivating influence, see Eugene C. Murdock, *One Million Men: The Civil War Draft in the North* (Madison: State Historical Society of Wisconsin, 1971), especially pages 154–69.

2. James Bamon ([Oil City, Pa.]) to H. Stroman, Apr. 5, 1865, Henry Stroman Papers, Ohio Historical Society.

3. For Delaware, Michigan, and Rhode Island, see Delaware—"Descriptive Books of Drafted Men, Aug. 1863–Mar. 1865," 3 vols., entry 3782; Michigan, Second District—"Descriptive Books of Drafted Men, 1863–1865," 3 vols., entry 5992; Michigan, Third District—"Descriptive Books of Drafted Men, 1863–1864 [1865?]," 1 vol., entry 6014; Rhode Island, First District—"Register of Drafted Men, 1863," 1 vol., entry 1331; and Rhode Island, Second District—"Descriptive Book of Drafted Men, 1863," 1 vol., entry 1348. All sources part of Record Group 110, National Archives.

4. Iowa, First District—"Descriptive Book of Drafted Men, Oct.–Dec., 1864," I vol., entry 6397; Iowa, Second District—[source is not designated, the manuscript title says "Medical Register of Examinations of Drafted Men, Nov. 1864–May 1865"], 1 vol., entry 6413; Iowa, Third District—"Descriptive Book of Drafted Men, Sept. 1864–Feb. 1865," 1 vol., entry 6429, and "Medical Register of Examinations of Enrolled Men, 1864–65," 1 vol., entry 6428; Iowa, Fourth District—"Medical Register of Drafted Men, Sept. 1864–Feb. 1865," 1 vol., entry 6450; Iowa, Fifth District—"Descriptive Book of Drafted Men [undated]," 1 vol., entry 6470; and Iowa, Sixth District—[very peculiar untitled source, part of records for Fort Dodge and Marshalltown], 1 vol., entry 6495. The records for Kansas and New Hampshire are more accessible and are clearly identified as "Descriptive Books." For Kansas's northern district see entry 6551, and for the southern district see entry 6552. For New Hampshire's First District set entry 645, for the Second District see entry 667, and for the Third District see entry 681. For New York's Thirtieth District, see "Descriptive Book of Drafted Men, Aug. 1863–June 1864," 1 vol., entry 2291, for the calls of 1863 and March 1864; and for the December 1864 call, see "Register of Drafted Men, Mar.–Apr. 1865," 1 vol., entry 2292. All sources are part of RG 110, NA.

5. Numerous sources, including Benjamin Gould's 1869 general categories, were used in constructing a matrix for the purpose of assigning an individual to a particular occupational group. The most beneficial and helpful was Theodore Hershberg and Robert Dockhorn's "Occupational Classification," *Historical Methods Newsletter* 9 (1976): 59–98. This important work, which relies on vertical categories, stems in part from earlier studies that examined occupations in North America in 1860. Among the more important of these is Theodore Hershberg et al., "Occupation and Ethnicity in Five Nineteenth-Century Cities: A Collaborative Inquiry," *Historical Methods Newsletter* 7 (1973): 174–216, a study in which five independent researchers attempted to establish comparable occupational scales in the five cities of Philadelphia; Hamilton; Ontario, King-

ston, Buffalo, and Poughkeepsie, New York. While these works did not answer all questions, they helped immensely in facilitating my work. After experimenting with a variety of general formats, the most appropriate was a version of the one that James McPherson developed for his table on Union soldiers.

6. Compare this range of occupations for drafted men to those for all recruits as described in Bell Irvin Wiley, *The Life of Billy Yank: The Common Soldier of the Union* (Baton Rouge: Louisiana State University Press, 1971), pp. 303–4.

7. James M. McPherson, *Battle Cry of Freedom: The Civil War Era* (New York: Ballantine Books, 1988), p. 608.

8. G. N. D. Evans, ed., *Allegiance in America: The Case of the Loyalists* (Reading, Mass.: Addison-Wesley Co., 1969), pp. 189–93.

9. Deferments created a multitude of administrative and political difficulties for twentieth-century draft officials. Three excellent studies cover this area in detail. For World War I, see John Whiteclay Chambers II, *To Raise an Army: The Draft Comes to Modern America* (New York: Free Press, 1987), pp. 153–63, 188–96. For the post–World War I era, see George Q. Flynn, "The Draft and College Deferments during the Korean War," *Historian* 50 (1988): 369–85; and his *Lewis B. Hershey: Mr. Selective Service* (Chapel Hill: University of North Carolina Press, 1985), especially pp. 81–82, 91–94, 105–16, 151, 193–215, 218–19, 234–35.

10. Chambers, *To Raise an Army*, p. 213; Flynn, *Hershey*, p. 79; and Myra McPherson, *Long Time Passing: Vietnam and the Haunted Generation* (Garden City, N.Y.: Doubleday & Co., 1984), pp. 402–3. For the most accurate calculations on Vietnam, see Chambers, p. 343, n. 34.

11. Robert E. Sterling, "Civil War Draft Resistance in the Middle West" (Ph.D. diss., Northern Illinois University, 1974), p. 163.

12. Peter Levine, "Draft Evasion in the North during the Civil War, 1863–1865," *Journal of American History* 67 (Mar. 1981): 816–34.

13. *OR*, ser. 3, 5:730–39.

14. *U.S. Stats.* 13:6–8.

15. Marguerite B. Hamer, "Luring Canadian Soldiers into Union Lines during the War Between the States," *Canadian Historical Review* 27 (1946): 155–56, 159–60; and William F. Raney, "Recruiting and Crimping in Canada for the Northern Forces, 1861–1865," *Mississippi Valley Historical Review* 10 (1923): 25–26, 28–30.

16. *The Tribune Almanac for the Years 1838 to 1868 Inclusive: Comprehending the Politicians Register and the Whig Almanac . . .* (New York: New York Tribune, 1868); and William Frank Zornow, *Lincoln and the Party Divided* (Norman: University of Oklahoma Press, 1954), p. 209.

17. Levine, "Draft Evasion," p. 828.

18. Conscription in America has been in limbo since 1973 when it was replaced with the All Volunteer Force. Even without the prospect of actually

being drafted, some American men continue to ignore the highly publicized legal requirement that they must register with the Selective Service System after their eighteenth birthday. The extent of this noncompliance has been estimated at between "7 and 25 percent." Michael Useem, "Conscription and Class," *Society* 18 (1981): 28.

19. Henry [n.p.], Sept. 23, 1861, to Lal [Laurel Summers], quoted in Hubert H. Wubben, *Civil War Iowa and the Copperhead Movement* (Ames: Iowa State University Press, 1980), p. 44.

20. Levine, "Draft Evasion," pp. 833–34.

21. For concerns with the modernization thesis, see Eric Foner, *Politics and Ideology in the Age of the Civil War* (New York: Oxford University Press, 1980), pp. 21, 33.

22. For the operations of the draft during America's *"Nation-State"* phase, see Chambers, *To Raise an Army*, especially pp. 6, 174–204, 266–67.

Chapter 5

To "Don the Breeches, and Slay Them with a Will!"

A Host of Women Soldiers

Elizabeth D. Leonard

Women were present in and around Civil War army camps in a variety of roles such as nurse and cook, but combat was supposed to be restricted to men. Nonetheless, four hundred or more women disguised themselves, passed physical exams described by one woman as "a firm handshake," and enlisted in one of the armies. Did they manage to avoid detection under the rigors of army life? If so, how did they do it? Elizabeth D. Leonard of Colby College answers these and other questions in this excerpt from All the Daring of the Soldier, *her 1999 study of women in the Union and Confederate armies.*

Hundreds of women . . . dressed as men, adopted male identities, and enlisted in the armies of the Union and the Confederacy during the Civil War. Needless to say, many women who envisioned a military role for themselves in connection with the war, particularly when wanting to defend their homes, did not ultimately enlist as soldiers, although some seemed to come quite close to doing so. A group of women in December 1864 wrote to the Confederate Secretary of War, James Alexander Seddon, requesting—probably not facetiously—that he sanction their organization of a "full regiment of *ladies*, between the ages of 16 and 40," to be armed and "equipped to perform regular service in the Army of the Shenandoah Valley," notably for purposes of local defense. "Our homes have been visited time and again by the vandal foe," wrote Irene Bell, Annie Samuels, and ten other women. "We have been subjected to every conceivable outrage & suffering," for which they blamed "the incompetency of the Confederate Army upon which we depend for defence." In consequence, wrote the women, "we propose to leave our hearthstones, to endure any sacrifice, any privation for the ultimate success of our Holy Cause." Should the Secretary of War approve their plan, Bell and the others concluded, "please favor us by sending immediately properly authenticated orders for the carrying out of our wishes. All arrangements . . . have been effected & we now only wait [for] the approval of the War department."[1]

Many other women, privately and publicly, expressed a similarly strong desire to join the army. In an 1862 letter to the Adjutant General of the Wisconsin National Guard, a Mrs. S. Ann Gordon asked if there was any way she might join the army as a nurse in order to be with her husband, a soldier in the 10th Wisconsin. Although she requested a nurse's position, Gordon clearly believed herself to be soldier material. "As most ladies are considered delicate," she told the Adjutant General, "excuse me for saying that for some weeks past I have accustomed myself to from two to 4 miles walk every day and endure it with very slight fatigue. I have not seen any sickness in twenty years, and I think I should make an enduring soldier." And Louisiana's Sarah Morgan was undoubtedly not the only woman to confide her martial aspirations to her diary: "Oh! if I were only a man," Morgan wrote. "Then I could don the breeches, and slay them with a will! If some few Southern women were in the ranks," she insisted, "they could set the men an example they would not blush to follow."[2] . . .

The vast majority of women who dressed as men during the war . . . did so in order to enlist . . . Sustaining an imposture as a male soldier was possible even over an extended period of time. As far as we know, not one of these women was discovered conclusively to be a woman by any observer during the period of her service. Fellow soldiers may have had some suspicions based on the women's relatively small stature, their beardlessness, their more highly pitched voices, and so forth, but in none of these cases is there any indication that such suspicions progressed any further. . . .

Certain features of mid-nineteenth-century military life and culture helped make cross-gender "passing" possible. For one thing, although in theory women had to overcome the obstacle of a physical examination in order to enlist in the army, in practice the recruitment exam was often quite perfunctory, and thus rarely constituted a serious barrier to a woman's enlistment. This is not to say that there were no army guidelines designed to make the examination process meaningful, for indeed there were. "In passing a recruit," one regulation stipulated,

> the medical officer is to examine him stripped; to see that he has free use of all his limbs; that his chest is ample; that his hearing, vision and speech are perfect; that he has no tumors, or ulcerated or cicatrized legs; no rupture or chronic cutaneous affection; that he has not received any contusion, or wound of the head, that may impair his faculties; that he is not subject to convulsions; and has no infectious disorder that may unfit him for military service.[3]

Moreover, after being examined as a raw recruit, the soldier who was accepted into the service was supposed to undergo a second examination upon joining his regiment.

But thanks to the combination of an equally inexperienced medical staff and the rush of so many soldiers to enlist, in the first part of the war in particular an army recruit rarely faced a physical examination "more rigorous than holding out his hands to demonstrate that he had a working trigger finger, or perhaps opening his mouth to show that his teeth were strong enough to rip open a minié ball cartridge."

According to historian Bell Wiley's research, of two hundred federal regiments who were the subject of an investigation by the watchdog United States Sanitary Commission towards the end of 1861, 58 percent were cited as failing to have made even a pretense of examining the health of their recruits at the time of their enlistment. At least one examiner had a reputation for being able to evaluate ninety recruits per hour. From this perspective alone, it is no wonder that women were often able to slip into the ranks undetected.[4]

Women soldiers who evaded or made it through the physical examination process soon discovered that many of the features of regular Civil War army life also provided effective shields against the discovery of their sex. Army life in the 1860s was significantly different from army life in the late twentieth century. For one thing, recruitment was rarely if ever followed by anything resembling modern-day boot camp with its intensive physical training. Rather, the focus was generally on learning how to drill. Wrote one Pennsylvania soldier after six months in the army: "The first thing in the morning is drill, then drill, then drill again.

Then drill, drill, a little more drill. Then drill, and lastly drill. Between drills, we drill and sometimes stop to eat a little and have a roll-call." In new units at least, "drilling" meant learning how to handle, load, and fire guns and how to parry and thrust with a bayonet, practicing simple maneuvers, and marching. In the early weeks of their military service, women soldiers' efforts, like those of their male comrades, centered on such gender-neutral exercises. Of course, women soldiers also had to learn to carry their own gear, which typically included a gun, a bayonet and scabbard, ammunition, blankets, a canteen, clothing, stationery, photographs, toiletries, and a mending kit, plus equipment for cooking and eating rations. But once they grew accustomed to the forty to fifty pounds of matériel they had to carry, as many men also needed to accustom themselves, women soldiers rarely had to fear that additional biologically based differences in physical strength would lead to their disclosure.[5]

Moreover, camp life, although intimate in some ways, allowed for sufficient freedom of movement to enable women soldiers to avoid notice when bathing and dealing with other personal matters. Civil War soldiers lived and slept in close proximity to one another, but they rarely changed their clothes. Furthermore, they passed the bulk of their time, day and night, out of doors, where they also attended to their bodily needs. Thus, a female soldier could often maintain a certain amount of physical distance from her comrades, which was particularly important in connection with her toilet. Prevailing standards regarding modesty in such matters worked in a woman soldier's favor, writes the editor of Sarah Rosetta Wakeman's papers, Lauren Burgess, "ensur[ing] that no one would question a shy soldier's reluctance to bathe in a river with his messmates or to relieve himself in the open company sinks [long trenches soldiers dug for sanitation purposes wherever they camped]."[6]

Of course, attending to one's personal needs on the march or in battle was a rather different matter. Though generally loose-fitting for the sake of easy sizing (and thus beneficial to the woman soldier trying to disguise her physical form), Civil War soldiers' uniforms consisted of many pieces, overlaid with a great deal of equipment—or "impedimenta," as Wiley calls it. Much of this clothing and equipment had to be removed if a woman did not want to soil herself, and at least one modern student of the phenomenon of women soldiers during the Civil War has argued persuasively that in order to avoid detection while on the march or on the field, women soldiers simply drank as little as possible given the weather conditions to which they were exposed, and if they could not get away to some private place to relieve themselves, just went ahead and did so in their clothing, as discreetly as possible, while on the move. Regarding the question of menstruation, one suspects that many women soldiers, who often became lean and athletic in the service, simply stopped menstruating. Those who continued to do so simply had to find ways to dispose of the evidence of their menstrual periods: bloody rags that they probably managed either to burn or bury themselves, or to combine surreptitiously with similar-looking "laundry" from soldiers wounded in battle.[7]

That there were so many young men and even boys in the ranks during the Civil War also helped women soldiers avoid exposure. Whereas armies composed only of fully mature men might have been less tolerant of the odd enlisted man whose build was slighter or whose cheeks were strangely smooth, Civil War armies drew their soldiers from a wide range of age groups. Despite various regulations to the contrary, untold numbers of boys seventeen and younger lied about their ages and joined the Union and Confederate armies as regular soldiers. The presence of so many youngsters who looked and sounded similar to women provided women soldiers with an added measure of security.[8]

Rigid codes of dress typical of the mid-nineteenth century also reinforced an assumption among Civil War soldiers that "if it wore pants, it was male."[9] Wrote one soldier after he discovered that a former comrade was a woman, "A single glance at her in her proper character leads me to wonder how I ever could have mistaken her for a man, and I readily recall many things which ought to have betrayed her, except that no one thought of finding a woman in a soldier's dress." In 1902 Captain Ira B. Gardner, formerly of the 14th Maine, recalled enrolling a woman soldier in his company who went on to serve for two years before he realized his mistake. "If I had been anything but a boy, I should have probably seen from her form that she was a female," Gardner wrote, but clearly the woman's clothes had been enough to deceive him.[10] Dominant mid-century notions about differences in men's and women's capabilities had a similar result: women were considered unfit for military service in consequence of their presumed physical, emotional, and intellectual weaknesses (though such presumed weaknesses clearly did not apply to working-class and slave women). Thus, few expected to find them in the

ranks or thought to look for them there. Interestingly, there is considerable evidence to suggest that women soldiers, who knew what signs to
watch for, recognized each other with relative ease.[11]

Almost certainly the bulk of women who served as soldiers during the
Civil War were never discovered. Some, like Jennie Hodgers, were discovered only years after their military service had come to an end.
According to a Chicago *Times-Herald* story published shortly after "his"
death, a coroner's examination revealed that Civil War veteran "Otto
Schaffer" was a woman. "Schaffer" had spent many years after the war
in Butler County, Kansas, living as a hermit. One day a major thunder-
storm caused "Schaffer" to take shelter in his cabin moments before a
bolt of lightning demolished it. Neighbors found the body on the floor
and called the coroner, who became aware of "Schaffer's" secret while
he was preparing the body for burial. Perhaps because "Schaffer" was
known to have participated in so many battles during the war, local
veterans rose to the occasion and gave "him" a soldier's burial, during
which they honored the veteran's remains with a final gun salute.[12]

Women soldiers sustained their impostures through all sorts of complicated situations and sometimes for the duration of their postwar lives.
Still, there were circumstances during the war under which exposure
became virtually unavoidable. Certainly any situation that caused her to
come under close scrutiny put a woman soldier's imposture in jeopardy.
One woman soldier is mentioned in the letter an Indiana cavalryman
wrote to his wife in February 1863: "We discovered last week a soldier
who turned out to be a girl," he wrote, and who had already been in
service for almost two years, during which time she was wounded twice.
"Maybe she would have remained undiscovered for a long time if she
hadn't fainted. She was given a warm bath which gave the secret
away."[13] . . .

Some women soldiers inadvertently gave themselves away by displaying behavior that aroused observers' suspicions about their sex. When
Sarah Collins of Wisconsin cut her hair, donned men's clothes, and
enlisted with her brother after the war broke out, she hoped to have an
opportunity to engage the enemy in battle. Instead, she failed to make it
out of town with her regiment. Described as a "robust girl" for whom
the soldier's life should have presented few challenges she could not
meet, Collins nevertheless aroused suspicion—and brought on her
dismissal—by her "unmasculine manner of putting on her shoes and

stockings." Similarly, shortly after the war, in his history of wartime Secret Service activities, Albert Richardson wrote of a twenty-year-old woman who served with the 1st Kentucky Infantry for three months before the regimental surgeon guessed that she was a woman. "She performed camp duties with great fortitude," wrote Richardson, "and never fell out of the ranks during the severest marches." Nevertheless, her "feminine method of putting on her stockings" gave her away. A particularly careless female recruit in Rochester, New York, unwittingly exposed herself as a woman when in a brief moment of awkwardness she was seen trying to pull her pants on over her head. Sources indicate that when Lizzie Cook of Iowa tried to enlist with her brother at St. Louis, she gave herself away by displaying surprisingly refined table manners. And despite being "inspected, accepted, and sworn in" with her regiment and participating fully in the regiment's establishment of its initial camp site near Cincinnati—"handling lumber, doing sentry duty, &c."—one young woman who followed her brother into the 3rd Ohio Infantry lasted only two weeks before she provoked suspicion by displaying an unusual degree of familiarity with him.[14]

Landing in a hospital as a result of illness or a battle wound was, not surprisingly, the most common precursor of discovery. In July 1862 seventeen-year-old Mary Scaberry of Columbus, Ohio, enlisted as "Charles Freeman" in Company F of the 52nd Ohio. Sixteen weeks later, when she was admitted to the general hospital at Louisville, Kentucky, the doctors diagnosed "Freeman" not only with "remittent fever" but also with "sexual incompatibility," and on December 13 Scaberry received her discharge. In July 1863 the feminist reform journal *The Sibyl*, which had published an article on Kady Brownell at New Bern, published one in which it described the discovery of a woman in the ranks of the 1st Kansas Infantry. The unnamed woman, who had been with the regiment for almost two years and who had reportedly participated in a dozen battles and skirmishes, had just died in the hospital, her sex having been revealed upon examination. The article described her as "rather more than average size for a woman, with rather strongly marked features" such that "with the aid of man's attire she had quite a masculine look." According to the article, the unnamed woman had a good reputation as a soldier, and was remembered by the men of her regiment with respect and affection for being "as brave as a lion in battle" and for never having failed to perform her duty under any conditions. "She must have been very shrewd," the article continued, "to have lived in the regiment so long and preserved her secret so well."[15] . . .

Many women soldiers' identities came to light after they were captured by the enemy. Such was the case with a woman who appears in the sources alternately as "Amy Clarke" and "Anna Clark." According to a December 1862 article in the Jackson *Mississippian*, Amy Clarke of Iuka, Mississippi, was thirty years old when she enlisted with her husband in a Confederate cavalry regiment, fighting with him until his death at the battle of Shiloh, whereupon she left the regiment and reenlisted in the 11th Tennessee. It was during her second period of enlistment, the article claimed, that Clarke was wounded in battle and captured by the federals, who discovered her sex and tried to put an end to her army career (in the same inconclusive manner that federal officials had attempted to put a stop to Confederate women's espionage activities) by sending her beyond the Confederate lines.[16] . . .

A woman soldier's sex necessarily came to light, of course, if—as happened on very rare occasions—she became visibly pregnant while in the service, though some continued to hide their true identity until the delivery of the child. In December 1864 the Sandusky, Ohio, *Commercial Register* reported a "strange birth" in the Confederate army. "We are credibly informed," wrote the article's Yankee author with obvious glee,

> that one day last week, one of the rebel officers in the "bull pen," as our soldiers call it: otherwise, in one of the barracks in the enclosure on Johnson's Island [prison on Lake Erie in Ohio], in which the rebel prisoners are kept, gave birth to a "bouncing boy." This is the first instance of a father giving birth to a child we have heard of; nor have we read of it "in the books."[17]

Death, of course, offered a belated opportunity for the detection of a woman soldier's true identity, but it did not guarantee it. . . . Most female soldiers' corpses underwent the same cursory burial on the field or on the grounds of the hospital as did those of their male counterparts. On July 17, 1863, however, when Brigadier General William Hays reported on the burial of the dead at Gettysburg, he noted that among those he counted was a "female (private) in rebel uniform." At least one woman's body went undiscovered at the Shiloh battleground in Tennessee until 1934, when Mancil Milligan unearthed the remains of several Civil War soldiers while planting in the flower bed of his home on the outskirts of the Shiloh National Military Park. Summoning the authorities, Milligan observed the excavation of the bones of nine soldiers, one of whom was determined to have been a woman, along with bits of the soldiers' uniforms and gear, and the ammunition that killed them. The bones, including those of the woman, were subsequently reinterred at the National Cemetery.[18] . . .

Because the information surrounding so many women soldiers' stories is so limited, it is often impossible to know precisely how an individual woman's imposture was revealed. An unidentified nineteen-year-old woman enlisted as "John Williams" in Company H of the 17th Missouri Infantry in October 1861, only to be discharged a few days later. Her service record reads simply, "Discharged (Proved to be a Woman)." In April 1862 at Natchez, Mississippi, a woman using the alias "William Bradley" mustered in to Company G of an organization of Louisiana volunteers known as "Miles's Legion." Though she signed on for the duration of the war, "Bradley" was discharged at the end of June. The remarks on her service record for June 30 indicate only that she was "mustered in through mistake, was of female sex."[19] . . .

Clearly a key reason why we know of the wartime service of so many women soldiers is that they received so much attention in the newspapers when their impostures were exposed. Indeed, newspaper notices relating to women's military service during the Civil War continued to appear years after Appomattox. In 1896 an article appeared in the St. Louis *Star* which considered the case of Mary Stevens Jenkins (alternately "Mary Owens Jenkins"). Jenkins, the article claimed, had been a Pennsylvania schoolgirl when the war broke out. Although a schoolgirl, Jenkins was also in love with a young man identified as William Evans, whom she followed into the army. For approximately two years Jenkins served with William Evans in Company K of the 9th Pennsylvania Infantry under the alias "John Evans." After William died in battle, Jenkins remained with the regiment and continued in the service, possibly being wounded on several occasions. It is not clear whether her sex was ever discovered while she was in the service: the sources disagree. In any case, after the war Jenkins married a coal miner named Abraham Jenkins. When she died, in about 1881, Jenkins was buried in a village graveyard in Ohio. Shortly thereafter, the St. Louis *Star* noted, when the story of her military service became widely known, Jenkins's grave was quickly decorated by local veterans "with honors equal to those bestowed upon any other of the grass-grown mounds."[20]

Snippets of material about various other women soldiers appear in a variety of sources, modern and otherwise. We learn, for example, about Lizzie Compton, whose sex was detected after she was wounded and who claimed, upon discovery, to have enlisted at the age of fourteen and to have served for eighteen months in seven different regiments, pursuant to the repeated discovery of her sex. We learn, too, of Margaret Henry and Mary Wright, Southern women discovered in uniform shortly before the end of the war, when they were captured by federal authorities while in the act of burning the bridges around Nashville; Catherine E. Davidson of Sheffield, Ohio, who after her discharge told interviewers that she had seen her lover killed at Antietam, where she herself sustained a wound; Satronia Smith Hunt, who enlisted with her husband in an Iowa regiment and who, after he died in battle, remained in the regiment until the end of the war, unwounded and her sex undetected; and Annie Lillybridge of Detroit, who enlisted in the 21st Michigan in order to be near her fiancé, but who managed to hide her identity even from him until she was disabled by a wound in her arm and was discharged following the discovery of her sex.[21] Especially if we assume that the majority remained undetected, it is clear that an impressive array of women joined the armies of the Union and the Confederacy in the guise of men, and that as long as they were able to sustain their impostures, they commonly fulfilled with fierce determination the responsibilities they had assumed as soldiers. As in the cases of women spies, resistance activists, army women, and daughters of the regiment, the individual women soldiers for whom we have the most substantial documentation are only a small proportion of those who felt compelled to "don the breeches" and serve as men.

NOTES

From Elizabeth D. Leonard, *All the Daring of the Soldier: Women of the Civil War Armies* (New York: Norton, 1999), 199–213, 218–25. Reprinted by permission.

"Don the breeches, and slay them with a will!" is a quote from the diary of Confederate enthusiast Sarah Morgan, who yearned to go to war as a soldier, in Francis Butler Simkins and James Welch Patton, *The Women of the Confederacy* (New York: Garrett & Massie, 1936; reprint, St. Clair Shores, Mich.: Scholarly Press, 1976), p. 74.

1. Irene Bell, Annie Samuels, et al. to "J. E. [*sic*] Seddon," December 2, 1864, in RG 109, Letters Received by the Confederate Secretary of War, 1861–1865, National Archives, Washington, D.C. See also New York *Evening Express*, May 29, 1861; and *Frank Leslie's Illustrated Newspaper*, April 30, 1861.

2. James B. Kennedy to the MINERVA list, September 29, 1995; Simkins and Patton, *The Women of the Confederacy*, p. 74.

3. George Worthington Adams, *Doctors in Blue: The Medical History of the Union Army in the Civil War* (New York: Henry Schuman, 1952), p. 12.

4. Lauren Cook Burgess, ed., *An Uncommon Soldier: The Civil War Letters of Sarah Rosetta Wakeman, Alias Pvt. Lyons Wakeman, 153rd Regiment, New York State Volunteers, 1862–1864* (Pasadena, Md.: MINERVA Center, 1994), p. 203; Bell Irvin Wiley, *The Life of Billy Yank: The Common Soldier of the Union* (Baton Rouge: Louisiana State University Press, 1952, 1971), pp. 23, 125; Adams, *Doctors in Blue*, p. 12.

With considerable crudeness, Henry Schelling of Company F of the 64th Illinois Infantry reportedly wrote to a friend on November 21, 1863, of a new recruit who had joined the regiment while it was on its way to Eastport, Tennessee, and who had failed to overcome the obstacle of the physical. "On examination," Schelling wrote, "he proved to have a Cunt so he was discharged. I was sorry for it, for I wanted him for a Bedfellow" (Thomas P. Lowry, *The Story the Soldiers Wouldn't Tell: Sex in the Civil War* [Mechanicsburg, Pa.: Stackpole Books, 1994], p. 35).

5. Wiley, *The Life of Billy Yank*, pp. 54, 49, 64. See also Burgess, *An Uncommon Soldier*, p. 3.

6. Burgess, *An Uncommon Soldier*, p. 3. See also Sylvia G. L. Dannett, *She Rode with the Generals: The True and Incredible Story of Sarah Emma Seelye, Alias Franklin Thompson* (New York: Thomas Nelson & Sons, 1960), pp. 56–57.

7. I thank Judith Bielecki, who reenacts as a private in the 20th Maine Infantry, for her comments on this question. On the nature of Civil War soldiers' uniforms, see Wiley, *The Life of Billy Yank*, pp. 58–65.

8. Burgess, *An Uncommon Soldier*, p. 4; Wiley, *The Life of Billy Yank*, pp. 298–300.

9. Burgess, *An Uncommon Soldier*, p. 3; Lauren Cook Burgess, "Typical Soldier May Have Been Red-blooded American Woman," *Washington Times*, October 5, 1991.

10. Report No. 929, 49th Cong., 1st sess. (to accompany H.R. 1172), p. 10; Burgess, *An Uncommon Soldier*, p. 3.

11. Burgess, *An Uncommon Soldier*, p. 3.

12. "The Dead Soldier Was a Woman," in RG 94, Records of the Adjutant General's Office, Administrative Precedent File ("Frech File") #3H36, National Archives, Washington, D.C.

13. Wiley, *The Life of Billy Yank*, p. 339.

14. Ethel Alice Hurn, *Wisconsin Women in the War Between the States* (Madison: Wisconsin History Commission, 1911), p. 103 (see also Mary Elizabeth Massey, *Bonnet Brigades* [New York: Alfred A. Knopf, 1966], p. 80; and Richard C. Hall, *Patriots in Disguise: Women Warriors of the Civil War* [New York: Paragon House, 1993], p. 19); Maysville, Kentucky, *Dollar Weekly Bulletin*, November 27, 1862; Albert D. Richardson, *The Secret Service: The Field, the Dungeon, and the Escape* (Hartford, Conn.: American Publishing, 1865), p. 175; "Hid Sex in the Army," in RG 94, Records of the Adjutant General's Office, Administrative Precedent File ("Frech File") #3H36, National Archives, Washington, D.C. (see also *New York Times*, April 4, 1915; and Jane Ellen Schultz, "Women at the Front: Gender and Genre in Literature of the American Civil War" [Ph.D. diss., University of Michigan, Ann Arbor, 1988], p. 285).

15. "Sarah E. E. Seelye Fought in the Civil War," in RG 94, Records of the Adjutant General's Office, Administrative Precedent File ("Frech File") #3H36, National Archives, Washington, D.C.; War Department Memorandum dated January 14, 1892, in RG 94, Records of the Adjutant General's Office, Administrative Precedent File ("Frech File") #3H36, National Archives, Washington, D.C.: Medical Record of Charles Freeman, in RG 94, Records of the Adjutant General's Office, Carded Medical Records, Mexican and Civil Wars, National Archives, Washington, D.C.; and Kentucky reg. #121 and Kentucky reg. #394, in RG 94, Records of the Adjutant General's Office, Hospital Registers, Civil War, National Archives, Washington, D.C.; "A Heroine," *The Sibyl* 8 (July 1863): p. 1157; *The Sibyl* 9 (January 1864): p. 1.

16. Jackson *Mississippian*, December 30, 1862. See also Simkins and Patton, *The Women of the Confederacy*, p. 80; Lowry, *The Story the Soldiers Wouldn't Tell*, p. 122; Schultz, "Women at the Front," pp. 289–90; and Massey, *Bonnet Brigades*, p. 81.

17. Sandusky, Ohio, *Commercial Register*, December 12, 1864. See also Burgess, *An Uncommon Soldier*, pp. 4–5; and Bell Irvin Wiley, *Confederate Women* (Westport, Conn.: Greenwood Press, 1975), p. 142.

18. W. E. Beard to General Marcus J. Wright, January 1, 1920, in RG 94, Records of the Adjutant General's Office, Administrative Precedent File ("Frech File") #3H36, National Archives, Washington, D.C.; Fred Brooks, "Shiloh Mystery Woman," *Civil War Times Illustrated* 17 (August 1978): p. 29. See also *Official Records*, ser. 1, vol. 27, pt. 1, p. 378.

19. Military Service Record of John Williams, in RG 94, Records of the Adjutant General's Office, Compiled Military Service Records, National Archives, Washington, D.C.; Military Service Record of William Bradley in RG 109, War Department Collection of Confederate Records, Compiled Military Service Records, National Archives, Washington, D.C.

20. "Served by Her Lover's Side," in RG 94, Records of the Adjutant Gen-

eral's Office, Administrative Precedent File ("Frech File") #3H36, National Archives, Washington, D.C. See also Betty Ingraham, "And of Mary Owen[s] Jenkins," *Civil War Times*, June 1959, p. 7 (I thank Philip A. Gonyar of Waterville, Maine, for sending me this article); and Lowry, *The Story the Soldiers Wouldn't Tell*, p. 121; DeAnne Blanton, "Women Soldiers of the Civil War," *Prologue* 25 (Spring 1993): p. 28; Massey, *Bonnet Brigades*, p. 80; Schultz, "Women at the Front," p. 290; *New York Times*, April 4, 1915.

21. On Compton, see Massey, *Bonnet Brigades*, p. 80, and Lowry, *The Story the Soldiers Wouldn't Tell*, p. 122; on Henry and Wright, see Massey, *Bonnet Brigades*, and Schultz, "Women at the Front," p. 288; on Davidson, see Schultz, "Women at the Front," p. 290; on Hunt, see Blanton, "Women Soldiers of the Civil War," p. 28; on Lillybridge, see *New York Times*, April 4, 1915, and John Laffin, *Women in Battle* (New York: Abelard-Schuman, 1967), p. 1.

For additional accounts, see Schultz, "Women at the Front," pp. 288, 286; and Laffin, *Women in Battle*, pp. 51–52.

Part II

How Soldiers Lived

Chapter 6

On the March

Carlton McCarthy

The historian Gerald Linderman has described a period of "hibernation" in the decade and a half following the Civil War: overwhelmed or exhausted or embittered by wartime memories, veterans and nonveterans entered into a tacit agreement not to speak about the war. As a result, few articles, novels, or reminiscences appeared in the late 1860s through the 1870s, but in the 1880s there was a remarkable reawakening of interest in the war — celebrations, retellings, and reunions enjoyed an extraordinary revival. In 1882, as this resurgence was beginning, Carlton McCarthy published his Detailed Minutiae of Soldier Life, *an account of life in the Confederate army. Barely into his teens when the war began, McCarthy nonetheless served in local units until he formally enlisted in the Richmond Howitzers of the Army of Northern Virginia in 1864. The purpose of his book was to "look at the individual soldier separated from the huge masses of men composing the armies," thereby revealing "the habits and characteristics of the individuals who composed the rank and file." In this selection McCarthy evaluates the miseries and rewards of army life on the march.*

Who does not know all about the marching of soldiers? Those who have never marched with them and some who have. The varied experience of thousands would not tell the whole story of the march. Every man must be heard before the story is told, and even then the part of those who fell by the way is wanting.

Orders to move! Where? when? what for?—are the eager questions of the men as they begin their preparations to march. Generally nobody can answer, and the journey is commenced in utter ignorance of where it is to end. But shrewd guesses are made, and scraps of information will be picked up on the way. The main thought must be to "get ready to move." The orderly sergeant is shouting "Fall in!" and there is no time to lose. The probability is that before you get your blanket rolled up, find your frying pan, haversack, axe, etc., and "fall in," the roll-call will be over, and some "extra duty" provided. . . .

This is the time to say farewell to the breadtray, farewell to the little piles of clean straw laid between two logs, where it was so easy to sleep; farewell to those piles of wood, cut with so much labor; farewell to the girls in the neighborhood; farewell to the spring, farewell to "our tree" and "our fire," good-by to the fellows who are not going, and a general good-by to the very hills and valleys.

Soldiers commonly threw away the most valuable articles they possessed. Blankets, overcoats, shoes, bread and meat,—all gave way to the necessities of the march; and what one man threw away would frequently be the very article that another wanted and would immediately pick up; so there was not much lost after all.

The first hour or so of the march was generally quite orderly, the men preserving their places in ranks and marching in solid column; but soon some lively fellow whistles an air, somebody else starts a song, the whole column breaks out with roars of laughter; "route step" takes the place of order, and the jolly singing, laughing, talking, and joking that follows no one could describe.

Now let any young officer who sports a new hat, coat, saddle, or anything odd, or fine, dare to pass along, and how nicely he is attended to. The expressions of good-natured fun, or contempt, which one regiment of infantry was capable of uttering in a day for the benefit of such passers-by, would fill a volume. As one thing or another in the dress of the "subject" of their remarks attracted attention, they would shout, "Come out of that hat!—you can't hide in thar!" "Come out of that coat, come out—there's a man in it!" "Come out of them boots!" The infantry seemed to know exactly what to say to torment cavalry and artillery, and generally said it. If any one on the roadside was simple enough to recognize and address by name a man in the ranks, the whole column would kindly respond, and add all sorts of pleasant remarks, such as, "Halloa, John, here's your brother!" "Bill! oh, Bill! here's your ma!" "Glad to see you! How's your grandma?" "How d'ye do!" "Come out of that 'biled shirt'!"

Troops on the march were generally so cheerful and gay that an outsider, looking on them as they marched, would hardly imagine how they suffered. In summer time, the dust, combined with the heat, caused great suffering. The nostrils of the men, filled with dust, became dry and feverish, and even the throat did not escape. The "grit" was felt between the teeth, and the eyes were rendered almost useless. There was dust in eyes, mouth, ears, and hair. The shoes were full of sand, and the dust, penetrating the clothes, and getting in at the neck, wrists, and ankles, mixed with perspiration, produced an irritant almost as active as cantharides. The heat was at times terrific, but the men became greatly accustomed to it, and endured it with wonderful ease. Their heavy woolen clothes were a great annoyance; tough linen or cotton clothes would have been a great relief; indeed, there are many objections to woolen clothing for soldiers, even in winter. The sun produced great changes in the appearance of the men: their skins, tanned to a dark brown or red, their hands black almost, and long uncut beard and hair, burned to a strange color, made them barely recognizable to the home folks.

If the dust and the heat were not on hand to annoy, their very able substitutes were: mud, cold, rain, snow, hail and wind took their places. Rain was the greatest discomfort a soldier could have; it was more uncomfortable than the severest cold with clear weather. Wet clothes, shoes, and blankets; wet meat and bread; wet feet and wet ground; wet wood to burn, or rather not to burn; wet arms and ammunition; wet ground to sleep on, mud to wade through, swollen creeks to ford, muddy springs, and a thousand other discomforts attended the rain. There was no comfort on a rainy day or night except in "bed,"—that is, under your blanket and oil-cloth. Cold winds, blowing the rain in the faces of the men, increased the discomfort. Mud was often so deep as to submerge the horses and mules, and at times it was necessary for one man or more to extricate another from the mud holes in the road. Night marching was attended with additional discomforts and dangers, such as falling off bridges, stumbling into ditches, tearing the face and injuring the eyes against the bushes and projecting limbs of trees, and getting separated from your own company and hopelessly lost in the multitude. Of course, a man lost had no sympathy. If he dared to ask a question, every man in hearing would answer, each differently, and then the whole multitude would roar with laughter at the lost man, and ask him "if his mother knew he was out?"

Very few men had comfortable or fitting shoes, and fewer had socks, and, as a consequence, the suffering from bruised and inflamed feet was terrible. It was a common practice, on long marches, for the men to take off their shoes and carry them in their hands or swung over the shoulder. Bloody footprints in the snow were not unknown to the soldiers of the Army of Northern Virginia!

When large bodies of troops were moving on the same road, the alternate "halt" and "forward" was very harassing. Every obstacle produced a halt, and caused the men at once to sit and lie down on the roadside where shade or grass tempted them; about the time they got fixed they would hear the word "forward!" and then have to move at increased speed to close up the gap in the column. Sitting down for a few minutes on a long march is pleasant, but it does not always pay; when the march is resumed the limbs are stiff and sore, and the man rather worsted by the halt.

About noon on a hot day, some fellow with the water instinct would determine in his own mind that a well was not far ahead, and start off in a trot to reach it before the column. Of course another and another followed, till a stream of men were hurrying to the well, which was soon completely surrounded by a thirsty mob, yelling and pushing and pulling to get to the bucket as the windlass brought it again and again to the surface. But their impatience and haste would soon overturn the windlass, and spatter the water all around the well till the whole crowd were wading in mud, the rope would break, and the bucket fall to the bottom. . . .

In very hot weather, when the necessities of the service permitted, there was a halt about noon, of an hour or so, to rest the men and give them a chance to cool off and get the sand and gravel out of their shoes. This time was spent by some in absolute repose; but the lively boys told many a yarn, cracked many a joke, and sung many a song between "Halt" and "Column forward!" Some took the opportunity, if water was near, to bathe their feet, hands, and face, and nothing could be more enjoyable. . . .

Men of sense, and there were many such in the ranks, were necessarily desirous of knowing where or how far they were to march, and suffered greatly from a feeling of helpless ignorance of where they were and whither bound—whether to battle or camp. Frequently, when anticipating the quiet and rest of an ideal camp, they were thrown, weary and exhausted, into the face of a waiting enemy, and at times, after anticipating a sharp fight, having formed line of battle and braced themselves for the coming danger, suffered all the apprehension and got themselves in good fighting trim, they were marched off in the driest and prosiest sort of style and ordered into camp, where, in all probability, they had to "wait for the wagon," and for the bread and meat therein, until the proverb, "Patient waiting is no loss," lost all its force and beauty.

Occasionally, when the column extended for a mile or more, and the road was one dense moving mass of men, a cheer would be heard away ahead,—increasing in volume as it approached, until there was one universal shout. Then some favorite general officer, dashing by, followed by his staff, would explain the cause. At other times, the same cheering and enthusiasm would result from the passage down the column of some obscure and despised officer, who knew it was all a joke, and looked mean and sheepish accordingly. But no *man* could produce more prolonged or hearty cheers than the "old hare" which jumped the fence and invited the column to a chase; and often it was said, when the rolling shout arose: "There goes old General Lee or a Molly Cotton Tail!"

The men would help each other when in real distress, but their delight was to torment any one who was unfortunate in a ridiculous way. If, for instance, a piece of artillery was fast in the mud, the infantry and cavalry passing around the obstruction would rack their brains for words and phrases applicable to the situation, and most calculated to worry the cannoniers, who, waist deep in the mud, were tugging at the wheels.

Brass bands, at first quite numerous and good, became very rare and their music very poor in the latter years of the war. It was a fine thing to see the fellows trying to keep the music going as they waded through the mud. But poor as the music was, it helped the footsore and weary to make another mile, and encouraged a cheer and a brisker step from the lagging and tired column.

As the men tired, there was less and less talking, until the whole mass became quiet and serious. Each man was occupied with his own thoughts. For miles nothing could be heard but the steady tramp of the men, the rattling and jingling of canteens and accoutrements, and the occasional "Close up, men,—close up!" of the officers.

The most refreshing incidents of the march occurred when the column entered some clean and cosy village where the people loved the troops.

Matron and maid vied with each other in their efforts to express their devotion to the defenders of their cause. Remembering with tearful eyes the absent soldier brother or husband, they yet smiled through their tears, and with hearts and voices welcomed the coming of the road-stained troops. Their scanty larders poured out the last morsel, and their bravest words were spoken, as the column moved by. But who will tell the bitterness of the lot of the man who thus passed by his own sweet home, or the anguish of the mother as she renewed her farewell to her darling boy? Then it was that men and women learned to long for the country where partings are no more.

As evening came on, questioning of the officers was in order, and for an hour it would be, "Captain, when are we going into camp?" "I say, lieutenant, are we going to ——— or to ——— ?" "Seen anything of our wagon?" "How long are we to stay here?" "Where's the spring?" Sometimes these questions were meant simply to tease, but generally they betrayed anxiety of some sort, and a close observer would easily detect the seriousness of the man who asked after "our wagon," because he spoke feelingly, as one who wanted his supper and was in doubt as to whether or not he would get it. People who live on country roads rarely know how far it is from anywhere to anywhere else. This is a distinguishing peculiarity of that class of people. If they do know, then they are a malicious crew. "Just over the hill there," "Just beyond those woods," " 'Bout a mile," "Round the bend," and other such encouraging replies, mean anything from a mile to a day's march!

An accomplished straggler could assume more misery, look more horribly emaciated, tell more dismal stories of distress, eat more and march further (to the rear), than any ten ordinary men. Most stragglers were real sufferers, but many of them were ingenious liars, energetic foragers, plunder hunters and gormandizers. Thousands who kept their place in ranks to the very end were equally as tired, as sick, as hungry, and as hopeless, as these scamps, but too proud to tell it or use it as a means of escape from hardship. But many a poor fellow dropped in the road and breathed his last in the corner of a fence, with no one to hear his last fond mention of his loved ones. And many whose ambition it was to share every danger and discomfort with their comrades, overcome by the heat, or worn out with disease, were compelled to leave the ranks, and while friend and brother marched to battle, drag their weak and staggering frames to the rear, perhaps to die pitiably alone, in some hospital.

After all, the march had more pleasure than pain. Chosen friends walked and talked and smoked together; the hills and valleys made themselves a panorama for the feasting of the soldiers' eyes; a turnip patch here and an onion patch there invited him to occasional refreshment; and it was sweet to think that "camp" was near at hand, and rest, and the journey almost ended.

NOTE

From Carlton McCarthy, *Detailed Minutiae of Soldier Life in the Army of Northern Virginia, 1861–1865* (Richmond: C. McCarthy, 1882), 41–55.

Chapter 7

The Life of the Common Soldier in the Union Army, 1861–1865

Fred A. Shannon

More than a decade before the appearance of Bell Wiley's first study of Civil War soldiers, Fred A. Shannon, then of Kansas State University, published "The Life of the Common Soldier in the Union Army." Though Shannon's title sounds similar to Wiley's, the former's emphasis differed. "The Life of the Common Soldier" became part of Shannon's Pulitzer Prize–winning Organization and Administration of the Union Army, 1861–1865. *Shannon's key source for this book was* The War of the Rebellion: A Compilation of the Official Records of the Union and Confederate Armies, *a 128-volume transcription of official correspondence and reports. The* OR, *as it is usually known, was published from 1880 to 1901 and is an extraordinarily rich source of information on decision making in the Civil War. Shannon's emphasis on wartime policies is apparent in this essay on soldiers' experiences.*

The lot of the private in the Union Army during the Civil War was established largely by two sets of conditions: first, those emanating from the policy of the government (federal and state) toward the army; and second, those resulting from the natural reactions of the soldier toward the unaccustomed conditions of army life.

As to governmental responsibility, it is fair to say that the private in the ranks was the least considered factor in the prosecution of the Civil War. This was perhaps not because of a conscious discrimination against him, nor because his worth was underestimated, but a consequence of the looseness of organization and lack of centralization in the control of the army, which resulted in a haphazard policy of military management, not only detrimental to the main task of restoring the Union, but incidentally subversive of the desirable aim of conserving the strength, efficiency, and lives of the troops. The soldier, especially in the first year of the war, was the victim of ignorant officers, of swindling contractors, and of unscrupulous federal inspectors of provisions; and throughout the war the army was burdened by an astounding stupidity in the ordnance bureau, unrelieved by keener understanding among superior officers of the War Department.

The effect of state control of recruiting and of civilian officers, indiscriminately selected, upon the army was little short of disastrous.[1] The reaction upon the men themselves was scarcely less pernicious. When a neighboring political boss or the village livery stable proprietor became captain of a company of his acquaintances, he could not be expected to command much respect from his subordinates, who often knew more of military tactics than he. Efforts to assume the dignity consonant with military rank were likely to excite ridicule, and frenetic efforts to display military knowledge were provocative of contempt.

Consequently the discomfiture of an officer was a treat to the privates, and the more important the officer the greater the fun. If the commanding general, recently graduated from the courthouse, were thrown from his horse, the situation could be made more delectable only if his landing place were a mud-puddle.[2] A command from a corporal was considered an impertinence and, if repeated, might even result in a reprimand from the offended person. Sergeants and corporals were mere necessary evils to facilitate drill, and were obeyed or not according to the way the soldiers felt about it.[3] The sergeant pleading with his squad and the private patronizing his captain were even made the subjects for illumination by popular cartoonists.[4] So seldom was a strict and capable disciplinarian found among the line officers that, whenever encountered, such a one became an object of universal hatred until his value in conserving the life of his command was demonstrated in battle.[5]

The ordinary officer, if diligent, usually kept just one or two jumps ahead of the men in the mastery of Scott's or Hardee's *Tactics*, the Army Regulations, and the Articles of War, but was none the less intolerant of the recruit whose knowledge was still more fragmentary and faulty.[6] Yet, when the blind thus led the blind, the situation was not always devoid of interest to the men in the ranks. If the blustering colonel of cavalry, as uncertain of the art of riding as of the science of military tactics, grasped for the saddle pommel to retain his seat, and in so doing lost his sheaf of unlearned orders in a gust of wind, a half-holiday for the regiment was a foregone conclusion. The situation, however, was likely to be reversed when a confused officer precipitated his men into a quagmire and then failed to locate in the index of his book citations to any order for extricating them again. Of course, improvisation was the final resort.[7] . . .

In the minutiae of administration, multitudes of things were left unlearned. Some army camps, in consequence, were scenes of indescribable filth, while ordinary sanitary measures were lacking in many. Some officers were thoroughly incompetent for the task of enforcing or even understanding the sanitary regulations. "I have ridden through a regimental camp," said an old officer, "whose utterly filthy condition seemed enough to send malaria through a whole military department, and have been asked by the colonel, almost with tears in his eyes, to explain to him why his men were dying at the rate of one a day."[8]

Lack of adequate clothing and camp equipage might often be charged to the War Department or the Quartermaster General's Bureau, but when soldiers failed to change their underwear for six weeks at a time in mid-summer, their officers were directly culpable. In some regiments, it seemed that there was collusion between colonels and quartermasters to cheat the men out of their allowances. Some men got full rations and others got almost nothing, while the officers were loafing around in Washington. At the same time other officers went to the opposite extreme of being too zealous in drilling and punishing men,[9] resorting to all the meaner forms of castigation for which the army was notorious, such as bucking and gagging and hanging by the thumbs, stopping short only of flogging, which, fortunately, had been abolished shortly before the war. . . .

The culmination of these conditions was disclosed in the worst crimes of the soldier: desertion, sometimes combined with treason, and mutiny. The 260,339 desertions reported from the ranks during the war[10] are eloquent testimony to laxity of discipline. These figures do not include ordinary absence without leave. At Camp Curtin, in 1862, when sentinels were armed merely with clubs, the soldiers came and went when they pleased. They "rushed the guards to go bathing in the river, and . . . did duty generally when it was convenient." Even a three days' absence to neighboring towns was not reported as desertion.[11] Actual mutiny was infrequent, and when encountered was handled severely, yet General George B. McClellan said, "I think the trouble arose rather from poor officers than from the men."[12]

Still worse than this travesty of discipline, in its discernible effect upon the soldier, was the deprivation and discomfort attendant upon the haphazard practice of army contracts which grew out of the hectic experiments of 1861.[13] While the government was throwing its scores of millions of dollars to sate the greediness of contractors and official inspectors, the soldiers were often stinted in the very necessities for existence. Though early regiments were often feasted and fêted when departing from their homes, though, for instance, food could be bought on the market so cheaply that eggs sometimes cost only a quarter for six dozen,[14] the era of plenty was usually short lived and the situation was soon reversed. Outside the open markets, whether provisions were purchased from neighboring farmers or came through the usual channels of the contractors, those who had things to sell believed in getting as much as possible for their produce, and none may accuse them of infidelity to their beliefs. The War Department had early opportunity to complain that subsistence per man was costing three times the necessary fourteen to twenty cents a day.[15] Even at such prices the food was often far from desirable. The staple article of diet, "salt horse," was scarcely better than the "embalmed beef" of later Spanish War fame, and the alternative of salt pork was rarely more agreeable. Both, in the absence of sufficient vegetables, were breeders of scurvy. Nor was the butter of variegated hue, distinctive odor, and titanic strength always a welcome addition to the diet.[16] . . .

In the matter of clothing the soldier did not find . . . ready recourse to his ingenuity for relief. He suffered from shortage of supply, poor methods of distribution, inferior materials and workmanship, and his own improvidence—the latter being largely the result of poor army organization and worse discipline.

The war was half over before the shortage of supply was eradicated.[17] In the meantime, while American manufacturers and contractors were trying to prevent foreign buying,[18] governors were procuring a varied assortment of clothing, bedding, and supplies from all available sources, much of the product being more notable for its cost than for uniformity, durability, or utility.[19] Volunteer assistance was solicited and generously rendered (in one instance, at least, actually by an express company). Soldiers' Aid Societies, composed of women possessed of laudable purpose but indifferent skill, sewed and knitted for the home recruits. Even society women deserted for a time their cards and teacups to knit socks of wondrous design,[20] until they tired of the fad. The shortage of blankets was actually remedied to some extent at one time, in 1862, by the request of the War Department that new recruits bring their own bedding with them when they enlisted.[21] All these irregular sources of supply were in addition to the numerous odds and ends which well-meaning relatives sent to the front to add to the burdens of the men.

Later in the war, when the War Department had sufficient supplies on hand, still the processes of distribution were so poor that frequently some regiments were in dire want while others were encumbered with a surplus. The Quartermaster General displayed great negligence, and probably favoritism, in the purveyance of camp equipage and clothing.[22] Neighbors of Illinois seem to have had some justification for the charge that Governor Richard Yates, who was always as insistent in his requests as he was profuse in his advice to the administration, received prior consideration in his requisitions for Illinois troops.[23]

Personal distribution in the regiments was scarcely any better. It sometimes consisted of a mad scramble upon a pile of clothing and shoes, where each took what he could get, trusting to the opportunity of trading if more suitable size and fit than chance afforded were desired.[24]

The uniforms of the army in 1861, supplied under such conditions as these, were as motley in hue as they were insecure in texture. Three regiments from the same state had no less than five distinct colors of uniforms: blue, gray, black and white striped, dark blue with green trimmings, and light blue. One of the regiments was caparisoned, each man with "a light blouse with green collar and patent leather belt, dark grey pants . . . , a black felt hat turned up at one side and fastened by a tin bull's eye, the size of a sauce plate," trimmed in the national colors.[25] Still other regiments affected the brilliant red, baggy breeches, and the turbans and fezzes of the Algerian Zouaves. Many of these outlandish outfits were still to be found in the army in 1862.[26]

The worst effect of this variegated display was that, when Union troops met Confederates likewise bedizened, it was difficult to distinguish between friend and foe, and fatal blunders resulted.[27] So frequently did such mishaps occur that the War Department had finally to ban all colors except the regulation light and dark blue, and by the winter of 1862–63 the army for the first time may technically be said to have been uniformed.[28]

Shortage of clothing is easily explained; inefficiency of distribution might reasonably be expected as one of the natural blunders of a non-military state in preparation for a great war; eccentricity of color and design can be forgiven; but the substitution of shoddy for genuine cloth was a crime against civilization, if not against the statutes. From the descriptions of Civil War shoddy of 1861, it must certainly have exceeded in rottenness anything since produced, 1917 and 1918 not excepted. A serious magazine article describes it as "a villainous compound, the refuse stuff and sweepings of the shop, pounded, rolled, glued, and smoothed to the external form and gloss of cloth. . . ."[29] Blankets were equally bad, frequently being only about a third the regulation size, so rotten that they were easily perforated by the fingers or toes of their occupants, of such light and open weave as to protect neither against cold or rain, and addicted to falling to pieces without previous warning.[30]

The testimony of the soldiers is eloquent of the uselessness of much of this material. Men on the first day's march "or in the earliest storm, found their clothes, overcoats, and blankets scattering to the winds in rags or dissolving into their primitive elements of dust under the pelting rain." One day they had brand new uniforms, the next day they were practically naked.[31] A Wisconsin regiment, ten days after it had been accoutered in bright new uniforms, had to be supplied again with blue overalls, in order that the soldiers might with decency be seen upon the streets.[32] Not a man in the "Iowa First," it was predicted by an observer, would "run from a lady or the enemy. For very shame's sake they would not dare turn aught but their faces to either."[33]

Elsewhere, even colonels were seen riding about on horseback in dressing gowns and slippers, and, in the Army of the Potomac, men were required to mount guard without trousers.[34] The Quartermaster General himself admitted that sentinels walked about Washington "in freezing weather in their drawers, without trowsers [sic] or overcoats," but he attributed this to lack of supply rather than to collapse.[35] Aprons made of flour sacks and worn behind to hide deficiencies in trousers, were reported to prevail in the army in Missouri, and some men even cut up their overcoats at the beginning of winter to make the more necessary garments.[36]

An equally painful account could be inscribed concerning the army shoes, which too frequently came apart the first day they were worn and rarely lasted a month. Stories of soldiers marching barefooted, or with their feet bound in rags or rawhide, are as numerous as the chronicles of fly-blown bacon and crawling cheese.[37] Often, even when shoes were in abundance, the soldiers preferred to go barefooted rather than torture themselves with the wares available; for, once inured to marching barefooted, the inconvenience was less than the agony of ill-fitting shoes. A motto of the army was, "Trust in God; But Keep Your Shoes Easy!"[38]

The worst of the story is that these flimsy garments were paid for by the soldiers themselves. Each private had a clothing allowance of $3.50 a month,[39] any unused balance coming to him as additional pay. But if, on the other hand, his clothing vanished in the usual way and new supplies had to be issued, anything beyond this meager allowance was deducted from the regular pay of $13 a month. Considering that a conservative estimate of equipment chargeable to this allowance was about $30 for a complete outfit, whether the best obtainable from Europe or the most fragile substitutes of the contractors,[40] it can readily be seen how soon the sutler or the government would be getting a dole from the monthly wage.

In none of the preceding particulars was official blundering more fatal in its effect than in the matter of munitions. In the decade prior to the war, the world had experienced a revolution in the manufacture of firearms. Before 1860, modern European governments had discarded the ancient muzzle-loading guns and had substituted for them breech-loading rifles using copper cartridges of almost present day pattern. Furthermore, repeating rifles of great accuracy and simplicity of design were being manufactured by various concerns in the United States before the war began. The most noted of these was the Spencer repeating rifle, which fired a magazine of seven cartridges and could be reloaded again in half a minute's time, even in the hands of a mounted trooper. These repeating rifles were not mere experiments, but were of proved merit, widely known, and popular, being especially prized by sharp shooters.[41]

When the most coveted of all these guns — the Spencer repeating rifle — was finally given a fair trial in the army in the last months of the war, it proved to be an invincible weapon. From the time troops were supplied with it, they not only won their engagements but they expected to win, just as the Confederates against whom it was used became disheartened at the dismal odds against them. The story became popular that the Confederates "were saying that the Yankees had now a gun that they loaded on Sundays and fired all the week."[42]

Yet the Ordnance Bureau consistently opposed the use of such guns until the war was nearly over. Even the Gatling gun, an engine of fearful destructive power, firing 250 shots a minute with deadly accuracy, was rejected by the War Department after its merits had been proved.[43] The reasons for refusing to use modern weapons were as puerile as they were profuse: the guns were too complicated; they cost too much; and anyway the soldiers would waste too much ammunition if given quick-firing rifles.[44]

So, instead of allowing the soldiers a fair fighting chance for their lives by arming them in modern style, the War Department bought all the cast-off junk of the European armies, dragged the flint- and fire-lock muskets of Revolutionary War vintage out of the arsenals, and encouraged domestic manufacturers to turn out hundreds of thousands of similar monstrosities, in order to save powder and lead and comfort the self-complacency of some doddering imbeciles at Washington. Some of the guns purchased were mere accretions of rust, of uneven caliber, sometimes with crooked barrels and defective locks. Others were so dangerous to their possessors that, as General U. S. Grant testified, the "men would hold them very tight, shut their eyes, and brace themselves for the shock."[45]

Yet the War Department clung to its prejudices and said that modern guns would be difficult for soldiers to handle. A sufficient commentary upon this oracular utterance was the proved inability of soldiers to manage the old-fashioned muzzle-loaders. Of 27,574 muskets collected from the field of Gettysburg, after the battle, 24,000 were loaded, 12,000 containing two unexploded charges each, and 6,000 were charged with from three to ten loads apiece. One musket had in it 23 loads, each being rammed down on the top of the preceding in regular order. The obfuscated soldiers, unable to manage their mediaeval guns after the first cartridge missed fire, had proceeded to go through the motions of loading and firing as long as the gun barrel held some remaining space.[46] Such stupidity would have been impossible for the possessor of a breech-loader.

But what does all this have to do with the daily life of the soldier? Simply this: since the War Department decreed that soldiers should not fire efficiently and rapidly, it followed that, in order to add to the effectiveness of the army, what was lacking in efficiency should be made up in numbers. It is fair to estimate that the fatuity of the War Department in this one particular made necessary the doubling of the size of the army and undoubtedly prolonged the war. While the daily life of the individual soldier might not have been greatly affected, the number of soldiers and the length of service was practically determined by the obtuse policy of the government in the matters of training and arming the troops. Though the War Department never admitted its blunders, it definitely proved its mistake when at the close of the war it adopted for universal use the very weapons which, for four years, it had denied a long-suffering army.[47]

Aside from such items as the above and other similar governmental factors, the daily life of the soldier was largely either of his own making or the consequence of the age in which he lived and the ordinary vicissitudes of army life. The newly mustered recruit first began to realize his new status when his company or regiment left home for concentration camp or the front. But leave-taking from home was not the same at all periods of the war. It varied from the brass band, verbose, and festive occasions visited upon the heroes of 1861, to the unheralded peregrinations to centers of high bounty in the mercenary era, or the grim visitations of draft officials.

In the early·days, ardent recruits looked forward with unrestrained eagerness to the hardships and battles which were to make of them the heroes they intended to become. Consequently they took with considerable seriousness the furor that was created over them. Speeches, gifts, parades, and the mild or more serious flirtations with young ladies, anxious to ease the pain of their departure, were accepted in the spirit of the gift and appreciated accordingly. Later recruits, realizing from experiences of their predecessors the humdrum realities of army life, were perhaps less hilarious but equally determined, and managed to be inducted into the mysteries of warfare with less display and attention than the boys of '61.

En route to camp the means of travel, at any stage of the war, were found to be poor enough at the best, so that long marches over poor roads, even in the shoes and uniforms of the contractors' era, were sometimes preferable to rattling day and night, herded together along with indiscriminate piles of cordwood and bacon, in cheerless box cars of diminutive design. Passage by steamboat was scarcely to be preferred in place of the box cars. It was often dangerous because the closely crowded conditions made it difficult for all to find place on the decks to lounge by day or sleep at night. With a whole regiment and all its equipage packed onto one river steamboat, the soldiers nearest to the rail were in constant peril of being jostled overboard, and those in the midst of the crowd equally in danger of being trampled under foot or suffocated, and all alike were likely to suffer on a cold, blustery, or snowy night.[48]

Once arrived in camp the recruits found themselves subjected to a new set of conditions. In Washington, early regiments were quartered wherever possible, in the Patent Office, the Capitol, the Georgetown College buildings, any place found vacant.[49]

Elsewhere tents of all shapes and descriptions were employed, culminating in the ubiquitous pup tent; vacant buildings were occupied; and finally rough wooden barracks of two-gable, "shot-gun" design were constructed. If quartered in tents, the men wrapped themselves in their blankets, covered sometimes by rubber ponchos, and slept on the ground. In the wooden barracks, they were corded along on shelves, in double rows of about twenty-five each, their heads toward the center, and so close together that when they turned over in the night it had to be by concerted endeavor and all at once. Barracks with accommodations such as these were built at an average cost of about two dollars an occupant, in a day when lumber at $10 a thousand feet was considered exorbitant in price and a fit subject for governmental investigation.[50] . . .

As to food, when freed from the domination of the contractors, the soldier in camp usually got all he wanted, though not always the things most savory to his palate; but in the field he took his chances at full-rations, half-rations, or no rations, forage, or hunger. The army ration, when received in full, was generous, though somewhat monotonous, and to foreign observers it seemed sinfully extravagant. How, even with their large appetites and wasteful methods of cooking, the soldiers could consume so large a quantity of food was totally beyond the comprehension of the Count of Paris.[51] When food was plentiful or foraging easy, the soldiers often lived in the lap of luxury, knowing that the next turn of the wheel of fortune might find them in the pangs of hunger or subsisting upon the loathsome wormy bacon, hardtack, or cheese still so vividly remembered by many a veteran.

They were often as much the victims of their own poor cooking as of the sins of the contractors, especially when they essayed the task of frying "slapjacks," made of flour and cold water fried in grease. Coffee of incredible strength and in immense quantities added to the gastronomic disturbances of the men, but it was the greatest reliance of the army when on a hard campaign, and was even voted a more necessary article of diet than was tobacco.[52]

Tableware for these repasts was simple and imposed no intricacies of etiquette upon the users. The sum total was a knife, fork, tin plate, tin cup, and spoon, the last named article being added to the list after a lapse of two years and a half of warfare.[53]

The daily routine of camp life was about as monotonous as the government rations. At sunrise came the morning gun or the reveille, a signal for the sleepy men to rise and arrange a simple toilet. Since they slept in their clothes and socks and wore their hair short and their beards long, it was usually sufficient to pull on a pair of shoes and shake the straws out of their whiskers, whereupon they were ready for roll call. Next came a short drill and then breakfast, where if no grace was said, according to the standards of the time, at least fervent remarks were often mumbled when food was bad and the spirits low. The rest of the day was occupied by inspection, meals, and more drill, sometimes splendidly executed when the young women of the neighborhood were out in full force and attractiveness to look on. After supper came fun and frolic until tattoo was sounded, whereupon the shoes came off again and all were expected to be in bed and quiet when taps sounded at ten-thirty.[54]

Nobody was at a loss for ways to occupy his time or amuse himself during leisure hours, in winter quarters, or on Sunday afternoons in camp when daily routine was suspended. Music and singing, debates about much or nothing, improvised glee club recitals, and dramatic efforts whiled away the evenings for those not tempted away by the major sins of the era, such as card playing, chuck-luck, or driving bargains for the wares of the occasional "bootleggers" in those camps where attempts at prohibition were made: Prayer meetings and inebriate revelling added to the din of idle hours, but if the former were scantily attended it was equally to the credit of the army that the latter class was not relatively numerous. Drunkenness, while frequently encountered, did not reach alarming proportions even in those regiments, where kegs of whiskey and barrels of beer were received almost daily from well-wishers at home. Yet some companies prided themselves on the hospitality displayed by the fact that they customarily had "from two to a dozen barrels of lager beer on tap."[55]

Of daytime sports, wrestling, sparring, baseball, horse racing, and fancy shooting were commonest, and, when these failed to entertain, straight poker could generally be depended upon to arouse interest. Practical jokes, especially when played upon petty officers, and any kind of escapades involving breach of discipline were the favorite pastime of many, especially in the era before camp guards were supplied with ammunition for their guns.[56]

Rainy days and bad weather put a damper on much of this fun, and at such times the homesickness of the men drove them to letter writing—especially love letters—watching for the mails, the reading and rereading of letters and newspapers from home, the printing of their own evanescent news sheets, voicing discontent and criticism of officers, longing for female companionship, or even to the composition of poetry dedicated to real or fancied houri.[57]

Of the unromantic side of camp life much could be said and volumes have been written, but to little purpose. The drudgery and misery of warfare is the side of which the soldier sees the most, of which he complains in his generation, and which his children promptly forget. "Sheridan's Ride," "Marching through Georgia," the heroic defense of Fort Sumter, Pickett's charge, "Maryland, My Maryland," and "Barbara Frietchie" are echoed in legend and song by succeeding generations, and buckets of gushing sentiment are spilled over the sentinel sleeping at his post. But all of these were grimly prosaic things as actually experienced.

Even the open-air life of the soldier did not have all the salubrious effect that was supposed to accompany it. Five men died of disease in the Civil War for every two who died of wounds received in battle.[58] Daily exposure, combined with crowded and ill-ventilated barracks, caused sickness and the easy spread of epidemics. Bad food and adulterated whiskey, imbibed as a substitute, took their daily toll, while the stagnant water drunk from southern swamps sometimes swept the pestilence of malaria through a camp, leaving only a remnant of live and able-bodied men.[59]

From such conditions and scores of similar ones the veterans of the Civil War were willing to admit at the close of the conflict that, while they had learned much, they had suffered more. It is only in the retrospect of a generation later—in the reminiscences, rather than in the diaries and letters of veterans—that the romantic side of the war is found to outweigh the hardships and discomforts.

NOTES

From Fred A. Shannon, "The Life of the Common Soldier in the Union Army, 1861–1865," *Mississippi Valley Historical Review* 13, no. 4 (March 1927): 465–82. Reprinted by permission.

1. F. A. Shannon, "State Rights and the Union Army," *Miss. Val. Hist. Rev.*, XII, 51–71.

2. Olynthus B. Clark (ed.), *Downing's Civil War Diary . . .* (Des Moines, 1916), 84; A. F. Sperry, *History of the 33d Iowa Infantry Volunteer Regiment, 1863–66* (Des Moines, 1866), 74.

3. Evan R. Jones, *Four Years in the Army of the Potomac: A Soldier's Recollections* (London, n.d.), 46.

4. *Harper's Weekly*, V, 320, 464.

5. William F. Scott, *Story of a Cavalry Regiment . . .* (New York, 1893), 14–15; S. H. M. Byers, *With Fire and Sword* (New York, 1911), 26–27.

6. Jones, *op. cit.*, 44; *Harper's Weekly*, VI, 542.

7. Scott, *op. cit.*, 15–16; Jones, *op. cit.*, 45; *Downing's Diary*, 16.

8. Thomas Wentworth Higginson, "Regular and Volunteer Officers," *Atlantic Monthly*, XIV, 355.

9. New York *Tribune*, July 17, 1861.

10. *The War of the Rebellion: A Compilation of the Official Records of the Union and Confederate Armies* (Washington, 1880–1901), Series III, Vol. V, 109. Hereafter this work is referred to as the *Rebellion Records*.

11. C. A. Ramsey, "The Story of the Headquarters Clerk and Sergeant Major," *Story of our Regiment: a History of the 148th Pennsylvania Volunteers, Written by the Comrades*, Joseph W. Muffly (ed.) (Des Moines, 1904), 336.

12. George B. McClellan, *McClellan's Own Story . . .* (New York, 1887), 99–100; New York *Tribune*, Aug. 17, 23, Sept. 16, 1861.

13. Shannon, *loc. cit.*, 59–61.

14. Cyril B. Upham, "Arms and Equipment for the Iowa Troops in the Civil War," *Iowa Journal of History and Politics*, XVI, 47; Theodore Winthrop, "New York Seventh Regiment: Our March to Washington," *Atlantic Monthly*, VII, 746; New York *Tribune*, April 22, 1861.

15. *Rebellion Records*, Series III, Vol. I, 586, 596–97.

16. For characteristic descriptions see G. Haven, "Camp Life at the Relay," *Harper's Monthly Magazine*, XXIV, 631; Franc B. Wilkie, *The Iowa First: Letters from the War* (Dubuque, 1861), 7, 69.

17. *Rebellion Records*, Series III, Vol. I, 582–83, 608–609, Vol. II, 355, 371–73; Charles A. Dana, *Recollections of the Civil War . . .* (New York, 1898), 162. Dana was at the time an assistant Secretary of War.

18. *Rebellion Records*, Series III, Vol. I, 583–86.

19. Augustus Louis Chetlain, *Recollections of Seventy Years* (Galena, Ill., 1899), 72; Upham, *loc. cit.*, 30, 38; New York *Tribune*, April 20, 1861; *Annual Message of Governor Ramsey to the Legislature of Minnesota, Delivered January 9th, 1862* (St. Paul, 1862), 27–28; S. H. M. Byers, *Iowa in War Times* (Des Moines, 1888), 45. Both of Byers's books are rabidly partisan in treatment where issues between the sections are concerned.

20. Benjamin F. Shambaugh (ed.), *Messages and Proclamations of the Governors of Iowa* (Iowa City, 1903–1905), II, 504; New York *Tribune*, April 23, May 24, Oct. 5, 22, Nov. 9, 1861; Upham, *loc. cit.* 31; Wilkie, *op. cit.*, 21–22.

21. *Rebellion Records*, Series III, Vol. II, 483.

22. *Ibid.*, 355–56.

23. Simon Cameron rarely denied his requests. *Idem*, Series III, Vol. I, 985 (index), "Illinois, Governor of, Correspondence, War Department" for citations. For protests from other governors, Upham, *loc. cit.*, 37; *Rebellion Records*, Series III, Vol. I, 163, 186.

24. Byers, *Iowa in War Times*, 496.

25. Upham, *loc. cit.*, 38; Wilkie, *op. cit.*, 14. For similiar descriptions see Julian W. Hinkley, *Narrative of Service with the Third Wisconsin Infantry* (Madison, 1912), 6.

26. Regis de Trobriand, *Four Years with the Army of the Potomac* (Boston, 1889), 83; *Harper's Weekly*, VI, 135, 137. For illustrations, *idem*, V, 353.

27. *Ibid.*, 562.

28. *Rebellion Records*, Series III, Vol. II, 803; New York *Tribune*, Feb. 18, 1862.

29. Robert Tomes, "The Fortunes of War: How They Are Made and Spent," *Harper's Monthly Magazine*, XXIX, 227–28; New York *Tribune*, May 1, 1861; Shannon, *loc. cit.*, 60.

30. Trobriand, *op. cit.*, 136; *Harper's Weekly*, V, 512; New York *Tribune*, May 1, Nov. 22, 1861.

31. Tomes, *loc. cit.*, 228.

32. Hinkley, *op. cit.*, 6–7.

33. Wilkie, *op. cit.*, 65, 84.

34. *Harper's Weekly*, V, 512; New York *Tribune*, July 17, 1861.

35. *Rebellion Records*, Series III, Vol. II, 803.

36. Upham, *loc. cit.*, 30–31; Chester Barney, *Recollections of Field Service with the Twentieth Iowa Infantry Volunteers* (Davenport, 1865), 107–108.

37. Choice examples are in Trobriand, *op. cit.*, 136; Wilkie, *op. cit.*, 94–95; Upham, *loc. cit.*, 41, 87; Barney, *op. cit.*, 100.

38. Winthrop, *loc. cit.*, 753; Barney, *op. cit.*, 109–10.

39. *Rebellion Records*, Series III, Vol. I, 153, 234; *U.S. Statutes at Large*, XII, 269.

40. See figures in *Downing's Diary*, 16, 90; *Rebellion Records*, Series III, Vol. II, 804, Vol. V, 286; Upham, *loc. cit.*, 33; Wilkie, *op. cit.*, 14.

41. Testimony as to the superior merit of various kinds of breech-loaders is abundant. The following accounts are particularly lucid: H.W.S. Cleveland, "Rifle Clubs," *Atlantic Monthly*, X, 303–10; Scott, *op. cit.*, 63, 183, 283–84; New York *Tribune*, June 2, 1861, Jan. 17, Aug. 4, 27, 1862; *Harper's Weekly*, V, 495; *idem*, VI, 239 advertisement; Wilkie, *op. cit.*, 88; Upham, *loc. cit.*, 27;

Louis Philippe Albert d'Orleans, Comte de Paris, *History of the Civil War in America* (Philadelphia, 1875–88), I, 300; Elbridge J. Copp, *Reminiscences of the War of the Rebellion* (Nashua, N.H., 1911), 431–32.

42. Scott, *op. cit.*, 283–84; Upham, *loc. cit.*, 27. Good illustrations are in the *Atlas to Accompany the Official Records of the Union and Confederate Armies* (Washington, 1891–95), plate no. 173.

43. "Richard Jordan Gatling," *Appleton's Cyclopaedia of American Biography* (New York, 1887), 617; Felix G. Stidger (ed.), *Treason History of the Order of the Sons of Liberty* (Chicago, 1903), 21. The Count of Paris, in his *Civil War*, I, 305–306, describes a similar machine gun of great effectiveness which he says was rejected after Lincoln himself tried it out and recommended its adoption.

44. *Rebellion Records*, Series III, Vol. I, 733–34; Anonymous, "Rifled Fire Arms," *Eclectic Magazine of Foreign Literature, Science and Art*, LIII, 561; New York *Tribune*, June 2, 1861; H.W.S. Cleveland, "The Use of the Rifle," *Atlantic Monthly*, IX, 300–306; Cleveland, "Rifle Clubs," *idem*, X, 303–10.

45. *House Report Number 2*, 37 Cong., 2 Sess., Part II, 1. Descriptions of foreign purchases and domestic supplies are in *Rebellion Records*, Series III, Vol. I, 1, 4, 7, 247, 293, 360, 418, 538–39; Hinkley, *op. cit.*, 89; Upham, *loc. cit.*, 21–24; Count of Paris, *op. cit.*, I, 298–99; Scott, *op. cit.*, 25; James A. Beaver, "The Colonel's Story," in *Story of Our Regiment*, 73–74.

46. Theodore T. S. Laidley, "Breech-Loading Musket," *The United States Service Magazine*, III, 69.

47. *Rebellion Records*, Series III, Vol. IV, 971–72; Vol. V, 142–43; "Gatling," *loc. cit.*, 617. The Chief of Ordnance who achieved the revolution was Brigadier General Alexander B. Dyer, the man who had done so much to bring the Springfield Armory to a high state of efficiency during the war.

48. For accounts of leavetaking and travel see Chetlain, *op. cit.*, 72–73; Jones *op. cit.*, 43–44; Wilkie, *op. cit.*, 47; New York *Tribune*, April 22, 1861; Byers, *With Fire and Sword*, 13; Barney, *op. cit.*, 172–75; Upham, *loc. cit.*, 44.

49. *Harper's Weekly*, V, 347; Winthrop, "Washington as a Camp," *Atlantic Monthly*, VIII, 105–108; New York *Tribune*, May 7, 1861.

50. Good descriptions and pictures of early quarters, tents, and barracks are found in: *Harper's Weekly*, V, 326, 331–32, 535; Trobriand, *op. cit.*, 79; Winthrop, "Washington as a Camp," *loc. cit.*, 111; Upham, *loc. cit.*, 43, 45–46; *Rebellion Records, Atlas*, plate CLXXIV; Count of Paris, *op. cit.*, I, 293; Scott, *op. cit.*, 4–5, 371; Barney, *op. cit.*, 36, 169–70; Wilkie, *op. cit.*, 41–42; Hinkley, *op. cit.*, 9; New York *Tribune*, Nov. 8, 1861, Jan. 13, 1862.

51. Count of Paris, *op. cit.*, I, 297. It consisted of one pound of biscuit or 22 ounces of bread or flour, 1¼ pounds of fresh or salt beef or ¾ pound of bacon for each man. To this was added for each 100 men, 8 gallons of beans, 10 pounds of sugar, 4 gallons of vinegar, 2 pounds of salt, 1¼ pounds of candles, and 4 pounds of soap.

52. Sperry, *op. cit.*, 61–62; Barney, *op. cit.*, 42.

53. *Rebellion Records*, Series III, Vol. III, 1030.

54. Practically all regimental histories, diaries, and reminiscences contain references to the daily routine. Frequent items can also be found in newspapers and magazines. Those especially consulted were Scott, *op. cit.*, 371–409; Wilkie, *op. cit.*, 36–39; Winthrop, "Washington as a Camp," *loc. cit.*, 111–13; Haven, *loc. cit.*, 630–32. One of the best accounts devoted solely to the daily life of the soldier is John D. Billings, *Hardtack and Coffee or the Unwritten Story of Army Life* (Boston, c. 1887).

55. Jones, *op. cit.*, 46, 119; Wilkie, *op. cit.*, 39–40, 48; Barney, *op. cit.*, 22; Scott, *op. cit.*, 17, are especially eloquent concerning the cheering influences of liquid refreshments. Jones, on p. 150, and Haven, *loc. cit.*, 631–32, deal also with the matter of evening entertainments.

56. Jones, *op. cit.*, 151–52; Sperry, *op. cit.*, 74; Wilkie, *op. cit.*, 33–35.

57. This phase is well described by Sperry, *op. cit.*, 82; Barney, *op. cit.*, 35; *Downing's Diary*, 134. A. M. Schlesinger's article, "The Khaki Journalists, 1917–1919," *Miss. Val. Hist. Rev.*, VI, 350–59, devotes some space to the soldiers' newspapers of the Civil War. Copious samples of soldier poetry are contained in Frank Moore (ed.), *The Rebellion Record: A Diary of American Events, with Documents, Narratives, Illustrative Incidents, Poetry, etc.* (New York, 1861–68), Vols. I–XI. A more compact work is his *Civil War in Song and Story, 1860–1865* (New York, 1889).

58. *Rebellion Records*, Series III, Vol. V, 664–65. The casualties in the Union Army totalled 359,528 divided as follows: killed in action, 67,058; died of wounds, 43,012; died of other causes, chiefly disease, 249,468.

59. Thomas T. Ellis, *Leaves from the Diary of an Army Surgeon; or, Incidents of Field, Camp, and Hospital Life* (New York, 1863), 23, 25; Scott, *op. cit.*, 19; *Downing's Diary*, 77, 128, 136–37, 139, 141, 142–43. The United States Sanitary Commission, organized by civilians, did much to correct camp conditions and relieve sickness and suffering, but the government failed to coöperate with it and, as often as not, placed actual hindrances in the way of its operation. As a result it never came to be as effective as it might have been under more favorable circumstances. The most complete work dealing with its activities is, Charles J. Stillé, *History of the United States Sanitary Commission: being the General Report of its Work during the War of the Rebellion* (Philadelphia, 1866).

Chapter 8

From Finery to Tatters

Bell Irvin Wiley

In this selection from The Life of Johnny Reb, *Bell Wiley provides a southern complement to Shannon's article. The common image of Confederate soldiers has them clad in all manner of homespun and captured clothing, but Wiley reminds us that there was a regulation Confederate uniform. The problem of ill-clad troops, as Wiley also reminds us, came from shortages in general and states' control over supplies in particular. Wiley's extensive use of Confederates' own testimony, as well as the* OR *and other sources, gives this selection a closer focus on the effects of inadequate supplies on soldiers (and on their ways of coping with the shortages).*

The Confederate private envisioned by Richmond authorities in 1861 was a nattily dressed person. . . .

But there was considerable difference between the clothing designated and that actually worn by the soldiers. This discrepancy came first from the inability of the Confederate Government to provide uniforms for the men who were called to arms. Captains who wrote in to Montgomery to inquire about equipment for companies in process of organization were informed that "the volunteers shall furnish their own clothes."[1] The reason was obvious: Jeff Davis and company had none in stock, nor were any to be forthcoming until contracts with Southern manufacturers should bear fruit, or purchasing operations in Europe could be completed; and this was to require a long time.

In the meantime volunteer companies did the best they could. Some received issues of clothing from state authorities, though these were faced with problems of supply very much like those of the central government.

A procedure widely followed during the early months of the war was for captains to take funds appropriated by local authorities or donated by philanthropists—who sometimes were the captains themselves—or contributed by the recruits, to purchase cloth from whatever source it might be obtained, and to have the uniforms made up by local tailors or seamstresses. In many cases the volunteers arranged individually for the fabrication of their outfits.

Women of the South responded nobly to the difficulties by organizing sewing clubs and knitting societies. As a general rule the aid rendered by the volunteer seamstresses was both timely and valuable, though there were numerous instances where coats, pants and socks turned out by the ladies indicated considerably more zeal than skill.[2]

The inevitable result of these devious sources and methods of supply was a miscellany that made mockery of the Richmond regulations. This is not to imply that the regalia worn by early volunteers were of poor quality. On the contrary many of the companies were resplendently clothed. Captain Alexander Duncan of the Georgia Hussars, a regiment hailing from Savannah, boasted that $25,000 was spent for that organization's initial outfit.[3]

In not a few instances, regiments went into Confederate service garbed in the flashy suits which they had worn for parade purposes as militia organizations. The Orleans Guard Battalion of New Orleans arrived at Shiloh while the battle was in progress, and went into the thick of the fight wearing blue dress uniforms. Fellow Rebels mistook the newcomers for Yankees and began to shoot at them. When the Guards realized the cause of their plight, they hastily turned their coats inside out so as to present a whitish color instead of blue; and thus they went through the battle.[4]

But blue was just one of many colors worn by soldiers of '61 and '62. The Emerald Guards of Mobile went to Virginia attired in dark green, a color adopted in honor of old Ireland, the land from which most of the members came.[5] Captain Patterson's company of East Tennesseans dressed themselves in suits of yellow to give meaning to their previously adopted designation of "Yellow Jackets."[6] The Granville Rifles of North Carolina sported uniforms featuring black pants and flaming red flannel shirts that must have made easy targets for Yankees considerably removed.[7] Some of the Maryland companies who espoused the cause of the Confederacy were clothed in uniforms of blue and orange. . . .

These flashy regalia contrasted markedly with other types observed in the streets of Richmond in the summer of 1861. Here might be seen a rugged Texan mounted on a high-pommel saddle, attired in homespun gray, peering disinterestedly from beneath the expansive brim of a western hat; there a native of the southern Appalachian area, ambling along in bearskin blouse, nondescript trousers and rawhide leggings. Occasionally one might encounter "the dirty gray and tarnished silver of the muddy-complexioned Carolinian; the dingy butternut of the lank, muscular Georgian, with its green trimming and full skirts; and the Alabamians from the coast nearly all in blue of a cleaner hue and neater cut."[8]

As the war went into the second and third years clothing became simpler and less diverse. Contributing to this change was the increasing ability of the quartermaster general to meet requisitions made upon the government for uniforms. By the end of 1862 Caleb Huse's purchasing operations had yielded substantial returns in trousers and cloth for coats. Contracts with domestic manufacturers were also beginning, after heartbreaking delays, to achieve a partial degree of fulfillment. In recognition of these developments Congress, on October 8, 1862, passed an act which modified the prior policy of allowing cash payments of fifty dollars a year to soldiers who clothed themselves, and announced the intention of the government to provide the uniform prescribed by regulations. . . .

Company officers were required to keep a record of clothing dispensed—two general issues a year were contemplated, one of winter uniforms in the fall, and the other of summer outfits in the spring—and soldiers who did not draw the full amount allowed were to be credited on the pay roll with the value of articles due them; on the other hand, those who overdrew their allowances were to be charged in like manner with items received in excess of the quantity authorized.[9]

Notwithstanding the intention expressed by the act of October 8, 1862, the clothing issued by government quartermasters deviated considerably from Army Regulations. Blue trousers, for instance, seem to have been the rare exception rather than the rule. Certainly the impression derived from soldier correspondence is that gray was the standard color for trousers as well as coats, and this impression is corroborated by wartime uniforms on display in various Confederate museums. But the cadet gray of 1861 and 1862 gradually gave way, as the blockade drove the South to an increasing dependence on her own resources, to a yellowish brown resulting from the use of dye made of copperas and walnut hulls. This peculiar tint was dubbed butternut, and so wide was its use for uniforms that Confederate soldiers were rather generally referred to by both Yanks and Southerners as "butternuts."[10]

In a few instances at least, undyed outfits were issued by the government. The Second Texas Regiment was the recipient of such an issue a few days before leaving Corinth for Shiloh. When the men beheld the whitish-looking garments exclamations of the most unorthodox character went up on every hand such as "Well, I'll be damn'!" "Don't them things beat hell?" "Do the generals expect us to be killed and want us to wear our shrouds?" After the battle a Federal prisoner was said to have inquired: "Who were them hell cats that went into battle dressed in their graveclothes?"[11] . . .

The intention implied by the Confederate Government in the law of October 8, 1862, of supplying the major portion of clothing for the army was destined to fall far short of fulfillment. The tightening of the blockade and the shortage of specie prevented the importation after 1863 of large quantities from Europe. The failure of importation was offset to a considerable extent by increased production of Southern factories. But the output of many of these establishments was gobbled up by state authorities, who insisted on outfitting their own soldiers and collecting commutation from the central government.

This would have been well enough if the supplies procured by each of the states beyond the needs of her own troops had been made available to Richmond authorities. But overzealous governors like Vance of North Carolina insisted on holding on to huge surpluses against the possible future needs of their own regiments while less fortunate Rebs suffered from deficiencies. North Carolina had forty textile factories in 1864, half as many as all the other Confederate states combined. She claimed the output of these almost exclusively for her own soldiers, despite the fact that she drew large quantities of wool and other raw materials from sister states.[12]

The most damning commentary on the disastrousness of such a shortsighted—though withal "constitutional" and well-meaning—policy is the fact that while Lee complained repeatedly of the raggedness and barefootedness of his men in the war's last winter, Vance hoarded in North Carolina warehouses "92,000 uniforms, great stores of leather

and blankets, and his troops in the field were all comfortably clad."[13]
This was State's Rights carried to its most costly extreme.

The combined—or perhaps it would be more accurate to say competing—efforts of Confederate and state authorities were unable to keep the majority of Confederate soldiers supplied with adequate and comfortable clothing. To meet deficiencies various expedients were invoked by Rebs themselves. One of these was to call on the folks at home. Letters to wives and parents, particularly those written during the winter months, were full of requests for garments of various sorts and for blankets.

In response to these importunities wives, mothers, and sweethearts, in co-operation sometimes with groups of slaves, brought forth spinning wheels and looms from outhouse and attic and set up home factories that rivaled the production of the more elaborate establishments of town and city. Jackets, trousers, hats, shirts, drawers, socks and other articles made by individual women and by soldiers' aid societies were packed in boxes and sent to camp on trains, or carried in small bundles by body servants or comrades on furlough.

Many soldiers preferred homemade clothing to that issued by the government, both for comfort and for durability. An Alabamian, who received garments from his wife regularly, wrote in the spring of 1864:

> "Bettie I send you a couple of shirts and a pair of drawers. Use them as you please. I had rather wear your make. The reason I drew them was that they are so much cheaper than you can make them. You can use them in making clothes for the children."[14]

Soldiers who were short of clothing frequently borrowed the needed articles from messmates or kinsmen. A striking instance of fraternal assistance is revealed by the letter of a Texan to his sister in 1863.

> "Me Joe and Grace all got together yesterday for the first time. Grace was the gladest fellow to see us that ever came a long he . . . is all most naked his Breeches is in strings all he has got fit to ware is a over shirt Joe gave him a par of drass [drawers] & shirt I gave him a par of breeches all I have except what I have on."[15]

When a Reb received fancy additions to his wardrobe from home-folk he was apt to be besieged for loans by socially minded fellows. A Mississippian wrote his mother in the spring of 1864:

"My Hat and boots are the admiration of all the Boys they all want them two of the Boys went out Courting the next day after I got here. I had to loan one my Hat and the other my overskirt."[16]

If a soldier had a little money to spare, he sometimes replenished his wardrobe by purchasing sundry items from comrades who were more amply supplied than himself. Now and then penny-wise Rebs capitalized on the near-nakedness of fellow soldiers by peddling among them at a profit clothing received from homefolk. A Virginian who had just returned from furlough with surplus apparel wrote to his wife:

"I sold my pants, vest, shoes, & drawers for sixtyone dollars so you see I am flush again. . . . You will have to make me more pants and drawers, if you can raise the material make two pair of pants & four pair of drawers & I will have A pair of pants & two pair of drawers for sale in that way will get mine clear . . . if you could make up a good supply of pants vests shirts and drawers, I could be detailed out to come after them."

A postscript was added cautioning her not to "tell any one what good pairs pants will bring in camp if they knew it they would go to peddling in clothes keep dark whether you make any for sale or not."[17] In some portions of the army the practice was followed of selling at auction the clothing of men who died in camp.[18]

A considerable portion of the Rebel clothing deficiency was supplied by the Federals. The cavalry branch of the service, because of its ability to make swift raids into Yankeedom, profited most in this respect. A Mississippian who was not inclined to exaggeration wrote his mother just after Christmas in 1862 that he had recently seen about six thousand cavalrymen pass his post and "every man had a complete Yankee Suit consisting of hats coats pants Jackets and boots."[19]

Infantrymen frequently did well by themselves in the wake of a battle. The writer's great-uncle told of a comrade who lost an arm on the night of the battle of Raymond, Mississippi, attempting to appropriate the uniform of one whom he thought to be a dead Yankee. The practice of reshoeing at the expense of dead and live Yankees was so common that the remark became trite among troops, "All a Yankee is worth is his shoes."[20]

Following the battle of Shiloh a newspaper correspondent wrote from Corinth that "other results of our victory are also everywhere visible. Unless he knew better, a stranger would mistake our army for first rate

Yankees. Fully three-fifths of the men are dressed in Federal hats and overcoats."[21]

The practice of wearing Union uniforms was apt to be disastrous if persisted in during a period of active campaigning. General orders were issued repeatedly enjoining the custom, but seemingly to no greater avail than to have a portion of the forbidden articles laid aside. In many companies the combination of butternut jacket and Yankee pants came to be so prevalent as to be considered in an unofficial way as the standard uniform.[22]

The following general order issued by Forrest in December 1864 indicates one method which was used to make practicable the wearing of captured clothing:

> "All men & officers belonging to this command who have blue yankee overcoats & clothing and who do not have them dyed by the 20th Inst The Coats Especially will be taken from them. . . . Division Commanders will order an inspection on the date above specified and see that this order is complied with. And in an instance when the Inspectors find the coats have not been dyed, they will be taken from the owners and turned over to the Qr M of The Division."[23]

But despite all the exertions of Confederate and state authorities, of soldiers and their families, and the enforced contributions of the Yankees, frazzled uniforms were much in evidence in Rebel ranks after the first half-year of conflict, and as a general rule raggedness increased as the war progressed. Rare indeed was that veteran who did not have occasion in 1863 and 1864 to inform his homefolk of embarrassing circumstances as to the seat of his britches.

"The 16th section of my uniform pants wore out," wrote one Reb to his wife, and another confided to his sister that he had been compelled to buy a new pair of trousers "as I had a 'flag of truce' hanging from a prominent part of my old 'uns."[24] But it remained for a Texan to sum up the situation in general. "In this army," he wrote from near Atlanta in June 1864, "one hole in the seat of the breeches indicates a captain, two holes a lieutenant, and the seat of the pants all out indicates that the individual is a private."[25] . . .

Practice in patching undoubtedly led to improved technique among Rebel seamsters, and some attained such deftness with scissors and needle as to abandon the more prosaic modes of repair for fancy designs. One morning Ben Lambert appeared at roll call displaying on the seat of his britches a large red flannel patch, shaped after the fashion of a heart. This example unloosed a plethora of aesthetic efforts among Lambert's comrades of the Richmond Howitzers, and soon trousers that had a short time before been showing white in the rear were splashed with figures of eagles, horses, cows and cannon. One artist depicted on one hip Cupid holding his bow, and just across on the other, in tribute to the Love God's dead-eye marksmanship, was a heart pierced with an arrow—all done in flaming red cloth.[26] Johnnies would have their fun, at the expense of their woes.

But there were many soldiers who either spurned the use of the needle or else felt unequal to its manipulation. Such men frequently invoked the assistance of women living in the environs of camp or sent tattered garments home for repair. In innumerable instances, however, Rebs took no remedial steps whatever, but simply wore their rags with the splendid indifference of seasoned campaigners.

To this spirit of indifference, indeed, must be attributed much of the raggedness which Confederates suffered. The beginning of almost every march was the occasion of a general discarding of surplus items of clothing, for veteran soldiers made a fetish of traveling light.

The observation of a Georgia captain in early 1863 was widely applicable. "The Company begins to look as ragged as ours ever did," he wrote; "the cause of it is that they have to toat their extra clothing and rather than toat it they wont have it."[27]

The tendency to get rid of extra garments was accentuated during the pressure of battle and of retreat. A Reb who during the withdrawal from the North Carolina coastal area in 1862 had lost everything but the sparse uniform he was wearing wrote significantly to his mother:

> "The fight we had the other day has taught me one thing, and that is never to carry anything more with me than I absolutely need and can carry on my back in case of necessity. It will not do to try to play soldier and gentleman at the same time. . . . You must take it rough."[28]

Doubtless it was this philosophy that caused many Rebs to forego without complaint some of the garments ordinarily deemed indispensable by civilized peoples. "I would like to have a pr socks," wrote a Mississippian to his mother in 1862, but "I can dispense with draw [er]s."[29]

A factor contributing markedly to the unhappy state of soldier wardrobes was the infrequency of launderings. Negro body servants and government-paid washerwomen may have been fairly ample for the laundry needs of the army in the early months of the war, but after 1862 most of the common soldiers had to do their own washing.[30] The situation was further complicated by a widespread scarcity of soap, dating from early in the war. In the summer of 1862 a Reb wrote disgustedly to his mother:

> "Soap seems to have given out entirely in the Confederacy & consequently it is almost impossible to have any clean clothes. I am with out drawers today both pair of mine being so dirty that I cant stand them."[31] . . .

It is not surprising frequently to find in wartime correspondence instances of Rebs going for two, three and four weeks without once removing their shirts, trousers or underclothing. And there were cases of considerably longer duration. A Georgian wrote his wife in 1864 that some of his comrades had gone for two months without stripping, and a Texan testified early in 1865 that "something ner half of the command has not changed shirts for 4 or 5 months."[32] An inevitable consequence of practices such as these was a premature rotting of clothing that could ill be spared.

Deficiencies in clothing varied, of course, from time to time and from organization to organization. North Carolina troops seem generally, as a result of the jealous exertions of their governor, to have fared better than those from other portions of the country. Border state troops probably suffered most of all, on account of inability of their home governments to supplement Confederate issues. An example of the extreme condition to which these orphan regiments might be reduced was the appearance at inspection on a cold November day in 1864 of a group of Missourians dressed in their drawers.[33]

Some articles of clothing were less scarce than others. Of socks, shirts and underclothing the central government seems to have had a fairly ample supply even in the winter of 1864–1865; want of these items must have been largely due, therefore, to failure of transportation or to delinquency of low-ranking quartermasters.[34] Overcoats and blankets were generally hard to get after the first year of war. Of the conflict's last winter a soldier stationed near Petersburg wrote: "I do not remember the issue of a single overcoat, and but a few blankets."[35] An Englishman who visited Lee's army during the Gettysburg campaign observed that many of the soldiers had blankets made of carpet strips, and that these gaily hued coverlets were adapted to use as overcoats in cool or damp weather by the cutting of holes in the middle, through which the men stuck their heads.[36] . . .

But the most pervasive and the most keenly felt of all deficiencies was that of shoes. The Rebel army was a walking army. Soldiers who followed Lee, Jackson, Bragg and other Confederate generals on their long and swift thrusts at the enemy won undying fame for themselves and their leaders. But the expenditure of leather entailed by these arduous marches was tremendous and, as circumstances proved, considerably beyond the producing and purchasing capacities of the South.

Shortage of shoes began to trouble generals and government officials before the war was a year old. Not long after, First Manassas Joseph E. Johnston informed Quartermaster-General A. C. Myers that his army needed shoes. Myers replied that "we have sent to Europe for shoes, and I have officers travelling over all the Confederate States purchasing shoes, making contracts with farmers for leather, and with manufacturers for making leather into shoes." He expressed apprehension, however, that he would not be able to meet the demands of increasing mobilization.[37] His fears proved to be well founded. Several thousand pairs of the European purchase arrived in due time on Confederate shores. Contracts with Southern factories yielded considerably more. But the approach of cool weather in 1862 found troops in decidedly greater need of shoes than they had been the previous year.

Shortly before Lee began his march into Maryland a newspaper correspondent estimated that forty thousand pairs of shoes were needed by the army.[38] This estimate may have been exaggerated, but there can be no doubt that thousands of Rebs failed to participate in the fighting of September 16–17 because the condition of their feet made it impossible for them to march with their comrades.[39] It may easily have been true that the difference between a victory and a draw for Lee at Antietam was his want of a few thousand pairs of shoes.[40] . . .

Congress took cognizance of the deplorable state of affairs by authorizing the detail of two thousand men to make shoes.[41] Extraordinary efforts such as this, plus the reduced wear incident to winter quarters, resulted in a general improvement of the situation in the early months of 1863. But the strenuous campaigns of Gettysburg and Chattanooga played havoc with the government's leather supply, and the winter months of 1863–1864 brought a chorus of complaints from all quarters. An Alabamian wrote to his homefolk from camp on the Rapidan:

"The weather is as cold as the world's charity. I counted out on inspection yesterday, thirty-one men in Battle's Brigade who did not have a sign of a shoe on their feet, yet they are compelled to perform as much duty as those who are well-shod."[42]

A Louisianian serving in the Army of Tennessee noted in his diary of January 3, 1864, that about one-half of the men in his company had refused to do duty on account of being barefooted.[43] In some portions of Lee's army, men gathered up hides from commissary butcheries, traded them for leather, and made their own shoes; and the products of their handwork were said to be considerably better than those obtained from government contractors.[44]

In the Army of Tennessee men tried making moccasins from the raw hides, but results were not satisfactory. One Reb said of his experiment, "I made myself a pair & made a nice Job too they fit Splendid But behold after two or three days drying around the fire they were about two inches too Short behind."[45] Another soldier complained that his rawhide sandals "stretch out at the heel . . . the[y] whip me nearly to death they flop up and down they stink very bad and i have to keep a bush in my hand to keep the flies off of them."[46]

During the early months of 1864 good factory-made shoes were at such a premium that a lieutenant of Johnston's army declared, "It is not safe to pull off shoes & go to sleep or one would wake up minus a pair."[47]

The nadir of deprivation of shoes, and of other clothes as well, seems to have been reached by men who accompanied Hood on the Tennessee campaign during the war's last winter. Many of the troops began the northward movement in November with shoes so worthless that, according to a Reb who went along, they would not endure a week's marching. Consequently hundreds were barefooted before they reached Columbia, Tennessee; and in some brigades, one-fourth of the men marched barefooted over frozen roads from Franklin to Nashville through blasts of sleet and snow, leaving behind them smears of blood.[48]

Retrogression after defeat on December 16 was accompanied by perhaps even greater distress. The rapid marching, necessitated by pressure of Yankee pursuers, took an increasing toll of sole leather. To protect their bleeding feet from the frozen ground men contrived shoes not only of rawhide, but of hats and coat sleeves as well. But these Rebs could still sing, and as they dragged themselves along they lifted their voices in an impromptu adaptation to the old tune "The Yellow Rose of Texas":

"And now I'm going Southward,
   For my heart is full of woe,
I'm going back to Georgia
   To find my 'Uncle Joe.'
You may sing about your dearest maid,
   And sing of Rosalie,
But the gallant Hood of Texas
   Played hell in Tennessee."[49]

And a remnant did go back, to draw in Mississippi some "sorry" government shoes and in the spring many of them followed "Uncle Joe" Johnston into North Carolina to fight their last battle at Bentonville. By their grim perseverance these veterans of the Army of Tennessee and their comrades of other commands, who marched and fought with ever-dwindling protection from rain and snow through four years of war, achieved for soldiers of the Lost Cause a fame no less lustrous than that won by the heroes of Valley Forge.

NOTES

From Bell Irvin Wiley, *The Life of Johnny Reb: The Common Soldier of the Confederacy* (Baton Rouge: Louisiana State University Press, 1978), 108–22. Reprinted by permission.

1. *War of the Rebellion Official Records of the Union and Confederate Armies* (Washington, 1880–1901), series 1, LI, part 2, 15.
2. Ibid., IV, 479; New Orleans *Daily Crescent*, May 4, 1861; F. B. Simkins and J. W. Patton, *The Women of the Confederacy* (Richmond, 1936), 18 ff; "War Reminiscences of Anne Pelham Finlay," typescript, Greenville, Mississippi, Public Library.
3. Randolph H. McKim, "Glimpses of the Confederate Army," F. T. Miller, editor, *Photographic History of the Civil War* (New York, 1911), VIII, 109.
4. Stanley Horn, *The Army of Tennessee* (Indianapolis, 1941), 140–141.
5. Kate Cumming, *A Journal of Hospital Life in the Confederate Army of Tennessee* (Louisville and New Orleans, 1866), 37.
6. H. M. Doak, "Reminiscences," 13, typescript, Tennessee State Library.
7. Oscar W. Blacknall, editor, "Papers of C. C. Blacknall," introduction, typescript, North Carolina Historical Commission.
8. T. C. DeLeon, *Four Years in Rebel Capitals* (Mobile, 1890), 96–97.
9. O. R. series 4, II, 229–230; III, 1039–1040.
10. Southern Historical Society *Papers*, XXXI (1903) 246; E. P. Thompson,

History of the Orphan Brigade (Louisville, 1898), 203; Miller, *op. cit.*, VIII, 120.

11. *Confederate Veteran*, XII (1904), 116. The issue of white uniforms to some conscript outfits caused stigma to be attached to their wear by volunteers. Members of the Twenty-sixth Louisiana had to be threatened with severe punishment before they would don the undyed regalia. Winchester Hall, *The Twenty-sixth Louisiana Infantry* (n.p., 1890), 59–60.

12. *O. R.*, series 4, III, 691–692, 1039–1040.

13. F. L. Owsley, *States Rights in the Confederacy* (Chicago, 1925), 126.

14. John Crittenden to his wife, March 24, 1864, typescript, University of Texas.

15. Frank Moss to his sister, Oct. 28, 1863, manuscript, University of Texas.

16. Jerome Yates to his mother, April 2, 1864, manuscript, Heartman Collection.

17. William H. Routt to his wife, March 13, 1863, manuscript, Confederate Museum, Richmond.

18. E. P. Becton to his wife, Dec. 14, 1862, typescript, University of Texas.

19. J. T. Terrell to his mother, Dec. 29, 1862, manuscript in private possession.

20. Charleston *Daily Courier*, Sept. 3, 1862.

21. Richmond *Daily Dispatch*, April 24, 1862.

22. DeLeon, *op. cit.*, 185.

23. Manuscript among L. M. Nutt Papers, University of North Carolina.

24. J. H. Puckett to his wife, April 15, 1863, manuscript, University of Texas; Thomas Caffey to his sister, Feb. 16, 1863, "War Letters of Thomas Caffey," Montgomery *Advertiser*, May 16, 1909.

25. Sebron Sneed to his wife, June 7, 1864, manuscript, University of Texas.

26. William M. Dame, *From the Rapidan to Richmond* (Baltimore, 1920), 36–37.

27. S. G. Pryor to his wife, Feb. 4, 1863. Typescripts, Georgia Archives.

28. James A. Graham to his mother, March 9, 1862, manuscript, University of North Carolina.

29. Andrew M. Chandler to his mother, Aug. 31, 1862, manuscript photostat in possession of Mrs. Ella Mae Chandler, West Point, Mississippi.

30. Bell Irvin Wiley, *Southern Negroes 1861–1865* (New Haven, 1938), 134.

31. R. W. Waldrop to his mother, Aug. 27, 1862, manuscript, University of North Carolina.

32. J. M. Jordan to his wife, June 27, 1864, typescript, Georgia Archives; T. B. Hampton to his wife, Feb. 3, 1865, typescript, University of Texas.

33. Maj. Henry C. Semple to his wife, Nov. 3, 1864, manuscript, University of North Carolina. Soldiers of the Army of Tennessee thought that partiality in clothing issues was shown by Richmond authorities to troops of Lee's command.

34. O. R., series 1, XLII, part 3, 1268–1269; series 4, III, 1039–1040; Lee to A. P. Hill, Jan. 20, 1865, manuscript, Confederate Museum.

35. J. F. J. Caldwell, *History of Gregg's and McGowan's Brigade* (Philadelphia, 1866), 196–197.

36. Fitzgerald Ross, *A Visit to the Cities and Camps of the Confederate States* (London, 1865), p. 31.

37. O. R., series 1, V, 785.

38. Charleston *Daily Courier*, Sept. 3, 1862.

39. O. R. series 1, XIX, part 2, 590–591.

40. The Richmond *Daily Dispatch* of October 9, 1862, carried a pungent editorial on the subject of clothing for Lee's army. In reference to the Antietam campaign the editor said: "Posterity will scarcely believe that the wonderful campaign which has just ended with its terrible marches and desperate battles, was made by men, one-fourth of whom were entirely barefooted, and one-half of whom were as ragged as scarecrows. . . . We cease to wonder at the number of stragglers, when we hear how many among them were shoeless, with stone bruises on their feet."

41. O. R., series 4, 11, 204.

42. Thomas Caffey to his mother, Nov. 12, 1863. Generals in command were evidently forced to require duty of barefooted men to prevent would-be shirkers from throwing away their shoes to avoid drilling and fighting. See O. R., series 1, XXX, part 4, 715.

43. Anonymous manuscript in Confederate Memorial Hall, New Orleans.

44. Richmond *Enquirer*, April 12, 1864. General Lee complained of the poor quality of some of the shoes issued by government quartermasters during the winter of 1863–1864. O. R., series 1, XXXIII, 1131–1132.

45. O. T. Hanks, manuscript photostat, University of Texas, 78.

46. John H. Hancock to his parents, Nov. 11, 1862, manuscript among Richard D. White Papers, North Carolina Historical Commission.

47. Robert M. Gill to his wife, July 30, 1864, manuscript in author's possession.

48. O. R., series 1, XLV, part 1, 735–736, 747.

49. Robert Selph Henry, *The Story of the Confederacy* (Indianapolis, 1931), 434.

Chapter 9

Fun, Frolics, and Firewater

James I. Robertson, Jr.

James I. Robertson, Jr., received a Ph.D. from Emory University, where he studied with Bell Wiley. Robertson, who now teaches at Virginia Tech, reflected Wiley's influence in his 1988 book Soldiers Blue and Gray, *a study meant to make use of material that was unavailable when Wiley was preparing his accounts. Like Wiley, Robertson divides his book into chapters corresponding to the facets of soldier life, and he largely lets the troops speak for themselves without extensive interpretations; unlike Wiley, Robertson combines Yankees and Confederates into a single volume. This selection describes the ways soldiers responded to one of the paradoxes of army life: liberated from some of the social constraints that limited masculine pleasure seeking, soldiers were nonetheless nostalgic for some of the trappings of home.*

The Civil War was barely a year old when Adam S. Rader of the 28th Virginia wrote from camp: "there is some of the most onerest men here that I ever saw and the most swearing and card playing and fitin and drunkenness that I ever saw at any place." Musician Henry E. Schafer of the 103rd Illinois voiced the same feeling more eloquently. "In our camps wickedness prevails to almost unlimited extent. It looks to me as though some men try to see how depraved they can be. Gambling, Card Playing, Profanity, Sabbath Breaking &c are among the many vices practiced by many of the men. . . . It is indeed wonderful what a demoralizing influence the vices of army life have upon the minds of a great many. It sometimes seems to me that the Almighty would never bless the efforts of our army to put down this rebellion while it is so depraved."[1]

Infrequently, soldiers confessed pleasure with the camp environment. The 4th Georgia's Louis Merz, who died at Antietam Creek, wrote in the war's first spring: "I'm just enjoying myself because the days of men are few and I want to be as merry as long as I can, and when we get home again I [will] make it all up."[2] Yet the overwhelming number of those who wrote letters or kept diaries were repelled by camp behavior: "the more wee see the more wee are convinced that this war is the most damnable curse that ever was brung upon the human family," a young recruit stated. Writing of "the vitiating influences of war," an Alabama private told the homefolk: "Few there are who have escaped the contagious effects of being mixed up with the vile and low. The bad are not reformed while the good are made bad." An Iowa sergeant was just as shocked. "I see enough every day to almost make one curse the race to which he belongs."[3]

An Ohioan correctly analyzed the population of an army camp. "Many of the men had not been much from home, and to say that they were homesick is to state the fact very mildly. Others, throwing off the restraints of home, acted more like wild colts than anything else. A very large majority were, however, steady, earnest men, as reliable in camp as out of it." Private Schafer commented that in service "almost every one thinks more about the best way to kill time than anything else."[4] Hence, the homesick, the "wild colts," and the earnest men spent the long inactive months in a multitude of camp activities. Most of them were peaceful in intent; some of them were not.

Letter-writing. . . . occupied many idle hours. So did reading—among those who could read. Printed matter was more in evidence in Northern army camps because reading materials were more available and the literacy rate was much higher. *Harper's Weekly* and *Frank Leslie's Illustrated Newspaper* were by far the most popular pictorial newspapers in the Union ranks, while the *American Review* and *Atlantic* were the more widely read magazines. Confederates enjoyed such serials as the *Southern Illustrated News, Southern Literary Messenger,* and *Field and Fireside. Waverly Magazine* was always in demand for its personal ads placed by young women seeking "a soldier correspondent."

The book in a revered class by itself in any Civil War army was the Bible. Chaplains and colporteurs alike scoured every outlet to keep soldiers supplied with testaments. Yet there were never enough to meet the demand. A few soldiers displayed a fondness for the classics, and they read Shakespeare or works in Latin and Greek. The ones who appreciated good literature, however, were so small in number as to appear out of place. Of the morale-building books that appeared in print during the war, the most memorable was Edward Everett Hale's 1863 story, *The Man without a Country.*

Those reading materials that generally flooded an army were twenty-five-cent thrillers, Beadle's famous "Dime Novels," and picture books offering "spirited and spicy scenes." An Indiana soldier thought such paperbacks, "miserable" and "worthless," but he added that they "were sold by the thousands." While some field missionaries reported disgustingly that "licentious books," and "obcene pictures" were to be found in encampments, more men North and South simply read what was available. A Baptist missionary observed early in the war that "the soldiers here are *starving* for reading matter. They will read anything." Charles Ross of the 11th Vermont gave credence to that statement. He once noted in his diary: "Have been reading all day in a bok I got of the Chaplin. It is a history of Missiens on the Haley island in the north sea."[5] . . .

Next to letter-writing, music was the most popular diversion found in the armies of the 1860s. Men left for war with a song on their lips; they sang while marching or waiting behind earthworks; they hummed melodies on the battlefield and in the guardhouse; music swelled from every nighttime bivouac. Singing was such a natural release of emotion that occasionally men hidden on outpost duty endangered themselves by raising their voices in song. It is hardly surprising, therefore, that no other event in the nation's history produced more enduring melodies than the Civil War. Never since has music been so integral a part of American military affairs.

Brass bands accompanied many units into service at the war's first year, and most of them were a joy to hear. A Midwesterner termed the musicians of the 8th New York "the gayest band I have ever seen. Their music fairly made me take the double shuffle right on the parade ground, before I thought where I was."[6] Often, however, the quality of the musicians was less than commendable. The scarcity of instruments, limited talent among band members, and weariness from campaigning led to inferior renditions on occasion. At the same time, many men possessed of good musical ability preferred instead to shoulder a musket alongside comrades rather than to defend home and country with a cornet.

As a result, an English officer visiting in Texas wrote of hearing one Confederate band "braying discordantly," while another Britisher observed that the performance of most bands was "wretched" and their "dismal noises an intolerable nuisance." Robert Moore of the 17th Mississippi once wrote that his regiment's band "has been practicing for more than a week but are not learning very fast. I think I am getting very tired of hearing the noise they make."[7] . . .

Regimental and brigade bands were nevertheless always welcomed by encamped soldiers in search of any entertainment. Yet for the most part, music in Civil War camps came from individual musicians. Any sizable body of men contained at least one fiddler of ability. Consequently, such foot-stomping tunes as "Arkansas Traveler," "The Goose Hangs High," "Billy in the Low Grounds," "Oh Lord, Gals, One Friday," and "Hell Broke Loose in Georgia" could be heard regularly. Many other soldiers were proficient with the harmonica, Jew's harp, or banjo. These performers would make music at the least invitation, while any two men could and usually did form an impromptu chorus.

Dancing was similarly popular with the generations of that day. In the autumn of 1862, a recruit in the 107th New York wrote his sweetheart: "I hope you will be favored with a few Hops this Winter So as to Keep in practice for I want to have one good old Dance when I get out of this War." Men in camp oftentimes staged company or regimental dances. They especially liked the cotillion and the Virginia reel. A Tarheel soldier described one of the all-male dances: "A handkerchief, if you had one, or a rag, of which there was no lack, tied around the left arm denoted the lady. We would trip the light fantastic toe on the greensward with as much zest as at home in the dance hall with the girls, but not with the same pleasure, affection and love, defined by one of our boys as 'an inward impressibility and an outward all-over-ishness.' "[8]

Civil War armies were deeply sentimental. This was so in great part because the overriding emotion of Johnny Rebs and Billy Yanks alike was loneliness. On a long march, regiments often broke out in song. The singing would eventually stop. Then, all along the ranks would come the cry: "I want to go home!"[9]

The truly popular songs in camp were not stirring airs that the folks back home (and generations of Americans thereafter) sang inspirationally. Rather, they were melodies with tones of sadness and homesickness.

The all-time favorite of Civil War troops was "Home, Sweet Home." Early in December 1862, two mighty armies gathered at Fredericksburg to do battle. Only the Rappahannock River separated the opposing hosts. One evening a Confederate band came to the front and played "Dixie." Immediately, across the way, a Union band responded with "John Brown's Body." The Confederates "retaliated" with "The Bonnie Blue Flag" and received "The Star-Spangled Banner" in return. The music ceased; silence descended over the battle arena. Then a lone Union bugler played the notes of "Home, Sweet Home." A New Hampshire soldier commented: "As the sweet sounds rose and fell on the evening air, . . . all listened intently, and I don't believe there was a dry eye in all those assembled thousands."[10] . . .

Each side had its own group of patriotic and happy melodies.

For the embattled South, and despite the fact that the song was written by Northerner Daniel Decatur Emmett for use in minstrel shows, "Dixie" became an unofficial national anthem. "It is marvelous with what wild-fire rapidity this tune of 'Dixie' has spread over the whole South," an Alabama recruit stated in May 1861. "Considered as an intolerable nuisance when first the streets re-echoed it from the repertoire of wandering minstrels, it now bids fair to become the musical symbol of a new nationality, and we shall be fortunate if it does not impose its very name on our country."[11]

"The Bonnie Blue Flag" ran a strong second in Confederate popularity. Western troops were fond of "The Yellow Rose of Texas." To belittle both the Southern diet and the soldiers from one particular state, Confederates teasingly sang:

> Just before the battle, the General hears a row.
> He says the Yanks are coming, I hear their rifles now.
> He turns around in wonder, and what do you think he sees,
> The Georgia militia, eating goober peas.

Union soldiers' letters and diaries make it clear that "John Brown's Body" (which gained stanzas on a seemingly monthly basis as the war progressed) was a beloved marching song.[12] In November 1861, Julia Ward Howe wrote new lyrics so as to give the majestic melody more dignity and power. Soldiers were slow in accepting the new words, but the resultant "Battle Hymn of the Republic" is the war's greatest musical legacy. . . .

One new and unforgettable bugle call emerged from the Civil War.

Federal General Daniel Butterfield enjoyed music. Shortly after the war commenced, he invented a bugle call for assembling his troops. The following spring, while campaigning on the Virginia peninsula, Butterfield summoned his bugler and whistled for him a little tune he had been muddling over of late. The general and the musician played with the tune, changed a little here and there, and then the bugler wrote the music on the back of an envelope. Thereafter, Butterfield directed, the tune was to signal lights-out at day's end, for he thought its melody denoted tired men settling down for sleep.

The bugler played the new song. Other buglers throughout the Union army picked up the tune. In time, it went west with troops. It soon became regulation. It has remained so since, for "Taps" does indeed signify the weary settling down to peaceful rest.[13]

A number of regiments gave their attention and love to mascots. "Old Abe," the bald eagle of the 8th Wisconsin, was the most famous of all. The 10th Maine had a dog, "Major," who "behaved well under fire, barking fiercely, and keeping up a steady growl from the time it went in [to battle] till we came out." The 104th Pennsylvania adopted a Newfoundland dog, a cat, and a tamed raccoon. Few of these animals survived the battles of which their regiment were a part.[14]

Physical activities were much in evidence at every encampment. Boxing, broad jumping, wrestling, footracing, hurdling, wheelbarrow racing, and occasional free-for-all scuffles were all popular pastimes. Of competitive sports, none was more visible in warm months than baseball. It was new and easy to play. High scores were the general rule; for even though the ball was soft, the base runner had to be hit by a thrown or batted ball before he was out. In one game between teams from the 13th Massachusetts and 104th New York, the Bay Staters won by a 66–20 score.

Another summertime diversion was animal chasing. A rabbit scurrying through a camp would create a riot of excitement. Any small mammal attracted attention. On November 4, 1861, Private Moore of the 17th Mississippi recorded in his diary: "This is Sunday in camp & a number of the boys are amusing theselves after squirrels. They have caught 3 or 4. I never heard such a noise in my life. Cpt. Duff was up a tree with a stick after a squirrel."[15] . . .

In wintertime, snowball fights became familiar sights. They generally were contests between individuals or small groups, but several "snow wars" of regimental and even brigade proportions took place. Snowball battles, a Virginia private observed, "were sometimes fought with such vigor as to disable the combatants. The result of such a battle was the capture of the defeated party's cooking utensils, and any food that might be contained in them." A particularly severe engagement erupted between the 2nd and 12th New Hampshire. In the action (according to a participant), "tents were wrecked, bones broken, eyes blacked, and teeth knocked out—all in *fun*."[16]

A good fistfight always attracted a large crowd, with betting on the outcome oftentimes spirited. Officers were inclined to ignore minor altercations between men and to let them settle their differences. Authorities usually intervened only if insubordination, striking an officer, or some other military violation was involved. Given such laxity, soldiers of a belligerent bent were quick to throw a punch when provoked.

Less athletically inclined soldiers sometimes concentrated on handiwork. This became a common diversion in hospitals and prisons as well as in camps. The men carved pipes from brierroot. Bones, sea shells, and soft wood were also raw materials for rings and other ornaments. A number of men became quite proficient at the art. An Indiana soldier sent two rings home in the space of a month, with one of the rings having an elaborately etched American eagle on its face.[17]

Checkers and chess were the most popular two-man games. Any large encampment had at least one Masonic lodge. Literary societies and debating clubs originated among the more educated men, with formal discussions ranging far afield in subject matter. A private debate was once held on the question, "Which Has the Most Influence on Man, to-wit Money or Women?" The latter argument was proclaimed the winner. One group in the Richmond Howitzers specialized in reversing the normal patterns of life. Known as the "Independent Battalion of Fusiliers," it met weekly and enjoyed such pursuits as: "In an advance, always [be] in the rear—in a retreat, always in front. Never do anything that you can help. The chief aim of life is to rest."[18]

Theatrical productions were sources of pleasure for large numbers of soldiers. Professional casts made an occasional visit into the field, but camp productions were the usual and more enjoyed of the presentations. The 48th New York and 45th Massachusetts acquired wide reputations for excellent stage plays on the Northern side. A troup from the Washington Artillery of New Orleans staged several productions during long wintry months. Its satires were so popular as to attract overflow audiences that included "some ladies from the adjacent country."[19]

Sometimes the presentations amounted to a community theater. At Plymouth, North Carolina, in 1862, a New York artillery regiment built a theater, the 5th Rhode Island constructed the stage scenery, and the 23rd Massachusetts supplied the cast. The audience consisted of all Union troops in the area. "Imagine Juliet," a Pennsylvanian commented, "with a sun-browned face, fierce mustache, and close-cropped hair, in a blue dress-coat, baggy blue pantaloons, and heavy brogans, wailing out her grief at the death of Romeo! Or Claud Melnotte saying to a fellow dressed in the same fashion, except a pair of cavalry boots in the place of brogans: 'We read no books that are not tales of love; we'll have no friends that are not lovers.' "[20] . . .

One of the most prevalent diversions in camp were bull sessions. Topics ranged from politics and the progress of the war to gossip about individual soldiers, reminiscences of childhood, boasts of the beauty of a wife or sweetheart, tales of pleasure from a visit to a "center of sin," and speculations about the future. The men of blue and gray utilized a variety of slang expressions that were a product of the ruralism from which most of the soldiers came. A brave soldier, for example, was "cool as a man hoeing corn" or "so cool water froze in his canteen." The panicky soldier was one who "jumped up and down like a bob-tailed dog in high oats." If only frightened, the man "mumbled like a treed coon." Asking a compatriot to have a drink was an offer to "change his breath." Occasionally, unknown words came forth—such as one soldier admitting: "I was squashmolished;" and another confessing: "I flumixed right in front of him."[21]

Many soldiers, related a private in the 10th Illinois, "would reel off yarns by the yard of their adventures both here and elsewhere, and build air castles, without number, as to what great things they would do when this cruel war was over." Stretching the truth became a source of pride. A Georgia private once noted: "Frank Reed wrote a letter home to Ben Cooper and if Frank cannot beat any man lying then I give it up. He wrote a right smart about me and made it a heap worse then it really is."[22]

Spreading rumors was a natural outgrowth of such conversation. "Every one tries to see what kind of rumor he can start," a member of the 21st Virginia stated, "so when our bodys are still we have our minds puzzled and harrassed by things from the reliable man." It was the same on the Northern side. "In camp," an Iowan stated, " 'Rumor' furnishes the morning and the evening news—some of it well founded, much of it baseless and imaginary."[23]

A Massachusetts soldier summarized the general course of a rumor. "After supper the men gathered around the fires for a smoke and to listen to the gossip of the regiment. It frequently happens that someone will invent a story, requesting the strictest secrecy, in order that it may travel the faster. In the course of twenty-four hours or so it will return, not exactly as it went forth, but so enlarged and exaggerated that you could scarcely recognize the original. Frequent repetition of this amusement very soon created such disbelief in camp stories, that it was difficult to get one well started except by the exercise of considerable ingenuity."[24] . . .

Some camp humor in the 1860s might appear adolescent by modern standards, yet in view of the limited recreational outlets for Civil War troops, anything that offered a laugh was eagerly sought. Suddenly, on a dull day, a soldier would loudly mimic a cow, donkey, or chicken—and, like echoes, hundreds of voices all over the camp would respond in similar sounds. These vocal exercises became very popular occurrences at nighttime. After all the men had bedded down and supposedly were reaching for sleep, one man would begin making loud noises. The chain reaction in the dark would then begin. A regiment quickly "represented the entire animal creation," a New Hampshire private wrote, and sometimes for hours "men together howled, crowed, bleated, barked, roared, squealed, yelled, screamed, sung, and laughed to the limit of vocal powers."[25]

Soldiers on both sides were chronic teasers. "The army laughs far more than it weeps," New Englander Millett Thompson asserted. "Camp jokes are common property." Visitors to army camp were popular prey. A civilian wearing one of the stovepipe hats fashionable in that era was likely to be greeted with: "Come down out of that hat and join the soldier-boys, and help whip the Yankees!" Other men would pick up the shout and add another, such as: "Come down! Come down! I know you are up there! I see your legs!" Should a gullible visitor enter camp and innocently ask the location, for example, of Company B, somewhere down the line would come the reply: "Here's Company B!" followed by dozens of the same shout from all over the encampment.[26] . . .

Practical jokes on compatriots were as frequent as drill. Hiding a musket, or stripping a man's tent while he was absent, were mild pranks. In wintertime, covering a chimney with boards was a sure bet to send the occupants of the hut choking and cursing into the cold air—and to a chorus of laughs and catcalls. Similarly, some jokesters would take several rounds of ammunition, place them inside a paper bag which, tied to a string, was lowered down the chimney of a log hut. In short time, several explosions would follow, and chaos inside momentarily prevailed. . . .

One recorded prank almost had fatal consequences. Members of the 103rd Illinois decided to take advantage of Mike Augustine, who thoroughly enjoyed smoking his pipe. They found the pipe half-full of tobacco and promptly laced the tobacco with gunpowder. Augustine returned to his tent and commenced smoking. A messmate told what happened next: "he said it was pleasant to have the privelige of taking a good old smoke, pretty soon it (the powder) ignited and blowed the fire & tobacco up in his face set his hair on fire, he jumped up leaped out of the tent, he flew around . . . I never laughfed so much in my life, the blamed fool thought some buddy had throwed a cartridge from the chimney."[27] . . .

Too often ignored in the literature is the seamier side of camp life. It beclouded every encampment. Peter Wilson of the 14th Iowa stated to his father after two years in service: "There is no mistake but the majority of soldiers are a hard set. It would be hard for you to imagine anything worse than they are. They have every temptation to do wrong and if a man has not firmness enough to keep from the excesses common to soldiers he will soon be as bad as the worst."[28]

The men of blue and gray were, in the main, a robust, plain-speaking and earthy folk. Much of army life in the 1860s aroused displeasure and frustrations. As a result, "profanity of the worst form from morning to night" characterized any gathering of troops. In June, 1862, Mississippi soldier T. J. Koger told his wife: "One of my greatest annoyances is my proximity to one tent of the Co. next [to] me, Co. F, in which are 9 or 10 [of] the most vile, obcene blackguards that could be raked up this side [of] the bad place, outside of a jail or penitentiary. From early morn to dewey eve there is one uninterrupted flow of the dirtiest talk I ever heard in my life. . . . those fellows have 'had no raising.' " A Union recruit confided in his journal: "Around me is the gibber of reckless men & I am compelled to Listen day and night to their profanity, filthy talk and vulgar songs. I have some conception how Lot felt in Sodom when he had to listen to and be cursed by the filthy conversation of the wicked."[29]

Some generals issued orders of admonition against profanity, and

Union army regulations expressly forbade it under fine of one dollar per offense. Such directives went against the tide of army behavior and were futile gestures. Only occasionally did a soldier express remorse over his language. When a member of an Ohio company illegally shot a buzzard, the lieutenant in the company called the men together and verbally fired "sulphurous expletives, the use of which is strictly forbidden by the Bible." A short while later, the officer again formed the company and "made a full apology for his lapse from self-control." The men cheered this free confession.[30] . . .

Gambling was almost as common among Johnny Rebs and Billy Yanks as profanity. It certainly was a universal time-killer in every camp. Betting was always in evidence at horse races, cockfights, boxing and wrestling matches, athletic contests, raffles, and any other competition that lent itself to waging money. Dice games were always popular, with "craps" heading the list. Close behind was "sweet-cloth" (or "bird-cage"), in which players bet on the various numbers that might appear when three dice were rolled from a cup. The man who had guessed the correct total beforehand won the pot.

Card games—"throwing the papers," they were sometimes called— were the overwhelmingly prevalent forms of gambling. It would not be too much of an exaggeration to paraphrase a biblical passage and state that "when two or three soldiers were gathered together, there did a deck of cards make its appearance among them and they did proceed to exchange their meager earnings." Virginian Alexander Hunter was convinced that five of every six soldiers played cards, "and some gambled day and night; draw poker of course being the game. When out of money, a man stayed in the game by resorting to the use of 'O. P.'s (order on the paymaster)."[31] . . .

So prevalent was gambling by 1864 that the Army of the James was known among Federals as the "Army of the Games." Officers as well as privates could be seen in camp "taking a twist at the tiger." Draw poker was the chief card game, but there were others: twenty-one, faro, euchre, keno, and a contest dubbed "chuck-a-luck." In February 1863, John T. Smith of the 13th Alabama solemnly informed his family: "You ought to hear your pious preacher curse. And you ought to see him bet on chuck-luck and farrer. Poor boy, I fear he is "forever fallen" from his high estate."[32]

Strict rules against gambling existed in the armies, and from time to time authorities sought to control the practice. General James H. Lane warned his North Carolinians that "gambling in this Brigade is prohibited and those caught at it will be severely punished."[33] The usual punishment was extra duty and forfeiture of a month's pay. So rarely was the prohibition enforced, however, that soldiers placed bets on the outcome of the cases involving men who were arraigned. No one seems to have regarded gambling as a serious offense. In February 1864, Federal General John C. Cleveland issued a directive: "Gambling within the limits of this division is prohibited. The attention of brigade and regimental commanders is called to the suppression of this evil."

Massachusetts soldiers read the order and "immediately concluded that the 'old man' had been 'roasted' the night before by some of his brigade and regimental commanders."[34]

The one development that could bring an abrupt halt to gambling was the call to battle. Men would promptly throw away cards, dice, and other gambling instruments so that, if wounded or killed, no "passports to sin" would be found on their persons. Avid gamblers could then be seen intently reading their Bibles as they awaited the command to form ranks.[35] Such repentance was generally short-lived. The more ardent gamblers who survived the battle would rush frantically into woods and fields in search of the discarded items.

A "minor sin" among an ever growing number of Civil War soldiers was the use of tobacco. Sutlers normally had a plentiful supply, both for chewing and for smoking, and it was moderately priced. If a youth had never been addicted to the use of tobacco at home, it required but a short period after enlistment for him to acquire a taste for the weed. Moreover, a Pennsylvania chewer observed, "the appetite always increases with the scarcity."[36]

A member of the 5th New York recalled how the men customarily shared the contents of packages from home. Yet "if there were any exception to this generosity, it would be in the case of tobacco; that was jealously guarded. It is said that many a man who was the fortunate recipient of a package or a plug of tobacco would carefully secrete it, and walk half a mile or more to a friendly patch of woods, that he might take a 'chew' unobserved. If known to be the possessor of such a luxury, his stock would be exhausted before he was an hour older."[37]

When tobacco was not available, soldiers resorted to a number of unsatisfactory substitutes. White-oak bark or dried tea leaves came into use regularly. Billy Yanks also learned to smoke coffee. "The fragrance is rather agreeable than otherwise," one man stated. "How the Yankees did enjoy smoking the Rebel tobacco!" Virginia Alexander Hunter exclaimed. "At the North they sold the soldiers a vile compound made of chickory, cabbage and sumac leaves ground together and christened tobacco. It burned the tongue, parched the throat, and almost salivated the consumer."[38] . . .

What triggered genuinely unpredictable behavior in army camps was consumption of alcohol.

Overimbibing in civilian life drove an untold number of men into the armies. Peter Welsh was a case in point. In his first letter to his wife after enlisting in the 28th Massachusetts, Welsh confessed: "you know i never would have left you only i was crazy from that acursed misfortune i fell intoo however, you need not be afraid of my drinking now for there is no licker alowed in the army nor no person is alowed to sell to soldiers and that is much the best."[39]

Welsh either was reassuring his wife with falsehoods, or else he was incredibly ignorant of in-ranks behavior. "Whiskey was the most troublesome enemy the army had to fight" in camp, a Pennsylvania officer asserted. "Through the instrumentality of 'red eye' and 'tribulated tanglefoot,' many a good fellow was brought to grief." No one evil so much obstructed an army "as the degrading vice of drunkenness," General George McClellan stated in 1862. "It is impossible to estimate the benefits that would accrue to the service from . . . total abstinence from intoxicating liquors. It would be worth 50,000 men to the armies of the United States."[40]

Thousands of soldiers had a far different perspective of the influence of whiskey. Removal of home restraints, the desire to be "one of the boys," the rationale that drinking in the army was first excusable and then necessary, loneliness, uncertainty about the future—these were some of the major factors that explain the high incidence of drinking in Civil War armies. "I can't get Liquor of any sort to drink" the 24th Virginia's John H. Morgan told his sister. "If I had some I think it would be an advantage to me sometimes." A member of the 13th Massachusetts was more philosophical. "The life of the common soldier is such an irksome guard that it is not to be wondered that he welcomes anything that will put a polish on the hard surface of his daily duties. There was nothing that so effectually removed the wrinkles from 'grim-visaged war' as a noggin of old rye."[41]

What created a problem, however, was overimbibing. A soldier in the 4th Louisiana wrote of a messmate: "I never knew before that Clarence was so much addicted to drinking. If he had been as fond of his mother's milk, as he is of whiskey, he would have been awful hard to wean." Ira Gillaspie of the 11th Michigan wrote from Kentucky in 1862: "One Tomey Crow was put in the guard house to keep until he gits sober. He is as tite as you pleas. I felt sorey for the oald fellow for shure. His oald wife died back in Mich. and he was acrying."[42]

Excessive drinking occurred more often in the Federal ranks because Billy Yank received periodic rations of whiskey, they were more frequently encamped near large cities, and they had more money with which to purchase beverages. In the early stages of the war, however, liquor was readily available in any locale. A recruit in the 4th South Carolina told how the trip from home to camp inspired much drinking. "It seems that every man in the regiment mistook himself for Commander-in-Chief of the regiment. Whiskey was plentiful and cheap; every man had as much as he wanted, and a great many had a great deal more than they needed."[43] . . .

Adding to the evil was the fact that being intoxicated was not a punishable military offense. However, just as in the case of profanity, any misconduct resulting from liquor could result in a military trial. Captain Joseph Newell of the 10th Massachusetts remembered one comical incident. "General [Don Carlos] Buell, upon riding up, left his horse in charge of a Company A man, while he went inside. The man, thinking the opportunity a good one to secure a hasty drink, jumped upon the horse's back and started for Graves' store, a mile away, the general's staff in hot pursuit. As the general's horse naturally made the best time, the man had secured his drink, and was on his way back, when he was overhauled by the provost guard. . . . For this little freak, the soldier had to perform a week's penance, mounted on the head of a barrel, carrying on his back a knapsack of sand."[44]

Most of the whiskey that made its way into camps was considered "mean" in those days and would be adjudged vile by modern standards. What was inside a bottle varied between raw, rough, and unknown. It contained a taste, and packed a wallop, that few men ever forgot. A soldier in the 14th Indiana analyzed one issue of whiskey as a combination of "bark juice, tar-water, turpentine, brown sugar, lamp-oil, and alcohol." Massachusetts cavalryman Ben Crowninshield recalled that the commissary whiskey "was new and fiery, rough and nasty to take."[45] . . .

A principal reason why drunkenness among the troops could not be effectively controlled was the prevalence of the same sin at officer level.

"The company is going down the hill," a private in the 2nd Michigan wrote his wife in the war's first winter. "The Capt. is *dead drunk* more than half his time. He doesn't get out of his tent to take command of the company more than two days in the week." Writing of an 1862 skirmish in Kentucky, an Illinois soldier made the simple statement: "Major Mellinger was so drunk that he fell off his horse." On one occasion an intoxicated Union corps commander walked straight into a tree in front of his tent, and then had to be restrained from arresting the officer of the guard on charges of felonious assault.[46] . . .

After soldiers had overimbibed sufficiently to dull common sense, fights inevitably followed. In December 1861, several members of the 5th New Jersey rejoined their regiment at a dramatic moment. "By the time we arrived the whiskey had begun to operate and a fight had commenced between two officers who were jealous of each other. Swords were drawn and sheathed again without any whiskey being spilt. This started the ball rolling between two companies and a regular old-fashioned free fight was the consequence for about half an hour, during which bloody noses and black eyes were freely given and received."[47]

Fatalities from drunkenness were not uncommon. A member of the 129th Illinois informed the homefolk in November, 1863: "One of the boys in the company died day before yesterday. He got into a row and got stabd so that he died in two days after. He was a tip top solder only he could get on a spree once in a while." Also in the Western theater, Sergeant Boyd of the 15th Iowa once wrote solemnly in his diary: "Col. Dewey of the 23d Iowa is *dead*. Old Whiskey at last laid him *out* as it is laying out many a thousand other men in this Army. It is killing more than the Confederates are killing."[48] . . .

Several regiments organized temperance societies in an effort to abolish the widespread consumption of whiskey. "The cause needs to be agitated in the army," Alburtus Dunham of the 129th Illinois declared, "for there is a great many that never drank a drop at home [who will] return tipplers, if they stay long."[49] Yet temperance movements almost without exception were short-lived undertakings that ended in failure.

Drinking, cursing, gambling, and similar vices were always present in camps North and South. They were escape vehicles from both horror and loneliness. All too quickly, a Billy Yank from Massachusetts explained, soldiering "was no longer an enthusiasm, nor a consciously difficult endurance; it had become ordinary every-day life . . ."[50]

Most Civil War soldiers who indulged freely in raucous camp activities just as freely relinquished them on returning home at war's end. Every army has its quota of rogues and weaklings, to be sure; but the evidence is overwhelming that the majority of Confederates and Federals were conscientious, devoted men possessed of simple but indelible virtues. They sought to do the best they could in an atmosphere over which they had no control. How well they met hardships and temptations during long months in camp varied with the individual. Nevertheless, an Iowa private spoke for all of them—indeed, for soldiers of all ages— when he declared: "There is one thing certain, the Army will either make a man better or worse morally speaking."[51]

NOTES

From James I. Robertson, Jr., *Soldiers Blue and Gray* (Columbia: University of South Carolina Press, 1988), 81–101. Reprinted by permission.

1. Adam S. Rader to Simon Rader, May 7, 1862, letter in the possession of James I. Robertson, Jr.; William A. Schafer to wife, Jan. 18, 1863, Schaeffer Papers, in possession of William A. Schaeffer III, Houston, TX.

2. Chattahoochee Valley Historical Society, *War Was the Place: A Centennial Collection of Confederate Soldier Letters* (Chambers County, AL: The Society, 1961), 20. A similar expression of contentment is in Nancy Niblack Baxter, *Gallant Fourteenth* (Traverse City, IN: Study Center Press, 1980), 36.

3. Joseph T. Glatthaar, *The March to the Sea and Beyond* (New York: New York University Press, 1985), 93; John T. Smith to family, Feb. 1, 1863, letter in possession of Melvin M. Scott, Falls Church, VA; Cyrus F. Boyd, *The Civil War Diary of Cyrus F. Boyd, Fifteenth Iowa Infantry, 1861–1863* Iowa City: State Historical Society of Iowa, 1953), 24. See also James I. Robertson, *Tenting Tonight: The Soldier's Life* (Alexandria, VA: Time-Life Books, 1984), 56.

4. L. W. Day, *Story of the One Hundred and First Ohio Infantry* (Cleveland: W. M. Bayne Printing Co., 1894), 19; Henry E. Schafer to wife, Apr. 9, 1865, Schaeffer Papers, in possession of Mrs. D. K. Brown, Vinton, VA.

5. Asbury L. Kerwood, *Annals of the Fifty-seventh Regiment Indiana Volunteers* (Dayton, OH: W. J. Shuey, 1868), 188–89; *Religious Herald*, May 8, 1862; Charles Ross, "Diary of Charles Ross," *Vermont History* XXX (1962), 135.

6. George H. Otis, *The Second Wisconsin Infantry* (Dayton, OH: Morningside, 1984), 135.

7. Arthur J. L. Fremantle, *Three Months in the Confederate States* (London: William Blackwood and Sons, 1863), 71; [Thomas E. Caffey] *Battle-fields of the South, by an English Combatant* (London: Smith, Elder and Co., 1863), II, 101;

Robert Moore, *A Life for the Confederacy* (Jackson, TN: McCowat-Mercer Press, 1959), 66.

8. Edwin Weller, *A Civil War Courtship: The Letters of Edwin Weller from Antietam to Atlanta* (Garden City, NY: Doubleday & Company), 14; William A. Smith, *The Anson Guards: Company C, Fourteenth Regiment North Carolina Volunteers, 1861–1865* (Charlotte: Stone Publishing Co., 1914), 163.

9. Robert Tilney, *My Life in the Army: Three Years and a Half with the Fifth Army Corps, Army of the Potomac, 1862–1865* (Philadelphia: Ferris & Leach, 1912), 53.

10. Leander W. Cogswell, *A History of the Eleventh New Hampshire Regiment, Volunteer Infantry, in the Rebellion War, 1861–1865* (Concord: Republican Press Assn., 1891), 64. For similar incidents, see Sheldon B. Thorpe, *The History of the Fifteenth Connecticut Volunteers in the War for the Defense of the Union, 1861–1865* (New Haven: Price, Lee & Adkins Co., 1893), 41; Marcus B. Toney, *The Privations of a Private* (Nashville: M. E. Church, South, 1907), 73.

11. Henry Hotze, *Three Months in the Confederate Army* (University: University of Alabama Press, 1952), 22.

12. For example, see S. Millett Thompson, *Thirteenth Regiment of New Hampshire Volunteer Infantry in the War of the Rebellion, 1861–1865* (New Haven: Price, Lee & Adkins Co., 1893), 106, 235.

13. Oliver W. Norton, *Army Letters, 1861–1865* (Chicago: O. L. Deming, 1903), 327–28.

14. John M. Gould, *History of the 1st-10th-29th Maine,* (Portland: S. Berry, 1871), 245; William W. H. Davis, *History of the 104th Pennsylvania Regiment, from August 22nd, 1861, to September 30th, 1864* (Philadelphia: J. B. Rogers, 1866), 14–15.

15. Moore, *A Life for the Confederacy*, 82.

16. Royal W. Figg, *"Where Men Only Dare to Go": The Story of a Boy Company (C.S.A.)* (Richmond: Whittet & Shepperson, 1885), 100–1; Martin A. Haynes, *A History of the Second Regiment, New Hampshire Volunteer Infantry, in the War of the Rebellion* (Lakeport, NH: The Author, 1896), 212.

17. E. H. C. Cavins to wife, Sept. 25, 1861, Cavins Collection, Indiana Historical Society.

18. William M. Dame, *From the Rapidan to Richmond and the Spotsylvania Campaign* (Baltimore: Green-Lucas Co., 1920), 23.

19. Figg, *"Where Men Only Dare to Go,"* 95.

20. James A. Emmerton, *A Record of the Twenty-third Regiment Mass. Vol. Infantry in the War of the Rebellion, 1861–1865* (Boston: W. Ware & Co., 1886), 161; John L. Smith, *History of the Corn Exchange Regiment, 118th Pennsylvania Volunteers, from Their First Engagement at Antietam to Appomattox* (Philadelphia: J. L. Smith, 1888), 378.

21. Jay Monaghan, "Civil War Slang and Humor," *Civil War History* III (1957), 125–33.

22. Ephraim A. Wilson, *Memoirs of the War* (Cleveland: W. M. Bayne Printing Co., 1893), 171; Chattahoochee Society, *War Was the Place*, 20.

23. John W. Worsham, *One of Jackson's Foot Cavalry* (Jackson, TN: Mc-Cowat-Mercer Press, 1964), xxi–xxii; George Crooke, *The Twenty-first Regiment of Iowa Volunteer Infantry* (Milwaukee: King, Fowle & Co., 1891), 17.

24. Charles E. Davis, *Three Years in the Army: The Story of the Thirteenth Massachusetts Volunteers from July 16, 1861, to August 1, 1864* (Boston: Estes and Lauriat, 1894), 29.

25. Thompson, *13th New Hamsphire*, 2.

26. Ibid., 542; Figg, *"Where Men Only Dare to Go,"* 98.

27. Henry Orendorff, *We Are Sherman's Men: The Civil War Letters of Henry Orendorff* (Macomb: Western Illinois University, 1986), 30.

28. Peter Wilson, "Peter Wilson in the Civil War," *Iowa Journal of History and Politics* XL (1942), 402–3.

29. John K. Bettersworth, ed., *Mississippi in the Confederacy* (Baton Rouge: Louisiana State University Press, 1961), I, 346; Glatthaar, *March to the Sea*, 96.

30. Wilbur F. Hinman, *The Story of the Sherman Brigade* (Alliance, OH: The Author, 1897), 225–26.

31. Alexander Hunter, *Johnny Reb and Billy Yank* (New York: Neale Publishing Co., 1905), 75.

32. Thompson, *13th New Hampshire*, 254.

33. General Order Book, 37th N.C. Troops, 1862–1863, Duke University.

34. Davis, *Three Years in the Army*, 307; John T. Smith to family, Feb. 1, 1862, Smith Letter, in possession of Mrs. D. K. Brown, Vinton, VA.

35. For example, see John W. Green, *Johnny Green of the Orphan Brigade: The Journal of a Confederate Soldier* (Lexington: University of Kentucky Press, 1956), 122.

36. Amos J. Judson, *History of the Eighty-third Regiment, Pennsylvania Volunteers* (Dayton, OH: Morningside, 1986), 164.

37. Tilney, *My Life in the Army*, 55.

38. Joseph K. Newell, *"Ours": Annals of 10th Regiment, Massachusetts Volunteers, in the Rebellion* (Boston: G. H. Ellis, 1893), 159; Hunter, *Johnny Reb and Billy Yank*, 244.

39. Peter Welsh, *Irish Green and Union Blue: The Civil War Letters of Peter Welsh* (New York: Fordham University Press, 1986), 17.

40. Davis, *104th Pennsylvania*, 38; McClellan order quoted in Bell I. Wiley, *The Life of Billy Yank* (Indianapolis, 1952), 252.

41. John H. Morgan to sister, Aug. 9, 1861, letter in possession of Melvin M. Scott, Falls Church, VA; Davis, *Three Years in the Army*, 299. A soldier in the 25th Georgia wrote his wife in November, 1861: "I thought I had quit liquor

but I find it is absolutely necessary to life & therefore drink mean whiskey that is worth about 40 cts a gallon at home that cost me $5 a gallon here." Theodorick W. Montfort, *Rebel Lawyer: Letters of Theodorick W. Montfort, 1861–1862* (Athens: University of Georgia Press, 1965), 30–31.

42. Robert D. Patrick, *Reluctant Rebel: The Secret Diary of Robert Patrick 1861–1865* (Baton Rouge: Louisiana State University Press, 1959), 115; Ira M. B. Gillaspie, *From Michigan to Murfreesboro: The Diary of Ira Gillaspie of the Eleventh Michigan Infantry* (Mount Pleasant: Central Michigan University Press, 1965), 22.

43. Jesse W. Reid, *History of the Fourth Regiment S.C. Volunteers, from the Commencement of the War until Lee's Surrender* (Greenville, SC: Shannon & Co., 1892), 11.

44. Newell, *10th Massachusetts*, 54.

45. William D. F. Landon, "Fourteenth Indiana Regiment: Letters to the Vincennes Western Sun," *Indiana Magazine of History* XXXIV (1938), 87; Benjamin W. Crowninshield, *A History of the First Regiment of Massachusetts Cavalry Volunteers* (Boston: Houghton, Mifflin and Co., 1891), 298–99.

46. Perry Mayo, *The Civil War Letters of Perry Mayo* (East Lansing: Michigan State University, 1967), 194–95; Charles E. Cort, *"Dear Friends": The Civil War Letters and Diary of Charles Edwin Cort* (n.p., 1962), 36; Thomas L. Livermore, *Days and Events, 1860–1866* (Boston: Houghton Mifflin Co., 1920), 297.

47. Alfred Bellard, *Gone for a Soldier: The Civil War Memoirs of Private Alfred Bellard* (Boston: Little, Brown and Co., 1975), 33. See also William S. Lincoln, *Life with the Thirty-fourth Mass. Infantry in the War of the Rebellion* (Worcester, MA: Noyes, Snow & Co., 1879), 126.

48. Arthur H. De Rosier, Jr., ed., *Through the South with a Union Soldier* (Johnson City: East Tennessee State University, 1969), 92; Boyd, *Civil War Diary*, 93.

49. De Rosier, *Through the South*, 45.

50. *Thirty-fifth Massachusetts: History of the 35th Massachusetts Volunteers, 1862–5* (Boston: Mills Knight, 1884), 220.

51. Wilson, "Peter Wilson in the Civil War," 403.

Part III

How Soldiers Fought

Chapter 10

The Negro as a Soldier

Thomas Wentworth Higginson

Prodded by antislavery activists and by mounting casualties among white troops, Union army officials enlisted a limited number of black soldiers in 1862; Abraham Lincoln's Emancipation Proclamation made recruitment of black troops official policy at year's end. In all, nearly 200,000 African Americans, about three-quarters of whom were former slaves, eventually joined the Union armed forces. Black soldiers received lower enlistment bonuses and less pay than white troops for most of the war, and army officials put white officers in charge of African American units. One of these officers was Thomas Wentworth Higginson, who prior to the war had been a minister and antislavery activist near Boston. In 1861 Higginson raised a regiment of white volunteers; the next year he was offered command of the First South Carolina Volunteer Infantry, one of the pre-emancipation black units, which he led until the war's end. Higginson knew about the considerable curiosity (and numerous misconceptions) regarding African American soldiers, so in this chapter of his wartime memoirs, Army Life in a Black Regiment, *he addresses a series of whites' questions about black troops.*

There was in our regiment a very young recruit, named Sam Roberts, of whom Trowbridge used to tell this story. Early in the war Trowbridge had been once sent to Amelia Island with a squad of men, under direction of Commodore Goldsborough, to remove the negroes from the island. As the officers stood on the beach, talking to some of the older freedmen, they saw this urchin peeping at them from front and rear in a scrutinizing way, for which his father at last called him to account, as thus: —

"Hi! Sammy, what you's doin', chile?"

"Daddy," said the inquisitive youth, "don't you know mas'r tell us Yankee hab tail? I don't see no tail, daddy!"

There were many who went to Port Royal during the war, in civil or military positions, whose previous impressions of the colored race were about as intelligent as Sam's view of themselves. But, for one, I had always had so much to do with fugitive slaves, and had studied the whole subject with such interest, that I found not much to learn or unlearn as to this one point. Their courage I had before seen tested; their docile and lovable qualities I had known; and the only real surprise that experience brought me was in finding them so little demoralized. I had not allowed for the extreme remoteness and seclusion of their lives, especially among the Sea Islands. Many of them had literally spent their whole existence on some lonely island or remote plantation, where the master never came, and the overseer only once or twice a week. With these exceptions, such persons had never seen a white face, and of the excitements or sins of larger communities they had not a conception. My friend Colonel Hallowell, of the Fifty-Fourth Massachusetts, told me that he had among his men some of the worst reprobates of Northern cities. While I had some men who were unprincipled and troublesome, there was not one whom I could call a hardened villain. I was constantly expecting to find male Topsies, with no notions of good and plenty of evil. But I never found one. Among the most ignorant there was very often a childlike absence of vices, which was rather to be classed as inexperience than as innocence, but which had some of the advantages of both.

Apart from this, they were very much like other men. General Saxton, examining with some impatience a long list of questions from some philanthropic Commission at the North, respecting the traits and habits of the freedmen, bade some staff-officer answer them all in two words, — "Intensely human." We all admitted that it was a striking and comprehensive description.

For instance, as to courage. So far as I have seen, the mass of men are naturally courageous up to a certain point. A man seldom runs away from danger which he ought to face, unless others run; each is apt to keep with the mass, and colored soldiers have more than usual of this gregariousness. In almost every regiment, black or white, there are a score or two of men who are naturally daring, who really hunger after dangerous adventures, and are happiest when allowed to seek them. Every commander gradually finds out who these men are, and habitually uses them; certainly I had such, and I remember with delight their bearing, their coolness, and their dash. Some of them were negroes, some mulattoes. One of them would have passed for white, with brown hair and blue eyes, while others were so black you could hardly see their features. These picked men varied in other respects too; some were neat and well-drilled soldiers, while others were slovenly, heedless fellows,— the despair of their officers at inspection, their pride on a raid. They were the natural scouts and rangers of the regiment; they had the two-o'clock-in-the-morning courage, which Napoleon thought so rare. The mass of the regiment rose to the same level under excitement, and were more excitable, I think, than whites, but neither more nor less courageous.

Perhaps the best proof of a good average of courage among them was in the readiness they always showed for any special enterprise. I do not remember ever to have had the slightest difficulty in obtaining volunteers, but rather in keeping down the number. . . . For instance, one of my lieutenants, a very daring Irishman, who had served for eight years as a sergeant of regular artillery in Texas, Utah, and South Carolina, said he had never been engaged in anything so risky as our raid up the St. Mary's. But in truth it seems to me a mere absurdity to deliberately argue the question of courage, as applied to men among whom I waked and slept, day and night, for so many months together. As well might he who has been wandering for years upon the desert, with a Bedouin escort, discuss the courage of the men whose tents have been his shelter and whose spears his guard. We, their officers, did not go there to teach lessons, but to receive them. There were more than a hundred men in the ranks who had voluntarily met more dangers in their escape from slavery than any of my young captains had incurred in all their lives. . . .

I used to think that I should not care to read "Uncle Tom's Cabin" in our camp; it would have seemed tame. Any group of men in a tent would have had more exciting tales to tell. I needed no fiction when I had Fanny Wright, for instance, daily passing to and fro before my tent, with her shy little girl clinging to her skirts. Fanny was a modest little mulatto woman, a soldier's wife, and a company laundress. She had escaped from the main-land in a boat, with that child and another. Her baby was shot dead in her arms, and she reached our lines with one child safe on earth and the other in heaven. I never found it needful to give any elementary instructions in courage to Fanny's husband, you may be sure. . . .

I often asked myself why it was that, with this capacity of daring and endurance, they had not kept the land in a perpetual flame of insurrection; why, especially since the opening of the war, they had kept so still. The answer was to be found in the peculiar temperament of the races, in their religious faith, and in the habit of patience that centuries had fortified. The shrewder men all said substantially the same thing. What was the use of insurrection, where everything was against them? They had no knowledge, no money, no arms, no drill, no organization,— above all, no mutual confidence. It was the tradition among them that all insurrections were always betrayed by somebody. They had no mountain passes to defend like the Maroons of Jamaica,—no impenetrable swamps, like the Maroons of Surinam. Where they had these, even on a small scale, they had used them,—as in certain swamps round Savannah and in the everglades of Florida, where they united with the Indians, and would stand fire—so I was told by General Saxton, who had fought them there—when the Indians would retreat.

It always seemed to me that, had I been a slave, my life would have been one long scheme of insurrection. But I learned to respect the patient self-control of those who had waited till the course of events should open a better way. When it came they accepted it. Insurrection on their part would at once have divided the Northern sentiment; and a large part of our army would have joined with the Southern army to hunt them down. By their waiting till we needed them, their freedom was secured.

Two things chiefly surprised me in their feeling toward their former masters,—the absence of affection and the absence of revenge. I expected to find a good deal of the patriarchal feeling. It always seemed to me a very ill-applied emotion, as connected with the facts and laws of American slavery,—still I expected to find it. I suppose that my men and their families and visitors may have had as much of it as the mass of freed slaves; but certainly they had not a particle. I never could cajole one of them, in his most discontented moment, into regretting "ole mas'r time" for a single instant. I never heard one speak of the masters except as natural enemies. Yet they were perfectly discriminating as to individuals; many of them claimed to have had kind owners, and some expressed great gratitude to them for particular favors received. It was not the individuals, but the ownership, of which they complained. That they saw to be a wrong which no special kindnesses could right. On this, as on all points connected with slavery, they understood the matter as clearly as Garrison or Phillips; the wisest philosophy could teach them nothing as to that, nor could any false philosophy befog them. After all, personal experience is the best logician.

Certainly this indifference did not proceed from any want of personal affection, for they were the most affectionate people among whom I had ever lived. They attached themselves to every officer who deserved love, and to some who did not; and if they failed to show it to their masters, it proved the wrongfulness of the mastery. On the other hand, they rarely showed one gleam of revenge, and I shall never forget the self-control with which one of our best sergeants pointed out to me, at Jacksonville, the very place where one of his brothers had been hanged by the whites for leading a party of fugitive slaves. He spoke of it as a historic matter, without any bearing on the present issue.

But side by side with this faculty of patience, there was a certain tropical element in the men, a sort of fiery ecstasy when aroused, which seemed to link them by blood with the French Turcos, and made them really resemble their natural enemies, the Celts, far more than the Anglo-Saxon temperament. To balance this there were great individual resources when alone,—a sort of Indian wiliness and subtlety of resource. Their gregariousness and love of drill made them more easy to keep in hand than white American troops, who rather like to straggle or go in little squads, looking out for themselves, without being bothered with officers. The blacks prefer organization.

The point of inferiority that I always feared, though I never had occasion to prove it, was that they might show less fibre, less tough and dogged resistance, than whites, during a prolonged trial,—a long, disastrous march, for instance, or the hopeless defence of a besieged town. I should not be afraid of their mutinying or running away, but of their drooping and dying. It might not turn out so; but I mention it for the sake of fairness, and to avoid overstating the merits of these troops. As to the simple general fact of courage and reliability I think no officer in our camp ever thought of there being any difference between black and white. And certainly the opinions of these officers, who for years risked their lives every moment on the fidelity of their men, were worth more than those of all the world beside.

No doubt there were reasons why this particular war was an especially favorable test of the colored soldiers. They had more to fight for than the whites. Besides the flag and the Union, they had home and wife and child. They fought with ropes round their necks, and when orders were issued that the officers of colored troops should be put to death on capture, they took a grim satisfaction. It helped their *esprit de corps* immensely. With us, at least, there was to be no play-soldier. Though they had begun with a slight feeling of inferiority to the white troops, this compliment substituted a peculiar sense of self-respect. And even when the new colored regiments began to arrive from the North my men still pointed out this difference,—that in case of ultimate defeat, the Northern troops, black or white, would go home, while the First South Carolina must fight it out or be re-enslaved. This was one thing that made the St. John's River so attractive to them and even to me;—it was so much nearer the everglades. I used seriously to ponder, during the darker periods of the war, whether I might not end my days as an outlaw,—a leader of Maroons.

Meanwhile, I used to try to make some capital for the Northern troops, in their estimate, by pointing out that it was a disinterested thing in these men from the free States, to come down there and fight, that the slaves might be free. But they were apt keenly to reply, that many of the white soldiers disavowed this object, and said that that was not the object of the war, nor even likely to be its end. Some of them even repeated Mr. Seward's unfortunate words to Mr. Adams, which some general had been heard to quote. So, on the whole, I took nothing by the motion, as was apt to be the case with those who spoke a good word for our Government, in those vacillating and half proslavery days.

At any rate, this ungenerous discouragement had this good effect, that it touched their pride; they would deserve justice, even if they did not obtain it. This pride was afterwards severely tested during the disgraceful period when the party of repudiation in Congress temporarily deprived them of their promised pay. In my regiment the men never mutinied, nor even threatened mutiny; they seemed to make it a matter of honor to do their part, even if the Government proved a defaulter; but one third of them, including the best men in the regiment, quietly refused to take a dollar's pay, at the reduced price. "We'se gib our sogerin' to de Guv'ment, Cunnel," they said, "but we won't 'spise ourselves so much for take de seben dollar." They even made a contemptuous ballad, of which I once caught a snatch.

> "Ten dollar a month!
> Tree ob dat for clothin'!
> Go to Washington
> Fight for Linkum's darter!"

This "Lincoln's daughter" stood for the Goddess of Liberty, it would seem. They would be true to her, but they would not take the half-pay. This was contrary to my advice, and to that of their other officers; but I now think it was wise. Nothing less than this would have called the attention of the American people to this outrageous fraud.

The same slow forecast had often marked their action in other ways. One of our ablest sergeants, Henry McIntyre, who had earned two dollars and a half per day as a master-carpenter in Florida, and paid one dollar and a half to his master, told me that he had deliberately refrained from learning to read, because that knowledge exposed the slaves to so much more watching and suspicion. This man and a few others had built on contract the greater part of the town of Micanopy in Florida, and was a thriving man when his accustomed discretion failed for once, and he lost all. He named his child William Lincoln, and it brought upon him such suspicion that he had to make his escape.

I cannot conceive what people at the North mean by speaking of the negroes as a bestial or brutal race. Except in some insensibility to animal pain, I never knew of an act in my regiment which I should call brutal. In reading Kay's "Condition of the English Peasantry" I was constantly struck with the unlikeness of my men to those therein described. This could not proceed from my prejudices as an abolitionist, for they would have led me the other way, and indeed I had once written a little essay to show the brutalizing influences of slavery. I learned to think that we abolitionists had underrated the suffering produced by slavery among the negroes, but had overrated the demoralization. Or rather, we did not know how the religious temperament of the negroes had checked the demoralization. Yet again, it must be admitted that this temperament, born of sorrow and oppression, is far more marked in the slave than in the native African.

Theorize as we may, there was certainly in our camp an average tone of propriety which all visitors noticed, and which was not created, but only preserved by discipline. I was always struck, not merely by the courtesy of the men, but also by a certain sober decency of language. If a man had to report to me any disagreeable fact, for instance, he was sure to do it with gravity and decorum, and not blurt it out in an offensive way. And it certainly was a significant fact that the ladies of our camp, when we were so fortunate as to have such guests,—the young wives, especially, of the adjutant and quartermaster,—used to go among the tents when the men were off duty, in order to hear their big pupils read and spell, without the slightest fear of annoyance. I do not mean direct annoyance or insult, for no man who valued his life would have ventured that in presence of the others, but I mean the annoyance of accidentally seeing or hearing improprieties not intended for them. They both declared that they would not have moved about with anything like the same freedom in any white camp they had ever entered, and it always roused their indignation to hear the negro race called brutal or depraved.

This came partly from natural good manners, partly from the habit of deference, partly from ignorance of the refined and ingenious evil which is learned in large towns; but a large part came from their strongly religious temperament. Their comparative freedom from swearing, for instance,—an abstinence which I fear military life did not strengthen,—was partly a matter of principle. Once I heard one of them say to another, in a transport of indignation, "Ila-a-a, boy, s'pose I no be a Christian, I cuss you so!"—which was certainly drawing pretty hard upon the bridle. "Cuss," however, was a generic term for all manner of evil speaking; they would say, "He cuss me fool," or "He cuss me coward," as if the essence of propriety were in harsh and angry speech,— which I take to be good ethics. But certainly, if Uncle Toby could have recruited his army in Flanders from our ranks, their swearing would have ceased to be historic. . . .

The extremes of religious enthusiasm I did not venture to encourage, for I could not do it honestly; neither did I discourage them, but simply treated them with respect, and let them have their way, so long as they did not interfere with discipline. In general they promoted it. The mischievous little drummer-boys, whose scrapes and quarrels were the torment of my existence, might be seen kneeling together in their tents to say their prayers at night, and I could hope that their slumbers were blessed by some spirit of peace, such as certainly did not rule over their waking. The most reckless and daring fellows in the regiment were perfect fatalists in their confidence that God would watch over them, and that if they died, it would be because their time had come. This almost excessive faith, and the love of freedom and of their families, all co-operated with their pride as soldiers to make them do their duty. I could not have spared any of these incentives. Those of our officers who were personally the least influenced by such considerations, still saw the need of encouraging them among the men.

I am bound to say that this strongly devotional turn was not always accompanied by the practical virtues: but neither was it strikingly divorced from them. A few men, I remember, who belonged to the ancient order of hypocrites, but not many. Old Jim Cushman was our favorite representative scamp. He used to vex his righteous soul over the admission of the unregenerate to prayer-meetings, and went off once shaking his head and muttering, "Too much goat shout wid de sheep." But he who objected to this profane admixture used to get our mess-funds far more hopelessly mixed with his own, when he went out to buy us chickens. And I remember that, on being asked by our Major, in that semi-Ethiopian dialect into which we sometimes slid, "How much wife you got, Jim?" the veteran replied, with a sort of penitence for lost opportunities, "On'y but four, Sah!" . . .

Still, I maintain that, as a whole, the men were remarkably free from inconvenient vices. There was no more lying and stealing than in average white regiments. The surgeon was not much troubled by shamming sickness, and there were not a great many complaints of theft. There was less quarrelling than among white soldiers, and scarcely ever an instance of drunkenness. Perhaps the influence of their officers had something to do with this; for not a ration of whiskey was ever issued to the men, nor did I ever touch it, while in the army, nor approve a requisition for any of the officers, without which it could not easily be obtained. In this respect our surgeons fortunately agreed with me, and we never had reason to regret it. I believe the use of ardent spirits to be as useless and injurious in the army as on board ship, and among the colored troops, especially, who had never been accustomed to it, I think that it did only harm.

The point of greatest laxity in their moral habits—the want of a high standard of chastity—was not one which affected their camp life to any great extent, and it therefore came less under my observation. But I found to my relief that, whatever their deficiency in this respect, it was modified by the general quality of their temperament, and indicated rather a softening and relaxation than a hardening and brutalizing of their moral natures. Any insult or violence in this direction was a thing unknown. I never heard of an instance. It was not uncommon for men to have two or three wives in different plantations,—the second, or remoter, partner being called a " 'broad wife,"—i.e. wife abroad. But the whole tendency was toward marriage, and this state of things was only regarded as a bequest from "mas'r time." . . .

The question was often asked, whether the Southern slaves or the Northern free blacks made the best soldiers. It was a compliment to both classes that each officer usually preferred those whom he had personally commanded. I preferred those who had been slaves, for their greater docility and affectionateness, for the powerful stimulus which their new freedom gave, and for the fact that they were fighting, in a manner, for their own homes and firesides. Every one of these considerations afforded a special aid to discipline, and cemented a peculiar tie of sympathy between them and their officers. They seemed like clansmen, and had a more confiding and filial relation to us than seemed to me to exist in the Northern colored regiments.

So far as the mere habits of slavery went, they were a poor preparation for military duty. Inexperienced officers often assumed that, because these men had been slaves before enlistment, they would bear to be treated as such afterwards. Experience proved the contrary. The more strongly we marked the difference between the slave and the soldier, the better for the regiment. One half of military duty lies in obedience, the other half in self-respect. A soldier without self-respect is worthless. Consequently there were no regiments in which it was so important to observe the courtesies and proprieties of military life as in these. I had to caution the officers to be more than usually particular in returning the salutations of the men; to be very careful in their dealings with those on picket or guard-duty; and on no account to omit the titles of the non-commissioned officers. So, in dealing out punishments, we had carefully to avoid all that was brutal and arbitrary, all that savored of the overseer. Any such dealing found them as obstinate and contemptuous as was Topsy when Miss Ophelia undertook to chastise her. A system of light punishments, rigidly administered according to the prescribed military forms, had more weight with them than any amount of angry severity. To make them feel as remote as possible from the plantation, this was essential. By adhering to this, and constantly appealing to their pride as soldiers and their sense of duty, we were able to maintain a high standard of discipline,—so, at least, the inspecting officers said,—and to get rid, almost entirely, of the more degrading class of punishments,—standing on barrels, tying up by the thumbs, and the ball and chain.

In all ways we had to educate their self-respect. For instance, at first they disliked to obey their own non-commissioned officers. "I don't want him to play de white man ober me," was a sincere objection. They had been so impressed with a sense of inferiority that the distinction extended to the very principles of honor. "I ain't got colored-man principles," said Corporal London Simmons, indignantly defending himself from some charge before me. "I'se got white-gemman principles. I'se do my best. If Cap'n tell me to take a man, s'pose de man be as big as a house, I'll clam hold on him till I die, inception [excepting] I'm sick."

But it was plain that this feeling was a bequest of slavery, which military life would wear off. We impressed it upon them that they did not obey their officers because they were white, but because they were their officers, just as the Captain must obey me, and I the General; that we were all subject to military law, and protected by it in turn. Then we taught them to take pride in having good material for non-commissioned officers among themselves, and in obeying them. On my arrival there was one white first sergeant, and it was a question whether to appoint others. This I prevented, but left that one, hoping the men themselves would at last petition for his removal, which at length they did. He was at once detailed on other duty. The picturesqueness of the regiment suffered, for he was very tall and fair, and I liked to see him step forward in the centre when the line of first sergeants came together at dress-parade. But it was a help to discipline to eliminate the Saxon, for it recognized a principle.

Afterwards I had excellent battalion-drills without a single white officer, by way of experiment; putting each company under a sergeant, and going through the most difficult movements, such as division-columns and oblique-squares. And as to actual discipline, it is doing no injustice to the line-officers of the regiment to say that none of them received from the men more implicit obedience than Color-Sergeant Rivers. I should have tried to obtain commissions for him and several others before I left the regiment, had their literary education been sufficient; and such an attempt was finally made by Lieutenant-Colonel Trowbridge, my successor in immediate command, but it proved unsuccessful. It always seemed to me an insult to those brave men to have novices put over their heads, on the ground of color alone; and the men felt it the more keenly as they remained longer in service. There were more than seven hundred enlisted men in the regiment, when mustered out after more than three years' service. The ranks had been kept full by enlistment, but there were only fourteen line-officers instead of the full thirty. The men who should have filled those vacancies were doing duty as sergeants in the ranks.

In what respect were the colored troops a source of disappointment? To me in one respect only,—that of health. Their health improved, indeed, as they grew more familiar with military life; but I think that neither their physical nor moral temperament gave them that toughness, that obstinate purpose of living, which sustains the more materialistic Anglo-Saxon. They had not, to be sure, the same predominant diseases, suffering in the pulmonary, not in the digestive organs; but they suffered a good deal. They felt malaria less, but they were more easily choked by dust and made ill by dampness. On the other hand, they submitted more readily to sanitary measures than whites, and, with efficient officers, were more easily kept clean. They were injured throughout the army by an undue share of fatigue duty, which is not only exhausting but demoralizing to a soldier; by the unsuitableness of the rations, which gave them salt meat instead of rice and hominy; and by the lack of good medical attendance. Their childlike constitutions peculiarly needed prompt and efficient surgical care; but almost all the colored troops were enlisted late in the war, when it was hard to get good surgeons for any regiments, and especially for these. In this respect I had nothing to complain of, since there were no surgeons in the army for whom I would have exchanged my own.

And this late arrival on the scene affected not only the medical supervision of the colored troops, but their opportunity for a career. It is not my province to write their history, nor to vindicate them, nor to follow them upon those larger fields compared with which the adventures of my regiment appear but a partisan warfare. Yet this, at least, may be said. The operations on the South Atlantic coast, which long seemed a merely subordinate and incidental part of the great contest, proved to be one of the final pivots on which it turned. All now admit that the fate of the Confederacy was decided by Sherman's march to the sea. Port Royal was the objective point to which he marched, and he found the Department of the South, when he reached it, held almost exclusively by colored troops. Next to the merit of those who made the march was that of those who held open the door. That service will always remain among the laurels of the black regiments.

NOTE

From Thomas Wentworth Higginson, *Army Life in a Black Regiment* (Boston: Fields, Osgood, and Company, 1870), 243–63.

Chapter 11

Heroes and Cowards

Bell Irvin Wiley

Recent attempts by Hollywood to be graphically realistic in portraying combat may cause readers of Civil War studies to ask, "What was it actually like to be in a battle?" Bell Wiley addresses this issue: each of his landmark books devotes a chapter to describing the battlefield experience, including emotions, sounds, sights, and smells. This selection from The Life of Johnny Reb *switches to the present tense to convey the drama of an infantry charge.*

When an encounter with the Yankees was expected certain preliminaries were necessary. One of these was the issue of extra provisions, accompanied by the order to "cook up" from three to five days' rations, so that time would not have to be taken for the preparation of food during the anticipated action. This judicious measure generally fell short of its object because of Johnny Reb's own characteristics: he was always hungry, he had a definite prejudice against baggage, and he was the soul of improvidence. Sometimes the whole of the extra ration would be consumed as it was cooked, and rarely did any part of it last for the full period intended. About the same time that food was dispensed the general in command would address his men for the purpose of firing their spirit and inspiring them to deeds of valor. Soldiers en route to Shiloh, for example, were thus charged by Albert Sidney Johnston:

> "I have put you in motion to offer battle to the invaders of your country. With the resolution and disciplined valor becoming men fighting, as you are, for all worth living or dying for, you can but march to a decisive

victory over the agrarian mercenaries sent to subjugate and despoil you of your liberties, property, and honor. Remember the precious stake involved; remember the dependence of your mothers, your wives, your sisters, and your children on the result; remember the fair, broad, abounding land, the happy homes, and the ties that would be desolated by your defeat.

"The eyes and the hopes of eight millions of people rest upon you. You are expected to show yourselves worthy of your race and lineage, worthy of the women of the South, whose noble devotion in this war has never been exceeded in any time. With such incentives to brave deeds and with the trust that God is with us, your general will lead you confidently to the combat, assured of success."[1]

Presently each man would be given a supply of ammunition. This was delayed as long as possible, so that the powder would not become dampened through carelessness of the men. If Confederates held the initiative, the issue of ammunition would take place the night before the attack; but if the Rebs were on the defensive, without any definite knowledge of the time of assault, the issue of cartridges had to take place at an earlier stage. The customary allotment to each fighter was from forty to sixty rounds, a round being a ball and enough powder for a single shot.[2]

Prior to their issue lead and powder for each load had, for convenience, been wrapped in a piece of paper with the bullet at one end, the powder behind it, and the other end closed with a twist or a plug to hold the powder in place. This improvised cartridge was cylindrical in shape, somewhat resembling a section of crayon. When Johnny Reb loaded his gun—usually a muzzle loader—he bit off the twisted end so that the powder would be exploded by the spark when the trigger was pulled, dropped the cartridge in the muzzle, rammed in a piece of wadding and waited for the opportunity to draw bead on a Yankee. Surplus rounds were kept in a cartridge box—a leather or metal container that hung from the belt—or in a haversack, or in trouser pockets. . . .

The day of battle finally comes. The men are roused from sleep at a very early hour, perhaps two or three o'clock. The well-known call to arms is an extended beat of the snare drum known as the "long roll." After the lines are drawn up officers inspect equipment, giving particular attention to ammunition, to see that all is in readiness.

Then a few words of advice and instruction: Do not shoot until you are within effective musket range of the enemy; fire deliberately, taking care to aim low, and thus avoid the overshooting to which you have been so markedly susceptible in previous battles. If you merely wound a man so much the better, as injured men have to be taken from the field by sound ones; single out a particular adversary for your fire, after the example of your sharpshooting forefathers at Bunker Hill and New Orleans. When possible pick off the enemy's officers, particularly the mounted ones, and his artillery horses. Under all conditions hold your ranks; avoid the natural but costly inclination to huddle together under heavy fire. When ordered to charge, do so at once and move forward rapidly; you are much less apt to be killed while going steadily forward than if you hesitate or retreat; but in case you have to fall back, do so gradually and in order; more men are killed during disorganzied retreat than at any other time; if your objective is a battery, do not be terrorized—artillery is never as deadly as it seems; a rapid forward movement reduces the battery's effectiveness and hastens the end of its power to destroy. Do not pause or turn aside to plunder the dead or to pick up spoils; battles have been lost by indulgence in this temptation. Do not heed the calls for assistance of wounded comrades or stop to take them to the rear; details have been made to care for casualties, and the best way of protecting your wounded friends is to drive the enemy from the field. Straggling under any guise will be severely punished. Cowards will be shot. Do your duty in a manner that becomes the heroic example your regiment has already set on earlier fields of combat.[3]

Orders to march are now given, and to the waving of colors and the stirring rhythm of fife and drum the regiments proceed to their appointed place in the line of battle. As the dawn mist clears away, a scene of intense activity is revealed on all sides. Surgeons are preparing their kits; litter bearers and ambulances are ominously waiting.[4] Arrived at their place in line, the men wait for what seem interminable hours while other units are brought into position. There is some talk while they wait, though less than earlier in the war. Comrades quietly renew mutual pledges to seek out those who are missing at the battle's end—for help if they are wounded and for protection of belongings and notification of homefolk if they are dead. A few men read their testaments, some mutter soft prayers—a devout captain is observed standing with Bible in hand reading aloud to his Mississippians, but this scene is unusual.[5] Here and there a soldier bites off a chew of tobacco and joins a host of comrades whose jaws are already working. Very rarely an officer or a private sneaks a swig of "How Come You So" to bolster his spirit for the ordeal ahead.[6] Everywhere suspense bears down with crushing force, but is indicated largely by silence.

Presently the rattle of musketry is heard in front. Skirmishers must have made contact with enemy pickets. All are alert. A signal gun is fired and the artillery joins in with accumulating fury. At last the command—"Forward!"—and an overpowering urge to make contact with the enemy. Soon lines of blue are discernible. Comrades begin to fall in increasing numbers. Now the shout, lost perhaps in the din of battle—"Charge!"—accompanied by a forward wave of officer's saber and the line leaps forward with the famous "Rebel yell."

This yell itself is an interesting thing. It was heard at First Manassas and was repeated in hundreds of charges throughout the war. It came to be as much a part of a Rebel's fighting equipment as his musket. Once, indeed, more so. Toward the end of an engagement near Richmond in May 1864, General Early rode up to a group of soldiers and said, "Well, men, we must charge them once more and then we'll be through." The response came back, "General, we are all out of ammunition." Early's ready retort was, "Damn it, holler them across." And, according to the narrator, the order was literally executed.[7]

The Confederate yell is hard to describe. An attempt to reproduce it was made a few years ago when Confederate veterans re-enacted battle scenes in Virginia. But this, by the very nature of things, was an inadequate representation. Old voices were too weak and incentive too feeble to create again the true battle cry. As it flourished on the field of combat, the Rebel yell was an unpremeditated, unrestrained and utterly informal "hollering." It had in it a mixture of fright, pent-up nervousness, exultation, hatred and a pinch of pure deviltry. Yelling in attack was not peculiar to Confederates, for Yanks went at Rebels more than once with "furious" shouts on their lips.[8] But the battle cry of Southerners was admittedly different. General "Jube" Early, who well understood the spirit of his soldiers, made a comparison of Federal and Confederate shouting as a sort of aside to his official report of the battle of Fredericksburg. "Lawton's Brigade, without hesitating, at once dashed upon the enemy," he said, "with the cheering peculiar to the Confederate soldier, and which is never mistaken for the studied hurrahs of the Yankees, and drove the column opposed to it down the hill." Though obviously invidious, the general's observation is not wholly inaccurate.[9]

The primary function of the rousing yell was the relief of the shouter.

As one Reb observed after a fight in 1864, "I always said if I ever went into a charge, I wouldn't holler! But the very first time I fired off my gun I hollered as loud as I could, and I hollered every breath till we stopped."[10] At first there was no intention of inspiring terror in the enemy, but the practice soon attained such a reputation as a demoralizing agent that men were encouraged by their officers to shout as they assaulted Yankee positions. In the battle of Lovejoy's Station, for instance, Colonel Clark cried out to his Mississippians, "Fire and charge with a yell."[11] Yankees may not have been scared by this Rebel throat-splitting, but they were enough impressed to set down in their official reports that the enemy advanced "yelling like fiends," or other words to the same effect.[12] . . .

But those Rebs who are now charging at the Yankees know that yelling is only a small part of their business. Yankee lines loom larger as the boys in gray surge forward. Now there is a pause for aiming, and the roar of countless muskets, but the individual soldier is hardly conscious of the noise or the kick of his weapon. Rarely does he have time to consider the effectiveness of his shot. He knows that scores of Yankees are falling, and his comrades as well, but he cannot attend to details of slaughter on either side. He drops to his knee, fumblingly bites off and inserts a cartridge, rams it home with a quick thrust of the rod, then rises and dashes forward with his fellows. On they go, these charging Rebs, feeling now that exaltation which comes after the fight gets under way. "There is something grand about it—it is magnificent," said Robert Gill of his experience under fire near Atlanta. "I feel elated as borne along with the tide of battle."[13]

Presently there is an obvious slowing down of the advance, as resistance increases and attacking ranks become thin. Artillery fire comes in such force as to shatter good-sized trees, and men are actually killed by falling limbs.[14] The lines of gray seem literally to bend beneath the weight of canister and grape, and yelling soldiers lean forward while walking as if pushing against the force of a wind.[15] Slaughter becomes so terrible that ditches run with blood.[16] The deafening noise is likened by one Reb to "a large cane brake on fire and a thunder storm with repeated loud thunder claps." The flight of shells (called "lamp posts" and "wash kettles" according to their size and shape) reminds Robert Gill of "frying on a large scale only a little more so"; and Maurice Simons thinks of a partridge flying by, "only we would suppose that the little bird had grown to the size of an Eagle."[17] Some of the men, unable to confront this holocaust, seek the protection of rocks, trees and gullies. Others of stronger nerve close the gaps and push onward.

The overwhelming urge to get quickly to the source of danger brings an end to loading and shooting. With one last spurt the charging troops throw themselves among their adversaries, gouging with bayonets, swinging with clubbed muskets, or even striking with rocks, fence rails and sticks.[18] Presently one side or the other gives way, and the charge is over.

But not the battle. Before the day's fighting is completed there will be several charges, each followed by lulls for reorganization. And perhaps the conflict, as at Gettysburg, will extend to a second and third day, each characterized by repetitions of attack over various portions of the field; or perhaps the main action, as at Fredericksburg, will be defensive, staving off repeated Federal assaults.

Moving to the charge, though by far the most dramatic part of the fighting, actually made up only a small portion of a soldier's experience in battle. There were hours of lying on the ground or of standing in line, perhaps under the heat of a broiling sun, while troops on other parts of the field carried out the tasks assigned them. Then there was endless shifting, to bolster a weak spot here, to cut off an enemy salient there, or to replenish ammunition. These and many other activities, coupled with repeated advances on enemy positions, took a heavy toll of the soldier's strength.

As the day wore on he was increasingly conscious of exhaustion. Though accustomed before the war to long hours of labor on the farm or extended jaunts in pursuit of game, he found fighting the hardest work he had ever done. Fatigue was sharpened by the fact that rest and food had been scarce during the days before the battle. By midafternoon his strength was often so depleted that he could hardly load and fire his gun, if indeed he was able to stand at all.[19] Those who fought at Shiloh may have joined in the postwar criticism of Beauregard for not pushing the battle as Sunday's sun sank in the west, but officers' reports made soon after the fight show that most of the men were so exhausted that further aggression was impossible.[20]

Increasing with the combatant's fatigue came intolerable thirst. Sweating in the grime and dust, he had emptied his canteen early in the day, hoping to refill it from some stream. But rarely was there any such chance. If he were lucky enough to reach a pond he was apt to find it so choked with the dead and wounded as to be unfit for use. But even so, that soldier considered himself lucky who could sweep aside the gory scum and quench his thirst by greedy draughts of the muddy water underneath.[21]

If the battle happened to be in winter, as at Murfreesboro, Fredericksburg, or Nashville, the suffering from thirst was not so intense. But the exposure to cold was hardly less severe. Discomfort was increased by damp weather, scarcity of clothing, and the inability to make fires. At Murfreesboro, for instance, soldiers lay in line of battle for nearly a week under a cold rain without fire.[22]

When the combat extended over several days, as was frequently the case, hunger was added to other discomforts. At Gettysburg Washington Artillerymen became so famished that a captain sent a detail to gather food from the haversacks of Federal dead.[23] Many other hungry soldiers were not so fortunate as to have this opportunity.

The coming of night usually brought a rest from fighting, but not from suffering. The disorganization which characterized Confederate battles often separated the soldier from his regiment.[24] The command of duty, plus a desire to know the lot of his friends, would cause him, tired to the point of prostration though he was, to set out on a tedious search for his fellows. When he found the scattered remnants of his company he would probably discover that some messmate, committed to his care by mutual pledge before the battle, was missing. Then he must make a round of the battlefield and the emergency hospitals, inquiring patiently, calling out the name of his friend, and scanning by candlelight the ghastly faces of dead and wounded. The quest might end in happy discovery, but more likely it would prove futile. At last the weary soldier would fall down on the ground. And in spite of the piteous cries of the wounded he would sink at once into heavy slumber.

The morrow of a battle, whether its duration was for one or several days, was in some respects more trying than the conflict itself. Scenes encountered in the burial of the dead were strange and appalling: there a dead Yankee lying on his back "with a biscuit in his hand and with one mouthful bitten off and that mouthful still between his teeth"; here "the top of a man's Skull Hanging by the Hair to a Limb some 8 or 9 feet from the ground"; yonder another "man Siting behind a large oak tree his head . . . shot off"; to the right a small, whining dog curled up in the arms of a dead Yankee, refusing to be coaxed from its erstwhile master; to the left a lifeless Reb sprawled across the body of a well-dressed Federal, the gray-clad's hand in the Northerner's pocket—a gruesome warning to those who are tempted to plunder during battle; farther on, the field is strewn with nude figures blackened and mutilated by a fire that swept across the dry foliage in the wake of the fight.[25] One of the burying party working in Federal-traversed territory is shocked to find that before his arrival "the hogs got a holt of some of the Yankey dead."[26] In any direction one chances to gaze lie heaps of disfigured bodies; to a rural-bred Georgian the scene following Fredericksburg suggested "an immense hog pen and them all killed."[27]

After a prolonged summer encounter the task was unusually repulsive. Wrote a soldier who helped in the burial of the Gettysburg dead:

"The sights and smells that assailed us were simply indescribable—corpses swollen to twice their original size, some of them actually burst asunder with the pressure of foul gases and vapors. . . . The odors were nauseating and so deadly that in a short time we all sickened and were lying with our mouths close to the ground, most of us vomiting profusely."[28]

While some were burying the dead, others were walking about picking up spoils. Trinkets of all sorts, such as Yankee letters, diaries, photographs, and pocket knives are much in demand as souvenirs to be sent home to relatives. "I am going to send you a trophie that come off the battle field at Gettysburg," wrote a Reb to his sister. "I got three pictures out of a dead Yankees knapsack and I am going to send you one. . . . The pictures are wraped up in a letter from the person whose image they are. . . . She signed her name A. D. Spears and she lived in Main somewhere, but I could not make out where she lived."[29] Occasionally Rebs laughed over the sentimental contents of such letters. Some soldiers profited financially from their plundering of battlefields. Following the Franklin engagement of December 1864 George Athey wrote:

"I got agood knapsack fuol of tricks whitch I sold $4.5 dolars worth out of it and cepe as mutch as I wanted."[30]

Articles essential to personal comfort were eagerly gathered up. After the Seven Days' Battles a Reb wrote exultantly:

"We have had a glorious victory with its rich Booty A many one of our boys now have a pair of Briches a nice Rubber cloth & a pair of Blankets also a pair or more of Small Tent Cloths."[31] . . .

If the battle ended in defeat, falling back might be so hurried as to leave the dead and wounded in Federal hands. This, added to the increased hardships of retreat and the disappointment of being whipped, caused the soldier's cup to overflow with bitterness.

But whether victorious or not, Johnny Reb began within a remarkably short time to recall and to enjoy the interesting and humorous detail of the combat. Campfire groups must have delighted in teasing Private Joseph Adams about losing his pants when a shell exploded near him at Murfreesboro; and there was doubtless plenty of laughter when M. D. Martin told how a shell cut off his two well-stocked haversacks and scattered hardtack so promiscuously that "several of the boys were struck by the biscuits, and more than one thought he was wounded."32

James Mabley could always get a good laugh with his story of the Reb at Chancellorsville who while in the act of drawing a bead on a Yank was distracted by a wild turkey lighting in a tree before him; the Federal was immediately forgotten, and in an instant the crack of this Reb's gun brought the turkey to the ground.33 . . .

Almost everyone could tell of a "close shave" when a bullet hit a knapsack, perforated a hat, or spent itself by passing through a bush immediately in front, to fall harmlessly to the ground in plain view. One soldier marveled at hearing through the din of battle the cry of John Childress as he fell: "I am killed, tell Ma and Pa goodbye for me."34

Then someone may have mentioned the tragic case of Jud and Cary Smith, Yale-educated brothers from Mississippi. While in the act of lying down under fire, the younger, Cary, putting his hand under his coat found his inner garments covered with blood; and with only the exclamation "What does this mean?" he died. Jud was so overwhelmed with grief that he spent the entire night muttering affectionate words over his brother's corpse. He passed the next day and night in unconsolable solitude. The third day was that of Malvern Hill, and when the first charge took place Jud kept on going after his comrades fell back under the murderous fire, and he was never seen or heard of again. After the father learned of the fate of his two sons he joined Price's army as a private soldier; when his regiment charged at Iuka, he followed the example set by Jud at Malvern Hill, and he likewise was never heard of again.35

But there was not much lingering on tragic notes. It was more pleasant to talk of how Jeb Stuart at Second Manassas beguiled the Yankees into exaggerated ideas of Rebel strength by having his men drag brush along the roads to stir up huge clouds of dust; or of how the Yankee General Banks was duped into abandoning several strong positions during his Red River campaign by such Confederate ruses as sending drummers out to beat calls, lighting superfluous campfires, blowing bugles, and "rolling empty wagons over fence rails"; or of how George Cagle, while lying on a ridge at Chickamauga, kept at work four or five muskets gathered from incapacitated comrades, and as Yankee bullets whistled overhead he simulated the activity of an artillery unit, giving such commands as "attention Cagle's Battery, make ready, load, take aim, fire"; of how Sergeant Nabors scared nervous Yankee prisoners who asked him at Atlanta if he were going to kill them by replying, "That's our calculation; we came out for that purpose."[36]

By no means was all of the fighting in the open field. Warring in trenches—Johnny Reb usually called them "ditches"—made its appearance in the spring of 1862 on the Virginia peninsula where Magruder's army was entrenched for a month. At Vicksburg, where Pemberton's troops were under siege for forty-seven days, soldiers spent most of the time in earthworks along the line, or in caves to the rear. During the Atlanta campaign Rebs of the Army of Tennessee saw considerable trench warfare. But by far the longest stretch of this sort of campaigning was done by Lee's troops, who spent the greater part of the war's last year in the ditches around Petersburg.

Occasionally the routine of trench fighting was broken by an assault of one army or the other, but the time was mostly spent in desultory exchanges of artillery and musket fire. The Federals, being the besiegers and having vastly superior resources, did the larger part of the firing. So unlimited, indeed, were their supplies of ammunition that they could make the countryside reverberate with repeated discharges of their heavy cannon.[37]

The defenders of Vicksburg were subjected to heavier fire than any other trench fighters in the war. Back of them lay the Mississippi, dotted with gunboats, and before them were the troops of Grant and Sherman well equipped with artillery. The besieged were deficient in both guns and ammunition. Hemmed in thus by superior forces and equipment, conscious of their inability to give effective retaliation, living on ever dwindling rations, suffering from a shortage of drinking water, and cut off largely from their friends, they were subjected day after day and night after night to a cannonading that was so severe at times as to make heads ache from the concussion.[38] . . .

In the trenches before Atlanta and Petersburg existence was not so perilous nor so gloomy as at Vicksburg. Common to all, however, was the intolerable heat of the summer sun. Some men sought alleviation by building little brush arbors along the trenches. The sultriness of the ditches became so unbearable at night that some of the men resorted to sleeping on the edge—and when the Federal batteries opened they would simply roll over to safety. But immunity from danger in the Atlanta and Petersburg trenches was only comparative. The killing and wounding of men by Federal sharpshooting and artillery fire were of such common occurrence as hardly to elicit notice save by the company to which the casualty belonged.[39]

The number of killed and wounded would have been much greater but for the skill of the men in side-stepping arched shots. "The mortars are thrown up a great height," wrote an Alabamian from Petersburg, "and fall down in the trenches like throwing a ball over a house—we have become very perfect in dodging them and unless they are thrown too thick I think I can always escape them at least at night." He added that the dugouts which they contrived at intervals along the trenches and which they were wont to call bombproofs were not impervious at all to mortar shells, and that "we always prefer to be out in the ditches— where by using strategy and skill we get out of their way."[40] So confident did the troops become of their ability to escape these lobbed shots of the Yankees that they would keep up a derisive yelling throughout a bombardment.[41]

During periods of truce ladies from Petersburg made several visits to the lines, walking down the ditches in their cumbersome hoop skirts to see how bombproofs were made, climbing upon the parapets to get a look at the Yankees, giggling and oh-ing at the strange sights confronting them. Both Federals and Rebs enjoyed these interludes in crinoline, but some of the latter could not refrain from mischievously expressing the wish that the Yanks would throw a few shells over to see if the fair visitors would shake with terror or raise the Rebel yell.[42]

But these tantalizing glimpses of Petersburg belles afforded only brief respite from the terrible filth, the smothering heat of summer and the cold of winter, the rain and mud of all seasons, the restricted movement and the countless other deprivations that made trench warfare the most unpleasant aspect of Confederate soldierhood. Open fighting with all its dangers was immeasurably preferable to such existence as this.

But what of valor and of cowardice on the field of battle? There were numerous manifestations of both, though many more of the former than of the latter. Deeds of Rebel bravery, individual and collective, were of such common occurrence as to be quite beyond all estimation. A few definite instances will serve as examples of the glory that lighted up the fields of Manassas, of Shiloh, of Antietam, of Gettysburg, of Spottsylvania—and of countless others. . . .

In his official report of Second Manassas Major J. D. Waddell, commanding Toombs' Georgians, said that he "carried into the fight over 100 men who were barefoot, many of whom left bloody foot-prints among the thorns and briars through which they rushed, with Spartan courage and really jubilant impetuosity, upon the serried ranks of the foe." Colonel E. C. Cook of the Thirty-second Tennessee Infantry reported after Chickamauga that one of his men, J. W. Ellis, who had marched for six weeks without shoes, "went thus into battle and kept up with his company at all times till wounded."[43]

At Chickamauga Private Mayfield was wounded in the thigh by a Minié ball and at the same time dazed by a shell. Litter bearers picked him up and were carrying him to the rear when he recovered from the shock and sprang to the ground with the remark, "This will not do for me," and rushed back to continue the fight. In this same engagement Private McCann fought gallantly until his ammunition was exhausted; then he picked up cartridge boxes of the dead and wounded and coolly distributed ammunition among his comrades. When the colonel commended his heroic conduct McCann asked that his bravery be cited in the official report of the battle. Shortly afterward he received a mortal wound and as he was borne dying to the rear, he turned smiling to his colonel and reminded him of the promise of honorable mention.[44]

Of all the brave those who were entrusted with the colors had the most consistent record. Almost every official report of regimental commanders mentions the courageous action of standard-bearers. To keep the flag flying was a matter of inestimable pride, and its loss to the enemy was an incalculable disgrace. Consequently men vied with each other for the honor of holding the cherished emblem aloft in the thickest of the fight.[45] The Federals, knowing the close association of morale and colors, and being easily able to single out standard-bearers because of their conspicuousness, were wont to concentrate an unusually heavy fire upon them. Literally thousands of those who aspired to the honor of carrying and guarding the flags paid for the privilege with their lives. . . .

Color Sergeant Rice of the Twenty-eighth Tennessee Infantry, downed by a bullet at Murfreesboro, still clung to the flag, holding it aloft as he crawled on his knees until a second shot brought death and delivered him of his trust. On another part of this bloody field Color Sergeant Cameron advanced too far ahead of his comrades and was captured. He tore the flag from its staff, concealed it on his person, carried it to prison with him, escaped, and brought it back to be unfurled anew above its proud followers.[46]

Murfreesboro likewise afforded the setting for perhaps the most extraordinary of all color-bearer feats. While this contest raged at its greatest fury the opposing lines came very near each other in that portion of the field occupied by the Nineteenth Texas Cavalry (dismounted). A Yankee standard carrier stood immediately to the front of the Texas Color Sergeant, A. Sims, waving his flag and urging the blue column forward. Sergeant Sims, construing this as something of a personal insult, rushed forward, planted his own flag staff firmly on the ground with one hand and made a lunge for that of his exhorting adversary with the other. At the moment of contact, both color-bearers, Yankee and Rebel, "fell in the agonies of death waving their banners above their heads until their last expiring moments." The Texas standard was rescued, but not until one who rushed forward to retrieve it had also been shot down.[47]

Confederate authorities sought to stimulate the men by offering medals and badges to those who were cited by officers. Unable to supply these emblems, Congress passed an act in October 1862 providing for the publication of a Roll of Honor after each battle which should include the names of those who had best displayed their courage and devotion. Such lists were read at dress parades, published in newspapers and filed in the adjutant general's office. As a further inducement commissions were offered to those who should distinguish themselves, and special inscriptions were placed on flags of those regiments that captured artillery or gave other proof of unusual achievement.[48] But the most effective incentive was probably that of personal and family pride. This was strikingly evidenced by the remark of a Georgian to his brother after Franklin: "I am proud to say that there was no one between me and the Yankees when I was wounded."[49]

Cowardice under fire, being a less gratifying subject than heroism, has not received much attention from those who have written or talked of the Confederate Army. Of the various sources of information on this obscure point the most fertile are the official reports of battles by commanders of units ranging from regiments to armies. But the most numerous of these reports—those submitted by regimental commanders—are characterized by a reluctance to admit wholesale cowardice because of possible reflections on the conduct of the commanders themselves. This reluctance sometimes resulted in misrepresentation of the rankest sort, as in the following case: After the attack on Battery Wagner, Morris Island, South Carolina, July 18, 1863, Colonel Charles W. Knight, commanding the Thirty-first North Carolina Regiment, said in closing his report, "It is useless to mention any officer or man, when all were acting coolly and bravely." In the body of his report he mentioned being repulsed, but there is absolutely no suggestion of bad conduct on the part of the regiment. But when Knight's superior, General William B. Taliaferro, reported the battle, he said: "The Thirty-first North Carolina could not be induced to occupy their position, and ingloriously deserted the ramparts. . . . I feel it my duty to mention . . . [their] disgraceful conduct."[50]

In the reports of higher ranking officers, who could admit bad conduct of portions of their commands with more impunity than colonels, and in the wartime letters and diaries of the common soldiers, much testimony on the subject may be found. This evidence shows clearly that Confederate soldiers were by no means immune to panic and cowardice.

At First Manassas a few Rebs fled into the woods when shells began to fly. There was disgraceful conduct at the beginning of McClellan's peninsula campaign, when General D. H. Hill wrote that "several thousand soldiers . . . have fled to Richmond under pretext of sickness. They have even thrown away their arms that their flight might not be impeded." At Seven Pines there were a few regiments that "disgracefully left the battle field with their colors." General W. H. C. Whiting in reporting the battle of Gaines's Mill said: "Men were leaving the field in every direction and in great disorder . . . men were skulking from the front in a shameful manner; the woods on our left and rear were full of troops in safe cover from which they never stirred." At Malvern Hill, General Jubal Early encountered "a large number of men retreating from the battle-field," saw "a very deep ditch filled with skulkers," and found a "wood filled with a large number of men retreating in confusion."[51] . . .

General Bushrod Johnson reported that at Murfreesboro troops on his right became demoralized and "men of different regiments, brigades, divisions, were scattered all over the fields," and that he was almost run over, so precipitate was their flight. Captain Felix Robertson said that he had never seen troops so completely broken as those demoralized at

Murfreesboro. "They seemed actuated only by a desire for safety," he added. "I saw the colors of many regiments pass, and though repeated calls were made for men of the different regiments, no attention was paid to them."[52]

At Chancellorsville and Gettysburg the conduct of the soldiers seems to have been exceptionally good. This may have been due in some part to vigorous efforts of General Lee and of the War Department early in 1863 to tighten up the discipline of the Army of Northern Virginia. The fighting before Vicksburg was marred by shameful conduct in the action of May 16, 1863, of which General Pemberton said: "We lost a large amount of artillery. The army was much demoralized; many regiments behaved badly," and Colonel Edward Goodwin reported of a small number of troops immediately in front of him:

"At this time our friends gave way and came rushing to the rear panic-stricken. . . . I brought my regiment to the charge bayonets, but even this could not check them in their flight. The colors of three regiments passed through. . . . We collared them, begged them, and abused them in vain."[53]

The wholesale panic which seized Confederate troops at Missionary Ridge was as notorious as it was mystifying. A soldier who took part in the battle wrote in his diary, "In a few minutes the whole left gave way and a regular run commenced." After a retreat of several hundred yards, this Reb's battalion rallied momentarily, "but it was in such a confused mass that we made but a feeble resistance, when all broke again in a perfect stampede." His conviction was that the troops acted disgracefully, that they "did not half fight."[54]

General Bragg in his official report of the fight said that "a panic which I had never before witnessed seemed to have seized upon officers and men, and each seemed to be struggling for his personal safety, regardless of his duty or his character." He added that "no satisfactory excuse can possibly be given for the shameful conduct of the troops on our left in allowing their line to be penetrated. The position was one which ought to have been held by a line of skirmishers against any assaulting column, and wherever resistance was made the enemy fled in disorder after suffering heavy loss. Those who reached the ridge did so in a condition of exhaustion from the great physical exertion in climbing, which rendered them powerless, and the slightest effort would have destroyed them." What stronger indictment could there be of any soldiery by its general-in-command![55] . . .

While the Atlanta campaign seems to have been remarkably free of demoralization under fire, there were at least two instances involving a considerable number of men. In a skirmish on June 9, 1864, a Texas cavalry unit that had a distinguished record in battle broke upon slight contact with the Federal cavalry, and fled in a manner described as disorderly and shameful by General Ross. Later, in the Battle of Jonesboro, August 31, 1864, an advancing brigade of Confederates halted without orders when it came to the Federal picket line, the men seeking shelter behind piles of rails. They seemed "possessed of some great horror of charging breastworks," reported Colonel Bushrod Jones, "which no power of persuasion or example could dispel."[56]

The last instance of large-scale panic during the war was at Nashville, December 16, 1864. On this occasion the division of General Bate, when assaulted about four o'clock in the afternoon by the Federals, began to fall back in great confusion and disorder. In a few moments the entire Confederate line was broken, and masses of troops fled down the pike toward Franklin. All efforts to rally the troops proved fruitless. General Bate in his official report leaves the impression that the rout, due to extenuating circumstances, cast little if any reproach upon his men. But General Hood, in chief command, was evidently of contrary opinion, as he says that Confederate loss in killed and wounded was small, implying that withdrawal took place without much resistance. He says further that the break came so suddenly that artillery guns could not be brought away.[57] Captain Thomas J. Key says in his diary that "General Bate's division . . . shamefully broke and fled before the Yankees were within 200 yards of them," and that there "then ensued one of the most disgraceful routs" that it had ever been his misfortune to witness.[58]

There were innumerable cases of individual cowardice under fire. When men are assembled in such large numbers, especially when many of them are forced into service, a certain proportion are inevitably worthless as fighters. Some of those who fled wanted earnestly to act bravely, but they had not the power to endure fire unflinchingly. This type is well exemplified by the Reb who covered his face with his hat during the battle of Fredericksburg, and who later, when told that his turn at the rifle pits was imminent, "made a proposition that he would go out from camp and strip" and let his comrades "get switches and whip him as much as they wanted" if they would obtain his release from the impending proximity to Federal fire.[59] A similar case was encountered by Colonel C. Irvine Walker. A man had been reported for cowardly behavior on the field. Walker called him to task and told him that he would be watched closely during the next engagement. When the time came the colonel went over to check his performance as the regiment advanced. "I found him in his place," reported Walker, "his rifle on his shoulder, and holding up in front of him a frying pan." The man was so scared that he sought this meager protection, yet he moved forward with his company and was killed.[60]

There can be no doubt that the trying conditions under which Confederate soldiers fought contributed to the bad performance of some of the field of battle. Men often went into combat hungry and remained long under fire with little or nothing to eat. Sometimes, as at Antietam and Gettysburg, they fought after exhausting marches. Many of those who participated in the routs at Chattanooga and at Nashville were without shoes. Often the Confederate artillery protection was inadequate. The superior number of the Federals made Rebel flanks unduly vulnerable, and flank sensitiveness was the cause of more than one panic. Casualties among line officers were unusually heavy, and replacement with capable men was increasingly difficult after 1863.

When all of these factors are considered, it is rather remarkable that defection under fire was not more frequent than it actually was. Those soldiers who played the coward, even granting that the offenders totaled well up in the thousands, were a very small proportion of the Confederate Army. Taken on the whole of his record under fire, the Confederate private was a soldier of such mettle as to claim a high place among the world's fighting men. It may be doubted that anyone else deserves to outrank him.

NOTES

From Bell Irvin Wiley, *The Life of Johnny Reb: The Common Soldier of the Confederacy* (Baton Rouge: Louisiana State University Press, 1978) 68–89. Reprinted by permission.

1. *War of the Rebellion: Official Records of the Union and Confederate Armies* (Washington, 1880–1901), series 1, X, part 2, 389.
2. Forty rounds was evidently the capacity of an ordinary cartridge box. After the battle of Gettysburg the War Department sent out a circular to army and departmental commanders enjoining the practice, except on special order of the general commanding, of issuing on the eve of battle twenty rounds of am-

munition, "over and above the capacity of the cartridge boxes." O. R., series 1, XXVII, part 3, 1091.

3. This summary of pre-battle instructions is derived from various sources. For examples, see O. R., series 1, X, part 2, 325–326, 535, and XI, part 3, 410–411. State pride was sometimes appealed to in these addresses. George Whitaker Wills to his sister, June 28, 1862, manuscript, University of North Carolina. General T. C. Hindman sought on one occasion to invoke hatred of the enemy as a pre-battle conditioner: "Remember that the enemy you engage has no feeling of mercy," he said. "His ranks are made up of Pin Indians, Free Negroes, Southern Tories, Kansas Jayhawkers, and hired Dutch cutthroats. These bloody ruffians have invaded your country, stolen and destroyed your property, murdered your neighbors, outraged your women, driven your children from their homes, and defiled the graves of your kindred." Broadside, dated Dec. 4, 1862, Emory University.

4. T. W. Montfort wrote to his wife from Ft. Pulaski, April 5, 1862: "There is something sad and melancholy in the preparation for Battle. To see so many healthy men prepareing for the worst by disposing of their property by will—to see the surgeon sharping his instruments & whetting his saw ... men engaged in carding up & prepareing lint to stop the flow of human blood." Typescript, Georgia Archives.

5. Journal of William P. Chambers, entry of May 18, 1864, Mississippi Historical Society Publications, Centenary Series, V, 321. This source will be cited hereinafter as P.M.H.S.

6. Robert M. Gill wrote to his wife from line of battle in Georgia, June 23, 1864: "I saw a canteen upon which a heavy run was made during and after the charge—I still like whisky but I do not want any when going into action for I am or at least was drunk enough yesterday without drinking a drop." Manuscript in author's possession.

7. H. Belo, *Memoirs* (Boston, 1904), 40.

8. For example, see O. R., series 1, XXX, part 2, 237.

9. O. R., series 1, XXI, 664. A Virginia veteran attributed the greater resonance of the Southern battle cry to the rural background of most Confederates. In isolated areas, he said, hallooing was a necessary means of communication, while in the cities and towns from which a substantial portion of Yankees came, there was hardly ever an occasion for shouting. In comparing the sounds of the two yells, he said that the Federal cheer was a repeated "hoo-ray," with prolonged emphasis on the second syllable, while the Confederate cry was a series of "woh-who—eys" with a heavy subsiding accent on the blended "who" and "ey," the effect being a sort of "whee." J. Harvey Dew, "The Yankee and Rebel Yells," *Century Magazine*, XLIII (1892), 953–955. Other veterans referred to the Yankee shout as a practiced "hurrah," or a concerted "hip, hip, huzza, huzza, huzza," and to the Rebel Yell as a "yai, yai, yi, yai,

yi," but nearly all stress the individual informal quality of the latter. W. H. Morgan, *Personal Reminiscences of the War of 1861–1865* (Lynchburg, 1911), 70; A. P. Ford, *Life in the Confederate Army* (New York, 1905), 58. Douglas Freeman told the writer in an interview that the Confederate cheer was a battle-field adaptation of the fox hunter's cry, which cry the Richmond *News Leader* designated in the Aug. 17, 1936, issue as a wild "y-yo yo-wo-wo." The writer leans toward the theory that the "who-ey" version was the one most commonly used.

10. Journal of William P. Chambers, entry of Aug. 4, 1864, P.M.H.S., Centenary Series, V, 332.

11. *O. R.*, series 1, XXXVIII, part 3, 922.

12. For example, see *ibid.,* series 1, XXXIV, part 1, 752.

13. Robert M. Gill to his wife, July 28, 1864.

14. *O. R.*, series 1, X, part 1, 583; XXXVI, part 1, 1093–1094.

15. Morgan, *op. cit.,* 200; E. D. Patterson, in his diary entry of June 28, 1862, says that at Gaines's Mill when he and his comrade went over a ridge they encountered such heavy fire "that the whole brigade literally staggered backward several paces as though pushed back by a tornado." Typescript in private possession.

16. *O. R.*, series 1, XXXVI, part 1, 1093–1094, General Samuel McGowan's report of the "Bloody Angle" phase of Spottsylvania Court House; McGowan says further that a 22-inch oak tree was cut down by the heavy musket fire, injuring several soldiers when it fell. *Ibid.*

17. John L. G. Wood to his aunt, May 10, 1863, typescript, Georgia Archives; Robert M. Gill to his wife, Oct. 6, 1863; diary of Maurice K. Simons, entry of May 31, 1863, manuscript photostat, University of Texas.

18. *O. R.*, series 1, XXX, part 2, 305, Gen. T. C. Hindman's official report of Chickamauga; XXXIX, part 1, 821, Maj. E. H. Hampton's report of Allatoona; XXXI, part 2, 726, 750–757, Gen. John C. Brown's and Gen. P. R. Cleburne's reports of Lookout Mountain; XXVII, part 2, 486–487, Maj. Samuel Tate to Gov. Z. B. Vance, July 8, 1863, concerning Gettysburg; A. C. Redwood, "Jackson's Foot Cavalry at the Second Bull Run," *Battles and Leaders of the Civil War* (New York, 1887–1888), II, 535–536; Walter Clark, editor, *North Carolina Regiments, 1861–1865* (Raleigh and Goldsboro, 1901), II, 376.

19. *O. R.*, series 1, XXXVIII, part 3, 689.

20. For condition of troops before and during the Shiloh fight see *O. R.*, series 1, X, part 1, 454, 464, 498, 499, 522, 547, 569–570, 586; and XVII, part 2, 641.

21. A young Georgian, writing of his experience at Manassas, said, "As we were retiring I stopped to take a mouthful of mud—scarcely could it be called water—my mouth was awfully hot and dry." New Orleans *Daily Crescent,* Aug. 8, 1861.

22. Thomas Warrick to his wife, Jan. 11–13, 1863, manuscript, Alabama Archives.

23. [Napier Bartlett], *A Soldier's Story of the War*, (New Orleans, 1874), 192–193.

24. For instances of scattering of regiments under fire, see O. R., series 1, X, part 1, 467, 584; XXV, part 1, 984–985; LI, part 2, 199. Also John Crittenden to J. S. Bryant, Jan. 29, 1863, typescript, University of Texas; and J. E. Hall to his father, June 3, 1862, manuscript, Alabama Archives.

25. W. W. Heartsill, *Fourteen Hundred and 91 Days in the Confederate Army* (Marshall, Texas, 1876), 159; O. T. Hanks, "Account of Civil War Experiences," 29, manuscript photostat, University of Texas; Henry L. Graves to his aunt, Aug. 7, 1862, typescript, Georgia Archives; G. A. Hanson, *Minor Incidents of the Late War* (Bartow, Florida, 1887), 36; O. R., series 1, XXX, part 2, 418.

26. J. W. Rabb to his mother, Jan. 14, 1863, manuscript photostat, University of Texas.

27. John L. G. Wood to his wife, Dec. 18, 1862, typescript, Georgia Archives.

28. Robert Stiles, *Four Years Under Marse Robert* (New York, 1903), 219–220.

29. Harmon Martin to his sister, Aug. 25, 1863, typescript, Georgia Archives.

30. George W. Athey to his sister, (no date, but Dec., 1864), manuscript, Alabama Archives.

31. Hanks, *op. cit.*, 35.

32. O. R., series 1, XX, part 1, 957; M. D. Martin to his parents, May 8, 1863, typescript in private possession.

33. James Mabley to his sister, May 16, 1863, manuscript, Emory University.

34. Diary of E. D. Patterson, entry of Aug. 31, 1863.

35. Stiles, *op. cit.*, 116–117.

36. O. R., series 1, XII, part 2, 736; W. W. Heartsill, *op. cit.*, 159; Robert M. Gill to his wife, July 25, 1864.

37. Diary of Maurice K. Simons, various entries, May 17–July 3, 1863.

38. *Ibid.* River water next to the east bank became contaminated with maggots from the great number of dead animals thrown in, and cisterns were either polluted or exhausted. O. R., series 1, XXIV, part 2, 392.

39. Diary of James J. Kirkpatrick, entry of Aug. 5, 1864, manuscript, University of Texas; Robert M. Gill to his wife, July 9, Aug. 16, 1864; Bolling Hall to his sister, Laura, Sept. 20, 1864, manuscript, Alabama Archives.

40. Crenshaw Hall to his father, Oct. 16, 1864, manuscript, Alabama Archives.

41. Crenshaw Hall to Laura Hall, Feb. 20, 1865. A Virginia officer charged

with building a redoubt on the Petersburg line kept a man posted to call out the Yankee shots. At each flash of their guns he would call out "down" and the men would fall flat in the trench. The Federals got on to the trick and resorted to the device of setting off a blaze of powder to deceive the Rebs, and then giving them the real load as they rose up from their shelter. C. G. Chamberlayne, editor, *Ham Chamberlayne — Virginian* (Richmond, 1932), 267–268.

42. J. E. Hall to Laura Hall, Oct. 15, 1864, Feb. 8, 1865; Crenshaw Hall to Laura Hall, Feb. 20, 1865.

43. O. R., Series 1, XII, part 2, 593; XXX, part 2, 379.

44. *Ibid.*, XXX, part 2, 190, 379–380.

45. *Ibid.*, XXV, part 1, 1003.

46. *Ibid.*, XX, part 1, 719, 852.

47. *Ibid.*, 931.

48. *Ibid.*, X, part 2, 528; XI, part 2, 992-993; XX, part 2, 494; Robert Ames Jarman, "History of Co. K, 27th Mississippi Infantry," 10, typescript in private possession.

49. James A. McCord to his brother, Dec. 3, 1864, manuscript photostat in private possession.

50. O. R., series 1, XXVIII, part 1, 418–419, 524.

51. Samuel E. Mays, compiler, genealogical *Notes on the Family of Mays* (Plant City, Fla., 1927), 36; O. R., series 1, XI, part 2, 563, 612; part 3, 506, 571.

52. O. R., XX, part 1, 761, 879.

53. *Ibid.*, XXIV, part 2, 88.

54. Anonymous diary of a Louisiana soldier, entry of Nov. 25, 1863, manuscript, Confederate Memorial Hall, New Orleans.

55. O. R., series 1, XXXI, part 2, 665–666; see also Bate's General Order of Nov. 28, 1863, *ibid.*, 744. News correspondent "Sallust" wrote from a point near the battlefield at midnight of November 25: "The Confederates have sustained today the most ignominious defeat of the whole war—a defeat for which there is but little excuse or palliation. For the first time during our struggle for national independence, our defeat is chargeable to the troops themselves and not to the blunder or incompetency of their leaders. It is difficult for one to realize how a defeat so complete could have occurred on ground so favorable." Richmond *Daily Dispatch*, Dec. 4, 1863.

56. O. R., series 1, XXXVIII, part 3, 835; part 4, 766–767.

57. *Ibid.*, XLV, part 1, 660, 747, 749, 750.

58. Wirt A. Cate, editor, *Two Soldiers* (Chapel Hill, 1938), 169.

59. W. A. Fletcher, *Rebel Private Front and Rear* (Beaumont, Texas, 1908), 84.

60. C. Irvine Walker to Ada Sinclair, July 28, 1864, typescript, University of Texas.

Chapter 12

The Confederate as a Fighting Man

David Donald

In the preface to The Life of Johnny Reb, *Bell Irvin Wiley writes that his purpose is "to give the man of the ranks . . . something of his rightful measure of consideration." Wiley makes no claim to a work of analysis and interpretation, though he does draw an occasional conclusion: in* The Life of Billy Yank, *for example, he argues that Union soldiers' performance improved during the war, and he asserts that "the similarities of Billy Yank and Johnny Reb far outweighed their differences." In this selection from a 1957 article, David Donald, emeritus professor at Harvard University, while acknowledging his debt to Wiley, takes issue with the latter of these assertions. Donald's premise is that the nature of southern society helps to explain both the way Confederate soldiers performed and the outcome of the war.*

The Confederate soldier was, in most important respects, not materially different from one of Xenophon's hoplites or Caesar's legionnaires. He enlisted for a variety of reasons; he was brave or he was cowardly; he fought till the end of the war or he was killed, wounded, or captured. If it is hard to generalize about him, it is even more difficult to think of him as unique. His story is that of all soldiers in all wars.

In basic attitudes he was very much like World War II GIs. The recent study of *The American Soldier* would puzzle him by its sociological lingo, but, if translated into layman's language, it would not surprise him by its conclusions. Like his GI descendants, the Confederate soldier agreed that the infantry was the most dangerous and difficult branch of service, and he preferred his own equivalent of the air force—the cavalry. Depending upon what the psychologists call his "personal esprit," his "personal commitment," and his "satisfaction with status and job," he would have expressed varying opinions when asked how well the Confederate army was run. He did not have any very clear idea as to what caused the Civil War, but, if questioned, he would very probably have responded as did ninety-one per cent of World War II soldiers who felt "whatever our wishes in the matter, we have to fight now if we are to survive."[1]

Johnny Reb was even more similar to Billy Yank, his opponent in the Union forces. In two fascinating and learned studies of the everyday life of Civil War soldiers Bell I. Wiley has amply proved that "the similarities of Billy Yank and Johnny Reb far outweighed their differences. They were both American, by birth or by adoption, and they both had the weaknesses and the virtues of the people of their nation and time."[2]

Yet contemporaries with opportunities to observe soldiers in both the opposing armies found the Southern fighting man subtly and indefinably different. He looked "the genuine rebel." That astute British diarist, Colonel Fremantle, found that "in spite of his bare feet, his ragged clothes, his old rug, and tooth-brush stuck like a rose in his buttonhole," the Confederate warrior had "a sort of devil-may-care, reckless, self-confident look, which is decidedly taking."[3]

Most impartial observers found a want of discipline among Confederate troops, a peculiar indifference to "their obligations as soldiers."[4] At the outset of the war, one participant later wrote, "The Southern army . . . was simply a vast mob of rather ill-armed young gentlemen from the country."[5] Six months before Appomattox the inspector-general of the Army of Northern Virginia concluded that things had not greatly changed: ". . . the source of almost every evil existing in the army is due to the difficulty of having orders properly and promptly executed. There is not that spirit of respect for and obedience to general orders which should pervade a military organization. . . ."[6]

The Southerners' want of military discipline is not surprising. Confederate soldiers were mostly recruited from the independent small farmers who composed the vast majority of the ante bellum Southern population.[7] They came from a society that was not merely rural but, in many areas, still frontier, and isolation of settlements, absence of established traditions, and opportunities for rapid social mobility encouraged a distinctive Southern type of self-reliance.[8] In the years before the Civil War political democracy triumphed in the South,[9] and demagogues repeatedly capitalized upon Southerners' resentments against the planter aristocrats. Even slavery was defended in terms of equalitarian ideals. "With us," said Calhoun, "the two great divisions of society are not the rich and poor, but white and black; and all the former, the poor as well as the rich, belong to the upper classes, and are respected and treated as equals. . . ."[10]

Southerners were citizens before they were soldiers, and they did not take kindly to military discipline. At the outbreak of the war they rushed to enlist, fearing the fighting would be over before they could get to the front. Instead of "fun and frolic,"[11] they soon learned that being a soldier meant drill, spit-and-polish, military discipline, and more drill. An Alabama enlisted man became disillusioned: "A soldier is worse than any negro on Chatahooche [sic] river. He has no privileges whatever. He is under worse taskmasters than any negro. He is not treated with any respect whatever. His officers may insult him and he has no right to open his mouth and dare not do it."[12]

Such a reaction was, of course, perfectly normal; it has happened in all American wars. Fifty-one per cent of our soldiers in World War II felt that discipline was "too strict about petty things" and seventy-one per cent thought they had "too much 'chicken' to put up with."[13] But the distinctive thing about the Confederate army is that Southern soldiers never truly accepted the idea that discipline is necessary to the effective functioning of a fighting force. They were "not used to control of any sort, and were not disposed to obey anybody except for good and sufficient reason given. While actually on drill they obeyed the word of command, not so much by reason of its being proper to obey a command, as because obedience was in that case necessary to the successful issue of a pretty performance in which they were interested. Off drill they did as they pleased, holding themselves gentlemen, and as such bound to consult only their own wills."[14]

They found routine training assignments tedious, and they shirked them. A Mississippi sergeant reported that his men objected to being put on details "because they said they did not enlist to do guard duty but to fight the Yankees. . . ."[15] When they did serve, they behaved with characteristic independence. Colonel Fremantle at first thought Confederate sentries "quite as strict as, and ten times more polite than, regular soldiers" when they challenged him as he entered Longstreet's camp. But when he complimented the Confederate commander, Longstreet "replied, laughing, that a sentry, after refusing you leave to enter a camp, might very likely, if properly asked, show you another way in, by which you might avoid meeting a sentry at all."[16]

On the march Southern troops were seldom orderly. Even Stonewall Jackson had trouble with stragglers,[17] and Lee's men moved "at a slow dragging pace" and were "evidently not good marchers naturally." In spite of repeated orders from headquarters, Confederates could never see the need for carrying heavy packs, and they were "constantly in the habit of throwing away their knapsacks and blankets on a long march." Particularly in the early years of the war, Southern soldiers found victory nearly as demoralizing as defeat, and after a battle "many would coolly walk off home, under the impression that they had performed their share."[18]

Toward their officers, and particularly toward their immediate superiors, they exhibited a typical democratic disrespect for authority. The whole highly stratified system of military organization, "in which hierarchies of deference were formally and minutely established by official regulation,"[19] was a denial of the principle of equality. Confederates disliked "the restrictions placed on the privates," when the officers were permitted to "go to town at option, stay as long as they please, and get gloriously drunk in and out of camp when it suits them to do so." Like one peevish Texan they felt that officers "are living better and wear better clothes than they did before the war." Officers had, another private echoed hungrily, "bacon to eat, Sugar to put in their coffee and all luxuries of this kind," while the common soldier had "the hardships to under go." Another Texan wrote home: ". . . I will stay and tuff it out with Col Young and then he can go to Hell . . . he has acted the dam dog and I cant tell him so if I do they will put me in the Guard House . . . but I can tell him what I think of him when this war ends . . . I will come [home] when my time is out or die I wont be run over no longer not to please no officers they have acted the rascal with me. . . ."[20] Clearly most Confederates would have agreed with the American soldier in World War II who grumbled: "Too many officers have that superior feeling toward their men. Treat them as if they were way below them . . . What's the matter with us enlisted men, are we dogs?"[21]

Such resentments against a caste system are normal among democratic citizen-soldiers. But where American troops in World Wars I and II had to vent their aggressions in grumbling and goldbricking, Confederates more often took direct action against their superiors. Confederate court martial records are full of such cases as that of Private George Bedell of Georgia, who called his commanding officer "a damned son of a bitch, a damned tyrant, a damned puppy, a damned rascal." If an officer persisted in acting like a martinet, his men might ride him on a rail until he promised "better behavior,"[22] or they might petition for his resignation.[23]

In fact, to an extent almost unparalleled in any other major war, the Confederate common soldier was the master of his officers. Southern armies were organized upon the principle that the men might voluntarily choose their commanders. The system grew up without much planning. The peacetime militia, a quasi-social, quasi-political organization, had always elected officers, and the Confederate army was constituted on the same basis. When volunteers enlisted, they chose from among themselves noncommissioned officers, lieutenants, and captains; in general the man who organized and helped outfit a company was elected its captain. "The theory was," as George Cary Eggleston noted, "that the officers were the creatures of the men, chosen by election to represent their constituency in the performance of certain duties, and that only during good behavior."[24] Only the high ranking field officers were appointed by Richmond.

A wartime emergency compelled the Confederate government to continue the inefficient elective system. At first Southerners had thought the war would be short, and most original Confederate volunteers enrolled for only twelve months' service. In December 1861 the Confederate Congress abruptly awoke to the fact that these troops, the mainstay of the Southern army, would be mustered out in the spring. To oppose McClellan's magnificently equipped Northern troops the South would have only a skeleton army. Hurriedly the Southern Congress passed a law to encourage reenlistment by granting furloughs and bounties to veterans who promised once more to volunteer. As a special inducement the measure provided that all troops who reenlisted should have the power to reorganize themselves into companies and elect new company officers; these companies, in turn, should "have the power to organize themselves into battalions or regiments and to elect their field officers." The law, as General Upton tersely remarked, should have borne the title, "An act to disorganize and dissolve the . . . Army."[25] . . .

The painful process of reorganization had a disastrous effect on military efficiency. The Confederate common soldier sharply reacted against discipline and order. The "men have defeated almost every good officer,"

T. R. R. Cobb lamented, "and elected privates and corporals to their places."[26] General E. P. Alexander agreed that ". . . the whole effect was very prejudicial to the discipline of the army."[27] General Beauregard in the West and General Joseph E. Johnston in the East united in reporting that their troops were "demoralized" by the elections.[28]

Though professional military men unanimously disapproved of the elective system, subsequent Confederate legislation retained it without material alteration. Until almost the end of the war Confederate companies were repeatedly disorganized by these political campaigns for military office. In September 1862 a Mississippi company saw "Great electioneering" with "Party lines . . . sharply drawn, two tickets . . . in the field, and the adherents of each . . . manfully working for success."[29] The following April the proud First Virginia Infantry was almost wrecked when recently added conscripts threatened to elect one of themselves lieutenant. That calamity was averted only when the colonel "told the Company in case any *raw recruit was elected* that he would instantly have him *examined* before the board," which weeded out incompetent officers.[30] As late as January 1864 Texas troops prepared to choose new commanders. "There is great wire-pulling among the officers just at this time," one Confederate wrote his wife. "Some that I know of will not *reign* again unless I am much mistaken."[31] . . .

Though militarily indefensible, the system was politically necessary, and it was retained until the closing months of the war. Confederate soldiers, liberty-loving citizens from a democratic society, cherished the right to elect their officers, and the politicians defended them. Soldiers "are not automatons," a Confederate congressman insisted, "dancing to the turning of some official organ grinder. The best *mind* and the best *blood* in the country are in the army, and much of both are found in the ranks. They have not lost the identity of the citizen in the soldier."[32] Even President Jefferson Davis justified the system: "The citizens of the several States volunteered to defend their homes and inherited rights . . . the troops were drawn from the pursuits of civil life. Who so capable to judge of fitness to command a company, a battalion or a regiment as the men composing it?"[33]

The election of officers unquestionably contributed to the chronic lack of discipline in Confederate forces, but it was also a reflection of the fact that Southern soldiers were unwilling to obey orders which struck them as onerous or commanders who seemed to them unreasonable. Like a tedious refrain, the theme of poor discipline runs through the official reports of all Confederate commanders. Even the Army of Northern Virginia, for all its intense devotion to Lee, was poorly controlled. When Lee took command in 1862, his troops were described as "an 'Armed mob' . . . magnificent material, of *undisciplined individuality,* and, as such, correspondingly unreliable and disorganized."[34] Three more years of fighting saw some improvement, yet in November 1864 Lee sorrowfully announced: "The great want in our army is firm discipline."[35]

Few Southern soldiers showed deference to the officers whom they themselves had elected, but some felt that there was another sort of rank which should be maintained and respected, namely, that of social position. "The man of good family felt himself superior, as in most cases he unquestionably was, to his fellow-soldier of less excellent birth; and this distinction was sufficient, during the early years of the war, to override everything like military rank."[36]

These upper-class Southerners belonged to that small group of planter, merchant, and professional families who still dominated the social and economic, if no longer the political, life of the region. Membership in this Southern aristocracy depended not merely upon wealth but upon family, education, good breeding, and intelligence. Nineteenth century equalitarian currents had eroded the political power once held by the Southern gentry, but they had left the plantation ideal untouched as the goal of social aspiration.[37]

The members of this upper class were dedicated Southerners, but they saw no reason why war should seriously alter their pattern of life. Some brought along slaves to serve as their personal attendants while in the army. Such was Tom, who cared for Richard Taylor, son of a former President of the United States, throughout the war. A "mirror of truth and honesty," Tom "could light a fire in a minute under the most unfavorable conditions and with the most unpromising material, made the best coffee to be tasted outside of a creole kitchen, was a 'dab' at camp stews and roasts, groomed . . . horses . . . , washed . . . linen, and was never behind time."[38] . . .

[Upper-class Southerners] might not be numerous, but they contributed to the want of discipline in the Confederate forces. They resented having to take orders. When one well-to-do private could not take "a dozen face and a smaller number of foot or bath towels" on campaign with him, he "actually wrote and sent in to the captain an elegant note resigning his 'position'."[39] "It is," wrote another of these snobs, "galling for a gentleman to be absolutely and entirely subject to the orders of men who in private life were so far his inferiors, & who when they met him felt rather like taking off their hats to him than giving him law and gospel."[40] When the gentleman-soldier found army regulations unduly restrictive, he was likely to defy them, and if he had good family connections, he was fairly certain not to suffer for his insubordination. A Mississippi judge complained that it was "but a mockery of form" to "convict a soldier of any offense, who has social position, friends, and influence."[41]

These Southern aristocrats were, of course, at a great disadvantage in competing in company elections. A planter's son had to be habile in concealing his social superiority and skilful in the arts of mass persuasion if he hoped to rise from the ranks through popular choice. All the class tensions and prejudices felt against him in civilian life carried over into military service, and the poorer soldiers were suspicious of "the genteel men," who "think all you are fit for is to stop bullets for them, your betters, who call you poor white trash."[42] A high Confederate administrator concisely summarized the social consequences of having elected officers: ". . . in our armies . . . to be an officer is not necessarily to be a gentleman.. . . ."[43]

If he was handicapped at the lower levels of advancement in the Confederate army, the Southern aristocrat found that the upper command posts were reserved almost exclusively for men of his class. Far more than the Confederate civilian administration, which had few claims to social distinction and included among the cabinet members a plantation overseer, the son of a keeper of a dried-fish shop, and a penniless German orphan immigrant,[44] the Southern army leadership was recruited from the most exclusive elements of ante bellum society. . . .

It was natural that the Confederacy should turn to this trained leadership when hostilities broke out. But it is significant that as the war wore on and deaths and resignations made new promotions possible, the South continued to recruit its military leaders from the same small aristocratic social stratum. Southerners appointed to high military rank in 1864 were, to be sure, much younger than the commanders chosen in 1861, and a significantly smaller proportion of them had been trained at West Point.[45] But in family background, wealth, and social position there was no real change. At the end of the war as at its beginning the Confederacy recruited its military chiefs from its finest families.

Though the Southern armies in the West were mostly raised from the rough, semi-frontier Gulf states, their commanders also came from the upper-class planter aristocracy. In the west as in the east, field officers were drawn almost exclusively from wealthy families, usually associated with planting, which had a long tradition of social leadership and military activity. Both groups of generals were well educated, though a somewhat higher proportion of those in the Eastern theater had attended the United States Military Academy.[46] From the point of view of social position, the two groups were virtually interchangeable.

The class line which separated field commanders from lower, elective officers was not completely impassable, but it was virtually so. The few who crossed it were made to feel conspicuous as social misfits. Nathan B. Forrest, the West's most daring cavalry leader, was never allowed to forget that he was "wholly without formal education" and that he had been in civilian life a trader in horses and slaves.[47] A Mississippi gentleman placed under Forrest indignantly expressed his "distaste to being commanded by a man having no pretension to gentility—a negro trader, gambler,—an ambitious man, careless of the lives of his men so long as preferment be *en prospectu*." "Forrest may be . . . the best Cav officer in the west", he added, "but I object to a tyrrannical, hotheaded vulgarian's commanding me."[48] Forrests in the Confederacy were few; the Southern army offered only limited opportunities for social mobility.

The Confederate army was, thus, at the same time an extraordinarily democratic military organization and an extraordinarily aristocratic one. The paradox was the reflection of the basic ambivalence of Southern society itself, which believed in the equality of all white men and simultaneously recognized sharp gradations between the social classes.

At the outbreak of the war this ambiguous Southern attitude toward democracy proved a major asset to the Confederate cause. There was little time to convert civilians into proper soldiers, and it was an advantage that Southern recruits were sturdy, independent-minded individualists. Their subaltern officers often lacked training and knew "nothing of details or how to look after the thousand wants which arise and must be met."[49] Even the West Pointers at first needed experience in handling large numbers of men. In 1861 when General R. S. Ewell, who had previously commanded a company of dragoons on the Indian frontier, was told that the countryside around Manassas was bare of supplies for his men, he sallied forth on a cattle hunt himself. Late in the day he returned to camp triumphantly leading one bull to the slaughter. When one of his fellow officers "observed that the bull was a most respectable animal, but would hardly afford much subsistence to eight thousand men," the general ruefully exclaimed, "Ah! I was thinking of my fifty dragoons."[50] In the circumstances it was just as well that Southern recruits were not army regulars.

At the same time it was a decided asset to have in the South recognized, trained leaders who merely required time and experience to develop into expert army commanders. There was some grumbling at times against the upper-class professional officers who preempted the high positions, particularly the staff officers, "young sprouts with bobtailed coats and vast importance, . . . who obviously thought the war was gotten up that they might dazzle the world by their talents."[51] Occasionally President Davis had to yield to popular prejudices and appoint political generals of no very great military knowledge or aptitude, such as "Extra Billy" Smith, former governor of Virginia, who "was equally distinguished for personal intrepidity and contempt for what he called 'tactics' and for educated and trained soldiers, whom he was wont to speak of as 'those West Pint fellows.' "[52] But the Confederacy never saw an organized attempt to oust the military experts comparable to the Northern Radical Republicans' campaign against the West Pointers in the Union army. In the South training, tradition, and social position kept qualified officers in control.

But what was an advantage in the opening days of the war became a serious handicap later. When both opposing armies were little more than armed mobs, the Confederate soldier, fighting on his own terrain, could ignore orders, rely on his wits, and still achieve victory. But as gigantic and highly disciplined Northern armies pressed forward, the Confederate, though still a magnificent individual fighter, was put at a disadvantage by his indifference to discipline. These differences must not be exaggerated; Northern armies too were shockingly undisciplined by modern standards. But the Confederacy, with its shortages of men and material, could scarcely afford the high price of individualism. In February 1865 General Lee sadly concluded: "Many opportunities have been lost and hundreds of valuable lives have been uselessly sacrificed for want of a strict observance of discipline."[53]

The rigidity of social structure which had provided the Confederacy with a secure, trained top command at the outbreak of the war also became a disadvantage as the conflict continued. The Confederate high command showed a remarkable continuity through the four years of war. While the Northern army was led successively by McDowell, McClellan, Pope, Burnside, Hooker, and Meade, the Southern forces in

Northern Virginia had only two generals-in-chief—Joseph E. Johnston and Robert E. Lee. As the war progressed and death or incapacity made room for fresh leaders there were, of course, new faces in the Confederate high command, but these were from the same social class, with the same kind of training and the same social outlook as their predecessors. Had the art of war remained unchanged, this continuity in Confederate leadership would have been only an advantage, but the Civil War, the first truly modern war, witnessed technological changes of an unprecedented nature—new kinds of rifles, new uses for artillery, new possibilities for railroad warfare. The Northern winning team of Lincoln, Grant, and Sherman came from a more openly structured society and was trained to improvise and adapt. Confederate leadership had an aristocratic hostility toward change.[54]

The Southerner as a fighting man, then, was a product of the paradoxical world that was the ante bellum South, devoted to the principles of democracy and the practice of aristocracy. And to compound the paradox, the Southerner's assets at the outbreak of the war became his liabilities by its conclusion. Historians in seeking the reasons for the collapse of the Confederacy have correctly pointed to inadequate Southern resources, poor transportation, unimaginative political leadership, and state rights. All these, and more, deserve to be taken into account, yet perhaps more basic to the Confederate failure was the fundamental ambivalence in the Southern attitude toward democracy. Because of that weakness the Southerner made an admirable fighting man but a poor soldier.

NOTES

From David Donald, "The Confederate as a Fighting Man," *Journal of Southern History* 25 (May 1959): 178–93. Reprinted by permission.

    1. Samuel A. Stouffer and others, *The American Soldier: Adjustment during Army Life* (Princeton, 1949), I, *passim*, especially 102, 432.
    2. Bell Irvin Wiley, *The Life of Billy Yank: The Common Soldier of the Union* (Indianapolis, 1951), 361. My indebtedness in these pages to Professor Wiley's massive researches is very great. His studies provide a vivid and detailed portrait of the Southern soldier.
    3. Arthur J. L. Fremantle, *Three Months in the Southern States: April, June, 1863* (Mobile, 1864), 293.

4. *Ibid.*, 123.

5. George Cary Eggleston, *A Rebel's Recollections* (Indianapolis, 1959), 69.

6. *The War of the Rebellion: A Compilation of the Official Records of the Union and Confederate Armies* (Washington, 1880–1901), series 1, XLII, part 2, 1276–77. Hereafter cited as *Official Records*.

7. Frank L. Owsley, *Plain Folk of the Old South* (Baton Rouge, 1949), *passim*.

8. W. J. Cash, *The Mind of the South* (New York, 1941), 4 ff.

9. Fletcher M. Green, "Democracy in the Old South," *Journal of Southern History*, XII (1946), 3–23.

10. Allan Nevins, *Ordeal of the Union* (4 vols., New York, 1947–1950), I, 419.

11. Wiley, *The Life of Johnny Reb: The Common Soldier of the Confederacy* (Indianapolis, 1943), 27.

12. Edmund Cody Burnett (ed.), "Letters of Three Lightfoot Brothers, 1861–1864," *Georgia Historical Quarterly*, XXV (1941), 389.

13. Stouffer *et al.*, *American Soldier*, I, 396.

14. Eggleston, *Rebel's Recollections*, 70–71.

15. Quoted in Wiley, *Johnny Reb*, 27.

16. Fremantle, *Three Months*, 247.

17. Douglas Southall Freeman, *Lee's Lieutenants: A Study in Command* (3 vols., New York, 1942–1944), I, 367.

18. Fremantle, *Three Months*, 226, 123.

19. Stouffer *et al.*, *American Soldier*, I, 55.

20. Quoted in Wiley, *Johnny Reb*, 236, 140.

21. Stouffer *et al.*, *American Soldier*, I, 372.

22. Quoted in Wiley, *Johnny Reb*, 49, 242.

23. John Q. Anderson (ed.), *Brokenburn: The Journal of Kate Stone, 1861–1868* (Baton Rouge, 1955), 162–63.

24. Eggleston, *Rebel's Recollections*, 71.

25. Emory Upton, *The Military Policy of the United States* (Washington, 1917), 460–61.

26. T. R. R. Cobb, "Extracts from Letters to His Wife, February 3, 1861–December 10, 1862," *Southern Historical Society Papers*, XXVIII (1900), 292.

27. E. P. Alexander, "Sketch of Longstreet's Division," *ibid.*, X (1882), 37.

28. *Official Records*, series 1, X, part 1, 779, and XI, part 3, 503.

29. William Pitt Chambers, "My Journal: The Story of a Soldier's Life . . . ," *Mississippi Historical Society Publications*: Centenary Series (1925), V, 248.

30. Joseph T. Durkin (ed.), *John Dooley: Confederate Soldier, His War Journal* (Georgetown, 1948), 89.

31. Frank E. Vandiver (ed.), "Letters from the Confederate Medical Service, 1863–65," *Southwestern Historical Quarterly*, LV (1952), 390.

32. Quoted in E. Merton Coulter, *The Confederate States of America, 1861–1865* (Baton Rouge, 1950), 329.

33. Dunbar Rowland (ed.), *Jefferson Davis, Constitutionalist: His Letters, Papers and Speeches* (10 vols., Jackson, 1923), IX, 543.

34. *Ibid.*, VII, 410.

35. *Official Records*, series 1, XLII, part 3, 1213.

36. Eggleston, *Rebel's Recollections*, 72.

37. For the power and prestige still retained by the planter aristocracy see Nevins, *Ordeal of the Union*, I, 416–19; Clement Eaton, *A History of the Old South* (New York, 1949), 444–54; and Roger W. Shugg, *Origins of Class Struggle in Louisiana* . . . (University, La., 1939), *passim*.

38. Richard Taylor, *Destruction and Reconstruction: Personal Experiences of the Late War* (New York, 1879), 63.

39. Robert Stiles, *Four Years under Marse Robert* (New York, 1903), 46–47.

40. Quoted in Wiley, *Johnny Reb*, 344.

41. *Official Records*, series 4, III, 709.

42. Bessie Martin, *Desertion of Alabama Troops from the Confederate Army: A Study in Sectionalism* (New York, 1932), 122; Hugh C. Bailey, "Disloyalty in Early Confederate Alabama," *Journal of Southern History*, XXIII (1957), 525.

43. *Official Records*, series 4, II, 949.

44. Burton J. Hendrick, *Statesmen of the Lost Cause: Jefferson Davis and His Cabinet* (Boston, 1939), 9.

45. The median age of generals, lieutenant-generals, and major-generals commissioned in 1861 was 51 years; the median age of those appointed in 1864 was 37. Of the 12 men commissioned at these ranks in 1861, 10 had attended the United States Military Academy; of the 29 commissioned in 1864, only 14 had been at West Point.

46. Of the 38 generals, lieutenant-generals, and major-generals clearly identified with the Western theater of operations, 57 per cent had attended the United States Military Academy; their mean age at the date of appointment to their highest rank was 40.7 years. Of the 50 top commanders identified with Eastern operations, 64 per cent had been at West Point; their mean age at achieving highest rank was 39.8 years. Generals like Samuel Cooper, who were identified with neither theater of action, and those like Joseph E. Johnston, who fought for long periods in both, have been omitted from these computations.

47. Thomas M. Spaulding in Allen Johnson and Dumas Malone (eds.), *Dictionary of American Biography* (22 vols., New York, 1928–1958), VI, 533.

48. Quoted in Wiley, *Johnny Reb*, 338.

49. Susan Leigh Blackford (ed.), *Letters from Lee's Army: Or Memoirs of Life in and out of the Army in Virginia* . . . (New York, 1947), 9.

50. Taylor, *Destruction and Reconstruction*, 38.

51. Blackford (ed.), *Letters from Lee's Army*, 12.

52. Stiles, *Four Years under Marse Robert*, 110.

53. Quoted in Wiley, *Johnny Reb*, 243.

54. I have developed this theme in more detail in my *Lincoln Reconsidered: Essays on the Civil War Era* (New York, 1956), 82–102.

Chapter 13

The Rebels Are Barbarians

Grady McWhiney and Perry D. Jamieson

*Like Donald, Grady McWhiney of Texas Christian University and Perry
D. Jamieson of the U.S. Air Force Support Office interpret the Confederate army's fate, but they find a different explanation. Where Donald
focuses on divisions within the Confederate army, McWhiney and Jamieson emphasize a unifying theme in southerners' ethnic heritage. The
authors are aware of the argument that the war's outcome was purely a
matter of quantities of and men and resources, reflected in one southerner's belief that "the enemy is superior to us in everything but courage." Yet they also remind us that in a number of instances, including
the Mexican War and Vietnam, the numerically inferior army was victorious. This selection is the concluding chapter of* Attack and Die
*(1982), McWhiney and Jamieson's controversial assessment of fighting
styles in the Civil War.*

It is significant that most of the Confederacy's military leaders practiced
in the 1860s the offensive tactics that they had seen work so well in
Mexico in the 1840s, but the tactical preferences of a few men—even
those in high command—could scarcely have prevailed if a majority of
the southern people had opposed offensive warfare. The simple fact is
that Southerners were aggressive.

They were culturally conditioned "for offensive war," explained a
Richmond newspaper in August 1862: "The familiarity of our people
with arms and horses gives them advantages for aggression, which are
thrown away by delay. Ten thousand Southerners, before the Yankees

learnt to load a gun, might have marched to Boston without resistance." Such confidence in their ability to drive the enemy was typical of Confederates, especially in the first years of the war. The cultural isolation of their society fostered a contempt for outsiders, particularly Yankees, and a romantic vision of southern self-prowess. Many a Southerner, contended a native of the South, "at all times feels able and prepared— cocked and primed, in his own vernacular—to flog the entire North." The common view in the antebellum South was that Northerners would not fight. "Such shameful cowards these Yankees are," proclaimed a Southerner. "I am sorry to hear of the times being so hard in old Blount [County, Alabama] but I think they will be better in 12 months & I have a good reason for thinking so," a young Confederate soldier wrote in October 1861. "Because we are going to kill the last Yankey before that time if there is any fight in them still. I believe that J. D. Walker's Brigade can whip 25,000 Yankees. I think that I can whip 25 myself."[1]

Combat was more highly esteemed in the Old South than in the Old North. "To such an extent does the military fever rage," observed one Southerner, "a stranger would conclude at least every other male citizen to be either 'Captain or Colonel, or Knight at arms.' Nor would he greatly err, . . . for . . . he would find more than every other man a military chieftain of some sort or other." Southerners were quick to anger and to fight. "I heard today of another instance of the barbarous manner which the Floridians have in settling difficulties," wrote a visitor. "Two men had a slight difficulty about some hogs. They became enraged & meeting each other both fired at the same time. The one was killed & the other dangerously wounded." Such encounters were customary. "Human life is a cheap commodity [in the South], and the blow of anger but too commonly precedes or is simultaneous with the word," explained a foreigner. "The barbarous baseness and cruelty of public opinion, dooms young men, when challenged, to fight," noted a traveler. "They must fight, kill or be killed, and that for some petty offence beneath the notice of the law. Established names only . . . may refuse to fight, but this is rarely done; to refuse is a stain and high dishonour." The southern habit of regarding a fighter—soldier or dueler—as a hero horrified many Northerners. "Cruel horrid custom thus to butcher & destroy men for the false code of honor," pronounced a Yankee preacher. Unlike Southerners, Northerners "were not so military in their habits," observed a contemporary, "because, though equally brave . . . , they were more industrious, more frugal, and less mercurial in their temperament. Religion was with them a powerful spring of action, and discouraged all wars except those of self-defence. The social and moral virtues, the sciences and arts, were cherished and respected; and there were many roads to office and to eminence, which were safer and more certain, and not less honourable, than the bloody path of warlike achievement."[2]

Their attitude toward combat was only one of the many ways in which Southerners and Northerners differed. Antebellum observers pointed out that Southerners practiced, as an Englishwoman put it, "a mode of life which differs entirely from that prevailing in the Northern States."[3] A wide range of eyewitnesses characterized Southerners as more hospitable, generous, frank, wasteful, lazy, lawless, and reckless than Northerners, who were in turn more reserved, thrifty, shrewd, disciplined, enterprising, acquisitive, careful, and practical than Southerners. The Old South was a leisure-oriented society where people favored the spoken word over the written and enjoyed their sensual pleasures—singing, dancing, eating, drinking, gambling, riding, hunting, fishing, and fighting. Family ties reportedly were stronger in the South than in the North; Southerners, whose values were more agrarian, wasted more time and consumed more tobacco and liquor. Yankees, on the other hand, were cleaner, neater, more orderly and progressive, worked harder, and kept the Sabbath better than Southerners.[4]

Yankee culture was in large part transplanted English culture; southern culture was Celtic—Scottish, Scotch-Irish, Welsh, Cornish, and Irish.[5] The Confederate diarist who wrote in 1863 that "the war is one between the Puritan & Cavalier" was close to the mark, and so was the English traveler who observed that "the slave-holding states appeared to stand in about the same relation to the free, as Ireland does to England; every thing appears slovenly, ill-arranged, incomplete [in the South]; windows do not shut, doors do not fasten; there is a superabundance of hands to do every thing, and little is thoroughly done."[6] . . .

This cultural dichotomy in America was not only the major cause of the Civil War but it explains why the war was fought the way it was. Because the American Civil War was basically a continuation of the centuries-old conflict between Celts and Englishmen, it is understandable that Southerners would fight as their Celtic ancestors had and that Yankees would follow the ways of their English forebears, even to the extent of recruiting foreigners and blacks to do some of their fighting for them.[7]

From the war's outset the Confederates fought in the traditionally Celtic way: they attacked. The best-known example of their recklessness was Gettysburg, where the Confederates lost nearly 23,000 men in three days of attacks. Losses were so severe at Gettysburg because the Confederates did just what the Federals wanted and expected them to do—attack strongly defended positions. "The plan of [Confederate General Robert E. Lee's] . . . attack seems to have been very simple," noted a foreign observer. Indeed it was; General Lee, reportedly a descendent of the Scottish military hero Robert Bruce, matched the raw courage of his men against the deadly fire of rifled muskets and artillery. The results can best be described in the words of participants in the slaughter. A Union soldier recalled that on the first day a line of Rebels "nearly a mile in length" attacked. "First we could see the tips of their color-staffs coming up over the little ridge, then the points of their bayonets, and then the Johnnies themselves, coming on with a steady tramp, tramp, and with loud yells." When they neared the Union position they were met by a "tornado of canister" that swept their line "so clean . . . that the Rebels sagged away. . . . From our second round on a gray squirrel could not have crossed the road alive."[8] . . .

Southerners lost the Civil War because they were too Celtic and their opponents were too English. The distinguished historian of the war's common soldiers, Bell I. Wiley, concluded that in many ways Johnny Reb and Billy Yank were quite different. Rebels fought "with more dash, *élan* and enthusiasm"; they were more emotional, more religious, more humorous and poetical, says Wiley. They also had a more "acute sense of the ludicrous, the dramatic or the fanciful." Yanks, on the other hand, were more practical, more materialistic, more literate, and they displayed "more of tenacity, stubborness en masse and machinelike efficiency."[9] These, and other distinctions that Wiley failed to mention, are significant. They suggest that the Civil War was a conflict between two distinct peoples and they also indicate the persistence over time of cultural patterns that seriously influenced, if they did not absolutely determine, the war's outcome.

All of the differences that Wiley recognized are cultural characteristics that separated not merely Rebels and Yankees but Celts and their historic enemies from antiquity to the American Civil War. Romans and Englishmen, like Yankees, were more practical, more materialistic, more literate, more tenacious, and more machinelike than the Celts they fought, just as the Confederates and their Celtic forebears were more emotional, foolhardy, romantic, and undisciplined than their opponents. . . .

Yankees viewed Southerners with fully as much contempt as Englishmen viewed Celts. Before the Civil War a Northerner, with typical Anglo-Saxon arrogance, advised Yankees to "mingle freely" with Southerners, "and . . . strive to bring up their habits, by a successful example, to the New England standard." When that proved impossible, stronger measures were recommended. "I believe," announced a saintly Northerner, "that the great conception of a Christian society, which was in the minds of the Pilgrims of the Mayflower, . . . is to displace and blot out the foul [South] . . . , with all its heaven-offending enormities; that . . . our vast and heterogeneous . . . population is either to be subdued and won to its principles and its blessings or to give place to the seed of the righteous." A Massachusetts soldier favored a policy of genocide toward Southerners. "I would exterminate them root and branch," he wrote just after the war. "They have often said they preferred it before subjugation, and, with the help of God, I would give it them. I am only saying what thousands say every day." In calls to exterminate Southerners and their "odious ways," Northerners sounded much like English Puritans who advocated the obliteration of their "barbarian" Celtic neighbors. It may be no coincidence that Irish-born reporter William Howard Russell described Federal Secretary of War Edwin Stanton as "excessively vain, . . . a rude, rough, vigorous Oliver Cormwell sort of man." Typically, Yankees referred to Confederates as dirty and ignorant, just as the English had spoken of the Irish, Welsh, and Scots. A Minnesotan called Confederate soldiers "vagabonds," while another Yank denounced them as "ruffians and desperadoes." Several Federals spoke of Southerners as "savages," and one Connecticut soldier informed his sister that the "Rebels are Barbarians and savages."[10] . . .

Much of what seemed to their enemies as barbaric—violence, sloth, and mirth—was literally part of the Celtic way of life. The Celts generally were pastoralists who thought that anyone who worked hard was crazy; it was easier to let animals make one's living and to spend time more pleasantly—eating, drinking, hunting, fishing, gambling, racing horses, dancing, and fighting. Polybius noted that the ancient Celts "slept on straw, usually ate meat and did nothing other than fight." Gerald of Wales wrote of the Welsh in the twelfth century: "They pay no attention to commerce, shipping or industry, and their only preoccupation is military training." The eighteenth-century traveler Thomas

Pennant pointed out that the Scots were "indolent to a high degree, unless roused to war, or to any animating amusement." So was the white antebellum Southerner, who was "fond of grandeur, luxury, and renown, of gayety, of pleasure, and above all of idleness," observed Alexis de Tocqueville; "nothing obliges him to exert himself in order to subsist; and as he has no necessary occupations, he gives way to indolence, and does not even attempt what would be useful."[11]

As their enemies were quick to point out, Celts shared certain warlike characteristics. They glorified war, seemed genuinely fond of combat, and usually fought with reckless bravery. "This people have no self-control," said the Roman writer Livy of the Celts. "They tear their banners out of the ground and set off." Strabo insisted that the "whole [Celtic] race is madly fond of war, high-spirited and quick to battle, and on whatever pretext you stir them up, you will have them ready to face danger, even if they have nothing on their side but their own strength and courage."[12]

A visitor to the Confederacy in 1861 found "revolutionary furor in full sway, . . . an excited mob, . . . flushed faces, wild eyes, screaming mouths, hurrahing for 'Jeff Davis' and 'the Southern Confederacy.' . . . Young men are dying to fight." One Southerner boasted that the Confederates could "beat the Yankees at the ordeal of dying. Fighting," he said, "is a sport our men always have an appetite for." Many Yanks agreed. One announced: "*A Confederate soldier would storm hell with a penknife.*" There is no record of Confederates attacking with only penknives, but General James R. Chalmers's Mississippi Brigade attacked at Murfreesboro with half the men in one regiment armed only with sticks, and, those in another regiment carrying rifles that were still too wet from the previous night's rain to fire. "The Rebles. . . . fight like Devills," admitted a Union soldier, and another Yank stated that the Confederates "outfight us . . . in every battle. I admire the desperation [with which they attack]." One observer noted that the Confederates "rushed upon the foe with an impetuosity and fearlessness that amazed the old army officers, and caused foreign military men to declare them the best fighters in the world."[13]

NOTES

From Grady McWhiney and Perry D. Jamieson, *Attack and Die: Civil War Military Tactics and the Southern Heritage* (Tuscaloosa: University of Alabama Press, 1982), 170–72, 178–85. Reprinted by permission.

1. *Daily Richmond Whig,* August 26, 1862; Daniel R. Hundley, *Social Relations in Our Southern States,* ed. William J. Cooper, Jr. (reissue, Baton Rouge, 1979), 224; John Washington Inzer, " 'The Yankees are the Meanest People on Earth,' " comp. Clarke Stallworth, in *Birmingham News,* November 4, 1980, B-1; T. B. Deaver to Thomas Hendricks, October 8, 1861, *Cherished Letters of Thomas Wayman Hendricks,* comp. Josie Armstrong McLaughlin (Birmingham, 1947), 86.

2. Hundley, *Social Relations,* 127–28; Henry B. Whipple, *Bishop Whipple's Southern Diary, 1843–1844,* ed. Lester B. Shippee (London, 1937), 29–30; Charles Mackay, *Life and Liberty in America, . . . in 1857–8* (New York, 1859), 173; William Faux, *Memorable Days in America . . .* (London, 1823), 187; Frederick Hall, *Letters from the East and from the West* (Washington, 1840, 287–88. The South's chivalric cult is emphasized in Rollin G. Osterweis, *Romanticism and Nationalism in the Old South* (New Haven, 1949).

3. Catherine C. Hopley, *Life in the South . . .* (2 vols., reissue, New York, 1974), I, 73–74.

4. See, for example, Thomas Ashe, *Travels in America . . .* (3 vols., London, 1808), I, 123; Carl David Arfwedson, *The United States and Canada, in 1832, 1833, and 1834* (2 vols., London, 1834), I, 364; II, 181; [Carlo Barinetti], *A Voyage to Mexico and Havana; including some General Observations on the United States* (New York, 1841), 29–30; James Silk Buckingham, *The Slave States of America* (2 vols., London, 1842), I, 286–87; Moritz Busch, *Travels Between the Hudson & the Mississippi, 1851–1852,* trans. and ed. Norman H. Binger (Lexington, 1971), 150–53; George William Frederick Howard, Earl of Carlisle, *Travels in America* (New York, 1851), 76–77; Michel Chevalier, *Society, Manners and Politics in the United States,* trans. Thomas Gamaliel Bradford (Boston, 1839), 149–50; Louis Auguste Felix, Baron de Beaujour, *Sketch of the United States . . . ,* trans. William Walton (London, 1814), 133–34; Ebenezer Davies, *American Scenes — and Christian Slavery: A Recent Tour of Four Thousand Miles in the United States* (London, 1849), 104, 208; Faux, *Memorable Days,* 35–36; William Kingsford, *Impressions of the West and South During a Six Weeks' Holiday* (Toronto, 1858), 53; Charles Joseph Latrobe, *The Rambler in North America . . .* (2 vols., London, 1835), I, 60–61, II, 5; Alexander Mackay, *The Western World; or Travels in the United States in 1846–47 . . .* (3 vols., London, 1849); I, 204; II, 134, 143; David W. Mitchell, *Ten Years in the United States; Being an Englishman's View of Men and Things in the North and*

South (London, 1862), 192; Charles G. Parsons, *Inside View of Slavery; or, A Tour Among the Planters* (Cleveland, 1855), 164; Alexis de Tocqueville, *The Republic of the United States of America, and Its Political Institutions*, trans. Henry Reeves (New York, 1858), 427, 560; Whipple, *Southern Diary*, 26, 43–44.

5. Forrest McDonald and Grady McWhiney, "The Antebellum Southern Herdsman: A Reinterpretation," *Journal of Southern History*, XLI (1975), 147–66; Grady McWhiney, "The Revolution in Nineteenth-Century Alabama Agriculture," *Alabama Review*, XXXI (1978), 3–32; Forrest McDonald, "The Ethnic Factor in Alabama History: A Neglected Dimension," ibid., 256–65; Grady McWhiney, "Saving the Best from the Past," ibid., XXXII (1979), 243–72; Forrest McDonald and Ellen Shapiro McDonald, "The Ethnic Origins of the American People, 1790," *William and Mary Quarterly*, XXXVII (1980), 179–99; Forrest McDonald and Grady McWhiney, "The South from Self-Sufficiency to Peonage: An Interpretation," *American Historical Review*, LXXXV (1980), 1095–1118.

6. T. Otis Baker Diary, October 8, 1863, T. Otis Baker and Family Papers, Mississippi Department of Archives and History, Jackson; Carlisle, *Travels in America*, 54–55.

7. Half a million of the Federal soldiers were foreign born and an additional 180,000 were blacks. E. B. Long and Barbara Long, *The Civil War Day by Day: An Almanac, 1861–1865* (Garden City, 1971), 705, 707. A foreign observer noted: "The Southerners . . . estimate highest the Northwestern Federal troops. . . . The Irish Federals are also respected for their fighting qualities; whilst the genuine Yankee and Germans (Dutch) are not much esteemed." Arthur J. L. Fremantle, *The Fremantle Diary . . .* , ed. Walter Lord (Boston, 1954), 133.

8. Fremantle, *Diary*, 210; William Winston Fontaine, "The Descent of General Robert Edward Lee from King Robert the Bruce, of Scotland," *Southern Historical Society Papers*, IX (1881), 194–95; Douglas S. Freeman, *R. E. Lee: A Biography* (4 vols., New York, 1934–1935), I, 160; Augustus Buell, *"The Cannoneer": Recollections of Service in the Army of the Potomac* (Washington, 1890), 63–64.

9. Bell I. Wiley, *The Life of Billy Yank: The Common Soldier of the Union* (Indianapolis, 1951), 358–61.

10. Abner D. Jones, *Illinois and the West* (Boston, 1838), 157; Julian M. Sturtevant, *An Address on Behalf of the Society for the Promotion of Theological Education in the West* (New York, 1853), 468–69; Wiley, *Life of Billy Yank*, 346; William Howard Russell, *My Diary North and South* (2 vols., London, 1863), II, 433; Wiley, *Life of Billy Yank*, 347–49.

11. T.G.E. Powell, *The Celts* (New York, 1958), 74–100; Anne Ross, *Everyday Life of the Pagan Celts* (London, 1970), 34–53, 87–109; Barry Cunliffe, *The Celtic World* (New York, 1979), 42–55; Lloyd Laing, *Celtic Britain* (New

York, 1979), 19–44, 131–57; Wallace Notestein, *The Scots in History* (reissue, Westport, 1970), 22–30, 92–96, 192–201; Gerald of Wales, *The Journey through Wales and the Description of Wales*, trans. Lewis Thorpe (reissue, New York, 1978), 233; Thomas Pennant, *A Tour in Scotland; 1769* (5th edition, London, 1790), 214; Tocqueville, *Republic of the United States*, 427.

12. Ross, *Everyday Life*, 74–77; Laing, *Celtic Britain*, 19–30; Cunliffe, *Celtic World*, 56–59; Gerhard Herm, *The Celts: The People Who Come Out of the Darkness* (New York, 1977), 1–13.

13. Russell, *My Diary*, I, 134–39; John B. Jones, *A Rebel War Clerk's Diary*, ed. Earl S. Miers (reissue, New York, 1958), 32; Bell I. Wiley, "The Common Soldier of the Civil War," *Civil War Times Illustrated*, XII, No. 4 (July 1973), 28; unpublished reports of Major J. O. Thompson, Forty-fourth (Blythe's) Mississippi Infantry, and Lieutenant Colonel T. H. Lyman, Ninth Mississippi Infantry, William P. Palmer Collection of Braxton Bragg Papers, Western Reserve Historical Society, Cleveland; Wiley, *Life of Billy Yank*, 351; Randolph A. Shotwell, *The Papers of Randolph Abbott Shotwell*, ed. J. G. de Roulhac Hamilton (2 vols., Raleigh, 1929), I, 314.

Chapter 14

The Infantry Firefight

Paddy Griffith

The Civil War saw the large-scale introduction of the rifled musket, a muzzle-loading weapon whose grooved barrel was capable of much greater accuracy than the smoothbore musket it replaced. It has long been accepted that the accuracy of rifled-musket fire made Civil War infantry charges exceptionally costly and increased the horror of battle for soldiers. Paddy Griffith, an independent scholar who lives in Nuneaton, England, questions this assumption. To Griffith, the key issue is not the accuracy of the weapon but rather the training of soldiers and their commanders. This selection from Battle Tactics of the Civil War *(1989) assesses small-arms firepower and offers alternative tactics that might have been more successful than those that were used.*

The characteristic mode of combat in the Civil War was the infantry firefight at close range. This was the usual result when an attacker had overcome his first fear of the enemy's rifles or fieldworks and had marched into contact. Sometimes a decision could be reached before this by long-range fire, and very occasionally it could be reached entirely by cold steel. More normally, however, there were clear winners and losers only after a period of intense musketry.

Two Theories of Infantry Fighting

... One very influential Civil War theory—in fact the most influential of all—envisaged infantry sheltering behind fieldworks, delaying the attack by obstacles and discouraging it by heavy fire. According to this theory the contest would almost inevitably be won by the static defender, because he would enjoy the advantage of protection while the attacker was presented as an easy target in the open.

... By 1864 troops imbued with this theory had become reluctant to press home their attacks, since they understood only too clearly what dangers they would have to run. Perhaps less obvious, however, are some of the purely logical difficulties for an attacker which such respect for entrenchments would entail. For example, the attacker who believes in fieldworks will naturally have built some of his own—and these will create a physical obstacle to his advance no less than a psychological reminder of the safety he is leaving. On some occasions soldiers were expressly forbidden to charge forward from their works even in favourable circumstances.[1] Then if the attacker does come close to the enemy he will perceive the latter's advantage in terms of protection from fire. Instead of moving forward, the attacker will himself wish to gain protection by going to ground and even digging in. Hence the contest will subtly have changed in structure from being an "attack" against a "defence" into a parallel contest of two entrenched units. Deprived of its dynamic, the battle will degenerate into an exercise in attrition and exhaustion.

Sometimes an attack would go forward, find it could make no progress, then retire a little to a somewhat safer place—at perhaps 300–400 yards from the enemy—and entrench.[2] On occasion some natural cover might be found closer than that, as in the Iron Brigade attack at Antietam: ...

> After a few rods of advance, the line stopped by a common impulse, fell back to the edge of the corn and lay down on the ground behind a low rail fence.[3]

This attack eventually moved forward after reinforcements arrived, but was then repelled in turn by the arrival of Confederate reserves. ...

One psychological reason for digging in so close to danger lay in the still greater danger, once one had come so close, which was assumed to lie in retreating back across open ground.[4] When one of the veterans of the Atlanta campaign described the difficulties and losses involved in coming close to the enemy, he culminated with the following snort of disgust:

... And then the slaughter of a retreat *there*! Oftentimes it is preferable to lie down and take the fire there until night rather than lose all by falling back under such circumstances.[5]

Perhaps this fear of retreat was linked to a horror of turning one's back on the threat. Even though the real danger from fire to a unit retreating from 200 to 400 yards from the enemy may not actually have been terribly great, it must have seemed crushing to a unit which had already suffered much while facing forward. A type of reverse ostrich syndrome may have applied, whereby the danger was bearable only while the men continued to watch it. Reluctance to abandon the wounded may also have played a part, as indeed may justifiable possessiveness for the ground won at such cost.

For whatever reason, Civil War units on the offensive did often settle down to a prolonged exchange of shots at close range with a defender, even without fieldworks being dug by either side. The following case from Second. Manassas is characteristic:

> ... it was a stand-up combat, dogged and unflinching, in a field almost bare. There were no wounds from spent balls; the confronting lines looked into each other's faces at deadly range, less than one hundred yards apart, and they stood as immovable as the painted heroes in a battle-piece ... and although they could not advance, they would not retire. There was some discipline in this, but there was much more of true valor.
>
> In this fight there was no manoeuvering, and very little tactics—it was a question of endurance, and both endured.[6]

This combat continued from "late in the afternoon" until at least 9 p.m.—perhaps three or four hours of close musketry. Another example comes from Murfreesboro:

> A few of the more venturesome Rebels reached a rail fence less than twenty yards from the muzzles of our muskets, but none ever returned. Others paused at a distance of seventy-five to a hundred yards, delivered their fire and dropped to the ground to load and fire again ...
>
> For at least half an hour this bloody angle at the edge of the cedars was held. ...[7]

A similar battle is recorded by one of the Union attackers at Champion's Hill in the Vicksburg campaign:

> The enemy had fallen back a few rods, forming a solid line parallel to our own, and now commenced in good earnest the fighting of the day. For

half an hour we poured the hot lead into each others' faces. We had forty rounds each in our cartridge boxes, and probably nine-tenths of them were fired in that half hour.[8] . . .

None of this adds up to firefights which were concluded rapidly, although it could sometimes happen. What we see more usually is a fairly protracted period of firing with only a limited forward movement by the attacker, if there is any at all. Maybe a conclusion could be reached in thirty or even fifteen minutes; maybe it took the $1\frac{1}{2}$–2 hours required for a regiment to fire off all its ammunition; or maybe it would drag on until night—however long that might be. The timespan was very variable, but the central thought behind many of these contests was that victory depended upon firepower, that the way to win was to blaze away into the enemy's face until he was too numb, or too exhausted, or too badly mauled to carry on. Then perhaps he would go away. This was the hope which kept men going in many of the assaults and slaughter pens of the first three years of war, and sometimes even in the year of demoralisation itself, 1864.

It was perhaps foolish for attackers to imagine that they could use firepower and protection more effectively than a prepared defender, and to that extent the eventual disillusionment with assaults was justified. Yet in battle after battle we find regiments hanging on at close range, slugging it out with presumably this hope in their minds. Perhaps it was a matter of pride in the imagined prowess of the unit, or simply fear of the disgrace of withdrawal. Probably there was a complex mixture of psychological pressures generated by the tensions of close combat itself. But, whatever the subliminal reasons may have been, the only rational theory of tactics that could be applied to these firefights was the static, attritional one of the engineers. The idea was to exchange shots and make both sides bleed, until the side with more men would be left the winner.

The alternative theory of tactics was the one implied by the European drill books, which may be termed the "infantry" as opposed to the "engineer" solution to the problem. According to this theory it was as ridiculous for a defender to stay cowering behind his earthworks as it was for an attacker to go to ground at the very moment when he had finally come near his objective. What was required instead was a fluid battle of attack and counter-attack in which firefights would be very short indeed, if they took place at all. The decision would not depend upon firepower and protection, according to this theory, but upon the bayonet and shock action.

"Shock action" is a much misunderstood term in the Civil War context, and the bayonet had been mercilessly mocked ever since General Sherman first realised that his army was shy of Johnston's trenchwork. In the high-handed verdict of history these traditional instruments have been derided as representing a theory of combat which no longer worked in practice, a theory relegated to the scrap heap by the supposedly more "scientific" conceptions of the engineers. Yet if we examine them here in a little detail we may perhaps discover that they were not quite as irrational or inappropriate as the polemicists would have us believe.

The key word, for both attack and defence, was not so much "bayonet" as "shock"! The defender would hide himself as best he could until the enemy was close, then spring up, shock him and charge into him, chasing him away. Conversely the attacker would attempt to come close to the defender, shock him into flight and then—once again—chase after him. This is what the British in the Peninsular War had generally understood by infantry tactics, and it was also the concept adopted by many French writers of the early nineteenth century—notably Marshal Bugeaud, the great mentor of the army which eventually fought so well in the Crimea and Italy. Both he and Wellington had seen that the important thing was to keep up the forward impetus of a formed body, regardless of whether their shock effect was gained by the bayonet alone, or by cheering, or by both of those allied to a short, sharp volley. This concept was perfectly familiar to the teachers at West Point, and it had worked well in Mexico in 1846,[9] but the lack of theoretical explanations in the drill manuals meant that it was rarely properly understood by the hastily improvised officers of the Civil War. In the absence of systematic guidance from above they tended to follow the most obvious—and superficially safest—line of action, using musketry from a protected position.

A great deal of misunderstanding has arisen from the fact that a "bayonet charge" could be highly effective even without any bayonet actually touching an enemy soldier, let alone killing him. One hundred per cent of the casualties might be caused by musketry, yet the bayonet could still be the instrument of victory. This was because its purpose was not to kill soldiers but to disorganise regiments and win ground. It was the flourish of the bayonet and the determination in the eyes of its owner that on some occasions produced shock,[10] just as on other occasions the same effect might be produced by noise or muzzle flash. It is only the believers in the attritional "engineer" or "fire-power" theories of tactics who have tried to portray the bayonet as a killing machine, in order to ridicule it.

A crucial element in shock action was the holding of fire until the enemy was at very close range. Not only would one's first volley be physically more damaging, but it would come as more of a surprise, especially if the enemy himself was unable to return the compliment at once. When he was subjected to a mass attack at Antietam, General Gordon reckoned that

> The only plan was to hold my fire until the advancing Federals were almost upon my lines. No troops with empty guns could withstand the shock. My men were at once directed to lie down upon the grass. Not a shot would be fired until my voice should be heard commanding "Fire!"[11]

In the event this plan worked well; the volley was very destructive and the counter-charge which followed it was effective, although it failed to completely break the opposition. The battle settled down into a protracted firefight after all. Rather more successful was the Orphan Brigade's use of a similar tactic near Resaca: "Our infantry reserved their fire until the enemy were in close range when we opened on them, almost every shot killing a man."[12] After this the attack made no further headway, although the defenders felt too weak to counter-attack it.

The use of shock on the defensive often exploited the classic "ambush" tactics of concealment and surprise. Shock tactics could also be used in the assault, however, without the benefit of concealment. A fortnight after its Resaca action the Orphan Brigade had to attack a hill. It was told to "Reserve your fire until forty yards of their line, then fire, each man taking careful aim and then rush upon them and give them the bayonet."[13] This was successful and, despite early Union shooting at longer range, the Confederates delivered their own fire only when they could see their enemies' buttons. The Federals broke as the attack came to ten yards of them. Then a number of them were shot in the back.

Nor was any of this new. As early as the Peninsula campaign of 1862 there had already been a fairly widespread use of shock tactics, especially in the Confederate army. At Gaines's Mill A.P. Hill's troops had stalled before the strong Union position when Whiting's division was fed through them in one of the war's more successful examples of the passage of lines. General Law tells us that his brigade was told not to halt at that point, but to take up the charge

> in double-quick time, with trailed arms and without firing. Had these orders not been strictly obeyed the assault would have been a failure . . . [A thousand men were hit as they advanced, but] not a gun was fired in reply; there was no confusion, and not a step faltered as the two gray lines swept swiftly and silently on; the pace became more rapid every moment; when the men were within thirty yards of the ravine, and could see the desperate nature of the work in hand, a wild yell answered the roar of the Federal musketry and they rushed for the works. The Confederates were within ten paces of them when the Federals in the front line broke cover, and leaving their log breastworks, swarmed up the hill in their rear, carrying away their second line with them in their rout.[14]

After this, once again, the main Confederate fire action came while the enemy was fleeing from them. . . .

There is certainly evidence to show that a unit which continued its charge without stopping could cause astonishment in the enemy's ranks, simply because such a tactic was so unexpected. Civil War soldiers regarded it as more natural to fight statically by fire, and did not know quite what to make of an attacker who held to some other theory. In Captain De Forest's first battle[15] his green troops started to receive infantry fire at about five hundred yards from the enemy trench. After marching forward through three volleys the colonel allowed them to relieve their feelings by opening fire and seeking cover on the ground, but then he insisted that they resumed their advance. This they did, still firing as they moved, although without regularity of drill. The enemy ran off when the range had closed to about one hundred yards. Prisoners later told the regiment that "We expected to see you come on in the usual style,—halt to fire and then advance again—not fire and come on all together . . . Your firing didn't hurt us . . . but your coming on and yelling scared us."[16] De Forest concluded that the position would not have been carried without both the firing in the advance and the rapidity of the advance itself. The firing raised friendly morale and spoiled the enemy's aim to the extent that only six men in the Union regiment were hit by musketry, while the speed of assault created the enemy's urgency to run away. A slower attack might have both inflicted and suffered more casualties—and it would have failed to carry the position because it would have lacked the essential ingredient of shock.

The essence of shock tactics was the deliberate acceptance of a higher risk in order to achieve a more decisive result. Holding fire until close range was psychologically difficult for most soldiers, because it left them longer in danger before doing anything in return, yet it was likely to be more effective than uncontrolled blazing away at long range. By the same token it took courage to continue an advance upon the enemy without alleviating the danger by lying down or halting at decently long range. Thus commanders who asked their men to use shock tactics were asking for an unnatural response to fear. It took exceptional leadership, or exceptionally high-quality soldiers, to make the system work. . . .

A further difficulty with shock tactics was that they demanded more coordinated action than the "engineer" tactics of firepower and protection. Even quite a small minority of soldiers opening fire prematurely could spoil the shock effect of a supposedly crushing volley, just as a minority of stragglers could make an attacking spearhead believe that it had been abandoned to its fate and was sticking its neck out too far. Sherman noted that this effect was particularly acute with skirmishers, who always had to contend with the loneliness of their open-order formation anyway. He said that even one or two men hanging back could bring a skirmish line's advance to a halt.[17] Nevertheless, the same phenomenon did also apply to the movements of a formed line. The impact was lost unless a regiment stuck together and moved with unanimity and common purpose, if not necessarily with drill-ground precision.

Unanimity of purpose could be spoilt by several different influences. In De Forest's battle, described above, it was almost spoilt by the inexperience of the troops. Only exceptionally firm leadership—and also probably the weakness of the enemy's position—carried them through. With excessively experienced troops, by contrast, there would be too many "old lags" in the ranks for bold ventures to be practicable. Whenever genuine risks were to be run—as opposed to operations which seemed risky to a greenhorn but were routine to a veteran—the unanimity of the regiment would tend to operate in the direction of security and safety.

Then again, pure chance might upset the balance in even the most total surprise. Consider the case of the Federal regiment at Second Manassas which used immaculate shock tactics only to find that ill fortune had pitted it against a rather special opponent. This is how the battle looked to one of the Confederates:

We neared the Chinn house, when suddenly a long line of the enemy rose from behind an old stone wall and poured straight in our breasts a withering volley at point-blank distance. It was so unexpected, this attack, that it struck the long line of men like an electric shock. But for the intrepid coolness of the colonel, the 17th Virginia would have retired from the field in disorder. But his clear, ringing voice was heard, and the wavering line reformed. A rattling volley answered the foe, and for a minute or two the contest was fiercely waged. . . . [18]

The ultimate outcome was that after a firefight lasting ten minutes at fifty yards' range the Union line withdrew—surely an undeservedly disappointing outcome to a perfect deadfall.

The simple fact is that shock tactics were always difficult to pull off successfully unless one's own troops were entirely reliable or the enemy's were markedly inferior.

In the Civil War especially, there was such a mixture of units at different phases of their "learning curve," on both sides, that it was impossible for a higher commander to make confident generalisations about the likely efficacy of any particular system of tactics. Thus Hood as a brigade commander could predict the efficacy of his unstoppable Texans, but Hood as an army commander was proved to be out of touch with reality when he applied the same standards to all his men. Civil War commanders found that each regiment had to be allowed to operate in the way to which it had become accustomed, in the hope that it would encounter the type of enemy it could "whip"—or at least "drive."[19] Shock tactics promised the biggest dividend if they could be made to work, but fire and protection tactics seemed to offer the greatest safety—even if they did not always deliver it in practice.

Musketry Rangers

An important feature of Civil War infantry fighting was the range of firing—both the range at which fire was first opened and the range at which an enemy could be persuaded to run away. These were rarely the same, although they might sometimes coincide—as we have seen—when shock tactics were being used. More normally an attacker would continue to advance some distance under fire before a decision was reached: he would observe a distinction in his mind between "maximum" and "decisive" range.

We have already seen many examples of protracted fire at very short range, and the conclusion appears to be unavoidable that this was the normal state of affairs in the Civil War.[20] We may nevertheless hope to refine our findings in a number of respects, since not all Civil War battles were the same. The terrain and the fields of fire were longer in some battles than in others, while the quality of the weapons improved quite significantly as the war went on. Early willingness to storm fortifications had sagged dramatically by 1864, and the incidence of strong fieldwork had correspondingly increased. There was also a difference in doctrine from one unit to another, from one commander to another, and from one theatre to another.

There is a major problem of evidence in all this, since armies unaccustomed to measuring ranges accurately, even in their prepared defensive positions, can scarcely be expected to cite accurate distances for confused battles which often took place on unfamiliar ground. Nevertheless, the literature is full of positive statements of the ranges at which fire was exchanged, so it may be worth taking them on trust. Even if this tells us no more than the ranges at which Civil War soldiers would in retrospect have *liked* fire to have been applied, it still represents knowledge of a sort.

In Gustavus Smith's book on Seven Pines there are seventeen usable references to the range of musketry fire, although unfortunately only three of them make the important distinction between "maximum" and "decisive" range (respectively 100 and 40 yards, 50 and 10 yards, 300 and 30 yards). The other ranges quoted are presumably those at which the bulk of each firefight took place, without necessarily telling us the range at which fire was opened or the range at which a decision was reached. In a good number of cases, however, it is specified that this was the range at which fire was opened.

The average range for the seventeen fights was 68 yards, or very considerably less than the 200 yards quoted by British experts as the battle range of the Brown Bess smoothbore musket.[21] There is only one reference in the Seven Pines sample to musketry at more than 200 yards, and that is the 300 yards maximum already mentioned. There is one reference to a firefight at 150-200 yards, but all the rest are described as taking place at 100 yards or less, with three at 100 yards, one at 75 yards and all the rest 50 or less. Twenty or thirty yards appears to be the most common combat range in this particular battle.

Seven Pines was not, of course, a "typical" Civil War action. It had rather more close country than was normal in Virginia—although it did also include some open fields. It was very much an "early war" battle, with a high proportion of smoothbore muskets and almost universally inexperienced regiments, yet it could show at least its fair share of fortifications. But as a representative battle for the early war period it could not easily be bettered.

In the course of my (admittedly somewhat random[22] research, however, I have come across forty-one other references to the range at which fire was delivered in the battles of 1861–2—the early war period. Of these 41 only five give both a "maximum" and a "decisive" range (400 and 25, 100 and 10, 150 and 25, 200 and 50, 400 and 75 yards respectively), but the general average works out at 122 yards, or almost twice the Seven Pines result. This includes only eight references to firing over 200 yards, and eight more between 101 and 200. Well over half of the references are therefore compatible with "Napoleonic" ranges of a hundred yards or less. If the seventeen references from Seven Pines are combined with the forty-one other "early war" results, we find the average range itself is only 104 yards.

If we look to 1863 as a putative transition point in the war—the mid-war period—we find that there were far fewer battles and therefore fewer references to range data. I happen to have encountered only ten, including two with both "maximum" and "decisive" figures (200 and 80, 40 and 20 yards). The average works out at 127 yards, with five references—exactly half—mentioning a range greater than 100 yards. The longest range mentioned is 250 yards, however, which contrasts with a reference to 500 yards in the early war sample.

In the late war period of 1864–5 I have encountered forty-five references to range, including six with both end points indicated (400 yards and "close", 300 and 50 yards, 300 yards and "close", 40 and 10, 120 and 10, and 200 and 30 yards. I have taken "close" to represent 20 yards in these cases). The average works out as a range of 141 yards, or rather more than for the two earlier periods, albeit still below the 200 yards quoted for the Brown Bess. In fact there are still only nineteen references to fire over 100 yards range—less than half the sample—with the longest ranges mentioned being 500 yards once and 400 yards four times. . . . Ranges did gradually lengthen as the war went on, but . . . they never lengthened very far. The difference between 68 yards for a smoothbore musket in a wood in 1862 and 141 yards for an Enfield fired across a clear glacis from an earthwork in 1864 is not particularly impressive, and the general difference between 104 yards for "early war" and 141 yards for "late war" is less impressive still. It is particularly striking that out of a sample of 113 references I have encountered only 17 which mention ranges longer than 250 yards, and none beyond 500. This contrasts with a well documented army corps volley at 1,000 yards at the Battle of Talavera in 1809, at a time when Monsieur C.E. Minié was still only five years old.

It is difficult to find any evidence at all to support the suggestion that Civil War musketry was delivered at ranges much longer than those of Napoleonic times, at least if one excludes the very tiny number of snipers who did occasionally fire beyond 500 yards. When it comes to the fire of formed bodies acting in concert, we have to admit that the arrival of the rifle musket actually made very little practical difference—whatever may have been its theoretical potential to revolutionise the battlefield.

It is possible to argue that the limited but nevertheless remorseless increase in battlefield ranges during the Civil War was the result of gradually improving weaponry, but it was more probably the spread of disillusionment later in the war that was really to blame. In every era of military history long-range fire is the preferred tactic of soldiers who have lost their taste for assaults at close quarters—and the example from Talavera, already cited, was very much a case in point.

We should also remember that there is a definite limit to the usefulness of long-range fire even today. Even with fully motivated troops the opportunities for fire over two or three hundred yards are rare in modern battle. Studies of the Second World War and the Korean War suggest that normal combat ranges were about 100 yards, and in Vietnam the figure was still lower.[23] There is therefore a fallacy in the notion that longer-range weapons automatically produce longer-range fire. The range of firing has much more to do with the range of visibility, the intentions of the firer and the general climate of morale in the army.

In the Civil War there was certainly a recognition that fire at excessive range would be wasted. In 1864 21st Virginia refused to imitate its neighbouring regiment, which fired at 400 yards, for this reason.[24] 35th Massachusetts in 1862, despite being armed with Enfields, considered that 300 yards was out of range of the enemy. Its main line lay down in the open at this distance, sending skirmishers nearer.[25] . . .

It may be true that advancing infantry perceived themselves to be at risk from musketry at longer ranges in the 1860s than they had done fifty years earlier, since undisciplined defenders opening fire at excessively long ranges may have caused bullets to fall harmlessly nearby. In particular, the peculiar whistling sound of the Minié bullet[26] must have made the fact of incoming fire more noticeable. Hence the "zone of fear" for an attacker was perhaps somewhat extended beyond Napoleonic norms. Nevertheless, it is clear from the record that the real effectiveness of musketry was negligible at all but point-blank range. Even at the noted "slaughter pens" at Bloody Lane, Marye's Heights, Kenesaw, Spotsylvania and Cold Harbor an attacking unit could not only come very close to the defending line, but it could also stay there for hours—and indeed days—at a time. Civil War musketry did not therefore possess the power to kill large numbers of men, even in very dense formations, at long range. At short range it could and did kill large numbers, but not very quickly.

Where we find a reference to both the "maximum" and the "decisive" range of fire, furthermore, we usually find that the latter is very short indeed. Out of my fourteen examples the average is 33 yards. This suggests that the existence of a wide field of fire may be regarded as irrelevant to the effect of musketry in the Civil War. All that was needed was a clear shot over perhaps the last 75 yards, as Captain Nisbet had arranged for his men at Resaca, or the last 55 yards, as General Griffin had contrived in the Wilderness.[27] This was the concept of tactics understood by Civil War officers who bothered to think about the matter—not some fancy idea of using the rifle musket's power at long range.

In order to determine the effect of open fields of fire upon the range of musketry it may be worth considering the case of Antietam, one of the most open battlefields of the war. I have found eleven references to range in this battle, giving an average of 107 yards. Only four ranges are longer than 100 yards, however, with the longest standing at 300 yards. Admittedly this was an "early war" battle in which considerable numbers of smoothbores were used, but even so the ranges are not as long as the terrain might lead one to expect. The contrast with the figures for the more wooded combat at Seven Pines is not dramatic.

It is rather harder to find such an open battlefield in the late war period, since trees and fortifications were then the normal rule. If we take the reasonably open terrain at Cold Harbor and Petersburg, however, we find ten references to range, with an average of 186 yards, and only two references to ranges below 100 yards; 400 yards is the longest, and it is mentioned twice. This does admittedly represent a considerable extension of the field of fire, although the average still falls short of the 200 yards claimed for the Brown Bess.

It was apparently even harder to find open fields of fire in the Western theatre than in the Eastern, since the overall average range in the West, from my sample, was exactly 100 yards. That in the East was 136 yards. However, my sample contains only 22 references to ranges in the West as opposed to 87 in the East (and 4 unclassifiable). This doubtless betrays a certain weighting of my sources in favour of the Virginia theatre, although it is also quite probable that fewer firefights actually did take place in the West—and certainly that any given individual was far less likely to see as many there as in the East.

Varieties of Attack

Now that we have established that Civil War earthworks were seldom barriers to movement, and that musketry was deadly only if maintained for a long period of time at short range, we can see that the success of the defence in this war was based largely on bluff. If two regiments opposing each other could often fire off their entire load of ammunition without reaching a conclusion, it is unlikely that a regiment holding a line could literally shoot down a massed attack. In the time the attacker needed to cross the last 33 yards—a minute at the outside—a defender who had already fired a few shots would be incapable of bringing down enough accurate fire to hit more than a small proportion of the assailants. The attacker would surely lose far fewer men if he pushed on without stopping than if he halted and tried to reach a conclusion by protracted volleying. If more Civil War regiments had understood this principle and possessed the military qualities needed to carry it out, we would doubtless have seen far fewer indecisive outcomes to the firefights.

Nevertheless, the bluff was usually effective and, for a variety of reasons, the attacker often did stop short of his objective. We even occasionally encounter the paradoxical spectacle of a regiment holding a position for some hours after it had used its ammunition.[28] Certainly a defender often fired high, not daring to lift his eyes above the protection of his works[29] but depending for his effect upon the flash and crash of the detonation, and the enveloping smoke which mercifully hid the scene from view.

On the attacking side there were many pressures acting against a resolute assault, apart from the enemy's appearance. The gruesome spectacle of the attackers' own wounded and dead would naturally create a deep impression, while the disintegration of drill would remove an important motor of unified action. The insidious doctrine that battles were supposed to be fought by firing must also have created a psychological barrier to forward movement—and in any case it was always easier to stand still doing something familiar than to venture into the unknown.

Some tacticians tried to overcome the natural inertia of units in combat by the use of shock tactics, as we have seen. Others, however, sought their salvation in inventive assault formations. Taking their cue from Napoleon, Jomini and the whole geometry of engineering science, commanders devised a range of different layouts intended to bring troops face to face with the enemy in a more than normally advantageous manner.

The basic infantry formation was a line of regiments deployed two men deep, with skirmishers ahead to prepare the way and supports a few hundred yards in the rear to cover for accidents.[30] In the classic European conception these intervals would be observed throughout the battle, and if the first lines needed succour they would be briskly replaced by the supports. In the difficult terrain of many Civil War battles, however, the succeeding lines tended to bunch too closely together until all became confused in a single shapeless mass. Attempts to meet the problem by adding additional support lines in the rear only made matters worse, as did the practice of closing the theoretical intervals between lines to 75 yards or so.

The use of columns instead of lines was more attractive in broken terrain, since they gave greater manoeuvrability, but the problem of excessive bunching remained. Once again, the attempts to solve the problem by throwing additional men at it—by making the columns deeper—was a failure. In any columnar assault formation the correct solution should have been to find ways to get the front ranks moving forward rather than to build up a mass of men behind them.

Some large assaults in columns or a succession of lines met with success[31]—enough to keep the idea alive throughout the war—but more often they were a failure. Most notably successful was Upton's attack at Rapahannock Station on 7 November 1863, repeated with much the same troops at Spotsylvania the following spring. The layout here was four successive lines each of three regiments—with the leading elements detailed to break outwards to the flanks once the enemy's first line had been cleared, and the rear line to hold back in reserve. This represented a move towards specialised assault drills of some sophistication, although it did not always work. A few weeks later at Cold Harbor Upton's attack was repulsed. . . .

French theorists such as Marmont, Jomini, Morand and Pelet looked not to heavier formations but to lighter ones. They wanted attacks to be made in a line of small columns—each no more than a regiment—with wide deployment distances between them and supports kept well to the rear until needed. This was a tactical conception which placed the responsibility for victory upon the individual regiment, and even the individual company. It did not submerge them in an anonymous mass of from ten to fifty thousand men thereby relieving them of any sense of personal trust or accountability for the result. To judge by the Civil War memoirs, troops most appreciated it when their regiment was left to fight its own battle in its own way, receiving support only when all else had failed. Many of the most brilliant actions of the war were conceived and executed on a small scale, drawing the best out of every individual soldier.

Doubtless Burnside at Fredericksburg or Pickett at Gettysburg would have replied that a large-scale enemy position could not be carried by a series of disjointed small-scale actions, even if each one of them could be guaranteed success. There were too many opportunities for local counter-attacks by the enemy to disrupt progress and reverse the advances piecemeal. Only a massive single move against the key point could be made to stick within the time-scale available. Any other policy would have initiated an uncontrollable series of scrappy little actions which might have continued for a week.

The answer to this superficially attractive argument is that by 1864 the American battles actually had started to have the character of a long series of small disjointed attacks, although by that time there was admittedly also a breakdown of unanimity and determination. Hence the best results could not be achieved by this approach, as they might have been if it had been applied earlier in the war. But at least by 1864 the higher commanders had learned to call off mass attacks which went wrong. Sherman at Kenesaw and Grant at Cold Harbor both called an end to the fighting considerably earlier than had Burnside at Fredericksburg.[32]

The trouble with these mass assaults was that they became disorganised by their own inner mechanisms, almost independently of enemy action. Hence the supposed advantage of superior numbers actually became a disadvantage, because no one was left free to fight in a scientific or carefully controlled manner. We therefore see the paradox that a smaller attack against a strong enemy position could be more effective than a large one. Once again, the best hope of safety lay in the apparently more dangerous course. If the time required turned out to be longer than the few minutes notionally needed for a "monstrous" column, then that was a cheaper price to pay than the failure and ruin which usually attended the latter. . . .

If "monstrous" columns represented the tactics of the past and light columns represented those of the present, it was still lighter and more dispersed formations that represented the tactics of the future. The idea of an attack entirely in skirmish order had been well known for at least a century before the Civil War, and frequently applied in Napoleonic times. Much of the discussion in the *chasseurs à pied* had concentrated upon it, and hence it was incorporated into Hardee as one possibility open to the Civil War commander. What was rather new in the 1860s, however, was the idea of basing an entire battle upon it, even in open ground without solid supports close at hand. This went beyond Hardee and reflected some of the more advanced thinking of the *chasseurs*.

At the beginning of the Civil War some regiments had adopted the so-called "Zouave rush" as their tactic.[33] Instead of advancing in a close line, stopping to fire from time to time, they charged forward in loose order at the quickstep and threw themselves flat between bounds, both to fire and to regain breath. Whenever they presented themselves as a target to the enemy, it was a difficult one to hit. This was an exciting and sensible way to fight, although it did perhaps suffer from a certain lack of ensemble for the final bound into the enemy's line. It was used with success by such diverse military organisations as the Garibaldini when they landed in Sicily in 1860, and by the Prussian Guard following their failure at St Privat in 1870.[34] In America it was identified with the way the Indians had fought, and was soon terminologically appropriated by New World nationalists. Instead of the "Zouave" rush it became the "Indian" rush.

Some authorities have claimed that the Indian rush eventually became the predominant assault tactic of the Civil War,[35] although the evidence for this appears slight. It may well be that "formless and indecisive skirmishing" was the predominant method of action in the war, but that is not quite the same thing.

There is admittedly a problem of definition in all this. To many observers almost any infantry which lost its drill-book precision, moved independently and used cover—with each man "yelling on his own hook and aligning on himself"—seemed to be behaving in an "Indian" manner. Already at Gaines's Mill one Union survivor was able to report that "The firing of the Texans was so accurate and their movements so cunning and Indian like that [I] never wish to make their acquaintance again"[36] In this battle the initial Texan attack had a certain amount of cover to exploit, but much of the way was across an open field, which surely precluded "cunning" movements. Nor was Hood anxious to see his men stop to fire, let alone indulge in stealthy stalking and sniping. We must conclude that this "Indian" behaviour of the Texans must have occurred somewhat later than their initial assault in close order, and was more in the nature of conventional skirmishing than a true Indian rush.

In 1864 on the Opequon, Captain De Forest had taken part in a static firefight in which he noted the deliberate and accurate fire of his opponents at a range of 200 yards. His conclusion was that the Army of Northern Virginia.

> . . . aimed better than our men; they covered themselves (in case of need) more carefully and effectively; they could move in a swarm, without much care for alignment or touch of elbows. In short, they fought more like redskins, or like hunters, than we.[37]

Once again, this perception seems to be based more upon Confederate skill in firing from cover than upon their offensive tactics, and the idea of a "swarm" suggests a skirmish movement more than a full-blown assault. At Winchester in 1864 "One of Jackson's Foot Cavalry" observed such an action from afar and applauded each bound that brought the skirmishers to a new piece of cover nearer to the Union line.[38] But it still did not produce a final charge to overrun the position . . .

Most Civil War battlefields were pulsating with skirmishers, especially by 1864. Anything between one and all ten companies of a regiment might be detailed for the duty, and often there might be two regiments sent forward from each brigade. Yet the standard procedure for these skirmishers was to do no more than probe the enemy, occupy his attention and maybe cause him some loss. At Fredericksburg 13th Massachusetts enjoyed especially fine drill training in skirmish movements, and prided itself upon its efficiency in this type of fighting. It advanced, drove off the enemy skirmishers by fire and then used all its ammunition against the enemy's main line—but it did not assault. It left that task to the heavy supports moving up from the rear, and gratefully retired once they had passed through.[39]

By 1864 we often find the same pattern repeated, but more often than not without the final appearance of heavy supports. Typically the skirmishers would move forward, probe the enemy entrenchments and find them too strong. They would then invoke this as a reason for cancelling the main attack before it even began. Sherman called such action "Indian war," but it is clear that it rarely contained any serious aspirations towards a decisive result.[40]

Without the dynamic of a genuine attack across the final 33 yards, we cannot really call skirmish action an assault technique. We are therefore left with relatively few examples of a true skirmisher attack, and still fewer of a thoroughbred Indian rush. Apparently one of the latter was performed by Sigel's men on the second day at Pea Ridge in Arkansas—a battle at which there were even some real Indians present. At Belmont Grant's men also moved to the attack from tree to tree.[41] But most of the other claimed instances of this technique ultimately appear to have been instances of something different after all.

At Beaver Dam Creek in 1862 there was at least one attack by a formed body which threw itself to the ground when the enemy fired his salvo, and then jumped up again to carry the position. But this was against a single artillery piece, where obviously the timing of each shot could be exactly predicted.[42] Against an infantry regiment giving a continuous fire at will such virtuosity would have been impossible.

One undoubtedly very significant Civil War assault technique which we have not yet considered is the trench raid. Take for example Captain Nisbet's exploit on the Kenesaw line in 1864, which stands in such stark contrast to the disastrous massed Union attack near the same spot a few days earlier. One night the Confederate picket line was manned with specially selected volunteers:

Armed with Colt's navy seven-shooters, self-cocking 44-calibre, they had instructions to crawl from our works and drop into the enemy's vidette pits, which were not more than fifty feet from our videttes. Each man was instructed to present his pistol to the vidette's head, and tell him (softly) he would blow his head off if he made any noise *and to do it* if need be.

The night was rainy and very dark. The scheme was successfully executed . . .[43]

After this some 200 shock troops rushed through to the now-unguarded front of the Union line, and captured the best part of a regiment of regulars before the alarm had been sounded or supports sent forward. The Confederates had their prisoners safely back in their own trenches before the counter-bombardment began . . .

Night and fog ought certainly to have been exploited more often by Civil War tacticians, as they have been in the twentieth century even to the extent of creating artificial fog in the shape of smoke screens. Night and fog are nonetheless notoriously tricky to manipulate, since it is a part of their nature to blind and befuddle friend as well as foe. In the Napoleonic period there had been many an enterprising commander who had hoped to win a trick by a night attack, only to find that it backfired upon him. Wellesley at Seringapatam and Abercrombie in North Holland had both experienced this, and each had sworn never to take such a risk again. Then in the Civil War there were repeated attempts to march at night which also caused disproportionately high resentment and confusion in return for disproportionately low mileage completed. When it came to actually fighting at night, furthermore, it was usually at the end of a long day of combat, when the opposed forces were already exhausted and ready for an excuse to cease fire. Bartlett Yancey Malone of 6th North Carolina made a dusk attack at Gettysburg—"But it was soon so dark and so much smoke that we couldn't see what we was a doing."[44] This was usually the way with such ventures.[45] Friendly units stood more than a normal chance of firing into other friendly units, and even if initial success was gained it was exceptionally difficult to consolidate—or to keep hold of one's prisoners—in the gloom. When Jackson wanted a night counter-attack at Fredericksburg it was forbidden by Lee as too risky, and at least one of the attendant staff officers concurred with heartfelt relief.[46] Ironically, it was to be in just such an operation a few months later that Jackson himself was accidentally shot by his own troops.

Woodland fighting was already very difficult to control without the added hazard of low visibility to increase the risk of confusion or panic. Nevertheless, steady troops could sometimes win significant advantages by fighting at night or in fog. One case of this was the combat of Lookout Valley near Chattanooga, fought at the dead of night. At first the Union troops succumbed to the normal sources of confusion, including stampeding mules and Confederates pretending to be Federals; but they were later successful when they renewed their assault, this time without firing until after the enemy had run off. Then a few weeks subsequently Lookout Mountain itself was stormed in force, in daytime but in thick clouds. The attack was more successful than had been hoped.[47]

Accelerating an Attack

Loss of impetus and failure to achieve shock were the main enemies of the Civil War tactician who wanted to cross the vital last 33 yards to come to grips with his foe. Instructions not to fire—or sometimes not even to load—were a common response to this need, although they were obeyed less often than the officers might have wished. The use of massed formations turned out to be even less successful, while raiding covered by night or fog was a specialised operation which could often go wrong. In many firefights commanders had to rely instead upon rather simpler expedients, which, although they were individually quite trivial, might in combination add up to something imposing enough to chase the enemy away.

The first consideration was the simple one that troops committed to a charge should be fresh and well in hand, preferably having eaten not long before. It was failure to observe this principle that had brought disaster to the British at New Orleans, as it was to bring equal disaster to many a Civil War regiment thrown carelessly into a fight in unpromising conditions. For example at Culp's Hill, Gettysburg, Stuart's brigade had been in action for six hours, and had run out of ammunition at least once, when it was asked to make a very difficult uphill attack against superior numbers in strong fortifications at right angles to its own line. The attack was made without any support from infantry or artillery, but under enfilading cannon fire.[48] If it failed we can scarcely attribute that to "newly improved musketry": it was due merely to neglect of the most basic rules of warfare. That some members of this attack came to twenty yards of the enemy line shows what might have been achieved by a better-planned operation.

Another obvious course of action was for an officer to make the maximum use of his vocal chords:

In battle the order to charge is not given in the placid tones of a Sunday-school teacher, but with vigorous English, well seasoned with oaths, and a request, frequently repeated, to give them that particular province of his Satanic Majesty most dreaded by persons fond of a cold climate.[49]

Modern studies of combat psychology have shown that constant chatter in a fighting unit helps to dispel the loneliness of fear, and to strengthen cohesion. Civil War officers who habitually shouted themselves hoarse in battle were therefore almost certainly doing the right thing, even though the deafening roar of combat might drown them out—and on at least one occasion a regiment advancing through a cotton field made earplugs for themselves to deaden the din.[50]

Nor was it only the officers who were supposed to shout, since whole regiments were encouraged to do so:

> At the same time you are ordered to yell with all the power of your lungs. It is possible that this idea may be of great advantage in forcing some of the heroic blood of the body into the lower extremities. Whatever may be the reason, it was certainly a very effective means of drowning the disagreeable yell of the enemy.[51]

The above may be termed the "defensive" use of yelling, to help one's regiment remember its identity. The "offensive" use could be still more effective, as a weapon to chase off the enemy. We read that in the Wilderness battle:

> ... the yellers could not be seen, and a company could make itself sound like a regiment if it shouted loud enough. Men spoke later of various units on both sides being "yelled" out of their positions.[52] ...

Another way to speed an attack was simply to lighten the men's load. The soldier on campaign tried to carry as little impedimenta as possible, but apart from his weapons there always remained an irreducible minimum of blankets, food, spare clothing and keepsakes. In each messing group there were communal cooking utensils which were particularly large and unwieldy. In the attack on Marye's Heights at Fredericksburg a company commander in 22nd Massachusetts reports:

> I turned to see if my company kept its formation intact, when Ned Flood, custodian of the treasured frying pan, held it out so as to catch my attention and asked by word and gesture, permission to drop it. I assented. With a serio-comical look of grief he cast it from him ... [53]

On many other occasions, however, Civil War units were ordered *en masse* to deposit their baggage either before entering battle or, more heroically, before launching into some especially daring venture once battle had been joined. "Packs down—charge!" was almost as stirring a cry to the weary warrior as the more conventional "Fix bayonets— charge!", and certainly signalled an even more serious intention. To throw down one's pack, especially if no arrangements were made for guarding or recovering it, was equivalent to instant destitution for the soldier. Only the most complete victory could make good the loss, so the troops could be expected to fight with the reckless abandon of those who have nothing further to lose.

The timing of a "packs down" order was a matter of delicate timing since if it was given prematurely, before the need arose, it would cause bitter resentment among the troops.[54] Even the best arrangements for retrieving personal baggage which had been dumped were notoriously unreliable, as 35th Massachusetts discovered when they had "their" packs forwarded from the Arlington training camp to the front at Antietam.[55] Conversely, a refusal to allow troops to jettison their equipment before a strenuous combat could cause equal resentment, not to mention some heavily overloaded soldiers whose combat value was thereby reduced.[56] Not only would they be more ready to run away than they might otherwise have been, but their first act upon doing so would be to jettison their hated baggage.

The battlefield would thus be doubly littered—partly by the soldiers moving into the fray, and partly from those running out of it. The man who could hold onto his pack throughout a battle could consider himself quite fortunate, although for the rest there would often be plenty of items available for salvage. If only one could reach the prisoners and casualties before the professional scavengers and "bummers" had a chance to ply their ghoulish trade, one could fit oneself out as good as new.

Before we leave this subject it may be as well to remember that the promise of plunder could itself be a spur to assaulting troops. The deprivations of campaigning life were considerable in this war, in which many soldiers went without a proper roof over their heads for their full three years' service, and whole armies sometimes starved. There was more than a grain of truth contained in General D. H. Hill's anecdote of the wounded Irish soldier at Chickamauga who urged on his companions by shouting "Charge them, boys! They have cha-ase [cheese] in their haversacks!"[57]

In Napoleon's day the motive of plunder had been no less great than in the Civil War, but the packs-off charge had been less common. At least a part of the reason for this must be found in the generally slower pace of battlefield manoeuvres, and hence the relatively lesser exertions demanded of an attacker. By the 1840s, however, the rise of *chasseur à pied* theories of the *pas gymnastique* had started to change this picture, and in the European wars of the 1850s it seems that the packs-off attack was already quite a normal feature. When we come to the 1860s we certainly find that the American armies often used Hardee's double quick time or even the dead run in the attack, and hence must have been more than ready to unburden themselves of their packs. They were attempting to manoeuvre around the battlefield faster than Napoleon's soldiers, faster than Scott's in Mexico and faster than Halleck had assumed was even possible for fragile militia troops.

After the war Upton retained the double quick time of 165-180 paces per minute in his tactical manual[58] so he, at least, must have felt it was worthwhile. He also retained the idea of jogging over much longer distances than a charge (4,000 paces in 25 minutes). Nevertheless, he appears to have been ambivalent about the tactical value of such high speeds, and like Ardant du Picq in France he apparently believed that a running unit would be especially fragile. He advised skirmishers that "the very ardor with which an enemy pursues a temporary advantage will surely secure his defeat, if boldly and unexpectedly confronted by the men whom he had supposed to be demoralised."[59] In a battalion attack Upton recommends a combination of gaits so that the colonel can maintain his control up to the final rush. The battalion should try to cross the beaten ground as fast as possible, but should not break into the double until all the men have a chance to arrive on the objective together.[60]

Such caution on the part of officers seems to have been commonplace in the Civil War itself. It was less difficult to persuade troops to run forward in the attack, apparently, than it was to keep them together under unified control. Captain De Forest's regiment, which had been so proud of its drill in its first battle, could maintain no more than "a loose swarm" in 1864 as it doubled a quarter of a mile forward over an open field to take up a firefight from a demoralised line. During this advance each individual apparently stopped occasionally for breath, and some attempted to stay under cover rather than to continue forwards.[61]

At Gettysburg Hood's troops found that their attempt to double forward 400 yards on a hot day left them exhausted for the fighting at the far end. At Seven Pines 17th Virginia doubled a mile and a half to the battlefield, regrouped and drew breath behind a woodpile, then made a charge. Whether it was because the men were blown or because fugitives retired through the ranks, the compactness of the regiment was lost. A few weeks later at Frayser's Farm the same regiment had been warned not to double forward until the enemy was in sight, but it did so anyway while there was still almost a mile yet to cross.[62] Presumably it was something similar to this which led Sergeant Hamlin Coe to make the startling comment about his battle at Adairsville in 1864 that "Although our regiment was broken and in disorder, they charged like tigers."[63]

It is at this point that the disciplined jogging of Hardee's double quick time must have merged into the formless mob tactics of a skirmish attack or even the elusive Indian rush itself. It is more than probable that many attacks which started off as orderly drill formations, well under the hands of their officers, degenerated into a swarm of individuals moving forward with enthusiasm but not cohesion. If these individuals eventually consolidated themselves into a thick skirmish line firing at the enemy from a distance, rather than sweeping over him in a unified movement, that was scarcely a surprising outcome. It showed that Hardee (and behind Hardee the whole *chasseur* movement) had been mastered only in part. It showed that a packs-down cheering charge at the *pas gymnastique* might work for Indians, Celts, or even (Halleck notwithstanding) for American militia in their first flush of enthusiasm, but that such tactics needed to be based upon a lot more specialised training if they were to work against formidable opposition.

This was never a problem that was properly identified in the course of the Civil War itself, nor was it very well identified elsewhere.[64] It was a major failing of the French *chasseur* school that for ideological reasons it gave inadequate attention to the weaknesses in its own formula, just as it was the fault of its opponents that they concentrated only on the style rather than the essence of what the *chasseurs* had to say. *Chasseur* tactics were actually enormously demanding, in terms of the assumptions of most nineteenth-century warfare, and they could not be transplanted easily or quickly upon an army which lacked either appropriate indoctrination or ammunition for target practice. Obviously one could not train men to shoot unless they were given hundreds of rounds to practise with, and one could not train them for the formal packs-down charge unless they went through the motions of it many times over in the roughest country available. None of this was practical in the Civil War, so the armies either improvised ineffectively or reverted to outdated tactics disastrously. They were not usually able to use the most modern tactics available to them—which ironically were incorporated in their own drill manuals—nor did they often hit upon the still more futuristic techniques of the trench raid or the infiltration.

NOTES

From Paddy Griffith, *Battle Tactics of the Civil War* (New Haven: Yale University Press, 1989), 137–63. Reprinted by permission.

1. For example, the Union defenders of Beaver Dam Creek, 1862—Robert U. Johnson and Clarence C. Buel, eds., *Battles and Leaders of the Civil War* (New York: The Century Co., 1884), 2, p. 329.

2. For example, the Union attack at Cold Harbor (Jennings C. Wise, *The Long Arm of Lee* (Lynchburg, 1915; reissued with introduction by L. Van Loan Naisawald, Oxford University Press, New York, 1959), p. 815); at Atlanta (Arthur L. Wagner, *Organisation and Tactics* (New York: Westermann, 1985), p. 94—two examples); at Spotsylvania (Donald L. Smith, *The Twenty Fourth Michigan of the Iron Brigade* (Harrisburg, PA: Stackpole, 1962), p. 192); at Cassville (Hamlin A. Coe, *Mine Eyes Have Seen the Glory* (Cranbury, NJ: Associated University Presses, 1975), p. 141). These cases are all suspiciously grouped together in "the year of demoralisation," and we are entitled to wonder just how energetically the attacks in question were actually pushed.

3. Donald Smith, p. 36.

4. Leslie Anders, *The Eighteenth Missouri* (Indianapolis, Kansas City and New York: Bobbs-Merrill, 1968), p. 226; Randolph H. McKim, *Soldier's Recollections* (New York: Longman Green, 1910), pp. 186, 206.

5. Henry S. Commager, ed., *The Blue and the Gray* (Indianapolis and New York: Bobbs-Merrill, 1950), p. 942.

6. *Battles and Leaders*, 2, p. 510.

7. Otto Eisenschiml and Ralph Newman, *Eyewitness — The Civil War* (New York: Grosset & Dunlap, 1956), 1, pp. 296–7.

8. Ibid., p. 441.

9. For European practice see my *Forward Into Battle* (Chichester: Bird, 1981), pp. 12–62. For Mexico, Perry D. Jamieson, "The Development of Civil War Tactics" (unpublished Ph.D. thesis, Wayne State University, Detroit, 1979), pp. 1–24.

10. Hence the paradox of "bayonet attacks" made without bayonets fixed— e.g. John J. Pullen, *The Twentieth Maine* (Philadelphia, PA: Lippincott, 1957), p. 119; Eisenschiml and Newman, 1, p. 441. John Buechler, " 'Give 'em the

Bayonet'—a Note on Civil War Mythology," in *Battles Lost and Won*, ed. John
T. Hubbell (Westport, CT: Greenwood Press, 1975), p. 137, uses a similar case
to argue the uselessness of the bayonet, not pausing to consider that soldiers
would surely feel it made more sense to lunge at an opponent with a bayonet
fixed than without.

11. Eisenschiml and Newman, 1, pp. 263–4.

12. Johnny Green, *Johnny Green of the Orphan Brigade*, ed. A. D. Kirwan
(University of Kentucky Press, 1956), p. 128.

13. Ibid., p. 123, The Orphan Brigade had already favoured this tactic in
earlier battles, ibid., pp. 30, 68, 159.

14. *Battles and Leaders*, 2, p. 363.

15. John W. De Forest, *A Volunteer's Adventures*, ed. J. H. Croushore (Yale
University Press, 1946; reprinted, New York: Archon Books, 1970), pp. 62–71.

16. Ibid., p. 70.

17. William T. Sherman, *Memoirs of General William T. Sherman By Himself* (London: King, 1875), 2, p. 395.

18. Quoted in Eisenschiml and Newman, 1, p. 236. See also George Wise,
History of the 17th Virginia Infantry (Baltimore, MD: Kelly Piet, 1870), p. 99,
for another account of the same action.

19. Herman Hattaway and Archer Jones, *How the North Won* (University
of Illinois Press, 1983), p. 235, for a fascinating discussion of Lee's use of
different phrases to describe his military aims, which normally fell short of
annihilating the enemy. For a (rather less concentrated) analysis of Grant's aims,
ibid., pp. 526–7.

20. Carl L. Davis, *Arming the Union — Small Arms in the Union Army* (Port
Washington, NY: Kennikat Press, 1973), p. xi specifically denies that the Civil
War battles were decided at short range but he does not, alas, support this claim
with evidence. Other authorities seem to favour quite close ranges—for example, Henderson said that most battles were fought under 100 yards (quoted in
Thomas V. Moseley, "The Evolution of American Civil War Infantry Tactics"
(unpublished doctoral thesis for University of North Carolina, Chapel Hill,
1967), p. 182) and John K. Mahon, "Civil War Infantry Assault Tactics," in
Military Analysis of the Civil War (Millwood, NY: KTO Press, 1977), p. 57,
claimed that attacks were stopped at 200–250 yards.

21. Hew Strachan, *From Waterloo to Balaclava* (Cambridge University Press,
1985), p. 32.

22. More systematic research still needs to be done on this—and many other
tactical questions—by, for example, a close analysis of the Official Records.
Systematic research into these questions is also needed for the Napoleonic era,
since much still remains obscure for that period of military history.

23. This point was ably made in Richard Munday's lecture, given in July
1985 at the Imperial War Museum for the Historical Breechloading Smallarms

Association. See also my *Forward Into Battle*, pp. 137–43 for a theoretical commentary on the search for long-range weapons.

24. J. H. Worsham, *One of Jackson's Foot Cavalry*, ed. J. I. Robertson Jr. (Jackson, TN: McCowat-Mercer, 1964), p. 170.

25. *Thirty-fifth Massachusetts: History of the 35th Massachusetts Volunteers, 1862–5* (Boston: Mills Knight, 1884), p. 169.

26. Rice C. Bull, *Soldiering*, ed. K. Jack Bauer (San Rafael, CA: Presidio Press, 1977), p. 45, among others, describes the whistling of Minié balls.

27. James C. Nisbet, *Four Years on the Firing Line*, ed. Bell I. Wiley (Jackson, TN: McCowat-Mercer, 1963), p. 188; Pullen, p. 181.

28. Nancy Baxter, *Gallant Fourteenth* (Traverse City, IN: Pioneer Study Center, 1980), p. 98, for 14th Indiana at Bloody Lane, Antietam; De Forest, pp. 184–6, for 12th Connecticut on the Opequon.

29. Wagner, p. 112.

30. Formations are discussed in Moseley, pp. 357–69; Jamieson, pp. 89–100; Wagner, p. 90.

31. Jamieson, pp. 104–8; Wagner, pp. 92–3.

32. A similar evolution during the First World War led commanders to call off attacks quickly in 1918, whereas in 1915–17 they had often allowed them to drag on for weeks after maximum results had been achieved (see Blaxland, G., *Amiens 1918*, London, 1968, p. 196).

33. The use of this tactic at Fort Donelson is discussed in *Battles and Leaders*, 1, pp. 422–4 and in Wagner, pp. 87–8.

34. G. M. Trevelyan, *Garibaldi and the Thousand* (London, 1909) for the battle (of) Calatafimi; E. Hoffbauer, *The German Artillery in the Battles Near Metz*, translated by Captain Hollist (London: King & Co., 1874), p. 102, for an early example of a "Prussian rush." Strachan, p. 27, mentions a "Sepoy Rush" used against the Sikhs in the 1840s.

35. Wagner, p. 87; Mahon, p. 63 (following Henderson); Moseley, p. 356 (although contradicted by his own p. 369).

36. Richard M. McMurry, *John Bell Hood and the War for Southern Independence* (University of Kentucky Press, 1982), p. 42.

37. De Forest, p. 190.

38. Worsham, p. 152.

39. Charles E. Davis, Jr., *Three Years in the Army* (Boston, MA: Estes & Lauriat, 1894), pp. 166–8. At Winchester this regiment actually had assaulted and carried a line of enemy trenches with skirmishers only—but the trenches were found to be unoccupied at the time (ibid., p. 30).

40. Quoted in Hattaway and Jones, p. 584. Note, however, that when a major assault *was* intended it was not uncommon for all skirmishers to be withdrawn completely—see, e.g., D. P. Conyngham, *The Irish Brigade and Its Campaigns* (Glasgow: Cameron & Ferguson, n.d. (1866?), p. 75; Bull, p. 133.

41. Jamieson, p. 121; Mahon, p. 61.
42. Eisenschiml and Newman, 1, p. 114.
43. Nisbet, pp. 203–4.
44. Bartlett Y. Malone, *Whipt 'Em Everytime* (Chapel Hill, NC, 1919); new edition, ed. by W. W. Pierson Jr. (Jackson, TN: McCowat-Mercer, 1960), p. 86. McKim, pp. 195–200, describes this action from the viewpoint of a neighbouring division, and it is clear that considerable success was achieved.
45. For example, twice in a night at Hazel Grove, Chancellorsville (Jennings Wise, pp. 488, 495); Wagner, p. 435 for Big Bethel.
46. G. Moxley Sorrel, *Recollections of a Confederate Staff Officer* (New York: Neale, 1905), p. 142.
47. Andrew J. Boies, *Record of the 33rd Massachusetts Volunteer Infantry* (Fitchburg, 1880), p. 48; *Battles and Leaders*, 3, p. 690.
48. McKim, pp. 199–205.
49. Charles Davis, p. 109.
50. Richard Wheeler, *Voices of the Civil War* (New York: Crowell, 1976), p. 235.
51. Charles Davis, p. 109.
52. Pullen, p. 185. On p. 191 we read of a whole army corps being yelled into retreat.
53. Steve Fratt, "American Civil War Tactics: The Theory of W. J. Hardee and the Experience of E. C. Bennett," in *Indiana Military History Journal*, vol. 10, no. 1, January 1985, p. 12.
54. Worsham, p. 152.
55. *Thirty-fifth Massachusetts*, p. 58. They received a very random selection from Casey's holdings in infantry accoutrements.
56. Ibid., p. 238; Benjamin F. McIntyre, *Federals on the Frontier*, ed. Nannie M. Tilley (Austin: University of Texas Press, 1963), p. 55.
57. Wheeler, p. 236. A variant is the Confederate joking before Gettysburg— "When we charge the intrenchments, boys, recollect the crackers inside" (McKim, p. 146).
58. Emory Upton, *A New System of Infantry Tactics, Double and Single Rank* (New York: Greenwood Press, revised., 1968) p. 20.
59. Ibid., p. 98.
60. Ibid., p. 143.
61. De Forest, pp. 182–3.
62. Jamieson, p. 120; George Wise, pp. 67, 80.
63. Coe, p. 131.
64. Only Ardant du Picq, in France, made a truly penetrating study of the problems associated with *chasseur* tactics.

Chapter 15

Leaving Their Mark on the Battlefield

Joseph T. Glatthaar

Thomas Wentworth Higginson's anecdotes tell us much about the character of the men in his African American regiment, but they leave a number of questions unanswered. How did black troops perform under fire? How did Confederates react when faced with African American soldiers? What was Union soldiers' attitude toward their black comrades? In his 1990 book Forged in Battle, *Joseph Glatthaar of the University of Houston examined soldiers' reminiscences and military records for his study of the United States Colored Troops, and in this selection he answers these and other questions about African Americans' combat performance.*

Despite the outstanding performance of black soldiers at Port Hudson, Milliken's Bend, and Fort Wagner, there was still a sense of uneasiness about blacks in combat. Their conduct had certainly not convinced everyone, and just because the Northern white population was coming around to the viewpoint that blacks in uniform could contribute to the war effort did not mean that they were willing to stand alongside black soldiers and slug it out against the Confederates. In addition to Rebel soldiers, black commands were battling generations of racial prejudice, and the lingering doubts were by no means easy to dispel. Thus, throughout the war, the USCT was under the spotlight of the Northern public, both in and out of military service.

Even among the white officers, nearly all of whom had previous combat experience, there was considerable consternation. The bulk of these commands had not devoted enough time to training, and in the back of their minds they were still unsure that the black race had the fortitude to stand up to the fire of the Confederates. Despite widespread acceptance of the notion of the innate savagery of the black race, Southern whites were held somehow to have subdued them, and some officers thought black soldiers might flee in the face of their former masters. As one lieutenant in the USCT recalled, "For so many years had the black man cowered beneath the lash of the oppressor, that his spirit was thought by all to have been crushed."[1]

Yet many white officers had good reason to dread risking their lives with such raw troops. On the eve of his first campaign with black soldiers, one lieutenant was the only officer in his company, and his regiment "had never fired a shot" in anger or on the practice range. Understandably, he was worried: "I was scared good and sure and would of given most any thing to of been at home with my dear Mother." Even units that had time to drill were not ready for combat. Too many white officers trained their men for parades to win the kudos of superiors and inspectors, but flashy drills did not prepare them adequately for battle. "Our regiment has been drilled too much for dress parade and too little for the field," a lieutenant complained, while a major in another regiment admitted his troops were able-bodied, muscular, and highly motivated, but the commander drilled them "more in what makes a good show, than in what will be needed in a fight." Indeed, very few officers entered their first engagement alongside black soldiers and had no apprehensions that they would perform well.[2]

With black troops, especially freedmen, this sense of anxiety was not quite so powerful. Many of them had already demonstrated unusual fortitude in their escape from slavery. As Colonel Higginson noted of his troops, "There were more than a hundred men in the ranks who had voluntarily met more dangers in their escape from slavery than any of my young captains had incurred in their lives." More importantly, they had motivations that enabled them to overcome these doubts better than did white soldiers. While whites fought for an impersonal restoration of the union, or even for the freedom of people they had never known and regarded as inherently inferior, blacks entered combat in search of freedom and justice for themselves and their families. One black sergeant commented that what his comrades lacked in military knowledge, at least early in their service, they compensated with commitment: "they had been to the armory of God and had received weapons of the heart, that made them daring and dangerous foes—men to be really reckoned with." For black soldiers, this was a crusade for the rights of themselves and their race, and the passions these goals generated helped them hurdle the obstacles of fear and doubt.[3]

Despite the lack of preparedness, these black units nonetheless found themselves in the thick of combat. The commander of the 39th U.S. Colored Infantry complained that the government threw his men into the field with almost no training whatsoever. Many of the men did not even know how to use their weapons. Some troops believed the ball went into the barrel first; others thought putting in two rounds was proper; and still others fired without taking aim, because no one had taught them. In the 8th U.S. Colored Infantry, a lieutenant wrote his sister that in the battle around Jacksonville, Florida, his troops had had so little rifle training that they could not defend themselves adequately, yet they held their ground. "We have had very little practice in firing, and, though they could stand and be killed, they could not kill a concealed enemy fast enough to satisfy my feelings." When they fell back on order, the men naturally bunched together and made an even easier target for the Confederates. The most amazing instance, however, was a company of recruits for the 52nd U.S. Colored Infantry. Confederate infantry and an artillery battery attacked them, and although the men had not been mustered into service, they begged their lieutenant not to surrender. The lieutenant vowed that they would "fight as long as there was a man of them left," and for three hours they somehow held the Confederate forces at bay.[4]

Naturally, there was a great deal of rhetoric around camp about what combat was going to be like and how individuals were going to perform, but as one enlightened soldier said to his comrades, they were all flapping their jaws: "You don't know notin' about it, boys. You tink you's brave enough; how you tink, if you stan' clar in de open field,—here you, and dar de Secesh? You's got to hab de right ting inside o' you. You must hab it served (preserved) in you, like dese yer sour plums dey 'serve in de barr'l; you's got to harden it down inside o' you, or it's notin'."[5]

Just as the sage soldier had predicted, all the campfire nerve did them no good as they approached battle for the first time. To reassure his comrades when they first heard the roar of battle, a sergeant who knew about combat from his previous service as a teamster told them. "You yeres dat music? How you likes it? It's to hear dat, and not to be skeered by it dat de guv'ment feeds you fer; dat's what dey gib you dese bu'ful shiny guns fer; no skulkin' now! Doan' ye dar to flinch!" Officers, too, tried to instill some confidence in their men. Like Colonel Shaw before the assault on Fort Wagner, most commanders tried to speak to their men about doing their duty just before a battle. And when both black and white troops were participating in the fight, officers in the USCT had an additional motivator. At Petersburg in 1865, Capt. Marshall Harvey Twitchell told his troops that they were fighting alongside the Sixth Army Corps, the best in the Army of the Potomac, and this was an opportunity to prove to the entire world whether they were men or fit only to be slaves. During these tense moments before coming under fire, a joke frequently worked wonders. While entering combat for the first time, a major in the 30th U.S. Colored Infantry instructed the men, "Now just imagine you are hunting for coons, and keep your eyes open." To this a soldier cracked, "Pears like 'twas de coons doin' de huntin' dis time," and the line erupted in laughter.[6] . . .

Clearly, the key was the sense of confidence troops had in one another and their officers. It took a sort of mystical chemistry that some officers were able to create during training while others needed actual combat experience, which pitted all the men together under the same adverse circumstances, to forge it. When troops felt they could rely on their officers and one another for support, they began to feel a bit more at ease in the combat arena. Often it was just one or two soldiers whom an individual could count on in desperate moments that gave him this self-assurance, and occasionally these bonds of comradeship crossed racial boundaries. After the war, an officer in the 19th U.S. Colored Infantry admitted, "I always found comforting in battle the companionship of a friend, one in whom you had confidence, one you felt assured would stand by you until the last. I can well remember our fight at Hatcher's Run. I had a sergeant, tried and true, who was at my elbow always. True, he was black; he was a pure African. No drop of white blood ever coursed his veins, but a hero in every sense of the word." The captain had regarded the man as reliable, and at the Battle of Yellow Tavern he sent him on a dangerous mission, which the black soldier successfully accomplished. That night, while trying to sleep on the picket line, the captain overheard an enlisted man tell the soldier that he would not thank the captain for sending him on such risky missions, that he would wind up dead. The soldier replied, "The captain will never send me where he thinks I will be killed, but if he would order me to go through hell, I'd die trying!" The next day the captain promoted the man to sergeant, and the bonds between them grew stronger with each passing day.[7]

Eventually, the sense of interdependence, of supporting one another in times of crisis, became so overwhelming that individuals felt an obligation to be with the unit in desperate times. Regardless of the inherent danger of combat, time after time they left their sickbeds to be with comrades for battle. A lieutenant in the 36th U.S. Colored Infantry, excused from duty for lameness, volunteered to charge through a swamp at the head of his company in the battle near New Market, Virginia, and suffered a breast wound. Another lieutenant, this one in the 5th U.S. Colored Infantry, was ill but wanted to be with his company for an assault. He fought alongside the men, and immediately after the battle he collapsed. Nor were things different with the enlisted men. One astonished officer noted in his diary that when the bugle sounded and the troops assembled for their first battle, "the sick list deserted the doctor," the opposite of what he had expected. "We have not had such full ranks since they fell in for pay," he quipped.[8]

Like most of their white counterparts in blue, the more battles they fought and the more losses they incurred, the stronger was their desire to see the war through to the finish. The allures of battle no longer enticed them; it became a matter of ensuring that their comrades had not died in vain. A black sergeant with exceptional writing skills explained the concept effectively when he asserted, "We had tasted of the dangers of battle, and this taste brought out the desire that we should fight to the finish. Some of our dear friends had laid down their lives already, and we reasoned that if it should be necessary for them to give such a sacrifice, that we were no better than they. So in our judgment, we were becoming calm, and in our determination, we were becoming more and more fixed."[9]

As the drum pounded or the bugle blared to alert the men to a coming battle, nearly all had a wrenching feeling in their stomachs. They rushed about, gathering gear and forming in position, while fear and bolts of panic raced through them. One veteran officer revealed to his parents; "That is a time when thought is active and for a little time my nerves refuse control but I soon become cool and I think I should then be prepared to act with coolness & deliberation." For those who were attacking, at least they knew roughly when the battle was going to begin. Defenders simply had to wait, and that was often the greatest agony.[10]

Once the battle began, most men settled into their work. Like their enemies, the Confederates, black soldiers had their own version of the Confederate attack cry, the "Rebel yell" that one officer termed "horrible howls." It had the twin psychological benefit of unnerving the defenders and releasing tension among the attackers.[11]

As the deafening roar and brutal scenes of the battlefield bombarded the troops' senses, they selectively tuned out much of the combat experience for psychological survival. Hours seemed like minutes. They performed their jobs almost mechanically, and after it was all over they had great difficulty recalling many of the specific events or feelings. In the attack on Petersburg in 1864 an officer who never cursed learned from those around him that he "swore all the way through the fight," but he did not remember it. "For myself," a lieutenant recorded in his diary after a battle, "I can truly say, I was oblivious of all danger. I had given up the hope of returning alive from this 'very Jaws of death,' and thought that it was only left for me to die facing the enemy." Many of them, particularly officers, were so preoccupied with their own duties that they saw very little. After a successful assault, a captain recalled that his command advanced across an open cornfield and charged the enemy works with a yell, but "I was too busy to see much beside the work before me." During the course of the battle he suffered an injury that made him partially lame, although "The Excitement of the charge & the work to do made me Entirely unconscious of it." The time to mourn losses was after the conclusion of the battle. During the fight, each man had an obligation to fulfill certain duties, and the survival of others depended upon it. Even though comrades fell, they had to keep at their posts.[12]

With the effective range of rifled muskets, the standard Civil War infantrymen's weapon, and the quality of field fortifications that troops learned to construct in the latter half of the war, most experienced soldiers preferred to fight on the tactical defensive. From behind breastworks, defenders were able to compensate for inadequate training or manpower inferiority, and it seemed logical that Federal authorities would use black units that way, especially considering the level of experience of their Confederate foe. Nevertheless, aside from the battles at Milliken's Bend, the infamous Fort Pillow, Wilson's Wharf, and a few other relatively minor engagements, the USCT seldom fought on the defensive.

Federal authorities much preferred to use black units as storming parties, or shock troops, to assault Confederate lines and punch holes through them. Most senior officers believed that employing black troops in charges was merely an effective utilization of their manpower. Because black units had not received enough training, from a tactical standpoint they were more capable of conducting assaults than anything else. Moreover, such attacks took advantage of white preconceptions of the black race. Permitting them to storm the enemy works and destroy everything in their path utilized what whites perceived as the greatest fighting quality of blacks, their innate savagery, to its fullest potential. "The most unbiased opinion," wrote the editors of the *New York Times*, "seems to be that they are best for a sudden dash, but are not good in a great disaster—not having the moral stamina to see long the horrible affects on the human body which shell or round shot produce."[13]

Nevertheless, military authorities did not consciously throw away the lives of their black troops on prejudiced grounds. Certainly many of them cared less for black than white lives; as one general officer wrote, "I shall feel less regret over the slain than if my troops are white," but in only one instance, at Fort Wagner, was there evidence that expendability was an issue. Commanders drew upon the forces they had available and employed them as they saw best. If they ordered black troops to make frontal attacks, it was an attempt to utilize their assets effectively, not to waste black soldiers for personal reasons.[14]

Even their own officers saw the value in using blacks for such assaults. They had doubts that black soldiers could stand up under sustained fighting, but in a short burst, an assault, they regarded their troops as excellent. In a sense, they viewed their men as wild and undisciplined in battle. "He rushed into a charge with terrible fierceness," described one of their officers, "but his impetuosity was apt to yield in long continued struggles." Another officer wrote to his wife, "I confess I am surprised at the dash and courage of these men. I have never felt sure of them before and even now I fear they would not have that steadiness under fire that many have but for a charge they cannot be beat." He compared their ability to assault with Thomas Meagher's Irish Brigade, notorious for its bravery, although many thought the courage of the Irishmen derived from their ignorance.[15]

The most famous charge involving black troops was the Battle of the Crater, or the Petersburg mine assault. Federals dug a long mine beneath the Confederate works and loaded it with gunpowder. On July 30, 1864, after one abortive attempt to light the charge, the mine exploded, creating a huge crater on the Confederate line. The original plan called for a black division to lead the assault, but for fear of political repercussions if the endeavor failed and black troops sustained huge losses, Maj. Gen. George Meade had a white division head the attack. As a result of mismanagement, Confederate obstinacy, and the difficulty of crossing the huge crater, the white troops soon bogged down and the Federals sent in the black division to exploit the break in the Confederate line. At first the black troops made good headway, but the Confederate artillery fire became so heavy that they could do nothing but hug the ground. Confederates then sealed off the breakthrough and fired on the attackers from the front and the flank. For the Federals, it appeared too dangerous either to retreat or advance, and throughout much of the day the black and white troops could do little more than hold their place. Eventually, the Confederates gathered enough forces to launch a counterattack, and most Federals, rather than surrender and risk their fate with their ene-mies, "after desperate resistance broke, and fell back in perfect disorder, [and] horrible slaughter," concluded an officer in the USCT. As the black commands rallied by units to tabulate losses, one officer wrote a friend, "I felt like sitting down & weeping on account of our misfortune." One regiment, the 29th U.S. Colored Infantry, entered the fight with 450 troops and exited with 128. In total, the black commands suffered more than 40 percent of the fatalities and 35 percent of the casualties, despite a preponderance of white soldiers in the engagement.[16]

Probably the most audacious assault by the USCT occurred at a railroad bridge over the Big Black River in Mississippi in late 1864. Confederate Lt. Gen. John Bell Hood had just begun his invasion of Tennessee, and by a roundabout railroad route he was able to draw supplies from southern Mississippi and Alabama. By destroying this railroad bridge, Federals would cut his supply line. The problem was that the railroad bridge was situated in an almost impenetrable swamp, and the only way over it was the railroad ties and trestles. At both ends of the span, some twenty-five feet high, the Confederates had erected a stockade and had allocated a large infantry force, estimated by one Union officer as "at least one regiment," to protect it. Although two previous attempts by the Federals with much larger forces had failed, authorities sent Maj. J. B. Cook and his 3rd U.S. Colored Cavalry to try his hand. Cook, who had to move rapidly as Confederates closed in on his raiding party, sent a dismounted company into the swamp on each side of the track with orders to work their way up near the bridge. "The men waded waist deep in mud and water a great part of the distance, which rendered progress extremely slow and tedious," an officer who commanded one of the companies in the swamp recorded. To occupy the attention of the defenders, Cook had his men advance toward the bridge, discharging a few rounds, and then fall back, luring the Confederate forces out of the near stockade to fire at the distant Federals. Eventually, the two companies worked their way to the riverbank, concealed themselves in thick underbrush, and awaited a bugle blast that signaled them to fire. The two companies caught the Confederates completely unprepared, and after they routed the Rebel forces outside the stockade, they peppered the portholes keep the Confederates inside from returning fire. Meanwhile, Cook's forces assaulted the stockade by charging along the narrow railroad tracks, and after a hand-to-hand battle, they drove the Confederates out. From the other side of the bridge, however, Confederates again poured a heavy fire into the 3rd U.S. Colored Cavalry, and after attempts to silence that stockade with musketry fire failed, Cook boldly led three companies in an assault over the narrow ties of the bridge and drove the Confederates into some woods on the other side. Planning ahead, Cook had directed one company to bring oil in its canteens, and the troops doused the bridge and piled on timber and brush as Confederates continued to harass them with fire from the woods. When some black troops lit the bridge, the entire structure went up in flames. Cook then had his men destroy part of the railroad track by lifting up the ties and hurling the entire structure, ties and rails, down the slope and into the swamp. As a reward for such outstanding service, Maj. Gen. E. R. S. Canby promoted Cook to lieutenant colonel and declared this "one of the most daring and heroic acts of the war" in a general order published throughout his military division.[17]

In fact, there were dozens and dozens of instances of brilliant performance by men in the USCT during combat. The most famous cases were Sgt. Anselmas Planciancois of what became the 73rd U.S. Colored Infantry, who promised his commander to carry the regimental colors in the assault on Port Hudson and return with them or explain why he failed to God: Sgt. William H. Carney of the 54th Massachusetts (Colored) Infantry, flag bearer who planted his colors on the Confederate parapet at Fort Wagner and carried them back despite wounds in his legs, breast, and arm; and Sgt. Maj. Christian A. Fleetwood of the 4th U.S. Colored Infantry, who saved the regimental colors after Confederates had shot two color guards and carried them heroically throughout the rest of the battle. Both Carney and Fleetwood were Medal of Honor winners, and deservedly so, along with thirteen officers and fourteen other enlisted men, yet there were many acts of bravery performed by men in the USCT that passed with little acknowledgment. At Chaffin's Farm, Orderly Sgt. William Strander, "scarce 20 years of age and as brave a boy as ever wore the diamond [the corps badge]," refused to seek medical attention despite a serious wound and insisted on continuing the fight. According to his commander, "with the blood streaming from his neck [Strander] followed me over the enemys works." During the Red River Campaign of 1864, acting First Sgt. Antoine Davis of the 92nd U.S. Colored Infantry suffered wounds in the head and breast but refused to leave the field. Not until a Confederate cavalryman felled him with a shot in the groin were Federals able to remove him from battle. Five days later, Davis died in a New Orleans hospital. After the 33rd U.S. Colored Infantry conducted a raid, a company commander reported that one soldier, wounded in the neck and shoulder, still carried two muskets from the field. Another man, with three wounds, one of which was in the head, refused to seek medical attention until his officers forced it upon him. And in the most unusual case, a soldier who had a bullet in his shoulder neglected to report to the surgeon and even performed guard duty until someone discovered his wound.[18]

What made the performance of the USCT so unusual, though, were the widespread and consistent levels of audacity and grittiness. Time after time black units as a whole acted bravely, because they were so afraid of accusations of cowardice. They fought aggressively, even recklessly, and no one could challenge their valor or commitment to the war. Black soldiers knew full well what was at stake, and they were willing to take greater risks in hopes of postwar rewards. "*Dat's just what I went for*," replied a soldier who had suffered two wounds when Higginson asked if a recent battle was more than he had bargained for.[19]

Of course, there were occasions when black units performed poorly and officers and men exhibited cowardice. At the Battle of Guntown, Mississippi, in June 1864, twenty-one of seventy-seven soldiers from a company in the 59th U.S. Colored Infantry threw away their rifles in the retreat. That same month back east, an officer went into combat twice with some unassigned recruits and had a mixed evaluation: "Some of our men acted very bravely last night and others acted very badly and even cowardly." The most serious case of cowardice involving black forces was when the commander at Fort Athens, Georgia, surrendered the entire garrison of over six hundred men, well fortified, without firing a shot, yet this was not the fault of the troops or even of subordinate officers.[20]

Most of the time, though, acts of cowardice were isolated instances. A major in the 34th U.S. Colored Infantry conveniently fell ill before two battles and left his place, even though the surgeon pronounced him fit for duty. In the 68th U.S. Colored Infantry, almost the exact same thing happened. A lieutenant colonel claimed he was ill, although the surgeon insisted that there "wasn't a d——d thing the matter with him." The regimental commander let him go to the rear, but not until he extracted a promise that if fighting began the lieutenant colonel would return to duty. During three days of combat, he was nowhere to be seen. A general court martial later dismissed him from the service, but the lieutenant colonel used his personal connections with two U.S. senators to get the decision overturned. In Virginia a court convicted a major of cowardice and tore off his insignia, broke his sword, ripped off his buttons, and drove him out of camp on an ox cart to the tune of the "Rogue's March" with all the troops present. And some cowards were not always so obvious. According to one officer who suffered a wound in the Battle of the Crater, among the patients in Chesapeake Hospital at Fort Monroe, Virginia, there were heroes, "But I see also some others here that I am sure will be sufferers all their life time—from cowardice."[21]

These acts of cowardice, however, were rare. In fact, one of the most significant problems USCT officers had was restraining their men in battle. With inadequate training, and a burning desire to prove themselves on the battlefield, the men were very difficult for officers to control. A lieutenant at the Battle of the Crater thought his men "were brave in their charge, but as a body, wholly unmanageable." Before the American Freedmen's Inquiry Commission, Higginson testified that "the most difficult thing in regard to them might be, for instance, to restrain them in such cases where they are required to charge with energy up a hill side," and sundry fights proved him right. In a skirmish at Vidalia, Louisiana, in 1864 the 6th U.S. Colored Heavy Artillery, fighting as infantrymen, broke up a Confederate assault, and only forceful action by the regimental commander "prevented them from breaking ranks to follow the enemy, their anxiety being great to do so." The eagerness of black troops in the battalion held in reserve was so "irrepressible" that the commander and all his line officers "were obliged to place themselves before their men with drawn swords, and threaten summary punishment to the first man who would attempt to quit the ranks to join their comrades fighting in the front."[22]

For Confederates, the prospect of fighting black soldiers was a bit frightening. Like their Northern enemies, Southerners cloaked their fears of slave violence with stereotyped descriptions of laziness, ignorance, and joviality. They had argued vociferously that slavery was good for blacks, that the institution was paternalistic, not cruel, yet deep down many knew that blacks despised enslavement. Nothing brought shudders to Southerners like the thought of armed slaves. For centuries they had kept blacks in a debased state, and now, in Union blue, blacks had a chance to strike back and destroy the oppressive institution. From the very beginning of black enlistment, the concept of fighting black soldiers worried Confederates. "I have talked with numbers of Parolled Prisoners in Vicksburg," wrote one Union officer to his mother, "and they all admit it was the hardest stroke that there cause has received—the arming of the negrow. Not a few of them told me that they would rather fight two Regiments of White Soldiers than one of Niggers. Rebel Citizens fear them more than they would fear Indians."[23] . . .

In part as an outlet for their frustration that blacks aligned with Union forces and in part as a means of intimidating blacks in uniform, to ruin the prospects of blacks developing into good soldiers by destroying their self-confidence and the regard Northerners had for the prowess of black troops, Confederates made a special effort to harass and abuse the USCT at every turn. A commander of a black regiment commented that Confederates fired at his troops regularly all night. They "seem to have a great animosity towards the colored soldier," he wrote. Maj. Gen. E. O. C. Ord informed Grant that in Virginia "the rebels on Warren's front called out to our men that they were going to shell Burnside's Niggers and they (Warren's men) must not mind it. They have shelled every morning since." In Louisiana a lieutenant reported that Confederate troops attacked their outposts and killed two black troops, then mutilated the bodies as a warning: "They were found in the morning with their ears cut off, and scalped and burned to a crisp." And the attack had the desired effect. Within a week the officer was complaining that his troops were "seeing Rebs where there were none" and shooting at cows and inanimate objects: "They get skeered and fire."[24]

Wartime atrocities against the USCT were commonplace, as Confederates first hoped to discourage blacks from enlisting and later sought revenge for their contributions to the Union Army. Initially they were frequent yet isolated incidents. In Louisiana after the Battle of Milliken's Bend a Confederate deserter reported that they had executed an officer and a few enlisted men, and not long afterward some Rebels beat some black troops and hung two others. Similar executions also occurred in Kansas and North Carolina.[25]

But as the war dragged on and Confederates became more and more frustrated, atrocities in battle escalated. In Arkansas at Poison Springs in 1864 Confederates struck some twelve hundred Federals from front and flank and forced them to give ground. Many of the wounded from the 79th U.S. Colored Infantry (New) fell into the hands of the Confederates, and "I have the most positive assurances from eye-witnesses that they were murdered on the spot," charged a Federal colonel. The black regiment suffered nearly twice as many troops killed as wounded, a rarity in the Civil War. At the Battle of the Crater, a Union officer ordered all troops in the crater to surrender, and a few kept up their firing. In retaliation, some Confederates began to bayonet wounded black soldiers, which in turn prompted blacks to counterattack with bullets, bayonets, and rifle butts. Eventually, a Confederate major managed to restore order, and he guaranteed adequate treatment for all prisoners, but if they resisted, he promised all would die. On the urgings of the Federal officers present, everyone then surrendered. In early October 1864 in the Battle of Saltville, Virginia, some fledgling black soldiers in the 5th U.S. Colored Cavalry launched a brilliant charge on Confederate works and drove their adversaries back. For two hours they held their position, but without support, authorities withdrew them at dusk. During the battle Confederates executed numerous black troops who fell into their hands, and wounded black soldiers insisted that their comrades take them in retreat. Despite efforts to collect everyone, some remained on the field, and over the next two days two separate parties of Confederate troops entered hospitals and executed seven wounded black soldiers in their beds.[26]

Without doubt, the most famous series of atrocities in the war occurred at Fort Pillow, some forty miles north of Memphis, in April 1864. There a force of 1,500 Confederate cavalrymen under the command of Maj. Gen. Nathan Bedford Forrest demanded the surrender of the fort, manned by some 550 Federals, nearly half of whom were black soldiers. When the Union commander refused, Forrest's forces stormed the fort and killed, wounded, or captured almost the entire garrison. Some two-thirds of all black soldiers at Fort Pillow lost their lives, while Confederates killed 36 percent of all white troops. After the fight, Federals charged Forrest's command with committing all sorts of atrocities against black soldiers who surrendered. Forrest and Confederate authorities claimed that no such thing occurred, that only black soldiers who continued to fight or tried to escape lost their lives. Eventually, the U.S. Congress's Committee on the Conduct of the War investigated the affair and concluded that Forrest's men had butchered black troops. Southerners, on the other hand, argued that the report was sheer propaganda, and that Forrest and his command had done nothing wrong. Testimony from both Federal and Confederate troops and civilians on the scene, however, indicates that Forrest's men did execute some black soldiers. No one will ever know how many men from the USCT lost their lives after they had surrendered, nor will anyone satisfactorily determine Forrest's role in the massacre.[27]

Southern guerrillas, too, proved to be a problem. Some Confederates and partisans surrounded a foraging party of twenty men from the 51st U.S. Colored Infantry under a lieutenant and forced them to surrender. They then murdered and mutilated the Federals, shooting the lieutenant through the mouth and leaving him for dead, although he lingered on for another ten days. In Kentucky some guerrillas attacked a guard of ten men from the 108th U.S. Colored Infantry, killed three of them, and then butchered their bodies. Six weeks later in Georgia, guerrillas killed three black troops from the 40th U.S. Colored Infantry and split their heads open with an ax. Such acts of violence did little for the Confederate war effort and only served to infuriate Federals.[28]

In his report after the battle at Fort Pillow, Forrest expressed hope that the "facts will demonstrate to the Northern people that negro soldiers cannot cope with Southerners." On the contrary, such atrocities solidified Northern support for the USCT and hardened attitudes toward Confederates within black units. They fought with a little more vigor, and they also decided that wartime atrocities was something "*at which two can play*," so wrote Brig. Gen. August Chetlain. At times they fought under the black flag, which warned the Confederates that they would neither take prisoners nor ask for any mercy for themselves; in other engagements, they acted without warning. An officer in the USCT wrote his wife that some troops in his regiment trapped ten Confederates and gunned down five of them. "Had it not been for Ft Pillow, those 5 men might be alive now. 'Remember Ft Pillow' is getting to be the *feeling* if not the word. It looks hard but we cannot blame these men much.*" During a scouting mission in Louisiana, a company of black cavalrymen discovered a party of guerrillas. The colonel of the expedition instructed his black soldiers to "Remember Fort Pillow," and the black horsemen captured and executed seventeen prisoners. In South Carolina a Confederate general complained that one of his privates had fallen into the hands of the 26th U.S. Colored Infantry. When the Confederates retook the ground, they found the private with six or seven bayonet wounds in him. A Maine cavalryman informed a friend at home that he had witnessed black troops executing a number of Confederates after they surrendered: "We had 200 niggers soldiers with us it did not make eny differance to them about the Rebs surrendering   they would shoot them down   the officers had hard work to stop them from killing All the prisoners   when one of them would beg for his life the niggers would say rember port hudson   it was the Same regiment that the rebs took part of and hung them over the walls." And in an assault at Fort Blakely, Alabama, where black units charged without orders, their conduct was not much different from the behavior of Forrest's command at Fort Pillow. According to a lieutenant in the USCT, when the black troops attacked, "the rebs were panic-struck. Numbers of them jumped into the river and were drowned attempting to cross, or were shot while swimming. Still others threw down their arms and run for their lives over to the white troops on our left, to give themselves up, to save being butchered by our niggers   the niggers did not take a prisoner, they killed all they took to a man." Many of their white officers simply overlooked such retaliation, while others did not endorse such conduct but proved incapable of putting a halt to it. In fact, the problem of blacks executing Confederates became so widespread that black chaplain Henry M. Turner complained publicly about these atrocities.[29]

Under such circumstances, both sides were extremely hesitant to surrender to one another, even when the situation demanded it. In a Federal attack along the Darbytown Road near Chaffin's Farm, Confederates had dug gopher holes and manned them with marksmen. They held their positions "until the inmates saw that we were black & close on them when they dropped all and ran." Black troops captured several South Carolinians in the fight, "who were badly scared lest the darkies should kill them," an officer wrote home. "Indeed all the rebels who fall into my hands remind me strongly of the fugitives who used to call at our house for aid—except that now the master begs favors from the slave and gets them too." During the extended siege of Petersburg, thousands of Confederates deserted to Federal lines, but very few came to the black units for fear of mistreatment. When they did accidentally surrender to commands in the USCT, both white officers and their black men enjoyed observing the "terrified" look once "they found out they had thrown themselves into the hands of the avenging negro."[30]

For black outfits, the possibility of execution if they fell into the clutches of the Confederates was an incentive to fight even more aggressively. Nevertheless, sometimes it was a question of surrendering or being annihilated, and then their officers opted to place their own lives and those of their men in the hands of the Confederate foe.

Needless to say, black prisoners of war had nowhere to hide, and they were exclusively at the mercy of the Rebels, who sometimes committed atrocities and other times treated them as ordinary prisoners. For their white officers, though, it was not always so obvious whom they commanded, and occasionally they had opportunities to protect themselves when captured in large battles by claiming they served in white units. In a fight in Tennessee in November 1864, two officers from the 44th U.S. Colored Infantry told their captors they served in their original white volunteer regiments and the scheme worked temporarily, but Confederates later executed them. At the Battle of the Crater, numerous officers in black units refused to acknowledge their service with the USCT, and their black troops covered for them. Some, however, had consciences that would not let them lie, or they were too proud of service alongside black soldiers to conceal it from anyone. After several whites provided false information to Confederate interrogators, one lieutenant indignantly barked out, "Lemuel D. Dobbs, Nineteenth Niggers by ——." Dobbs as well as others who admitted service in the USCT received bad treatment at the hands of the Rebels, but it was no worse than any other Union soldier who surrendered at the Crater. Other times, soldiers in gray intended to teach USCT officers a lesson, but their own officers refused to tolerate such conduct. When Lt. Joseph K. Nelson surrendered and told his captors that he was an officer in the 111th U.S. Colored Infantry, a Confederate soldier shoved a revolver in his face and said, "You are one of those G—— d—— nigger officers, are you?" Fortunately a Confederate officer intervened and ordered the man away before the soldier could do anything.[31]

Like all soldiers who entered combat, officers and men in the USCT had to deal with the prospect of death, and they appeared to cope with it well. White officers and Northern blacks had made a conscious decision to enter the USCT, well knowing the increased risks, and many former slaves, with religion as their anchor, had long ago adopted the view that God would repay them for all sacrifices and hardships on earth with rewards in heaven, and this belief continued to sustain them throughout their military careers. One officer thought a number of his men "were perfect fatalists in their confidence that God would watch over them, and that if they died, it would be because their time had come." Along similar lines, a lieutenant explained to his mother that Confederate threats to hang white officers did not worry him: "If a man is born to be hung he will not be shot." Others claimed no insight into fate. They merely regarded the goals of the war as worthy of the risk to their lives. "If I fall in the battle anticipated," a black sergeant wrote a friend, "remember, I fall in defence of my race and country." In a dramatic scene that left a lasting impression on the commander, a lieutenant told his troops prior to an advance. "Boys, it may be slavery or Death to some of you today," to which a black soldier replied, "Lieutenant, I am ready to die for Liberty." Moments later, a ball pierced the soldier's heart.[32]

Statistically, during the last two years of the war black troops suffered one-half the fatalities in combat per one thousand men that white volunteers did, but this information is misleading. Because military authorities assigned black commands to peripheral duties and reserved the combat jobs in main armies for white soldiers, black troops fought in comparatively few major battles, even in 1864. But when they did have an opportunity to fight, they almost always battled tenaciously. On numerous battlefields black commands suffered proportionately higher casualties and performed as well, if not better, than more experienced white units. No doubt part of the reason for advances of black troops beyond those of whites, and higher casualties, was inexperience. One advantage veteran troops had was to recognize when attacks were hopeless and when retreats were essential for survival. Veterans learned to conserve their own lives to fight the next day. Yet black troops had to prove to whites that they were inferior to no one, and combat served as the primary arena. They consciously took on extra risks, and lost many lives because of it, in hopes that their labors on the battlefield would reap benefits to the survivors, their families, and future generations. As an officer in the 100th U.S. Colored Infantry explained after the Battle of Nashville, it was sad to walk over the battlefield and see hundreds of bodies of black and white men, clad in blue, killed in battle; but in a peculiar way, the sight was also uplifting, because "the blood of the white and black men has flowed freely together for the great cause which is to give freedom, unity, manhood and peace to all men, whatever birth or complexion." No doubt, amid the tragedy of combat sprouted hope among black soldiers, so alluded a sergeant and former slave at the end of 1864: "The bones of the black man are at present time whitening the battle-fields, while their blood, simultaneously with the white man's, oozes into the soil of his former home."[33]

Given their aggressive conduct in battle, officers and men in the USCT certainly suffered their share of wounds. Varying in seriousness from nicks to those that inflicted fatal injuries, wounds were at times the most harrowing experience of war. One captain in command of a skirmish line during a Confederate attack sustained a wound in his left forearm, then in the right shoulder, and finally in the right forearm, which pierced an artery. For nine hours he lay on the field with no water or medical care and bullets and shells flying all around him. All he could think about was home and the possibility of being a cripple for life. He prayed for water to ease his thirst and for nightfall, when his comrades could come out and rescue him.[34] . . .

In most cases wounded soldiers received medical attention right near the front line. As units assembled for battle, it was the duty of operating physicians within a brigade or division to assemble a surgeon's booth, some three hundred yards to the rear, and preferably in a protected area, where they removed balls, stopped the bleeding, and dressed wounds temporarily. They also administered morphine as a pain killer and some whiskey as a "stimulant." Ambulances then transported the wounded to "flying" or field hospitals, where they received more thorough medical attention. Providing they were able to travel, patients with injuries that were likely to keep them from duty for more than ten days then went to a base or general hospital.[35]

Combat units regarded it as critical to have at least two physicians. One had to set up the surgeon's booth, hang out a lantern, and then send a messenger to the front to guide the stretcher-bearers to the operating area. The other physician went to the front to give water and sometimes whiskey to the wounded and have the stretcher-bearers remove the injured men from the field of battle. This was an important job, particularly in the USCT, as a surgeon stated: "*I know what will*

*become of the white troops who fall into the enemy's possession, but I
am not certain as to the fate of the colored troops."* Yet it was also a
dangerous duty that cost the USCT numerous physicians. Although one
assistant surgeon tried to reassure his wife that he would not be "rushing
into battle" because "I am one of the biggest cowards in the world &
then my province is not to fight," there were considerable risks. Another
surgeon more candidly explained to his mother that he did his best not
to expose himself recklessly, not only because he feared injury but also
because he was not "doing his full duty to my men if I expose myself,
when my services may be exceedingly necessary to them." Nevertheless,
he had a three-pound shot pass just over his head, "much disarranging
my ideas & causing me to skedaddle swiftly."[36] . . .

For operating surgeons, the work was frantic. After one battle a
surgeon wrote home that he had attended two hundred wounded and
performed thirty-five to forty "capital" operations,—that is, leg and arm
amputations, at all possible spots,— "besides as many more resections."
He even had to remove about one-half of a soldier's upper jaw without
chloroform because he feared the man would swallow too much blood
and choke. Another surgeon, whose regiment suffered two hundred
killed and wounded in one day, wrote, "For the last sixty-four hours I
have had but ten hours sleep. I worked twenty-two hours yesterday."
Serving with a combat regiment in Virginia in 1864, he labored so
intensively that, he confessed, "It is rarely I sleep nights I am so nervous." One month later, the pressure of surgery and overwork resulted
in dizzy spells.[37]

With elementary equipment, the most prominent item being a saw,
and little understanding of sanitation and sterilization, these surgeons
operated on their patients in desperate hope of saving lives. Huge, soft
chunks of lead inflicted horrible wounds, and clothing and dirt introduced with the projectile produced infections and gangrene. One surgeon
told his father, also a doctor, that out of one soldier's back he removed
"a piece of shell weighing a pound, completely embedded in the flesh."
Many surgeons were quick to sacrifice limbs to save lives, while others
agonized over the decision, particularly with arms, because some men
could lose a considerable amount of bone and still retain use of the limb.
Miscalculation with amputations, however, often resulted in the death
of patients from infections and hemorrhage. In search of lead and bits of
clothing, surgeons sometimes cut substantial holes in patients and poked
and pried until they secured the foreign objects. At times, patients could

not decide whether the injury or operation was more painful. "The fact is I've lain now seven days," complained an officer, "wounded in both thighs by the enemy & wounded in the rear by the surgeon who cut a ball out—by the rear." Other times, because of the location of the ball, surgeons could only remove clothing fragments and dress the wound. One such instance occurred when a ball entered the left shoulder of a man and pierced his lung. Miraculously, he recovered, although he carried the ball around, lodged in him permanently.[38]

One of the least visible and most private injuries in the Civil War was combat stress. Fighting in relatively compact formations, with buddies all around to help ease the tension and buoy the confidence, combat stress seldom afflicted black troops, just as it was rather uncommon in white volunteer units. But for white officers in the USCT the situation was different. As models for black soldiers, these whites had to try to suppress their very natural fears and uncertainties concerning both their troops and themselves and portray a sense of confidence and composure. Worse yet, they entered combat under the added pressure of fighting with troops whom they regarded as inexperienced, improperly trained, and not wholly trustworthy. And because they felt a keen sense of isolation, surrounded by dozens and dozens of blacks, many of them had no viable outlet for their emotions. The night after the Battle of Chaffin's Farm, a captain who led thirty-two men into the fight and returned with only three others, all black, began to feel depressed. "I experienced a tingling, prickly sensation, as though a thousand little needles were jagging my flesh. The air seemed oppressive, and I breathed with difficulty." The captain realized he was in trouble and sought help from the regimental surgeon. That night the surgeon drugged the captain to enable him to sleep and the next day sent him to the corps hospital for ten days. Although doctors diagnosed his problem as intermittent fever, the captain knew better: "The strain on me was so great through the day, that when the excitement passed over and quiet came, my nervous organization broke down temporarily. That was all." Ten days of rest, along with a liberal amount of quinine, "toned me up again," and he returned for duty. Another officer, this one in the 54th Massachusetts (Colored) Infantry, also suffered from combat stress after the attack on Fort Wagner, and his regimental surgeon did a much better job of determining his problem: "*His brain has been seriously affected by isolation and exhaustion during the recent field operations on James [Morris] Island so that an absence from the department is necessary to prevent permanent disability.*" A third officer also experienced some combat stress, yet doctors refused to acknowledge his problem. As a foreigner who had just joined his unit before the Virginia Campaign of 1864, he had not integrated into the command. Exposure to the scenes of battle several days after they had taken place horrified him, and the officer soon found service with black troops unrewarding. With the added burdens of fighting, regular campaign duties, and some homesickness, he became so depressed that he could not get up out of bed. When he finally sought medical attention, the doctor found nothing physically wrong with the officer and ordered him back to duty. That evening the officer vented his spleen in his diary, "The meanness of the medical department in the army here, no assistance, no sympathy, no help." Three weeks later he admitted that joining the USCT had been the greatest blunder of his life and even mentioned suicide as an alternative.[39]

Despite the temptation to compare the combat performance of black and white units in the Union Army, such efforts are utterly unfair. By the time the Federal government decided to enlist black soldiers, hundreds of thousands of white troops already had substantial battlefield experience, and as fledgling black soldiers "saw the elephant" for the first time, they faced a veteran Confederate Army. Most high-ranking Union officers preferred to use black troops for fatigue and noncombat duty and rely on the veteran white commands for combat. Thus, black units had little time for drill and were often relegated to rear-area occupation duties or secondary and tertiary campaigns. While black soldiers had powerful reasons for military service, such as the elimination of slavery, revenge for generations of bondage, and a chance to demonstrate to whites the fallacy of prejudice, they also suffered the humiliation of unequal pay and bounties and virtually no promotions to the officer corps. Along with shouldering the additional burden of the welfare of their families in the transition from slavery to freedom, it is a tribute to their commitment to the war effort that the desertion rate of black soldiers in the Union Army was almost identical to whites.[40]

On several occasions, the performance of black commands outshone that of white volunteer units. In South Carolina the 7th U.S. Colored Infantry came to the rescue of a veteran white regiment that had run out of ammunition. As the black troops marched in behind the line, veteran white soldiers broke and fled under the weight of a Confederate assault. The men of the 7th U.S. Colored Infantry turned toward the Confederates and advanced boldly, with white Federal troops pouring through their formation, and filled the gap in the Federal line to repulse the attack. At the Battle of Brice's Crossroads in June 1864, Forrest's command routed a Federal force and black troops blocked the Confederates while their white comrades escaped. With almost no assistance from white volunteers, two black infantry regiments and a black light artillery battery battled the advancing graycoats for three days, sometimes in hand-to-hand combat, and even ran out of ammunition, but saved the command of Brig. Gen. Samuel D. Sturgis. Out of 1,350 men, the black brigade suffered well over 800 casualties. On yet another occasion, the 600 recruits who composed the 5th U.S. Colored Cavalry were so raw that a black sergeant admitted he did not even know the names of his men when they first entered combat. En route to Saltville, these troops silently endured insults, harassment, and derogatory remarks about their lack of fighting prowess from the white volunteers. In the battle, of the 400 black soldiers who saw combat, the Confederates killed or wounded 118, and the black regiment penetrated deepest into the Rebel works. According to a captain in the 13th Kentucky Cavalry, a regiment that so opposed the enlistment of blacks that some of its men nearly murdered a recruiting officer for the USCT, he and his comrades "never saw troops fight like they did. The rebels were firing on them with grape and canister and were mowing them down by the Scores but others kept straight on." The captain admitted he "never thought they would fight till he Saw them there." In support, Col. James S. Brisbin wrote, "I have seen white troops fight in twenty-seven battles, and I never saw any fight better" than his black soldiers. Brisbin also noted that "On the return of the forces[,] those who had scoffed at the colored troops on the march out were silent."[41]

As they earned more and more combat experience, those raw recruits were transformed in attitude and performance into veterans. They neither shunned battle nor craved it; combat became an obligation. Black troops still regarded it as a great opportunity to prove themselves to whites on both sides of the line, and they continued to fight aggressively, yet their previous battlefield experience had taught them warfare's serious side and they acted a bit less recklessly. More importantly, they learned to cope with dangers and fears of combat, and confidence in their own ability to handle its rigors grew. When a Confederate army approached Fort Pulaski. Tennessee, manned by the 14th U.S. Colored Infantry, a black soldier told his regimental commander, "Col'nel, dey

can't whip us: dey nebber git the ole Fourteenth out of heah, nebber."
Several weeks later, in Virginia, another black regiment got into a nasty
fight as most of the men fired two hundred rounds at the Confederates.
Unfortunately, the residue from all the black gunpowder they used got
the muskets so dirty that troops were unable to ram down charges and
had to clean them while under heavy fire. Nevertheless, they retained
their composure, which thoroughly impressed one of their officers: "the
men however, coolly sat down, dismounted their pieces and cleaned
them, after which they resumed firing."[42]

Once they fought alongside white troops and demonstrated their combat prowess, black soldiers went a long way toward neutralizing the
distrust and disdain whites had for them. After the garrison at Paducah,
Kentucky, held off Forrest's larger force, the post commander confessed.
"I have been one of those men, who never had much confidence in
colored troops fighting, but these doubts are now all removed, for they
fought as bravely as any troops in the Fort." Nothing could have felt
better than to hear the three hearty cheers some white troops gave to the
14th U.S. Colored Infantry after their stellar conduct at Decatur, Alabama, or the reception three black regiments received after their successful assault on the works outside Petersburg in June 1864. "You ought
to have heard the 'Bully for you's the Cavalry (Kautz's) favored the boys
with," an officer wrote his wife. When Hancock's Corps from the Army
of the Potomac arrived and relieved his regiment, these veterans congratulated the black soldiers and treated them with respect. "A few more
fights like that," predicted the officer, "and our Cold [Colored] boys will
have established their manhood if not their Brotherhood to the satisfaction of even the most prejudiced."[43]

In the late stages of the war, the USCT really began to make its
presence felt. Nearly one in every eight soldiers in the siege of Petersburg
was black, and at the Battle of Nashville, where Maj. Gen. George H.
Thomas's troops crushed the Confederate Army of Tennessee and put a
halt to Lt. Gen. John Bell Hood's Tennessee invasion, black forces
played a major role despite their comparatively small size. On the first
day of fighting, the two black brigades attacked the Confederate right to
draw resources away from the main Federal thrust on the Rebel left
flank, which was successful. During the second day, black and white
troops swarmed up the slick slopes of the Confederate position on Over-
ton Hill. "I can hear the voices of the officers as they called out, 'Close

up those ranks,' " recalled an officer in the USCT, "as great gaps were made in them by howitzer and grape shot guns loaded to the muzzle." Although they did not break the Confederate line, these troops again forced the Confederate high command to transfer men to its right, which weakened the left and facilitated its fall to Federal attackers. Black units sustained 630 casualties out of 3,500 men in the victory.[44]

An even better example of black troops acting decisively in a major engagement was the Battle of Fort Blakely, Alabama, in April 1865. There a division of black troops occupied the extreme right of the Union line, and in the late afternoon, because of Confederate inactivity, they received permission to advance their skirmishers. Although Confederate troops fought vigorously, Rebel skirmishers fell back quickly into their own trenches. According to one officer in the USCT, "As soon as our niggers caught sight of the retreating figures of the rebs the very devil could not hold them their eyes glittered like serpents and with yells & howls like hungry wolves they rushed for the rebel works   the movement was simultaneous regt.   [regiment] after regt. and line after line took up the cry and started until the whole field was black with darkeys." Similar in some respects to the famous Union assault up Missionary Ridge near Chattanooga, Tennessee, in November 1863, the black troops seized the opportunity and pursued the Confederates so closely that the defenders could not fire on them without fear of hitting their own men. Moments after the unscheduled charge, Federal troops around the line launched a planned assault, although word had never reached the black division and the Federals carried the Confederate works everywhere.[45]

These and other outstanding battlefield performances by the USCT appeared to open new avenues to the black soldiers. In Virginia, where black units did some of their best fighting, an officer may have exaggerated a bit when he wrote his daughter that white troops "say the Darkies are Bully fellows to fight and all the prejudice seems to be gone," but he nevertheless conveyed the changing attitude among white volunteer units toward the USCT. Another USCT officer who had just come to Virginia from service in South Carolina and Florida also noted the more liberal racial atmosphere: "The colored troops are very highly valued here & there is no apparent difference in the way they are treated. White troops & blacks mingle constantly together & I have seen no single Evidence of dislike on the part of the soldiers. The truth is they have fought their way into the respect of all the army." Elsewhere progress was slow albeit steady. White troops were looking at black soldiers in a completely different light than they had some two years earlier.[46]

Such changes boded well for the future. Both white officers and their black soldiers believed that no one would ever again doubt the combat abilities of the black race. "The long contended point of negro fighting qualities is now forever settled," wrote one officer in the USCT. "They have proven themselves good soldiers, as well as ardent fighters." In fact, a few antiblack stalwarts now insisted that they "fight too well," noted Brig. Gen. Daniel Ullmann. Some of these individuals had actually recommended to Ullmann that "We must not discipline them, for if we do, we will have to fight them some day ourselves." Moreover, black troops and some white officers had reason to hope that a new era of race relations and civil rights was dawning, with blacks attaining all the rights and privileges of the white race. "The future of the colored soldier seems open more and auspiciously, both for himself and the country," concluded a chaplain. Such elevation, argued a captain, would also have a positive effect on white society: "They have raised themselves and all mankind in the scale of manhood by their bold achievements for I hold that, as water seeks a common level, so does the raising of a certain class of the people must of necessity raise the whole community!"[47]

NOTES

From Joseph T. Glatthaar, *Forged in Battle: The Civil War Alliance of Black Soldiers and White Officers* (New York: Free Press, 1990), 143–68. Reprinted by permission.

Abbreviations

Repositories

AAS	American Antiquarian Society
BL, UMI	Bentley Library, University of Michigan
CWM, LC	Civil War Miscellany, Library of Congress
CWMC, MHI	Civil War Miscellaneous Collection, U.S. Army Military History Institute
CWTIC, MHI	Civil War Times Illustrated Collection, U.S. Army Military History Institute
EU	Emory University

ILSHL	Illinois State Historical Library
LC	Library of Congress
MAHS	Massachusetts Historical Society
MHI	U.S. Army Military History Institute
MNHS	Minnesota Historical Society
NA	National Archives
OHS	Ohio Historical Society
RIHS	Rhode Island Historical Society
SC, CL, UMI	Schoff Collection, Clements Library, University of Michigan
SHC, UNC	Southern Historical Collection, University of North Carolina
SSC	Sophia Smith Collection, Smith College
UAR	University of Arkansas
UIA	University of Iowa
VTHS	Vermont Historical Society
WRHS	Western Reserve Historical Society
YU	Sterling Library, Yale University

Other Abbreviations

AAR	After Action Report
AGO	Adjutant General's Office
CMSR	Compiled Military Service Records
GO	General Orders
HQ	Headquarters
MOLLUS	Military Order of the Loyal Legion of the United States
RG	Record Group

1. William Eliot Furness, "The Negro As a Soldier," *Military Order of the Loyal Legion of the United States-Illinois*, 2, 457–88, pp. 457–58.

2. William Baird, "Reminiscences," pp. 64–65. William Baird Papers, BL, UMI; Danl to friends at home, 2 June 1864. Densmore Family Papers, MNHS; Oliver Norton to Father, 1 May 1864. Oliver Willcox Norton, *Army Letters, 1861–1865* (Chicago: O. L. Deming, 1903), p. 202. Also see Danl to Friends, 17 June 1864. Densmore Family Papers, MNHS.

3. Thomas Wentworth Higginson, *Army Life in a Black Regiment* (Boston: Beacon Press, 1962), p. 246; Alexander H. Newton, *Out of the Briars: An Autobiography and Sketch of the Twenty-ninth Regiment Connecticut Volunteers* (Philadelphia: A.M.E. Book Concern, 1910), p. 39. Also see Jas. Rogers to ?, 1 Feb. 1863. James S. Rogers Papers, SSC, Smith College; Seth Rogers to ?, 5 Feb. 1863. MOLLUS Collection, MHI; Ullman to Stanton, 6 June 1863. "The Negro," p. 1298. RG 94, NA.

4. Oliver Norton to Sister L, 29 Feb. 1864. Norton, *Army Letters*, pp. 198–99; L. Grim to Aunt, 1 Feb. 1865. Wise-Clark Family Papers, UIA. Also see

Maj. Quincy McNeil to Brig. Gen. Jno. A. Rawlins, 13 Aug. 1864. Ira Berlin, Joseph P. Reidy, and Leslie S. Rowland, eds., *Freedom: A Documentary History of Emancipation, 1861–1867* (New York: Cambridge University Press, 1982), II, pp. 602–3; Oliver Norton to Father, 1 Mar. 1864. Norton, *Army Letters*, p. 202; C.G.G.M. to Father, 28 Feb. 1864. Charles G. Merrill Papers, YU.

5. Higginson, *Army Life*, p. 25.

6. F. S. Bowley, *A Boy Lieutenant* (Philadelphia: Henry Altemus Company, 1906), pp. 47–48, 69–70. Also see Luis F. Emilio, *A Brave Black Regiment: History of the Fifty-fourth Regiment of Massachusetts Volunteer Infantry* (Boston: Boston Book Company, 1894), pp. 77–78; M. H. Twitchell, "Reminiscences," p. 76. M. H. Twitchell Papers, VTHS.

7. Frank Holsinger, "How Does One Feel Under Fire?" *MOLLUS-Kansas*, 1, pp. 300–301. Also see Stuart to Sister Emma, 16 May 1865. Morris Stuart Hall Papers, BL, UMI; A. S. Fisher to dear afflicted Captin, 31 July 1863. A. S. Fisher Papers, Gettysburg College.

8. John Habberton diary, 7 Apr. 1864. John Habberton Papers, MHI. Also see Jos. J. Scroggs diary, 29 Sep. 1864. CWTIC, MHI: HQ. Dept. of Virginia & North Carolina. 11 Oct. 1864. George R. Sherman Papers, RIHS.

9. Newton, *Out of the Briars*, p. 47. Also see A. S. Fisher to dear afflicted Captin, 31 July 1863. A. S. Fisher Papers, Gettysburg College.

10. Henry to Parents & all, 24 July 1864. Henry M. Crydenwise Papers, EU. Also see James H. Richard, "Service with Colored Troops in Burnside's Corps," *Personal Narratives, Rhode Island Soldiers and Sailors Historical Society* (series 5, no. 1), pp. 40–41.

11. Edward W. Bacon to Kate, 31 Oct. 1864. Edward W. Bacon Papers, AAS.

12. John McMurray, "A Union Officer's Recollections of the Negro as a Soldier," ed. Horace Montgomery, *Pennsylvania History*, 28 (April 1961), p. 36; Joseph J. Scroggs diary, 29 Sep. 1864, CWTIC, MHI; Lewis to Mother, 17 Aug. 1864. Lewis Weld Family Papers, YU. Also see Lewis to Amelia, 20 Jul. [1863]. Carter Woodson Papers, LC; Stuart Hall, "Reminiscences," p. 40. Morris Stuart Hall Papers, BL, UMI.

13. *New York Times*, 8 Jan. 1865.

14. August V. Kautz to Mrs. Savage, 29 Mar. 1865. August V. Kautz Papers, ILSHL. Also see Testimony of Nathaniel Paige, Special Correspondent of the *New York Tribune*, before AFIC. "The Negro," pp. 2586–87. RG 94, NA.

15. George E. Sutherland, "The Negro in the Late War," *Military Order of the Loyal Legion of the United States-Wisconsin*, 1, 164–88, p. 180; [Gus] to Wife, 21 Jun. 1864. Charles Augustus Hill Papers, Richard S. Tracy Collection.

16. Albert Rogall diary, 30 July 1864. Albert Rogall Papers, OHS; D. E. Proctor to Harvey, 1 Aug. 1864. David E. Proctor Papers in possession of Chester L. Somers. Also see William Baird, "Reminiscences," p. 20. William

Baird Papers, BL, UMI; *War of the Rebellion: Official Records of the Union and Confederate Armies* (Washington, 1880–1901), I, 40, pt. 1, pp. 46, 137, 246–49; *Memorial of Colonel John A. Bross* (Chicago: Tribune Book and Job Office, 1865), p. 17.

17. Edwin M. Main, *The Story of the Marches, Battles and Incidents of the 3rd USCC* (Louisville: Globe Print Co., 1908), pp. 200–203; GO No. 81. Hdqrs. Military Division of the West Mississippi. 9 Dec. 1864. OR I, 45, pt. 1, p. 778. Also see AAR of Col. E. D. Osband, 4 Dec. 1864. OR I, 45, pt. 1, p. 781–82.

18. Joseph J. Scroggs diary, 29 Sep. 1864. CWTIC, MHI. Also see Benjamin Quarles, *The Negro in the Civil War* (Boston: Little, Brown and Company, 1953, pp. 15, 214, 219; Lt. Col. Joseph B. Mitchell, *The Badge of Gallantry: Recollections of Civil War Medal of Honor Winners* (New York: The Macmillan Company, 1968), p. 139; AAR of Lt. Col. Jno. C. Chadwick, 13 June 1864. OR I, 34, pt. 1, p. 444; Dr. Seth Rogers to ?, 27 Jan. 1863. MOLLUS Collection, MHI; George R. Sanders to Mrs. Burnham, 15 July 1863. Burnham File, Civil War Miscellaneous Papers, YU.

19. G. A. Rockwood to Sir, 31 Oct. 1864. 890 R 1864. Letters Received, AGO. RG 94, NA; T.W.H. to James, 24 Nov. 1862. T. W. Higginson Papers, AAS. Also see AAR of Col. S. J. Crawford, 20 May 1864. Stanton to ?, 16 June 1864. Lt. Col. I. C. Terry to Lt. Proudfit, ND. "The Negro," pp. 3107–9, 3164 3420, RG 94, NA; Extract of Annual Report of 51st U.S. Colored Infantry for 1863. "The Negro," p. 2143, RG 94, NA.

20. C. P. Lyman to ones at home, 19 June 1864. Carlos P. Lyman Papers, WRHS. Also see List of Camp and Garrison Equipage Lost in George W. Strong Papers, UIA; Maj. S. W. Pickens et al. Statement, 17 Oct. 1864. Berlin et al., *Freedom*, II, pp. 553–56.

21. Danl to Brother, 24 July 1864. Densmore Family Papers, MNHS; Gus to Wife, 3 Aug. 1864. Charles Augustus Hill Papers, Richard S. Tracy Collection. Also see Reports of Surg. Daniel D. Hanson and Lt. Col. W. W. Marple. Pension File of B. Ryder Corwin. RG 15, NA; Danl to Brother, 11, 30 Aug. 1864. Danl to Friends at home, 5 Oct. 1864. Densmore Family Papers, MNHS; Proceedings of GCM. Trial of J. H. Clendening. LL 3110. RG 153, NA; Richard, "Service with Colored Troops," pp. 22–23; Lewis to Mason, 7 Oct. 1864. Lewis Weld Family Papers, YU; John McMurray, *Recollections of a Colored Troop* (Brookville, PA: n.p. 1916), p. 35. Albert Rogall diary, 19 Aug. 1864. Albert Rogall Papers, OHS; Foster to Bvt. Brig. Gen. Brice, 12 Dec. 1864. Letters Regarding Recruiting, Division of Colored Troops. RG 94, NA; Henry Whitney Journal, no date. Whitney Family Papers, Rutgers U; CMSR of Chap. Alvah R. Jones, 10th USCI. RG 94, NA. These were white men.

22. Bowley, *Boy Lieutenant*, p. 12; Testimony of Col. T. W. Hinson before AFIC. "The Negro," pp. 2551–52. RG 94, NA; AAR of Lt. Col. Hubert A. McCaleb, 9 Feb. 1864. OR I, 34, pt. 1, p. 130. Also see Sutherland, "The Negro

in the Late War," p. 182. Higginson, *Army Life*, p. 112; AAR of Col. T. W. Higginson, 1 Feb. 1863. Berlin et al., *Freedom*, II, p. 524.

23. Ben F. Stevens to Mother, 12 Aug. 1863. Richard N. Ellis, ed. "The Civil War Letters of an Iowa Family," *Annals of Iowa*, series 3, 39, no. 8 (Spring 1969), 561–85, p. 582. Also see Jas. Rogers to ?, 18 Mar. 1863. James S. Rogers Papers, SSC, Smith College; Saxton to Stanton, 4 Apr. 1863. "The Negro," pp. 1168–69. RG 94, NA.

24. Lt. Col. Theo. Trauernicht to Mussey, 23 Oct. 1863.

Letters Received, 2nd USCI. RG 94 NA; E.O.C. Ord, to Grant, 20 Aug. 1864. "The Negro," p. 2754. RG 94, NA; Samuel D. Barnes diary, 24 Apr., 1 May 1864. CWM, LC.

25. See AAR of Brig. Gen. Geo. B. Andrews, 6 Aug. 1863. OR I, 26, pt. 1, p. 240; Jas. to Wife, 5 Mar. 1864. Peet Family Papers, MNHS; Lt. Commander E. K. Ewen to Act'g Rear Admiral David D. Porter, 16 June 1863. Affidavit of Sgt. Samuel Johnson, 11 July 1864. Col. Jno. Logan to Col. E. B. Ewell, 3 Sep. 1863 and Col. Frank Powers to Col. Jno. Logan, 2 Sep. 1863. Col. Williams to Maj. T. R. Livingston, 21 May 1863. Berlin et al., *Freedom*, II, pp. 574–75, 581, 584–85, 588–89.

26. AAR of Col. J. M. Williams, 24 Apr. 1864. OR I, 34, pt. 1, p. 746. Also see F. S. A. Bowley, "The Petersburg Mine," *Military Order of the Loyal Legion of the United States-California*, War papers, no. 3, pp. 14–15; AAR of Col. James Brisbin, 20 Oct. 1864. Report of Surg. William H. Gardner, 13th Kentucky Infantry, of the shooting of Union prisoners, 26 Oct. 1864. OR I, 39, pt. 1, pp. 554–55, 557.

27. For the most recent and probably the best account of Fort Pillow, see John Cimprich and Robert C. Mainforth, Jr., "Fort Pillow Revisited: New Evidence about an Old Controversy," *Civil War History*, 28, no. 4 (Dec. 1982), pp. 293–306 (percentage losses are on page 295). For testimony about the massacre, see OR I, 32, pt. 1, pp. 519–40. For Forrest's side of the story, see OR I, 32, pt. 1, pp. 586–619.

28. See Notes of George N. Carruthers. CWM, LC; Return of the 51st USCI for Feb. 1864. "The Negro" p. 3018. RG 94, NA; Stuart to Sister Emma, 14 Feb. 1865. Morris Stuart Hall Papers, BL, UMI; Maj. Cochrane (?) to Foster, 9 Jan. 1865. Letters Sent by the Commissioner, RG 393, NA; Walter Chapman to Parents, 17 July 1864. Walter A. Chapman Papers, YU; Extract from the Annual Return of the 108th USCI, 1864. Capt. Ben S. Nicklin to Maj. B. H. Polk, 10 Oct. 1864. "The Negro," p. 3302. RG 94, NA; W. C. Ream to Cousin Tillie, 11 Feb. 1864. Wise-Clark Family Papers, UIA.

29. Maj. Gen. N. B. Forest to Col., 15 Apr. 1864. OR I, 32, Pt. 1, p. 610; AAR of Brig. Gen. August Chetlain, 14 Apr. 1864. "The Negro," p. 3072. RG 94, NA; Gus to Wife, 6 May 1864. Charles Augustus Hill Papers, Richard S. Tracy Collection; Lieut. Anson S. Hemingway to ?, 17 May 1864. Lydia Min-

turn Post, ed., *Soldiers' Letters From Camp, Battle-field and Prison* (New York: Bunce & Huntington, Publishers, 1865), p. 366; E. R. Manson to Friend John, 19 Oct. 1864. E. R. Manson Papers, Duke U.; Walter Chapman to Parents, 11 Apr. 1865. Walter A. Chapman Papers, YU. Also see Alonzo Rembaugh to Capt., 28 Feb. 1864. Loomis-Wilder Papers, YU; Brig. Gen. B. H. Robertson to Maj., 14 July 1864. "The Negro," p. 3200. RG 94, NA; H. M Turner to Mr. Editor, 30 June 1864. Christian Recorder, 9 July 1864.

30. Edward W. Bacon to Kate, 26 Sep., 31 Oct. 1864. Edward W. Bacon Papers, AAS. Also see Hen [Marshall] to Hattie, 25 Nov. 1864. SC, CL, UMI; AAR of Col. A. G. Draper, 15 May 1864. "The Negro," pp. 3114–16. RG 94, NA; George R. Sherman, "Reminiscences," p. 9. George R. Sherman Papers, RIHS.

31. Richard, "Service with Colored Troops," p. 29; Joseph K. Nelson, "Reminiscence," p. 47. CWMC, MHI. Also see Stuart Hall, "Reminiscences," pp. 41–2. Morris Stuart Hall Papers, BL, UMI; William Baird, "Reminiscences," pp. 20, 79–81. William Baird Papers, BL, UMI; Hall, "Mine Run to Petersburg," p. 24; George R. Sherman, "Reminiscences." George R. Sherman Papers, RIHS.

32. Higginson, *Army Life*, pp. 255–56; M. Miller to Mother, 27 Jul. 1863. Minos Miller Papers, UAR; J. H. Welch to Brother in Christ, 15 Oct. 1863. *Christian Recorder*, 24 Oct. 1863; Thomas J. Morgan, PNRISSS. Ser. 3, No. 13, p. 29. Also see Sam to Father, 13 Sep. 1863. Evans Family Papers, OHS.

33. GO. No. 5, HQ. 100th USCI. 2 Feb. 1865. "The Negro," pp. 3512–513. RG 94, NA; Thomas B. Webster to Editor, Dec. 1864. *Christian Recorder*, 7 Jan. 1865. Also see *The Medical and Surgical History of the War of the Rebellion*. Pt. First, Medical Volume and Appendix, pp. xl–xli; McMurray, *Recollections*, p. 59; N. P. Hallowell, "The Negro as a Soldier," in *Selected Letters and Papers of N. P. Hallowell* (Peterborough, NH: Richard R. Smith Co., Inc., 1963), p. 37.

34. See Holsinger, "How Does One Feel Under Fire?" pp. 303–4.

35. See J. R. Weist, "The Medical Department in the War," *Military Order of the Loyal Legion of the United States-Ohio*, II, 71–95, p. 84; Ch. G. G. Merrill to Father, 2 Aug. 1864. Charles Merrill Papers, YU.

36. Rufus S. Jones to *Christian Recorder*, 20 Mar. 1864. *Christian Recorder*, 16 Apr. 1864; J. O. More to Lizzie, 23 Feb. 1864 and Charles to Father, 23 June 1864. Charles Merrill Papers, YU. Also see George W. Adams, *Doctors in Blue: The Medical History of the Union Army in the Civil War* (New York: Henry Schuman, 1952), pp. 66–67; Ch. G. G. Merrill to Father, 2 Aug. 1864. Charles Merrill Papers, YU; Lewis to wife, 2 May 1864. Jonathan Lewis Whitaker Papers, SHC, UNC.

37. [Francis] to Aunt Margie, 1 Aug. 1864. Sarah Swan Weld Blake, ed., *Diaries and Letters of Francis Minot Weld* (Boston: [Stetson Press], 1925), p. 166; Charles to Annie, 16 June 1864. Ch. G. G. Merrill to Father, 1 Aug.

1864. Charles Merrill Papers, YU. Also see Charles to Mother, 8 Sep. 1864. Charles Merrill Papers, YU.

38. Charles to Father, 3 July 1864. Charles Merrill Papers, YU; Jas. C. Beecher to Kinsley, 8 Dec. [1864]. Edward W. Kinsley Papers, MAHS; Hattie to Tillie, 13 June 1865. Wise-Clark Family Papers, UIA. Also see Ch. G. G. Merrill to Father, 18 Jan. 1864[5]. Charles Merrill Papers, YU.

39. McMurray, *Recollections*, pp. 61–2; Surgeon's Certificate for Maj. J. W. M. Appleton, by Surg. Charles E. Briggs. CMSR for J. W. M. Appleton. RG 94, NA; Albert Rogall diary, 14 June 1864. Albert Rogall Papers, OHS. Also see Carded Medical Records of John McMurray. RG 94, NA; Albert Rogall diary, 8 10, 11 June, 1 July 1864. Albert Rogall Papers, OHS. Rogall had no Carded Medical Records at NA. For comments on the sense of isolation, see J. H. Mead to Ellen, 31 Mar. 1865. Mead Family Papers, UIA; Sam to Father, 8 Jun. 1864. Evans Family Papers, OHS.

40. See *OR* III, pp. 668–70. Also see Ella Lonn, *Desertion During the Civil War* (Gloucester, MA: Peter Smith, 1966). Some sixty-seven black troops deserted per one thousand, whereas sixty-three white troops per one thousand deserted. Authorities recruited the bulk of the white units on the local level, while that was not really the case with black soldiers, and that alone could easily account for the difference.

41. Jeff [Hoge] to Tillie, 4 Nov. 1864. Wise-Clark Family Papers, UIA; AAR of Col. James S. Brisbin, 20 Oct. 1864. *OR* I, 39, pt. 1, p. 557. Also see Col. John Shaw, Jr. to Bvt. Lt. Col. George Lee, 15 Aug. 1866. "The Negro," p. 3199. RG 94, NA; AAR of Col. Ed. Bouton, 17 Jun. 1864. Testimony of Col. Edward Bouton in the Sturgis hearings. *OR* I, 39, pt. 1, pp. 125–27 and 213–14; Bowley, "The Petersburg Mine" p. 14; Affidavit of Sgt. Samuel Walker, undated. Pension File of George Turner, Co. G, 5th USCC. RG 15, NA.

42. Thomas J. Morgan, "Reminiscences of Service with colored Troops in the Army of the Cumberland," *Personal Narratives, Rhode Island Soldiers and Sailors Historical Society*, series 3, no. 13, p. 32; Edward W. Bacon to Kate, 31 Oct. 1864. Edward W. Bacon Papers, AAS. Also see G. A. Rockwood to Sir, 31 Oct. 1864. 890 R 1864. Letters Received, AGO. RG 94, NA.

43. AAR of Col. S. G. Hicks, 6 Apr. 1864. *OR* I, 32, pt. 1, p. 549; Gus to Wife, 15 June 1864. Charles Augustus Hill Papers, Richard S. Tracy Collection. Also see Higginson, *Army Life*, p. 123; GO No. 50. HQ, 14th USCT. 23 Nov. 1864. Berlin et al., *Freedom*, II, p. 559.

44. Stuart Hall, "Reminiscences," p. 40. Morris Stuart Hall Papers, BL, UMI. Also see *OR* I, 46, pt. 1, p. 61; Joseph T. Glatthaar, "Hood's Tennessee Campaign," *The March to the Sea and Beyond: Sherman's Troops in the Savannah and Carolinas Campaigns* (New York: New York University Press, 1985), pp. 191–93, 199–201; *OR* I, 45, pt. 1, pp. 59, 103.

45. Walter Chapman to Parents, 11 Apr. 1865. Walter A. Chapman Papers,

YU. Also see Henry to parents & all, 10 Apr. 1865. Henry M. Crydenwise Papers, EU; AAR of Brig. Gen. John P. Hawkins, 16 Apr. 1865. OR I, 49, pt. 1, p. 287.

46. John Pierson to Daughter, 3 Oct. 1864. SC, CL, UMI; Lewis to Mother, 17 Aug. 1864. Lewis Weld Family Papers, YU. Also see Hunter to Gov. Andrew, 4 May 1863. Ullmann to Stanton, 6 June 1863. Dana to Stanton, 22 June 1863. Thomas to Stanton, 7 Nov. 1864. "The Negro," pp. 1219–20, 1298, 1343, 2819. RG 94, NA.

47. L. Grim to Aunt Tillie, 27 June 1864. Wise-Clark Family Papers, UIA; Ullmann to William C. Bryant, 7 Mar. 1864. "The Negro," p. 2412. RG 94, NA; Sam S. Gardner to Sir, 13 Apr. 1865. 339 G 1865. Letters Received, AGO. RG 94, NA; C. P. Lyman to ones at Home, 21 June 1864. Carlos P. Lyman Papers, WRHS.

Chapter 16

The Nature of Battle

Earl J. Hess

John Keegan's Face of Battle, *which appeared in 1976, challenged historians to take a fuller and more analytical approach to the experience of battle. Keegan examined three pivotal European engagements, describing soldiers' fatigue, hunger, and confusion in the smoke and noise of combat, and argued that these conditions, plus concepts such as honor and courage, were as important as commanders' decisions in the outcome. Earl J. Hess of Lincoln Memorial University is the first historian to make extensive use of Keegan's insights in studying the Civil War. Hess's 1997 book* The Union Soldier in Battle *explores the distinctive features of combat in the Civil War, and devotes special attention to the "will to combat." This selection examines the ecology of battle-the terrain, fighting at night, fortifications, seasonal versus continual campaigning, and other circumstances, as experienced by Union soldiers.*

Sherman Was Right

Having crossed the gulf of experience from the status of a green volunteer to that of a veteran, the Northern soldier was in a position to know and understand battle. That knowledge brought with it a deep appreciation of chaos, for that was one of the most pervasive aspects of combat. The sights, sounds, and emotions assaulted their senses, nearly wrecked their ability to perceive coherent patterns in the world around them, and forced them to confront an alien experience for which most of them had no prior reference points. Battle created an environment that most soldiers described with images of dissonance, confusion, and frightening, nearly demonic fear. Combat tested their sensory, their emotional, and even their moral abilities to the fullest. They came to know that Sherman was right when he said, "War is hell."

Soldiers experienced what Captain James Franklin Fitts of New York termed "the awful demonism of battle" every time they entered combat. "Oh that horrible tempest of fire in those few moments!" vividly recalled Ebenezer Hannaford of his experience in the battle of Stones River. "Then the incessant din of musketry, the ringings in one's ears, the smell and the smoke of gunpowder, the defiant cheers, the intensity of intellection, the desperation even at last!" After enduring his first battle, Pennsylvanian Jacob Heffelfinger concluded that "the horrors of war more than counterbalance the glory."[1] . . .

Battle was a comprehensive physical experience of the senses that surrounded the soldier with a lethal, chaotic environment. He had no control over that environment and often had great difficulty controlling his emotional response to it. Historian Eric J. Leed, in writing of World War I, described the soldier's perception of himself as an autonomous player in a world that could be manipulated. He was used to living this role in civilian life but found that in the trenches of the Western Front, those safe assumptions were no longer valid. The result could be a breakdown of something essential to morale.[2]

The Civil War soldier never quite became entrapped in the kind of physical environment of combat that the unlucky veterans of World War I found themselves in, yet he and all soldiers in combat faced the same problem: how to deal with an environment over which he had little control. Chaos was the theme most consistently used by Northern soldiers in their descriptions of combat. On all levels—from the smoke-enshrouded vision of the individual to the confused movements of companies struggling through brush-entangled terrain—the soldier struggled against chaos and strove to create a coherent vision of battle.

Soldiers often found that combat wrecked the most reassuring element of order in military life: the linear tactical formations that were the foundation of movement on the battlefield. "It is astonishing how soon, and by what slight causes, regularity of formation and movement are lost in actual battle," mused David L. Thompson of the 9th New York. "Disintegration begins with the first shot. To the book-soldier all order seems destroyed, months of drill apparently going for nothing in a few minutes." Thompson admitted that the presence of the enemy was the most important factor in the breakdown of order in the ranks, but it was also caused by vegetation and the terrain. A clump of trees, for example, could cause one portion of a line to lag behind the rest, skewing the whole or even resulting in the line losing its direction and advancing to a point its commanders had not intended.[3]

As Thompson indicated, the chaos of battle was not caused solely by the dangers of flying lead threatening frail bodies; it was also the result of the natural arena on which Civil War battles took place. The South occupied a vast geographic area with a variety of terrain and natural growth. Generally, about half the land on any given battlefield was covered with vegetation, ranging from open woods to thickets of scrub trees choked with dense brush and briers. Maps of several battlefields large and small—from Wilson's Creek, Pea Ridge, and Prairie Grove in the Trans-Mississippi; to Shiloh, Corinth, and Chickamauga in the west; to Second Bull Run, the Wilderness, and Five Forks in the east—show a mixture of open fields, choked thickets, and grand forests. Long battle lines typically spanned this mixture, part of them moving freely in the open and the rest struggling through jungle matting. Infantry units clawed their way through woods until they burst out into fields and then wormed their way once again through thick growth. Civil War field armies were so large that they could not fit onto the small farms and pastures of the South but sprawled across the landscape. Theodore Lyman, an aide on Major General George Meade's staff, commented on the difficulties of keeping the 5th Corps line straight during the early phases of the Petersburg campaign. It "was not straight or facing properly. That's a chronic trouble in lines in the woods. Indeed there are several chronic troubles. The divisions have lost connection; they cannot cover the ground designated, their wing is in the air, their skirmish line has lost its direction, etc., etc."[4]

Vegetation had an enormous impact on Civil War tactics. It broke up formations, nullified the power of shock on the battlefield, and allowed firepower to dominate the action. This greatly intensified the problem of controlling the movements of individual regiments, brigades, and divisions. Lateral coordination broke down, leaving units unsupported on their flanks and commanders frustrated over the lack of control they could exercise over their own men. Vegetation severely limited visibility, thus reducing the range of rifle fire. Soldiers often had to wait until the enemy was seventy-five, forty, or even twenty yards away before catching glimpses of gray-clad figures. Heavy growth often nullified the effectiveness of artillery fire, for projectiles that hit trees lost considerable velocity and were deflected from their course. Most important, thick vegetation hid targets, and Civil War artillerymen could fire only at what they saw. It also made the cavalry even more irrelevant on the battlefield than it had already become due to the rifle musket. On open ground, cavalry was decimated by rifle fire when it attempted to launch mounted assaults against infantry; in brush-entangled terrain, cavalrymen had no chance to employ shock tactics against infantry.

Trees, bushes, and grasses of all kinds were such ever-present elements on the battlefield that they became unintended targets. Civil War battle had an enormous, awe-inspiring effect on vegetation, ripping the natural growth like a great reaping machine. Soldiers were nearly as astonished by this as by the destruction of human bodies. Lieutenant Colonel Alexander W. Raffen of the 19th Illinois looked with amazement at the field of Chickamauga several months after the battle. "The trees in some places are cut down so much by the artilerly that it looks as if a tornado had swept over the field, all the trees and stumps are pluged all over with bullits it is astonishing to think that any one could have come of safe without being hit." Such destruction led an Indiana soldier to remark of Shiloh, "Thare is some places that it Looks as if a mouse could not get threw alive."[5] . . .

Few soldiers could actually enjoy seeing nature destroyed, partly because it meant that the stable placement of natural objects around them was also destroyed. Their sense of disorder and the inability to control their immediate environment was heightened when they saw great trees shorn and splintered. It was physical proof that nothing, not even the "monarchs of the forest," could withstand combat unscathed. And it was not only the trees that suffered; astonishingly, even bushes, underbrush, and blades of grass were clipped as if by shears and scissors in the storm of rifle fire that swept the battlefield. . . .

It seemed rather odd to Northern soldiers that trees, bushes, and grass could become casualties of war. That is why so many of them commented on this aspect of combat. Indeed, considering the small size of field armies and the usually short duration of engagements in America's previous wars, the Civil War was the only conflict fought on American soil in which the natural environment was decimated by artillery and small-arms fire. The destruction of natural growth was yet another example of the bizarre chaos generated by battle. Nothing was safe from the lethal fire unleashed by massed formations of determined men.[6]

Virtually no man was safe from that lethal fire either. One of the great untold stories of the Civil War was the tragic deaths of Union soldiers from what twentieth-century writers would call "friendly fire." The Union army made no attempt to determine how many of its members became victims at its own hand. Much of it was the result of poor artillery fire and faulty equipment. The ever-observant Theodore Lyman of Meade's staff noted the frequency of this occurrence: "Not a battle is fought that some of our men are not killed by shells exploding short and hitting our troops instead of the enemy's, beyond. Sometimes it is the fuse that is imperfect, sometimes the artillerists lose their heads and make wrong estimates of distance."[7]

The majority of friendly casualties, however, resulted from small-arms fire. "A lot of Maine Conscripts fired into us the other day wounding several of the boys," complained William Ketcham of the 13th Indiana. Nervousness and lack of training led to the unintended deaths of thousands. Musing on the death of a "wicked profane boy" who nevertheless was a "good soldier" (he was struck in the back of the head by a Federal ball while standing picket duty), Thomas White Stephens of the 20th Indiana complained, "It is a shame that men can not keep cool in time of battle, but fire into one another." The religious Stephens took this philosophically, but many others were greatly embittered by such an unexpected loss of their comrades.[8]

None of the green volunteers who flocked to the recruiting stations in 1861 could have guessed that battle would consume men in this fashion. As they came to know it, some of the glory went out of the sacrifice, and the soldier's awareness of the chaotic nature of battle increased. He had to be concerned not only with fire to the front but also with the potential of fire to the rear.

Beyond the disorder caused by tangled terrain and friendly fire, the ultimate chaos of combat occurred when soldiers engaged in hand-to-hand fighting. When soldiers were exchanging blows with clubbed muskets or lunging at each other with bayonets and swords, all order broke down. Officers found it impossible to direct or control their men, and soldiers found themselves surrounded on all sides by an enemy who was close enough to knock them down with their fists. Hand-to-hand combat created an environment of brute survival unequaled by any other form of battle. . . .

Few civilians realized that battle seldom involved close-range fighting. It was the most personalized form of warfare, and soldiers avoided it.

To kill the enemy at a distance was safer and easier. Depersonalized combat represented the true nature of modern warfare; making the killing easier to do and to endure. "We hear a great deal about hand-to-hand fighting," complained Henry Otis Dwight of the 20th Ohio during the Atlanta campaign. "Gallant though it would be, and extremely pleasant to the sensation newspapers to have it to record, yet, unfortunately for gatherers of items, it is of very rare occurrence. . . . When men can kill one another at six hundred yards they generally would prefer to do it at that distance than to come down to two paces."⁹

The chaotic elements of battle were also evident in night fighting. It was nearly as rare as hand-to-hand combat because of the difficulties it posed. Although field commanders could operate effectively without seeing the enemy, they had to see their own units and the terrain. Darkness cut the typically poor visibility of the common soldier down to nearly nothing, increasing his sense of confusion and fear. Thus when night fighting did occur, it was usually incidental to daylight operations, the fighting continuing beyond dusk until exhaustion or the impenetrable darkness forced an end to it.

A few commanders planned and executed night operations to achieve surprise. One of the more famous such battles occurred on the night of October 28–29, 1863, at Wauhatchie, in the valley of Lookout Creek near Chattanooga. Union forces had just opened a new supply route into this beleaguered city and had barely assumed positions to safeguard the flow of supplies when Confederates under Lieutenant General James Longstreet attacked them in the dark. Some of the toughest fighting was done by Brigadier General John W. Geary's division of the 12th Corps. His command was struck from the north, the opposite direction from which it expected an attack, at 12:30 A.M. "The moon was fitful and did not afford light sufficient to see a body of men only 100 yards distant," wrote Geary. The darkness covered the Rebels' approach. When they opened fire, it startled Geary and his staff members, who were overseeing the formation of an improvised battle line. The general and about twenty horsemen rode furiously out of the way, cutting through the ranks of the 149th New York, which was marching to take its place in the line. Several wagon teams and ambulances also shattered the formation of the New York unit. For three hours Geary's division fought in a twilight world lit only by musket flashes. Artillerymen and infantrymen directed their fire at these fleeting lights, their only indication of the location of the enemy. To add to the confusion, Geary's teamsters fled their posts and allowed mules and horses to scatter all over the field; some of them were hit by stray balls, and their crumpled bodies dotted the area. Despite the complications, Geary's command held the little knoll that had become the focal point of its position. Night fighting may not have been an effective way to conduct an offensive, but it certainly intensified the swirling chaos of battle.[10] . . .

Northern soldiers knew that chaos was a key and unavoidable characteristic of battle. But as they came to know combat, they also came to know the utter frustration of striving mightily to achieve few results, for another key and unavoidable characteristic of Civil War battle was indecision. Commanders and members of the rank and file learned through hard experience that the war was not to be won by a single great engagement but by a long, seemingly endless series of campaigns to grind down the Confederate armies. The naive assumptions of 1861 were replaced by the hardened acceptance of costly, determined offensives that would take the lives of tens of thousands of Northern men but inevitably would take the life of the slave empire as well.

In Search of Victory

Northerners had the precedents of earlier conflicts to bolster their belief that the war against the rebellion would be short. The war with Mexico had lasted only a year and a half and had resulted in minimal loss of life, and American armies had driven deep into the heartland of Mexico. An even more encouraging historical example was the series of wars between France and a host of European allies from 1792 to 1815. Napoleon's wars, in particular, demonstrated that massed armies could still win quick battlefield victories that convinced their opponents to negotiate peace.

But Northern volunteers did not appreciate the unique situation they faced. The army had an unprecedented task: to eradicate a government and subdue a large, hostile population scattered over a vast geographic area—in short, to reclaim half the United States. No previous American war had been like this one. It was a twentieth-century conflict being fought by an eighteenth-century military force. American politicians had crafted an army designed for wars of short duration and limited goals, consisting largely of green troops who had to be mobilized, armed, and trained after the war began and before any significant fighting took place. Long delays and bitter setbacks were inevitable.

These strategic and policy factors greatly lengthened the Civil War, but tactical factors were just as important in frustrating Northern hopes for a quick victory. As indicated earlier, the defining characteristic of Civil War combat was the indecisive nature of battle. During the Revolutionary War, it had been possible for one army to nearly annihilate another in only an hour of fighting, as at the battle of Cowpens. During the Napoleonic conflicts, much larger armies had fought much longer, yet one of them could break up, scatter, and render its opponent militarily ineffective. The latter scenario was uncommon during the Civil War; the former was impossible.[11]

Historians have long attributed this dramatic change in tactics to the adoption of the rifle musket by the American army in the 1850s. It was more accurate and had a greater range than the smoothbore musket of previous wars. With the smoothbore, the army that took the tactical offensive had as good a chance of victory as the army that took the defensive. Because the volume of fire was limited, shock was as important as firepower in deciding victory. A spirited assault by infantry in a column or line could overwhelm the defender before his musketry could stop it. Historians have argued that the rifle musket made firepower dominant on the battlefield, tipping the tactical balance in favor of the defense.[12]

Even if the defender was outnumbered or attacked from three directions simultaneously (as happened at the battle of Atlanta), the defender had an excellent chance of doing more damage to the attacker than he received. While retreating, an army could maintain its fighting integrity by deploying, halting a pursuit, and continuing to withdraw. The introduction of breech-loading and magazine weapons, such as the Spencer and Henry, further increased the rate of fire a soldier could deliver on his target, but these advanced weapons were not distributed widely enough among Northern regiments to replace the Springfield and Enfield rifle muskets as the primary arms of the Union soldier.[13]

The range of fire, ironically, remained consistent. Pre–Civil War armies fired their smoothbore muskets at ranges of less than a hundred yards. Northern soldiers continued that practice, although they had weapons capable of hitting targets at five times that distance. This was partly due to the rugged terrain and dense vegetation that reduced visibility. More important, habit dictated their decisions to wait until the enemy was close by. Thomas L. Livermore, a veteran of two New Hampshire regiments, recalled that any officer who ordered his men to fire as far as the true range·of the rifle musket "would have been looked upon as light-headed."[14]

The short range did not lessen the defender's ability to repel an attack as long as the rate of fire was high. The maximum firing rate of the rifle musket, three rounds per minute, was possible only under ideal conditions, but even when circumstances were less than perfect, Civil War soldiers could pour in fire. Charles C. Paige of the 11th New Hampshire Infantry was able to shoot 200 rounds over a four-hour period during the battle of Fredericksburg—nearly one round per minute. He had to stop halfway through the battle and swab the barrel with his handkerchief. Later, he accidentally fired off his ramrod and had to find an abandoned one to replace it. Yet Paige and his comrades were able to maintain this rate of fire despite these problems. "They fired with great deliberation and coolness, and stood at their posts in an unbroken line till ordered to retire," their colonel proudly reported.[15]

When the terrain and vegetation allowed the troops to fire at longer ranges, they could maximize the damage done to attacking forces. At the battle of Franklin, Confederate divisions advanced over open, rolling ground for a mile before they attacked heavy fortifications. The Federals were ready for them and opened fire as soon as they could. Andrew Moon of the 104th Ohio scampered over the battlefield that night before his regiment pulled out of the works. "Well, for 400 yards in front, I could hardly step without stepping on dead and wounded men. The ground was in a perfect slop and mud with blood and, oh, such cries that would come up from the wounded was awful."[16]

The linear tactical formations used in the Civil War have been blamed for some of the indecision on the battlefield. They presented massed targets for men firing modern weapons at short ranges. Only the skirmishers—few in number and deployed with several yards between them—could take cover and fight as individuals. The battle line was effective against short-range, smoothbore muskets. The only way to deliver a significant volume of fire onto an attacker was to mass men in broad, shallow formations and fire in unison. It has long been portrayed, however, as a tactical formation whose day had passed.[17]

More recent studies have shed new light on the roles of the rifle musket and linear tactics in the Civil War. Given the normally short ranges at which battles occurred and the similar rate of fire compared with the prewar smoothbore, the rifle musket did not significantly alter the tactical picture. Also, linear formations were exactly the right tactics for the rifle musket. The weapon that would foster a change in tactical formations was the breechloader or a magazine-fed weapon, such as the Sharps carbine or the Spencer repeater. These weapons dramatically increased the rate of fire of the individual soldier and made massing personnel on a broad front unnecessary. Single soldiers or groups of men could take cover and deliver heavy volumes of fire from prone positions. These weapons, which were not widely used in the Civil War, demanded loose-order formations, which would become common following Appomattox.[18]

The most important reason that Civil War battle was indecisive was the lack of training among field commanders, who found it difficult to effectively manage huge armies that sprawled across the rugged landscape of the battlefield. This was the fault of the military system of the country and was felt on both strategic and tactical levels. It was not surprising that the tiny professional army was incapable of adequately training the gargantuan volunteer force, for it was dwarfed by the sheer size of it. Because the volunteer regiments were organized by the state governments, politics and favoritism dictated the creation of this unique force. With only 16,000 officers and men, the regular army could not mold a force that would number nearly 300,000 by the summer of 1862. At best, it could only try to ensure that soldiers were properly uniformed, armed, and drilled in the intricate maneuvers of linear formations. Far too often, volunteer officers had no regular officers to serve as mentors. Most of them had to study on their own, reading drill manuals the night before trying out the next maneuver on their unsuspecting men. No matter how inspired by ideology or adventure, no army of this type could be expected to win a large, complicated war quickly.[19]

Far worse than the regular army's inability to thoroughly train the volunteers was its failure to properly train its own personnel. West Point was not a true military school. Rather than rounding out the cadets' knowledge with intensive study of strategy, tactics, logistics, administration, and planning, the curriculum focused on subjects its graduates could use in civilian society, such as engineering. Given the country's traditional distrust of a large professional army, a holdover from the days of the Revolution, West Point could not get the support to turn out well-trained generals. Many West Point graduates in the Union army rose above their training, but none could claim to have been adequately prepared for commanding large forces in the field.[20]

The most serious deficiency in academy training lay in administration. The army had no general staff to plan strategy or properly coordinate logistics. Although the administrators generally worked wonders in the areas of supply and communications, it was done without the aid of a modern administrative apparatus similar to the kind being perfected in Prussia.[21]

In addition to the institutional deficiencies of the service, Civil War commanders faced a nearly insurmountable difficulty on the tactical level that heavily contributed to battlefield indecision. The huge size of their field armies led to a chronic problem: lack of control. Linear tactics had been perfected by the small armies of the eighteenth century, which usually numbered ten thousand to thirty thousand in strength. Napoleonic armies were greatly expanded in size, but massed linear tactics were still effective because field commanders interspersed columns into the battle line. This broke up the linear formations into shorter segments that were still connected to each other. The mix of column and line diversified the formations, giving generals the option of delivering both shock and firepower. The result was added flexibility.[22]

Civil War commanders relied almost solely on the line. There was little experimentation with column formations, probably due to the shortcomings of their West Point training. The size of their field armies was equal to that of Napoleon's, but they failed to use his innovations. The result was that on dozens of battlefields, lines stretched for miles over rough, broken terrain and through dense thickets. Generally, a battle line of ten thousand men covered one mile. The thick vegetation that smothered many battlefields was hardly a fit environment for even a small unit, yet armies of nearly one hundred thousand men formed battle lines nearly ten miles long across this imposing terrain.

It was impossible to maintain control over armies deployed under such conditions. The result was a persistent breakdown of coordination between regiments, brigades, divisions, and corps. On the offensive, units found it difficult to coordinate their movements and far too often engaged in piecemeal attacks that the enemy easily stopped. The breakdown of lateral coordination reduced the shock effect of the assault and enabled the defender to better use his firepower to overwhelm the attacker. On the defensive as well, a breakdown of lateral coordination could endanger a field army if the attacker managed to maintain his control. The problem of lateral coordination was so pervasive that it even infiltrated the inner ranks of the regiment. On many battlefields, a regimental commander's control over his ten companies broke down, and the basic unit of Civil War field armies fragmented into tiny pieces while advancing on or defending a position.[23]

Consequently, field officers on all levels of command often relied on small-unit action. They sent one or two regiments or brigades to do work better left to divisions or corps. This was particularly true in the first half of the war, when both officers and men were relatively untried in maneuvering under fire. In battle after battle, men were forced to wait and watch as a single regiment went forward alone and unsupported against a force several times its number, with the predictable result.[24]

On the defensive, the field commander's habit of relying on individual regiments and brigades was often effective in blunting an attacker's momentum. At the battle of Perryville, the 21st Wisconsin was placed at least seventy-five yards in front of the rest of Starkweather's brigade, which held a key hill in the face of a driving assault by Maney's brigade. The Wisconsin men were exposed between the opposing lines, battling four Tennessee regiments with only marginal fire support on their flanks. They quickly lost over one hundred men and were forced to retire. Michael Fitch, a member of the regiment, wrote: "The enemy had lapped both flanks and were in addition firing in front. The regiment was compelled to retreat over a high fence and up the face of a bare hill which the enemy could sweep with terrific effect." Its ranks were broken during the retreat but rallied behind the cover of Starkweather's fresh regiments atop the hill. Despite their exposed, outnumbered condition, the Wisconsin men had delivered enough fire to temporarily halt Maney's brigade. Given the inherent power of the defensive, piecemeal deployment could be effective but unusually costly.[25]

Not surprisingly, flanking movements designed to bypass a strongly defended position were risky. If coordinating the movements of units that were within sight and sound of each other was difficult, one can only imagine how hard it was to coordinate the movements of units that were marching thousands of yards, even miles, from each other. Frontal attacks often became the simplest, but deadliest, maneuver a field commander could use. The extensive reliance on frontal assault also contributed to the dominance of firepower, not shock, on the battlefield. Defenders could more easily detect frontal attacks and get ready for them. Given the effectiveness of the rifle musket, one of the few ways an attacker could employ shock was to strike unexpectedly and on the flank or rear of a surprised and unprepared enemy.[26]

Even when Civil War armies achieved some success in reducing the fighting capacity of their enemy, they usually failed to capitalize on it. Generals were notorious for not adequately following up tactical victories. There were a number of reasons for this, including the impact of vegetation. Recalling the Atlanta campaign, William T. Sherman wrote that "habitually the woods served as a screen, and we often did not realize the fact that our enemy had retreated till he was already miles away." The exhaustion of the troops was a common factor as well. Field commanders typically had to employ all available men during the course of a battle, leaving no sizable rested reserve to fully exploit a tactical success.[27] . . .

Northern soldiers found themselves fighting a war with little possibility of quick victory on the battlefield. They would have to pay a deadly price for their nation's insistence on maintaining a small, poorly trained professional army in peacetime. The only thing they could do was to obey orders and move forward into yet another costly and probably futile assault that should not have taken place. The volunteer army had no institutional means of self-examination. There were no military commissions charged with finding out why battle was indecisive and offering recommendations for dealing with the problem. The regular army was too small, poorly trained, and overwhelmed with other duties to fulfill that important role.[28]

By 1864, in response to the persistent deadlock on the battlefield, Northern commanders developed a policy of continuous campaigning, a major innovation in the course of American military history. This led to another innovation, the use of sophisticated field fortifications. The first innovation failed to make battle decisive, but it did wear down the Confederate army in a strategy of exhaustion that shortened the war. The second innovation was a major reason that the tactic of continuous campaigning did not lead to dramatic breakthroughs on the battlefield. The North would win the war with continuous campaigning, but its casualty rate would mount exponentially. Although the horrors of constant fighting and trench warfare would be lessened in the western theater compared with the eastern, the last year of the Civil War would dramatically foreshadow the nature of warfare in the twentieth century.

Continuous campaigning was a new experience for Northern soldiers. During the first three years of the war, operations had centered on the pitched battle, a distinct engagement lasting from a few hours to a few days, each engagement separated by weeks if not months of preparation, maneuvering, and idleness. The Army of the Cumberland, for example, spent six months recuperating from the horrible battle of Stones River before resuming the series of campaigns along the railroad line that penetrated the southeastern portion of the Confederacy. Nearly all field armies entered winter camps rather than exhaust themselves by struggling over mud-engulfed roads. In Europe, where geographic distances were shorter and improved road systems offered armies a greater opportunity to achieve strategic gains in a shorter time, seasonal campaigning did not unnecessarily prolong conflicts. But in America, with its dirt roads and great geographic expanses, seasonal campaigning prolonged the fighting and loss of life. Ulysses Grant's promotion to commander of all Federal armies in March 1864 changed this pattern. Grant intended to apply continuous pressure on the two major Confederate armies in Virginia and Georgia in order to wear down their strength and prevent them from taking the strategic offensive into territory already cleared of Rebel troops. The war would be more vigorously pursued, and losses would be great for the immediate future, but the war would be shortened and fewer lives sacrificed in the long term.[29]

As a result, the campaigns of 1864–1865 would be a new and terrible experience for the Northern soldier. The pitched battles of 1861–1863 had been extremely costly. That would not change. Essentially, Grant's strategy would pack several battles with the intensity of Gettysburg and Chickamauga into a compressed time span, each one linked by only a few hours or days of maneuvering into new positions while under the guns of an alert and desperate enemy. The war would shift into over-drive, and the pressures placed on the common soldier would dramatically intensify.

The practice of continuous campaigning fostered another key feature of modern warfare: the extensive use of earthen field fortifications. Earthworks had been widely used from 1861 through 1863, but primarily to protect fixed assets such as towns, artillery emplacements, and river passages. The nature of pitched battles, which lasted only a few hours or a few days, discouraged the construction of even temporary earthworks in the field—soldiers usually had no time to dig them and lacked the incentive to rely on them if they knew that the battle would end soon.

When armies remained in longer contact with each other, both the time and the incentive appeared. Living, fighting, even marching within sight of the enemy placed a premium on protection. Soldiers learned to construct earthworks quickly, often doing so while under fire. Henry Dwight of the 20th Ohio explained this tactical development in an article published in 1864. "Wherever the army moves, either in gaining the enemy's work, or in taking up a new line of attack, the first duty after the halt is to create defensive fortifications. . . . It is now a principle with us to fight with movable breast-works, to save every man by giving him cover, from which he may resist the tremendous attacks in mass of the enemy."[30] . . .

The effect of this continuous campaigning on the men was dramatic. Previous pitched battles had been traumatic experiences, but the rank and file had always had an opportunity to recuperate between confrontations. Now they had no time to physically rest or to recover their spirits. Campaigning in the field was never easy; now it drove the men to the breaking point. Continuous marching, digging entrenchments, skirmishing, repelling or launching frontal assaults, hastily burying the dead, and beginning the cycle of combat all over again was the rule for months.

The effect of Grant's campaign, in particular, was overwhelming. "Many a man has gone crazy since this campaign began from the terrible pressure on mind & body," reported Captain Oliver Wendell Holmes, Jr. The relentless fighting at Spotsylvania created an exhaustion that severely hampered combat effectiveness. At the Mule Show Salient, two Federal regiments moved up to relieve a third regiment late in the day's fighting. As a modern historian described it:

> They took their position along the crest, standing in mud halfway to their knees, with bodies all around them. From there, they fired at the top of the Confederate works until they were numb with fatigue. Some of them sank down into the bloody mud and fell asleep under fire. Their officers, who were just as tired as the men, moved among the prostrate forms, shaking them and shouting at them to resume their places on the firing line. In many cases the officers were exhorting dead men, but they were too numb with exhaustion to know it.[31] . . .

The citizen soldiers of the North became instant experts on military engineering. In both Virginia and Georgia, men learned how to strengthen the basic trench with embellishments. Traverses (embankments attached to a trench) were built at an angle to the earthwork to prevent the enemy from outflanking it and pouring a destructive fire into the position. In front of the main trench, men built elaborate obstructions of tree branches, palisades of sharpened stakes, or even wire entanglements—anything to trip up an attacking enemy. Trench lines were constructed to take full advantage of the lay of the land, even incorporating rocky outcroppings into the trench's parapet for added strength. Sometimes trenches were constructed to form a defense in depth, forcing the enemy to deal not just with one trench line but with several lines placed a few yards behind one another. Modern trench warfare, eerily prescient of World War I, became a fact of military life.[32]

Field fortifications hardened the life of the Northern soldier. They fixed the lines in close proximity, intensifying the already fierce nature of Civil War combat. Early in the Petersburg campaign, enterprising Federals devised a plan to dig a mine under no-man's-land, blow up a Confederate fort, and advance through the gap in the Rebel defenses. On July 30, 1864, the mine exploded, creating a crater 30 feet deep, 60 feet wide, and 170 feet long. The attacking divisions went in with inadequate preparation, and the men were awestruck at the sight of the hole and its horrors. The attack was stalled. "Every organization melted away, as soon as it entered this hole in the ground, into a mass of human beings clinging by toes and heels to the almost perpendicular sides. If a man was shot on the crest he fell and rolled to the bottom of the pit." Men struggled for life within a few yards of enemy guns for many hours while the crater became a hellhole. Major Charles Houghton of the 14th New York Heavy Artillery described the scene: "The sun was pouring its fiercest heat down upon us and our suffering wounded. No air was stirring within the crater. It was a sickening sight: men were dead and dying all around us; blood was streaming down the sides of the crater to the bottom, where it gathered in pools for a time before being absorbed by the hard red clay."[33]

The worst example of how fortifications could turn a very small space into a hell of flying metal and desperate survival occurred on May 12 at Spotsylvania. The Mule Shoe Salient, a large bulge in Lee's lines, became the object of a powerful attack by the Federals. Rain fell, keeping the powder smoke low over the battlefield as the Unionists lodged themselves against the outer slope and ditch of the entrenchments while the Rebels clung to the inner slope. The two armies were separated only by an earthen parapet. "Like leeches we stuck to the work," wrote a Federal, "determined by our fire to keep the enemy from rising up." For twenty-three hours the men fought savagely. "So continuous and heavy was our fire that the headlogs of the breastworks were cut and torn until they resembled hickory brooms. . . . The dead and wounded were torn to pieces by the canister as it swept the ground. . . . The mud was half-way to our knees, and by our constant movement the dead were almost buried at our feet." When the inconclusive fighting ended, the men were awestruck by the sight of the horribly mangled corpses. Many were "nothing but a lump of meat or clot of gore," according to Thomas Hyde, a 6th Corps staff member. One man found the body of an acquaintance that had been so riddled there was no untouched spot larger than four square inches. Another man had to rely on the color of a beard and the torn pieces of a letter to identify a friend, for the body "no longer resembled a human being but appeared more like a sponge."[34]

In Georgia, the use of field fortifications also intensified soldiers' suffering. John W. Geary's men of the 20th Corps, who were in action from Resaca to the outskirts of Atlanta, knew this as well as anyone. Geary's division took up positions in the valley of Mud Creek, near Kennesaw Mountain, on June 16, 1864. According to Geary, the stream was aptly named:

> After dark commenced a series of very severe rain-storms, which lasted, with occasional short intermissions, for several days and nights. Our skirmish pits were filled with water, and the occupants suffered much from cramps. All the troops bivouacked in fields of soft, low ground, and without adequate shelter, suffering much from these rains, which were accompanied by chilly winds. Muddy Creek and its small tributaries became swollen to the size and power of torrents, and the low ground adjoining, part of which were unavoidably occupied by my troops in line, were flooded with water.[35] . . .

For all the horror, discomfort, and disease in the trenches, field fortifications made continuous campaigning possible. Only by digging in could the armies maintain close contact for long periods of time. In addition, living in the trenches itself had a debilitating effect on the Confederates, who were chronically short of men and supplies. During the latter stages of the Petersburg campaign, which lasted eleven months, Lee's army suffered a desertion rate as high as 8 percent per month. Pinned to the cold, bare earth with inadequate food and outnumbered by its opponents, the Army of Northern Virginia suffered an attrition rate between battles that foreshadowed the slow hemorrhage commonly endured by field armies between offensives during World War I.[36]

Ironically, field fortifications also strengthened the power of defense. They provided additional cover for troops and offered a difficult physical obstacle to attacking forces. When defenders enhanced their trenches with obstructions placed in front to trip up enemy troops, they multiplied their ability to hold a position by many times. It would take even more force, determination, and bloodshed to subdue the Rebels than fighting in the open had demanded.

Yet there was no alternative. This new method of pressuring the enemy was the key to the North's military victory. Given the nature of combat in the Civil War, the North could have fought on indefinitely as long as its armies continued the tired routine of fighting, withdrawing, and fighting again. The Rebels had to be ground down in a process of applying continued pressure before peace and the Union could be restored.

This was the environment of combat that the Northern soldier entered. The nature of battle during the Civil War was such that the warrior could expect little opportunity to participate in quick or decisive engagements. Instead, he had to find his way through a vast, often cruel experiment in modernization. The military world in which the Civil War took place was changing, and the average soldier had little opportunity to affect the course of that experiment or even to fully understand it.

NOTES

From Earl J. Hess, *The Union Soldier in Battle: Enduring the Ordeal of Combat* (Lawrence: University Press of Kansas, 1997), 45–60, 64–72. Reprinted by permission.

1. James Franklin Fitts, "In the Ranks at Cedar Creek," *Galaxy* 1 (1866): 538; Ebenezer Hannaford, "In the Ranks at Stone River," *Harper's New Monthly Magazine* 27 (November 1863): 813; Jacob Heffelfinger Diary, June 29, 1862, *Civil War Times Illustrated* Collection, U.S. Army Military History Institute.

2. Eric J. Leed, *No Man's Land: Combat and Identity in World War I* (New York, 1979), 132–36.

3. David L. Thompson, "With Burnside at Antietam," in *Battles and Leaders of the Civil War*, vol. 2 (New York, 1956), 660.

4. Maps and descriptions of the cluttered vegetation on Civil War battlefields can be found in many studies, such as William L. Shea and Earl J. Hess, *Pea*

Ridge: Civil War Campaign in the West (Chapel Hill, 1992); John J. Hennessy, *Return to Bull Run: The Campaign and Battle of Second Manassas* (New York, 1993); and Robert Garth Scott, *Into the Wilderness with the Army of the Potomac* (Bloomington, 1992). The maps published in the *Atlas to Accompany the Official Records of the Union and Confederate Armies* (Washington, 1891–1895) are extremely helpful as well. George R. Agassiz, ed., *Meade's Headquarters, 1863–1865: Letters of Colonel Theodore Lyman from the Wilderness to Appomattox* (Boston, 1922), 173–74.

5. Raffen to Grace, March 22, 1864, Alexander W. Raffen Papers, Illinois State Historical Library; Thomas to sister, April 19, 1862, James S. Thomas Papers, Indiana Historical Society.

6. In addition to artillery and small-arms fire, the clear-cutting of fields of fire in front of defensive positions devastated the natural environment. Captain Marcus M. Spiegel of the 67th Ohio was awed by the wholesale nipping of the woods at Harrison's Landing after the Seven Days campaign. "You can possibly have no Idea of the slashing of trees there has been done since we came here; 8 or 10 miles of a wild and picturesque forest has been leveled to the ground and the trees felled every way mixed, so as to keep the enemy from using any Artillery and Cavelery against us." Frank L. Byrne and Jean Powers Soman, eds., *Your True Marcus: The Civil War Letters of a Jewish Colonel* (Kent, 1985), 126.

7. Agassiz, ed., *Meade's Headquarters*, 202.

8. William Ketcham to Pa, October 30, 1864, John Lewis Ketcham Papers, Indiana Historical Society; Thomas White Stephens Diary, June 7, 1864, State Historical Society of Missouri; Earl J. Hess, ed., *A German in the Yankee Fatherland: The Civil War Letters of Henry A. Kircher* (Kent, 1983), 100.

9. Henry Otis Dwight, "How We Fight at Atlanta," *Harper's New Monthly Magazine* 29 (October 1864): 665; John Buechler, " 'Give 'em the Bayonet'—A Note on Civil War Mythology,"*Civil War History* 7 (June 1961): 128–32.

10. *War of the Rebellion: A Compilation of the Official Records of the Union and Confederate Armies* (Washington, D.C., 1880–1901), vol. 31, pt. 1, 112–16, 133, 135; (hereafter cited as *OR*).

11. Herman Hattaway and Archer Jones, *How the North Won: A Military History of the Civil War* (Urbana, 1983), 47.

12. Ibid.

13. Earl J. Coates and Dean S. Thomas, *An Introduction to Civil War Small Arms* (Gettysburg, 1990), 13–29.

14. Thomas L. Livermore, "The Northern Volunteers," *Journal of the Military Service Institution of the United States* 12 (September 1891): 934.

15. Charles C. Paige Memoir, 24, 27, Wendell W. Lang, Jr., Collection, U.S. Army Military History Institute; *OR*, vol. 21, 329.

16. *Annette Tapert, The Brothers' War: Civil War Letters to Their Loved*

Ones from the Blue & Gray (New York, 1989), 227. There are numerous ways to determine the range at which Civil War soldiers commonly fired their weapons. Many mentioned this information in their reports and personal correspondence. Paddy Griffith, *Battle Tactics of the Civil War* (New Haven, 1989), 145–50. Battlefields such as Chickamauga have many markers, erected by veterans of the fighting, that precisely place the location of regiments and thus vividly demonstrate the closeness of the opposing lines.

17. Grady McWhiney and Perry D. Jamieson, *Attack and Die: Civil War Military Tactics and the Southern Heritage* (Tuscaloosa, 1982), 31–32.

18. Griffith, *Battle Tactics of the Civil War*, 73–90.

19. Bell Irvin Wiley, *The Life of Billy Yank: The Common Soldier of the Union* (Baton Rouge, 1952), 17–30. For useful commentary on the deficiencies of the volunteer army, see Thomas Wentworth Higginson, "Regular and Volunteer Officers," *Atlantic Monthly* 14 (September 1864): 348–57, and Allan Nevins, ed., *A Diary of Battle: The Personal Journals of Colonel Charles S. Wainwright, 1861–1865* (New York, 1962), 273.

20. Hattaway and Jones, *How the North Won*, 11–14.

21. Ibid., 102–7.

22. Brent Nosworthy, *The Anatomy of Victory: Battle Tactics, 1689–1763* (New York, 1992), 86; Gunther E. Rothenberg, *The Art of Warfare in the Age of Napoleon* (Bloomington, 1980), 153–54.

23. Evidence of the breakdown of lateral control can be found throughout the battle reports in OR. Additional evidence can be found in soldiers' personal accounts. For an analysis of this phenomenon in one battle, see Shea and Hess, *Pea Ridge*, 128–33, 313–16. See also Griffith, *Battle Tactics of the Civil War*, 140–45.

24. See, for example, the discussion of the Confederate assaults at Stones River in James Lee McDonough, *Stones River: Bloody Winter in Tennessee* (Knoxville, 1980), 148–49.

25. Kenneth A. Hafendorfer, *Perryville: Battle for Kentucky* (Louisville, 1991), 260–68.

26. Albert Castel, "Mars and the Reverend Longstreet: Or, Attacking and Dying in the Civil War," *Civil War History* 33 (June 1987): 103–14.

27. William T. Sherman, *Memoirs*, vol. 2 (New York, 1875), 885.

28. Griffith, *Battle Tactics of the Civil War*, 190.

29. Hattaway and Jones, *How the North Won*, 515–19.

30. Dwight, "How We Fight at Atlanta," 664.

31. Mark DeWolfe Howe, Jr., ed., *Touched with Fire: Civil War Letters and Diary of Oliver Wendell Holmes, Jr., 1861–1864* (Cambridge, 1946), 149–50; William D. Matter, *If It Takes All Summer: The Battle of Spotsylvania* (Chapel Hill, 1988), 257.

32. Edward Hagerman, *The American Civil War and the Origins of Modern*

Warfare (Bloomington, 1988), index; Griffith, *Battle Tactics of the Civil War,* 123–35.

33. William H. Powell, "The Battle of the Petersburg Crater," in *Battles and Leaders of the Civil War,* vol. 4 (New York, 1956), 551, 553–54; Charles H. Houghton, "In the Crater," in ibid., 562.

34. G. Norton Galloway, "Hand-to-Hand Fighting at Spotsylvania," in *Battles and Leaders of the Civil War,* vol. 4 (New York, 1956), 172–73; Thomas W. Hyde, *Following the Greek Cross or, Memories of the Sixth Army Corps* (Boston, 1894), 202; Matter, *If It Takes All Summer,* 266–67.

35. OR, vol. 38, pt. 2, 131.

36. James M. McPherson, *Battle Cry of Freedom: The Civil War Era* (New York, 1988), 821.

Part IV

How Soldiers Felt

Chapter 17

Trials of Soul

Bell Irvin Wiley

*The psychology of military service has always been important to those
who deal with soldiers. Morale, an especially obvious aspect of soldier
psychology, is intertwined with most features of army life, from combat
performance to desertion. Morale is a vital interest of commanders in
the field, authorities in the centers of power, and loved ones at home,
and it has also occupied historians. Each of Bell Wiley's pioneering
studies of Civil War soldiers includes a chapter on morale, portraying it
as a complex, changeable product of individual experience and national
fortunes. This selection is from* The Life of Johnny Reb.

The South entered the war in the spring of 1861 with high spirit. The
people were, with few exceptions, thoroughly convinced of the rightness
of their cause—the defense of their homes against tyrannous and godless
invaders. They were overwhelmingly confident of success. Men of the
South, they thought, accustomed to an active outdoor life, were more
robust than factory- and shop-bred Northerners. Southerners were also
deemed tougher in temper than Yankees.

Overweening certainty of Rebel superiority was shown in wartime
textbooks for the common schools. Johnson's *Elementary Arithmetic*,
published in North Carolina, proposed these problems for patriotic
youngsters:

"(1) A Confederate soldier captured 8 Yankees each day for 9 successive
days; how many did he capture in all? (2) If one Confederate soldier kill
90 Yankees how many Yankees can 10 Confederate soldiers kill? (3) If

one Confederate soldier can whip 7 Yankees, how many soldiers can whip 49 Yankees?"[1]

Southerners generally believed that the majority of Northerners were opposed to fighting, and those who were so foolish as to essay conflict with brave secessionists could not stand up under the rigors of battle. The war would doubtless be a short one, but short or long, most of the South's young men wanted to have a part in it—and many of the old ones.

In the flood tide of patriotism which rose during the first months of war there was an irresistible rush to arms. "All Mississippi is in a fever to get to the field, and hail an order to march as the greatest favor you can confer upon them," wrote Governor Pettus to President Davis in May 1861.[2] Everywhere men formed themselves into companies and regiments, with or without authorization, and importunately demanded immediate transfer to camps of instruction, or better still to prospective seats of war. Letters from state officers and from private citizens flooded Richmond authorities asking for induction into Confederate service, for arms and for assignment to active duty. Secretary of War Walker informed President Davis in July 1861 that applications on file in his office left no doubt "that if arms were only furnished no less than 200,000 additional volunteers for the war would be found in our ranks in less than two months."[3]

Some volunteers were so imbued with ardor that they not only equipped themselves, but also refused to take pay for their army services.[4] The revival-meeting type of zeal which characterized the first days of the Confederacy was further expressed by recruits choosing to sleep in the open when tents were available, and taking over the lowlier duties of army life. In a few instances this ardor ran to fantastic extremes. After one of the early battles a group of prowling Rebs came across a trunk full of United States currency. Such was the rampant state of their patriotism that, according to the recollection of one of them, they "scorned the filthy lucre and consigned it to the flames, only reserving a little as mementoes."[5]

Naturally the first swell of enthusiasm did not continue for long. In fact signs of defection made their appearance while ardor was still at flood stage. These were in connection with the length of service pledged by volunteers. When the war began Richmond authorities accepted troops for a twelve months' period, with equipment to be furnished by

the War Department. Shortage of accouterments, combined with ma-
turer consideration, caused Davis and his associates to revise this policy
and to equip at Confederate expense only those volunteers who should
enlist for three years, or the duration of the war. Twelve-month volunteers would be received, but only on condition that they provide their
own equipment.

Announcement of this policy a short time after the fall of Fort Sumter
aroused a widespread cry of protest. Some men of moderate means
objected on the score that in view of the small compensation of soldiers
they could not afford to pledge themselves to so lengthy a service. Non-
slaveholders complained that rich men could enlist for the one-year
period because of ability to equip themselves, while they, because of
their lack of means, were required to enlist for three years or not at all.[6]
Thus before a battle was fought, selfishness and class strife were fouling
the pure waters of patriotism.

As weeks turned into months enthusiasm for military service gradually dwindled, and long before the passage of the first conscription act
of April 1862 the initial flood of volunteering had ebbed to a mere
trickle. The first draft law gave new life to volunteering, but it was of a
spiritless sort, occasioned primarily by the desire of men subject to
conscription to escape the odium attached to forced service. Each subsequent conscription act was followed by a similar reaction. By August
1863 General Daniel Ruggles was constrained to write that "the spirit
of volunteering has ceased to exist," and the great bulk of available
evidence verifies the approximate correctness of his observation.[7]

After the first enthusiasm had spent its force, not even conscription
could bring the South's available man power into military service. The
policy of forcing enlistment by law was never more than a meager
success. Its chief benefit was to hold in the army at critical times men
whose volunteer periods were about to expire, and to stimulate the
immediate enlistment of a small portion of civilians subject to draft.

Coercive acts of the Confederate Congress were subjected to sabotage
on every hand. State governors insisted on the exemption of local defense
troops, and thousands of militiamen of conscription age thus escaped
Confederate service. Provincial-minded executives like Georgia's Joe
Brown and North Carolina's Zeb Vance went so far as to demand
immunity from draft of many petty officials, including justices of the
peace, on the claim that they were essential to the discharge of governmental functions. They also encouraged resistance to conscription by

declaiming the unconstitutionality of draft laws; and some state justices added their influence by issuing writs of habeas corpus on behalf of those held for their violation. Local physicians handed out certificates of disability with great nonchalance which, until the law was rectified, conscription officers were bound to accept at face value, even when presented by the most robust individuals. In many communities public sentiment was so lethargic or so hostile during the last two years of the war as to defeat all efforts to compel slackers to service. Granted that the policy of conscription was impaired by defects in administrative machinery and personnel, the main cause of its failure must be found in the dwindling morale of the people.[8]

One of the most striking evidences of this was the practice of evading military service by substitution. As early as the fall of 1861 the War Department permitted release from the army of volunteers who presented able-bodied proxies to serve in their stead. The first conscription act sanctioned the practice. A conscriptee, when summoned to a camp of instruction, might take a substitute with him; if the proxy upon examination proved to be of sound body and not subject to military service on his own account, the "principal" was permitted to return home and the substitute accepted in his place. Only one substitution a month was allowed in each company, but this provision was frequently violated.

Objections to substitution were voiced soon after the policy was initiated, and the protest grew with the declining fortunes of the Confederacy. But the practice increased. Newspapers carried bids for the service of proxies, ranging from about $500 in 1862 to several thousand dollars in the latter part of 1863. Occasionally men not liable to conscription, induced by the lucrative hire and by the bounty which Richmond authorities allowed to enrollees, advertised their availability as substitutes.

Transactions were handled with the detached formality incident to regular trade, by banks, factors and merchants; laws of supply and demand eventually led to the setting up of substitute brokerages. Such a business was naturally accompanied by endless fraud and deceit. Men who were hired as substitutes frequently deserted, sometimes to multiply their gains by repeated substitutions under different names. By connivance with examining authorities, persons of unsound bodies were unlawfully accepted as proxies. Under the best conditions men thus inducted into service were not good soldier material. Many were aliens having little interest in the fortunes of the Confederacy. Most of them were mainly concerned with getting as much money and rendering as little service as possible. In a great many cases, by devising fraudulent papers, men who had no substitutes at all remained out of service on the pretext of having engaged them.

Substitution was originally designed to mitigate the apparent harshness of conscription, for it must be remembered that before the Confederacy's first law a general draft had never been resorted to in America. It was thought too that essential talent for home production would find the necessary release from army service. But the policy did not turn out as expected. Granted, as Howell Cobb pointed out, that a considerable number of men who availed themselves of proxies were substantial and patriotic citizens, all too frequently they were of another sort.[9] In numerous cases men who were released from service resorted to speculation and profiteering. Many of them revealed their true character by fleeing to the North when eventually ordered into the army or by procuring for "a consideration" some petty clerkship in the government offices at Richmond.

The presence of able-bodied men at home in large numbers, especially after Vicksburg and Gettysburg, was in itself the source of great dissatisfaction to men in the army and to their families; disgruntlement was particularly strong among the poorer classes who saw additional proof of their growing conviction that this was "a rich man's war and a poor man's fight." After frequent and futile efforts to purge the substitute system of its defects and abuses, Congress early in 1864 took the bull by the horns and abolished it. But even then there were many hangovers in the form of judicial claims of unconstitutionality.[10]

The number of men who purchased exemption from military service by substitution while the system was in force cannot be ascertained because the War Department records are inadequate. In the summer of 1863 General Bragg estimated the total at 150,000, but this outright guess was probably extravagant.[11] Secretary of War Seddon in his report to the President of November 1863 ventured an estimate of "not less certainly, than 50,000."[12] Seddon's figure is probably conservative. However that may be, the spectacle of nearly as many men as constituted Lee's effective force in the Army of Northern Virginia in the fall of 1863 escaping military responsibilities under the guise of purchased proxies— most of whom rendered poor service or none at all—is a shameful reflection on Confederate patriotism.[13]

While the morale of soldiers seems always to have been better than that of civilians, the army experienced a growing defection of spirit as the conflict went on. Expressions of war-weariness began to creep into their letters after Rebs had undergone only a few months of service. By that time it had become apparent that the Yankees were not to be whipped in one campaign, and camp life had lost the glamor of novelty.

Disillusionment sometimes found its first expression in advice to friends and relatives against volunteering. "I still advise you, and as strongly as ever," wrote an Alabamian to his brother in the spring of 1862, "to not come to the war. I tell you you will repent it if you do I do believe. You have no idea of what it is to be a soldier. . . . and be you assure[d] that if I had your chance to stay out of it I would do [so]. I do think that you would do very wrong to come unless they draught you."[14]

But the most thorough case of disillusionment encountered by the writer was that of a young Mississippi aristocrat. In April 1861 this man wrote his sister that he had failed of admittance to the Washington Artillery because of his low stature but was drilling in New Orleans with a group of prospective infantrymen. "I am better-fitted for a soldier than anything else," he exulted. "I believe I am brave and not afraid to meet an enemy. . . . I am anxious to go—for I honestly and candidly believe that one Southern man is a match for any two Northern fanatics. . . . If they conquer us we can[t] be anything but rebellious provinces—And if we conquer them we will make them our slaves. . . . If I live I will hand down the name of Mandeville to posterity and to history—And if I perish it will be said I did so gallantly & not from a shot in the back. . . . When I go it will be to make a name."

He succeeded in getting in service a short time later and was sent to Virginia, where he was exposed to some strenuous marching. In August 1861, less than five months after having professed such enthusiasm for soldiering, he wrote his homefolk: "It is the opinion of the people here that we will be home by the first of October & I hope so for I am heartily tired of this life."[15] He died early in 1863, but whether under such circumstances as to make lustrous the name he bore is not known. . . .

Some soldiers seem to have experienced the depths of depression during the first winter, for then they felt homesickness at its worst, and they were not yet toughened to the hardships of war. As they became accustomed to separation from loved ones and more thoroughly inured to the discomforts of army life, they suffered less acutely, and consequently bore subsequent winters in camp with more fortitude than the first.

For most of the Rebs, however, greater depths of gloom were yet to come. Resort to conscription in April 1862 was a severe blow to their morale. Many objected to the policy as unconstitutional; others resented deeply the fact that the law deprived them of the privilege of visiting homefolk at the end of their year of volunteered service; still others found fault with the list of exemptions. Not a few saw in forced service an admission of despair on the part of government authorities. The reaction of a South Carolinian serving at Yorktown was typical:

> "The Conscript Act will do away with all the patriotism we have. Whenever men are forced to fight they take no personal interest in it. . . . My private opinion is that our Confederacy is gone up, or will go soon. . . . A more oppressive law was never enacted in the most uncivilized country or by the worst of despots."[16]

Active campaigns in the spring, summer and fall of 1862 buoyed morale considerably, but going into winter quarters again, with its implication of another season of conflict, led to an unprecedented wave of war weariness. A Texan wrote his sister from Arkansas in late November, 1862, that he had "enough of Yanks." "I would to God," he added, "that I could do my share of fightin and come home though I see no chance for that." But he consoled himself with the observation, "There is one thing Sure the war cant go on always I will either go up the flew or come home before a graitwhile."[17] . . .

This second winter's wave of despondency overwhelmed some who hitherto had shown great enthusiasm for army life. A case in point is that of E. J. Ellis of Louisiana. On June 9, 1862, Ellis had written to his mother:

> "This war has done me good in many ways—It has taught me patence and endurance & 'to labor & wait'. . . . it has learned me to be less particular in a great many things—when I see dirt in my victuals, I take it out and eat on—If I taste it, I swallow & eat on. . . . If my bed is hard & my head not high enough, I content myself with the idea that it might be worse & go to sleep. . . . I think I have seen the dark side of soldiering and although it is tolerably hard, yet there aint any use of calling it intolerable."

In eight months this Reb's consoling philosophy had petered out, and he was singing a very different tune. "The fact is," he said in commenting on a slight but incapacitating injury suffered by a fellow soldier at Murfreesboro, "I would like first rate to get such a wound. . . . Oh! wouldn't it be nice to get a 30 days leave and go home and be petted like a baby, and get delicacies to eat . . . and then if I ever run for a little office I could limp and complain of the 'old wound.' "

The passage of another month found him still harboring this idea, though the desired wound was increasing in seriousness. If "some friendly bullet" would "hit me just severely enough to send me home for 60 or 90 days," he wrote wistfully, "I would gladly welcome such a bullet and consider the Yankee who fired it as a good kind fellow."[18] . . .

While soldier Ellis was pining for a wound, an Alabama comrade was speculating on the war's termination. "If the soldiers were allowed to settle the matter," he wrote in February 1863, "peace would be made in short order," and he expressed the hope that he and his family might eat watermelons together the next summer[19] But instead of watermelon cuttings on home lawns, the summer of 1863 brought Vicksburg and Gettysburg. And before the year's end Bragg's Chattanooga battles filled the cup of Confederate disaster to overflowing. Many soldiers came now to despair of ultimate success.

A Georgia Reb home on sick furlough wrote to his brother in camp that his leave had already been extended twice, and if it was not renewed a third time he thought he would just stay at home anyhow. "There is no use fighting any longer no how," he said, "for we are done gone up the Spout the Confederacy is done whiped it is useless to deny it any longger."[20] . . .

No doubt some of those who succumbed to defeatism at this stage of the war were men who had never felt any strong enthusiasm for the struggle. But that troops of consistently good morale were also affected is seen in the case of Charles Moore, a young Louisianian. Moore, who served with the Army of Northern Virginia, was of unusual buoyancy of spirit. His diary fairly exudes cheerfulness and optimism during the first two years of war. A serious wound at Gettysburg, followed by amputation of his leg, evokes not a word of complaint or of pessimism. But on February 26, 1864, he enters in his journal the despairing note "no use of us fighting," and this was his first hint of despondency.[21]

Governmental and military authorities exerted themselves greatly to stay the tide of pessimism which besieged Rebel camps during the war's third winter. President Davis visited the Army of Tennessee and regaled the soldiers with optimistic sentiments. Confederate and state political leaders followed his example by visiting and addressing this and other portions of the Southern fighting force. The system of furloughs was broadened by some commanders. Sham battles were staged on grand and realistic scale to fire enthusiasm for spring campaigns.[22]

Officers high and low used the technique of suggestion and example with great effectiveness to induce en masse re-enlistment of men whose three-year terms were to expire in the spring of 1864. True, the continued service of these men was required by a recently enacted conscription law, but the gesture of voluntary action was desired as a fillip to general morale. A favorite device of officers to inspire pledges to further service was the assembling of men for dress parade, addressing them in patriotic vein, moving the flags up a few paces ahead, and then asking all those who were willing to re-enlist for the duration of the war to step up to the colors. When the lead was taken, whether by few or many, the impulse for all to follow suit was usually overwhelming.

Such action was recognized in a manner calculated to arouse the patriotism of other units. For example, on February 3, 1864, Lee promulgated General Order Number 14, in which he said: "The commanding general announces with gratification the reenlistment of the regiments of this army for the war. . . . This action gives new cause for the gratitude and admiration of their countrymen. . . . It is hoped," he added significantly, that "this patriotic movement, commenced in the Army of Tennessee will be followed by every brigade of the Army of Northern Virginia, and extend from army to army until the Soldiers of the South stand in one embattled host determined never to yield." He then proceeded to name the batteries, regiments and brigades that had initiated the movement "so honorable to themselves and so pleasing to the country."[23] Congress added the weight of its influence by voting resolutions of thanks to various organizations as they renewed their commitments. In the Army of Tennessee, furloughs at the rate of one to every ten men present for duty were promised to regiments that re-enlisted.[24]

The response of the soldiers delighted the officers. The enthusiasm that accompanied the pledging ceremonies was often unrestrained. Instead of promising renewal of service for three years or the duration, a few regiments of Johnston's army suggested avowal of forty- and fifty-year periods, while the Twentieth Mississippi Regiment proposed re-enlistment for ninety-nine years or the war.[25]

[One example is provided by] the testimony of a sergeant in the Forty-sixth Mississippi Regiment, Army of Tennessee. On March 31, 1864, he wrote in his journal: "On the night of the 25th a meeting of the . . . men of the regiment was called to consider the subject of reenlisting for the war. . . . We reenlisted . . . by adopting some very bold resolution of the original fire eating sort (but which I endorse) and were mustered in for the war." But he added significantly, "I am compelled to say that it was the immediate prospect of obtaining furloughs that induced many of the men to reenlist."[26]

There can be no doubt, however, that the various expedients invoked during the winter of 1863–1864 had a good effect on army morale. Grant's failure to take Richmond during the following summer also raised the general spirit. But the evacuation of Atlanta, followed by the march of Sherman's hosts through the heart of the Southland and Hood's overwhelming disaster at Nashville, caused so deep a depression in Confederate camps as to set at naught every effort to boost morale.[27]

The increasing despondency is vividly reflected by the tone of letters coming from camp. "The soldiers are badly out of heart," wrote a Georgian from Charleston in January 1865, "for they have been a suffering for nearly four long years and there is no prospect of doing better."[28] An Alabamian in Lee's army who had previously testified to the good spirits of his comrades observed about the same time that "the successful and . . . unopposed march of Sherman through Georgia, and the complete defeat of Hood in Tennessee, have changed the whole aspect of affairs."[29] A soldier of the Army of Tennessee returning from furlough in mid-January was struck by the depression that had overtaken his fellow soldiers. "When it comes to discussing the prosecution of the war," he said, "they are entirely despondent, being fully convinced that the Confederacy is gone."[30]

Several factors, in addition to reversals on the field of battle, contributed to the decline of morale in the Confederate Army. Important among these was the poor quality and meager quantity of the rations. Rebs proved in countless instances that men can march and fight well on empty stomachs, but even so, the long continuing and gradually increasing shortage of food, particularly of meat, was depressing.

"If I ever lose my patriotism, and the 'secesh' spirit dies out," wrote a private to his homefolk in October 1862, "then you may know the 'Commissary' is at fault. Corn meal mixed with water and tough beef three times a day will knock the 'Brave Volunteer' under quicker than Yankee bullets."[31]

This Reb was hitting close to a bull's-eye. In the spring of 1863 some of Bragg's troops refused to drill because of the reduction of their fare to bread made of meal and water. They were put in the guard-house, but one of their officers expressed apprehension that the Federals might ultimately triumph by starvation of the Southern armies.[32] . . .

Even more depressing than their own hardship was the knowledge that wives, children and parents at home were deprived of sufficient food and clothing. An Alabamian wrote to his wife in October 1863 that he was going to try to get a furlough, but if he failed in his efforts he intended to come home anyhow, "for I cant Stand to here," he said, "that you and the children are Sufren for Bread."[33] And thousands of Rebs were moved by just such sentiments to set out for home without benefit of either furlough or discharge.

The conviction of soldiers that they and their families were being swindled by speculators, most of whom were thought to be slackers, was another factor working strongly against morale. The high prices that naturally followed inflation of the currency were widely believed to be the result of shady manipulations by heartless profiteers.

A Mississippian in Lee's army fairly boiled with rage when he heard that in his own community draft dodgers were "cramed down in every hole and corner speculating and extortioning on those who try to live honest." "I believe," he said, "that such things are going on all over the C. S.," and that "impressing officers have pressed that to which they have no right for the intention of speculation." He decried the effect of such wrongdoing on the prospects of victory for, he opined, "the Old Book says that man can not serve both God & Mamon."[34] Doubtless most soldiers had exaggerated ideas about the prevalence of speculation, but whether they were right or not, their belief had a demoralizing effect on their patriotism.

Failure to receive their pay was another blow to the resolution of the men. The payment allowed by law for infantry and artillery privates was eleven dollars a month.[35] Even under normal conditions this was a miserly sum, but with the constant depreciation of money values the amount shrunk in 1864 and 1865 to the merest pittance. Congress failed to adjust wages to meet inflation. In fact no boost in pay was provided at all until June 1864, when the dilatory legislators at Richmond finally voted an increase of seven dollars a month for all non-commissioned officers and privates.[36] Payment was slow, and when it actually came the money was worth only a fraction of its original value. This fact did not escape pay-conscious Rebs. On March 4, 1864, William P. Chambers recorded in his journal:

> "Yesterday we were paid up—wages to Jany. 1, 1864 and commutation for clothing for the year ending Oct. 8; 1863. As the 'old issue' of Confederate notes will soon be worthless, it seems the Treasury Department is very anxious to get rid of it—hence the large installment of wages we received."[37]

Letters and diaries of soldiers, as well as official communications of commanding officers, show that it was not unusual for pay to be six months behind, and in some instances troops went for a year without receiving any money from the government. In despair of getting their pay, not a few Rebs set up an informal business among their comrades in order to make enough money to buy tobacco, stationery and other conveniences. Some peddled eggs obtained from sources that probably would not have borne official investigation; others bought and sold fruit and vegetables. Still others had whiskey, food, clothing and other items sent to them from home for vending in camp. In the fall of 1862 such bargaining became so rife in the Army of Northern Virginia that General Lee issued a prohibitive order.[38]

For the most part discontent over delayed payment was expressed in mere grumbling—which according to one general was the soldier's greatest luxury—but in two cases at least it led to insubordination. A regiment of Pemberton's command in South Carolina gave notice in March 1862 that it would not obey an order to move to the support of Albert Sidney Johnston in Tennessee until it was paid; and two Mississippi companies stacked arms in February 1864 when the signal was given for dress parade, and announced that no more duty of any kind would be performed until they received at least a part of the wages due them.[39] . . .

The transfer of men to places far from their homes was a common cause of desertion. This was not true early in the war, because it was generally thought that the struggle would be short, and a trip to Virginia or Kentucky was regarded by Louisianians, Texans and others as a sort of holiday excursion. Nor were single men as much affected as those who were married. But after it became apparent that the war was to be long, and that various portions of the South were to be invaded, the thought of being far away from families who were helpless and in danger caused many a Reb to cast longing and uneasy glances toward home.

The question of furloughs also entered into the situation, for leaves seemed harder to get when the distance was great, and even if an absence of forty days was granted poor transportation cut short the stay at home. Then, too, homesickness from natural causes seemed to bear some relation to distance. However sound these latter deductions may be, there can be no doubt that after 1861 men objected strongly to transfers that took them far from home. An order of troop removal from Western Virginia to the vicinity of Richmond in December 1862 provoked wholesale desertion.[40] . . .

Another cause that contributed greatly to the decline of soldier morale was the consolidation of military units. With the dwindling of regiments, brigades and divisions through casualties and absences to small fractions of their full strength in 1863 and 1864, some adjustment had to be found. Recruiting was resorted to, to fill up the ranks, but with slight success. Conscripts and substitutes were frequently scorned by veteran volunteers, and these enrollees dreaded the prospect of being put in with men who would taunt and despise them.[41]

So with the failure to build up skeleton outfits by recruiting, Richmond authorities considered it necessary to combine them. But such a policy ran counter to the pride which old soldiers felt in their organizations, and this pride was too deep-seated to be readily laid aside. A regiment such as the Second Texas Infantry, for instance, jealous of the awe in which it was held by opposing Yankee outfits—as evinced after parole at Vicksburg by the respectful and admiring tone adopted by Federals when they said, "There goes the Second Texas!"—would naturally be unwilling to lose its identity, its battle flags and its hardwon reputation for gallantry on numerous fields of battle, by consolidation late in the war with a miscellany of regiments garnered perhaps from states other than the glorious Lone Star Republic.[42] And when such fusions were pushed down their throats, consequences were apt to be disastrous. . . .

In numerous cases officers testified to the harmful effect on morale of such combinations. "Both officers and men bitterly object," wrote an inspector of Gordon's division in 1864; "strange officers command strange troops," and "old organizations feel that they have lost their identity and are without the chance of perpetuating the distinct and separate history of which they were once so proud."[43]

The dismounting of cavalry outfits aroused even more discontent than the consolidation of infantrymen. Yet the heavy loss of horses through battle casualties, overuse and undernourishment made it necessary sometimes to convert cavalrymen into foot soldiers. The mere proposal of such an action, however, would almost invariably cause a wave of desertion.[44]

The matter of furloughs was a tremendous source of discontent. Any request for leave had to run a long gamut of approvals, and frequently action came only after months of delay. While soldiers waited they naturally chafed. When their requests were finally acted on they were generally refused. This led to a conviction that those in authority were heartless and unreasonable.

Then, there always seemed to be grounds for finding partiality in cases where furloughs were granted, and these were seized upon and magnified by those who were disappointed. Married men complained that single comrades were preferred, and vice versa; poor men were convinced that wealthy men were favored, privates grumbled that officers received a disproportionate share of leaves.

But the greatest dissatisfaction came from the failure of military authorities to grant furloughs which had been promised as rewards for re-enlistment, for procuring recruits and for returning deserters. The answer of those in authority to such complaints was that change in the military situation, increase of desertion, or overstaying of leaves that had been granted made impossible the fulfilment of agreements as made. But to homesick soldiers who after long effort had earned promise of a visit with homefolk, all such excuses seemed utterly invalid. The natural reaction was to "go anyhow," and thousands did.

Mistreatment by officers, fancied or real, in matters other than furloughs was often a factor in demoralization. One Deter Jochum wrote to his mother in 1864:

> "The tiranny of officers is as great as can be the numerous desertions which occur at every retreat of ours is mainly caused by the tyranny of officers with their high pay they enjoy themselves no matter how high the prices while the poor soldier suffers."[45]

Sensitiveness to authority was unusually keen among the less literate classes of Rebs. The sharpness of reaction in such cases is vividly illustrated by a Texan's letter to his homefolk:

> "We see hard times, and you can guess it is tolerable bad for me as I am Not allowed the chance of a dog I have come to The conclusion that I will

stay and tuff it out with Col Young and then he can go to Hell for my part you know that if any one will try to do I can get along with Them but when they get Hell in their Neck I cant do any thing with them and so I don't Try if a man treats me well I will stick up to Him till I die and then see that my spirit helps him when I am gone to my long Home but he has acted the dam dog and I cant tell him so if I do they will put me in the Guard House . . . but I can tell him what I think of him when this war ends and as to go with him I wont do it to save his life . . . I will come [home] when my time is out or die I wont be run over no longer not to please no officers they have acted the rascal with me . . . I am so sick of war that I dont want to heare it any more till old Abes time is out and then let a man say war to me and I will choke him."[46]

Extravagant words, obviously, but there can be no doubt of the depth of his resentment and dissatisfaction, or of numerous parallels among fellow soldiers.

No small portion of the dissatisfaction in the Confederate Army must be attributed to the drabness of camp routine. Most Rebs were country bred, and to men accustomed to the freedom of field and farm an existence regulated in every detail by drum beats and bugle blasts was particularly distasteful.

"Oh how tiresome this camp life to me," wrote a Mississippian, in 1864, "one everlasting monotone, yesterday, today & tomorrow."[47]

Another had written several months previously, "I sometimes get very much vext at . . . [drill] orders and am all must fit to bite my lips. So very much so that I dont think I will ever waunt to hear of one a gain. nor hear the naim of officer dril are [or] Soldier gard or detail eny more after peace is made. Oh how glad I will be when the day comes that We . . . never . . . hear the Tap of a drum a gain which bids us rise and drill."[48]

Added to military disaster, deprivation of food, clothing and pay, highhandedness of officers, loss of regimental identity, and the intolerable boredom of camp were still other factors tending to demoralize. Some soldiers whose spirit remained strong under all other hardships were revolted by the apparently futile slaughter of the war's last years; others were crushed by the repeated lamentations of their homefolk; still others were broken by the stench and filth of their surroundings; not a few were dispirited by squabbling and inefficiency among commanding officers and governmental authorities; and most depressing of all were the multiplying evidences of greed, selfishness, and ebbing patriotism that permeated army and citizenry alike after the summer campaign of 1863.

Declining morale revealed itself in several ways besides those already noted. One of these was the evading of responsibility by feigning sickness. This subterfuge, referred to as "playing old soldier" by Rebs, made its appearance early in the war.

In June 1861 William R. Barksdale wrote from a camp near Harper's Ferry that "many are reported sick who have little or nothing the matter but only desire to avoid drill. It reminds me of Jake and his chills to see some of these fellows drooping about here trying to look sick."[49] In spite of the efforts of officers and surgeons to put a stop to such shamming, it continued to flourish throughout the war. The prospect of a hard march, of a turn on picket, or of some other unpleasant duty almost invariably produced a swelling of the sick lists.

A less frequent resort to avoid service was the self-infliction of an injury of some sort. One Reb shot himself in the foot, and another in the hand, to escape service. A Louisianian amputated some of his fingers. A South Carolinian secured sick leave by making his arm sore, and extended his sojourn in the infirmary by tampering with the wound. Another South Carolinian managed to keep himself hospitalized for the greater part of the war by aggravating the infection of a toe.[50]

But physical disabling was a serious business. A much more common ruse to evade service was that of getting detailed to some softer assignment than soldiering. "When a person gets a Government contract or agency," wrote Lee to Seddon in 1863, "his first endeavor appears to be to get his friends out of the army in order to help him. Then there are hundreds who go home on sick furloughs, and while there look out for places to which to be detailed, and forward petitions, stating in strong terms the necessity, &c, inclosing surgeons' certificates showing their competency for that work and no other. . . . There are some regiments reduced almost to insignificance by these details."[51]

After adoption of conscription many would-be slackers sought release from the army by claiming exemption on the basis of age, of election to state office, or of coming under the provision allowing immunity from service for ownership of fifteen or twenty slaves. And in numerous cases, by resort to the writ of habeas corpus, such shirkers were successful in obtaining discharges.[52]

A favorite practice was to secure transfer, by regular means or otherwise, to free-booting cavalry outfits or to state organizations in which duties were comparatively light. The prevalence of this practice is convincingly attested by the frequent complaints of departmental commanders and of other high-ranking officers that leaders of independent scouts, partisan rangers and home guards had recruited large numbers of infantry absentees. Such irregularities were invalidated and denounced repeatedly by Richmond authorities, but return of one of these infantrymen to his regular connection involved difficulties so vast that it was seldom accomplished. And the indications are that literally thousands of demoralized Rebs used these shady attachments to effect their escape from the full service due the Confederate Government.

Another method of dodging duty was abuse of the furlough system. Some soldiers, particularly those of partisan ranger companies, connived with their captains to secure leaves without authority from higher officers. Others purchased furloughs from comrades who had legally received them, for considerations ranging from twenty-five dollars to a horse. Others "bought" recruits—i.e. paid men to enlist in their outfits—so that they might secure the forty-day furlough authorized for each addition to the army. Still others told their parents to write letters to commanding officers telling of woeful conditions at home. And some Rebs went so far as to write their own furloughs, and "got by" with it.

Once arrived at home, they found great temptation to prolong the leave. And in countless instances some means of extension were found. A favorite technique was to get a local doctor to write a note saying that the absentee was ill, attaching a certificate of disability, and to mail this to army headquarters; another device was to overstay the furlough for a few days, then on reaching camp to tell of broken-down transportation, the rising of swollen streams or some other hindering act of man or God. Such events were actually frequent enough to make the stories plausible.

By far the most striking manifestation of sagging morale was the increase in the number of soldiers improperly absent from places of duty. Included among these were: first, men absent without leave, such as convalescents who failed to report for duty as ordered, troops who straggled from the ranks on the march, and those overstaying their furloughs; second, soldiers absent with leave, but not in accord with policies authorized by highest authorities; third, men absent under improperly granted detail; fourth, troops serving with organizations other than those to which they were regularly assigned; and fifth, men who without benefit of disguising techniques deserted to the enemy or to the protecting fastnesses of native mountains, swamps and forests.[53]

Unwarranted absentees, as all those who took leave of their assigned duties without proper authorization may be conveniently called, became a source of concern for Confederate leaders very early in the war. Their number was considerably boosted by the announcement in the spring of 1862 that all soldiers between eighteen and thirty-five years of age whose one-year terms of enlistment were about to expire would be held to continued service by conscription. This forcing of unwilling men to prolonged army connection, and induction after April 1862 of draftees whose spirits were already damaged by exposure to such epithets as slackers and conscripts, further enhanced the lists of improper leave-takers. General Lee was deprived of from one-third to one-half of his effective fighting force on the Antietam campaign by straggling; after his return to Virginia he wrote to Davis that "desertion and straggling . . . were the main causes of . . . retiring from Maryland."[54] Remedial legislation was sought by the President, and state governors were asked to co-operate in bringing shirkers to justice. But these efforts were only temporarily effective.

After the disasters of July 1863 leave-taking waxed greater in volume and boldness. Pemberton's men flocked home in such numbers following their parole at Vicksburg that Davis was forced to forego his desire to hold them together pending exchange, and instead to give the general leave-taking a semblance of validity by granting wholesale furloughs.[55] In the wake of Gettysburg the highways of Virginia were crowded daily with homeward-bound troops, still in possession of full accouterments; and, according to one observer, these men "when halted and asked for their furloughs or their authority to be absent from their commands, . . . just pat their guns defiantly and say 'this is my furlough,' and even enrolling officers turn away as peaceably as possible."[56]

The Assistant Secretary of War estimated at this time that the number of soldiers evading service by devious means, but chiefly by unauthorized absence, reached 50,000 to 100,000.[57]

Once arrived in their home country, these men from the mountains of North Carolina, Georgia, Virginia, Tennessee and Arkansas, from the piny woods of Alabama and Mississippi and from the lowlands of Florida, were wont to organize themselves into armed bands. In this way they were able to defy, with few exceptions, all efforts of Confederate authorities to bring them to justice. Secret societies, with imposing signs and rituals, were also formed for self-protection and for urging the cessation of war; to this latter end connivance with Federals, even to the extent of making friendly signs in battle to avoid being shot, was furthered.[58]

Many of the deserters were consistent Union sympathizers conscripted into the army against their will. Such was the case with a Georgia private who wrote his father in 1863:

> "I am this day as strong a Union man as ever walked the soil of Va. I would hate to desert but if I ever get a good chance I will be sure to do it. I never expect to kill a Union man."[59]

Others were persons who, because of extreme youth or of little learning, had never gained a clear idea of what the war was about and consequently had little concern as to its outcome or little conception of the seriousness of desertion. Still others felt that they had to choose between continuing army service and returning home to rescue families from starvation, and they chose the latter. Some were cowards, but there were many whose bravery had been proved on the field of battle.

The defeats and privations of 1864 were accompanied by an alarming increase of unwarranted absenteeism. General Lee wrote apprehensively of the thinning of his ranks in August, and Secretary Seddon observed in September that "desertion is committed almost with impunity."[60] President Davis, according to the Richmond *Enquirer* of October 6, "emphatically announced the startling fact that two-thirds of the army are absent from the ranks."

The three months preceding Appomattox saw an ever mounting tide of leave-taking. Small groups of men assigned to picket duty slipped away nightly from their posts all along the Virginia front; scores of others took advantage of the cover of darkness to crawl from the trenches. In the retreat from Nashville Hood's troops straggled by the hundreds, never to rejoin their commands. Across the Mississippi 400 of General Price's men deserted in one day of February 1865.[61] Between February 26 and March 8, 779 men deserted from the Army of Northern Virginia, according to a report of General Lee, and from March 15 to 25, 1,094; in one instance an entire brigade deserted en masse.[62]

John S. Preston, Superintendent of the Bureau of Conscription, stated in February 1865 that there were over 100,000 deserters scattered throughout the Confederacy, and compilations from other sources indicate that his estimate is conservative.[63] But, as stated previously, figures for desertion tell only part of the story; unfortunately, due to lack of data covering absence other than desertion, the complete tale cannot be told.

There is significant information, however, in a composite tabulation prepared by the War Department from the last returns sent in by the various armies. This compilation shows a total of 198,494 officers and men absent and only 160,198 present in the armies of the Confederacy on the eve of surrender.[64] The figure for absentees includes of course those excused for wounds, sickness and other legitimate purposes, but even so, it is shamefully large. Interpreted most generously, available evidence is such as to merit the observation that months before Appomattox the Confederacy's doom was plainly written in the ever swelling tide of men who were unpatriotically taking leave of their comrades-in-arms.

But in the midst of all the defection that cursed the Confederacy, and in the face of increasing hardship, there were a large number of Rebs whose spirit remained strong. It is pleasant to turn from the woeful subject of evasion to consideration of those who stood firm at their posts of duty.

Morale seems to have been considerably better among the upper and middle classes than it was among less privileged groups. This better spirit can be attributed not so much to the greater material stake involved as to intangible factors of education, travel, experience and self-confidence. A broad background led to a more wholesome point of view and to greater adaptability. Aristocratic organizations like the Washington Artillery, the Mobile Cadets and the Richmond Blues were able to maintain a consistently higher morale than were the toughest of mountaineer troops.[65] And desertion was noticeably worse among soldiers of lower classes than it was among those of moderate and superior means.[66] But there were, of course, innumerable instances of strongheartedness among the humblest of Rebs.

A patriotic and optimistic attitude on the part of friends and relatives at home was a powerful stimulant to soldier morale. The will to persevere must have been strengthened by a note such as that penned by Mollie Vanderberg to her sweetheart in the army:

"Dear Henry,

"I feel more lonely and sad than I have been in some time—perhaps tis because the last companie have taken off nearly all of the gentlemen I respect in Texas. . . . Oh! that I knew what the termination of this awful conflict would be. Henry I want to see you but dont you come—join for the War if tis forty years if you get killed tis the most honorable death—if you escape *I will rejoice. I will love thee still.*" [67]

Likewise, the attitude of a father such as that of C. L. Stephens must have been an effective deterrent to desertion. "I have not tolde you Pa's sentiment about this war," wrote Stephens to his cousin in March 1865. "Some time he is in mighty good spirits and at another time he is out of heart but he does not believe in desertion atall be told me when I was at home [on furlough] that he did not want none of his boys to desert and ly in the woods . . . that he had reather [lose] our wate in gold than for any of us to runaway . . . I had rather die than to runaway myself." [68]

But the morale of many Rebs remained good in spite of expressions of gloom on the part of homefolk, as shown by statements of mild censure in letters sent home. "I am sorry . . . the people at home are whipped," wrote a Georgian to his father, in the spring of 1864; "Yes more than whipped. Some are both whipped and defeated. The army lacks a great deal of being whipped." [69] Several months later while dark clouds of defeat were overcasting Confederate skies a Mississippian observed to a fellow soldier, "Citizens seem very gloomy and desponding about our cause but this Army still retains its high spirits: we are all sanguine." [70]

Statements of soldiers about the general morale of the army cannot be accepted at face value when addressed to homefolk, because optimistic letters were sometimes merely attempts at lightening depression. But there is considerable significance in the very fact that men in the army must often rouse the lagging spirits of those at home.

The dogged and cheerful performance of duty in the most trying circumstances repeatedly testified to the staunch-heartedness of a portion of the army from beginning to end of the conflict. After the strenuous campaign about Yorktown in the spring of 1862 General J. B. Magruder reported that "from April 4 to May 3 this army served without relief in the trenches. Many companies of artillery were never relieved during this long period. It rained almost incessantly; the trenches were filled with water; the weather was exceedingly cold; no fires could be allowed; the artillery . . . of the enemy played upon our men almost continuously day and night; the army . . . subsisted on flour and salt meat, and that in reduced quantities, and yet no murmurs were heard . . . patriotism made them indifferent to suffering, disease, danger, and death." [71]

After the terrible ordeal of Vicksburg, where men lived for forty-seven

days and nights under almost constant shelling, nourished by the scanti-
est of rations and by maggot-infested water, officers of several units
testified to a dauntless spirit. Colonel Ashabel Smith of the Second Texas
infantry said that "up to the last moment of siege the men bore with
unrepining cheerfulness" the overwhelming hardships which they experienced. "When I think of their buoyant courage under these circumstances," he added, and "the alacrity with which they performed every
duty, it appears to me no commendation of those soldiers can be too
great."[72] . . .

One reason for this high morale in the face of great want was the
inurement of the men to hardship, accompanied by a sort of do-or-die
reaction. An Alabama captain noticed this tendency in his company.
After the terrible suffering experienced by Longstreet's command in the
war's third winter, he wrote to his father:

> "If anyone had told me before the war that men could have borne for
> month after month . . . what we have, I would have thought it all talk.
> And I recollect when we first came into the service we grumbled at fare
> that we would now think the greatest luxuries."[73] . . .

Even in the midst of all the shirking and defeatism that marked the
last year of war there was much disapproval of the widespread defection.
"Let a man try to 'play out' now by feigning disability," wrote a participant in the Atlanta campaign, "and he is jeered at and when exposed
by the Surgeons he is greeted with shouts of derision."[74] A Louisianian
aired his opinion against the seekers of soft appointments. "I have a
profound contempt," he wrote, "for all men croakers who are hunting
easy places at home to avoid the dangers of the battle field."[75] And, of
course, good soldiers everywhere denounced the mounting tide of desertion that encompassed them.

Even in the hour of defeat the spirit of some was unyielding. Scores
of Lee's men slipped away from Appomattox to avoid the intolerable
humiliation of formal capitulation. And when General Bryan Grimes
announced the surrender to his command, one Reb threw away his
musket and with upraised hands cried out, "Blow, Gabriel! Blow! My
God, let him blow, I am ready to die." Another grasped his leader by
the hand in farewell and sobbed, "Good-by, General; God bless you, we
will go home, make three more crops, and try them again."[76]

Most soldiers of good morale were subject to occasional lapses of
spirit, but there was one Reb of such consistent and high patriotism as

to merit special mention. This man was J. T. Terrell, of Aberdeen, Mississippi. Though of superior background and education, he left military school to enlist as a private in the spring of 1861; and while he undoubtedly could have secured a lieutenancy through his influence, he never held a commission.

His letters fairly overflow with buoyancy from beginning to end of his service. On November 16, 1862, for instance, he wrote his mother:

"A soldier's life never was hard to me I can get along anywhere and under any circumstances. I have been in camp so long that I feel perfectly at home, and if I was anywhere else I . . . would have a natural feeling of not being in my proper place."

To his mother's suggestion after his sojourn in a Northern prison in 1862 that a substitute might be procured for him, he responded:

"I can say I do not want any as I think it is the duty of every man to bear an equal part in this struggle. . . . I think all men that own property to any extent and especially negro property Should take a part in this war as it has a tendency to encourage the poorer classes."

Just after re-enlistment for the duration of the war by his regiment in early 1864, he exulted:

"I tell you we are not by any means subjugated or despondent. There is life in the old land yet."

Two months later while on his way to participate in the defense of Atlanta, he wrote encouragingly to his mother:

"Hold up your hand and behold the Sky as it brightens. Day is fast dawning upon our infant Confederacy."

After the lapse of a few weeks he boasted:

"Our army is buoyant, enthusiastic, and hopeful in feeling. There is no better army anywhere nor is there any that is better officered. You need not fear the result when the Shock comes."[77]

Two and one-half months later "Tom" Terrell was dead—his brain pierced by a sharpshooter's bullet while on picket before Atlanta. After a few days his father at Quincy plantation in Mississippi received a letter from the hands of his soldier son's Negro body servant, Gabriel, telling of the tragedy. The missive, written by one of Tom's comrades on the very day of his death, is an eloquent testimony to unfaltering devotion to duty:

In the Ditches Atlanta Ga.

Aug 22 1864

Col. B. M. Terrell

My Dear Friend It becomes my duty to inform you of the death of your noble and gallant son. . . . Tom was a favorite with the whole regiment and all concur in saying that he was the best soldier in the regiment There can be said more for him than can be said for one in Ten thousand, he has never missed a roll call a drill a tour of duty never been absent a day without leave never reported to a surgeon nor has he ever slept out of camp unless on duty the loss of such men can not be supplied. Tom was strictly moral I never saw him out of humor in my life. . . .

Very respectfully your friend

G. W. Pennington[78]

If this tribute be accurate, Tom Terrell was truly "the good soldier" of the "lost cause."

How tragic for the Confederacy that there were not more like him. In the months that followed his death, the morale of both citizens and troops came to be in ever sharper contrast to the loftiness of spirit exemplified by Terrell, until on the eve of Appomattox evaders and absentees far outnumbered soldiers who were present for duty.

At the time of surrender an Alabama private addressed his captain on the sad fate that had overtaken the Southland. "Who was the cause of it?" he asked. "Skulkers Cowards extortioners and Deserters not the Yankees that makes it woss."[79] And in light of the shirking that surrounded him, this lowly Reb's observation carries an impressive conviction of truth.

NOTES

From Bell Irvin Wiley, The Life of Johnny Reb: The Common Soldier of the Confederacy (Baton Rouge: Louisiana State University Press, 1978), 123–50. Reprinted by permission.

1. L. M. Johnson, An Elementary Arithmetic Designed for Beginners (Raleigh, 1864), 34, 38, 44.

2. War of the Rebellion: Official Records of the Union and Confederate Armies (Washington, 1880–1901), series 4, I, 277.

3. *Ibid.*, 497.

4. *Ibid.*, 380.

5. Undated but postwar letter of J. M. Montgomery to Victor Montgomery, manuscript in private possession.

6. O. R., series 4, I, 352–353, 380.

7. *Ibid.*, series 1, XXIV, part 3, 1053–1054.

8. This summary of conscription is based primarily on data from the fourth series of the Official Records of the Union and Confederate Armies. Extensive and scholarly treatments of the subject are to be found in A. B. Moore, Conscription and Conflict in the Confederacy (New York, 1924), and Frank L. Owsley, *States Rights in the Confederacy* (Chicago, 1925). A thorough survey of judicial aspects of the question is available in William M. Robinson, Jr., Justice in Grey (Cambridge, 1940).

9. O. R., series 4, III, 48–49.

10. This account of substitution is drawn principally from series four of the Official Records, from Professor Moore's excellent chapter on the subject in his Conscription and Conflict in the Confederacy, and from J. B. Jones, A Rebel War Clerk's Diary (Philadelphia, 1866). William M. Robinson, Jr., has helpful comments on judicial harangues over substitution in his Justice in Grey.

11. O. R., series 4, II, 696.

12. *Ibid.*, 997.

13. Exception should be made of some men, not subject to military service, who engaged substitutes as a gesture of patriotism. The number of such cases, however, was so small as to be of insignificant proportion to the aggregate of proxies. See O. R., series 4, III, 12, General Order No. 3, Adjutant General's Office. Men and officers reported as "present for duty" in Lee's army in April 1863 aggregated 64,799. *Ibid.*, 530.

14. Joseph A. E. Boyd to "De" Boyd, April 12, 1862, manuscript, Alabama Archives.

15. Theodore Mandeville to Rebecca Mandeville, April 22, Aug. 17, 1861, manuscript, Louisiana State University.

16. J. W. Reid, *History of the Fourth Regiment of South Carolina Volunteers* (Greenville, S.C., 1892), 76.

17. Frank Moss to "Lou" Moss, Nov. 27, 1862, manuscript, University of Texas.

18. E. J. Ellis to his mother, June 9, 1862, Feb. 15 and March 18, 1863, manuscript, Louisiana State University.

19. John Crittenden to his wife, Feb. 20, 1863, typescript, University of Texas.

20. John R. Hopper to his brother, Sept. 9, 1863, manuscript, Heartman Collection.

21. Diary of Charles Moore, manuscript, Confederate Memorial Hall.

22. "I witnessed the other day a fight between the divisions composing Hardee's Corps. It was the grandest affair I ever witnessed. . . . One part presented the Confederate States Army and one the Yankees army. The Yankees made the attack. They marched up with banners flying to the tune of Yankee Doodle. As soon as the Confederates charged them they fled apparently in the . . . wildest confusion. Five rounds to the man was expended. The battle lasted about three hours. Nearly the whole of Hood's corps witnessed it." John R. Crittenden to his brother, April 9, 1864.

23. *O. R.*, series 1, XXXIII, 1144–1145; see also *ibid.*, XXXII, part 2, 571–582.

24. *Ibid.*, XXXII, part 2, 582, 665, *et passim.*

25. J. T. Terrell to his mother, March 12, 1864, manuscript in private possession.

26. P.M.H.S. Centenary Series, V, 311–312.

27. There were some who took a pessimistic view of the situation even after Grant's setbacks in the Wilderness. On June 13, 1864, Sgt. William H. Phillips wrote his parents: "We hav bin in the habit of Driving away Every army of the North that has ever come close to Richmond But I am afraid that old Grant is rather too much for us this time he cant [can] outnumber Genl Lee so fare I think it will be hard to get him away this time, if Grant would Keep fighting of us we soon get him so weak that we could Drive him away but he has stoped and fortified himself and is waiting for us to fight him." Manuscript Duke University. General Stephen D. Lee noted a deleterious effect of the unsuccessful defense of Atlanta on fighting qualities. "The majority of the officers and men were so impressed with the idea of their inability to carry even temporary breastworks," he wrote, "that when orders were given for attack, and there was a probability of encountering works . . . they did not generally move to the attack with that spirit which nearly always assures success." O.R., series 1, XXXIX, part 1, 810.

28. J. J. Hardy to his cousin, Jan. 24, 1865, typescript, Georgia Archives.

29. Thomas Caffey to his sister, Jan. 15, 1865, "War Letters of Thomas Caffey," Montgomery Advertiser, May 16, 1909.

30. P.M.H.S. Centenary Series V, 356.

31. Robert W. Banks to his homefolk, Oct. 22, 1862, typescript in private possession.

32. Crenshaw Hall to his father, May 27, 1863, manuscript, Alabama Archives.

33. Thomas Warrick to his wife, Oct. 26, 1863, manuscript, Alabama Archives. Private Andrew J. Patrick of the 37th Mississippi Regiment wrote his wife, Oct. 26, 1862: "I would not mind living hard if I node you was not suffering but you are there and I am here and cant tend to you." On November 2, 1862, he wrote further on the subject: "I am uneasy about you and the

children getting something to eat . . . there is already a heap of men gone home and a heap says if their familys gets to suffering that they will go if they have to suffer [punishment]." Typescripts in private possession.

34. H. A. Stephens to his sister, Jan. 1, 1864, manuscript in private possession; T. B. Barron of the Fiftieth Virginia Regiment wrote to his parents, Aug. 8, 1863: "It is truly hard for the soldier to content himself in the field . . . when he sees his government give the speculator the advantage of him & his family speculation will cause desertion & desertion will be our ruin." Manuscript, Confederate Museum.

35. For scale of pay prescribed by Congress by an act of March 6, 1861, see *O. R.*, series 4, I, 130.

36. *O. R.*, series 4, III, 492. The Georgia Legislature petitioned Congress for an increase to $20 per month of the pay of privates in April 1863, but to no avail. *Ibid.*, II, 485.

37. P.M.H.S. Centenary Series, V, 308.

38. *O. R.*, series 1, XIX, part 2, 722.

39. *Ibid.*, VI, 408; P. M. H. S. Centenary Series, V, 298.

40. T. B. Hampton to his wife, Dec. 15, 1862, typescript, University of Texas.

41. *O. R.*, series 4, III, 48–49.

42. *Ibid.*, series 1, XXIV, part 2, 393–394. For detail of reaction of officers and men to such a proposal, see petition of Johnson's brigade in *ibid.*, series 1, XLII, part 2, 1264–1265.

43. *O. R.*, series 1, XLIII, part 1, 609–610, report of Major Moore, and indorsement of Assistant Adjutant and Inspector General *Peyton*; see also *ibid.*, XXXII, part 2, 778–779.

44. *Ibid.*, series 1, XLI, part 4, 1112–1113.

45. Deter Jochum to his homefolk, Jan. 30, 1864, manuscript, Confederate Memorial Hall.

46. W. M. Moss to his sisters, Dec. 28, 1863, manuscript, University of Texas.

47. Orville C. Bumpass to his wife, Oct. 22, 1864, manuscript, Evans Memorial Library.

48. C. W. Stephens to his sister, Jan. 30, 1864, manuscript in private possession.

49. William R. Barksdale to his brother, June 11, 1861, manuscript in private possession.

50. Richmond *Enquirer*, Nov. 3, 1863; Correspondence of Medical Director of General Hospitals in Virginia, 1864–1865, Confederate Archives, chapter VI, volume 365, p. 214, manuscript, National Archives; General Orders and Circulars, Department of South Carolina, Georgia and Florida, *ibid.*, chapter II, volume 43, p. 329–330; diary of C. M. Horton, entry of July 7, 1863, manu-

script, Confederate Memorial Hall. Henry C. Semple to his wife, Dec. 19, 1862, manuscript, University of North Carolina; Alfred W. Bell to his wife, Sept. 17, 1864, manuscript, Duke University.

51. *O. R.*, series 1, XXV, part 2, 639.

52. Robinson, *op. cit.*, 252–254; *O. R.*, series 4, II, 465; III, 68–69.

53. Confederate authorities attempted on occasion to differentiate between deserters and other unwarranted absentees, and historians have been constrained in some instances to follow their example. But the line of demarcation is so thinly drawn and so variable as to be largely arbitrary. At what point, for example, did a man who overstayed his furlough, or a convalescent who failed to report for duty, become a deserter? And in what category was the infantryman to be placed who, without ample authority, secured transfer to a cavalry company? The purpose of this study is better served by classifying as unwarranted absentees deserters and all other soldiers who absented themselves by irregular devices from the service to which they were assigned.

54. *O. R.*, series 1, XIX, part 2, 597, 605, 622; Philip Slaughter, Sketch of the *Life of Randolph Fairfax* (Richmond, 1864), 33, quoting a letter of Fairfax from Bunker Hill, Va., Oct. 3, 1862; Richmond *Daily Dispatch*, Sept. 26, 1862, Jan. 14, 1864; Douglas S. Freeman, *R. E. Lee* (New York, 1934), II, 411–412. A factor contributing to straggling was, as Freeman points out, the exhausted and shoeless condition of many of the troops.

55. *O. R.*, series 1, XXIV, part 3, 1007, 1010, 1018.

56. *Ibid.*, series 4, II, 721.

57. *Ibid.*, 674; an editorial in the Richmond *Daily Dispatch* of Jan. 11, 1864, said: "Nearly half our military force is scattered over the country, and if returned to its proper position not another man would be needed in the field." Three days later the Dispatch editor reverted to the subject of straggling with this inquiry: "Where was the balance of the 110,000 men on Bragg's muster roll when he fought the battle of Chickamauga with less than 40,000? . . . Where are the stragglers and deserters who swarm in the mountains and infest the lower country like locusts?"

58. *O. R.*, series 4, III; 397–398, 802–803; series 1, XXXII, part 3, 681–682; XXXIX, part 2, 588–589; Ella Lonn, *Desertion During the Civil War* (New York, 1928), 62–105; Georgia Lee Tatum, *Disloyalty in the Confederacy* (Chapel Hill, 1934), 24 ff.

59. J. M. Jordan to his father, Feb. 14, 1863, typescript, Georgia Archives.

60. *O. R.*, series I, XLII, part 2, 1175–1176; series 4, III, 689–690. The Richmond *Daily Dispatch* of Jan. 26, 1865, quoted a correspondent of the Atlanta Appeal: "If one-half of the men of the Confederacy capable of bearing arms would cease to shirk their duty . . . and . . . come to the front we could expel the invaders from our soil within six weeks."

61. Lonn, *op. cit.*, 23.

62. *Ibid.; O. R.,* series 1, XLVI, part 2, 1265, 1293.

63. *O. R.,* series 1, LI, part 2, 1065; Lonn, *op. cit.,* 30.

64. *O. R.,* series 4, III, 1182. Returns are for varying dates, ranging from Dec. 31, 1864, to April 17, 1865, for different armies of the Confederacy.

65. T. C. DeLeon, *Four Years in Rebel Capitals* (mobile, 1890), 142.

66. Lonn, *op. cit.,* 123.

67. Mollie Vandenberg to C. H. Clark, March 11, 1862, manuscript in private possession.

68. C. L. Stephens to E. A. Stephens, March 5, 1865, manuscript in private possession.

69. James L. G. Wood to his father, March 31, 1864, typescript, Georgia Archives.

70. J. Joe Evans to John Holliday, Jan. 7, 1865, manuscript in private possession.

71. *O. R.,* series 1, XI, part 1, 408–409.

72. *Ibid.,* XXIV, part 2, 392–393.

73. Bolling Hall to his father, April 15, 1864, manuscript, Alabama Archives.

74. Robert M. Gill to his wife, April 16, 1864, manuscript in author's possession.

75. Joseph Renwick to his wife, April 14, 1865, manuscript, Louisiana State University.

76. Pulaski Cowper, complier, *Extracts of Letters of Maj. Gen. Bryan Grimes* (Raleigh, 1883), 122–123.

77. J. T. Terrell to his parents, Nov. 16, 1862, March 12, May 2, June 6, 1864.

78. Manuscript in private possession.

79. J. M. J. Tolly to James R. Hall, April 22, 1865, manuscript, Alabama Archives.

Chapter 18

A Study of Morale in Civil War Soldiers

Pete Maslowski

The narratives written by most historians of Civil War soldiering reflect their best judgment about the patterns and tendencies among the letters, diaries, and official records they have read. A few historians use an alternative approach, reporting a "content analysis" of their sources: they tabulate how many sources mention, for example, patriotic motives for enlisting and how many do not. This method depends on the historian's judgment in question-framing to much the same degree as does a conventional narrative; it should be seen as an additional level of detail that features minor as well as major themes in soldiers' testimony. In this selection from a 1970 article, Pete Maslowski of the University of Nebraska, Lincoln, compares World War II soldiers' attitudes with those expressed in Civil War soldiers' diaries, memoirs, and letters.

Tolstoy wrote in *War and Peace:* "In warfare the force of armies is the product of the mass multiplied by something else, an unknown x . . . x is the spirit of the army, the greater or less desire to fight and face dangers on the part of all the men composing the army, which is quite apart from the question whether they are fighting under leaders of genius or not, with cudgels or with guns that fire thirty times a minute."[1]

This intangible entity, this x, is the heart of a military machine. Just as a doctor can understand a great deal about a patient by examining his heart, so too can the historian tell a great deal about an army by investigating this quantity. The problem is to establish criteria whereby x may be measured with a high degree of certainty. Samuel A. Stouffer, et al., in the first two volumes of their monumental work, *The American Soldier, Studies in Social Psychology in the World War II*, formulated such criteria by demonstrating several ways in which high—or low—morale was manifested in the attitudes of World War II American soldiers.[2]

The authors of *The American Soldier* hinted that their guidelines might be applied profitably to soldiers in other wars. Indeed, this essay was in part inspired by their observation: "If by some miracle a cache should be found of manuscript material telling of the attitudes toward combat of a representative sample of, say, a hundred men in Stonewall Jackson's army, the discovery would be of interest to Civil War historians." Actually, no "miracle" is necessary to provide an abundance of relevant source material since diaries, letters, and memoirs of Civil War soldiers abound in almost every library. Much of this material has been used before. Bell I. Wiley, for example, relied on it almost exclusively when doing his studies of the commom soldier. His results were generally "literary" and qualitative; by applying Stouffer's criteria to similar sources the conclusions which emerge should be more quantitative, or, if you will, "scientific."

Classifications and Methodology

Although the criteria which will be used in judging the spirit and morale of Civil War soldiers were suggested by similar topics discussed in *The American Soldier*, there must be an essential difference in methodologies. Stouffer *created* his data by using a questionnaire—almost a public opinion poll—approach, supplemented by interviews and observations. This system is direct and readily adaptable to statistical analysis. On the other hand, the data used in this study already *had been created*, and so the method must be much more indirect and less adaptable to concise statistical analysis. For example, Stouffer asked directly on a questionnaire, "In general, how well do you think the Army is run?" and then followed this with a list of explicit responses such as, "It is run very well; It is run pretty well; It is not run very well; It is run very poorly; Undecided." In the study presented here it was assumed hypothetically that a question like this was asked, and then an answer was sought. Of course, very few such precise remarks as "I think the army is run very well" were found. The conclusions of this paper, accordingly, must be more ambiguous and flexible than those of *The American Soldier*. If Stouffer was prudent in warning his readers to place emphasis on trends and patterns as a whole rather than on specific percentages, the warning seems to be doubly prudent here.

In this treatise several attitude and morale classifications gleaned from the pages of *The American Soldier* were applied to the letters and/or diaries of 50 men who fought in the Civil War. Twenty-five of these men were from the South, and 25 from the North. These will be known henceforth as Group I (Southerners) and Group II (Northerners).[3]

The number of variables involved in a random selection of 50 Civil War soldiers who wrote of their experiences is great. For this study only two variables were held constant. First, each man enlisted as a private and attained no permanent rank higher than Captain, and very few reached this rank. Essentially, then, all 50 could be termed "common soldiers." Secondly, all the men were from rural environments; hence, they probably had some similarities of background and upbringing. No attempt has been made to control such factors as age, marital status, education, whether a man fought in the eastern or western theater, or the length of time spent in the service.

Orientation and Commitment

One of Stouffer's most interesting attitude classification dealt with orientation toward and personal commitment to the War. He concluded that World War II soldiers did *not* view the war in terms of ideological principles or causes. Their commitment was a defensive one in that they merely accepted the War as a necessary evil imposed on them by an aggressor nation.

What about Civil War soldiers? Why did they march off to fight and then continue to endure the slaughter? What thoughts sustained them as they slept in the mud, ate hardtack, and marched out periodically to kill and be killed? When Civil War troops stole a few moments to jot down a line or two in their diaries did they discuss the meaning of the war or did they talk about such "base" things as payday and the excitement they encountered on a battlefield?

References to three different criteria, or subheadings, were regarded as indicative of high ideological commitment. These three, with examples of each, are as follows:

1) Love for one's country: "I love peace but I love my country more."[4] "But always with me the first thing was duty to my country and comfort next."[5]

2) Belief in a better world to come in the future if victory was achieved: ". . . but there is a better time coming, perhaps, for me with others. Perhaps not for me, but for others. Someone will see better times at least."[6]

3) Belief that there were certain basic issues at stake in the War and it was worthwhile fighting for the benefits which would accrue from a favorable settlement of these issues. Among the issues were slavery ("In the heat of battle, the powder and sweat gave us soon the complexion of the black man for whose freedom we were fighting."[7]); the tariff ("The tariff was also a question which divided the sections."[8]); freedom and liberty ("But I am engaged in the glorious cause of liberty and justice, fighting for the rights of man—fighting for all that we of the South hold dear."[9]); and state rights ("We only fought for our State rights, they for the Union and power. The South fell battling under the banner of State rights, but yet grand and glorious even in death."[10]). The very few references to these supposedly vital issues were startling. Less than one-sixth of the men, for instance, made any comment relating to slavery.

References to four other criteria were assumed to be illustrative of a lack of ideological orientation and commitment. These are:

1) Fighting to gain glory and to "save face" both among fellow soldiers and at home: "Well we have earned our reputation, and although it has cost us something and may cost us some of our best men yet, still I think it will pay to keep it up, cost what it will."[11] "I Glory in the honor and pride of a solgers [*sic*] life."[12]

2) Fighting for adventure and excitement. There were no direct comments to the effect that a man enlisted for the sheer excitement and adventure he expected to encounter in the War. Yet, in reading the diaries and letters one gets the definite impression that some of the soldiers were preoccupied with adventure-seeking, while for others an exciting event at least served to relieve the drudgery of army life and thereby make it more endurable. There is a great deal of indirect evidence bearing on this criterion. When men were enlisting they sometimes commented on the intense excitement which pervaded the atmosphere. Once in the service, raids and battles, foraging, rumors, and other excitement-inducing features of army life were the subjects of continual com-

ment. During periods of inactivity there were numerous complaints about the monotony of army life. The quantity of this indirect evidence is so large that this factor has to be accorded considerable weight in any analysis.

Here are several sample statements: "Nothing but positive orders would have induced me to cease firing. I never experienced such excitement and rapture."[13] "During our march, on the previous night, I suggested to young Calmes, a member of the company, that we ride ahead of the advance guard and look for an adventure."[14] "We are delighted to hear for a change and any new adventure will be welcome."[15]

3) Financial and economic considerations: "The great excitement in the army is now about pay. Half of the men in our Regiment are men of families and most of them depend on their wages to support their families."[16] "One important feature in the life of a soldier was the matter of his pay."[17]

4) Fighting just to get the War over with in order to return home to loved ones and "the old way of life:" "Time drags lazily on but each day makes our term of service one less day."[18] "We are all ready to go to the last; we want to wind the thing up and get home if we live ever to go back."[19]

For each of the 50 men considered, a separate page contained a list of these seven criteria. Each time a statement was found which was applicable to one of these criteria a check was made opposite its listing on the page. Hence it was a simple matter of addition to determine each soldier's ideological outlook.

Neither the Southerners (Group I) nor the Northerners (Group II) displayed high ideological orientation and commitment. In Group I only 12 per cent of the men made more statements representative of high ideological commitment than low ideological commitment, while 64 per cent had more references indicative of low ideological orientation than they did of high ideological orientation. The remaining 24 per cent were even in their comments one way or the other. In Group II the corresponding percentages are 8, 88 and 4. The conclusion is that, like Stouffer's World War II soldiers, the Civil War soldiers studied here were notoriously deficient in ideological orientation. And on each of the specific criteria Northerners and Southerners were very much alike in their orientation. A quick glance at several of the separate sub-headings will illustrate this.

In Group I, 52 per cent of the men made between one and five statements which were illustrative of "love for one's country," four per cent made six or more comments relating to it, and 44 per cent made no mention of anything that could be construed as love for one's country. For Group II the corresponding percentages are 64, 12, and 24. In regard to the meaning and worthwhileness of the War, 64 per cent of the men in Group I made between one and five relevant comments, 8 per cent made six or more, and 28 per cent made no applicable statements. The corresponding percentages for Group II are 52, 4, and 44. Finally, the comments indicative of excitement and adventure as a factor in orientation broke down this way: 52 per cent of the writings in Group I contained between one and five applicable references, 8 per cent six or more, and 40 per cent contained no apt comments. The corresponding percentages for Group II are 48, 16, and 36. Thus, for all three of these criteria the distinct trend for both Groups is this: The majority (in one instance, only 48 per cent) of the writings included between one and five pertinent statements, a large number made no applicable references, and a much smaller number contained six or more germane comments.

The data for the other sub-headings of this classification showed, with but a few minor deviations, the same high degree of similarity between Northerners and Southerners.

The fact that the men of these two Groups were so much like the troops Stouffer studied, and that they were so similar to one another, raised an interesting question in regard to Wiley's conclusion about the orientation of Civil War soldiers. In the concluding chapter of *The Life of Billy Yank*, Wiley states that "Soldier attitudes as revealed in their letters and diaries leave the impression that Billy Yank was not so deeply concerned with the War as Johnny Reb. Financial considerations seem to have figured more conspicuously in his participation in the conflict, and he appears to have felt less of personal commitment and responsibility."[20] The data found in this study do not support this general statement. As far as orientation and commitment go, *neither* side possessed a high ideological orientation or awareness; and the *patterns and tendencies* in all of the individual subheadings in the orientation classification were identical, with, as mentioned, only minor deviations. Further, if, as Wiley writes, "Billy Yank was fighting to subdue a revolt against national authority and to free the slaves; Johnny Reb was fighting to establish an independent government, but he also was fighting for a peculiar way of life, for the defense of his home, and as it often seemed to him, for life itself," Billy Yank and Johnny Reb did not seem to be particularly cognizant of this themselves. Or, if they were conscious of it, they did not commit their awareness to paper.

Combat

A second morale classification to which Stouffer devoted considerable time and energy was attitude toward combat. Under this classification the present study found pertinent information on two criteria. One of these was a man's confidence in his physical and mental stamina, especially during combat. Essentially, this boiled down to how many times a soldier mentioned that he was or was not tired or fatigued by carrying out his military duties. It is assumed that the less a soldier complained the better his morale, and vice versa. Examples were numerous: "In fact we have so much skirmishing and working this week that I am almost broken down."[21] "I have come to the conclusion that I can march as far as most any man in the regiment."[22] "I was on Guard duty, had no rest for four days and nights, am almost exhausted for want of rest."[23]

Only 16 per cent of the Southerners (Group I) had confidence in their stamina, 60 per cent did not, and 24 per cent either made no pertinent statements or else an equal number of positive and negative references on the subject. For the Northerners (Group II) the percentages are 28, 48, and 24. Once again there is very little difference between the soldiers, Reb or Yank: In both Groups most of the soldiers complained of being tired and exhausted more than they commented to the contrary, though Rebs were slightly more prone to carp than their Northern counterparts.

The second sub-heading was whether or not a soldier was willing and eager for combat. Willingness, naturally, would be an indication of high morale; lack of eagerness an indication of lower morale. Most of the relevant statements concerning this matter were direct and to the point one way or the other: "In a few days I was 'spoiling for a fight,' and so were the rest."[24] "I am anxious for the fight to come off."[25] "I hope I will not have to go into another fight as long as I live, for the more I go into the more I dread them."[26]

In Group I, 56 per cent showed a willingness for combat, 20 per cent did not, and 24 per cent either had no apt references or else an equal number of positive and negative responses on the subject. For Group II the corresponding percentages are 44, 20, and 36. In both groups, then, there was a definite willingness to fight, but with a very slight edge in eagerness going to the Rebs.

In a survey applied to 6,280 soldiers, which was designed to determine whether or not a soldier was willing for combat, Stouffer asked two questions. The first was, "Which of the following best tells the way you feel about getting into an actual combat zone?" This was followed by seven possible gradated responses. 2,970 of the men showed a willingness for combat, 2,624 did not, and 686 had no opinion or answer. The second question was, "Which of the following best describes your own feeling about getting into combat against the Germans?" This was followed by five gradated responses. 4,202 of the men expressed a willingness to fight, 1,763 did not, and 135 had no answer. Thus, in both World War II soldiers and Civil War troops—both Reb and Yank— there was a decided overall willingness for combat.

Wiley may well be overstating the case when he writes that "Moreover, the men who wore the gray fought with more dash, *elan* and enthusiasm . . . Their penchant for recounting the details of combat in home letters suggests that they derived a greater thrill from fighting." True, the data presented here do indicate that Southerners were slightly more willing to "butt heads" with the enemy than Northerners, but the difference is not as dramatic as Wiley's statement suggests.

Military Leadership

Despite Tolstoy's intimation that x is not necessarily related to leadership, Stouffer found that attitudes toward military leadership were quite significant in the morale of World War II combatants. Three subheadings in this classification proved fruitful when the writings of Civil War soldiers were applied to them.

The first criterion questioned whether or not a soldier had confidence in his officers. The assumption is that such confidence would be illustrative of high morale. Pertinent statements took two different forms. Some [named specific officers: soldiers] "would be very uneasy about our situation if Gen. [*sic*] Lee was not in Command."[27] "Suffice it that the army is in good spirits and have confidence in 'Rosy.' "[28] ". . . we are out of Banks' Dep't [*sic*]. I hope we may never go near it again."[29] Others were far more general in scope: "Had great confidence in our officers."[30] "This state of things has been brought about by the laziness and incompetency of our company officers."[31]

In presenting the data for this subheading, repetition cannot be avoided: Southerners and Northerners were remarkably similar. In Group I, 40 per cent of the men thought their officers were competent, 24 per cent did not, and 36 per cent had no comments or an equal number of references one way or the other. For Group II the corresponding percentages are 52, 20, and 28. If anything, there is a slight tendency for Northerners to fare better under this criterion.

The second sub-heading under military leadership dealt with the question of whether or not a soldier's officers "served by example." What this boiled down to in an overwhelming majority of the cases was: Did the officers take their place in the front ranks or were they cowards? It is easy to imagine the depressing effect a cowardly officer could have on the spirit of a common soldier. "When we 'went in' on the above mentioned position old Capt. [sic] Reddish took his place in the ranks and fought like a common soldier."[32] "At this moment, when we had the advantage of position, the cowardice of our advance detachment commander, Lieut. Col. [sic] Park, caused him to order a retreat."[33] "The officers, of course, fared no better than the men—all took the same medicine."[34]

In Group I, 80 per cent and in Group II, 60 per cent of the soldiers studied were satisfied with the personal example displayed by their officers. No one in Group I thought badly of the example set by his officers, and 20 per cent either had no comments or else an equal number of positive and negative responses. In Group II eight per cent were dissatisfied and 32 per cent made no references or else an equal number of pro and con responses. Although both Groups exhibit the same trend in regard to this criterion, it does seem that Group II was not as opinionated about the example set by its officers as was Group I.

The final sub-heading in this classification was designed to discover whether or not a soldier believed that his officers took a personal interest in, and stood up for him. Logically, an officer who took such an interest in his men could be expected to induce higher spirits in them than could a more egocentric officer. This criterion included a whole medley of responses because, basically, any pro or con statement about an officer's behavior which was not applicable to one of the other two sub-headings was included here. "He was not only our beloved Captain, but was comrade, friend, yea, brother and father to us all."[35] "But the officers got busy and went up town and bought, with their own money, some-thing for us to eat."[36] "It seems to us that it is the delight of some officers to see the poor soldier suffer."[37]

The trend that emerged here is identical to that of the previous sub-heading. In Group I, 56 per cent of the men thought their officers took a personal interest in them, only 4 per cent did not, and 40 per cent made no pertinent comments or else an equal number of statements one way or the other. In Group II the corresponding percentages are 36, 24, and 40. Both Groups contained more men who thought their officers took pretty good care of their needs and desires than thought the oppo-site; yet, again, the men of Group II did not regard their officers as favorably as the men of Group I.

The evidence put forth in these last two sub-headings indicates that Southerners did indeed think more highly of their officers during the War than did Northerners. However, the subheading dealing with the question of general competence of officers presents a real enigma because on this issue Northerners were more favorably disposed toward their officers than were Southerners. Thus, if the emphasis is placed on the absolute percentages in each of these three sub-headings there appears to be a contradiction in the evidence. If, however, the emphasis is fo-cused on the general *trends or patterns* in these sub-headings—both individually and collectively—the supposed contradiction disappears and the strong resemblance between the men in the blue and the gray in their awareness of their officers is highlighted.

Not only were Rebs and Yanks similar to each other in regard to leadership, but they also were very much like Stouffer's World War II soldiers on this score. For example, a large majority of Stouffer's soldiers were satisfied with the example set by their officers. In one study which examined attitudes toward officers according to length of time in com-bat, 60 per cent or more of the men in five different groups of privates, pfcs, and noncoms believed their officers were "willing to go through anything they asked their men to go through." Another survey showed that 70 per cent of the front line troops felt that all or most of their officers were willing to set good examples. In this same study 61 per cent of the front line troops thought all or most of their officers took a personal interest in them. And finally, a study of six companies with pre-determined high morale showed that in all six of them two-thirds or more of the men believed their officers were interested in the men, understood their needs, and were helpful to them.

Conclusion

In their attitudes toward leadership and combat and in their orientation and commitment to the War in which they fought, Civil War and World War II soldiers were amazingly similar. A number of other characteristics and attitudes affecting morale were also considered in the original study. These were: 1) discipline; 2) promotions; 3) personal esprit, that is, the soldier's expressed sense of well-being; 4) satisfaction with army job and status; 5) approval or criticism of the army. Like those three classifications reviewed in some detail here, each of these classifications was divided into several criteria or subheadings, all of which were suggested by analogous headings in *The American Soldier*. In all but one instance a high degree of correlation between the soldiers of both Wars was maintained. The contiguity in attitudes of American soldiers separated by a span of 80 years is indeed striking.

The one exception to this contiguity concerned promotions. Stouffer found that World War II troops did not think very highly of the system of promotions—his data showed an unmistakable trend toward an unfavorable view of the promotions policy. On the other hand, the data gathered in this study showed that less than 10 per cent of either Group I or Group II was dissatisfied with the promotions system, while about 50 per cent of each Group was satisfied with the system.[38] This discrepency is probably related to differences in military organization between 1860 and 1940. Several differences, for example, are readily apparent. One is that in a good many instances (at least early in the War) Civil War soldiers were able to elect their own officers. World War II troops were not given the privilege of participating in the election of their own officers. A second is that Civil War soldiers never had to endure ROTC and Officer Candidate School officers. These officers, who were often regarded as "outsiders," came in for more than their share of scorn and contempt. A third difference is that army organization during World War II not only permitted, but also seemed to encourage a wide official and social gap between commissioned and enlisted personnel. This gap seemed considerably narrower in Civil War armies.

This data on promotions during the Civil War is not in harmony with Bell Wiley's statement, "Still another indication of the Northern soldier's more practical bent was his greater concern about rising in the military hierarchy; certainly his letters and diaries are more replete with comment about promotions." Rebs and Yanks were approximately *equal* in their concern with advancement. If anything, Rebs were slightly more vocal on the subject than Yanks.

Wiley also concluded that "Johnny Rebs seem to have taken more readily to soldiering from their prior mode of life . . ." This conclusion does not seem warranted by the data collected in this study which showed, for instance, that Southerners were consistently in worse mental condition and consistently enjoyed army life less than Northerners.[39] Wiley's assertions that a Rebel's "cheerfulness outweighed his dejection" and that "Adaptability and good nature, in fact, were among his most characteristic qualities" may need substantial revision.

On a number of other issues our data concurred fully with Wiley's findings. In fact, his final verdict that, "In sum, it may be stated that the similarities of Billy Yank and Johnny Reb far outweighed their differences" generally seems to be true; and if Southerners and Northerners by and large resembled each other, it is also true that they closely resembled World War II soldiers on almost all of the attitudes under consideration.

This general conformity, however, should not obscure the fact that this study has raised some interesting and provocative questions in regard to Wiley's conclusions. These center around the issues of personal orientation and commitment, promotions, and mental well-being, but branch out to include such topics as military leadership and willingness for combat where expected differences were not so large and clear-cut as to make them conclusive. Were Civil War soldiers personally aware of the stakes involved in the conflict? Where they at all motivated by high ideological considerations? Were Yanks or Rebs more concerned with promotions? Did Southerners really enjoy fighting more than Yanks? How great was the difference in Southern and Northern attitudes toward their officers? Questions like these still need more definitive answers before we can fully understand the Civil War soldier in the ranks. The method employed here, if projected on a larger and more complex scale, might well provide some of the answers. Certainly the strong correlation between the results set forth here and those obtained by Stouffer suggest this may be the right path to follow.

NOTES

From Pete Maslowski, "A Study of Morale in Civil War Soldiers," *Military Affairs* 34 (December 1970): 122–26. Reprinted by permission.

1. Leo Tostoy, *War and Peace* (Translated by Constance Garnett), (New York: McClure, Phillips and Co., 1904) III, Part XIV, p. 268.

2. Samuel A. Stouffer, et al., *The American Soldier, Studies in Social Psychology in World War II* (Princeton, New Jersey: Princeton University Press, 1949, 4 vols.). Individual page references to these volumes will not be cited. All information used in the present study is contained in Volumes I and II.

3. In the original study two additional Groups were considered. Group III consisted of twenty-five memoirs or reminiscences written by Southerners; Group IV consisted of twenty-five memoirs or reminiscences written by Northerners. In no instance did the examination of these two Groups result in data contradictory to that derived from Groups I and II. In essence, then, these observations were derived initially from a sample group of 100, not 50, men.

4. James I. Robertson, Jr. (ed.), "An Indiana Soldier in Love and War: The Civil War Letters of John V. Hadley," *Indiana Magazine of History* (September, 1963) LIX, p. 230.

5. Wirt Armistead Cate (ed.), *Two Soldiers, The Campaign Diaries of Thomas J. Key, C.S.A., and Robert J. Campbell, U.S.A.* (Chapel Hill, N.C.: The University of North Carolina Press, 1938) p. 128.

6. Margaret Brobst Roth (ed.), *Well Mary: Civil War Letters of a Wisconsin Volunteer* (Madison, Wis.: The University of Wisconsin Press, 1960) p. 113.

7. J. S. Clark, *Life in the Middle West, Reminiscences of J. S. Clark* (Chicago: The Advance Publishing Company, no date given) p. 54.

8. Augustus Pitt Adamson, *Brief History of the Thirtieth Georgia Regiment* (Griffen, Ga.: The Mills Printing Co., no date given) p. 9.

9. John G. Barrett (ed.), *Yankee Rebel, The Civil War Journal of Edmund DeWitt Patterson* (Chapel Hill, N.C.: The University of North Carolina Press, 1966) p. 14.

10. Sam R. Watkins, *"Co. Aytch" Maury Grays First Tennessee Regiment or a Side Show of the Big Show* (Jackson, Tenn.: McCowat-Mercer Press, 1952) p. 49.

11. Stephen E. Ambrose (ed.), *A Wisconsin Boy in Dixie: Selected Letters of James K. Newton* (Madison, Wis.: The University of Wisconsin Press, 1961) p. 63.

12. Aurelia Austin (ed.), "A Georgia Boy With "Stonewall" Jackson, the Letters of James Thomas Thompson," *The Virginia Magazine of History and Biography* (July, 1962) 70, p. 322.

13. Edward W. Spangler, *My Little War Experiences with Historical*

Sketches and Memorabilia (York, Pa.: York Daily Publishing Company, 1904) p. 34–35.

14. John N. Opie, *A Rebel Cavalryman with Lee, Stuart, and Jackson* (Chicago: W. B. Conkey Company, 1899) p. 127.

15. J. W. Gaskill, *Footprints Through Dixie, Everyday Life of the Man Under a Musket on the Firing Line and in the Trenches, 1862–1865* (Alliance, Ohio: Bradshaw Printing Company, 1919) p. 58.

16. Ambrose, *A Wisconsin Boy in Dixie*, p. 158.

17. Leander Stillwell, *The Story of a Common Soldier of Army Life in the Civil War, 1861–1865* (no location given: Franklin Hudson Publishing Co., 1920) p. 270.

18. Mabel Watkins Mayer (ed.), "Into the Breach, Civil War Letters of Wallace W. Chadwick," *The Ohio State Archaeological and Historical Quarterly* (April-June, 1943) LII, p. 165.

19. Roth, *Well Mary*, p. 56.

20. All quotations from Bell Irvin Wiley used in this study are from either his *The Life of Billy Yank, the Common Soldier of the Union* (New York: The Bobbs-Merrill Company, 1951) p. 360–361; or *The Life of Johnny Reb, the Common Soldier of the Confederacy* (New York: The Bobbs-Merrill Company, 1943) p. 347.

21. George D. Harmon (ed.), "Letters of Luther Rice Mills—A Confederate Soldier," *The North Carolina Historical Review* (July, 1927) IV, p. 298.

22. George C. Osborn (ed.), "The Civil War Letters of Robert W. Banks," *The Journal of Mississippi History* (July, 1943) V, p. 143.

23. John D. Barnhart (ed.), "A Hoosier Invades the Confederacy, Letters and Diaries of Leroy S. Mayfield," *Indiana Magazine of History* (June, 1943) XXXIX, p. 178.

24. Susan Williams Benson (ed.), *Berry Benson's Civil War Book, Memoirs of a Confederate Scout and Sharpshooter* (Athens, Ga.: University of Georgia Press, 1962) p. 77.

25. Bell Irvin Wiley (ed.), "The Confederate Letters of John W. Hogan," *The Georgia Historical Quarterly* (September, 1954) XXXVIII, p. 188.

26. Henry McGilbert Wagstaff (ed.), "Letters of Thomas Jackson Strayhorn," *The North Carolina Historical Review* (October, 1936) XIII, p. 332.

27. Harmon, "Letters of Luther Rice Mills," p. 305.

28. A. Piatt Andrew, Jr. (ed.), *Some Civil War Letters of A. Piatt Andrew, III* (Gloucester, Mass.: privately printed, 1925) p. 79.

29. Ambrose, *A Wisconsin Boy in Dixie*, p. 107.

30. H. M. Povenmire (ed.), "Diary of Jacob Adams, Private in Company F, 21st O.V.V.I.," *Ohio Archaeological and Historical Publications* (1929) XXXVIII, p. 646.

31. Willain H. Runge (ed.), *Four Years in the Confederate Artillery, the*

Diary of Private Henry Robinson Berkeley (Chapel Hill, N.C.: The University of North Carolina Press, 1961) p. 25.

32. Stillwell, *The Story of a Common Soldier*, p. 61.

33. Thomas Francis Galwey, *The Valiant Hours* (Harrisburg, Pa.: The Stackpole Company, 1961) p. 12.

34. William Valmore Izlar, *A Sketch of the War Record of the Edisto Rifles, 1861–1865* (Columbia, S.C.: August Kohn, 1914) p. 22.

35. Howell Carter, *A Cavalryman's Reminiscences of the Civil War* (New Orleans: The American Printing Co., Ltd., no date given) p. 77.

36. Stillwell, *The Story of a Common Soldier*, p. 25.

37. D. G. Cotty, *Four Years Campaigning in the Army of the Potomac* (Grand Rapids, Mich.: Dygert Bros. & Co., 1874) p. 169.

38. The remaining percentage in each Group either had no comments about promotions or else had an equal number of positive and negative references.

39. In Group I, 16 per cent indicated they were in good mental condition, 56 per cent in bad mental condition, and 28 per cent had no relevant comments or an equal number of positive and negative responses. For Group II, on the other hand, these percentages were 32, 40, and 28. Again, in Group I only 40 per cent seemed to enjoy army life, 36 per cent did not, and 24 per cent had no comments or an equal number of pro and con responses. The corresponding percentages in Group II were 88, 8, and 4.

Chapter 19

Christian Soldiers
The Meaning of Revivalism in the Confederate Army

Drew Gilpin Faust

While army life was creating barriers between soldiers and the civilian world, there were also reminders of home that offered to lessen the changes caused by soldiering. Religion was prominent among these reminders, particularly in the South. Revivals periodically swept through the Confederate armies, peaking in the winters, when fighting diminished, and producing an estimated 150,000 converts among the approximately 900,000 Confederate troops. Evangelical religion, which predominated in the South, was exceptionally well suited to easing the stresses of the war. In this selection from a 1987 article, Drew Gilpin Faust of Harvard University explains why southern soldiers were especially drawn to evangelical preaching.

From the fall of 1862 until the last days of the Civil War, religious revivalism swept through Confederate forces with an intensity that led one southerner to declare the armies had been "nearly converted into churches."[1] A remarkable phenomenon in the eyes of contemporary observers, these mass conversions have been largely ignored by modern scholars.[2] The attention recent historians have devoted to other manifestations of nineteenth-century Evangelicalism makes this neglect of Civil War religion seem all the more curious, for scholarly findings about the relationship between revivalism and the processes of social and cultural transformation suggest that an exploration of army Evangelicalism should yield important insights into the meaning of the South's experience in an era of profound dislocation and change.[3] . . .

Although the southern religious press reported scattered conversions of soldiers from the time fighting broke out, Confederates did not begin to identify what one Evangelical called a "genuine and mighty work of grace" until the fall of 1862. [4] At first confined to the Army of Northern Virginia, and always strongest there, significant religious awakenings spread to the Army of Tennessee and to the Trans-Mississippi forces in 1863 and 1864.[5] One observer later calculated that as many as 150,000 soldiers were "born again" during the war, but even if far fewer actually converted, thousands more participated in the revival without themselves undergoing the dramatic personal experience of grace.[6] . . .

When the timing of battle permitted, chaplains and lay preachers organized a prodigious schedule of services—sometimes as many as five or six meetings a day. During a six-week lull in the fighting in Virginia during the summer of 1864—a time when the military situation made invocation of divine help particularly appropriate—one brigade chaplain scheduled daily prayers at sunrise, an "inquiry meeting" each morning at eight, preaching at eleven, prayers for the success of the Confederate cause at four, and preaching again at night.[7]

Brigades in which the revival spirit was vigorous often constructed chapels, especially in winter quarters when the men were likely to spend several months in one place. In January 1865, for example, a Virginian reported that his brigade had erected churches every six to eight hundred yards along the lines. In summer soldiers built outdoor chapels in the woods. Split logs served as benches; a wooden platform became the altar; iron-mesh baskets held firewood to illuminate the gatherings. Even places for two thousand worshippers were often not sufficient. "The interest manifested," one soldier reported, "was so great that the seats were taken in the afternoon by such men as were not on duty. When night relieved from duty those who had been drilling, the men stood up in immense numbers around those who were seated." When observances were held indoors, the smaller number of places made competition even more intense. "Men may sometimes be seen an *hour before services* running to the house, in order that they may procure seats. They come from regiments two miles off." Men of the Army of Northern Virginia packed one brigade chapel like "herrings in a barrel."[8]

The revival spawned as well a major Confederate publishing endeavor. In spite of paper and labor shortages, nearly two hundred million pages of tracts were distributed to soldiers during the war. Several denominations also published religious newspapers for the troops, and the Confederate Bible Society, founded in 1862, hoped to supply every soldier with his own New Testament. When revivalists were unavailable, tracts served as substitutes. "These little preachers," as the *Confederate Baptist* called them, could be read over and over—in the tent, on a march, or even in the heat of battle—and were often cited as themselves responsible for conversions. The popularity of tracts and papers grew throughout the war, and Stonewall Jackson was reputed to keep a supply on hand to use as rewards for his men. One Baptist missionary thought that much of the appetite for the publications arose because "the soldiers here are *starving* for reading matter. They will read anything." But even if their appeal originated in the monotony of camp life, the tracts achieved remarkable effectiveness as an "instrument" in saving souls. Together with the exhortations of missionaries and chaplains, religious publications kept the army's revivalist fervor at a remarkably high pitch.[9]

Curiously, the evangelical fervor of the Confederate troops was not paralleled by enthusiasm at home, and, as self-righteous southerners loved to charge, "nothing like this occurred in the Yankee army."[10] Despite the widespread perception of the conflict as a holy war, southern civilians, even church members, were not experiencing God's grace in substantial numbers. The coldness of established congregations throughout the war years troubled southern clergy, who attributed their failures to the preoccupation of their flocks with the secular realities of politics and economic survival. But surely the Confederacy's soldier-converts were even more concerned with the actualities of war. For them, perhaps, the ever-present threat of death gave battle a transcendent, rather than primarily worldly, significance, or possibly the enthusiasm within the army reflected Evangelicals' concerted efforts with the troops.

The comparison with soldiers' experiences in the northern army is more problematic, for revivals did occur with some frequency among Yankee troops. Most nineteenth-century observers, as well as twentieth-century scholars, have remarked, however, upon significant differences in the scale and in the intensity of army religion North and South. Abraham Lincoln himself worried that "rebel soldiers are praying with a great deal more earnestness . . . than our own troops . . ." A number of explanations for this contrast seem plausible. The greater homogeneity of religious outlook within the overwhelmingly evangelical and Protestant southern army was certainly significant. The more profound stresses on southern soldiers, who because of shortages of manpower and materiel served for longer periods of time, with fewer furloughs, and with greater physical deprivation, undoubtedly played a role as well, for it was as the war increased in duration and intensity that revivalism began to spread.[11] . . .

The mobilization of the southern clergy to confront the wartime challenge paralleled the mobilization of Confederate military resources. Identifying both the hazards and the opportunities that war offered the church, ministers worked to devise a strategy for conquering army camps, and, not incidentally, for making religion—and its preachers— a central force in the creation of the new nation. With the successes of the church among the troops, a chaplain declared to a gathering of his colleagues, "the foundation for a wide religious power over the country is now lain. . . . We, then, here and now, stand at the fountain head of the nation's destiny. We lay our hands upon its throbbing heart. Never again shall we come so near having the destiny of a great nation in our own hands."[12]

But opportunity was not achievement. The role of the preacher in Confederate armies was neither clearly defined nor greatly respected. Chaplains had no official military rank, received poor pay and only a private's rations. To combat the "low repute" in which the post was held, ministers and many churches lobbied throughout the war for legislative improvement in the chaplain's situation, but their efforts met with only limited success. Most denominations supplemented meagre army salaries in order to encourage qualified men to serve, but many regiments and even brigades—perhaps as many as half—never had an official minister. In June 1861 Virginia Baptists decided to augment government efforts by employing colporteurs to distribute tracts and to discuss religious subjects with the men. Several Protestant denominations also sent itinerant civilian missionaries to the troops, and these preachers usually cooperated closely with official chaplains in the effort to spread the divine word to every part of the army. Denominational differences were all but forgotten in what became an ecumenical movement to bring Christ to the camp. Baptists preached without insisting on baptism as a requirement for the forgiveness of sin; Protestant soldiers flocked to services conducted by Catholic chaplains. Evangelist J. William Jones remarked that war had brought "a truce to denominational bickerings—there are no sectarian sermons preached and no sectarian tracts circulated, but all seem to work together to make men Christians . . ."[13]

In the fall of 1862 these religious labors began to bear fruit, as circumstances came to the aid of the southern churches. The timing of evangelical successes during the war offers important clues to the meaning of the conversion experience. By late 1862 many initial illusions had begun to disappear; after more than a year of "hard service," as one chaplain explained, "the romance of the soldier's life wore off, a more sober and serious mood seemed to prevail in the camps." Conscription had begun the previous spring, and by fall soldiers without the romantic zeal and optimism of the original volunteers had joined the ranks. Perhaps most significantly, however, revivals first broke out among troops retreating from Maryland after the Confederate loss at Antietam, which represented not only the first major southern defeat in the eastern theater but the bloodiest single battle day of American history as well. The experiences of slaughter and military failure surely had their impact in encouraging the "serious reflection and solemn resolve" that preceded evangelical commitment. There was great "eloquence" in the "din" and "carnage" of the field. "We are so much exposed," one soldier observed, as he explained why he had quit "light trashy novels" for the Bible, "we are likely to be called off at any moment."[14]

During the rest of the war the most dramatic outbursts of religious enthusiasm followed fierce and bloody battles—especially losses. The "great revival along the Rapidan" in the late summer and fall of 1863 swept through troops encamped for the first time since their retreat from Gettysburg. The pattern was clear to contemporary observers. As one army correspondent explained in 1863 to the *Confederate Baptist*, "There have been always among us, some pious men, but until that time nothing like a general revival or even seriousness. The regiment had just returned from the disastrous Pennsylvania expedition, and a few days before had the closest and most desperate encounter with the enemy that they had ever had. The minds of the men were fresh from scenes of danger and bloodshed and were forced thereby to contemplate eternity, and in many cases, to feel the necessity of preparation." In the West, Vicksburg and Chattanooga had a similar effect. Individual experiences of grace were closely connected to the wider search for God's favor implicit in the divine gift of military victory. As one recently converted soldier wrote in a letter home, he hoped the revival in his camp would bring "a great blessing nationally as well as Spiritually."[15]

Religion thrived, however, not just on growing personal and national insecurity, not just on individual and collective fear of the Yankees, but on anxieties related to social realities within the Confederate army itself. Chaplains, missionaries, and colporteurs had begun to make clear that rather than hinder military effectiveness, they could do a great deal to enhance it. Officers previously indifferent, if not openly hostile, to religion in the camps came to encourage piety and to provide spaces and occasions for the evangelization of their troops. "It is an interesting fact," observed Baptist preacher J. J. D. Renfroe in November 1863, "that most of our officers have undergone some change on the subject of chaplains. . . . when they first started out it made no difference with them what sort of man they had for chaplain, or whether they had any at all; but now you will not talk with an officer ten minutes about it until you will discover that he does not want a chaplain simply to 'hold service,' but he wants a man who will promote the religious good of his regiment. I have had irreligious officers to tell me that a good chaplain is worth more for the government of troops than any officer in a regiment." Colonel David Lang communicated his satisfaction that his chaplain's efforts in the fall of 1863 were "making good soldiers of some very trifling material."[16]

Despite the notable and inspiring exceptions of Robert E. Lee, Stonewall Jackson, and other pious commanders, army evangelism had its greatest impact among the common soldiers. Missionaries, chaplains, and even Jackson himself complained repeatedly of the religious indifference of the officers. The rhetoric of the Confederate revival, the themes of its sermons and its tracts, suggest one obvious explanation of why so many southern leaders encouraged piety among their troops while they remained largely aloof. "Irreligious colonels," the *Religious Herald* explained, "seek the cooperation of a good chaplain in their desire to render their regiment as efficient as possible." Religion promised significant assistance in the thorny problem of governing the frequently intractable Confederate troops.[17]

From the outset the Confederate army experienced great difficulties with discipline, for the southern soldier was most often a rural youth who had every expectation of becoming—if he was not already—an independent landholding farmer. Despite the uneven distribution of wealth and particularly of slaveownership in the prewar South, the common man ordinarily had no direct experience with political or social oppression, for he lived in a democratic political and social order where decentralization minimized perceptions of sharp stratification between planters and plain folk. The prevalent ideology of republicanism had encouraged rich and poor whites alike to cherish their "independence" and autonomy, emphasizing a sharp contrast between their status and that of enslaved blacks. But the army was to demand a hierarchy and a discipline that the prewar situation had not, even if practices such as election of officers might seem to symbolize the soldier's willing contractual surrender of control over his own life. Previously masterless men were compelled in the army to accept subordination for the first time, and many recruits complained bitterly about this change in expectations and circumstances. As one young soldier wrote home in the summer of 1861, "we are not lowd to go to the Shops without a permit and we are not lowd to miss a drill without a furlo sickness or permit, we are under tite rules you dont no how tite they are I wish I coul see you and then I could tell you what I thought of campt life it is very tite rules and confinen."[18]

Religion promised considerable assistance in easing this difficult transition. Élie Halévy, E. P. Thompson, and others have described the role of Methodism in the transformation of English workers into an industrial proletariat, and more recently Anthony F. C. Wallace has explored the influence of evangelical Protestantism upon laborers in nineteenth-century Pennsylvania textile mills. In the South of the 1860s the role of religion was somewhat different, for young rural Confederates were going to war, not to the factories. But the requirements of industrialized work and industrialized warfare are alike in important ways—in their demand for new levels of discipline, regularity, and subordination. Daniel T. Rodgers has described a process of "labor commitment— . . . by which new industrial employees adjusted deeply set rural loyalties and work habits to the disrupting demands of factory labor." In their identity shift from farmers to soldiers, young southerners needed to make analogous changes in internal values and expectations. A soldier "must be trained," insisted the *Religious Herald*, "and willing to submit to thorough training. . . . There is a *moral* requirement as important as the material one—an inward man as indispensable as the outward one. . . ." Religious conversion and commitment could serve as the vehicle accelerating and facilitating this necessary personal transformation. Both southern military and religious leaders recognized that Evangelicalism could contribute to internalizing discipline and enhancing the efficiency of the Confederate soldier; the church could help to mold disorganized recruits into an effective fighting force. "A spirit of subordination and a faithful discharge of duty," the *Biblical Recorder* summarized, "are [as] essential to the good soldier" as they are to the good Christian.[19]

The term "efficiency" appeared again and again in evangelical rhetoric. The Christian soldier would be an efficient soldier because he would not be afraid to die; he would be obedient and well disciplined because he would understand the divine origin of earthly duty. One army chaplain offered a striking illustration of the *"military power of religion.* In a brigade of five regiments, where there has recently been a glorious revival, two of the regiments, which had not shared in the revival, broke, while the three which had been thus blessed stood firm. . . ." A missionary of the Army of Tennessee made an even more dramatic claim. "Preaching," he asserted, had "corrected" one of "the greatest evils of our army, in a military point of view . . . —that of straggling." The servant of God, he explained, learned that he must execute all earthly as well as all spiritual obligations "conscientiously," and that meant keeping up with your regiment even if you were ill or had no shoes. A colonel of the South Carolina Volunteers emphasized the point when he congratulated a colporteur on the usefulness of his tracts, which he found "of incalculable service in encouraging the soldier to a continuation of his hard duties, and making him feel contented with his lot."[20] The Reverend R. N. Sledd no doubt won similar approval from Confederate military leaders when he insisted to a congregation of common soldiers about to depart for war that "it is . . . not only wise, but necessary to your efficiency, that for the time you surrender your will to that of your officers, . . . This lesson of submission to control is a difficult one for many to learn; but until you have completely mastered it, . . . you are not prepared to behave yourself the most valiantly and the most efficiently in the field of conflict." Significantly, religious leaders stressed the profitable management of time as well as the adoption of regular personal habits, and often chose the bourgeois language of commerce and the marketplace to emphasize the productive uses of religion. A correspondent to the *Religious Herald* suggested in 1863 that chaplains on the field make themselves easily identifiable by wearing badges emblazoned with the epigraph, "Godliness is profitable unto all." Another article reported an imaginary dialogue between an officer and a recently converted private who assured his superior, " 'I used to neglect your business; now I perform it diligently'."[21]

But the virtues religion inculcated did not just appear on the battlefield. Evangelicalism also sought to ease the conflict over appropriate values and behavior that was disturbing many Confederate camps. Soldiers who had lived in isolated circumstances in the overwhelmingly rural South had found little necessity to adjust to the lifestyles of other groups. Many complaints in their wartime diaries and letters sound very much like the earlier reactions of genteel Yankees first confronting the squalid realities of life among the lowly in the urban North. Confederate army camps played a role analogous to that of northern cities in juxtaposing classes and cultures in what was to many a new and alarming propinquity. "One of my greatest annoyances," a Mississippian wrote to his wife, "is my proximity to one tent of the Co[mpany], next [to] me . . . in which are 9 or 10 [of] the most vile, obscene blackguards that could be raked up this side [of] the bad place, outside of a jail or penitentiary. From early morn to dewey eve there is one uninterrupted flow of the dirtiest talk I ever heard in my life. . . . those fellows have 'had no raising'."[22]

In the army the evangelical cause took on a new urgency because of the "great trial" imposed on numbers of refined southerners who found themselves required to tent next to "such abounding wickedness" as was represented by some of their comrades. Separated before the war by the decentralized, overwhelmingly rural nature of southern life, privileged and less privileged whites came to know each other in new and unsettling ways within the Confederate camps. And with this knowledge came not the rapprochement of different social groups so often hailed as the outcome of the English experience in the trenches of World War I. Instead, in a South that had throughout the antebellum period stressed the republican equality of all white men, this wartime experience brought an emerging awareness of class. "Cannot something be done to lessen the unnatural distance that is gradually and rapidly creeping in between officers and men?" one tract demanded. *The Soldier's Paper* worried in similar terms, "Let not our private soldiers feel that they have ceased to be men because they are soldiers. Let them not imagine that they are degraded to mere machines because they are fighting in the ranks . . . let them feel that they still have friends in their officers." A correspondent in the *Confederate Baptist* in 1863 was more explicit still in a discussion of the plight of the common fighting man oppressed by his superiors. "CLASSES—," he reflected. "We were struck with a remark made to us by a private in the army. He said, 'before the war, there were only white men and negroes among us; now there are white men, negroes and soldiers'." It could not but have been chillingly symbolic for the troops marched out in June 1862 to witness the punishment of army deserters with thirty-nine lashes and branding on the cheek—a characteristic form of correction for runaway slaves throughout the antebellum period. White men previously above corporal punishment seemed as soldiers to occupy a new status in which even the most cherished distinctions between freeman and black slave were fast disappearing. As the *Confederate Baptist* protested in 1863, "That any officer of the Confederate army should inflict upon a fellow soldier, a punishment which is peculiar to slaves, is enough to make us blush for our country. Is the poor man a negro, and is he fighting only for the privilege of having a different master?"[23]

The social significance of the revival impulse is perhaps most strikingly revealed to a twentieth-century observer by the unexpected centrality and importance of the evangelical campaign against profanity, which one chaplain hailed as "*the* national sin." Although one response to such a curious claim might be admiration for the level of virtue such a minor indictment implies, evangelical preoccupation with swearing deserves fuller explanation. By the mid-nineteenth century public profanity was becoming largely a class sin, found most often, as one tract explained, among the "common" and the "ill bred." In an 1860 analysis of social classes in the South, for example, native Alabamian Daniel R. Hundley defined "low, vulgar and obscene" speech as characteristic of one particular element of the region's lower orders.[24] But what might now be regarded as the seemingly harmless "profanity of the privates" attracted enormous attention from Evangelicals. Swearing, they declared repeatedly, was dangerous because it was a "useless sin." Unlike gluttony, venality, or lust, it had no rational objective. The swearer risked damnation for no purpose. "You commit the utter folly of . . . ruining your souls, for nothing at all!" To swear was "to incur guilt, without delight." In an age and within a religious movement increasingly dedicated to the advancement of utilitarian values, swearing represented an "*irrational*," "unprofitable," inefficient vice; it simply did not "pay." In its purposeless affront to piety it seemed to carry with it a dangerous "spirit of rebellion against conscience, society and God" Swearing was "disinterested sin—sin committed only from the love of sin." It was a direct and overt attack on religion and social order rather than a sin committed out of moral weakness in the face of irresistible temptation. A quintessential embodiment of loss of control and rejection of deference, profanity became a symbolic as much as a substantive enemy of the army revivals.[25] . . .

Yet such a view of the role of Confederate religion—as manipulative and hegemonic—is partial and one-dimensional. Recent scholarly work has justly insisted that monolithic emphasis on the aspects of social control within evangelicalism must not distort its larger meaning or impugn the authenticity of revivalists' piety and sacred commitment by casting them simply as conspirators seeking to enhance their own social power. Most advocates of the order and discipline central to the revivalistic impulse sincerely believed that their goals were above all to fulfill God's design and only secondarily to serve the needs of men. The perceptions of the common Confederate soldiers who were the targets of army revivalists' efforts is less clear. Certainly the impact of the evangelical message among the troops was profound, as the large number of conversions attests. And many of these converts readily accepted the notion of a regenerate life as one of discipline and self-control, for soldiers frequently wrote home that revivals had made it impossible to find a cardplayer or a profane swearer in the regiment. It seems likely, however, that the cynicism of some reductionist twentieth-century social control historians may have been shared by at least some nineteenth-century soldiers. The suspicion and hostility toward evangelical hegemony expressed by the plain folk who participated in the antimission movement in the prewar South had not, in all probability, entirely disappeared, even though there is scant surviving evidence of its existence in the Confederate army. The revivals could not in any case have completely succeeded in transforming southern soldiers into a tightly disciplined fighting force, for complaints about insubordination continued throughout the war and even increased as the desertion rate rose dramatically in 1864 and 1865.[26]

Common soldiers may well have ignored much of the rhetoric of control in tracts and sermons to appropriate from the evangelical message truths that they found more meaningful. The notion of a disciplined and deferential Christian soldier undoubtedly had a greater appeal to religious and military leaders than to the common fighting man instructed that it was his "business..to die." Yet Evangelicalism met important needs for the soldiers themselves as well as for their military masters. Like religion among black slaves or working-class Methodists, army evangelism did what E. P. Thompson has described as a "double service," appealing in different ways both to the powerful and to the powerless. In the Old South the Christianity preached by masters to their bondsmen was quite different from that embraced by the slaves.[27]

Similarly, common Confederate soldiers used religion in their own ways, focusing on the promise of salvation from death as well as upon the reality of an evangelical community that recreated some of the ideals of a lost prewar world. The experience of conversion served as the basis for a shared equality of believers and an Arminian notion of ultimate self-determination that in profound ways replicated the antebellum republican order that military hierarchy and command had obliterated. There was, as the *Religious Herald* observed in 1863, a sense of real "homogeneity and fellow-feeling" within the brotherhood of believers.[28] The comradeship of the regenerate encouraged as well the group solidarity that modern military analysts have identified as critical to the maintenance of morale. Converts formed Christian Associations within their brigades and regiments to assume communal responsibility for evangelical discipline, and, in the words of the constitution of one such organization, "to throw as many strengthening influences around the weak . . . as it is possible to do. . . ." The associations ran Bible and reading classes, established camp libraries of tracts and religious newspapers, but, perhaps most significantly, confronted the fear of death—and of dying abandoned and alone—that haunted so many soldiers. The believers of the Seventh Virginia Infantry covenanted, for example, to "care specially for each other in all bodily or mental suffering, to show each other respect in case of death. . . ." In practice this usually meant that association members would try to identify comrades disabled on the field of battle in order to provide them either with medical care or with Christian burial.[29]

On a more individual level, evangelical religion provided psychological reassurance to southern soldiers struggling with the daily threat of personal annihilation. In its Christian promise of salvation and eternal life, conversion offered a special sort of consolation to the embattled Confederate. In striking ways accounts of camp conversions parallel descriptions of what in World Wars I and II was first known as "shell shock," then as "combat exhaustion" or "combat stress." Shaking, loss of speech, paralysis of limbs, uncontrolled weeping, and severe emotional outbursts often appeared among twentieth-century soldiers when they reached safety after military action. Similar behavior characterized many Confederate converts who found Christ in the emotion-filled revival meetings held in the intervals between Civil War battles. The fiercest encounters brought the largest harvests of souls, just as the most desperate fighting of World Wars I and II yielded the highest incidence of combat stress. These similarities in nineteenth- and twentieth-century soldiers' responses suggest that analogous psychological processes might well have been involved.[30] . . .

The language of post-Freudian self-scrutiny used by World War I participants was not available to Civil War soldiers. But their silences are eloquent. Their speechlessness was part of a process of numbing, of the denial that is a widespread human response to stress. "We hurry," one soldier wrote, "through the dreadful task apparently unconscious of its demoralizing influences and destructive effects." The war, another confirmed, "is calculated to harden the softest heart." The majority came to act as "unconcerned as if it were hogs dying around them." A correspondent writing to the *Religious Herald* in 1862 understood well, however, "the true fountain" of this apparent indifference. Soldiers' unconcern, he explained, was "the result of an effort to *banish*, not to *master*, the fear of death. . . . the expedient of the ostrich [who acts]. . . . as though refusing to look on a peril were to escape from it."[31]

Modern-day analysts of combat stress point out, however, that such denial has its limits, that numbness and indifference can only be retained for so long. Eventually extreme stress results in the appearance of symptoms in virtually everyone. Often denial begins to be interrupted by what psychiatrists call "intrusions," nightmares or irrepressible and unwelcome daytime visions of stress-producing events. One Confederate soldier who had previously told his wife that he had found the battle of Shiloh indescribable wrote again several weeks later, "I've had great and exciting times at night with my dreams since the battle; some of them are tragedies and frighten me more than ever the fight did when I was awake. . . ." Another soldier was obviously more profoundly affected, for, as a friend described him, he began reliving battles in his everyday life. "He became more and more alarmed, and, at last, became so powerfully excited—to use his own words—he felt as if some one was after him with a bayonet, and soon found himself almost in a run, as he moved backwards and forwards in his beat."[32]

Many psychiatrists believe that reliving stress-producing experiences in this way serves to work through and eventually to resolve material repressed in the denial phase. The appearance of intrusions, therefore, signals the emergence of overt conflict that, even though profoundly disruptive, may ultimately enable an individual to cope with and to transcend a traumatic experience. Revivals often explicitly encouraged such intrusions and exacerbated internal tension in the effort to induce the religious conversion that would dissolve all stress in the promise of divine salvation. In order to shake soldiers' personal defenses, preachers and tracts insisted, "Death stares you in the face. The next battle may be your last." The soldier, one revivalist explained, had to be "forced to feel how frail and uncertain is life." The crisis was unavoidable; numbness and denial could be no real or lasting protection. In "the GREAT CONSCRIPTION there is no discharge . . . Are you ready to take your place with them who will have the victory? . . . Or will your place be in that vast division of death's army, which shall assemble only to be defeated, accursed and punished forever?"[33]

Significantly, the rhetoric of camp sermons was often designed to encourage a metaphorical reliving of battlefield experiences by casting religion as the equivalent of military conflict. Exhorters focused overwhelmingly on the issue of salvation and its frightening alternative, thus calling forth the feelings associated with the life-and-death struggle that soldiers actually confronted each day. Preachers manipulated already existing fear, stressing the nearness of death and its terrors for the unconverted. But at the same time that revivalists exacerbated the tension and helplessness soldiers felt in the face of battle, they emphasized that the men did retain a dimension of choice; even amidst the barrage of bullets, they could decide for God. As one tract demanded of those who had not yet exercised this option, *Why Will You Die?* Death, its author implied, was a matter of personal will and could be consciously rejected in favor of eternal life. Just as the common soldier concerned about social issues of mastery and subordination within army life could have the symbolic comfort of electing his own captain, so he might psychologically escape from his sense of victimization by choosing Christ as the "Captain of [his] . . . salvation." He might transcend the ultimate and profound loss of control over his destiny that battle involved by making an existential commitment, by enlisting as a Christian soldier under the "banner of the Cross." The decision for Christ restored the illusion of free will. And with the return of a sense of control often comes, as contemporary psychiatrists have observed, the ability once again to cope.[34]

Ultimately, revivalists insisted, this was not a war of North against South, but one of goodness versus evil, of God against Satan. Evangelical rhetoric invited soldiers to relive the emotions of the battlefield, to express the resulting tensions, then to resolve them in the promise of eternal life—the only real assurance of safety from war and from the more general inevitability of death.[35]

This process of conversion is in its general outlines remarkably similar to influential twentieth-century psychiatric notions of appropriate therapy for combat exhaustion or other traumatic stress. During World War II American military physicians in North Africa used drugs and hypnosis, as Civil War revivalists used their tracts and sermons, to revive "partially or completely forgotten traumatic battle episodes." As a result of this effort "repressed battle experience was restored to consciousness, thus losing most of its previous potential to evoke anxiety." Patients were encouraged to explore emotions that had been denied and to release unmanageable anxiety through abreaction.[36]

Civil War conversions and twentieth-century treatments for combat stress should not, of course, be seen as identical or interchangeable processes. The pious would object to such a rationalization of belief, while psychologists would regard such an equation as an undue mystification of the scientific. Undoubtedly they would point as well to the important differences in the populations under study and to their contrasting contexts and circumstances. Yet the similarities in soldiers' responses in the two eras are difficult to ignore, especially in the way they point to the profound dislocation experienced by so many Civil War soldiers. Like combatants in more recent wars, Confederate soldiers found themselves personally unprepared to cope with the ways that battle threatened both their existence and their identity. Adjustment and survival required personal transformation. The cult of the Lost Cause in the postwar years and the numerous continuities between Old South and New should not lull us into forgetting that in significant ways the Civil War created new men. . . .

In the crucible of war, the consensus that had characterized antebellum white society was to break down. Demands for mobilization of men and resources created troubling wartime divisions over the operation of conscription and impressment laws and over the distribution of newly scarce necessities of life. And when economic deprivation emerged as an unfamiliar reality for white southerners, social divisions that had been only intermittently visible in the prewar years intensified until they threatened the Confederacy's very survival. Individualistic southern yeomen found it difficult to adjust to the hierarchy required by war and to what many viewed as the disproportionate sacrifices expected of them.

These growing conflicts appeared within the context of army religion as differences of personal and cultural values over issues such as temperance, cleanliness, profanity, and self-discipline. But ultimately the frictions became much more overt, as they were expressed first in wartime desertions and disloyalties and later in the class-based political activity of the postbellum years.[37]

Yet Evangelicalism remained central within this strife even after Appomattox. The postwar era was a time of dramatic growth for southern churches, for the revival spirit seemed to follow soldiers home from the camps. On the one hand, Evangelicalism became, as Charles Reagan Wilson has argued, the language of defense for the old order and the Lost Cause. Yet at the same time the New South vision of modernity and industrial progress also assumed an evangelical idiom. By the 1890s the church seemed so closely allied with the business class that North Carolina Populists directly attacked religious discipline as an instrument of the class hegemony that they perceived to have grown so oppressive in the years since the close of the war. But these Populists did not reject Evangelicalism entirely. Instead, like common soldiers three decades before, they too had their uses for revivalism and an alternative vision of its significance, not so much as a form of discipline but as a means of empowerment.[38] The broader significance of army religion may thus be the way in which it points to the importance of the experience of war itself in establishing a framework for the social and political conflicts of a New South. In the Confederate army, as in the South of the postwar years, the protean nature of the evangelical message permitted its adherents to appropriate it to satisfy very different purposes and needs. Revivalism served at once as an idiom of social strife and a context for social unity in an age of unsettling transition; it became a vehicle both for expression and resolution of conflict about fundamental transformations in the southern social order.

The identity crisis of the Confederate soldier adjusting to distressing new patterns of life and labor was but a microcosm of the wartime crisis of a South in the throes of change. Military service inaugurated for many southerners a new era characterized by a loss of autonomy and self-determination that even peace would not restore. In the postwar years a southerner was far more likely to be a tenant and far less likely to be economically self-sufficient than he had been in the antebellum period. He might even follow his experience of military wage labor with that of factory employment, as the cotton mill campaign drew thousands of white southerners into industry.[39]

But perhaps the most profound transformation for many Confederate soldiers was deeply personal. In the past decade we have been made sharply aware of the lingering effects of another lost war upon its veterans years after their return to civilian life. Irrational outbursts of violence and debilitating depression are but two characteristic symptoms of what psychiatrists have come to see as a definable "post-Vietnam" syndrome. Southerners deeply scarred by their experiences of horror in the world's first total war may have been affected in similar ways. Perhaps part of the explanation for the widespread violence of the postwar South should be psychological; Klan activity, whitecapping, and lynching may have been a legacy of soldiers' wartime stresses as well as a political response to new and displeasing social realities.[40]

In the clues that it offers to the profound impact of battle and to the social origins of a new South, revivalism is central to the Confederate experience. The Civil War challenged both the South and her fighting men to be "born again."

NOTES

From Drew Gilpin Faust, "Christian Soldiers: The Meaning of Revivalism in the Confederate Army," *Journal of Southern History* 53, no. 1 (February 1987): 63–90. Reprinted by permission.

1. "Rev. A. E. Dickinson's Annual Report to the General Association of Va.,"*Confederate Baptist*, June 24, 1863. I would like to thank the Stanford Humanities Center, the several audiences who made helpful comments on preliminary versions of this paper, and especially Lizabeth Cohen, Steven Hahn, Randall Miller, Reid Mitchell, Charles Rosenberg, and Morton Sosna for their suggestions and criticism.

2. For example, James M. McPherson's excellent recent overview of the war does not mention the revivals. See *Ordeal by Fire: The Civil War and Reconstruction* (New York, 1982). The best discussion of the revivals is still Bell Irvin Wiley, "Consolations of the Spirit," Chap. 10 in *The Life of Johnny Reb: The Common Soldier of the Confederacy* (1943; rpt. ed., Baton Rouge, 1978), but in my view Wiley underestimates their significance. See also Gorrell Clinton Prim, Jr., "Born Again in the Trenches: Revivalism in the Confederate Army" (unpublished Ph.D. dissertation, Florida State University, 1982), for a recent but largely

unanalytical account. Equally unanalytical are G. Clinton Prim, Jr., "Revivals in the Armies of Mississippi During the Civil War," *Journal of Mississippi History*, XLIV (August 1982), 227–34; Herman Norton, "Revivalism in the Confederate Armies," *Civil War History*, VI (December 1960), 410–24; John Shepard, Jr., "Religion in the Army of Northern Virginia," *North Carolina Historical Review*, XXV (July 1948), 341–76; Sidney J. Romero, *Religion in the Rebel Ranks* (Lanham, Md., New York, and London, 1983); and Benjamin Rice Lacy, Jr., *Revivals in the Midst of the Years* (Richmond, 1943). Two accounts published shortly after the war by participants are useful. See J. Wm. Jones, *Christ in the Camp: or Religion in Lee's Army* (Richmond, 1887); and William W. Bennett, *A Narrative of the Great Revival in the Southern Armies . . .* (Philadelphia, 1877). A work that appeared after the completion of this essay deals in some detail with the role of religion during the war, although it does not devote particular attention to its significance in the Confederate army. See Richard E. Beringer, Herman Hattaway, Archer Jones, and William N. Still, Jr., *Why the South Lost the Civil War* (Athens, Ga., and London, 1986). For my reservations about their viewpoint see Drew Gilpin Faust, "Reassessing the Lost Cause of the South," *Books/Leisure, Philadelphia Inquirer*, June 29, 1986, pp. 1, 8–9.

3. For a useful overview of this literature see Leonard I. Sweet, "The Evangelical Tradition in America," in Leonard I. Sweet, ed., *The Evangelical Tradition in America* (Macon, Ga., 1984), 1–86.

4. Jones, *Christ in the Camp*, 336 (quotation). For examples of early reports of conversions see *Religious Herald*, August 29, 1861, September 12, 1861, October 17, 1861, April 17, 1862, June 5, 1862, August 21, 1862.

5. See Jones, *Christ in the Camp*, Appendix II, 535–624; Lacy, *Revivals in the Midst of the Years*, 119; James Cooper Nisbet, *Four Years on the Firing Line*, ed. by Bell Irvin Wiley (1914; rpt. ed., Jackson, Tenn., 1963), 175; "Great Trans-Mississippi Revival," *Southern Christian Advocate*, August 25, 1864; and *Confederate Baptist*, June 1, 1864.

6. Jones, *Christ in the Camp*, 390. For an assessment of different estimates of numbers of converts see Herman Norton, *Rebel Religion: The Story of Confederate Chaplains* (St. Louis, 1961), 64.

7. Jones, *Christ in the Camp*, 504. See also the preaching schedule of John DeWitt McCollough, March through May, 1862, Journal, John DeWitt McCollough Papers (South Caroliniana Library, University of South Carolina, Columbia).

8. *Christian Observer*, January 26, 1865; John H. Worsham, *One of Jackson's Foot Cavalry . . .*, ed. by James I. Robertson, Jr. (1912; rpt. ed., Jackson, Tenn., 1964), 113–14 (first quotation); *Religious Herald*, February 11, 1864 (second quotation), October 10, 1861; R. S. Webb to his mother, April 16, 1864, Webb Family Papers (Southern Historical Collection, University of North Carolina, Chapel Hill; repository hereinafter cited as SHC); *Central Presbyte-*

rian, April 2, 1863 (third quotation). See also Samuel P. Lockhart to Ellen Lockhart, March 14, 1864, Hugh Conway Browning Papers. (William R. Perkins Library, Duke University, Durham, N.C.; repository hereinafter cited as Duke),

9. *Confederate Baptist*, May 16, 1863 (first quotation); *Religious Herald*, May 8, 1862, October 10, 1861 (second quotation); James W. Silver, ed., *A Life for the Confederacy, as Recorded in the Pocket Diaries of Pvt. Robert A. Moore* . . . (Jackson, Tenn., 1959), 95. On tracts see Romero, *Religion in the Rebel Ranks*, 163; James W. Silver, *Confederate Morale and Church Propaganda* (Tuscaloosa, Ala., 1957); and Wiley, *The Life of Johnny Reb*, 177. Much of the research for this paper was made possible by the availability on microfilm of almost all surviving Confederate tracts and sermons as well as most other extant printed Confederate material. See *Confederate Imprints* (New Haven, 1974).

10. *Religious Herald*, April 8, 1864 (quotation). On the lack of religious fervor on the home front see "Revivals at Home," *Southern Christian Advocate*, September 8, 1864; *Biblical Recorder*, June 17, 1863; *Army and Navy Messenger*, March 1, 1864; William Flinn to William Letcher Mitchell, April 24, 1863, William Letcher Mitchell Papers (SHC).

11. John G. Nicolay and John Hay, eds., *Complete Works of Abraham Lincoln* (12 vols.; New York, 1905), VIII, 29–30 (quotation). On comparison with religion in the northern armies see Bell Irvin Wiley, *The Life of Billy Yank: The Common Soldier of the Union* (New York and Indianapolis, 1952); William Warren Sweet, *Methodism in American History* (New York, Cincinnati, and Chicago, 1933), 287.

12. B. W. McDonnald, *Address to Chaplains and Missionaries* (Petersburg, Va., 1863), 8 (first part of quotation), 13 (second part of quotation).

13. Jones, *Christ in the Camp*, 360, 365 (quotation); *Southern Presbyterian*, June 25, 1863; *Southern Churchman*, December 18, 1863; *Biblical Recorder*, December 9, 1863, February 5, 1862; T. Conn Bryan, ed., "Letters of Two Confederate Officers: William Thomas Conn and Charles Augustus Conn," *Georgia Historical Quarterly*, XLVI (June 1962), 177; Stephen Cocke to Charles T. Quintard, April 25, 1863, and William Bennett to Charles T. Quintard, March 25, 1863, Charles Todd Quintard Papers (Duke); "The Office of Evangelist," *Central Presbyterian*, April 3, 1862; Joseph T. Durkin, ed., *Confederate Chaplain: A War Journal of Rev. James B. Sheeran, . . . 14th Louisiana, C.S.A.* (Milwaukee, 1960), 57; *Confederate Baptist*, May 20, 1863. Episcopalians and Presbyterians expressed some doubts about evangelical fervor but were for the most part won over by the revivals' power and effectiveness. See William S. Lacy to Bessie L. Dewey, September 23, 1863, Drury Lacy Papers (SHC); and Abner Crump Hopkins Diary, March 16, 1863, Abner Crump Hopkins Papers (Virginia Historical Society, Richmond). As one Episcopal paper rationalized, "anything is better than the quietness of moral death. . . ." *Southern Churchman*,

June 5, 1863. Some members of the more literalistic denominations indicated concern about the doctrinal compromises implicit in cooperation. See for example *Biblical Recorder*, July 30, 1862, December 9, 1863, January 16, 1864, and October 19, 1864. On hostility to chaplains see *Confederate Baptist*, November 4, 1863; and R. S. Webb to his mother, February 13, 1864, Webb Family Papers. On lobbying for improved status see for example *Southern Christian Advocate*, February 19, 1863; and *Central Presbyterian*, January 11, 1862. On chaplains generally see W. Harrison Daniel, "An Aspect of Church and State Relations in the Confederacy: Southern Protestantism and the Office of Army Chaplain," *North Carolina Historical Review*, XXXVI (January 1959), 47–71; Frank L. Hieronymus, "For Now and Forever: The Chaplains of the Confederate States Army" (unpublished Ph.D. dissertation, University of California, Los Angeles, 1964); Bell Irvin Wiley, " 'Holy Joes' of the Sixties: A Study of Civil War Chaplains," *Huntington Library Quarterly*, XVI (May 1953), 287–304; Sidney J. Romero, "The Confederate Chaplain," *Civil War History*, I (June 1955), 127–40; Romero, *Religion in the Rebel Ranks*; James W. Silver, "The Confederate Preacher Goes to War," *North Carolina Historical Review*, XXXIII (October 1956), 499–509; Norton, *Rebel Religion*; Charles Frank Pitts, *Chaplains in Gray: The Confederate Chaplains' Story* (Nashville, 1957); Arthur Howard Noll, *Doctor Quintard: Chaplain C.S.A. and Second Bishop of Tennessee* (Sewanee, Tenn., 1905); Joseph Cross, *Camp and Field: Papers from the Portfolio of an Army Chaplain* (Macon, Ga., 1864); Donald E. Everett, ed., *Chaplain Davis and Hood's Texas Brigade . . .* (1863; rpt. ed., San Antonio, 1962); Randolph H. McKim, *A Soldier's Recollections: Leaves from the Diary of a Young Confederate . . .* (New York, 1921); A. D. Betts, *Experiences of a Confederate Chaplain, 1861–1864*, ed. by W. A. Betts (n.p., n.d.); Durkin, ed., *Confederate Chaplain*; Jones, *Christ in the Camp*; and Bennett, *A Narrative of the Great Revival*.

14. Bennett, *A Narrative of the Great Revival*, 246 (first quotation); Jones, *Christ in the Camp*, 272 (second quotation); *Religious Herald*, August 21, 1862 (third quotation); *Central Presbyterian*, November 6, 1862; *Religious Herald*, October 23, 1862, November 27, 1862; *Biblical Recorder*, September 2, 1863; *Camp Nineveh* (Petersburg, Va., [186–]); Everett, ed., *Chaplain Davis*, 107; Addams to Dear Brother, January 5, 1863, William Miller McAllister Papers (Duke) (fourth quotation). On conversions after the Wilderness see *Southern Christian Advocate*, July 28, 1864. On Antietam see Stephen W. Sears, *Landscape Turned Red: The Battle of Antietam* (New Haven and New York, 1983). Wiley overlooks these 1862 outbursts but emphasizes the significance of Gettysburg in the 1863 revivals. Wiley, *The Life of Johnny Reb*, Chap. 10.

15. *Confederate Baptist*, April 6, 1864 (first quotation); Mat[hew]. A[ndrew]. Dunn to Nora, August 22, 1864, in Weymouth T. Jordan, ed., "Mathew Andrew Dunn Letters," *Journal of Mississippi History*, I (April 1939),

110–26 (second quotation on p. 125); Jones, *Christ in the Camp*, 245; *Religious Herald*, September 3, 1863.

16. *Confederate Baptist*, November 4, 1863 (first quotation). See also *Religious Herald*, November 5, 1863, August 21, 1862; and David Lang to Cousin Annie, September 13, 1863, in Bertram H. Groene, ed., "Civil War Letters of Colonel David Lang," *Florida Historical Quarterly*, LIV (January 1976), 359 (second quotation). Cromwell's army was frequently cited as evidence of the military effectiveness of religion; see *Religious Herald*, July 31, 1862. Note the observation of one officer who felt that a town regiment was always twice as efficient as one from the country; cited in Horace H. Cunningham, *Field Medical Services at the Battle of Manassas (Bull Run)* (Athens, Ga., 1968), 25.

17. Jones, *Christ in the Camp*, 501, 465–66; Durkin, ed., *Confederate Chaplain*, 50–51; *Confederate Baptist*, May 16, 1863; *Religious Herald*, August 21, 1862 (quotation). On religion and officers see also Thomas Hart Law, July 20, 1863, Journal, Thomas Hart Law Papers (South Caroliniana Library); and William S. Lacy to Bessie L. Dewey, September 23, 1863, Lacy Papers. Other religious generals included Leonidas L. Polk, John B. Gordon, Daniel H. Hill, Ambrose P. Hill, John B. Hood, and Joseph E. Johnston.

18. James S. Beavers to Isham Sims Upchurch, July 2, 1861, Isham Sims Upchurch Papers (Duke) (quotation). On discipline see David Donald, "Died of Democracy," in David Donald, ed., *Why the North Won the Civil War* (Baton Rouge, 1960), 77–90; Everett, ed., *Chaplain Davis*, 150–51; also Jefferson Davis's call for greater discipline, quoted in the *Confederate Baptist*, November 12, 1862; and "Address of General D[aniel]. H[arvey]. Hill, Reunion of the Virginia Division Army of Northern Virginia Association," *Southern Historical Society Papers*, XIII (January-December 1885), 261. The Confederate army contained a significantly greater proportion of previously masterless men than did the northern army. By 1870, when the first complete occupational census was taken, 60 to 70 percent of the northern labor force worked under masters. Agricultural areas of the North, and the white South generally, averaged well below this. Daniel T. Rodgers, *The Work Ethic in Industrial America, 1850–1920* (Chicago and London, 1978), 37. See also David Montgomery, *Beyond Equality: Labor and the Radical Republicans, 1862–1872* (New York, 1967), 30; and Eric Foner, *Free Soil, Free Labor, Free Men: The Ideology of the Republican Party Before the Civil War* (New York, 1970), 32. Both the less detailed 1860 census (which lacks complete occupational data) and data collected by Bell Wiley indicate marked prewar differentials as well. Also note that 20 percent of the Confederate army was made up of draftees and substitutes as compared with 8 percent of the Union forces; see McPherson, *Ordeal By Fire*, 359, 182. On the devotion of the southern common people to their personal independence see J. Mills Thornton III, *Politics and Power in a Slave Society: Alabama, 1800–1860* (Baton Rouge and London, 1978); and Steven Hahn, *The Roots of Southern Populism: Yeo-*

man Farmers and the Transformation of the Georgia Upcountry, 1850–1890 (New York and Oxford, 1983).

19. E. P. Thompson, *The Making of the English Working Class* (New York, 1963); Thompson, "Time, Work-Discipline, and Industrial Capitalism," *Past & Present*, XXXVIII (December 1967), 56–97; Anthony F. C. Wallace, *Rockdale: The Growth of an American Village in the Early Industrial Revolution . . .* (New York, 1978); Élie Halévy, *Histoire du peuple anglais au XIXe siecle* (Paris, 1913). Daniel T. Rodgers, "Tradition, Modernity, and the American Industrial Worker: Reflections and Critique," *Journal of Interdisciplinary History*, VII (Spring 1977), 656 (first quotation); Herbert G. Gutman, *Work, Culture, and Society in Industrializing America: Essays in American Working-Class and Social History* (New York, 1976); Bruce Tucker, "Class and Culture in Recent Anglo-American Religious Historiography: A Review Essay," *Labour/Le Travailleur*, VI (Autumn 1980), 159–69; *Religious Herald*, July 31, 1862 (second quotation); *Biblical Recorder*, July 10, 1861 (third quotation). See also *Central Presbyterian*, February 6, 1862; *Christian Observer*, June 30, 1864; *Army and Navy Messenger*, May 1, 1863. On the weakness of the work ethic in the South see C. Vann Woodward, "The Southern Ethic in a Puritan World," Chap. 1, in *American Counterpoint: Slavery and Racism in the North-South Dialogue* (Boston and Toronto, 1971), especially 29 and 42. As E. P. Thompson has noted the relevance of timepieces to industrial work, David Landes has similarly related their development and dissemination to industrialized warfare. David S. Landes, *Revolution in Time: Clocks and the Making of the Modern World* (Cambridge, Mass., and London, 1983).

20. W. H. Christian, *The Importance of a Soldier Becoming a Christian* (Richmond, [186–]), 3; Jones, *Christ in the Camp*, 380–81 (first quotation); *North Carolina Presbyterian*, August 4, 1862; *Confederate Baptist*, July 6, 1864 (second quotation), May 16, 1863 (third quotation). On the religious cure for desertion see John Paris, *A Sermon: Preached Before Brig.-Gen. Hoke's Brigade, . . . Upon the Death of Twenty-Two Men . . . Executed in the Presence of the Brigade for the Crime of Desertion* (Greensborough, N. C., 1864), 12. On the severe military problem presented by persistent straggling see *The War of the Rebellion: A Compilation of the Official Records of the Union and Confederate Armies* (70 vols. in 128; Washington, 1880–1901), Ser. I, Vol. XIX, Pt. 1, 1026; and Worsham, *One of Jackson's Foot Cavalry*, 151.

21. R. N. Sledd, *A Sermon; Delivered in the Market Street M. E. Church, Petersburg, Va., Before the Confederate Cadets, on the Occasion of Their Departure for the Seat of War, Sunday, Sept. 22d, 1861* (Petersburg, 1861), 14 (first quotation); *Religious Herald*, April 23, 1863 (second quotation), June 11, 1863 (third quotation).

22. T. J. Koger, June 22, 1862, quoted in John K. Bettersworth, ed., *Mississippi in the Confederacy: As They Saw It* (Baton Rouge, 1961), 346. See also the

volunteer cavalry colonel who early in the war resigned because of "the uncontrollable wickedness of soldiers in camp." John N. Waddel, *Memorials of Academic Life: Being an Historical Sketch of the Waddel Family* . . . (Richmond, 1891), 398; A. Curtis to Matthias Murray Marshall, December 20, 1862, Matthias Murray Marshall Papers (Duke); Samuel P. Lockhart to Emeline Lockhart, May 11, 1862, July 27, 1862, Browning Papers; Unidentified to Dear Willie on back of Dr. G. McAllister to Dear Clara, October 26, 1861, McAllister Papers.

   23. *Religious Herald*, quoted in E. M. Boswell, "Rebel Religion," *Civil War Times Illustrated*, XI (October 1972), 28 (first and second quoted phrases); *A Kind Word to the Officers of our Army* (Charleston, [186–]), 2 (third quotation); *Soldier's Paper*, February 15, 1864 (fourth quotation); *Confederate Baptist*, October 21, 1863 (fifth quotation); Addams to Dear Brother, June 12, 1862, McAllister Papers; *Confederate Baptist*, April 8, 1863 (sixth quotation). For an outstanding treatment of the role of class in the Confederacy see Armstead Louis Robinson, "Day of Jubilo: Civil War and the Demise of Slavery in the Mississippi Valley, 1861–65" (unpublished Ph.D. dissertation, University of Rochester, 1977).

   24. *Swearing* (Raleigh, [186–]), 2 (first quotation); the same phrase appears also in [Jabez Lamar Monroe Curry], *Swearing* (Raleigh, [186–]), 2; [Mrs. Frances Blake Brokenbrough], *A Mother's Parting Words to Her Soldier Boy* (Petersburg, Va., [186–], 5 (second quotation); D[aniel]. R. Hundley, *Social Relations in Our Southern States* (1860; rpt. ed., Baton Rouge, 1979), 226, 239–40 (third quoted phrase). Also see literary treatments of antebellum southern language in which swearing is restricted to a particular, often morally depraved segment of the lower class, or, as in William Gilmore Simms's *Woodcraft*, soldiers. Simms, *Woodcraft, or Hawks about the Dovecote: A Story of the South at the Close of the Revolution* (1854; rpt. ed., New York, 1961). See also A. B. Longstreet, "Georgia Theatrics," and "The Fight," in *Georgia Scenes: Characters, Incidents . . . in the First Half Century of the Republic* (1835; rpt. ed., Gloucester, Mass., 1970); Merrill Maguire Skaggs, *The Folk of Southern Fiction* (Athens, Ga., 1972), 23; and Shields McIlwaine, *The Southern Poor-White from Lubberland to Tobacco Road* (Norman, 1939), 50.

   25. Sylvanus Landrum, *The Battle is God's* . . . (Savannah, 1863), 12 (first quoted phrase); R[obert]. L[ewis]. Dabney, *Swear Not* (Petersburg, Va., 1863), 1 (second quoted phrase and third quotation); *Southern Christian Advocate*, February 5, 1863 (fourth quoted phrase); *Profane Swearing* (Charlotte, N.C., 1864), 3 (fifth quoted word); J[eremiah]. B[ell]. Jeter, *Don't Swear!* (Raleigh, [186–]), 1 (sixth quoted word); *Why Do You Do It?* (Richmond, [186–]), 1 (seventh quoted word); J. N. Andrews, *Why Do You Swear?* (Raleigh, [186–]), 6 (eighth quotation); J. C. Mitchell, *A Sermon Delivered in the Government Street Church* (Mobile, 1861), 20 (ninth quoted phrase). See also *The Bold Blasphemer. A Narrative of Facts* (Richmond, [186–]); B[enjamin]. M[organ].

Palmer, *National Responsibility Before God* . . . (New Orleans, 1861); Sam'l Barnett, *The Tongue* (Richmond, [186–]); *The Silly Fish* (Columbia, S.C., [186–]); and "Profane Swearing," *Biblical Recorder*, August 20, 1862. On the social role of swearing see K. C. Phillipps, *Language and Class in Victorian England* (Oxford and New York, 1984), 54; Robert Graves, *Lars Porsena: Or the Future of Swearing and Improper Language* (New York, 1927), 37n; Ashley Montagu, *The Anatomy of Swearing* (New York, 1967), 224, 226, 237; Henry Cecil Wyld, *A History of Modern Colloquial English* (1920; rpt. ed., Oxford, 1936), 386; Eric Partridge, *Words at War, Words at Peace: Essays on Language in General and Particular Words* (1948; rpt. ed., Freeport, N. Y., 1970).

26. See Adam to Harriet C. Lewis, November 1, 1864, Harriet C. Lewis Papers (Duke); James N. Riddle to Dear Sisters, August 11, 1863, James N. Riddle Papers, *ibid.* On social control and religion see Lois W. Banner, "Religious Benevolence as Social Control: A Critique of an Interpretation," *Journal of American History*, LX (June 1973), 23–41. On opposition to Evangelicalism see 23–44.

27. *The Sentinel*, 1 (first quotation); Thompson, *The Making of the English Working Class*, 354–55; Eugene D. Genovese, *Roll, Jordan, Roll: The World the Slaves Made* (New York, 1974).

28. For an excellent portrait of the quality of the evangelical community see Rhys Isaac, *The Transformation of Virginia, 1740–1790* (Chapel Hill, 1982), 161–72; *Religious Herald*, September 3, 1863.

29. On the importance of the primary group in battle see S. L. A. Marshall, *Men Against Fire: The Problem of Battle Command in Future War* (New York, 1947); Richard A. Gabriel and Paul L. Savage, *Crisis in Command: Mismanagement in the Army* (New York, 1978); and Anthony Kellett, *Combat Motivation: The Behavior of Soldiers in Battle* (Boston, 1982). For a sensitive consideration of the place of religion in another army see Charles Royster, *A Revolutionary People at War: The Continental Army and American Character, 1775–1783* (Chapel Hill, 1979), 13–23. *Constitution, By-Laws, and Catalogue of Members of the Christian Association of the Stonewall Brigade* (Richmond, 1864), 2 (first quotation); *Religious Herald*, June 4, 1863 (second quotation). See also Edmund Cody Burnett, ed., "Letters of a Confederate Surgeon: Dr. Abner Embry McGarity, 1862–1865," *Georgia Historical Quarterly*, XXIX (September 1945), 182–83; W. Harrison Daniel, "The Christian Association: A Religious Society in the Army of Northern Virginia," *Virginia Magazine of History and Biography*, LXIX (January 1961), 95–96; Daniel, "The Southern Baptists in the Confederacy," *Civil War History*, VI (December 1960), 397; Robert Emory Park, "War Diary of Capt. Robert Emory Park, Twelfth Alabama Regiment. January 28th, 1863-January 27th, 1864," *Southern Historical Society Papers*, XXVI (January–Frank to K. M. Frank, April 16, 1864, Alexander Frank Papers (Duke); Prim, "Born Again in the Trenches," 52. Religion also no doubt benefited from sol-

diers' close personal ties. See Rodney Stark and William Sims Bainbridge, "Networks of Faith: Interpersonal Bonds and Recruitment to Cults and Sects," *American Journal of Sociology*, LXXXV (May 1980), 1376–95; John Lofland and Rodney Stark, "Becoming a World-Saver: A Theory of Conversion to a Deviant Perspective," *American Sociological Review*, XXX (December 1965), 862–75.

30. Leo H. Bartemeier, Lawrence S. Kubie, Karl A. Menninger, John Romano, and John C. Whitehorn, "Combat Exhaustion, Part I," *Journal of Nervous and Mental Disease*, CIV (October 1946), 358–89; "Part II," *ibid.* (November 1946), 489–525; Jones, *Christ in the Camp*, 281; *North Carolina Presbyterian*, September 20, 1862; *Central Presbyterian*, September 24, 1863; *Soldier's Visitor*, February 1864; *Biblical Recorder*, December 10, 1862; Prim, "Born Again in the Trenches," 40. See also William Sargant, *Battle for the Mind: A Physiology of Conversion and Brain-Washing* (Garden City, N. Y., 1957). A study of post-traumatic stress in Vietnam soldiers estimates that half of all veterans suffer from the syndrome and that stress disorders existed unrecognized in combat veterans well before World War I, when they first drew sustained attention. Herbert Hendin and Ann Pollinger Haas, *Wounds of War: The Psychological Aftermath of Combat in Vietnam* (New York, 1984), 6, 9.

31. On indifference see the first page of *The Soldiers' Almanac* (Richmond, 1863), 9: "WARNING TO SOLDIERS. Guard against unfeeling recklessness. By unfamiliarity with scenes of violence and death, soldiers often become apparently indifferent to suffering and anguish, and appear to be destitute of the ordinary sensibilities of our humanity." See also William L. Nugent to his wife, September 7, 1863, in Bettersworth, ed., *Mississippi in the Confederacy*, 354 (first quotation); Dunn to his wife, October 13, 1863, in Jordan, ed., "Mathew Andrew Dunn Letters," 112 (second quotation); H[ugh]. H[arris]. Robison to his wife, November 11, 1861, in Weymouth T. Jordan, ed., "Hugh Harris Robison Letters," *Journal of Mississippi History*, I (January 1939), 54 (third quotation); *Religious Herald*, July 24, 1862 (fourth quotation), See also N. M. Osborne, Jr., to my dear Aunt, June 28, 1863, Elizabeth Moorman Smithson Papers (Duke).

32. On combat stress see Mardi Jon Horowitz, *Stress Response Syndromes* (New York, 1976); Norman Q. Brill, "Gross Stress Reaction. II: Traumatic War Neurosis," in Alfred M. Freedman and Harold I. Kaplan, eds., *Comprehensive Textbook of Psychiatry* (Baltimore, 1967), 1031–35; Peter G. Bourne, *Men, Stress, and Vietnam* (Boston, 1970); Roy R. Grinker and John P. Spiegel, *Men Under Stress* (Philadelphia, 1945); Abram Kardiner and Herbert Spiegel, *War Stress and Neurotic Illness* (New York and London, 1947); Nolan D. C. Lewis and Bernice Engle, *Wartime Psychiatry: A Compendium of the International Literature* (New York, 1954); E. E. Southard, *Shell-Shock and Other Neuropsychiatric Problems . . .* (Boston, 1919); Albert Deutsch, "Military Psychiatry: The Civil War, 1861–1865," in American Psychiatric Association, *One Hundred Years of American Psychiatry* (New York, 1944), 367–84; Peter Watson, *War*

on the Mind: The Military Uses and Abuses of Psychology (New York, 1978), 60 (first quotation); and *Camp Nineveh*, 4 (second quotation). See also Jones, *Christ in the Camp*, 289, and for a description of symptoms of "congestion of the brain" in a fearful soldier, James K. Street to My Dear Ninnie, May 8, 1863, James K. and Melinda East (Pace) Street Papers (SHC). See also Stephen Cocke to Charles T. Quintard, April 25, 1862, Quintard Papers.

33. *Confederate Baptist*, June 17, 1863 (first quotation); *Religious Herald*, March 20, 1862 (second quotation); *Biblical Recorder*, October 8, 1862 (third quotation).

34. *Why Will You Die?* (Petersburg, Va., [186–]); and A. M. Poindexter, *Why Will Ye Die?* (Raleigh, [186–]); E[dwin]. T[heodore]. Winkler, *Duties of the Citizen Soldier. A Sermon . . . Before the Moultrie Guards* (Charleston, 1861), 14 (first quotation); [Brockenbrough], *Mother's Parting Words*, 2 (second quoted phrase). J[ohn]. C[owper]. Granbery, *An Address to the Soldiers of the Southern Armies* (Raleigh, [186–]), 8; *Are You Prepared?* (Raleigh, [186–]), 1. On the role of loss of control in inducing stress see Horowitz, *Stress Response Syndromes*.

35. For the identification of religion as war see other examples: *Can I Be Religious While I Am A Soldier?* (Richmond, [186–]); Charles F[orce]. Deems, *"Christ in You"* (Raleigh, [186–]), 2; *Bread Upon the Waters, or a True Story of Lucknow* (Petersburg, Va., [186–]), 2; [Herbert T. Bacon], *The Countersign* (Richmond, [186–]); *The Muster* (Charleston, [186–]); B[asil]. Manly, Jr., *Halting on this Side of Jordan . . .* (Raleigh, [186–]).

36. Brill, "Gross Stress Reactions," 1032 (first quotation); Albert J. Glass, "Psychotherapy in the Combat Zone," *American Journal of Psychiatry*, CX (April 1954), 727 (second quotation). On guilt and its role in war neuroses see Bartemeier *et al.*, "Combat Exhaustion"; Southard, *Shell-Shock*, 256; Joseph Lander, "The Psychiatrically Immunizing Effect of Combat Wounds," *American Journal of Orthopsychiatry*, XV (July 16, 1946), 536–41. On suggestibility in early stages of combat stress see Glass, "Psychotherapy in the Combat Zone," 726. For a discussion of guilt as a standard vehicle of conversion see Edmund S. Morgan, *Visible Saints: The History of a Puritan Idea* (New York, 1963); Murray G. Murphey, "The Psychodynamics of Puritan Conversion," *American Quarterly*, XXXI (Summer 1979), 135–47; and John Lofland and Norman Skonovd, "Conversion Motifs," *Journal for the Scientific Study of Religion*, XX (December 1981), 373–85.

37. On social conflict see Paul D. Escott, " 'The Cry of the Sufferers': The Problem of Welfare in the Confederacy," *Civil War History*, XXIII (September 1977), 228–40; Hahn, *The Roots of Southern Populism*, 86–133; Stephen E. Ambrose, "Yeoman Discontent in the Confederacy," *Civil War History*, VIII (September 1962), 259–68; Georgia Lee Tatum, *Disloyalty in the Confederacy* (Chapel Hill, 1934); Ella Lonn, *Desertion During the Civil War* (New York,

1928); Bessie Martin, *Desertion of Alabama Troops from the Confederate Army: A Study in Sectionalism* (New York and London, 1932); Maurice Melton, "Disloyal Confederates," *Civil War Times Illustrated*, XVI (August 1977), 12–19.

38. On the postwar period see Charles Reagan Wilson, *Baptized in Blood: The Religion of the Lost Cause, 1865–1920* (Athens, Ga., 1980); Rufus B. Spain, *At Ease in Zion: A Social History of Southern Baptists, 1865–1900* (Nashville, 1967); Hunter Dickinson Farish, *The Circuit Rider Dismounts: A Social History of Southern Methodism, 1865–1900* (Richmond, 1938); and Ernest Trice Thompson, *Presbyterians in the South: 1861–1890* (3 vols.; Richmond, 1973), II. On Populists and religion see Frederick A. Bode, *Protestantism and the New South: North Carolina Baptists and Methodists in Political Crisis, 1894–1903* (Charlottesville, Va., 1975); Bode, "Religion and Class Hegemony: A Populist Critique in North Carolina," *Journal of Southern History*, XXXVII (August 1971), 417–38; and Robert C. McMath, Jr., *Populist Vanguard: A History of the Southern Farmers' Alliance* (New York, 1975), 75.

39. See Hahn, *Roots of Southern Populism*, 137–289; Forrest McDonald and Grady McWhiney, "The South from Self-Sufficiency to Peonage: An Interpretation," *American Historical Review*, LXXXV (December 1980), 1095–1118; and Broadus Mitchell, *The Rise of Cotton Mills in the South* (Baltimore, 1921).

40. Hendin and Haas, *Wounds of War*. See also the striking descriptions of postwar southern "lethargy and listlessness" that sound much like other, less violent manifestations of post-Vietnam syndrome, in Dan T. Carter, *When the War Was Over: The Failure of Self-Reconstruction in the South, 1865–1867* (Baton Rouge and London, 1985), 271. See also David Herbert Donald, "A Generation of Defeat," in Walter J. Fraser, Jr., and Winfred B. Moore, Jr., eds., *From the Old South to the New: Essays on the Transitional South* (Westport, Conn., 1981), 3–20.

Chapter 20

From Volunteer to Soldier
The Psychology of Service

Reid Mitchell

Morale is a significant part of soldier psychology, but historians have considerably broadened their examination of Civil War soldiers' inner life. David Donald's "Confederate as a Fighting Man" hinted at the ways regional culture limited the effects of military experience, but historians in the 1980s began to emphasize the sharp psychological changes wrought by the war. Civil War Soldiers (1988), by Reid Mitchell, an independent scholar living in New Orleans, exemplifies this expanded psychological investigation of army life. In this selection, Mitchell explores soldiers' alienation from the folks at home.

The Civil War experience changed men; its subjective component matched its physical reality. Most men who were soldiers for any period of time underwent a psychological transformation. Those men who volunteered for an extended period—three years or the war—tended to lose their prewar identities. Citizens who had been volunteers turned into soldiers. And even if they escaped death, the volunteer soldiers could not escape feeling occasionally like helpless victims—more often than they admitted they were also killers. The wartime experience created new identities. . . .

Men had valued their autonomy so much that they went to war when they felt it was threatened. Military life itself, however, proved a powerful threat to men's self-esteem. Military discipline required that their autonomy be curtailed; the conditions of camp life were frequently degrading; and in the process of becoming soldiers men found themselves increasingly cut off from civilian life. In order to retain their self-esteem under these conditions, volunteers came to pride themselves on their ability to endure and to view soldiers as superior in their patriotism to all those who would not enlist. In short, men who congratulated themselves on their autonomy now congratulated themselves on their willingness to part with it. This willingness was the evidence that one truly deserved autonomy.

Americans found military regimentation hard to accept. North or South, the soldier of the 1860s was most likely an independent farmer or a farmer's son. His work had been regulated by the weather, the cycle of the growing year, and the remote but all important authority of the market. The authority immediately over him was personal—not the "feudal" authority of the planter, but the patriarchal rule of a father or an older brother who bossed him until such time as he could set up his own farm, and whose authority derived from his place in the family. Besides his relative freedom from discipline in the workplace, the volunteer had been brought up in a political culture that celebrated personal autonomy and democracy. In the North, of course, the Republican Party was based largely on the defense of free labor and free men; and in the South the Democratic Party, with its sometimes paranoid denunciations of corruption and with its thoroughly egalitarian rhetoric, outlived the commercially oriented Whig Party. Finally, American political thinkers had always viewed the military with suspicion; a Confederate soldier could still use eighteenth-century terminology and refer to an officer as a member of the old "standing army."[1]

If regimentation was difficult for most Americans of the 1860s to bear, it was particularly onerous for a Southern white man. For him, subordination and regulation were not simply abstractions in a republican demonology. He had seen them during his life—perhaps every day. The rules and restrictions of the army reminded the Confederate of the humiliation of slavery and of the degraded position that blacks held in his society.[2]

Southerners of all classes referred to military discipline as a form of slavery. Edwin Fay, a Louisiana soldier and perpetual grumbler, had not been in the Confederate army long when he decided, "No negro on Red River but has a happy time compared with that of a Confederate soldier." One regulation in particular drew the ire of Fay and other Confederates: when a soldier wanted to leave camp he had to obtain a pass.

The spectacle of white men carrying passes drew the amused attention of at least one Southern slave and probably more. Sgt. C. E. Taylor wrote his father in July 1861 what a black in Corinth, Mississippi, said after he witnessed a guard demand to see Taylor's pass. "He said it was mighty hard for white folks now. He said he had quit carrying a pass and his master had just commenced to carry them." J. C. Owens summed up the resemblance between slavery and soldiering when he wrote, "I am tired of being bound up worse than a negro."[3]

Northerners, too, could feel the comparison between the soldier and the slave. A soldier doing common labor might say he "worked like a nigger." Another soldier wrote from Virginia, "We keep very comfortable *for soldiers*. But its nothing like *white* living." Allen Geer became homesick contemplating the difference in his life after enlisting: "yesterday a freeman—today a slave." The true difference between his slavery and that of slaves in the South was that his obedience was, in a sense, not coerced. "A sense of duty and patriotism made me obedient to all the discipline."[4]

Besides the image of the slave, men used that of the machine to explain their position in the army. One war-weary Northern officer wrote his mother, "The interest I once took in Military is almost gone. I do my duty like a machine that has so much in a day to do anyway." One veteran remembered that the doctor in the hospital looked upon his patients as "so many machines in need of repairs." He explained, "In War men are looked upon and considered as so many machines. Each machine is expected to perform a certain amount of service. If the machine becomes weakened or impaired by service, care is taken that it be mended and restored so that it may again do its duty. But if, in the arduous service and dangers to which it is exposed, the life or moving force is destroyed, then a trench and covering of earth hides the remains, and that is all. This, of course, looks very heartless, but War is relentless and cruel, and so long as War lasts, and men will take up arms against one another, this State of things will continue." The machine and the slave were two metaphors for entities without wills of their own. The soldier was a third. But the machine goes beyond the slave and soldier: it is not even human.[5]

What the men of the 1860s feared in war was not simply curtailment of their freedom. They were willing to give up some freedom long enough to defend a larger freedom. The volunteers also feared what might best be called dehumanization. Many experiences common to soldiering during the 1860s and in other times served to increase such fears. For example, after the war one Confederate soldier recalled that the first time one discovered lice on one's person it was "a very mortifying and humiliating experience." Significantly, his company became lice-ridden during what they regarded as their first military humiliation, the retreat from Yorktown in 1862. "Up to this time we had maintained our self-respect and decency." "I well remember the feeling of humiliation with which we made the discovery we were inhabited. . . ." "We were inhabited"—what could violate one's autonomy more than losing control even of one's flesh? In camp lice were inescapable because of the proximity of large numbers of men with varying habits of personal cleanliness. On the march they were inescapable because men could not wash their clothes or their bodies. Inescapable or not, they made men feel degraded. Infestation, associated with sloth and poverty, became a hallmark of the soldier.[6]

Along with lice and filth, of course, went material deprivation in general. Deprivation is comparative; the war experience probably affected enlisted men worse than officers, Confederates worse than Federals, blacks worse than whites. And whether or not a man judged conditions as onerous in part depended on the conditions of his life before the war. Yet for those Americans of middle-class values, military life produced an intense psychological strain.

Soldiers as seemingly different as an Alabama officer and a Connecticut sergeant shared the same reactions to filth and deprivation. The Alabamian wrote his sister about his desire to return home, however briefly: "And then I could put on a white shirt and have my shoes blacked and ride on horseback or perhaps be exalted to a seat in a buggy and then I could sit down in a chair like a white man, and eat at a table like a white man and feel for a little while like a white man once again!!" The sergeant expressed similar longings. The Union siege of Port Hudson during the summer of 1863 was a particularly grueling experience. The heat of a Louisiana summer, the monotony of a siege, and the constant deadly Confederate sniping all combined to drive men close to distraction. The sergeant told his commanding officer "that if I could only go off somewhere and have a good cry, put on some clean clothes, get a letter from home, that I would be ready to come back and die like a Christian." Both of them valued cleanliness and neatness; more importantly, both found their absence defiling.[7]

Sickness, sometimes minor, sometimes fatal, plagued the country dwellers North and South as they crowded into military camps. Measles, mumps, and colds were common diseases. Life in the army proved more difficult than anticipated. One Confederate warned his uncle that "the camp life is a hard life to live" and asked him to tell the other male members of the family not to volunteer, "for I Dont think that they could stand it for it is hard to do [.]" Another Georgia soldier wrote from his first camp, "There some dying every day on either side the death bells ringing in my ears constant[.]"[8]

Death by disease was not what men had volunteered for. Disease was a far more impersonal enemy than the savage foe men had gone to war to fight. What made such camp deaths even worse was the increasingly matter-of-fact attitude toward them: they were common, barely worth noting. A North Carolina soldier wrote from his first camp that "ef a man dies there is not much sed about it[.]" Anonymous death was not glorious.[9]

One irony of the Civil War was that the hospital, a symbol of concern and care, that even now evokes among the literary-minded memories of Walt Whitman, became a symbol of indifference and dread for many soldiers. A Confederate soldier from Marion, Alabama, wrote home from a hospital in Richmond, "If a man Lives he Lives and if he Dies he Dies A Dog is thought more of Down in Marion than A Solger is hear." And a Union soldier observed, "I had rather risk a battle than the Hospitals." More so than one's company, the hospital represented military bureaucracy and the dehumanization of the American soldier.[10]

Even at its best, medical practice of the 1860s was faulty and barbaric. Particularly after a battle, when surgeons spent a long night in ill-lit hospital tents amputating the arms and legs of wounded men in an assembly-line procedure, medical care impressed the soldiers not only as dubious and painful, but as dehumanizing. One Confederate visited a military hospital after First Bull Run and saw "piles of arms and legs laying about just as you have seen rags and papers laying about a floor where a little child has been playing." The spectacle of men being reduced to their component parts was not a reassuring one.[11]

During the war, however, medical practice was not at its best. Frequently, soldiers came to feel that their doctors were incompetent and uncaring. Perhaps they judged too harshly the men who worked in such miserable conditions. Nonetheless, the belief that the army or the government could not provide decent medical treatment encouraged the soldier's sense of neglect. . . .

One last thing that horrified soldiers when they considered military hospitals was the treatment of the dead. Indeed, the Civil War soldier thought burial of great—perhaps ultimate—significance. The dead were entitled to their due. They deserved not just recognition of their valor and patriotism, but proper treatment of their corpses—a decent burial. The anonymous wounded suffered from neglect in the hospital; so did the anonymous dead. One Union soldier wrote from the hospital, "The way the teamsters who bury them treat the bodies is shameful. I have seen them if the coffins were a little short get into them with their boots on, and trample them in even stepping on their faces."[12]

Such treatment of the dead was not limited to hospitals. The wholesale nature of death during the war left many a man an anonymous, neglected corpse. One Northern soldier wrote his sister, responding to her letter telling of her sorrow at attending a soldier's funeral, "if you would haf to see so many dead brother Soldiers laying on the field thousands of them and also thousand of wounded and no body to bury them while the engagement lasts and sometimes they are left lay altogether on top of the earth that is a sad affair." His emotion prevented him from finishing his thought clearly. Men wanted their bodies to be respected after death; they wanted proper burials. One Confederate thought after the disastrous Gettysburg campaign, "the worst of all was we did not get to bury our dead."[13]

For the soldiers of the Civil War, the enemy's treatment of the slain was as important an indicator of their moral worth as their treatment of the living. The faces and hands of dead men sticking out of their graves shocked a Union soldier who visited the Bull Run battlefield. He could not understand how "people calling themselves enlightened should take so little pains to bury their foe." He said the Confederate dead had been buried properly, but the Union slain covered with just a little dirt; some were not buried at all. This was another example of enemy savagery.[14]

But savagery was not limited to the enemy. A Confederate visited the Bull Run battlefield in the fall of 1861 and discovered that the Yankee graves had been dug up "and their skeletons & clothing . . . scattered all around." People seeking Union buttons as souvenirs had disinterred the corpses. Visiting the battlefield at Maryland Heights, some Union soldiers discovered a dead Confederate who had not been buried properly— "only some stones thrown on him." A few of the soldiers took some hair from the corpse as a souvenir. Two who desired more exciting relics knocked some teeth from the corpse's mouth. One man in the party wrote, "the way they acted with him was enough to make a dog sick let alone a man."[15]

When the soldier saw the dead of his own side, he might react with horror or with a learned indifference. Viewing the enemy dead might produce rejoicing at their defeat or sympathy for the suffering they and their families underwent. The sight of the dead also often brought out a strong physical disgust. Some soldiers, upon seeing their own or enemy dead, felt sick at their souls, reminded of their own mortality. Others faced with corpses revealed troubled consciences. And still others abused the dead bodies of their enemies, as if to demonstrate finally the inhumanity of their foes. . . .

Each man knew he might soon become one of the anonymous corpses that littered battlefields or were buried near a hospital. The only way to endure such a thought was to try to ignore the humanity of the men who died. Men became numb. One Confederate officer cited as an example of the callousness war produced in men that "We cook and eat, talk and laugh with the enemy's dead lying all about us as though they were so many hogs." It was easier, of course, to deny the humanity of the enemy. No one could stand perpetual sensitivity to the ubiquity of death. Denying the humanity of the dead, however, was one more way in which the soldier's own sense of self was degraded, both as one who is aware of the humanity around him, and as one who is likely to join the ranks of dead soldiers.[16]

So-called primitive cultures use ritual to set their warriors apart from the broader society; the warrior may be said to be "dead" to that society until he has returned from war and been ritualistically cleaned. The ways in which the Civil War soldier was set apart and reincorporated into society were not self-conscious rituals, although the uniforms, parades, flag presentations, and the other paraphernalia of service have ritualistic overtones. But the psychological results of wartime conditions—living in filth, subject to unaccustomed discipline, surrounded by the diseased, wounded, and dead—set the soldier apart from civilian society in a manner as profound as any ritual. The soldier learned his difference from the civilian. It is less clear that the broader society acknowledged the distinction.[17] . . .

Early in the war their fellow citizens willingly gave the soldiers the respect they demanded. The passage of volunteers through a town was a cause of celebration. Just as their hometowns had sent the troops to war with lavish public ceremony, other communities welcomed their patriotic defenders. For example, the Oglethorpe Light Infantry received the warmest greetings as they proceeded from Savannah to the Virginia war front. They marched through the streets of Petersburg to the tunes of brass bands, with the eyes of lovely women on them, and banners waving over their heads. The ladies called them the "company of bachelors"—the soldiers were sixteen to twenty-five, without a married man among them. ". . . indeed, we looked like boys," one wrote his mother, "with our handsome blue uniforms & smooth faces." They were great favorites everywhere they went[18] . . .

These receptions cheered the volunteers—who felt they deserved them. The public placed the value on the soldier that military life threatened to deny them. As the war continued, however, the sight of a soldier became commonplace. Civilians no longer thronged to meet the soldiers. In fact, as civilians went about their daily pursuits, they did not simply take soldiers for granted—they looked down on them. Or so the soldiers came to feel.[19]

Soldiers began to hear stories of civilian disdain; they began to complain of their treatment on their furloughs home. Cpl. Rudolphe Rey of the 102nd New York Volunteers received a discouraging letter from a fellow soldier who had lost a leg. Upon his return home, the crippled soldier reported that all his friends acted as if they could not remember him; he swore he would be able to support himself without their aid. He warned Rey that if he wore his uniform home while on leave, he could travel with a railroad car to himself. Another New York soldier said much the same thing: at home, "Soldiers and dogs go together."[20]

It might be thought that indifference toward soldiers was characteristic of a money-grubbing, unchivalrous North and not the militaristic South. As early as 1862, however, a Virginia Confederate observed that "six months ago a soldier was the greatest thing in the world but now they are worse than the devil not countenanced by nobody at all but the soldiers." Confederate soldiers, campaigning near Jackson, Mississippi, in June 1863, heard rumors that "The City Council in compliance with the solicitations of many citizens attempted some time since to pass an ordinance forbidding *soldiers the use of the pavement* and *sidewalks* and forcing them to walk in the middle of the streets. The motion was defeated by a majority of *only Three* votes." When the soldiers marched through the city, they would cry out, "Boys, don't get on the sidewalk!" and "Corporal of the Guard, here's a soldier on the sidewalk!" and the citizens nervously assured them, "Yes, you *can* walk on the sidewalks."

"The Boys would frequently ask them 'where the Yankees walked while they were here'? They would cry out good-humoredly while passing a crowd of Ladies and Gentlemen, 'Here's the boys that cant walk on the pavements.' *We* can fight for you though.' " Whether the proposed civic ordinance existed or not, it is significant that the soldiers so readily believed that it did.[21] . . .

One source of discontent was the soldiers' feeling that the people did not understand how difficult their job was. Both sides went to war expecting a quick victory; both sides were quickly, but not thoroughly, disillusioned. Soldiers who were themselves reluctant to admit that the war would not end with the next big battle were likely to be sensitive to accusations that victory could easily be achieved with different strategy, different commanders, and different armies. Even though all soldiers reserved the right to grumble about the mistakes of their superior officers, most resented it when home folks judged the operations of the army in the field unfavorably. In part, of course, such judgments were felt to reflect not only on the commanders but on the men as well. Furthermore, the soldier felt that civilian judgments were made in ignorance. The folks at home had no concept of the difficulties experienced by the soldiers in the field. A Pennsylvania lieutenant wrote home testily, when civilians were complaining that McClellan allowed Lee to escape after Antietam, that if men there "think the Rebble army can be Bagged let them come & bagg them. . . . Bagging an army is easy to talk about." The men who remained at home had forfeited their right to criticize those who had marched away to war.[22] . . .

Another, more onerous grievance was the difference between the economic positions of the soldier and the civilian. Many civilians did well during the war, particularly in the North. Soldiers and their families, conversely, often suffered. With furloughs home and the surprisingly frequent exchange of mail between the front and home, soldiers were perfectly well informed as to the economic success of those they had left behind.[23]

A particular problem arose when the soldier thought that the people at home were not fair to his family or were grasping and picayune in money matters while he risked his life for the cause. John Pierson, a Union officer, reacted angrily when he learned that one of his creditors in Pontiac, Michigan, dunned his wife. "Those left at home in the quiet pursuit of their business," he told his daughter, "can well aford to wait.

The business I am engaged in is a game of heads and I may loose mine and his is in no danger unless they chose to get up a war at home. . . ."[24]

When the man continued to hound his wife, Pierson wrote her "any man that is so avaricious as to dun a woman for a small demand he may have against her Husband while he is in the Army helping to Suppress this Montrous Rebelion is mean enough to make a false bill and ought to lose and honest one." He assured her, "If I get home Pontiac will not suffer much on my account if I get killed they may come where I am and collect. . . ."[25]

The issue was not simply one of personal debts. It was also one of forgone opportunities for profit in the wartime economy. Henry Seys, the Union abolitionist, summed up the soldiers' fears and pride well when he wrote his wife from Chattanooga: "True I sometimes think why should *I* care so much of what, is my duty to my country? Why not do as others, stay at home and fatten in purse on the blood of the land?" In ten years, he predicted, "the parvenu, made rich by lucky speculation, or some swindling contract" would "elbow from place the soldier broken down or maimed, by long exposure or ghastly wound received on some battle field or lonely picket post. . . ." But he answered his question by saying that he served because his childhood education and his concern for the respect of his own children made him patriotic both "in *deed* as well as word." He asked his wife to teach their children that "their duty to the land of their birth is next to their duty to God."[26]

Those soldiers who believed that their immediate family had become indifferent to them probably felt the most wretched sense of abandonment. In May 1862 an officer in the Army of the Potomac, then located near Richmond, complained, "I am tired of soldiering and were it not for us being just where we are, I would not stay a day longer not careing whether you wanted me home or not I cannot understand why you deserve [desire?] me to stay I see other letters to young men from their parents, begging and imploring of them to come home this makes me feel sad and sometimes I think I am not wanted at home by my parents[.]" He was killed not long after, at the battle of Seven Pines.[27]

Civilian disdain was as potent a source of degradation as military life. Still, the soldiers' resentment of civilian contempt and indifference was not always unambiguous. Sometimes they feared it was deserved. Soldiers knew that military life might indeed transform men into beasts and this could inform a soldier's reactions to civilians. For example, in the fall of 1862 a Union soldier in Illinois suffered from the usual camp diseases and decided to treat himself with "some fresh air and a good bed to sleep in. . . ." He went to a farm near camp to request a place to stay for the night; the "old lady" was obviously suspicious and reluctant to shelter him but the soldier persuaded her to relent. When he wrote his parents, he explained, "The people here are suspicious of soldiers just as Ma is of pedlars and dont like to put them into their beds and I cannot blame them either some of the soldiers have not pride enough to keep themselves halfway decent. Some of them seem to think that being a soldier is a license for a man to make a brute of himself."[28] . . .

So while men sometimes prided themselves on their patriotism and soldierly qualities, they also worried about the changes military service had made in their fellows when they compared the men around them to their families back home. The psychological transformation caused by war sometimes upset men more than anything else. Lyman C. Holford, a Wisconsin soldier, wrote in his diary, "a little after dark I saw something which was a little the worst of any thing I have yet seen in the army. Some of the boys of the 24th Mich (a new Regt lately attached to our Brigade) found a cow which had been dead for several days and being a little meat hungry they went to work and cut meat from the cow and carried it to camp and ate it." It was not just the spectacle of dead animals and rotten meat that disgusted Holford; as a veteran of battle he had seen far worse. What disgusted Holford was seeing men reduce themselves to hyenas. Somehow the dehumanization implicit in that selfish and sickening act was greater than that of killing and wounding in battle, for it showed men turned into beasts.[29]

Dehumanizing treatment was inflicted from outside; it might be resisted. Psychological transformation was more insidious. The changes that soldiering made in men might be impossible to eradicate. The Assistant Surgeon of the 12th Michigan observed, "Soldiering is certainly not beneficial to the mind, and the large lists of sick do not look as if it improved the bodily health much. I think it certainly engenders laziness." He attributed this laziness to "the alternation of very hard work, which is compulsory, and nothing at all to do, with very few resources for amusement." Laziness, unfortunately, might become a permanent part of the volunteer's personality. The surgeon feared, "When the war is over if that happy time ever comes, I believe the greater part of them will join the regular service, from sheer unfittness for anything else."[30] . . .

In some cases, men were surprised by the direction of the moral transformation engendered by war. One Confederate soon learned that "War is a strange scale for measuring men." He described a fellow soldier, from whom nobody expected very much, who "made as good a soldier as there was in the Regiment. Cool and brave in battle and always on hand and never shirking duty in camp." This man proved a far better soldier than "others who occupied honorable positions in society." A New York regiment enlisted one of its soldiers after finding him sleeping drunkenly in a lumberyard. "He was dirty filthy and covered with vermin." They exchanged his rags for a new uniform. John Fleming remembered that "Strange as it may appear, that man became very steady, and one of the cleanest men and best soldiers we had." While such improvements in character were no doubt welcome, they also served to reinforce the distance felt between civilian life and the life of the soldier. These reformations were only extreme examples of how little one's peacetime identity seemed to relate to one's soldiering.[31]

The families back home shared the fears that the Civil War experience would change men beyond recognition. Soldiers frequently reassured wives and parents in their letters that they would not change or that their love was constant, apparently responding to the distressed queries of their loved ones. Such fears found their expression whether those they possessed wanted to admit them or not. A dream about her husband terrified one Georgia woman. She dreamed he had gone mad and had to be brought home. "I thought you would not speak to me. I thought all you wanted to do was to fill up the roads with logs and brush so that Lincoln's Army could not pass through the country, it pestered me worse than any dream I ever dreamed before but I hope there is nothing of it." Such a dream revealed the fear on the woman's part that the war, which ironically was often cast as a defense of the home, would alienate husbands and fathers from their families.[32]

In most cases the transformation experienced by Civil War soldiers was not as dramatic or as clear-cut as that from drunkard to model soldier, devoted husband to madman, or man to beast. Men found that the war called forth a broad array of emotional responses. One of the most perceptive analysts of the psychology of soldiering was a Union soldier, James T. Miller. While Miller's letters home reveal him to be a man particularly concerned with the ways war was influencing his character, his observations probably applied to men less articulate and introspective.

The battle of Chancellorsville sparked Miller's self-scrutiny. In May 1863 he wrote home, "i can hardly make it seem possible that three short weeks ago that i was rite in the thickest of a terrible battle but such is a soldiers life. . . ." Miller confessed that such a life had its appeal "for a brave reckless man who has no family even in war times it has a good many charms and i think i can begin to understand something of the love an old sailor has for his ship and dangers of the Ocean." The appeal, in part, may have been aesthetic. A month after Chancellorsville, Miller explained to his parents, "steadyness under fire is the great beauty of a soldier[.]" One is reminded that Robert E. Lee, watching the advance of Burnside's troops at Fredericksburg, said, "It is well that war is so terrible; we should grow too fond of it."[33]

Miller analyzed at length the emotions experienced by the soldier. He admitted the danger inherent in war, but explained "in regard to the danger I have passed through that part is very pleasent[.]" Soldiers amused themselves after battle by sitting around campfires and laughing over stories of "hairbreadth escapes" told in a "gay reckless carless way." An observer "would be very apt to think that we were the happiest set of men" he had ever seen.

"But if you should go with us to the battle filed and see those that are so gay thier faces pale and thier nervs tremblings and see an ankziety on every countenance almost bordering on fear," Miller said, "you would be very apt to think we were all a set of cowardly poltrouns[.]" The soldiers should be imagined this way "just before the fight begins and the enemy is in sight and the dul ominous silence that generaly takes place before the battle begins[.]" The soldier does not fear the dangers he has been through already, but he fears those that are to come.

Once skirmishers had been deployed, and the firing of cannons and small arms had begun, Miller observed that the soldiers' expressions changed remarkably. They could now "see the solid columns of the foe advance in plain sight every man seeming to step as proudly and steadily as if on parad and even while the artilery tears large gaps in thier line still on they come hardly faltiring for a moment[.]" This spectacle of war left the men still pale, "but see the firm compressed lips the eye fixed and [persevering?] and blood shot and the muscels rigid and the veins corugated and knoted and looking more like fiends than men[.]" When the order to charge came, "away we in to the very jaws of death and never for one moment faltering but yeling like devils up to the mouths of the Canon and then to hear the wild triumphant cheer[.]" Yet in a few hours these men who had resembled devils would be ministering to the wounded left on the field, both friends and enemies, "with the kindness and tenderness of a woman[.]" Miller concluded that "by the time you have seen this you will begin to think that a soldier has as many carackters as a cat is said to have lives[.]"[34]

Miller's description points to the fact that a soldier could not be well-defined in simple terms—either as patriotic hero or as savage beast. The war demanded a full range of responses from men. Miller understood that "a soldiers life is a sucession of extreems, first a long period of inactivity folowed by a time when all his energies both mental and phsical are taxed to the utmost[.]" The rapid and extreme changes that men underwent increased the anxiety created by the war: No one "character" would serve for a man in such an environment.[35]

This was true in other ways. The Massachusetts college student, Samuel Storrow, wrote home about the various physical tasks in which military life required proficiency. "When I get home I shall be qualified for any position, either that of a boot black, a cleaner of brasses, a washer-(wo)man, cook, chambermaid, hewer of wood & drawer of water, or, failing in all these I can turn beggar & go from door to door asking for 'broken vittles'. In all these I should feel prefectly at home by long practise therein." Storrow was middle class and was perhaps more amused—or chagrined—by his new roles than most soldiers were. But the occupations he lists were all notable for their lack of dignity. Most of them were associated with servants and other dependents; beggars commanded even less respect; and "hewer of wood & drawer of water" was a Biblical phrase that usually denoted a slave. These demeaning roles were unwelcome additions to one's image as a soldier and hero; they were ways in which military life broke down civilian ideas of status and identity.[36]

Another contradiction experienced by the soldier was that between his image of the volunteer as the preeminently virtuous patriot and the reality of the men with whom he shared army life. Where he had expected to find paragons, he found mortal men. Both the Union and Confederate armies had their share of petty thieves, drunkards, slackers, and other lowlife.

The camp was simultaneously immoral and virtuous, full of temptation and full of piety. Christopher Keller of the 124th Illinois was shocked by the temptations to vice open to men when they first went into camp after his regiment was raised in the fall of 1862. Apparently the other men of his company were shocked as well, for they soon voted to have their captain teach a regular Bible class. Shortly after their arrival Keller wrote a description of his camp that caught the two contrary impulses displayed there. "My bunkmate is reading his bible and in the bunk below they are having a prayer meeting on a small scale while others are cutting up, some swearing, some laughing, some writing, and others reading." He concluded that camp was "the place to see human nature in all its different varieties."[37] . . .

The contradiction between image and reality, the excitement and fear of combat, the psychological exhaustion caused by the extremes in a soldier's life, the dehumanization of the army, even the risk of bestialization—the volunteer had to suffer all these to fight for his cause. It is not surprising that he sometimes felt resentful of those who had remained at home and that he acquired a new identity as a soldier. It is not even surprising that some soldiers did act like the beasts that most soldiers feared they might become.

After the surrender of Confederate Gen. Joseph E. Johnston's army, Union Gen. W. T. Sherman marched his victorious soldiers north from Bennett Place, North Carolina, to Washington, D.C. Along the way they stopped to visit the battlefields of the east, where the Army of the Potomac had long struggled with Robert E. Lee's forces. Robert Strong's company passed through the Wilderness, where one of the greatest battles of the war had been fought. "Right in the line of breastworks stood a lone house," Strong remembered. "When we passed the house it was occupied only by women, not a single living man. They were surrounded by the bones of thousands of dead men."

The women in the house came to the door to watch the Union soldiers march by. One of Strong's fellow soldiers had picked up a skull from the battlefield. He greeted the women and asked them, "Did you have any friends in this fight?"

One of them replied her brother had been killed in the battle.

"Here is his head," the soldier said, and "tossed the skull in among them."[38]

The soldiers of the Civil War did not escape the psychological terror most associated with war: the full shock of the horrors of combat. A surgeon with the Army of the Ohio expressed both the romanticism that led some men willingly to war and the reality ultimately encountered. Joshua Taylor Bradford felt "the attraction of war and *fascination* of its *pomp* and *glitter*" as the army marched in February 1862, "with banners flying and music filling the air with melody." The army passed crowds of spectators, cheering it on. Nine days later, as Buell's columns left behind sick men who had fallen out, the surgeon commented on the pathos of war. And in March, when he visited military hospitals in Nashville and saw "hundreds, yea, thousands, in their narrow *bunks*, some dead Some dying, and many tossing the 'wild and fevered limbs in delerious forebodings,' " he found the sight "a sermon preached to the understanding, more potent than words." He called it "a humiliating evidence of war." A month later he participated in the battle of Shiloh.[39] . . .

Many soldiers awaited their first battle impatiently; they felt eager to prove their courage and to defeat the enemy. One Confederate wrote a friend, "I want to be in one Battle, just for the curiosity of the thing." An Illinois soldier fretted that the war might be over before he had a chance to fight in battle. "I sometimes feel as if the war was to end now I would never dare to say I had been a soldier. I do not feel as if I had earned it." He explained his desire to participate in a battle by saying, "I hope we will have something to do not because I *want* to get into a fight but if there is fighting to do I am willing to bear my share so as to have this war over as soon as possible so I if alive can return home. . . ."[40]

The disillusionment that followed such eagerness is predictable. One Union soldier had complained when he was promoted to Ordnance Sergeant as it diminished his chance of fighting; "when I think of you & the babies I am almost glad for what would you do if I should be kiled but that is not what I came for I came to fight & kill and come back[.]" A year and a half later he wrote his wife, "it makes me laugh to see the papers talk about this regiment and that and that the men ar eager for a chanc to get at the enemy all in your eyes, thare is none that wants to fight or will if they can keep clear of it."[41]

The actual experience of battle horrified some men. One Confederate wrote home after his first battle, "I have bin in one battle and that satisfied me with war and I would beg to be excused next time for I tell you that there cannons and the shot and shell flying as thick as hail and the grape and cannister flying between the shot and shells." The battle had been furious; "there was a [patch] of woods behind the gun that we was at work at and to look back through the woods and it looked like the trees were falling faster than a hundred men could cut them down with axes and the ground was torn all to peaces holes large enough to bury a horse and so thick that I did not see how a man escaped for it looked like there was not room any where for a man to stand up nor lay down without being hit by a shot or shell[.]" A Union soldier who survived the inferno at Cold Harbor simply noted, "God has spared me this time I pray he will spare me to return to you alive & well. I shan't reinlist."[42]

Shiloh was the first great battle in which many western soldiers participated. One Confederate, who told of seeing the branches of springs all colored with blood, wrote a correspondent, "you could never form an idea of the horrors of actual war unless you saw the battlefields while the conflict is progressing." He explained that "Death in every awful form, if it really be death, is a pleasant sight in comparision to the fearfully and mortally wounded. Some crying, oh, my wife, my children, others, my Mother, my sisters, my brother, etc. any and all of these you will hear while some pray to God to have mercy and others die cursing the 'Yankee sons of b——s.' "[43]

One Union soldier wrote after Shiloh, "I have seen since I have been here what I never saw before and what I never want to witness again." George W. Crosley, an Iowan, admitted he could not describe the battle, but tried to evoke the quality of the corpse-strewn field after the fighting had ceased by telling his correspondent to "call to mind all the horrible scenes of which you ever saw or heard, then put them all together and you can form some faint conception of the scene I witnessed in passing over this bloody Battlefield of Pittsburgh Landing."[44]

Yet horror did not entirely overwhelm men during their first battle; they responded in other ways as well. Crosley recalled that during the battle of Shiloh he did not fear death because he knew "I was in the performance of the noblest duty—except the worship of God that a man is ever permitted to perform here upon earth." And one thing that kept him from fear was the image of the woman he loved: "My dear Edna I have thought of you a hundred times while engaged in Battle. Your image would rise before me in the heat of conflict. . . ."[45]

Many men felt bolstered by such images. Shepherd Pryor, a Confederate, admitted to his wife that he thought of her and their children all through his first battle. A devout man, he thanked God he "had the nerve to stand it," but confessed, "I felt bad thinking I might be shot dead every moment[.]" The association of family with the bloodshed of battle might seem incongruous. But the men of the Civil War era quite sincerely regarded their participation in the war as an extension of their duty to protect their family. It was appropriate then that when that defense reached its moment of greatest stress, in battle, men should remember their sweethearts, wives, and children. Of course the duty for which these remembrances steadied men was that of killing.[46]

Both Crosley and Pryor also received consolation from their religious faith while they were in battle. This was not uncommon among Civil War soldiers. American Christians were particularly prone to attribute escape from death in battle to providential intervention, the result of prayer and devotion. "I have not Received as much as a sratch," R. F. Eppes wrote after the Seven Days Battles. "Surely God has been with mee hee has kept me in the hollow of his hand Surely he has heard theese heart pleadings of those near and dear ones at home for the Fervent Effectual Prairs of the Writious availeth much." Just as men might think of their loved ones to strengthen them in battle, they might also think of God.[47]

Other men found themselves caught up in the compulsions of battle from the first. One Confederate ran across a field with his company under Union fire in his first engagement; he positioned himself behind a tree where the soldier next to him was wounded. While they crossed the field, he "expected to get shot every step." But once he had gotten into a place he could return fire in relative safety, he "did not think of any thing but shooting yankees." Joseph Cotten was grateful for having been at Bull Run, even though Providence had prevented him from actually firing his gun. He described the battle as "sublime." Looking forward to at least "one more great struggle," he thought that it would suffice to win Confederate independence.[48]

Adjusting to battle meant more than facing and overcoming fear. As long as the soldier concentrated on the possibility—often probability, occasionally near-inevitability—of death, he could think of himself as a suffering patriot or a victim of war. Soldiers could not, however, free themselves from the moral burden of killing other men, for that was the nature of war. Despite the cruelty of the foe, some soldiers had trouble reconciling themselves to the idea that going to war for liberty meant killing their fellowmen. One expected savages, dupes, and mercenaries to murder without thought—the enemy was far more bloodthirsty than the legitimate ends of war demanded. But to embrace killing personally was to give way to impulses that society had long demanded be kept under strict self-restraint. Needless to say, different men felt very differently about the bloodshed of the Civil War.

When his company was first issued ammunition, Confederate Edmund DeWitt Patterson meditated, "These are the first 'Cartridges' that I have ever seen, and is it possible that we are actually to *kill men? Human beings?* . . . Yes, this is war and how hardened men must become." Richard M. Campbell made a diary entry as he hid in the bush watching for Union soldiers while on picket near Williamsburg: "My gun lies near at hand & my orders are to shoot whoever of my fellow man shows himself in front of the line. Such are the ways of war. It is a terrible scourge to any nation." The tension of the wait and of holding still wearied Campbell as if he "had been taking active exercise all day."[49]

In May 1863 Hugh Roden confessed that his fellow Union soldiers admired the late Stonewall Jackson a great deal. He explained, "there was something so daring a[nd] Noble in his way of fighting that made his enemys love him." Nonetheless, he said, "those men that praise him and his daring would not hesitate a moment if they had the Chance to send a Ball through his *heart*." The soldiers welcomed Jackson's death as they would the death of any rebel. "A soldier praised Bravery no mater where found a soldier will shake hands with the enemy one moment and shoot him the next—Such is war."

Roden recognized this mixture of respect and cold-blooded killing as only one of the psychological strains combat placed upon the soldier. War's "sickening sights" saddened men, yet its excitement made them "unconscious of danger." In battle "everything *home life* everything that is dear" was forgotten and a man changed into "a Blood thirsty Being." "all his Better feelings forsake him[.]" He reached the condition where he not only could kill his fellowmen, men whose bravery he respected, but where he rejoiced in their deaths.[50]

Other soldiers showed more hesitation in embracing their role of killers. Numa Barned, who had fraternized with rebels against orders, said, "I don't know that I ever shot any one or dont want to know." He had shot at many Confederates but in battle his policy was "as long as I can see a man head in front of me I will shoot and never look at the consequences." If he knew he had shot a man he would not admit it; "I do not want any man's blood on my hands." Having volunteered to be a soldier, Barned seemed to think he could kill and not be a killer if he only remained ignorant of the deaths he caused. During the battle of Arkansas Post, Henry C. Bear thought of his wife's Dunkard convictions against war, but shot at the Confederates as much as anyone else did. But when the battle was over, and he and the rebel prisoners had shaken hands and shared a meal of bread and meat, he wrote his wife, "I hope I did not hit any person if they are Rebles."[51]

Hatred was one way soldiers reconciled themselves to killing. A Southern soldier wrote in 1863 that he hoped they could drive the Yankees from Virginia "without having to kill them, but if it is impossible to move them, I hope that we may slay them like wheat before the sythe in harvest time." He had some Christian scruples about his animosity toward the Northerners, but confessed, "if it is a sin to hate them, then I am guilty of the unpardonable one." After his first battle, Michael Donlon was no longer "afraid of the Rebel guns, for i have had one trial of them and I shot 4 men." He told his brother that he must not judge him a murderer for these killings, "for it wer my duty to Shoot as many of the Devils as I could and so i did."[52]

Sometimes the eagerness with which men approached battle surprised even themselves; it could represent a strange reversal of emotion. A Union soldier remembered a counterattack he participated in during the battle of Gettysburg: "Charge we did drove the foe like chaff before the wind. Strange it does seem to be these men that a few moments before was driving our Men Now threw Down their arms & begged for mercy at our hands they said they could not stand our fire Strange too, our men that A Short time before seemed to be almost Dead was now as full of life and vigor as men could be As for myself, I never felt better then I did when making that grand charge"[53]

Other men felt no such excitement while in battle. William Nugent, a Confederate, wrote, "You have frequently heard of the wild excitement of battle. I experience no such feelings. There is a sense of depression continually working away at my heart, caused by a knowledge of the great suffering in store for large numbers of my fellow men, that is entirely antagonistic to any other emotions. It is doubtless true that I feel exhilarated when the enemy is driven back and our troops are cheering and advancing. Still I cannot be happy as some men are in a fight. I believe the whole machinery of war is indefensible on moral grounds, as a general proposition, and nothing but a sense of duty and the sacredness of our cause, could at all buoy me."[54]

Nonetheless, a soldier's lack of enthusiasm for battle made little difference so long as his loyalty remained constant. Duty and patriotism were as successful as hatred and bloodlust in motivating men to fight. The soldier who did not relish combat continued to fight—out of "a sense of duty"; because of "the sacredness of our cause." John Frederic Holahan, a Union soldier, explained that he belonged "to Uncle Sam, mentally, morally, and physically." Part of his obedience lay in fighting. He belonged to Uncle Sam "*Morally*—for my virtues and vices must correspond to that of my fellows; I must *lie* to rebels, *steal* from rebels and *kill* rebels;—Uncle Sam making vicarious atonement for these sins." Both the Confederate Nugent and the Federal Holahan resigned their moral sense to the greater cause, trusting that that would absolve them of any moral blame. And they continued to fight. Thus they reconciled their Christian morality with their patriotism and tried to soldier without becoming a soldier. Thus they resisted the final transformation from citizen to killer. Perhaps those men who embraced the warrior's role had an easier time of it.[55] . . .

The Civil War volunteer . . . was certain that his cause was just. It was not simply the cause of the king—or of Uncle Sam. In a democratic society the volunteer had helped make the decision to go to war. The cause of the Union or of the South was bound up with one's community, one's home and family, and one's God. That is what allowed men like Nugent and Holahan to fight when they feared fighting was immoral, and that was why the Civil War volunteer not only submitted to his transformation into a soldier, but took pride in it. Ultimately, the worth of the cause was the worth of the soldier.

In 1864 a soldier reflected on the death of his comrades. He believed the people back home said of those who died for their country, "He was nobody but a soldier. We will enjoy the rights that he died for. We care not who suffers death for the good of the country. We will undo all that they can do." The men who said such things must shut up or be silenced. The soldier threatened, "The day is fast coming when such men will have to curtail the cowardly and unruly tongues that hang in their heads or they will fill a grave more degrading than that of a soldier."[56]

In order to make war, men had transformed themselves—from citizen to soldier. Men who had changed themselves, who felt increasing resentment toward civilian society, predictably demanded that society at large be changed. Part of the soldiers' transformation was learning to endure—

and value—discipline. That was not the only discipline they thought war required. The soldiers began to ask that those who stayed at home be disciplined as well.

The soldiers feared that the enemy, so much less scrupulous than they, had a significant—perhaps overwhelming—advantage making war. Their society was free and open, the enemy's tyrannically efficient. Their society let dissent, even treason, have its voice; the enemy's was united—perhaps by deceit and force, but nonetheless united. The soldier's belief in the repressiveness of enemy society not only informed his attitudes toward the enemy: it was a justification of the war he fought. Indeed, this belief protected his faith in representative institutions—no democracy would wage the unjust war that the enemy waged. But democracy had two flanks, and this defense left one uncovered. What if democracy was not compatible with making war successfully? Men wanted to fight the other's tyrannical society, but they worried that a successful war would require them to emulate their enemy's tyranny. And as they made their own sacrifices, they became less reluctant to advocate discipline for those who stayed behind.

One of the most important mechanisms for enforcing support for the war was conscription. First the Confederacy, then the Union had to draft men into the army. This was a radical departure from earlier American practice—and it was one that soldiers in the field generally welcomed. After all, they had already volunteered and they were not too concerned if the stay-at-homes were forced to come into the field. Besides, whatever the constitutional scruples offended by the act, the soldiers knew that the larger their army, the better the chances for victory. Few resolved the issue as straightforwardly as Confederate Edwin H. Fay did, but many would have shared his sentiments: "I think the act tyrannical but am satisfied it is the speediest way to put an end to the war." Fay was particularly pleased that the act would bring in "strong young speculators under 35."[57]

Since Northern soldiers fought not only for liberty but for a strong national government to defend it, they had fewer qualms about conscription. Some of them welcomed it as confirmation of the government's power. One officer believed that "the enforcement of this Draft is of more vital importance than the most brilliant victories in the Field." He did not want the war to end without "the Governments rights to the Services of all her Citizens" confirmed. "The *Individual* power of the

Government to *Command* her Subject must go hand in hand with that other fact that all the just Powers of the Government are derived from the governed."[58]

Men in the battle lines very easily wrote of bringing the stay-at-homes into the army: men who would not fight for their rights must be made to do so. But while most soldiers were eager that shirkers be drafted, they were also reluctant that their brothers, sons, or fathers be exposed to the hardships of military life. Sergeant Jewett, who advocated drafting those who would not enlist, told his brother, "I am glad that father is too old to be drafted, and that you are too young, and I hope Bill won't be taken, as I think one is enough from our family, and don't want any more to go out of it." His attitude was far from unique. A soldier could advocate conscription—"No *man* can stay at home *now*"—at the same moment he rejoiced that his own brother was exempt. He might advise his brothers, "Do as I tell you, do not do as I did," and tell them to stay home. E. J. Lee was disappointed when the young men in Union Parish did not join the army, but he wrote his friends advising them not to volunteer and hoped they would avoid conscription—"you could not stand the fairs and hardships of a soldier." A Virginia soldier wrote his sister in 1864 that "Pa had Better stay at home." Another soldier told his father to lie about his age and stay out of the army: "there are a plenty of men who do it." James T. Binion of the 10th Georgia begged his brother to stay out of the army.[59]

These men were not simply being hypocritical. They saw themselves as representing their families. After their family had provided one son for the cause, it should not be called upon to provide another, until less patriotic families had done their part. Soldiers saw conscription as an instrument that would enforce equity. All would benefit from victory; all should share the burdens of war equally. As far as the volunteer was concerned, the draft was not unfair to those whom it affected; rather, their absence from the army was unfair to those who had volunteered. The refusal of those at home to enlist made the draft necessary.

In soldiers' eyes, this refusal reflected a larger problem: a lack of total commitment to the war on the part of those outside of the army. Enforcing the draft was one way to demonstrate the nation's power to prosecute the war. Another way would be to silence those who spoke against the war. Soldiers began to demand that those who did not fight would not speak; "it is real mean to stay at Home and discuss war affairs." Political dissent could destroy the people's will to fight. Soldiers were never sure of anyone's patriotism apart from the army; in fact, fellow soldiers often shocked them by indifference or war-weariness. Civilians back home, particularly men who did not emulate the soldier's sacrifice, could not be relied upon. Furthermore, civilians might go so far as to infect the army itself with their fecklessness, destroying its will to fight. Samuel Storrow felt "perfectly sick at heart" when his fellow soldiers expressed defeatism. "To hear *men* avow openly and boldly their conviction that the restoration of the Union by force of arms is hopeless, that the war is worse than useless, that all this outpouring of noble blood is a fruitless sacrifice and will meet with no fit recompense, this and more of the same kind of talk have I been listening to." He called this mental cowardice. Soldiers sought its origins in civilian society, in politics and newspapers.[60]

Henry Pippitt indignantly wrote his mother upon the receipt of two newspapers, asking that she never send them to him again. Instead, she should send him loyal papers. He gave her a rule of thumb for recognizing a secesh newspaper: if the paper said "the Confederates have crossed the Potomac," instead of "the rebels have crossed the Potomac," it was a secession paper. If Pippitt's identification of disloyal newspapers lacked sophistication, it still represented the profound distrust soldiers had for newspapers. Men feared dissent in civilian society; newspaper editors spread that poison. Both Confederate and Union soldiers lamented the ways newspapers undermined morale within and without the army. Soldiers faulted newspapers for lying, for criticizing the war effort, and for demoralizing both the army and the general public. One Confederate complained that when the newspapers attacked the government, "they do it in such a way as, if believed, to undermine all confidence in them." After all, "confidence is indispensible to success. How can our people be expected to make the heavy sacrifices now required of them if they believe that imbecility presides at Richmond and madness governs at our Army Headquarters?" When newspapers threatened the will to make war, they became dangerous. Suppression was required. Samuel Eells, an anti-Copperhead soldier, welcomed the order forbidding circulation of the Chicago *Times* in his department of the army; the paper was nothing but "a great source of consolation" to rebels. Soldiers forgot that previously they claimed the enemy's denial of freedom of the press had been prime evidence of despotism. Now they saw an unbridled press as an aid to the destruction of the liberties for which they fought.[61]

In the North, Peace Democrats became known as Copperheads. Many soldiers did not view them as a legitimate opposition. For them, those who wanted to end the war with anything less than total victory were traitors, and their dissent dangerous. One soldier warned that "the Copperheads of the North had better crawl down on there neese and hide themselves"—the Union army had enough men to take care of the rebels and whip all the traitors at home, Others called for the government silencing "rebels at home" or sending the soldiers to do so: "we would make short work of it if we only had the chance."[62]

Sgt. Caleb Blanchard complained of the way the Democrats in his regiment grumbled about the war. When he heard soldiers criticizing the administration or predicting Southern victory, he "told them to shut their head and stop talking treason or they would be handled as traitors." He explained that "to hear them talk so" was "against my liberty and rights." Blanchard could not silence the Democrats at home as well. In March 1863 he wished that "a portion of our army could be at home and shoot the traitors there." "it will not be safe from them to show their faces when the union patriots get back." He blamed the Copperheads for the lack of volunteers in 1863 and wished that the Northern Copperheads would reveal their true allegiance by joining the Confederate army. Three months later, during Lee's invasion, Blanchard longed for "an army of a million men in the North" to "march through and make peace there annihilite the copperheads."[63] . . .

Northern volunteers were more prone to detect disloyalty in their commanding officers than Southern soldiers were in theirs. This was particularly true of the period before emancipation became a policy and the need to break the Southern will became commonly accepted. Joseph Lester believed "our Generals are tinctured with the same leaven the Rebels are." They wished to replace "Republican Institutions" with monarchy, destroy "Free Thought and Speech," and extend slavery.[64]

"Disloyalty"—if that is the right word to use—in the Confederacy went to further extremes than it did in the North and was met with more stringent repression. A Confederate in north Georgia reported the hanging of a local parson who had helped organize an anti-war meeting. "his olest daughter was up hear when he was hung & I supoze taken him home[.]" The Confederate government had arrested other local men for the same offense of disloyalty. The Confederate government was remarkably careful about freedom of speech in many ways—its record was considerably better than that of the Union—but when faced with strong Unionist insurgency, it retaliated viciously.[65]

Soldiers tried to justify the denial of rights to dissenters by arguing that they had lost them by their unpatriotic behavior. Douglas Cater said of Confederates at large, "There are those who deserve liberty and peace. There are those who do not." Another Confederate said of the people at home, "if it was not for the women & children they ought to be under Lincoln." A Northern general wrote that "The man who doesn't give hearty support to our bleeding country in this day of our country's trial is not worthy to be a descendant of our forefathers, and he ought to be denied the protection of our laws and shipped at once to South America, where they will have a government that suits them." Dissenters, whether or not they cherished their own rights, did not have the right to give up the rights of soldiers and their families. Soldiers wanted them punished.[66]

The vengeance soldiers took against the people at home was rhetorical: it served to relieve feelings of bitterness, but was not acted on. While their governments did repress dissent—the Confederacy far less so than the Union—soldiers themselves almost never engaged in violence against their own citizens, no matter what their threats. Still, as the war went on, they habituated themselves to the notion of repression. Power joined liberty as a fundamental American value.

How much this habit of thought, even though it was rarely acted on, influenced postwar political behavior is a matter of speculation. In the South both Republicans and Populists, white and black, would be suppressed violently by a society intent on forcing unity. In the North the years following the war would witness state-sponsored violence against the labor movement and "foreign" anarchists and socialists. The men who wielded repressive power would see themselves as tough-minded realists free from sentimentality. Perhaps tough-mindedness was a legacy of the Civil War.

But the appeal of power during the Civil War was not unalloyed. Power was to be a tool of the righteous, for the righteous had to discipline the wicked. The erring section must be punished; the traitors at home must be forced to obey; even the patriot volunteer must be subject to military discipline. The war itself could be seen as God's chastisement of His disobedient American children. "It is Gods inexorable Law," a Northern volunteer explained, "that wrong 'doing' must receive Punishment, whether it is Nations or Individuals, and our Sin has found us out, and the Penalty is being meted out to us." A Confederate private believed that when a nation became too proud, "War has been the means which the Great Creator has resorted to, to humble that Nation." Northern and Southern soldiers alike could agree the ultimate cause of the Civil War was American sin.[67]

NOTES

From Reid Mitchell, *Civil War Soldiers: Their Expectations and Their Experiences* (New York: Viking Penguin, 1988), 56–89. Reprinted by permission.

Abbreviations

AHS	Atlanta Historical Society.
CHS	Connecticut Historical Society.
DUKE	Duke University.
EMORY	Emory University.
LC	Library of Congress.
LHC	Louisiana Historical Center. Louisiana State Museum.
MHS	Massachusetts Historical Society.
NYHS	New-York Historical Society.
SCHOFF	Schoff Collection, Clements Library. University of Michigan.
SHC	Southern Historical Collection, University of North Carolina, Chapel Hill.
TULANE	Tulane University.
UG	University of Georgia, Athens.
USAMHI	U.S. Army Military History Institute.
UT	University of Texas, Austin.
WM	The College of William and Mary in Virginia.

1. Charles A. Wills to Mary J. Wills, May 10, 1863. Mary J. Wills Papers. WM.

2. David Donald discusses Confederate attitudes toward authority in his essay, "The Southerner as Fighting Man," in Charles G. Sellers, ed., *The Southerner as American* (New York, 1960), 72–88.

3. Bell Irvin Wiley, ed., *"This Infernal War": The Confederate Letters of Sgt. Edwin H. Fay* (1958), 51, 162. C. E. Taylor to father, July 14, 1861, Confederate States of America Records, UT. J. C. Owens to Susannah Owens, April 26, 1863, Confederate Papers (Miscellaneous). SHC.

4. George Bates Starbird to Marianne Starbird, April 2, 1864. Starbird Letters. SCHOFF. Jacob J. Frank Diary, July 26, 1862. LC. Mary Ann Anderson, ed., *The Civil War Diary of Allen Morgan Geer, Twentieth Regiment, Illinois Volunteers* (1977), 2. See also Samuel Storrow to parents, December 4, 1862. Samuel Storrow Papers. MHS.

5. David C. Bradley to mother, June 21, 1863. Civil War Miscellany Papers. USAMHI. John Fleming, *Civil War Recollections*, 226, 384. NYHS.

6. "Some of Our Hardships," Ms. in Charles Fenton James Papers. SHC. A Northern soldier stationed in Florida wrote, "We have been very busy since coming down here in the first place we had to tear down all the old Quarters that the N.H. regt left and then build new again you should have seen the Quarters left by the N.H. Regt I would suppose any white folks above staying in such filthy Quarters you would by staying in the bunks say one hour be so covered with fleas that you could pick them off your clothes by the dozen   I am not troubled with the dear little creatures much in the way of biting but they will get next to my hide and drill in squads." Orra B. Bailey to wife, May 30, 1863. Orra B. Bailey Papers. LC.

7. Paul Vaughan to sister, August 3, 1863. Paul Vaughan Papers. SHC. John Crosby to Abby J. Crosby. June 4, 1863. John Crosby Papers. CHS.

8. J. W. Allen to uncle, October 16, 1861. Confederate Miscellany. EMORY. Matthew Bone to William Bone, October 14, 1861. Adams Collection. UG. H. H. Green to J. M. Davis, May 28, 1862. Malcolm Letters. UG.

9. Neill McLeod to Elisabeth McLeod, July 19, 1862. Neill McLeod Papers. SHC.

10. John A. Hall to A. M. Morrow, May 15, 1862. Confederate Miscellany. EMORY. John Crosby to Abby J. Crosby. May 1 [1863]. John Crosby Papers. CHS.

11. War Journal, August 19, 1861. Albert Moses Luria Papers. SHC.

12. Thomas S. Howland to mother, June 10, [?] Thomas S. Howland Papers. MHS.

13. Daniel Faust to sister, May 7, 1863. Harrisburg Civil War Round Table Collection. USAMHI. B. H. Coffman to wife, July 12, 1863. Civil War Miscellany Papers. USAMHI.

14. George H. Allen Diary, December 27, 1862. UT. For a Confederate account of exposed bodies left from the battle of Fredericksburg, see Joseph Hilton to mother and father, March 23, 1863. Confederate Miscellany. EMORY.

15. Alexander Smith Webb to mother, October 31, 1861. Webb Family Papers. SHC. Frank Appleton Badger to mother, October 2 [5?], 1862. Alfred M. Badger Papers. LC.

16. Norman D. Brown, ed., *One of Cleburne's Command: The Civil War Reminiscences and Diary of Capt. Samuel T. Foster, Granbury's Texas Brigade, C.S.A.* (Austin, 1980), 115.

17. The soldier's feeling of being set apart—liminality—has long been characteristic of the warrior experience. The soldier has long been seen as both the representative of his society and as a figure foreign to organized society. Traditionally, war is seen as teaching a knowledge that cannot be communicated. The

best discussion of this is Eric J. Leed, *No Man's Land: Combat and Identity in World War I* (Cambridge, 1979), 1–38.

18. S. H. Baldy to mother, May 31, 1861. Confederate Miscellany. EMORY.

19. John William DeForest's *Miss Ravenal's Conversion from Secession to Loyalty*, a fine novel written by a Union officer, touches upon this phenomenon and reveals particular bitterness about the place of the veteran in postwar America. For an account from another war, see Ford Madox Ford's *Parade's End*. Soldiers serve as a standing moral rebuke to civilians in times of crisis; one suspects that much of the contempt shown them by civilians springs from the need to project outward the emotions produced by one's own failure to participate in the great struggle. See also Charles Royster, "The Nature of Treason': Revolutionary Virtue and American Reactions to Benedict Arnold," *The William and Mary Quarterly*, 3rd Series, XXXVI (April 1979), 163–93, for a discussion of civilian attitudes during the American Revolution.

20. Rudolphe Rey to Miss Lizze DeVoe, June 14, 1865. Rey Papers. NYHS. George Starbird to Marianne Starbird, October 21, 1863. Starbird Letters. SCHOFF.

21. Habun R. Foster to Charles A. Wills, September 11, 1862. Mary J. Wills Papers, WM. Rufus W. Cater to Cousins Laurence and Fannie, June 1, 1863. Douglas J. and Rufus W. Cater Papers. LC.

22. Benjamin F. Ashenfelter to father, September 26, 1862. Harrisburg Civil War Round Table collection. USAMHI.

23. Susan Previant Lee and Peter Passell, in their analysis of Claudia Goldin and Frank Lewis, "The Economic Cost of the American Civil War," *Journal of Economic History* 35 (June 1975), 304–309, reveal some of the limitations of economic history by admitting it cannot explain why the soldiers of both armies fought for so much less money than they should have received in light of "risk premiums" and "loss of future wages." They suggest, in the case of the Union army, "the difference between the actual human capital loss and the required risk premium paid reflected unmeasured non-material benefits the soldiers received in fighting for their cause(s)." *A New Economic View of American History* (New York, 1979), 224–25. It would be disingenuous of me, however, to pretend that the Confederate and Union soldiers were not very much concerned with money; resentful of better-paid officers, bounty-jumping volunteers, and stay-at-homes who earned enough to buy their way out of the army, the soldiers worried about economic matters frequently. Patriotism does not blind, nor are those who experience it insensible to everything else.

24. John Pierson to daughter, March 26, 1863. John Pierson Letters. SCHOFF.

25. John Pierson to Joanna, July 15, 1863. John Pierson Letters. SCHOFF. See also the letter of a Pennsylvania laborer. "I also feele sorry That I could not send you some Money yet the pay day is past for over a month ago   But as

long as we are marching and fighting wee wont Draw any money and it would-ent do To draw any money now for wee couldnot send any home in any safety at at preasant for the is no express from here but I hope wee will soon get into camp and get our money. I know you would need it veary Bad But I hope your friends will not lieve you suffer you must do the Best you can   I hope every-thing will come rite after all for all that Abel Herrold wouldent Trust you that flower I ecspect the cause is becase he is a copper head and they cant any Thing Better be exspected of such a man as he is for that is coper head princiapels. The time I Boated for him I had to wait 18 months for 40 dollars of my pay and he wont trust 5 dollars for a couple of weeks" John Carvel Arnold to wife, June 5, 1864. John Carvel Arnold Papers. LC.

26. Henry H. Seys to Harriet Seys, October 23, 1863. Henry H. Seys Letters. SCHOFF.

27. John Rogers to family, May 15, 1862. Rogers Family Papers. Harrisburg Civil War Round Table Collection. USAMHI.

28. Christopher Howser Keller to George and Esther Keller, October 3, 1862. Christopher Howser Keller Letters. SCHOFF.

29. Lyman C. Holford Diary, November 4, 1863. LC.

30. S. H. Eells to friends, June 25, 1862. S. H. Eells Papers. LC.

31. Harry Lewis to Mrs. John E. Lewis, August 20, 1863. Harry Lewis Papers. SHC. John Fleming, *Civil War Recollections*, 50. NYHS.

32. Pellona Alexander to Manning P. Alexander, April 14, 1862. Manning P. and Pellona David Alexander Letters. UG.

33. James T. Miller to Joseph Miller, May 24, 1863. James T. Miller to Robert and Jane Miller, June 6, 1863. Miller Brothers Letters. SCHOFF.

34. James T. Miller to William Miller, June 8, 1863. Miller Brothers Letters. SCHOFF.

35. James T. Miller to Robert and Jane Miller, February 18, 1863. Miller Brothers Letters. SCHOFF.

36. Samuel Storrow to parents, December 4, 1862. Samuel Storrow Papers. MHS.

37. Christopher H. Keller to Caroline M. Hall, September 14, 1862, September 21, 1862; to George and Esther Keller, September 14, 1862. Christopher H. Keller Letters. SCHOFF.

38. Ashley Halsey, ed. *A Yankee Private's Civil War by Robert Hale Strong* (Chicago, 1961), 205.

39. Joshua Taylor Bradford Diary, February 7, 16, 23; March 6, 1862. LC.

40. George M. Decherd to Friend Rehum, January 6, 1862. James W. Redding Family Papers. UT. Bela St. John to brother, May 10, 1863; Bela St. John to parents, July 25, 1862. Bela Taylor St. John Papers. LC.

41. John S. Willey to wife, July 14, 1861; February 6, 1863. Norman Daniels Collection. Harrisburg Civil War Round Table Collection. USAMHI.

42. Habun R. Foster to Mary J. Wills, July 26, 1862. Mary J. Wills Papers. WM. George Henry Bates to William Bates, June 2, 1864. George Henry Bates Letters. SCHOFF.

43. Andrew Devilbliss to Mary, April 16, 1862. Civil War Miscellaneous Series. TULANE.

44. James Henry Hall to Richard M. J. Hall, May 2, 1862. SCHOFF. George W. Crosley to Edna, April 10, 1862. Civil War Miscellany Papers, USAMHI.

45. George W. Crosley to Edna, April 10, 1862. Civil War Miscellany Papers. USAMHI.

46. Shepherd Green Pryor to Penelope Tyson Pryor, October 6, 1861. Shepherd Green Pryor Papers. UG.

47. R. F. Eppes to wife, July 13, 1862. Confederate Papers (Miscellaneous). SHC.

48. A. W. Smith to mother, June 17, 1862. Civil War Miscellaneous Series. TULANE. Joseph Cotten to uncle, August 30, 1861. Joseph Cotten Papers. SHC.

49. John G. Barrett, ed., *Yankee Rebel: The Civil War Journal of Edmund DeWitt Patterson* (Chapel Hill, 1966), 6. Richard M. Campbell Diary, 25. AHS. See also Byron Densmore Paddock Diary, January 1, 1863. SCHOFF.

50. Hugh Roden to George Roden, Sr., November 12, 1862. Roden Brothers Letters. SCHOFF. See also Henry Pippitt to mother, June 20, 1864: "Mother when you go into battle you dont think of being killed all you think of is push a head and kill all you can of the rebs." Henry Pippitt Letters. SCHOFF.

51. Numa Barned to A. Barned [n.d], 1862. Numa Barned Letters. SCHOFF. Wayne C. Temple, ed., *The Civil War Letters of Henry C. Bear: A Soldier in the 116th Illinois Volunteer Infantry* (Harrogate, Tenn., 1961), 30.

52. H. C. Kendrick Papers, fragment, 1863. SHC. Later Donlon and a Confederate soldier exchanged shots while Donlon was on picket. Donlon wounded the rebel in the leg and the Union soldiers caught him. Donlon asked the prisoner for a ring he was wearing "and he gave it to me to remember him with as I had given him a mark he would take to the grave." Donlon sent the ring to his mother to wear until he returned from the war—something he never did, as he died at Andersonville Prison. Michael Donlon to brother, January 14, 1864, May 21, 1864. Civil War Miscellany Papers. USAMHI.

53. Benjamin F. Ashenfelter to Father Churchman, July 29, 1863. Harrisburg Civil War Round Table Collection. USAMHI.

54. William M. Cash and Lucy Somerville Howorth, eds., *My Dear Nellie: The Civil War Letters of William L. Nugent to Eleanor Smith Nugent* (Jackson, Miss., 1977), 185–86.

55. John Frederic Holahan Diary, November 3, 1862. Private possession.

56. Margaret Brobst Roth, ed., *Well Mary: The Civil War Letters of a Wisconsin Volunteer* (Madison, 1960), 111.

57. Bell Irvin Wiley, ed., *"This Infernal War": The Confederate Letters of Sgt. Edwin M. Fay* (1958).

58. George Anthony to Ben Anthony, August 15, 1863. George Tobey Anthony Letters. SCHOFF.

59. George O. Jewett to Deck, July 20, 1862. George O. Jewett Papers. LC. Samuel Storrow to parents, February 27, 1863. Samuel Storrow Papers. MHS. E. J. Lee to J. G. Taylor, October 13, 1861; May 20, 1862. Lee Collection. UT. John Thomas to sister, June 17, 1864. Confederate States of America Archives. Army-Miscellany. Officers and Soldiers Letters. DUKE. John to My Dear Pa, August 31, 1864. DUKE. James T. Binion to brother, July 30, 1861. EMORY.

60. Charles H. Richardson Diary, June 10, 1863. LC. Samuel Storrow to parents, January 22, 1863. Samuel Storrow Papers. MHS.

61. Henry Pippitt to Rebecca Pippitt, August 14, 1864. Henry Pippitt Letters. SCHOFF. Franklin Gaillard to Maria, August 12, 1863. Franklin Gaillard Papers. SHC. Samuel Henry Eells to aunt, February 12, 1863. Samuel Henry Eells Papers. LC.

62. Andrew J. Sproul to Fannie, July 4, 1863. Andrew J. Sproul Papers. SHC. Orra Bailey to wife, March 13, 1863. Orra Bailey Papers. LC.

63. Caleb Blanchard to wife, February 11, 1863; March 22, 1863; April 15, 1863; June 11, 1863. Caleb Blanchard Papers. CHS. See also Caleb Blanchard to wife, February 8, 1863; February 26, 1863; March 5, 1863; March 11, 1863; August 15, 1863.

64. Joseph Lester to father and sisters, November 1, 1862. Joseph Lester Papers. LC.

65. James Barfield to wife, April 21, 1864. Confederate Miscellany. EMORY.

66. Douglas Cater to Fannie, June 24, 1864. Douglas J. and Rufus W. Cater Papers. LC. Shepherd Green Pryor to Penelope Tyson Pryor, February 23, 1862. Shepherd Green Pryor Papers. UG. James I. Robertson, Jr., ed., *The Civil War Letters of General Robert McAllister* (New Brunswick, N.J., 1965), 106.

67. Joseph Lester to father and sisters, November 1, 1862. Joseph Lester Papers. George Boyd Smith Diary, 5. LC.

Chapter 21

Emotional Responses to Combat

Joseph Allan Frank and George A. Reaves

Joseph Allan Frank, emeritus professor at the University of Ottawa, and the late George A. Reaves of Shiloh National Military Park used content analysis to examine letters and diaries of men who fought at Shiloh in April 1862. This battle was a baptism of fire (a time to "see the elephant," a contemporary phrase that gives Frank and Reaves's study its title) for most of the soldiers involved. This selection from "Seeing the Elephant" (1989) explores emotional reactions to combat by soldiers on both sides.

The range of emotions that were engendered by battlefield stresses are as varied as the number of soldiers in any army (B. I. Wiley 1978: 29–30), but recent studies have concluded that the predominant emotion was fear[1] its "symptoms" in combat include a "violent pounding of the heart," "a sinking feeling in the stomach," "cold sweat," "nervousness," "shaking hands," "repeating meaningless acts," "losing control of bowels," and "urinating in pants" (Stouffer 1949: II, 201; see also Woolridge 1968: 9). Fear—along with the enemy—had to be defeated. On the battlefield, the soldier is in a two-front war: on one front, he fights the enemy, and on the other front, he struggles with himself to hold his fear in check. In his psychological struggle, his mood races through a series of wild oscillations in reaction to the changing situation on the battlefield. Through it all, he tries to hold on, to keep control. Moods change from moment to moment in response to the rapid succession of terrifying stimuli. Going through his baptism of fire, Sam Watkins of the 1st

Tennessee gave some idea of this flood of emotions, ranging from sadness to dazed awe and then to elation.

> Men were lying everywhere in every conceivable position . . . some waving their hats and shouting to go forward. It all seemed to me a dream; I seemed to dream; I seemed to be in a sort of haze, when siz, siz, siz, the minnie balls from the Yankee line began to whistle around our ears. . . . Down would drop just one fellow and then another, either killed or wounded, when we were ordered to charge bayonets. I had been feeling mean all the morning as if I had stolen sheep, but when the order to charge was given, I got happy. I felt happier than a fellow does when he professes religion at a big Methodist camp-meeting (1962: 42). . . .

Beyond self-control, there are, of course, degrees of courage. Based on his experiences as a medical officer in World War I, Lord Charles Moran set up a scale of valor, which is equally applicable to classifying the combat behavior of the Civil War volunteers. Moran's scale of valor had four levels. First, there were those who simply did not feel fear. Second, there were the men who did feel fear, but did not show it. Third, there were soldiers who showed it but did their duty. And finally, there were men who felt fear, showed it, and shirked their duty (1966: 3).

More than two-thirds of the recruits expressed passive-defensive reactions, involving fear, awe, or surprise during their baptism of fire. Their responses to the baptism of fire put them in Moran's second and third categories of courage. This was no different from the reaction of World War II veterans, 65 percent of whom expressed the same type of emotion (R. Holmes 1986: 205).

On the other hand, less than a third of Shiloh's recruits claimed that they felt calm, steadfast, angry, or elated during their first contact with the enemy, fitting into Moran's highest category of courage in battle. This suggests that only one in three of the raw troops turned out to be what Egbert defined as active and effective fighters. This raises questions about Linderman's suggestion that the early volunteers were exceptionally motivated combatants because of a Victorian ethos equating fearlessness and bravery (Linderman 1987: 18). Egbert defined a good fighter not merely as one who managed to fire his weapon (Marshall 1947), but one who also provided leadership during assaults, got men to fire, encouraged them to stay in the firing line, calmed them and increased their confidence, took aggressive action against the enemy by volunteering for hazardous missions, and fired effectively at the enemy.

He performed supporting tasks under fire, such as caring for the wounded and bringing up ammunition. The good fighter also led the men by getting them into position. He set the standard for good conduct by taking aggressive action and remaining cool throughout (Egbert 1954: 3, 8). Most of the Shiloh volunteers did not attain this level of fearlessness and effectiveness in battle. Their emotional response to combat was much the same of soldiers in later wars. . . .

There was only one honorable escape from the dilemma of fear versus duty and that was being lightly wounded. Elisha Stockwell, 14th Wisconsin, was slightly injured just as the unit took up positions for an assault. He was struck in the arm by a spent cannonball. He showed his wound to his lieutenant, who told him he did not have to participate in the attack and that he was excused to return to Pittsburg Landing. Stockwell admitted he "was as tickled as a boy let out of school," when he learned he was out of it with a "million dollar wound" (Abernathy 1958: 20–21). Few were so lucky.

The decisive moment of the Shiloh volunteers' baptism of fire occurred just as they emerged from their initial daze and began to perceive the effects of the enemy fire. At that moment, they suddenly became conscious of the dangers around them. Panic swept them up, ebbed, and then engendered a paralytic undertow. Many factors instilled a feeling of terror: there were the rumors of encirclement, the detonations of the heavy guns, the close misses, the sight of comrades struck down, and finally, there was the frightening sight of the enemy deploying ominously in their front. . . .

Most surmounted the urge to flee and stayed in the line to meet the enemy. However, others such as George McBride were overcome by fear. He and the 15th Michigan had the misfortune to bear the brunt of the Confederate attack at the very opening moments of the battle. Even thirty years later he could vividly relive the scene as the Confederate onslaught battered the green troops of the 6th Division. He remembered looking terror-stricken at the shot bouncing along the ground throwing up little clouds of dust and at the sight of men falling all around them. It "impressed me with a desire to get out of there. I recollect," he continued, "that the hair now commenced to rise on the back of my head . . . and I felt sure that a cannon-ball was close behind me, giving me chase as I started for the river. In my mind, it was a race between me and that cannon-ball" (McBride 1894: 9).

Many situations elicited panic. The demoralizing effect of shirkers was often mentioned. Shirkers were resented not for their weakness, but for their corrosive effect on morale. Levi Wagner was with one of the units from Buell's army that had to pass through numerous panicked soldiers at the landing as it moved up. As he and the 1st Ohio disembarked, they were engulfed with dire imprecations on the fate that awaited them if they proceeded farther. " 'For God's Sake, don't go out there or you will all be killed,' " were "cheering words for raw men," he recalled (Papers). Yet no unit broke completely; even after the 53rd Ohio fled, many of its companies continued to function as independent units.

Other situations corroded morale as well: near misses from enemy fire, wounds and pain, seeing comrades fall, and fatigue could cause the volunteers to lose control and withdraw from the fight. There was also the terrifying sight of enemy regiments resolutely deployed for an attack. Even without a shot fired, this sight was a supremely frightening spectacle, leading to the suggestion that the majestic evolutions of compact masses of infantry had as much effect on green troops as the actual shooting. Watching such a display on Prentiss' left, Leander Stillwell conceded, "I am not ashamed to say . . . that I would willingly have given a general quit-claim deed for every jot and title of military glory falling to me . . . if I only could have been miraculously . . . set down . . . a thousand miles away" (1920: 44). Seeing the formidable ranks of enemy battalions preparing to march on the 11th Iowa Infantry, Henry Adams thought it was "an impossibility to stand such a force" (Diary, n.d.).

Even more terrifying was enemy artillery unlimbering in one's front. Seeing the enemy gunners go through their preliminaries, knowing that in a few minutes they would be taking fire was a sobering experience. Young crouched behind what cover was handy and watched in horrified anticipation as an enemy battery wheeled into position on a little hill in front of Shiloh Chapel, just opposite his position. There was a wounded man caught in the no-man's land between the unit and the Confederate gunners. "In agony of alarm, [the helpless soldier] . . . saw the men loading their guns. The cannon seemed to be aimed right in his face. He called out . . . 'Don't shoot me!' And even while he spoke he saw flames belch from the guns" and he disintegrated in the smoke (1894: 102).

A brush with death was another event that could shatter morale and cause panic. A close call could put some of the green soldiers *hors de combat* just as much as an actual wound. Henry Stanley was attacking with his Arkansas regiment, when he was sent sprawling by a Union bullet in the stomach. He thought he was finished and would now die in agony from one of the worst-feared wounds, but he soon regained some composure and discovered that the bullet had only slammed into his belt buckle leaving it bent and cracked, but had not pierced him. However, it was just as effective. Stanley's nerve was as shattered as his belt buckle, and he crawled to cover leaving the rest of the 6th Arkansas to sweep on (Laurie 1985: 44) . . .

Others were less fortunate, for them there was the awful assessment of the extent of their injury as they waited in dread for the pain to begin to well up and the effects of the stress-generated anesthesia [endomorphine] to subside. They were physically immobilized by their injuries or were in such pain that they could no longer function. If ambulatory, they sought shelter nearby or ambled befogged toward succor. Ultimately, where possible, they were gathered up and brought to the captured Union camps where the Confederate surgeons set up makeshift aid stations. On the Union side, they ended up at the landing, and there they sat or lay waiting. The least fortunate ones languished in no-man's-land.

Seeing casualties all around as they headed into action also eroded morale. Men who fought with units that took above average casualties (over 25 percent) evinced aggressive combat attitudes half as often as soldiers from outfits that had suffered light casualties.[2] The results coincide with World War II studies that found a high correlation between low morale and high casualty rates (Hicken 1969: 247). This effect was registered by Sergeant Edwin Payne as his Company A, 34th Illinois passed through Savannah with Colonel Edward Kirk's 5th Brigade of McCook's division. The town was already filled with wounded. "We saw long rows of white cots . . . visible in an empty store building as we . . . marched by raising in the mind many questions as to whether or not their lot was not better than ours who were yet to take the chances of the battle the next day" (1902: 16).

Finally, along with the experiences of watching in fearful anticipation as the enemy deployed, the shattering effect of a brush with death, and the sight of the wounded, combat morale was also eroded by sheer fatigue. A soldier in battle may reach the point where he is emotionally and physically exhausted. He simply cannot take any more. At this moment, men may begin drifting away from the firing line as a response to the stress (R. Holmes 1986: 229). Withdrawal may not be a tumultuous panic, but simply a gradual pullback by men who have reached the limits of their endurance. This began to occur by late afternoon of the first day. Exhausted by the physical exertions and tired from the psychological stress of combat, the volunteers were fought out by late afternoon. Contrary to modern wars, the time that Civil War soldiers spent in the firing line was relatively short, but it was very intense fighting. At the end of the first day's fighting, the troops were so tired that they could not carry out further sustained operations. Unit cohesion had become extremely fragile. Sleep was the only way to restore morale. Even if the opposing forces had any organized forces available, fatigue had nullified what fighting morale remained after fear and wounds had taken their toll. The men collapsed in sleep even in a driving rain. "Never was I so tired as this night," George Hurlbut confided to his diary (April 7, 1862).

Plunged into the turmoil and terror of their first battle, the outcome of the volunteers' two-front war against their enemy and against their own fear was in doubt on both "fronts." Their social values and instinct pulled in opposite directions: the one to steadfastness and effective action, and the other toward flight and survival.

Despite the overwhelming terror inherent in the new environment of battle, some soldiers evinced active fighter attitudes such as calm, elation, or rage. Captain William Bradford was commanding Company A of the 57th Indiana as it joined in the Union counterattack of April 7. He told his wife, "I was perfectly astonished at myself. I never became excited, I do not know that it changed the beat of a pulse" (To wife, April 10, 1862). Others, such as Stanley, felt a sense of elation and aggressive excitement when the order to fix bayonets was given to the 6th Arkansas, and with it came the opportunity for release from the tension (Laurie 1985: 44; and B. I. Wiley 1978: 72–73). Yet others such as George Gates became enraged and fought all the harder. When Gates saw the first comrade shot, he declared. "I was so enraged . . . I could have tore the heart of the rebel out could I have reached him" (To parents, April 8, 1862). Bradford's calm, Stanley's excitement, and Gates' anger were all positive responses to battle stress, and they all exemplified emotions that were associated with the third of the respondents of the men who expressed active-aggressive responses to their initiation in battle.

These responses were reinforced by certain situations. Among the most supportive were ties with friends and the sense of confidence they had in their territorially recruited units (Kellett 1982: 98, 286–87). This type of regiment embodied both political and community bonds with military traditions, such as esprit de corps and devotion to comrades.

The volunteer regiment was thus a source of overlapping powerful loyalties. Lord Moran contended that good civilians made good soldiers. Fortitude in battle transcends military, organizational commitments. "Fortitude," he argued, "has its roots in morality." Responsible men who do their duty at home will also do so on the battlefield. Courage in battle is thus a character trait, a "moral quality." The individual volunteer's personal conscience and the choice he made between fight or flight determined his development as an effective soldier (Moran 1966: 160). By inference therefore, an army of volunteers composed of men who for a large part enlisted out of a sense of patriotic duty would be more resilient than an army of mercenaries or conscripts. . . .

Some men were consumed by combat narcosis: a feeling of surging power and anger as they were swept along with their units. This sensation was facilitated by the relatively close formations of nineteenth-century warfare, in which collective emotions could spread more quickly. Olney experienced the feeling when his unit drove off a Confederate attack. The victory "exhilarated us," he recalled. It swept them up in a wave of savage excitement. "We had tasted blood and were thoroughly aroused. . . . The very madness of blood-thirstiness possessed us. To kill, to exterminate the beings in front of us, was our whole desire" (1885: 586). Victory also spurred on the elan of J. W. Green's Kentuckians as they swept the Union defenders before them. They plunged on thinking that "we would capture Grant's entire disorganized army," and were "greatly disappointed that we were not pushed forward" when evening wrung down the curtain (Diary, April 6, 1862). . . .

Yet underlying the active fighter's emotions was always a strong sense of patriotic commitment. There was a belief in "the cause." It was not formally articulated as an ideology, nor was it frequently mentioned, but it was there. Nationalism was such a powerful force that even recent immigrants had absorbed it. Leander Stillwell remembered asking his friend Charles Oberdieck, a recent arrival from Hanover, what he thought of the situation as their line collapsed along the Sunken Road. Was it all up, were they going to surrender at the landing, Stillwell asked Oberdieck. " 'I yoost tells you how I feels,' " replied the Hanoverian. " 'I no care anything about Charley [referring to himself]; he no haf wife nor children, fadder nor mudder, brudder nor sister; if Charley get killed, it makes no difference; dere vas nobody to cry for him, so I dinks about myselfs; but I tells, you I yoost den feels bad for de Cause!' " (Stillwell 1920: 50).

Emotional responses by the volunteers ran the gamut of human emotions from awed passivity to terror and panicky flight, to calm, exhilaration, and vengeful rage. Broadly speaking, the range of emotions can be divided into active-aggressive responses and passive-defensive responses. Among the fifty-one respondents in the three armies, Grant's army had the highest proportion of aggressive responses, Buell's men registered the lowest proportion of aggressive emotions, and A. S. Johnston's was in-between. The figures are puzzling, because Johnston's men had been the attackers and Buell's were probably the best trained, yet Grant's men evinced the most-frequent active-fighter emotions, despite the mauling they had sustained. However, Grant's men were the most successful of the three armies and they went into action with a higher feeling of confidence. When comparing the enlisted men and the officers, the results were not as surprising. The officers expressed aggressive reactions to the battle more frequently than the enlisted men.[3] This is attributable to the higher motivations and greater responsibilities that went with their rank. Officers, by necessity, could less afford to fall victim to passive emotions and abandon their responsibilities. The concerns for their command allowed them less occasion to think of their own fears, lapse into passivity, or let surprise paralyze them.

NOTES

From Joseph Allan Frank and George A. Reaves, *"Seeing the Elephant": Raw Recruits at the Battle of Shiloh* (Westport: Greenwood, 1989), 111–19. Reprinted by permission.

1. In his seminal study of the reaction of 300 members of the Abraham Lincoln Brigade, *Fear in Battle* (Washington, D.C.: The Infantry, 1944), John Dollard found that the vast majority of the men experienced fear in combat. Dollard's sample of highly motivated Lincoln Brigade volunteers in the Spanish Civil War were, however, veterans with at least a year of fighting when they were polled (see also Samuel L. A. Marshall, *Men Against Fire* (New York: William Morrow and Co., [1947] 1966): 149; Peter Watson, *War on the Mind: The Military Uses and Abuses of Psychology* (New York: Basic Books, 1978): 213).

2. Thirty-six soldiers left behind descriptions of their emotions in battle.

3. Fifty men commented on this with officers expressing active-aggressive reactions at almost twice the rate of the enlisted men.

References

Abernathy, Byron R., ed. *Private Stockwell, Jr. Sees the Civil War*. Norman: University of Oklahoma Press, 1958.

Adams, Henry Clay. Civil War Journals, 1861–65. University of Iowa Library.

Ates, F. S. Papers. Shiloh National Military Park.

Bradford, William S. Letters. Indiana State Library.

Caldwell, John W. Diary (Typed). U.S. Army Military History Institute.

Egbert, Robert L. et al. *The Characteristics of Fighters and Non-Fighters*. Fort Ord, Calif.: Human Research Unit No. 2, 1954.

Gates, F. S. Papers. Shiloh National Military Park

Green, John Williams. Diary, 1861–65. Filson Club, Louisville, Kentucky.

Hicken, Victor. *The American Fighting Man*. London: Macmillan, 1969.

Holmes, Richard. *Firing Line*. Harmondsworth, UK: Penguin Books, 1986.

Hurlbut, George. Diary, 1862. Western Reserve Historical Society.

Kellett, Anthony. *Combat Motivation: The Behavior of Soldiers in Battle*. Boston: Kluwer Nijhoff, 1982.

Lathrop, Barnes F. "A Confederate Artilleryman at Shiloh." *Civil War History*, Vol. 8. No. 4 (1962), pp. 373–85.

Laurie, Clayton. "Two-Sided Adventure." *Civil War Times Illustrated*, Vol. 24, No. 4 (June 1985), pp. 40–47.

Linderman, Gerald F. *Embattled Courage*. New York: Free Press, 1987.

Loudon, Dewitt Clinton. Papers. Ohio Historical Society.

Marshall, Samuel L. A. *Men Against Fire*. New York: William Morrow and Co., [1947] 1966.

McBride, George W. "My Recollection of Shiloh." *Blue and Gray*, Vol. 3 (1894), pp. 8–12.

———. "Shiloh, After Thirty-Two Years." *Blue and Gray*, Vol. 3 (1894), pp. 303–10.

Moran, Charles Lord. *The Anatomy of Courage*. London: Constable, 1966.

Olney, Warren. "The Battle of Shiloh: With Some Personal Reminiscences." *The Overland Monthly*, Vol. 5 (1885), pp. 577–89.

Payne, Edwin Waters. *History of the Thirty-Fourth of Illinois Infantry*. Clinton, Iowa: Allen, 1902.

Stillwell, Leander. *The Story of a Common Soldier of Army Life in the Civil War*, 1861–1865. N.p.: Franklin Hudson, 1920.

Stouffer, Samuel L. et al. *The American Soldier: Vol II: Combat and Its Aftermath*. Princeton, NJ: Princeton University Press, 1949.

Wagner, Levi. Recollections. U.S. Army Military History Institute.

Watkins, Samuel R. *Co. Aytch: A Confederate Soldier's Memoirs*. New York: Collier Books, [1881–2] 1962.

Wiley, Bell I. *The Life of Johnny Reb*. Baton Rouge: Louisiana State University Press, 1978.

Woolridge, William O. "Combat." *Army Digest*, Vol. 23 (January 1968), pp. 6–11.

Wright, Charles. *A Corporal's Story: Experiences in the Rank of Company C, 81st Ohio Vol. Infantry*. Philadelphia: State Historical Society, 1887.

Young, Jesse Bowman. *What a Boy Saw in the Army*. New York: Hunt and Eaton, 1894.

Chapter 22

"Dangled over Hell"
The Trauma of the Civil War

Eric T. Dean, Jr.

The Vietnam War has given us a new sensitivity to the psychological damage that war can inflict. For years after the war ended, news reports featured Vietnam veterans, tormented by memories of the war, on a violent rampage; experts created a new label, "post-traumatic stress disorder," to describe the veterans' syndrome. Some scholars, however, have questioned whether the nature of recent combat and soldiers' reactions to it are unique to Vietnam. Eric T. Dean, Jr., an independent scholar who lives in New Haven, Connecticut, is prominent among these skeptics. This selection from Shook Over Hell *(1997), his exploration of post-traumatic stress following the Civil War, describes the trauma of battle in terms that allow comparisons to the aftereffects of Vietnam.*

In post-Vietnam America, the key word in considering the psychological state of returning veterans is "trauma." Specifically, what hardships and trials did the veteran undergo during his service in the military? Was he placed in situations in which he experienced anxiety and fear? Was he exposed to combat, to the death and mutilation of his fellow warriors, or to the spectacle of enemy soldiers being slaughtered in battle or, as prisoners, being summarily executed? Did he encounter disease or discomforts that might have weakened his psychic defenses or exacerbated his sense of alienation and unease about being sent far from home and given the anomalous task of killing other human beings? Did his bonds to fellow soldiers or to civilians at home somehow ameliorate his problems and prevent psychological breakdown? Did an eventual warm homecoming "wash away" disturbing memories of pain and death?

In comparing the trauma experienced by the Civil War soldier with that of the Vietnam veteran or any combatant in modern twentieth-century armies, one is struck first of all by the physical hardships that soldiers encountered in what one man characterized as a "destroying manner of living." Although the Civil War has been portrayed as the first modern or industrial war in which machinery such as locomotives and rifled muskets or ironclad warships and naval torpedoes were engaged, the infantryman in this war moved from one place to another mainly on foot. He sometimes covered ten and twenty miles a day, or even more in the case of a forced march when troops had to be maneuvered quickly to come to the aid of embattled and endangered comrades or to defend or seize key positions.[1] . . .

Men were frequently marched through suffocating dust and under the blazing sun throughout the day, with minimal and sometimes seemingly no breaks allowed. A New York volunteer remembered that on a forced march of thirty miles in the fierce heat of summer, the men had thrown away overcoats, blankets, and even their knapsacks. Nonetheless many became violently ill from the exertion, some having convulsions and others dying from heatstroke. Another soldier recalled that during such a forced march he had to stop and vomit "every once in a while and my head ached dreadful." He vomited eight or ten times during the day, and the last time threw up blood. . . . The scenery on these marches was not always calculated to lighten the mental burden consequent to such physical exertion, as is demonstrated by the letter of one Rebel soldier to his wife: "i am well as common except for a bad cold and march most to death. . . . Mi dear wife i want you to pray for me i hop i will se you agin. . . . I have walked over more ded yankes than i ever want to do agin." Within two weeks this man was killed at the Battle of Antietam.[2]

Confederate troops in particular also had to deal with the problem of inadequate (or no) footwear. One Rebel surgeon lamented in a letter to his wife that she could hardly believe what the army had recently endured: "Most of our marches were on graveled turnpike roads, which were very severe on the barefooted men and cut up their feet horribly. When the poor fellows could get rags they would tie them around their feet for protection." Sometimes these forced marches lasted into or throughout the night, and soldiers literally learned to walk while asleep or would sometimes collapse from fatigue and sleep at that spot for hours, oblivious to all attempts to rouse them and force them to continue. A Massachusetts volunteer wrote: "I doubt if our ancestors at Valley Forge suffered more from cold than we did. . . . [I] often found that I had been sound asleep while my legs were trudging along."[3] . . .

Such was the centrality of marching to the experience of the Civil War soldier that when some men were eventually issued disability discharges, it was not uncommon for the examining surgeon to give as the reason for such separation the fact that the man was no longer able to carry a knapsack or keep up with the army on the march. In the years following the war, Union veterans frequently claimed "sunstroke" and "hard marching" as the basis for military disability pensions—and these claims were often granted. All who had been through the experience knew exactly how trying and destructive it could be.[4]

When the hard-marching Civil War soldier reached his destination, conditions did not improve, for a constant fact of life in the Civil War era was that all soldiers, Northerners as well as Southerners, were routinely exposed to the elements. These men were expected to sleep out in the open on the ground in the middle of winter or in the midst of a driving rainstorm, oftentimes with only one blanket or the equivalent of a pup tent to fend off the damp and cold or the frost and snow. One Indiana soldier wrote in his diary: "Rained nearly all last night, woke up two or three times before day, the water was running under us so that we had to get up and sit shivering around the fire until morning." Another Hoosier volunteer's diary revealed similar circumstances: "Last night very cold, did not sleep well . . . woke from a dream crying. . . . Day rainy and gloomy. . . . Have the blues." As a Michigan volunteer reflected: "We had atuf time Last night. it rained all night and when I got up this morning my bed was wet thru this is what a soldier has got to stand." Regarding winter conditions, in letters and diaries, Civil War soldiers frequently mention waking up covered with frost or snow, and with both their boots and clothes, and even their very bodies, seeming to be frozen, requiring several hours to thaw out. Under such circumstances, a Confederate who was called to fall out in the middle of the night recalled: "I had gotten chilled and my teeth were glued together and a feeling of complete wretchedness came over me as I took my place in the ranks to march to the front." One irony was that when railroad cars were made available to transport Civil War troops, the conditions could be all the more difficult, as when men were transported on open cars throughout the night in a driving rainstorm: "We have bin shiped several hundard miles and we have done the most of it of nights right through the rain and cold on top of freitcars I have bin allmost chilled to death & have shook for hours & worse than if I had ague . . . then when we got to lay down we had to lay down wet through and cover up with a wet blanket." In pension claims after the war, one frequently encounters the expression "exposure in the army" as the claimed basis of a disability such as rheumatism or mental prostration. In reviewing the conditions that these men had to endure, one begins to understand exactly what this "exposure" was and how it shattered men's constitutions and health—a situation from which many never recovered.[5]

Soldiers shivering in the rain or snow had the added anxiety, of course, resulting from the ever-present danger of being killed by the enemy. One Confederate assigned to protect Missionary Ridge as Federal troops massed for an attack in the vicinity of Chattanooga during the winter of 1863 recalled later that he would never be able to forget the hard fight itself or the suffering endured by his comrades in the three or four weeks preceding the battle. Because the men had no tents, they had to use their blankets stretched on poles to keep the rain off; since few had more than one blanket, this left the Confederate soldiers nothing with which to cover themselves or to place over the freezing ground. They suffered intensely: "You could hear the boys praying and wishing for the fight to come if it was coming, anything to get out of the suspense and suffering caused by lack of rations and shelter." He noted that at night the only fire allowed was a few coals over which the men would warm their fingers and toes, because the light from any more substantial fire would inevitably attract the attention of enemy snipers.[6] . . .

In light of the frequent rain, mud was another of the elements with which Civil War soldiers had to contend, and memoirs and letters are filled with depressing accounts of men, animals, and equipment mired in the muck. On occasion the situation was so bad that equipment sank halfway into the ooze, and had to be abandoned. One Hoosier infantryman characterized camp at Cheat Mountain in West Virginia as "this infernal mountain which is the meanest camping ground that I have ever seen," noting that the mud was not less than shoe-top deep. Another Hoosier volunteer, sent to the front shortly after the Battle of Shiloh in April of 1862, was appalled by the stench of dead bodies, and struggled with his comrades to move an artillery piece up to a bluff. The men were literally masses of sticky mud moving around, and were so tired that they were ready to lie down in the mud to sleep, which they had to do eventually anyway: "There was not a dry spot in the Country about to make camp on. Mud mud *every* where."[7] . . .

Although the marching, rain, snow, damp, and mud clearly had a depressing effect on the spirits and health of men in Civil War armies, the psychological and physical effect of these conditions probably did not compare with the impact of infectious disease. Paul Steiner has noted that the Civil War was a form of "biological warfare" in which several hundred thousand men died of disease; because accounts of the Civil War often focus on the dash and verve of famous commanders, it is easy to forget the basic pedestrian fact that for every battle death, two men died of disease in the Civil War. Exact statistics are not available, but by most estimates about 164,000 Confederates and 250,000 Federals died of disease during the war. In the absence of a sound understanding of public health or effective medical therapies, diseases such as cholera, typhoid, malaria, smallpox, measles, mumps, scurvy, and tuberculosis, in addition to a variety of "camp fevers" and chronic diarrhea, were prevalent, frequently spread without restraint, and took a substantial toll. Although diseases such as typhoid and smallpox killed large numbers of men, dysentery and diarrhea were the great nuisance, affecting 78 percent of the soldiers annually. At times, up to two-thirds of a regiment might be on sick call at the same time, and historians have estimated that there were approximately 10 million cases of sickness (6 million for the Union Army and 4 million for the Confederates) during the Civil War, with every participant falling ill an average of four to six times.[8]

Medicine was still in its dark ages during the Civil War era, and the great advances in sanitation, germ theory, medical education and medical training, as well as the emergence of the hospital as the modern technological palace of healing, were all in the future. Of all the great advances of the nineteenth century, only anesthesia was available at this time; Koch and Pasteur were still conducting experiments in their laboratories, and Lister's precepts regarding the use of disinfectants were not yet established. Asepsis was almost half a century away, meaning that Civil War surgeons operated with germ-infested instruments; the infectious agents of disease were unknown, with the result that there was no conception that certain diseases could be communicated by air, water, or in the case of inadequate cleanliness, by touch. Moreover, tragically, the Civil War was marked by an almost total absence of any significant medical discovery or addition to existing knowledge. Civil War medical men operated in ignorance and continued to make the same mistakes throughout the war, which often led to unnecessary suffering and death. Writing in 1905, a Civil War veteran recalled that in his youth a doctor had—astonishingly—denied him any water during his bout with typhoid; of this ignorant and dangerous treatment, the veteran observed: "Darkness & fog surrounded the medical profession. The doctors were then feeling their way thru their duties, as a blind man gropes his way along a strange street." Confidence in the medical profession was not great in the Civil War era, as indicated by the comment of one soldier: "Dr. seems to have been the executioner indirectly."[9] . . .

It is no shock, then, that Civil War letters and diaries report the frequent deaths in camp of soldiers from disease (in one man's words, the "fangs of disease") and the depressing effects of illness and death on the troops. One soldier wrote home: "Sickness causes more deaths in the army than Rebel lead. . . . A man here gets sick and unless he has a strong constitution he sinks rapidly to the grave." A typical diary of a Union soldier reported: "June 1, 1862: Sunday, On guard. Had the tooth ache. Thomas Shepherd died. June 2, 1862: In camp very warm. Harry Arnold died." Another Federal noted that the unit was losing a man a day on average, and that the roll of the muffled drum and the blank discharge of a dozen muskets served as a solemn reminder to the entire camp that another soldier had gone to his last bivouac. Civil War soldiers could be haunted by the deaths of comrades, especially when they died far from home and did not receive decent burials. Years after the war, Ben R. Johnson of the 6th Michigan Infantry wrote of the disease and death he had witnessed in the swamps of Louisiana, something that he would never forget:

> The enemy [was swamp fever]. . . . His slimy, cold, and merciless hand bore down upon us until we moaned in our anguish and prayed for mercy . . . many comrades were stricken down in the midst of life and laid away under the accursed soil of the swamp. . . . Ask any living member of the old 6th if they remember Camp Death, and ten chances to one he will tell you its fearful perils are engraved upon memory's tablet as with a pen of iron. I wonder when I look back how any of us boys from the clime of Michigan ever escaped from the doom that hung over us in that hades of the swamp.[10]

Also hardly calculated to ease the mental stress and anxiety of Civil War soldiers was the fact that pay was often in arrears, and that, especially for Confederate soldiers, food was chronically in short supply. As one Southerner wrote his wife: "The main topic of conversation among the men is what they could eat if they had it."[11]

As devastating as marching, exposure to the elements, and disease could be, the major psychological trauma that Civil War soldiers encountered related to the terror of battle. One of the ironies of the experience of fighting men in the Civil War was that green recruits were often terribly worried that the war would end before they had a chance to experience combat; as one Confederate recalled: "I was tormented by feverish anxiety before I joined my regiment for fear the fighting would all be over before I got into it." In a similar vein, a Hoosier volunteer reminisced: "We really conceived the idea that if we could only get to the front with our six guns the whole affair would soon be settled to the entire satisfaction of our side. . . . A horrible fear took possession of all of us that the war would be over before we got to the front." Veterans, however, assured one Union Army novice that there would be sufficient action ahead: "They always advised us not to worry about not having plenty of chances to meet the enemy as we would soon get enough and plenty when spring came."[12]

Indeed, the glories of war regarded from afar were one thing, but as troops were assembled and moved to the front to enter combat, men began to experience the worst sort of nerve-wracking anxiety, fear, and tension imaginable. It was particularly difficult for men—especially new recruits—to be within earshot of the battlefield, to hear the bullets, exploding shells, and screams of the combatants without yet being engaged. One Union man commented: "The real test comes before the battle." Rice Bull depicted the terrific anxiety of the moment as his unit awaited the order to move forward at the Battle of Chancellorsville and, while waiting, witnessed terror-stricken Union troops fleeing from the battlefield for the rear. These men had thrown away everything that was loose—guns, knapsacks, caps, and coats: "Nothing could stop them. They were crazed and would fight to escape as though the enemy were close to them. We were ordered to stop them but we might as well have tried to stop a cyclone. . . . One can hardly conceive of the terror that possessed them . . . their panic was nerve-wracking to troops new to the service."[13] . . .

Some men on the line before battle could look merely solemn or even calm, but the reaction of another Union soldier seemed more typical when he recalled that a feeling of horror, dread, and fear came over him: "I was faint. . . . A glance along the line satisfied me that I was not alone in my terror; many a face had a pale, livid expression of fear." A Michigan volunteer remembered: "Some may say they never had any fear that may be true but it was not so with me I was scared . . . I was scared good and sure." Sometimes this fear was so intense that men would fall to the ground paralyzed with terror, bury their face in the grass, grasp at the earth, and refuse to move. Officers would scream and cajole and beat on these men, even striking them with bayonets, or, in extreme instances, resort to shooting them—but with no effect. Before one battle, a Union soldier noticed one man who was trembling so badly that he could not stay on his feet or hold his gun, and another who had great beads of sweat on his forehead and a fixed stare on his face. A third man threw his head back and, with mouth wide open, sang a hymn at the top of his lungs; it was understood that he was simply trying to steady himself under the well-nigh unendurable strain. Instances of men being so terrified before a battle that they lost control of their bowels were not unknown.[14]

Once men actually entered combat and began to fire their weapons, however, there was a radical transformation as fear and anxiety evaporated and gave way to rage, anger, and a sense of disembodiment. One Federal soldier recalled: "As soon as the first volley was fired all dread and sense of personal danger was gone." As the line surged forward in one assault, a Union officer noted great hysterical excitement, the eagerness to go forward, and a reckless disregard of life: "The soldier who is shooting is furious in his energy. . . . The men are loading and firing with demoniacal fury and shouting and laughing hysterically." Another Union soldier participating in such an attack heard his comrades shrieking like demons . . .

Commenting on this rage as well as an obliviousness to personal danger, Franklin H. Bailey of the 12th Michigan Infantry wrote to his parents: "Strange it may seam to you, but the more men I saw kiled the more reckless I became; when George Gates . . . was shot *I was so enraged* I could have tore the heart out of the rebel could I have reached him."[15] These wild emotional extremes could push some men to the breaking point on the battlefield itself, as in the case of one young Confederate: "I witnessed a sight I have never forgotten a member of the 14 Miss, a young boy looked to be about 15 was calling on his regt for Gods sake to reform and charge the Yankees again the tears were rolling down his face and I think he would have gone alone if an officer had not taken him to the rear."[16]

Numerous Civil War soldiers testified to the sense of disembodiment they felt during battle: when the firing began, they became oblivious of their own bodies and needs, and focused entirely on the action at hand in the battle. The matters of food, water, and comfort were forgotten. When men were wounded, it frequently came as a complete surprise: in memoirs or letters they would describe the feeling of a sting, a "strange sensation," a feeling of being struck with an axe or a board, or of being inexplicably whirled around or knocked off their feet; sometimes the realization of having been hit came only when a soldier was no longer able to lift an arm, or when his vision was suddenly blurred by his own blood flowing into his eyes from a head wound:

> By far the larger number felt, when shot, as though some one had struck them sharply with a stick, and one or two were so possessed with this idea at the time, that they turned to accuse a comrade of the act, and were unpleasantly surprised to discover, from the flow of blood, that they had been wounded. About one-third experienced no pain nor local shock when the ball entered. A few felt as though stung by a whip at the point injured. More rarely, the pain of the wound was dagger-like and intense; while a few, one in ten, were convinced for a moment that the injured limb had been shot away.[17]

Such shell or gunshot wounds could quickly bring a man back to the reality of his own body and a sense of vulnerability, leading in some cases to panic, terror, and the fear of dying: "When hit, he thought his arm was shot off. It dropped, the gun fell, and, screaming that he was murdered, he staggered, bleeding freely, and soon fell unconscious." Those who fought on rarely experienced such vulnerability, however, and in some cases, men became so engrossed in the action that they refused to leave the front when their unit was relieved. A Confederate soldier recalled the scene after one battle: "[O]n every living face was seen the impress of an excitement which has no equal here on earth."[18]

The demoniacal appearance of the men—enraged, blackened faces, screaming, firing their rifles in a frenzy, grappling in hand-to-hand combat—was matched by the surreal aspect of the battlefield, its smoke, smell, noise, confusion, and havoc. Smokeless gunpowder had not yet been developed, so after the firing began, the Civil War battlefield was frequently enshrouded in a pall of smoke and sulphurous vapor, which severely limited one's field of vision and added to one's sense of confusion and disorientation. Appalling sounds assaulted one's senses from all directions in what one man described as the "awful shock and rage of battle," and others characterized as "that howling acre," a "portrait of hell," or a "rumbling, grinding sound that cannot be described. . . . The dreadful pounding and concussion from the cannonading was such that blood gushed out of the nose and ears of one Indiana infantryman at the Battle of New Hope Church in Georgia, and numerous Civil War soldiers were permanently deafened from exposure to the concussion of cannon fire.[19]

At Chickamauga, the "rattle of musketry was dreadful and to see the men lying dead and dying on the field and being run over by artillery and lines of men it was perfectly appalling." At Spotsylvania Courthouse, "it was an awful din. The air seemed full of bullets." The cacophony of zipping bullets and bursting shells created such a maelstrom that it was impossible to shout orders so that one could be heard. An Ohio soldier recalled an atmosphere hideous with the shrieks of the messengers of death at the Battle of Franklin: "The booming of cannon, the bursting of bombs, the rattle of musketry, the shrieking of shells, the whizzing of bullets, . . . the falling of men in their struggle for victory, all made a scene of surpassing terror and awful grandeur." Of the sights and sounds of battle, one Northerner concluded: "The half can never be told—language is all too tame to convey the horror and the meaning of it all."[20]

Nor should one overrate the ability of men infuriated and obsessed with battle to screen out all horror of death. Although men concentrated on the task at hand and put personal safety aside, they still witnessed and reacted to—even if belatedly—horrific scenes of slaughter, and these sights and memories took an eventual toll. In the Civil War, innovations in weapons (particularly the rifled musket and an array of antipersonnel artillery charges) had extended the range of deadly fire on the battlefield and allowed defenders, ensconced in trenches or behind abatis and breastworks, to mercilessly shred the ranks of assaulting troops; in spite of this, however, Civil War commanders still frequently attempted to storm enemy fortifications by means of frontal assaults. The results could be deadly as attacking columns were torn and blasted by the defenders: "Brains, fractured skulls, broken arms and legs, and the human form mangled in every conceivable and inconceivable manner. . . .

At every step they take they see the piles of wounded and slain and their feet are slipping in the blood and brains of their comrades."[21] At times the horror and shock overwhelmed men, who would flee from the battlefield in terror, for sights of the wounded could be devastating:

> A wounded man begged piteously for us to take him to the rear; he was wounded in the neck, or head, and the blood flowed freely; everytime he tried to speak the blood would fill his mouth and he would blow it out in all directions; he was all blood, and at the time I thought he was the most dreadfull sight I ever saw. We could not help him, for it was of no use, for he could not live long by the way he was bleeding.[22]

The Civil War has sometimes been portrayed as almost gentlemanly, an unfortunate war between brothers in which Union and Confederate soldiers routinely chatted with each other and exchanged newspapers or tobacco for coffee. Such incidents surely did take place, but not on the battlefield. There frenzy drove and impelled soldiers to commit acts of violence and cruelty toward their fellow men. Participating in the assault on Confederate positions at Spotsylvania Courthouse on May 12, 1864, Robert S. Robertson of the 93rd New York Infantry recalled a scene of violent chaos when the Rebel line was finally broken:

> The 26th Mich. was the first to reach the breastworks, and as the line scaled the bank it was met by a volley from close quarters & recoiled with fearful loss, but only for an instant, for we pushed on, and the works were ours. The men, infuriated and wild with excitement, went to work with bayonets and clubbed muskets, and a scene of horror ensued for a few moments. It was the first time I had been in the midst of a hand to hand fight, and seen men bayonetted, or their brains dashed out with the butt of a musket, & I never wish to see another scene.[23] . . .

Cases of atrocities in which prisoners of war were killed in cold blood, furthermore, were certainly not unknown in the Civil War: in some instances, the motivation was racial as Confederates killed captured African-Americans, or Northerners retaliated by killing captured Rebels. In one such instance, Union men took a Confederate prisoner only to notice a "Fort Pillow" tattoo—Fort Pillow having been the scene of the Confederate massacre of dozens of Union troops, who had surrendered, but were nonetheless slaughtered: "As soon as the boys saw the letters on his arm, they yelled, 'No quarter for you,' and a dozen bayonets went into him and a dozen bullets were shot into him. I shall never forget his look of fear." In describing the Battle of Gettysburg, Wladimir Krzyzanowski wrote that the men with their powder-blackened faces and fierce expressions looked more like animals than human beings and that they indeed had an animal-like eagerness for blood and the need for revenge. He concluded that this "portrait of battle was a portrait of hell. This, indeed, must weigh heavily on the consciences of those who started it. Terrible, indeed, was the curse that hung over their heads."[24]

The vicious disregard for human life evident at pitched battles such as Shiloh, Gettysburg, and Spotsylvania Courthouse was particularly pronounced in the guerrilla warfare that raged constantly behind the lines in Tennessee, Kentucky, Missouri, and Kansas; this guerrilla warfare is particularly relevant in assessing the claims of some that the Vietnam War was singular in the history of American warfare. Rebel guerrillas routinely blew up trains and destroyed Union property throughout the war, and in early 1865, Franklin H. Bailey of the 4th Michigan Cavalry wrote to his mother that "bushwhackers" would kill any Union soldier who strayed from his unit. Another Michigan man observed that his camp—despite being "behind the lines"—was every bit as dangerous as a battlefield: "Our lives are in danger every moment without having the satisfaction of even defending ourselves. Those Bushwhackers fire on you as they would on sparrows." In innumerable incidents, guerrillas would single out and murder African-American soldiers or shoot and kill Union troopers out foraging; they would place dead animals in ponds to poison the water and then threaten to kill anyone who removed the carcasses; utilizing their spies, they would take care not to attack an adequately guarded train, but would strike and kill unsuspecting Union soldiers and civilians on trains, boats, and elsewhere when the opportunity permitted. In Missouri and Kansas, atrocities were all too common, such as the incident in Lawrence, Kansas, in August of 1863, when marauding Rebels under the leadership of William C. Quantrill shot and killed over 150 civilian Union men and boys in cold blood. The legendary James brothers, Frank and Jesse, got their start as Confederate "raiders" or guerrillas—"murderers" in the Union Army's lexicon—in the Civil War.[25]

Under such circumstances, reprisals were common in which entire towns were shelled and destroyed or plundered in retaliation for guerrilla activity. As was the case in Vietnam, Union soldiers were frequently fired upon, but the guerrillas would scatter before they could be engaged; in these cases, Northern infantrymen would burn and pillage all houses and towns within reach: "[W]e burned all their houses & everything they

had & we boys hooked everything we could carry & some things we
could not." When Union soldiers found army mail in a house, they
burned down the house in which they found the mail in addition to
adjacent houses, and "throwd women and children out of dores and
plaid hell Generaly." In other instances, when the Union Army determined that a house had been used to harbor guerrillas or if Union men
were killed in the vicinity, these houses, or even all houses within a
certain radius, would be torched and the occupants ordered to leave the
district. Union retaliation went beyond the destruction of property; when
guerrillas were captured, they were frequently hanged with or without a
trial.[26] . . .

Did Union soldiers feel guilt over such acts of violence committed
during the war? Regarding the mere observation of these executions, one
notes occasional comments in letters and diaries such as "entirely beyond
the pale of civilization" or "awful." Regarding the feelings of Union men
who actually did the hanging or shooting, the case of John A. Cundiff
of the 99th Indiana Infantry is suggestive of an answer. Cundiff had
apparently been detailed to shoot a Confederate prisoner during the war,
and in the years after the war, he was convinced that Rebel spies
or relatives of the dead Confederate were after him. Affidavits taken
by Pension Bureau officials in 1893 and 1894 revealed the following
behavior:

> He has always claimed that the rebels had spies out to kill him, and would
> take his gun and blanket and stay in the woods for days and nights at a
> time, and would leave the house at night and sleep in the fence corners.
> . . . He told me one day that two or three of his neighbors were rebels
> from the south (there were some new people came in then) & that they
> were going to kill him but that he put his axe under his bed at night to
> defend himself.[27]

Cundiff's troubling memories of having shot Rebel prisoners calls to
mind the atrocities and "abusive violence" that psychologists frequently
discuss in reference to Vietnam veterans. . . .

Historians have often claimed that World War I was the watershed in
psychological casualties during warfare, that such casualties were minimal before 1914 and epidemic in numbers thereafter. This argument is
based on two assertions. First, soldiers of World War I, compared with
soldiers from the nineteenth century, had less training and regimentation
to shield them from the horrors of war: they are viewed as industrial,

"deskilled" workers/soldiers. Second, and more important, the advent of high-powered explosives shifted the nature of warfare to a situation in which as many as 70 percent of casualties resulted from artillery fire, and this killing occurred at long range, leading to a sense of dread and helplessness in infantrymen subjected to this type of bombardment. An army surgeon commented on the eve of World War I: "[T]he mysterious and widely destructive effects of modern artillery fire will test men as they have never been tested before. We can surely count then on a larger percentage of mental diseases, requiring our attention in a future war." In considering the experience of soldiers in the Civil War era, attention must therefore be paid to the attitude of infantrymen to artillery fire. A review of the evidence quickly reveals that Civil War soldiers were indeed terrified at the prospect and actuality of such bombardment, and experienced considerable psychological fear and anxiety as a result.[28]

In his first exposure to combat, Rice Bull noted the terrifying noise of a shell overhead, which, "hissing and shrieking," tore through the branches and leaves of a tree; Bull noted that the shell made everyone jump and duck. This was a nervous habit few ever fully overcame, and perhaps the basis of what may have become startle reactions, a classic symptom of PTSD, in some of these men. Other Union soldiers who witnessed artillery duels wrote of "screaming metal," which made the earth groan and tremble; one recalled that through the murk, he heard hoarse commands, the bursting of shells, and cries of agony:

> We saw caissons hit and blown up, splinters flying, men flung to the ground, horses torn and shrieking. Solid shot hit the hill in our front, sprayed battalions with fountains of dirt, and went plunging into the ranks, crushing flesh and bone. . . . The shock from a bursting shell will scatter a man's thoughts as the iron fragments will scatter the leaves overhead.[29]

The Union cannonading at Fredericksburg was so awful that the ground shook and even rabbits left their dens in the earth and came into the camps, trembling with fright. A Federal at the Battle of Chickamauga was stunned at the carnage wreaked by Union artillery on Confederate ranks, as a cannonball wiped out four lines of Rebels, making a space large enough to drive and turn around a six-mule team: "It was terrible to behold. It seemed like they had almost annihilated them." Predictably, a Confederate wrote that men subjected to artillery bombardment never forgot how to hug the ground. In addition to solid shot, Civil War

soldiers particularly feared what was called canister, a load of antipersonnel shrapnel (three-quarter-inch iron balls) fired from cannons at
close range on charging infantry; these projectiles frequently dismem-
bered or disemboweled attacking soldiers.[30]

Men subjected to long-range bombardment lost the ability to calculate time objectively. Recalling a seemingly interminable Rebel artillery
bombardment at Gettysburg, one Northerner commented that the thunder of the guns was incessant as the whole air seemed to be filled with
rushing, screaming, and bursting shells: "Of course, it would be absurd
to say we were not scared. . . . How long did this pandemonium last?
Measured by our feelings it might have been an age. In point of fact it
may have been an hour or three or five. The measurement of time under
such circumstances, regular as it is by the watch, is exceedingly uncertain
by the watchers." Another Union soldier reflected that in the space of a
mere two seconds on the approach of a shell, thoughts and images of all
types of possible mutilation and death occupied the minds of men, and
that if one wrote for an entire day afterward, one could not completely
express these myriad fears and terrors as they had run through the mind
the instant before impact.[31] . . .

Aside from dead soldiers or mangled bodies, what were the psychological repercussions of this horrific cannon fire? Artillery and high explosives produced a number of psychiatric casualties in the Civil War
that seemed at times almost identical to the hysterias, mutism, and
uncontrollable shaking produced by the barrages on the Western Front
in World War I. One nurse recounted the case of a man buried alive in
the terrific explosion of a Union mine at Petersburg in 1864, when Union
sappers had attempted to breach the Confederate defenses by placing a
huge load of high explosives in a mine shaft under the Rebel lines: "[He]
was buried alive in the explosion of the mine at Petersburg and has lost
hearing, speech and almost all sensation. He has a piteous expression of
face and makes signs, as best he can, of gratitude for even a look of
sympathy." Another man almost struck by a shell fragment which narrowly missed his head "went all to pieces, instantly" and was described
as completely "demoralized, panic-stricken and frantic with terror." In
a similar incident, a man who had been chattering away before a shell
shrieked overhead and landed nearby was left completely speechless.
When shelling began in another instance, an officer begged a companion:
"For Gods sake don't leave me."

Perhaps the most striking case, however, is that of Albert Frank.

Sitting in a trench near Bermuda Hundred in the vicinity of Richmond, Virginia, Frank offered a drink from his canteen to a man sitting next to him. Frank kept the strap around his own neck and extended the canteen to the other man's mouth for him to take a drink, but at just this moment a shell decapitated the other man, splattering blood and brain fragments on Frank. The shell continued on, exploded to the rear of the trench, and in no way directly injured Frank. That evening, Albert Frank began to act strangely, and a fellow soldier advised that he go to the bomb shelter; once there Frank began screaming, ran out the other door, and went over the top of the breastworks toward the enemy. His fellow soldiers, alarmed, went looking for him, and eventually found him huddled in fear. On the way back to Union lines, he seemed to go mad: "[H]e would drop his gun, and make a noise like the whiz of a shell, and blast and say 'Frank is killed.' " Because he had completely lost control, his comrades tied him up that night to restrain him and took him to the doctor the next day. There he was declared insane, and sent to the Government Hospital for the Insane in Washington, D.C.[32]

Also deeply affected after artillery fire was John Bumgardner of the 26th Indiana Light Artillery. At Dalton Hill, Kentucky, he was knocked down by the concussion of an exploding shell, and other soldiers at the scene noticed that he was shaken and pale; after returning to camp, he was morose and sullen and continued to tremble for weeks. He talked constantly about fighting when there was no enemy in sight, and would suddenly start yelling: "There they come men run boys run they are after us." He was eventually sent to the insane asylum at Lexington, Kentucky.[33] The Civil War experience seems to confirm the theory that soldiers in a passive position of helplessness—such as those subjected to artillery bombardments—feel intense terror and anxiety, and may be at great risk for psychological breakdown. Although the experience of World War I might have intensified this phenomenon, it certainly did not originate it.

While exposure to artillery fire and the sights and sounds of a battle in progress could be unnerving in the extreme, perhaps the most horrific aspect of the Civil War experience was the scene of the battlefield after the firing had subsided. Mangled men, dead and dying, littered the landscape; the wounded would frequently plead for water and medical attention, and an occasional man, terminally wounded, would beg to be shot and put out of his misery. One North Carolina soldier wrote that after the heat and excitement of the battle ended and the smoke cleared away, the battlefield presented a harrowing scene that beggared description: "The grim monster death having done its terrible work leaves its impress on the faces of its unfortunate victims . . . now wrapt in the cold embrace of death." A Confederate described the scene at Chickamauga as ghastly, with hundreds of dead on the field, their faces upward and some with their arms sticking up as if reaching for something. According to a Maine volunteer, the dead were lying about as thickly as if they were slumbering in camp: "[T]he sight was most appalling . . . the horror of such a picture can never be penned." A Rebel recalled that after the Battle of Seven Pines in 1862 many Union wounded were too weak to pull themselves out of ditches, which were full of water because of inordinately heavy rains; judging by the sounds he heard, these men seemed to be drowning and strangling to death: "The cries of the wounded Yankees sound in my ears yet."[34]

After fierce fighting in Georgia in 1864, a Rebel walked over the field and saw the dead piled four deep. Some guns were still standing on end, their bayonets having been driven through the bodies of victims, giving ample evidence of the awful conflict that had gone before. Of the field at Shiloh, a Hoosier noted that dead men seemed to be everywhere: "You could find them in every hollow, by every tree and stump—in open field and under copse—Union and Rebel, side by side—in life foes, in death, of one family." The psychological effect of these scenes could be devastating, as evidenced by one Confederate, who characterized the battlefield at Franklin, Tennessee, as one vast slaughter pen: "After gazing on it I felt sick at heart for days afterwards. . . . The men were so disheartened by gazing on that scene of slaughter that they had not the nerve for the work before them." In a similar vein, a Northerner wrote: "It was a scene that I wish never again to behold. I have had enough of War." Nor did these impressions fade with time; a Union soldier wrote decades after the war that the Shiloh battlefield had shocked and disheartened him: "Tho it now lacks but two days of forty two years since that morning, the picture has not faded in the least . . . it was a rude awakening to the realities of an active War Service." He characterized this scene as the "real stuff good & strong." After attempting to describe such a scene, a Michigan volunteer ended a letter to his sister: "I cannot comment more, nor dwell on the subject. *I am so unwell.*"[35]

As with recruits aching for a fight, Civil War soldiers had a great curiosity to see what a battlefield looked like. One such experience was usually satisfactory, as indicated by the account of Calvin Ainsworth of the 25th Iowa Infantry:

I went over the field of battle as soon as possible after the surrender. At some points it was terrible. My eyes never beheld such a sight before. I hope they may never again. In some places the dead lay very thick, not more than 3-5-10 feet apart; some were shot in the head, others in the breast and lungs, some through the neck, and I saw 3 or 4 torn all to pieces by cannon balls; their innards lying by their side,. . . . It is indeed a sickening sight, . . . I had often wished that I could be in one battle and go over a battle field. My curiosity has been gratified. I never wish to see another.[36]

Twentieth-century research into psychiatric disorders associated with military service has indicated that soldiers attached to the Graves Registration Detail (that is, those who handle dead bodies) often experience psychological problems related to this work, and, in the Civil War era, duty with burial details could indeed produce psychological distress. One man noted that he helped to bury the dead after a battle, and it was, to say the least, a disagreeable job: "i helped to bury Some that was tore in pieces and throwed in every direction one leg here and another there wee Just had to gather up the pieces and fix them away the best wee could wee caried a hundred and fifty together and dug a big ditch. . . . i never want to See another battle field." The bodies of the dead would sometimes lie on the field for several days before they were buried, creating an unbearable stench. Particularly during the summer, this would result in scenes of sunbaked and putrefied bodies: "These corpses were so black that we, at first glance, thought they were negroes; but they had lain in the hot August sun all the day before and all this day and had been burned black and were in a state of loathsome corruption and covered with living vermin. . . . Our task of burying these poor fellows was loathsome and disgusting."[37] The attempts of Civil War soldiers to describe the carnage of the battlefield seemed time and again to end with phrases such as "pen cannot properly describe this valley of death, it was too horrible"; "the horrors of a battle field cannot be described, they must be seen"; "[t]he most shocking sight I ever saw"; "ghastly"; "O what a sight, it almost makes me shudder to think of it"; "I am shure I would not want you to witness the sight I did."[38]

Last of all, in assessing the psychological trauma to which Civil War soldiers were exposed, one should consider the ritual execution of deserters. In the Vietnam era, executing deserters would have been an utter impossibility—completely unthinkable. In the Civil War, however, hundreds of such men were shot to death by the military, and these executions were staged in ceremonies calculated to terrify the men remaining in the ranks, so as to discourage others from engaging in such behavior. The temptation to desert did, of course, exist, as one might imagine after considering the situation regarding marching, exposure to the elements, lack of adequate clothing and food, the prevalence of disease, and the horrors of battle.[39]

When executions were staged, the men in the regiment were lined up on three sides, and the condemned man was placed on top of his coffin and brought to the grounds by wagon; after the man was shot to death by the firing squad, the entire company of men was paraded by the bullet-riddled body. At times, the man executed would then be buried on the spot and the ground above smoothed over with no marker, to further terrify onlookers with the prospect not only of death, but eternal oblivion. On most occasions, men who were forced to witness these executions were appalled and deeply disturbed. One Confederate soldier witnessed an execution at which the condemned man begged piteously for his life, but was nonetheless tied to a stake and shot; the Rebel observer called it "one of the most sickening scenes I ever witnessed . . . [it] looked more like some tragedy of the dark ages, than the civilization of the nineteenth century." A Union soldier who witnessed such an execution wrote in his diary: "I call it murder in the first degree in taking his life. I don't think I will ever witness another such a horror if I can get away from it. I have seen men shot in battle but never in cold blood before." A New Hampshire volunteer was equally stunned: "I venture to say it was [a scene] never to be forgotten while life lasted, with any who witnessed it. There the body lay, the clothing stripped from the breast revealing it perforated with bullets." Writing forty years after the end of the war, a Hoosier veteran remembered that it had taken him a long time to mentally recover from the shocking sight of an execution he had witnessed so many years before: "To me it was a dreadful thing to see a human being sat on a box, blindfold & his life taken in such a savage barbarous manner. I have long since disbelieved in capital punishment, & this affair was, I think, the forerunner of this disbelief." Another Civil War soldier summed up the entire experience: "War is horrid beyond the conception of man."[40]

NOTES

From Eric T. Dean, Jr., *Shook over Hell: Post-Traumatic Stress, Vietnam, and the Civil War* (Cambridge: Harvard University Press, 1997), 46–69. Reprinted by permission.

1. Francis Wayland Dunn, diary entry of October 30, 1862, Bentley Historical Library, University of Michigan, Ann Arbor ["destroying manner of living"].

2. C. Macfarlane, *Reminiscences of an Army Surgeon* (Oswego, N.Y.: Lake City Print Shop, 1912), p. 55 [forced march]; Robert Watson memoirs, entry of July 4, 1863, Florida State Archives, Tallahassee [vomiting]; Thomas Clark to his wife, Martha Ann, September 7, 1862, Florida State Archives, Tallahassee [killed at Antietam].

3. Spencer Glasgow Welch. *A Confederate Surgeon's Letters to His Wife* (Marietta, Ga.: Continental Book Co., 1954; originally published in 1911), p. 31; John G. Perry, *Letters from a Surgeon of the Civil War*, ed. Martha Derby Perry (Boston: Little, Brown and Co., 1906), p. 144.

4. Disability discharge papers, September 10, 1862, federal pension file of Wesley Lynch [A 35 Ind. Inf.], National Archives.

5. Aurelius Lyman Voorhis journal, entry for December 5, 1862, Indiana Historical Society [shivering]; Andrew Jackson Smith diary, entries for January 2, December 19, and December 25, 1864, Indiana Historical Society [blues]; David R. Trego to his brother, October 3, 1863, Bentley Historical Library [wet bed]; Wash Vosburgh to Ella, January 30, 1863, Nina L. Ness Collection, Bentley Historical Library [covered with snow]; John Johnston memoirs, p. 29, Confederate Collection, Tennessee State Archives [wretched feeling]; James N. Wright to his brother, Squire, November 17, 1864, John Johnson Papers, Indiana Historical Society [freight cars].

6. Henry W. Reddick, *Seventy-Seven Years in Dixie: The Boys in Gray of 61–65* (Santa Rosa, Fla.: II. W. Reddick, 1910), p. 21. Wash Vosburgh to Ella, May 12, 1864, Nina L. Ness Collection, Bentley Historical Library.

7. Carroll Henderson Clark memoirs, p. 9, Confederate Collection, Tennessee State Archives [equipment abandoned; breadth of mud]; Augustus M. Van Dyke to his parents, August 12, 1861, Indiana Historical Society [Cheat Mountain], DeWitt C. Goodrich memoirs, p. 114, Indiana Historical Society [at Shiloh].

8. Paul E. Steiner, *Disease in the Civil War: Natural Biological Warfare in 1861–1865* (Springfield, Ill.: Charles C. Thomas, 1968). The *Medical and Surgical History of the War of the Rebellion*, Medical History, pt. I, vol. I (Washington, D.C.: U.S. Government Printing Office, 1870), indicates that for Union troops (white and black), there were 6,454,834 cases of disease, with 195,627

deaths from disease. In general, see Courtney Robert Hall, "Confederate Medicine: Caring for the Confederate Soldier," *Medical Life*, 42 (1935): 445–508; William M. Straight, "Florida Medicine and the War between the States," *Journal of the Florida Medical Association*, 67 (8) (August 1980): 748–760; Alfred Jay Bollet, "To Care for Him That Has Borne the Battle: A Medical History of the Civil War," *Resident and Staff Physician*, 35 (November 1989): 121–129; James O. Breeden, "Confederate Medicine: The View from Virginia," *Virginia Medical Quarterly*, 118 (4) (Fall 1991): 222–231; and John Ochsner, "The Genuine Southern Surgeon," *Annals of Surgery*, 215 (5) (May 1992): 397–408.

9. In general, see George W. Adams, *Doctors in Blue: The Medical History of the Union Army in the Civil War* (Dayton, Ohio: Morningside Press, 1985), and Horace H. Cunningham, *Doctors in Gray: The Confederate Medical Service* (Gloucester, Mass.: Peter Smith, 1970). DeWitt C. Goodrich memoirs, pp. 9–10, Indiana Historical Society [primitive state of medicine]; Andrew Newton Buck to Myron and Susan, January 28, 1862, Buck Family Papers, Bentley Historical Library [executioner].

10. Roderick Gospero Shaw to his sister, October 8, 1863, Florida State Archives, Tallahassee [fangs of disease]; Henry G. Noble to Ruth, February 26, 1863, Bentley Historical Library [Rebel lead]; Chauncey H. Cooke, *Soldier Boy's Letters to His Father and Mother, 1861–5* (privately published, 1915), p. 23 [muffled drum]; Ben C. Johnson, *Soldier's Life: Civil War Experiences of Ben C. Johnson*, ed. Alan S. Brown, Faculty Contributions, ser. VI, no. 2 (Kalamazoo, Mich.: Western Michigan University Press, 1962), pp. 48–49.

11. James J. Nixon to his wife, May 11, 1864, P. K. Yonge Library of Florida History, University of Florida, Gainesville.

12. Col. James L. Cooper memoirs, p. 4, Confederate Collection, Tennessee State Archives; DeWitt Goodrich memoirs, p. 106, Indiana Historical Society; Rice C. Bull, *Soldiering*, p. 36.

13. Abner R. Small, *The Road to Richmond: The Civil War Memoirs of Major Abner R. Small of the Sixteenth Maine Volunteers, Together with the Diary Which He Kept When He Was a Prisoner of War*, ed. Harold Adams Small (Berkeley: University of California Press, 1939), p. 185 [real test]; Bull, *Soldiering*, p. 51.

14. Elbridge J. Copp, *Reminiscences of the War of the Rebellion, 1861–1865* (Nashua, N.H.: Telegraph Publishing Co., 1911), pp. 134–135 [horror and dread]; William Baird memoirs, p. 16, Bentley Historical Library [Michigan volunteer]; Perry, *Letters from a Surgeon*, p. 168 [screaming officers; singing soldier]; Small, *The Road to Richmond*, p. 71 [trembling soldier]; Major and Surgeon S. C. Gordon, "Reminiscences of the Civil War from a Surgeon's Point of View," in Military Order of the Loyal Legion of The United States, Maine Commandery, *War Papers* (Portland, Maine: Lefavor-Tower, 1898–1919),

p. 143 [trembling soldiers]; George T. Ulmer, *Adventures and Reminiscences of a Volunteer, or a Drummer Boy from Maine* (1892), p. 28 [loss of control of bowels].

15. Charles A. Fuller, *Personal Recollections of the War of 1861* (Sherburne, N.Y.: News Job Printing House, 1906), p. 20 [first volley]; Major Rufus R. Dawes [*Service with the Sixth Wisconsin Volunteers*], quoted in Henry Steele Commager, ed., *The Blue and the Gray: The Story of the Civil War as Told by Participants* (New York: Bobbs-Merrill, 1950), p. 213 [demoniacal fury]; Robert S. Robertson, *Diary of the War,* ed. Charles N. Walker and Rosemary Walker (Fort Wayne, Ind.: Allen County-Fort Wayne Historical Society, 1965), pp. 181–182 [shouts which startle the dead]; Franklin H. Bailey to his parents, April 8, 1862, Bentley Historical Library.

16. William Lewis McKay memoirs, p. 37, Confederate Collection, Tennessee State Archives.

17. William A. Ketcham memoirs, p. 4, Indiana Historical Society [forgot personal needs]; B.S.P., "Battle Impressions," in *The Soldier's Friend,* July 1867, p. 1 [sense of disembodiment]; Bull, *Soldiering,* p. 57 [sharp sting]; Copp, *Reminiscences of the War of the Rebellion,* p. 337 [blow from club]; Fuller, *Personal Recollections of the War of 1861,* p. 95 [arm ceased to function]; William E. Sloan diary, September 19, 1863, Confederate Collection, Tennessee State Archives [terror of the wounded]; Robertson, *Diary of the War,* p. 183 [legs knocked out]; James L. Cooper memoirs, p. 39 [felt like struck with board], Confederate Collection, Tennessee State Archives; S. Weir Mitchell, George R. Morehouse, and William W. Keen, *Gunshot Wounds and Other Injuries of Nerves* (Philadelphia: J. B. Lippincott & Co., 1864), p. 14 [by far].

18. Mitchell et al., *Gunshot Wounds,* p. 87 [case study of David Schively, E 114 Pa. Inf.; staggered]; James L. Cooper memoirs, p. 22 [excitement], Confederate Collection, Tennessee State Archives.

19. George E. Ranney, "Reminiscences of an Army Surgeon," in *War Papers Read before the Michigan Commandery of the Military Order of the Loyal Legion of the United States,* vol. 2 (Detroit: James H. Stone & Co., 1898), p. 189 [awful shock and rage of battle]; Small, *The Road to Richmond,* p. 133 [the Battle of the Wilderness as "that howling acre"]; Alfred A. Atkins to parents, February 11, 1864, Georgia State Archives [rumbling, grinding noise]; David Ballenger to his mother, May 8, 1863, South Caroliniana Library [Chancellorsville]; declaration of January 2, 1900 [blood gushing], federal pension file of Thomas B. Hornaday [E 70 Ind. Inf.], National Archives. For a typical pension claim for deafness induced by cannonading, see federal pension file of Elijah Wingert [D 118 Pa. Inf.], National Archives.

20. William B. Miller diary, entry for September 19, 1863 [Chickamauga]; Robertson, *Diary of the War,* p. 182 [Spotsylvania]; Gus F. Smith, "Battle of Franklin," in *War Papers Read before the Michigan Commandery of the Mili-*

tary Order of the Loyal Legion of the United States, p. 262 [awful grandeur]; Copp, *Reminiscences of the War of the Rebellion*, p. 242 [the half].

21. *John Dooley War Journal* (Washington D.C., 1945), p. 23, quoted in Horace H. Cunningham, *Field Medical Services at the Battles of Manassas (Bull Run)*, University of Georgia Monographs, no. 16 (Athens, Ga.: University of Georgia Press, 1968), p. 87.

22. Austin C. Stearns, *Three Years with Company K: Sergt. Austin C. Stearns, Company K, 13th Mass. Infantry (Deceased)* ed. Arthur A. Kent (Rutherford, N.J.: Fairleigh Dickinson University Press 1976), p. 109 [wounded man].

23. Robertson, *Diary of the War*, p. 182.

24. Joseph T. Glatthaar, *Forged in Battle: The Civil War Alliance of Black Soldiers and White Officers* (New York: Meridian Books, 1991), pp. 155–158 [racially motivated atrocities]; Robert Hale Strong, *A Yankee Private's Civil War* (Chicago: Henry Regnery Co., 1961), p. 16 [Fort Pillow]; Bull, *Soldiering*, pp. 155, 136[deadly sniper fire]; Wladimir Krzyzanowski, *The Memoirs of Wladimir Krzyzanowski*, trans. by Stanley J. Pula, ed. James S. Pula (San Francisco: R & E Research Associates, 1978), p. 49.

25. Franklin H. Bailey to his mother, January 3, 1865, Bentley Historical Library; Victor E. Comte to wife Elise, May 12, 1863, Bentley Historical Library [sparrows]; Elvira J. Powers, *Hospital Pencillings: Being a Diary while in Jefferson General Hospital, Jeffersonville, Ind., and Others at Nashville Tennessee, as Matron and Visitor* (Boston: Edward L. Mitchell, 1866), p. 107 [Negro soldiers killed]; Elijah P. Burton, *Diary of E. P. Burton, Surgeon 7th Reg. Ill. 3rd Brig. 2nd Div. 16 A.C.* (Des Moines, Iowa: Historical Records Survey, 1939), p. 26 [forager killed]; David Wiltsee diary, February 28, 1862, Indiana Historical Society [dead animals]; Michael Fellman, *Inside War: The Guerrilla Conflict in Missouri during the American Civil War* (New York: Oxford University Press, 1989), p. 25 [Quantrill raid]. See also Stephen V. Ash, "Sharks in an Angry Sea: Civilian Resistance and Guerrilla Warfare in Occupied Middle Tennessee, 1862–1865," *Tennessee Historical Quarterly*, 45 (3) (Fall 1986): 217–229; and Gary L. Cheatham, " 'Desperate Characters': The Development and Impact of the Confederate Guerrillas in Kansas," *Kansas History*, 14 (3) (Autumn 1991): 144–161.

26. Horace Charles to unknown, October 23, 1862, Bentley Historical Library [burned houses]; Victor E. Comte to Elise, May 12, 1863, Bentley Historical Library [burning and plundering in retaliation]; William R. Stuckey to unknown, April 27, 1863 [captured mail], Indiana Historical Society; Russell F. Weigley, *Quartermaster General of the Union Army. A Biography of M. C. Meigs* (New York: Columbia University Press, 1959), pp. 307–308 [retribution after Union soldier killed]; Judson L. Austin to wife, Sarah, July 11, 1863, Nina L. Ness Collection, Bentley Historical Library [summary execution]; Reddick, *Seventy-Seven Years in Dixie*, p. 35 [six bushwackers executed].

27. Joseph Dill Alison diary, entry for May 19, 1861, P. K. Yonge Library of Florida History, University of Florida, Gainesville [pale]; John H. Sammons, *Personal Recollections of the Civil War* (Greensburg, Ind.: Montgomery & Son, n.d.), p. 13 [awful]; for the Cundiff case, see affidavits of Henry C. Coffin, May 8, 1893, Harrison Walters, May 8, 1893, Harvey R. Benshan (guardian), June 5, 1894, John A. Jordan, June 6, 1894, James H. Pebworth, June 6, 1894, and L. B. Ashby, June 6, 1894, federal pension file of John A. Cundiff [H 99 Ind. Inf.], National Archives.

28. See Edward A. Strecker, "II. Military Psychiatry: World War I, 1917–1918," in J. Hall, G. Zilboorg, and H. Bunker, eds., *One Hundred Years of American Psychiatry* (New York: Columbia University Press, 1944), pp. 385–416, 385; Harold Wiltshire, "A Contribution to the Etiology of Shell Shock," *Lancet*, 1 (June 17, 1916): 1207–1212; and Eric J. Leed, *No Man's Land: Combat and Identity in World War I* (New York: Cambridge University Press, 1979), pp. 163–192; R. L. Richards, "Mental and Nervous Disease in the Russo-Japanese War," *Military Surgeon*, 26 (1910): 177–193; 179 [mysterious].

29. Bull *Soldiering*, p. 41; Small, *The Road to Richmond*, pp. 105, 185 ["screaming metal"].

30. Robertson, *Diary of the War*, p. 73 [rabbits]; William B. Miller diary, September 19, 1863 [Chickamauga]; William Lewis McKay memoirs, p. 37, Confederate Collection, Tennessee State Archives ["hugging the ground"]; Calvin Ainsworth diary, p. 42, Bentley Historical Library [canister]. For an explanation of varieties of Civil War artillery, see Wayne Austerman, "Case Shot and Canister: Field Artillery in the Civil War," *Civil War Times Illustrated*, 26 (5) (September 1987): 16–48.

31. John Gibbon, *Personal Recollections of the Civil War* (New York: G. P. Putnam's Sons 1928), pp. 147–149 [sense of time]; Charles B. Haydon, *For Country, Cause, and Leader: The Civil War Journal of Charles B. Haydon*, ed. Stephen W. Sears (New York: Ticknor & Fields, 1993), p. 306 [two seconds].

32. Jane S. Woolsey, *Hospital Days* (New York: D. Van Nostrand, 1970), p. 112 [man buried at Petersburg]; William Meade Dame, *From the Rapidan to Richmond and the Spottsylvania Campaign* (Baltimore: Green-Lucas Co., 1920), p. 122 [demoralized man]; Ferdinand Davis memoirs, pp. 127–128, 141, Bentley Historical Library [man rendered speechless; terrified officer]; declaration of Albert Frank, June 7, 1884, and affidavit of Henry Moody, October 15, 1884, federal pension file of Albert Frank [B 8 Conn. Inf.], National Archives. For Frank's admission to the Government Hospital for the Insane, see admission number 1707, November 17, 1864, National Archives. For a case of aphonia, see William W. Keen, S. Weir Mitchell, and George R. Morehouse. "On Malingering, Especially in Regard to Simulation of Diseases of the Nervous System," *American Journal of Medical Sciences* 48 (July–October 1864): 367–394, 383.

33. Affidavits of Allen M. Bridges, February 3, 1888, and Thomas McMa-

hon, February 1, 1888, federal pension file of John Bumgardner [26 Ind. L.A.], National Archives.

34. P. L. Ledford, *Reminiscences of the Civil War, 1861–1865* (Thomasville, N.C.: News Printing House, 1909), p. 67 [grim monster death]; Washington Ives, *Civil War Journal and Letters of Serg. Washington Ives, 4th Florida C.S.A.* (Jim R. Cabanniss, privately published, 1987), p. 44; Ulmer, *Adventures and Reminiscences of a Volunteer*, pp. 40–41 [slumbering camp]; Samuel Elias Mays, *Genealogical Notes on the Family of Mays and Reminiscences of the War between the States* (Plant City, Fla.: Plant City Enterprise, 1927), p. 65 [drowning Yankees].

35. Gervis D. Grainger, *Four Years with the Boys in Gray* (Dayton, Ohio: Morning-side Press, 1972; originally published in 1902), p. 21 [bayonets]; Jesse B. Connelly diary, p. 33, Indiana Historical Society [one family]; James L. Cooper, pp. 50–51, Confederate Collection, Tennessee State Archives [Franklin]; J. M. Coleman to Mrs. R. B. Hanna, April 29, 1862, Robert B. Hanna Papers, Indiana Historical Society [enough of war]; DeWitt C. Goodrich memoirs, pp. 113–115, Indiana Historical Society [Shiloh]; Stephen Lampman Lowing to sister, Mary, May 17, 1862, Bentley Historical Library [unwell].

36. Calvin Ainsworth diary, pp. 23–24, Bentley Historical Library.

37. Samuel Futterman and Eugene Pumpian-Mindlin, "Traumatic War Neuroses Five Years Later," *American Journal of Psychiatry*, 108 (1951–1952): 417 [soldiers in graves registration units at risk for traumatic war neuroses]; James E. McCarroll et al., "Symptoms of Posttraumatic Stress Disorder Following Recovery of War Dead," *American Journal of Psychiatry* 150 (12) (December 1993): 1875–1877; Patricia B. Sutker et al., "Psychopathology in War-Zone Deployed and Nondeployed Operation Desert Storm Troops Assigned Graves Registration Duties," *Journal of Abnormal Psychology*, 103 (2) (1994): 383–390 [psychological aftermath of war-zone participation involving the task of handling human remains was profound]; James H. Jones to his parents, January 9, 1863, Indiana Historical Society [pieces of bodies]; William G. Le Duc, *Recollections of a Civil War Quartermaster: The Autobiography of William G. Le Duc* (St. Paul, Minn.: North Central Publishing Company, 1963), p. 77 [unendurable stench]; John Johnston, p. 99, Confederate Collection, Tennessee State Archives [loathsome task].

38. Rufus W. Jacklin, Records of the Military Order of the Loyal Legion of the United States, Michigan Commandery, 1885–1937, p. 14 [valley of death]; Robertson, *Diary of the War*, pp. 23–24 [horrors]; Curtis Buck to unknown, May 23, 1864, Buck Family Papers, Bentley Historical Library [shocking sight]; Eli Augustus Griffin diary, entry of May 3, 1864, Bentley Historical Library [ghastly]; Franklin H. Bailey to parents, April 8, 1862, Bentley Historical Library [shudder]; Judson L. Austin to wife, September 12, 1863, Nina L. Ness Collection, Bentley Historical Library [you would not want to witness].

39. In *Desertion during the Civil War* (Gloucester, Mass.: Peter Smith, 1966), Ella Lonn estimates that there were 103,400 Confederate deserters and 278,644 Union deserters from 1863 to 1865. In *Stop the Evil: A Civil War History of Desertion and Murder* (San Rafael, Calif.: Presidio Press, 1978), p. 77, Robert I. Alotta concludes that nearly 60,000 Union deserters returned to duty, and that the actual number of deserters apprehended and brought to trial is unknown.

40. Joshua Hoyet Frier memoirs, Florida State Archives, Tallahassee [dark ages]; William B. Miller diary, pp. 320–321, Indiana Historical Society [murder]; Ferdinand Davis memoirs, pp. 63–64, Bentley Historical Library [shock]; George M. Fredrickson, *The Inner Civil War: Northern Intellectuals and the Crisis of the Union* (New York: Harper and Row, 1965), p. 85.

Part V

What Soldiers Believed

Chapter 23

The Values of Civil War Soldiers

Michael Barton

Michael Barton of Pennsylvania State University at Harrisburg ex-
plained at the outset of his 1981 book, Goodmen: The Character of
Civil War Soldiers, *that his primary purpose was the systematic study of*
national character rather than the Civil War, but his findings were cited
more often by historians than by social scientists. Reviews were mixed,
ranging from "a model of the new social history" to "absurd," demon-
strating how divisive this method of historiography can be. What follows
is a chapter from Goodmen *demonstrating how content analysis can be*
performed and its results presented. Barton compares the "core values"
of northern and southern soldiers. Ruling out alternative explanations
for his results, he finds that northern and southern soldiers had common
values but different styles of expressing them.

This chapter will seek to discover whether Northern and Southern soldiers expressed moral values differently—making this search through a
content analysis of the core values expressed in the published Civil War
diaries of one hundred soldiers. . . .

A brief description here of the methodology should make the data
which follow more immediately comprehensible.

Content analysis is, in effect, a systematic method of sorting and
counting written evidence. It makes explicit what many historians do
implicitly. First, one selects the categories into which the content of the
documents will be sorted. The categories for this phase of the study
come from Robin Williams's modern theory of values.[1] Williams has

written that core American values are (1) Achievement, Success, and Competition, (2) Activity and Work, (3) Moral Judgmental Orientation, (4) Humanitarian Mores, (5) Efficiency and Practicality, (6) Materialism and Passive Gratification, (7) Progress and Optimism, (8) Equality, (9) Freedom and Liberty, (10) External Conformity, (11) Science and Secular Reason, (12) Nationalism and Patriotism, (13) Democracy, (14) Individualism, and (15) Racism and Group Superiority. Williams's list was adapted slightly for this study: the category "Other Values" was added, "Religion" was added, and "Racism" was deleted. Six content analysts, or coders, studied Williams's definitions of those core values, and then each coder read a share of the published diaries of twenty-five Northern officers, twenty-five Southern officers, twenty-five enlisted Northerners, and twenty-five enlisted Southerners. Officers were separated from enlisted men to allow the study of social class differences in core values.

Whenever a coder found the core value of Achievement, for example, in a diary, he would mark the coding sheet for that diary in that category and write down the statement which revealed that value. However, when all the coders' notes were pooled and tallied, they did not pay attention to the absolute number of times each core value was used in each diary; instead, they only counted each core value as either "present" or "absent" in each diary. The final data were thus less precise but more reliable—there would be no arguments over the exact number of core values used in a diary. Also, if differences among the four groups of soldiers still appeared after using this conservative system of counting, then the coders would feel more confident that those differences were valid.

It is important to mention here that this content analysis has not dealt with the intensity of expression of any one man's values nor with their order of importance in his diary. It does not lead to an artful commentary on all the intricacies of any one man's values. It does not tease out the subtle differences among the value-laden remarks of various soldiers. The method is, obviously, a blunt instrument. But it is one way of making a systematic, quantitative comparison of value expression in two populations. It is a general solution to the general question, How different was the Old South?

The first column of Table 1 shows the general order in which the core values were expressed. The most interesting fact about this over-all distribution is that those core values which are often said to be most "American" and characteristic of much of our history—Freedom,

TABLE I
Distribution of Core Values

Core Value	Total (N = 100)	Percentage of Soldiers Expressing the Value at Least Once			
		Section		Rank	
		Northern (N = 50)	Southern (N = 50)	Officers (N = 50)	Enlisted (N = 50)
Moralism	100	100	100	100	100
Progress	79	72	86	84	74
Religion	76	68	84	84	68
Achievement	69	60	78	78	60
Patriotism	67	60	74	72	62
Materialism	55	48	62	52	58
Humanitarianism	53	38	68	62	44
Activity	51	50	52	60	42
Efficiency	45	34	56	46	44
Other Values	38	24	52	42	34
Freedom	31	24	38	38	24
Equality	24	20	28	26	22
Individualism	24	16	32	34	14
Conformity	12	10	14	16	8
Science	10	8	12	14	6
Democracy	10	6	14	16	4

Equality, Individualism, and Democracy—occur least frequently. They are expressed by one-third of the soldiers at most and by as few as one tenth. Those core values which are expressed most often—Moralism, Progress, Religion, Achievement, and Patriotism—by two-thirds of the soldiers or more, are not so much ideological concepts as psychosocial traits.

But one could attack the significance of this distribution by arguing that the first set of ideological values is not likely to be expressed in diaries by its very nature, while the second set of psychosocial values is, by its nature, more likely to be expressed in diaries. Thus, this distribution might be revealing more about the nature of Civil War diaries than the nature of Civil War diarists. Nevertheless, it appears that there was less overt commitment to the ideological core values of Freedom, Equality, Individualism, and Democracy than might have been expected from ... American histories [that] emphasized the great importance of those ideological values, but the current results suggest that those values ranked second in the lives of American men. The psychosocial values of Moralism, Progress, Religion, Achievement, and Patriotism appear to have been more practically important.

Columns 2 and 3 of Table 1 show how the core values were expressed by Southerners and Northerners. Treating each pair of scores as a statistical trial, the difference between the series of scores of the two groups of soldiers, applying a two-tailed sign test, is significant at the .002 confidence level.[2] This means that there are only two chances out of a thousand that Southerners would have exceeded Northerners in the use of all sixteen values purely by accident. Therefore, Southern dominance in the use of the core value system is a trustworthy finding.

While these North-South differences are not the most significant findings, there are differences in those values which were not expected: Southerners appear more likely to value Achievement, Humanitarianism, Efficiency, Materialism, Freedom, Equality, Science, and Democracy than Northerners. This appears to contradict the historical clichés about the natures of the two regions, clichés which held Northerners famous for all characteristics. Before drawing any conclusions from this rather surprising finding, a further breakdown of these results is in order.

The core values were expressed by officers and enlisted men in the pattern revealed in columns 4 and 5, Table 1. The difference between the series of officer and enlisted scores, using the two-tailed sign test, is again statistically significant at the .002 level. The dominance of the officers is not surprising, since one might expect leaders to be more value-conscious than followers, by virtue of the officers' training and experience, their perceived obligation to uphold and teach values to their enlisted men, and their role requirements in general.

The final breakdown of the data, as seen in Table 2, shows how the

TABLE 2

Distribution of Core Values among the Four Groups

	Percentage of Soldiers Expressing the Value at Least Once			
Core Value	Northern Officers (N = 25)	Northern Enlisted (N = 25)	Southern Officers (N = 25)	Southern Enlisted (N = 25)
Moralism	100	100	100	100
Progress	72	72	96	76
Religion	80	56	88	80
Achievement	68	52	88	68
Patriotism	76	44	68	80
Materialism	52	44	52	72
Humanitarianism	48	28	76	60
Activity	64	36	56	48
Efficiency	48	20	44	68
Other Values	36	12	48	56
Freedom	28	20	48	28
Equality	28	12	24	32
Individualism	28	4	40	24
Conformity	16	4	16	12
Science	12	4	16	8
Democracy	8	4	24	4

four groups of soldiers—Northern officers, enlisted Northerners, Southern officers, and enlisted Southerners—differed in their frequency of value expression. The two-tailed sign test reveals the following probabilities for the relationships among the four groups:

	Southern officer	Southern enlisted	Northern officer
Southern enlisted	.302		
Northern officer	.266	.744	
Northern enlisted	.002	.002	.002

There are no statistically significant differences among the series of scores of Northern officers, Southern enlisted men, and Southern officers, but Northern enlisted men stand out as being significantly different from each of those three groups. The number of times enlisted Northerners use core values is so low that it is possible to conclude that they are significantly different from each of the other groups in respect to "system usage."

Comparison of the scores of the four groups of soldiers on each core value rather than on use of the whole system yields the following statistically significant results (significance in this case determined by a one-tailed sign test and a confidence level of .10):

(1) Southern officers used ten of the sixteen values—Progress, Religion, Achievement, Patriotism, Humanitarianism, Efficiency, Other Values,* Freedom, Individualism, and Democracy—significantly more often than Northern enlisted men.

(2) Enlisted Southerners used eight of the values—Religion, Patriotism, Materialism, Humanitarianism, Efficiency, Other Values,* Equality, and Individualism—significantly more often than Northern enlisted men.

(3) Northern officers used six of the values—Religion, Patriotism, Activity, Efficiency, Other Values,* and Individualism—significantly more often than Northern enlisted men.

(4) The remaining significant relationships are: Southern officers using Progress, Achievement, and Democracy more often than Southern enlisted men; Southern officers using Progress and Humanitarianism more often than Northern officers; and Southern enlisted men using Materialism more often than Northern officers.

*The most frequently mentioned Other Values were Peace, Home, Family, and Justice.

There are no significant differences among the four groups of soldiers on the frequency of use of Moralism, Conformity, and Science. Thus, in twenty-four of the thirty significant relationships Northern enlisted men are dominated by some other group. They are dominated by all other groups on five values—Religion, Patriotism, Efficiency, Other Values, and Individualism.

We have established the saliency of the variables of section and rank on of the expression of core values. Southerners express them more often than Northerners, and officers more often than enlisted men. Moreover, when the effects of these two variables are combined, Southern officers and Northern enlisted men tend to be the most dissimilar groups; indeed, enlisted Northerners are unique. However, before discussing these findings at length, the possibility that two other variables—education and achievement motivation—might have had a significant influence on core value expression must be explored.

Education is a difficult variable to assess because there are twenty-nine cases of missing data. In Table 3 the distribution does not include the missing data. The sample is highly skewed in favor of highly educated men. "College" refers to all those diarists who were college stu-

TABLE 3
Core Values and Education

Core Value	Percentage of Soldiers Expressing the Value at Least Once	
	College (N = 43)	Noncollege (N = 28)
Moralism	100	100
Progress	77	79
Religion	81	79
Achievement	72	75
Patriotism	70	71
Materialism	60	57
Humanitarianism	51	68
Activity	53	54
Efficiency	42	50
Other Values	37	43
Freedom	44	14
Equality	28	21
Individualism	26	25
Conformity	16	7
Science	12	7
Democracy	12	4

(Missing Data: Twenty-nine cases)

dents, graduates, or professional men when they joined their army; "noncollege" refers to those men who were known not to have a college or professional background when they joined their army. The value orders for the two groups are roughly similar—Moralism, Progress, Religion, Achievement, and Patriotism rank near the top in both groups, while the ideological values of Freedom, Equality, Individualism, and Democracy rank near the bottom. College soldiers dominate noncollege soldiers on those ideological values, especially in regard to Freedom. Noncollege soldiers, on the other hand, dominate Humanitarianism. Those particular differences might be worth some investigation, but when the two groups are compared in respect to their use of the whole system (again treating each pair of scores as a statistical trial), no significant difference between them emerges.

The missing educational data can be manipulated in two ways. The first involves re-coding all the missing data as being noncollege, on the assumption that the editor of the diary or the diarist would have mentioned such education if the author had attained it. When the data are manipulated in this way, college soldiers have a higher frequency of expression of twelve of sixteen values; a two-tailed sign test gives a confidence level of .118, which approaches the acceptable level of .10, but the findings are not statistically significant. Moreover, that result occurred only because of a most drastic manipulation of the missing data, which may have been an unreasonable re-coding.

The other manipulation requires splitting the twenty-nine cases of missing educational data proportionately and randomly between the college and noncollege groups; treating the distribution of the known sample as reliable, 61 percent of the missing cases are assigned to the college group and 39 percent to the noncollege group. This would be considered a more reasonable re-coding than the previous one. The results of the second manipulation show the least differentiation between the two groups. The two-tailed sign test indicates that there is a nearly perfect probability that the scores could have achieved this distribution by chance alone. Thus education seems to have had no effect on the use of the value system in Civil War diaries. The bias in favor of high education in the sample of diarists is an interesting fact, but not a poisonous one for the research.

That education seems to have had no effect on valuation may be an artifact of the diaries' having been written during the war, when section and rank were bound to have more power over valuation temporarily. But it is also possible that a key insight may be drawn from this result: perhaps schooling only supported the evaluative habits which had already been established by one's social rank and section of the country, and perhaps that is all schooling was intended to do in the past.

Examining value expression according to the soldiers' "Rank Progress" (that is, whether he was always enlisted, always an officer, or progressed from the enlisted to the officer ranks) gives the distribution displayed in Table 4. Rank Progress is employed here as a measure of achievement motivation in order to explore its relation to core value expression, the assumption being that those soldiers who made the most significant increases in rank may have been the highest achievers, and that they also may have expressed values most often. However, the two-tailed sign test indicates that the high achievers (Enlisted to Officer) do not differ significantly from the other two groups in frequency of core value expression:

Enlisted-to-officer versus Always enlisted $p = .180$
Enlisted-to-officer versus Always officer $p = .608$
Always enlisted versus Always officer $p = .008$

TABLE 4
Core Values and Rank Progress

| Core Value | Percentage of Soldiers Expressing the Value at Least Once | | |
	Always Enlisted (N = 39)	Enlisted to Officer (N = 23)	Always Officer (N = 29)
Moralism	100	100	100
Progress	74	78	86
Religion	67	74	90
Achievement	59	78	72
Patriotism	67	70	69
Materialism	56	70	41
Humanitarianism	46	43	69
Activity	41	39	69
Efficiency	46	43	41
Other Values	33	48	38
Freedom	26	26	41
Equality	23	22	28
Individualism	15	35	28
Conformity	8	9	24
Science	3	9	14
Democracy	5	9	17

(Missing Data: Nine cases)

In fact, those who were always enlisted differ significantly from those who were always officers, and this is an even stronger indicator of the impact of status differences on core value expression. Thus, the psychological characteristic of need for achievement has little influence on valuation in general, at least compared to section and rank. It is interesting to note, however, that on the specific values of Achievement, Materialism, and Individualism, soldiers advancing from the enlisted to officer ranks have the highest scores.

Returning to our main results, it is still necessary to explain the fact that Northern enlisted men (the modal type of American male) tended not to use the core value system so frequently as the other three groups. It could be that enlisted Northerners were using a different core value system than the one we measured them against, but that possibility is remote, since the enlisted Northerners' Other Values were not different from the remaining three groups' Other Values. Moreover, only three enlisted Northerners expressed statements which were coded as Other Values.

The possibility that the answer lies in the enlisted Northerners' different ordering of the core values is also unsatisfactory. Comparison of the four groups' rankings of the core values (based on the number of men in each group who used each value) shows that the four orders are quite similar. These results are in Table 5. Spearman's coefficient for rank-order correlation shows that the four rank-orders are almost in perfect agreement. Spearman scores on the six possible rank-order paired comparisons range from .86 to .96 (1.0 is a perfect correlation), and all six Spearman scores are significant at a confidence level of .01. Thus, it appears that enlisted Northerners simply used the core value system much less often than the other soldiers. Pursuit of an explanation for that "flattened valuation," may be aided by a look at the ways the soldiers kept their diaries. Table 6 shows various characteristics of the four groups' diaries. In this sample of published documents, Southerners kept diaries for a longer period of time than Northerners, and they also wrote the longest diaries. (Variations in page size or words per page were standardized for these computations.) Those figures could lead to the conclusion that all the results are merely a function of the quantity of written material which was coded rather than its quality. However, the last items in Table 6 undercut that conclusion. The former shows that, the sheer quantity of writing aside, the coders judged the Southern-

TABLE 5
Rank Order of Core Values among Four Groups

	Rank According to Frequency of Use			
Core Value	Northern Officers (N = 25)	Northern Enlisted (N = 25)	Southern Officers (N = 25)	Southern Enlisted (N = 25)
Moralism	1	1	1	1
Religion	2	3	3.5	2.5
Progress	4	2	2	4
Patriotism	3	5.5	6	2.5
Achievement	5	4	3.5	6.5
Materialism	7	5.5	8	5
Activity	6	7	7	9
Humanitarianism	8.5	8	5	8
Efficiency	8.5	9.5	10	6.5
Freedom	11	9.5	9	11
Equality	11	11	12.5	10
Individualism	11	13.5	11	12
Conformity	13	13.5	14.5	13
Science	14	13.5	14.5	14
Democracy	15	13.5	12.5	15

TABLE 6
Characteristics of Diaries

	Northern Officers (N = 25)	Northern Enlisted (N = 25)	Southern Officers (N = 25)	Southern Enlisted (N = 25)
Average Months Per Diary	7.9	9.4	12.8	11.6
Average Number of Pages Per Diary	31.8	25.5	42.7	36.0
Type of Literary Style				
Verbose	48%	32%	96%	64%
Plain	24%	20%	0%	20%
Log	28%	48%	4%	16%
Number of actual core values expressed per page	.68	.41	.69	.69

ers to be verbose and the Northern enlisted men to be log-keepers. The last item shows that, when the soldiers are compared on the actual number of core values used per page, all the rates are remarkably similar except for the enlisted Northerners, who are simply not as expressive. These two results indicate that the four groups' scores on the use of the core value system are a function of the qualities of the diarists, not simply the amount of material they wrote.

In summary, a content analysis of one hundred diaries of Civil War soldiers shows that the ideological values of Freedom, Equality, Individualism, and Democracy were less often expressed than the more prosaic values' of Moralism, Progress, Religion, Achievement, and Patriotism. The analysis also shows that the soldiers did not use many other values outside this system, and that they expressed Robin Williams's core values in about the same order of frequency no matter what their section or rank. These results suggest that Southerners and Northerners shared the same core value system, a proposition which has been supported by a number of historians.

But some significant differences have also been uncovered among the soldiers. Southern officers expressed those core values most frequently, and enlisted Northerners expressed them much less frequently than any other group. These results were not due to how much the diarists wrote, nor to their level of education. Here is support for the proposition that Northerners and Southerners had different emotional styles in spite of their common value system.

NOTES

From Michael Barton, *Goodmen: The Character of Civil War Soldiers* (University Park: Pennsylvania State University Press, 1981), 23–33.

1. Robin M. Williams, Jr., *American Society; A Sociological Interpretation*, 3rd ed. (New York: Knopf, 1970), pp. 438–504.

2. The sources for all the statistical tests used throughout the book are Hubert M. Blalock, Jr., *Social Statistics*, rev. 2nd ed. (New York: McGraw-Hill, 1979); Sidney Siegel, *Non-Parametric Statistics for the Behavioral Sciences* (New York: McGraw-Hill, 1956); Jum G. Nunnally, *Psychometric Theory*, 2nd ed. (New York: McGraw-Hill, 1978); and Norman H. Nie, C. Hadlai Hull, Jean G. Jenkins, Karin Steinbrenner, and Dale H. Bent. *SPSS; Statistical Package for the Social Sciences*. 2nd ed. (New York: McGraw-Hill, 1975).

Chapter 24

Embattled Courage

Gerald F. Linderman

It is well known that there was a tremendous rush to take up arms as the Civil War began. Driven by patriotism, the desire to prove their manhood, and a determination to get in on what they believed would be a quick victory, tens of thousands of young men enlisted on both sides. As the war lengthened and the need for troops intensified, however, these motivations proved inadequate; both sides' adoption of a draft acknowledged that enlistment enthusiasm had run its course. We estimate that each side lost approximately 10 percent of its troops to desertion and was hampered by uncounted stragglers, but we also know that each side had conscription officers and provost marshals to pursue reluctant soldiers, plus firing squads to execute deserters. What motivated those soldiers who did fight on? Was it fear of punishment? In this selection from Embattled Courage, *his influential 1987 study of soldiers' motivations, Gerald F. Linderman of the University of Michigan describes values that require suspension of twenty-first-century skepticism, and finds that these values changed during the Civil War.*

Courage at the Core

A young private of the Richmond Howitzers, Carlton McCarthy, recognized immediately how the soldier was expected to bear himself in the

Civil War: "In a thousand ways he is tried . . . every quality is put to the test. If he shows the least cowardice he is undone. His courage must never fail. He must be manly and independent."[1]

Numberless other soldiers joined Carlton McCarthy in filling their journals, their letters home, and their memoirs with the moral values they knew to be at issue in the conflict between North and South: manliness, godliness, duty, honor, and even—among the best-educated on both sides—knightliness. At their center stood courage.

Such words often seem irrelevant to contemporary thought. Americans continue to invoke "honor" and "courage" on ceremonial occasions—the Fourth of July, perhaps Memorial Day—but do so with a sense that they are not terms with which we need contend in our daily lives. When they are employed by a government agency, a specialized group, or others who would enlist them in behalf of their limited enterprises, we are often skeptical of their appropriation. The terms retain their old aura of importance, but their meanings seem elusive and their usages vaguely discredited. On the eve of the Civil War, however, Americans had hardly begun to confront the industrial transformation that would enlarge experience, multiply the categories of knowledge, and introduce processes requiring behaviors so much more complex that the older, obvious line separating the "right" and the "wrong" would grow indistinct. Prior to the rush of moral relativism that followed in the wake of industrialization and urbanization, conduct remained subject to standards both broad and precise, measures of comportment thought as easily applicable to the pursuits of war as to those of peace.

The constellation of values in 1861, with courage at its center, was not a perfect circle. Not all other values were equidistant from courage. Some stood very close and were almost identical with courage; others were distant and shared with courage only one or two components. But they all served, albeit in varying degrees, to support in the mind of the volunteer soldier the centrality of courage.

Manliness was only slightly removed from courage. Indeed, many soldiers used "courage" and "manhood" interchangeably. A Georgia soldier found in the "grand-glorious" sight of Tennessee regiments intrepidly repulsing Sherman's attack at Kennesaw Mountain "the sublimity of manhood." A Texas private, disappointed at his failure to act courageously in the field at Gettysburg, spoke plaintively of his efforts "to force manhood to the front." Many soldiers called combat the test of manhood. They often spoke of courage as the "manliest" of virtues.

In corroboration, the 1861 edition of Noah Webster's *American Dictionary of the English Language* identified as virtues "much valued" by Americans, "chastity in females" and "bravery in men." A failure of courage in war was a failure of manhood. A Union staff officer warned that cowardice robbed the soldier of all his manhood. Another Federal apologized for his pusillanimity at Antietam with the statement that it had been the only battlefield "I could not look at without being unmanned."[2]

In the minds of numerous Civil War soldiers the connection between courage and godliness was almost as intimate as that between courage and manliness. Many thought of their faith as a special source of bravery; religious belief would itself endow one with courage. Such conviction especially permeated the more homogeneous Confederate armies, whose largely Protestant rank-and-file noted that those of their commanders whose spirituality was most ardent were those who possessed, in the words of a Southern artilleryman, "the most intense spirit of fight."[3] Robert E. Lee, Stonewall Jackson, and J. E. B. Stuart, with their fervor for combat and their equanimity under fire, seemed to demonstrate that God bestowed courage directly on those of great faith.

Others' courage might be enhanced obliquely via a related conviction that God protected those who believed in Him. Many a soldier was certain, in the words of a South Carolinian, that God's "unseen hand" had carried him safely through a furious battle. A Louisiana sergeant, Edwin Fay, the target of Federal balls that narrowly missed, did not "believe a bullet can go through a prayer," for faith is a "much better shield than . . . steel armor." The common understanding was that the more complete the soldier's faith, the greater would be God's care. Perfect faith seemed to offer the possibility of perfect safety. If only my comrades and I possessed Stonewall Jackson's faith, a Confederate reasoned, we would find it unnecessary to give thought to our personal safety.[4]

Such conviction of God's direct interposition was itself an inducement to courage, for soldiers agreed that a prime enemy of courage in battle was the apprehension rooted in fear for one's safety. Accordingly, it was common to find in both armies on the eve of battle numbers of men who sought to shore up their courage by attempting to reinforce their religious faith. George Armstrong Custer was one who felt that by professing his belief he consigned himself to God's keeping. His anxiety, he wrote his wife, Libbie, was thereby dispelled. Because his fate thenceforth rested "in the hands of the Almighty," he was made brave.[5] One could not always tell, of course, if one's faith were sufficient to ensure survival, but with the outcome resting with God, soldiers felt relieved of a burden that would otherwise inhibit heroic action. "Leave all to Him" was a formula on which many drew for battle courage.

Those of less substantial faith often promised greater attentiveness to religious prescriptions in return for divine protection. Bargaining with God, soldiers approaching battle threw away their decks of cards and vowed that if they were allowed to live they would never again gamble or utter a profane word or smoke a pipe, that they would control their tempers or carry to the spring all their comrades' canteens or share food with others or go to services or live moral lives or declare publicly for Christ or become ministers.[6]

Godliness bore not only on individual survival but on the outcomes of battles. A conviction of wide currency was that God would ensure the victory of the army whose collective faith was sturdiest, a notion requiring no complex extension of logic. As William Poague, an officer in Virginia's Rockbridge Artillery, expressed it, he and most of his men had placed themselves in God's hands: While "the good Lord [shields] our heads in the hour of peril," the Confederates would be wounding and killing Yankees, making inevitable the enemy's defeat on the field. Indeed, soldiers on both sides professed confidence that the benefactions of godliness would manifest themselves on every social level—that the faithful soldier would survive combat; that the army of greatest faith would win the battle at hand; that the cause whose adherents possessed the faith indomitable would prevail in the war. When at the battle of Stone's River Federal troops realized that the Confederates had begun to retreat, a member of the 64th Ohio began to sing the Doxology. "Praise God from whom all blessings flow" was taken up first by his comrades, then by the regiment, and then ran up and down the line.[7]

As courage and godliness were linked, so were cowardice and disbelief. The Catholic chaplain of the 14th Louisiana was convinced that none were more cowardly than those who failed to renew their faith and relieve themselves of mortal sin by taking the sacraments prior to battle. A Protestant soldier of the 47th Illinois was equally certain that the Bible enjoined courage: The soldier's "standard of manhood is high, and he found it in the Book his mother gave him: 'If thou faint in the day of adversity, thy faith is small.' " Such thought found a deft summation in the words of George Cary Eggleston, who, though Indiana born, fought for the Confederacy. Cowardice, he said, "is the one sin which may not be pardoned either in this world or the next." In the mind of the soldier, godliness sustained courage and victory; doubt underwrote cowardice and defeat.[8]

Duty would seem a value more comprehensive than courage, but that inclusiveness denied it the focus and force of courage as a prescription for behavior in war. A precise definition of duty is difficult. Civil War soldiers, particularly those of officer rank, spoke as if they knew their duty, but they seldom felt it necessary to discuss or dissect it. They most often referred to duty to country, but generally the objects and the degrees of obligation remained elusive. Webster's 1861 dictionary identified duty as "that which a person is bound to pay, do or perform," but to whom or to what? Duty to God? To the Northern or Southern cause? To the Union or Confederate government? To one's unit, the regiment? To one's comrades? To one's family at home? There had been in the American experience no encounter with feudalism, and thus there remained at mid-century not even a residue of a hierarchy of duties. The prewar period, moreover, had been a time of expansive individualism, and duty was one of those categories in which individual definitions varied—and prevailed. Though men felt duty's weight, its nature remained amorphous. What emerged, however, was an impetus to persist— to remain at soldiering, to continue to heed combat orders, to persevere in battle. Whatever the individual might conceive to be the object of his duty, the principal way to satisfy it was to act courageously. As the Brahmin Stephen Minot Weld made clear when, wrestling with prebattle suspense, he conceded that "I had all I could do to keep myself up to my duty," actions that met duty's demands also met the claims of courage.[9]

Honor too yielded to the centrality of courage but was of a still different quality. Courage, as we shall see, possessed clear definition, but within the meaning of honor—as within duty's—there were broad areas of intangibility, at least to the mind of the twentieth-century observer. The compilers of Webster's dictionary, failing—or perhaps assuming it unnecessary—to define honor, instead described it. The most important of the fourteen annotations they devoted to it represented honor as "True nobleness of mind; magnanimity; dignified respect for character, springing from probity, principle, or moral rectitude; *a distinguishing trait in the character of good men.*" While courage had to be demonstrated, honor did not. Notions of honor so suffused the opening of the war that the honorable nature of the soldier—especially the Northern and Southern volunteers of 1861–62—was widely assumed. In the works of the South's writer-soldier John Esten Cooke, participation in the war was held to be in itself a mark of honor. An accompanying assumption, held most prominently by those in command positions, was that the forthcoming conflict would in its essence be a contest between gentlemen. Such convictions created for the soldier a task unlike that imposed by the requisites of courage. Assumed to be honorable, he had to act so as to escape any imputation of dishonor. It was not a simple matter; one risked dishonor in many ways—by employing coarse language, by exhibiting disrespect for women, by dropping from the line of march—but by far the gravest lapses—fleeing from battle, for example—were those that revealed cowardice. Thus the single most effective prescription for maintaining others' assumption that one was a man of honor was to act courageously. Seldom could the soldier with a reputation for courage be thought dishonorable, so incompatible did those traits seem. Perfect courage was thus the best guarantor of an honorable reputation.[10]

The linkage between honor and courage manifested itself in Civil War soldiers' frequent references to the "honorable death"—inevitably the courageous death—and the "honorable wound"—inevitably suffered in the course of courageous action.

Wounded at Ball's Bluff, Oliver Wendell Holmes, Jr., contemplated with joyful pride the prospect of dying a "soldier's death."[11] The soldier's desire to uphold his society's values shines forth in such responses, especially when the honorable wound is contrasted with the "million-dollar wound" so prominently referred to during World War II. Clearly, Civil War soldiers gave highest importance to the context in which the wound was sustained, whereas the twentieth-century soldier first measured its severity—serious enough to require evacuation home, not so serious as to kill or disable permanently. The former was prized as a badge of honor and the latter, in a war of vastly different combat experience and broader-based armies less susceptible to middle-class values, as a passport from jeopardy.

Honor more than other values within the soldier's moral constellation possessed aspects that did not attach themselves to courage but were nevertheless critical to the good soldier—the sanctity of one's word of honor, for example. That it should so frequently have been offered with good intent and accepted by others without suspicion struck close to how nineteenth-century Americans thought of themselves. Today it seems remarkable that they so trusted the personal pledges of others— enemies in war—that they would build on that confidence arrangements critical to the war effort. Prisoners of war, for example, were often paroled pending exchange. Ulysses Grant released the Vicksburg garrison on parole. Each was liberated solely on the basis of his assurance that he would not return to soldiering until informed that a captive held by his own side had been released, freeing both to return to duty. In the interim the paroled soldier was expected to proceed on the basis of his word of honor—to go home or, in a few cases where states forbade the return of parolees, to report to one of the detention camps maintained by his own side.

After his division had led the disastrous charge at Gettysburg, George Pickett was angered by orders assigning its remnant to guard Northern prisoners, so "I instructed my Inspector-General to parole the officers and give them safeguard to return [to Northern lines], binding them to render themselves prisoners of war at Richmond if they were not duly recognized [as exchangeable] by their government."[12] There was no mockery in the expectation that a Northern officer released in Northern territory would, if unexchanged, make his way to the enemy's capital and report for incarceration. . . .

Intrinsic to a gentlemen's war was the conviction that enemies no less than comrades merited honorable treatment. Accordingly, prisoner interrogations were gentle affairs based on the proposition that a soldier had no right to ask questions whose answers would compromise the integrity of the prisoner or damage his cause. Francis Amasa Walker, a future president of the Massachusetts Institute of Technology, was captured by rebels during Wilderness combat in 1864. His captors were "exceedingly cordial," so much so that he was able to escape. Swimming the Appomattox River, however, he landed among other Confederates, whose colonel asked him whether anyone had escaped with him. Bristling, Walker retorted, "Of course you do not expect me to answer that question." The colonel did not press him.[13] . . .

Knightliness might be described less as a distinct value than as an extension and an exaggeration of honor. Its influence was not broad. The men in the ranks paid it little heed, and serious interest confined itself to two narrow social strata: the Southern upper class, especially Virginia gentlemen, and New England Brahmins. Here its impact was intense, and each group wielded in its section of the country an influence far beyond its numbers.

Those who aspired to knightliness imposed on warfare a set of romantic images derived from the writings of Sir Walter Scott, especially his Waverly novels. George Cary Eggleston found that the libraries of Southern planters, although "sadly deficient in the literature of the present," contained Scott's novels "in force, just as they came, one after another, from the press of the Edinburgh publishers." John Esten Cooke had had Scott—"his ultimate literary ancestor"—read to him as a child. Five hundred miles to the north the boy Oliver Wendell Holmes, Jr., had enthusiastically lost himself in the Waverly adventures. Mark Twain would later charge, not entirely in jest, that Scott should be held responsible for the Civil War.[14]

To those imbued with knightliness, warfare seemed a joust and the soldier a knightly warrior or holy crusader, an exemplar of brave and noble manhood. Their influence at the outset of the war tended primarily to intensify certain aspects of courage's war. Knightliness elaborated and sharpened the appeal of the honorable death; as its principal incarnation, J. E. B. Stuart, put it, "All I ask of fate is that I may be killed leading a cavalry charge."[15] Fascination with the duel accentuated the attractiveness of individualized combat. The idealization of the mounted warrior wrapped the cavalry, especially the Confederate horse, within an aura of romance. The chivalric ideal—*sans peur et sans reproche*—both enhanced the soldier-knight's determination to do his duty without regard for consequences and harshly increased the onus attached to his feelings of fear. The accent on gallantry and courtesy strengthened ties between enemies. Had the impulse to knightliness been able to sustain itself, the Civil War would have been a most polite war.

Manliness, godliness, duty, honor, and knightliness constituted in varying degrees the values that Union and Confederate volunteers were determined to express through their actions on the battlefield. But each, as an impulse to war, remained subordinate to courage. Young Americans would most often cite "duty" as having prompted them to enlist and "honor" as having held them to soldiering through their terms of enlistment, but the pursuit of courage—and its obverse, the flight from cowardice—proved the ultimate sanction. Courage served as the goad and guide of men in battle. . . .

Unraveling Convictions

As Civil War battles revealed by degrees that bravery was no guarantor of victory, that rifled muskets and defensive works could thwart the most spirited charge, soldiers sensed the insufficiency of courage and began to move away from many of their initial convictions.

One of the first tenets to be discarded was the one holding that exceptional combat courage deserved special protection, even to the point of suspending efforts to kill the bravest of the enemy. Indeed, certain commanders had opposed such deference almost from the outset. Stonewall Jackson always urged special attention of another sort to the enemy's most courageous soldiers:

> At the battle of Port Republic [June 9, 1862] an officer commanding a regiment of Federal soldiers and riding a snowwhite horse was very conspicuous for his gallantry. He frequently exposed himself to the fire of our men in the most reckless way. So splendid was this man's courage that General Ewell, one of the most chivalrous gentlemen . . . at some risk to his own life, rode down the line and called to his men not to shoot the man on the white horse. After a while, however, the officer and the white horse went down. A day or two after, when General Jackson learned of the incident, he sent for General Ewell and told him not to do such a thing again; that this was no ordinary war, and the brave and gallant Federal officers were the very kind that must be killed. "Shoot the brave officers and the cowards will run away and take the men with them."[16]

While Ewell continued to uphold courage as the primary virtue wherever demonstrated. Jackson focused on the way courage bonded enemies, and he wanted no part of anything that might vitiate the combativeness of his troops. He also comprehended, as few did so early in the war, that to obliterate the most courageous of the foe was to demoralize those whose discipline drew on their example. . . .

That logic soon made targets of the enemy's color-bearers, soldiers whose courage had won them positions of honor as carriers of the regimental standards around which men might be inspired to charge or to rally. By the time of Fredericksburg, a Confederate officer was ordering his men, "Now, shoot down the colors," and by 1865 it had become acceptable practice to direct fire upon color-bearers even as they lay on the ground. ("And how we did keep pouring the bullets into them, the flags for a mark! . . . The flags continued to tumble and rise.") Often every member of the color guard, ordinarily one corporal from each of the regiment's ten companies, was shot down before the battle was over. Early in the war soldiers had coveted such positions. By 1863, though by then additional incentives were offered—in the 20th New York, exemption from guard and picket, company drills and roll call; duty of no more than three hours a day—few any longer volunteered. In such brusque ways, soldiers discovered that a war of attrition left less and less room for concessions to the enemy's courage.[17]

A related casualty was the conviction that courageous behavior imparted battlefield protection. Experience taught the opposite: The cowards either remained at home or found ways to avoid battle; the bravest "went farthest and stand longest under fire"; the best died. In, January 1863 General Frank Paxton of the Stonewall Brigade complained: "Out of the fifteen field officers elected last spring, five have been killed and six wounded. . . . In these losses are many whom we were always accustomed to regard as our best men." Three months later he again found it "sad, indeed, to think how many good men we have lost. Those upon whom we all looked as distinguished for purity of character as men, and for gallantry as soldiers, seem to have been the first victims." After thirty days of Wilderness combat, Colonel Theodore Lyman of Meade's staff deplored Grant's strategy: "[T]here has been too much assaulting, this campaign! . . . The best officers and men are liable, by their greater gallantry, to be first disabled."[18]

Those in the ranks noted the phenomenon principally by its result: a decline in the quality of their leadership. John Haskell, an artillery commander in Lee's army, was bitter that those who took such care to protect their own lives, "the dodgers," by virtue of their seniority had been promoted to replace dead or disabled officers who had "taken no pains" to preserve their lives. By such routes soldiers moved far from their original conceptions of ostentatious courage as protection and assurance of victory to the realization that it was instead an invitation to death. A few might attempt to find a new virtue in that reality—Charles Russell Lowell, contemplating the death in battle of Robert Gould Shaw, decided that the best colonel of the best black regiment *had to die*, for "it was a sacrifice we owed"—but most simply felt its demoralization.[19]

Godliness as a protective mantle shared the same decline. For every story in the war's first months about a pocket Bible that had stopped an otherwise fatal bullet, there was in later years a matching tale of the opposite implication—that, for example, of the Union colonel who told his men that the replica Virgin Mary around his neck would protect him, and minutes later was mortally wounded. Hunter said of the Confederate rank-and-file in 1864–65: "The soldiers naturally distrusted the efficacy of prayer when they found that the most devout Christians were as liable to be shot as the most hardened sinner, and that a deck of cards would stop a bullet as effectively as a prayer book."[20]

Doubt that the original equations were still valid sometimes arose in mundane fashion. A Massachusetts soldier noticed that those who persevered to complete arduous marches with the column were often "rewarded" by being placed on guard duty before the stragglers reached camp. Blackford, who like other Confederate cavalrymen was required to furnish his own mount, realized that if one were forthrightly courageous in battle, one's horse was more likely to be killed. From month to month replacements became more and more difficult and expensive to procure, and failure to find one resulted in reassignment to the infantry. "Such a penalty for gallantry was terribly demoralizing."[21]

Though disconcerting, such challenges to the notion that courage permitted the soldier to control his life and death were pinpricks set beside the challenges presented by the failed charge. The rapidity with which great numbers of men were killed at Antietam and the ease with which they were cut down at Fredericksburg and Gettysburg produced gloomy reflection as soldiers contemplated a war that had inexplicably recast its actors as victims. Minds groped to comprehend why courage had failed to secure victory and in the face of such disastrous results began, hesitantly and diversely, to move away from conventional thought and language.

Lieutenant William Wood of the 19th Virginia was one of the 15,000 who made Pickett's charge. Prior to the attack he and his men were ordered to lie down, exposed both to a boiling sun and to the fire of Federal artillery batteries. (A Napoleon cannon could hurl a 12-pound ball a mile.) When they were brought to attention to begin the attack, some of the men immediately dropped of "seeming sunstroke," but for the charge itself Wood had only praise. It was a "splendid array" and a "beautiful line of battle." But it failed: "Down! down! go the boys." As he reached that spot of ground beyond which no Confederate could go, he suffered a sense of personal shame: "Stopping at the fence, I looked to the right and left and felt we were disgraced." The assault's failure bluntly told him that he and his comrades had not done enough, and yet he knew that they had done everything they had earlier been sure would carry the victory. The result was a paralyzing disbelief: "With one single exception I witnessed no cowardice, and yet we had not a skirmish line [still standing]." Courage should have conquered![22] . . .

Even before the assault at Cold Harbor, soldiers entering their fourth year of war understood perfectly what the result would be. They knew that the Confederates had had thirty-six hours in which to prepare their positions and that by that stage of the war *any* attack under such circumstances was doomed. Charles Wainwright thought it absurd that Grant should simply repeat here the order "which has been given at all such times on this campaign, viz: 'to attack along the whole line.' " On the eve of battle, Union soldiers who had glimpsed some part of the Southern defenses or heard them described by the "news-gatherers" were, Wilkeson reported, depressed: "Some of the men were sad, some indifferent; some so tired of the strain on their nerves that they wished they were dead and their troubles over . . . and though they had resolved to do their best, there was no eagerness for the fray, and the impression among the intelligent soldiers was that the task cut out for them was more than men could accomplish." Indeed, numbers of soldiers wrote their names on small pieces of paper and pinned them to their coats, in a hope, signaling hopelessness, that their bodies would not go unidentified. On June 15, 1864, when Grant's army finally reached the James at a cost of 60,000 casualties, a number equivalent to the size of Lee's army at the outset of the campaign, the Union regular Augustus Meyers felt the "gloomy and depressing effect" of such "awful sacrifices without any advantages." Ira Dodd became convinced that following its attacks in the Wilderness and at Cold Harbor, the Army of the Potomac was never again the same.[23]

Not all soldiers felt compelled to abandon or even to modify early-war views. George Stevens of the 77th New York was one who remained steadfast: "Never was heroic valor exhibited on a grander scale than had been manifested by the Army of the Potomac throughout this long struggle, in which every man's life seemed doomed. [T]heir illustrious valor and never failing courage must sooner or later meet with their reward."[24] But change was afoot. Northern civilians might invoke the courage of the attackers at Cold Harbor as if it continued to constitute a substitute for victory, but soldiers contemplating the deaths of friends, their own narrow escapes, and the seeming uselessness of such charges began to speak of "futile courage" and said no more of "sublime courage."

Swelling conviction of courage's insufficiency bred new doubts about commanders whose virtues encompassed but did not extend beyond bravery. James Nisbet was unhappy when Hood replaced Johnston, for he considered Hood "simply a brave, hard fighter." Thus, in courage's depreciating currency, the ultimate accolade had fallen to faint praise. Hood might possess "a Lion's Heart," but it came to count more that he had "a Wooden Head." On the other side that summer, Theodore Lyman, too, noted changing attitudes toward those diminishing numbers of officers whose impulse was to "dash in": "You hear people say, 'Oh, everyone is brave enough; it is the head that is needed.' "[25]

No longer was courage strong enough to stand alone and thus to serve as its own reward. At the outset both sides had considered medals unnecessary. That notion was akin to the view of some Southern gentlemen and respectable organizers of Union regiments that their own willingness to remain "humble" privates constituted the highest expression of self-effacing patriotism. External signs of virtue or achievement were unimportant, and medals were in any case the insignia of an effete and vainglorious European militarism. But as the war evolved and the centrality of courageous behavior began to erode, agitations arose in both armies for the formal recognition of bravery.[26]

In November 1862 the Confederate Congress authorized the President to bestow medals and badges of distinction on soldiers who had demonstrated special battle courage. Officers were to be cited for individual acts, while the men of each company were to select one of their number for a decoration. Little was done, however. Jefferson Davis was uninterested, and in any case medals were difficult to fabricate in a Confederacy whose resources were being stretched thinner every day. As a substitute of sorts, names were to be inscribed on a Roll of Honor to be read at dress parades, but, given the accelerating tempo of combat, few regiments were able to make time for such a ritual. Fighters increasingly grew to regret that the political leadership seemed simply to assume the Southern soldier's courage and made so little effort to reward extraordinary instances of it. William Owen dined at a Richmond restaurant with English friends, including a Captain Hewitt of the Royal Navy who had won a Victoria Cross at Inkerman. After hearing Hewitt's story, the Confederate complained, "What a pity our boys have no V.C.'s to look forward to! They are doing things every day that deserve decorations."[27]

Regret became vexation in the case of another device that some wished to employ to recognize special courage: promotions for valor. Apparently neither Davis nor Lee permitted them, a stance that raised some anger among the rank-and-file. John Haskell told of two Confederate soldiers who had performed on the battlefield with great bravery. Both had suffered wounds. Their superiors granted them sick leave but sent them off with no word of commendation. When they reached their homes on a stretch of North Carolina coast occupied by Union forces, both took the oath of loyalty and remained out of the war, a loss, Haskell was sure, to be counted against a stingily unappreciative high command.[28]

The situation on the Union side was different but, from the men's perspective, hardly more favorable. Medals and promotions came much more frequently than in the Confederate service—too often for many observers. When the 27th Maine's tour of duty was about to expire just prior to the battle of Gettysburg, President Abraham Lincoln authorized the award of the Medal of Honor to each soldier who would reenlist. Three hundred agreed to remain on duty as "emergency troops," but medals were issued in error to all 864 members of the regiment. The 27th Maine had seen no battle before Gettysburg; its remnant played no role at Gettysburg. Similarly, so many brevet (i.e., honorary) promotions were awarded, Augustus Meyers complained, that they "seemed to lose dignity" and became objects of ridicule. His friends in the ranks began to refer to mules as "brevet horses" and to camp followers as "brevet soldiers." Such awards, moreover, seemed seldom to recognize battlefield bravery. *Field* promotions were almost as rare as in the Confederate Army.[29] . . .

Another consequence of the new complexity of combat experience following the displacement of the simple courage of 1861–62 was that it allowed distinctions impermissible earlier. With the awareness that the peripheries of battle could be just as trying as combat itself and that the moral nature of the individual determined far less than supposed, those strict definitions of the courageous and cowardly began to blur and to merge. In early September 1862, at the outset of Lee's first invasion of the North, Alexander Hunter recorded that there was still "no sign of our commissary wagons and not a mouthful of food had the men that day. Some of our best soldiers were left [behind] on account of sickness, and many began to straggle from ranks to seek in farm-houses along the route something to allay their gnawing hunger. . . . [E]ach one was a serious loss, for we never saw any of them until after the campaign." Soldiers without shoes also fell out, and other straggling could be traced to the weakness of the body—diarrhea, fever, anemia—rather than the weakness of the will.[30] Those remaining in the ranks, all of whom had at least brushed with illness and hunger, thus came to temper their views of those who dropped out. Courage was not always at issue. Men could be lost for reasons reflecting no cowardice.

From the shared sense that the rigors of war were broader and the terrors of combat sharper than expected, a readiness to narrow the definition of cowardice arose. Burdette reported that a private in the 47th Illinois was a good soldier in every way but one: Despite all his efforts to "play the man," he ran from every battle! When he later returned, each time with an excuse no one believed, many in the regiment were angry at first, but they came to realize that he measured well against those who feigned illness or exhaustion, stopped to tie shoes during the charge, arranged hospital details, or in other ways avoided or moved themselves beyond the range of charges of cowardice. He marched into every battle. He was brave until blood appeared, and then he fled. "He was beaten in every fight but he went in" every time. "This man was a coward," but "a good coward." Burdette realized that such a formulation begged questions each day growing more difficult: "But who are the cowards? And how do we distinguish them from the heroes? How does God tell?" Uncertain, he agreed that the man should not be punished, joining others whose anger dissipated as they concluded that "God never intended that man should kill anybody." Angered by a soldier who faltered several times during a charge at Fredericksburg, Abner Small pulled him to his feet and called him a coward, but when the man in obvious agony explained that "his legs would not obey him," Small apologized. Soldiers, he concluded, "were heroes or cowards in spite of themselves." Long Bill Blevins of the 21st Georgia knew that his captain was authorized to detail one man as company cook, and he asked for the job: "Captain, I can't stand the shooting, and I'm afraid I might run,—and disgrace my name." The incident was reported without censure. Perhaps soldiers were coming to feel the disdain of one unable to master his fear less than the relief that another had confessed, in actions or words, to the fear that all shared.[31]

By 1864 the new tolerance for men whose behavior would earlier have brought condemnation had achieved informal incorporation in the military justice system. Colonel Rufus Dawes of the 6th Wisconsin was summoned to head the Fifth Corps's examining board. There "cowards met no mercy. They were dismissed and their names published throughout the land, a fate more terrible than death to a proud spirited soldier."

But the board broke with the past in acknowledging that the war was now one in which brave men could be overcome by fear for their lives: The "unexampled [Wilderness] campaign of sixty continuous days, the excitement, exhaustion, hard work and loss of sleep broke down great numbers of men who had received no wounds in battle. Some who began the campaign with zealous and eager bravery, ended it with nervous and feverish apprehension of danger in the ascendancy. Brave men were shielded if their records on other occasions justified another [chance], which ordinarily resulted well." Cowards would continue to meet no mercy, but when did a man become a coward? When he faltered a second time? A third time?[32]

Experience that altered soldier definitions of cowardice perforce modified definitions of courage. The most dramatic example was the final dissolution of the previously vital linkage between courage and the charge.

On November 26, 1863, General George Gordon Meade launched an offensive against Lee's Army of Northern Virginia. The Union commander was outmaneuvered, however, and his Army of the Potomac quickly ran up against the Confederates strongly posted in the small valley of Mine Run, Virginia. On November 28, Meade probed Lee's position and prepared a large-scale assault. Meanwhile, Federal rank-and-file had an opportunity to judge for themselves the strength of the defenses. "All felt that it would be madness to assault," Robert Carter of the 22nd Massachusetts said; "I felt death in my very bones all day." George Bicknell of the 5th Maine wrote that there was not "a man in our command who did not realize his position. Not one who . . . did not see the letters [of] death before his vision. . . . [N]ever before nor since had such an *universal* fate seemed to hang over a command." Fortunately, one who agreed was Gouverneur Warren, the commander of the Second Corps; completing a reconnaissance, he reported to Meade that, contrary to his earlier judgment, he considered an attack hopeless. Some members of Meade's staff, thinking perhaps that so much of their planning was going for nothing, insisted that the Confederate works could be carried, but Meade canceled the assault and on December 1 ordered his army back across the Rapidan, a retreat into winter quarters.[33]

Observers quickly characterized Meade's brief campaign as failed, maladroit, and weak-willed, but the Union ranks celebrated their commander's decision as if it were a great victory. "The enemy is too strong!

We shall not charge!" "Oh," Bicknell sighed, "such a sense of relief as overspread those men, cannot even be imagined." Lyman praised his superior's courage in ordering withdrawal: Meade had only to "snap his fingers" and there would have been "ten thousand wretched, mangled creatures" lying on the valley's slopes—and praise of Meade for having "tried hard." Earlier in the war audacity in attack had caught much of what men thought important in that word "courage"; now at the close of 1863, to some, courage, turned on its head, had become the will to renounce the charge.[34]

NOTES

From Gerald F. Linderman, *Embattled Courage: The Experience of Combat in the American Civil War* (New York: Free Press, 1987), 7–16, 156–63, 166–68. Reprinted by permission.

1. Carlton McCarthy, *Detailed Minutiae of Soldier Life in the Army of Northern Virginia, 1861–1865* (Richmond: J. W. Randolph & English, 1888), 208.

2. (Georgian) James C. Nisbet, *Four Years on the Firing Line* (Chattanooga, TN: The Imperial Press, 1914), 299; (Texan) William A. Fletcher, *Rebel Private, Front and Rear* (Beaumont, TX: Press of the Greer Print, 1908), 76; Noah Webster, *An American Dictionary of the English Language* (Springfield, MA: G. and C. Merriam, 1861), 559; Horace Porter, "The Philosophy of Courage," from *The Century Magazine* 36 (June 1888), 250; George B. Sanford, *Fighting Rebels and Redskins*, ed. E. R. Hagemann (Norman: University of Oklahoma Press, 1969), 181. See also Allan Peskin, *Garfield: A Biography* (Kent, OH: Kent State University Press, 1978), 120. James A. Garfield congratulated his men on their victory at Middle Creek, Kentucky: "Soldiers of the Eighteenth Brigade! I am proud of you. . . . With no experience but the consciousness of your own manhood, you have driven [the enemy] from his stronghold."

3. Robert Stiles, *Four Years Under Marse Robert* (New York and Washington: The Neale Publishing Company, 1903), 110.

4. Jesse W. Reid, *History of the Fourth Regiment of S.C. Volunteers* (Greenville, SC: Shannon & Company, Printers, 1892), 24; Edwin H. Fay, *"This Infernal War": The Confederate Letters of Sgt. Edwin H. Fay*, ed. Bell I. Wiley (Austin: University of Texas Press, 1958), 34; William T. Poague, *Gunner with Stonewall* (Jackson, TN: McCowat-Mercer Press, 1957), 66.

5. George A. Custer, *The Custer Story: The Life and Intimate Letters of*

General George A. Custer and His Wife Elizabeth, ed. Marguerite Merington (New York: Devin-Adair, 1950), 95.

6. Alexander Hunter, *Johnny Reb and Billy Yank* (New York and Washington: The Neale Publishing Company, 1905), 53; Stiles, 142–43; Wayland F. Dunaway, *Reminiscences of a Rebel* (New York: The Neale Publishing Company, 1913), 35.

7. Poague, 140; Wilbur F. Hinman, *The Story of the Sherman Brigade* (Alliance, OH: Printed by the author, 1897), 357.

8. James B. Sheeran, Confederate Chaplain: A War Journal, ed. Joseph T. Durkin, S.J. (Milwaukee: Bruce Publishing Company, 1960), 6; Robert J. Burdette, *The Drums of the 47th* (Indianapolis: Bobbs-Merrill Company, 1914), 47; George C. Eggleston, *A Rebel's Recollections* (New York: Hurd & Houghton; Cambridge, MA: The Riverside Press, 1875), 197.

9. Webster, 374. Among the examples offered are duty as obedience to princes, magistrates and laws; obedience, kindness, and respect to parents; fidelity to friends; reverence to God. Stephen M. Weld, *War Diary and Letters of Stephen Minot Weld 1861–1865*. 2d ed. (Boston: Massachusetts Historical Society, 1979), 300.

10. Webster, 559. Emphasis in original. John O. Beaty, *John Esten Cooke, Virginian* (New York: Columbia University Press, 1922), 95.

11. Oliver Wendell Holmes, Jr., *Touched with Fire: Civil War Letters and Diary of Oliver Wendell Holmes, Jr., 1861–1864*, ed. Mark De Wolfe Howe (Cambridge: Harvard University Press, 1946), 27.

12. George E. Pickett, *Soldier of the South: General Pickett's War Letters to His Wife*, ed. Arthur Crew Inman (Boston and New York: Houghton, Mifflin Company, 1928), 73, 75.

13. James P. Munroe, *A Life of Francis Amasa Walker* (New York: H. Holt & Company, 1923), 75, 79, 81–86.

14. George C. Eggleston, "The Old Regime in the Old Dominion," from *Atlantic Monthly* 36 (November 1875), 615; Beaty, 161; Mark De W. Howe, *Justice Oliver Wendell Holmes: The Proving Years, 1870–1882* (Cambridge: Belknap Press of Harvard University Press, 1963), 10; Rollin G. Osterweis, *Romanticism and Nationalism in the Old South* (New Haven: Yale University Press, 1949), 26.

15. Eggleston, *Rebel's*, 123.

16. Hunter H. McGuire, *The Confederate Cause and Conduct in the War Between the States*; as quoted in Stiles, 245–46.

17. Dunaway, 57–58; Berry Benson, *Berry Benson's Civil War Book: Memoirs of a Confederate Scout and Sharpshooter*, ed. Susan W. Benson (Athens: University of Georgia Press, 1962), 183; Enos B. Vail, *Reminiscences of a Boy in the Civil War* (Brooklyn, NY: Printed by the author, 1915), 89.

18. Ira S. Dodd, *The Song of the Rappahannock* (New York: Dodd, Mead & Company, 1898), 251; Elisha F. Paxton, *The Civil War Letters of General Frank "Cull" Paxton, CSA, a Lieutenant of Lee and Jackson*, ed. John G. Paxton (Hillsboro, TX: Hill Junior College Press, 1978), 70, 78; Theodore Lyman, *Meade's Headquarters, 1863–1865: Letters of Colonel Theodore Lyman from the Wilderness to Appomattox*, ed. George R. Agassiz (Boston: The Atlantic Monthly, 1922), 148.

19. John C. Haskell, *The Haskell Memoirs*, ed. Gilbert E. Govan and James W. Livingood (New York: Putnam, 1960), 56–57; Edward W. Emerson, *Life and Letters of Charles Russell Lowell* (Boston and New York: Houghton, Mifflin & Company, 1907), 288–89.

20. Washington Davis, *Camp-Fire Chats of the Civil War* (Chicago: Lewis Publishing Company, 1888), 80; Hunter, 685.

21. Robert G. Carter, *Four Brothers in Blue* (Austin: University of Texas Press, 1978), 335–36; William W. Blackford, *War Years with Jeb Stuart* (New York: C. Scribner's Sons, 1945), 203.

22. William N. Wood, *Reminiscences of Big I*, ed. Bell Irvin Wiley (Jackson, TN: McCowat-Mercer Press, 1956), 45–46.

23. Lyman, 142–43; Charles S. Wainwright, *A Diary of Battle: The Personal Journals of Colonel Charles S. Wainwright, 1861–1865*, ed. Allan Nevins (New York: Harcourt, Brace & World, 1962), 405, 411; Frank Wilkeson, *Recollections of a Private Soldier in the Army of the Potomac* (New York and London: G. P. Putnam's Sons, 1886), 127; Augustus Meyers, *Ten Years in the Ranks, U.S. Army* (New York: Arno Press, 1979), 320; Dodd, 239.

24. George T. Stevens, *Three Years in the Sixth Corps* (Albany, NY: S. R. Gray, 1866), 358, 360.

25. Nisbet, 305; Lyman, 139.

26. McCarthy, 29; 29; Jacob D. Cox, *Military Reminiscences of the Civil War*, 2 vols. (New York: C. Scribner's Sons, 1900), I: 14; Francis A. Lord, *They Fought for the Union* (Harrisburg, PA: Stackpole Company, 1960), 229.

27. Nisbet, 141–42; William M. Owen, *In Camp and Battle with the Washington Artillery of New Orleans* (Boston: Ticknor & Company, 1885), 305.

28. Hunter, 577; Haskell, 59.

29. Lord, 229; Joseph B. Mitchell, *The Badge of Gallantry* (New York: The Macmillan Company, 1968), 7–9. In 1916 a board of review struck all 864 names from the rolls of the Medal of Honor; Meyers, 308.

30. Hunter, 268, 270.

31. Burdette, 101–8; Abner R. Small, *The Road to Richmond*, ed. Harold A. Small (Berkeley: University of California Press, 1939), 70–71; Nisbet, 64.

32. Rufus R. Dawes, Service with the Sixth Wisconsin Volunteers, ed. Alan T. Nolan (Madison: State Historical Society of Wisconsin, 1962), 299–300.

33. Carter, 375; George W. Bicknell, *History of the Fifth Regiment Maine*

Volunteers (Portland, ME: H. L. Davis, 1871), 287–88. Emphasis in original. Lyman, 56; Thomas F. Galwey, *The Valiant Hours: Narrative of "Captain Brevet," an Irish-American in the Army of the Potomac*, ed. W. S. Nye (Harrisburg, PA: Stackpole's, 1961), 177.

34. Bicknell, 287; Lyman, 57–58, 273.

Chapter 25

On the Altar of My Country

James M. McPherson

Some historians dispute Linderman's interpretation of soldiers' values, agreeing that modern readers must suspend disbelief when they read Civil War soldiers' expressions of patriotism, but questioning whether values changed as the war went on. James M. McPherson of Princeton University examined hundreds of soldiers' letters and diaries for his 1997 book For Cause and Comrades; *in this selection McPherson discovers greater differences between Yankees and Confederates than between early and later stages of the war.*

The emphasis on primary group cohesion that emerged in studies of combat motivation after World War II had a significant corollary: the unimportance of patriotic or ideological convictions. The detailed analysis of *The American Soldier* quoted one G.I.: "Ask any dogface on the line. You're fighting for your skin on the line. When I enlisted I was as patriotic as all hell. There's no patriotism on the line. A boy up there 60 days on the line is in danger every minute. He ain't fighting for patriotism." A British officer said that "it would be foolish to imagine that the average British or American soldier went into battle thinking he was helping to save democracy. . . . He never gave democracy a thought."[1] Another study of World War II soldiers found that "considerations of ideology, patriotism, and politics seem remarkably remote from the concerns of the front-line soldier." Questionnaires administered by social scientists to American soldiers found that their "convictions about the war and its aims" ranked low among various reasons for fighting. Indeed, among enlisted men there was "a taboo against any talk of a flag-waving variety."[2]

Likewise, American soldiers in Vietnam dismissed ideological and patriotic rhetoric as a "crock," "crap," "a joke." Some of these same American soldiers, however, explained the extraordinarily high combat motivation of enemy soldiers by reference to *their* ideological convictions. The North Vietnamese, said one American, were "the toughest fighters in the world" because "they knew what they were fighting for." A black American machine gunner described a North Vietnamese soldier as the bravest man he had ever seen "because he really believed in something."[3] One student of the American army in Vietnam insisted that primary group cohesion alone cannot motivate men to fight: on the contrary, it might cause them to refuse combat in order to ensure group survival. "Primary groups maintain the soldier in his combat role only when he has an underlying commitment to the worth of the larger social system for which he is fighting." Nevertheless, the primacy of group cohesion and the relative unimportance of ideology remain the orthodox interpretation. In the heat of combat, writes a British military analyst, "the soldier will be thinking more of his comrades in his section or platoon than of 'The Cause,' Democracy, Queen and Country."[4]

Most American soldiers in World War II and Vietnam were draftees or professional regulars; most soldiers in the Civil War were volunteers. Did that make a difference? Some historians think not. "American soldiers of the 1860s appear to have been about as little concerned with ideological issues as were those of the 1940s," according to Bell Irvin Wiley, the foremost student of Johnny Reb and Billy Yank.[5] Another scholar who examined the letters, diaries, and memoirs of fifty enlisted men concluded that "the Civil War soldiers studied here were notoriously deficient in ideological orientation." An analysis of Tennessee soldiers based on questionnaires completed in the early 1920s by surviving veterans concluded that "few Tennesseans were conscious of the major issues of the Civil War, and fewer still had any concept of the South's goals." In 1992 the commander of the New York chapter of the Sons of Union Veterans said that "it wasn't because our fathers knew what they were fighting for that they were heroes. They didn't know what they were fighting for, exactly, and they fought on anyway. That's what made them heroes."[6]

Research in the letters and diaries of Civil War soldiers will soon lead the attentive historian to a contrary conclusion. Ideological motifs almost leap from many pages of these documents. A large number of those men in blue and gray were intensely aware of the issues at stake and passionately concerned about them. How could it be otherwise? This was, after all, a *civil war*. Its outcome would determine the fate of the nation—of two nations, if the Confederacy won. It would shape the future of American society and of every person in that society. Civil War soldiers lived in the world's most politicized and democratic country in the mid-nineteenth century. They had come of age in the 1850s when highly charged partisan and ideological debates consumed the American polity. A majority of them had voted in the election of 1860, the most heated and momentous election in American history. When they enlisted, many of them did so for patriotic and ideological reasons—to shoot as they had voted, so to speak. . . .

Newspapers were the most sought-after reading material in camp—after letters from home. Major metropolitan newspapers were often available only a day or two after publication, while hometown papers came weekly when the mail service functioned normally. "I receive the 'Chronicle' regularly," wrote a lieutenant in the 50th Ohio to his brother back home in 1863. "The boys all want to read it. . . . The officers subscribed $4.75 each for papers for the benefit of the boys. [We] get *four daily* papers, all loyal and right on politics"—that is, Republican. In January 1862 a private in the 17th Mississippi stationed near Lees-burg, Virginia, wrote in his diary: "Spend much time in reading the daily papers & discussing the war question in general. We allways close by coming to the conclusion that we will after much hard fighting succeed in establishing our independence."[7] . . .

Some European officers who attached themselves to Civil War armies expressed astonishment at this phenomenon. One of them was Gustave Paul Cluseret, a graduate of St. Cyr and a French army officer for two decades before he wangled a brigade command under General John C. Frémont in 1862. Looking back on his American adventure a few years later, Cluseret wrote that "if the American volunteers accomplished prodigies of patience, energy, and devotion it is because they fought with knowledge of the cause. In the midst of the messiest business one could hear the squeaking voice of the 'news boy' over the sound of the fusil-lade, crying 'New York Tribune, New York Herald.' The soldier paid up to 10 cents for the newspaper . . . After reading it . . . there would be a redoubling of his zeal and drive." The discipline of European regulars, concluded Cluseret (a radical who would support the Paris Commune in 1871), could never have produced "the sentiment of abnegation and the force of resistance" that his brigade of Union volunteers "obtained through their love of liberty and country."[8]

Several regiments or brigades established debating societies while in winter quarters. A thrice-wounded sergeant in the 20th Illinois stationed near Vicksburg described some of the debates in his brigade during the winter of 1863–1864.

> *November 30:* "Took part on the affirmative of Resolved that the Constitutional relations of the rebel states should be fixed by Congress only.... Witnessed some rare outbursts of untutored eloquence."
>
> *December 14:* "Had an interesting debate at the Lyceum on the subject of executing the leaders of the rebellion. Made my speech on the negative. The affirmative carried by just one vote in a full house."
>
> *December 24:* "Discussed the question of reducing rebel states to territories."
>
> *Dec. 31:* "Sergeants Rollins & Need discussed ably the rights of the South. Sergt. Miller expanded on the revolution of ideas."[9]

In the Army of the Potomac, the debate topic in one brigade during November 1863 was "Do the signs of the times indicate the downfall of our Republic?" This topic must have been popular, for a soldier in the 103rd Illinois of Sherman's army reported a debate on the same proposition in February 1864. Not surprisingly, the negative carried the day in both debates, as did the affirmative in a debate the following winter at the convalescent ward of a Union army hospital in Virginia: "Resolved that the present struggle will do more to establish and maintain a republican form of government than the Revolutionary war."[10]

Some officers were not pleased with these disputatious activities. "A soldier [should have] naught to do with politics," wrote an Ohio colonel. "The nearer he approaches a machine ... the more valuable he becomes to the service."[11] ... None other than Ulysses S. Grant noted with pride after the war that "our armies were composed of men who were able to read, men who knew what they were fighting for." The same could be said for Confederate soldiers. If the assertion of John Keegan that "the Blue and the Gray [were] the first truly ideological armies of history" is an exaggeration, it is closer to the truth than Bell Wiley's remark that they were "as little concerned with ideological issues" as G.I.s in the 1940s were alleged to have been.[12] . . .

When the war began, the Confederacy was a distinct polity with a fully operational government in control of a territory larger than any European nation save Russia. Although in the minds and hearts of some Southern whites, American nationalism still competed with Confederate nationalism, the latter had roots several decades deep in the antebellum ideology of Southern distinctiveness.[13] Thus it seemed natural for many Confederate soldiers to express a patriotic allegiance to "my country." "Sink or swim, survive or perish," wrote a young Kentuckian who had cast his lot with the Confederacy, "I will fight in defense of my country." Another Confederate Kentuckian insisted in August 1862 that "we should yield all to our country now. It is not an abstract idea. . . . We have no alternative: we must triumph or perish." A sergeant in the 8th Georgia told his family in 1863 that "if my heart ever sincerely desiered any thing on earth . . . it certainly is, to be useful to my Country. . . . I will sacrifice my life upon the alter of my country." He did, at Gettysburg.[14]

Sacrifice on the "alter" (a frequent misspelling) of one's country was a typical phrase in soldier letters. So were the words written by a Missouri Confederate soldier to his wife in 1862 that she should take comfort in "knowing that if I am killed that I die fighting for my Country and my rights." Two months later she learned that this grim foreboding had come true. A lieutenant in the 47th Alabama wrote his wife in 1862: "I confess that I gave you up with reluctance. Yet I love my country [and] . . . intend to discharge my duty to my country and to my God." He too never returned to his wife and two children he missed so much.[15]

The conflict between love of family and love of country troubled some married Confederate soldiers. A homesick Arkansas sergeant wondered "why can I not be better satisfied here for surely my duty is to serve my country but I am restless. . . . [Not] money nor anything else could keep me from home and my little family except love of country and freedom for which I think every man ought to bear almost anything."[16] Many soldiers reconciled their dual responsibilities to country and family by the conviction that in fighting for the one they were protecting the other. A yeoman farmer from Alabama who had seven children wrote home from his cavalry battalion after one of the children had died in 1862: "If it were not for the love of my country and family and the patriotism that burn in my bosom for them I would bee glad to come home and stay there but I no I have as much to fite for as any body else."[17] . . .

The urge to defend home and hearth that had impelled so many Southerners to enlist in 1861 took on greater urgency when large-scale invasions became a reality in 1862. A Shenandoah Valley farmer serving with the 10th Virginia Cavalry learned that the Yankees had entered his county in April 1862. "I intend to fight them to the last," he assured his wife. "I will kill them as long as I live even if peace is made I never will get done with them."[18] . . .

Tennesseans and Louisianians who saw large parts of their states including the principal cities fall to the "insolent invader" in the spring of 1862 felt a redoubled commitment to the Cause. A captain in the 16th Tennessee wrote after the surrender of Fort Donelson that his men were "now more fully determined than ever before to sacrifice their lives, if need be, for the invaded soil of their bleeding Country. . . . The chivalrous Volunteer State will not be allowed to pass under Lincoln rule without . . . the fall of a far greater number of his hireling horde than have yet been slain at the hands of those who are striking for their liberties, homes, firesides, wives and children." . . . More succinctly, a Louisiana planter from Bayou La Fourche serving with his artillery unit in northern Mississippi wrote to his wife after the fall of New Orleans that "now I must fight to return to you."[19]

By 1863 much of Mississippi had also come under Union occupation, causing a thirty-three-year-old private in the 37th Mississippi, a former schoolteacher, to vent his spleen in diary entries: "Let me liberate my home from the varlet's tread, and then . . . my country shall be freed from the fiendish vandals who thirst for the extermination of a people who are actuated by motives as far above those that influence and characterize the enemy as is the soaring Eagle above the most insignificant reptile."[20]

Some Northern soldiers acknowledged the extra incentive that animated Confederates fighting in defense of hearth and home. "There is much more dash in the Southern troops and more real war spirit," wrote a lieutenant in the 12th New York, "for they feel they are fighting for their homes."[21] . . .

The morale advantage of fighting for one's neighborhood could be a two-edged sword, however. This point first became evident among pro-Southern troops from border states that had fallen under Union control. Their principal desire was to regain their states for the Confederacy, a goal that did not necessarily fit with the overall purposes of Confederate strategy. An officer in the 8th Missouri Battalion stationed in Arkansas became convinced by the summer of 1862 that Missouri "is to be abandoned in this struggle. . . . Dont you think it too great a tax on ones patriotism to be asked to abandon all he has for the sake of [a] government that wilfully throws away the country that holds remains of his friends—the graves of his father's?"[22]

Similar bitterness boiled up in regiments from Confederate states partly controlled by Union forces. Soldiers in the 2nd Arkansas resented their assignment to Georgia when much of their own state was under enemy occupation. They vowed to fight to the last "provided they are transferred to Arkansas," declared a captain in the regiment, "but not under any other circumstances." When the Army of Tennessee retreated (for the second time) from its namesake state in the Tullahoma campaign of 1863, hundreds of Tennessee soldiers deserted. "It is very mortifying that so many should have left," lamented an officer in the 1st Tennessee. "It is caused by the fact that the Army has no confidence in [Braxton] Bragg and thought he was giving up their homes without proper attempt to defend them."[23] One of the reasons for General John Bell Hood's quixotic invasion of Tennessee in November 1864 was a hope to revitalize the morale of troops from that state. Instead, after the devastating defeats at Franklin and Nashville forced Hood to retreat to Mississippi, few Tennesseeans remained with the now almost nonexistent Army of Tennessee.

Many Confederate soldiers understood, however, that the best way to defend their state was to win the war, even if that meant fighting on a front a thousand miles from home. The war experience molded an incipient Southern nationalism into the genuine article. "No amount of description can convey the most remote idea of the hardships" of soldiering, wrote a private in the 21st Mississippi serving in Virginia, but "I am perfectly content to remain five years or until there is not a Yankee south of the Mason & Dixon's line." A sergeant in the 16th Mississippi, also part of the Army of Northern Virginia, likewise expressed his intention "never to lay down my rifle as long as a Yankee remains on *Southern* soil."[24] A private in the 9th Tennessee insisted that he was fighting "for our *national* rights. . . . We will fight them until Dooms Day or have our independence. I believe that we will be one of the greatest nations on the Globe." A University of Georgia student who left school to enlist wrote his sweetheart from Virginia in 1862 assuring her that the Confederacy would "become a nation among the nations of the earth, designed to fulfill a glorious destiny."[25]

This glorious destiny was much on the mind of twenty-one-year-old "Sandie" Pendleton, Stonewall Jackson's right-hand staff officer, when he wrote to his father (who was chief of artillery for the Army of Northern Virginia) in 1862 that "our men are thinking too much of a whole skin, and too little of their country and the future. What difference does a few hours more or less here of life make in comparison with the future destiny of the people?" Pendleton lived and died by this creed of Confederate nationalism; he was killed at Fishers Hill in 1864.[26]

Patriotism and nationalism were also powerful sustaining motivations for Union soldiers. This truth has sometimes been difficult to grasp. Southern motives seem easier to understand. Confederates fought for independence, for a way of life, for their homes, for their very survival as a nation. But what did Northerners fight for? Why did they persist through four years of the bloodiest conflict in American history, which cost 360,000 Northern lives?

Puzzling over this question in 1863, Confederate War Department clerk John Jones wrote in his diary: "Our men *must* prevail in combat, or lose their property, country, freedom, everything. . . . On the other hand the enemy, in yielding the contest, may retire into their own country, and possess everything they enjoyed before the war began." A Texas private likewise insisted that "we are fighting for matters real and tangible . . . our property and our homes," while Yankees fought only for "matters abstract and intangible." Even an Illinois colonel seemed to agree with this assessment. "We are fighting for the Union," he wrote in 1864, "a high and noble sentiment, but after all a sentiment. They are fighting for independence and are animated by passion and hatred against invaders. . . . It makes no difference whether the cause is just or not. You can get up an amount of enthusiasm that nothing else will excite."[27]

It is perhaps true that Northern nationalism was more "abstract and intangible" than its Southern counterpart. But it was nonetheless just as real and as deeply felt. Union soldiers did not think that they could "retire into their own country" if they lost the war "and possess everything they enjoyed before the war began." Most of them believed that they would no longer have a country worthy of the name. "If we lose in this war, the country is lost and if we win it is saved," wrote a New

York captain in 1863. "There is no middle ground." Another captain, in the 12th New Jersey, spelled out this idea in more detail in a letter to his brother and sister in January 1863, a time of profound Northern discouragement. "Though my nightly prayer is for peace," wrote this veteran, " 'tis for an honorable peace. I would rather live a soldier for life [than] see this country made a mighty sepulcher in which should be buried our institutions, our nationality, our flag, and every American that today lives, than that our Republic should be divided into little *nothings* by an inglorious and shameful peace."[28] . . .

Sometimes the Victorian idioms in which soldiers expressed their patriotism became almost cloying. One wonders what the mother of a Pennsylvania cavalry corporal thought of a letter from her son in 1863 that listed his duties in the following order: "first my God, second my country, third my mother. Oh my country, how my heart bleeds for your welfare. If this poor life of mine could save you, how willingly would I make the sacrifice." Enlisted men in two renowned regiments, the 1st Minnesota and the 5th Iowa, used phrases that by 1862 had become clichés. "Thousands of precious lives will have to be sacrificed" to "support the best Government on God's footstool . . . the best Government ever made." A fifty-four-year-old captain in the 85th New York, a farmer from the dairy belt, wrote his wife in 1863 that "if I never get home you will not say my life has been thrown away for naught. My country, glorious country, if we have only made it truly the land of the free . . . I count not my life dear unto me if only I can help that glorious cause along."[29]

Glorious cause. Lives sacrificed on the country's altar. Hearts bleeding for the country's welfare. Some modern readers of these letters may feel they are drowning in bathos. In this post-Freudian age these phrases strike many as mawkish posturing, romantic sentimentalism, hollow platitudes. We do not speak or write like that any more. Most people have not done so since World War I which, as Ernest Hemingway and Paul Fussell have noted, made such words as *glory, honor, courage, sacrifice, valor,* and *sacred* vaguely embarrassing if not mock-heroic.[30] We would justly mock them if we heard them today. But these words were written in the 1860s, not today. They were written not for public consumption but in private letters to families and friends. These soldiers, at some level at least, *meant* what they said about sacrificing their lives for their country.

Our cynicism about the genuineness of such sentiments is more our problem than theirs, a temporal/cultural barrier we must transcend if we are to understand why they fought. Theirs was an age of romanticism in literature, music, art, and philosophy. It was a sentimental age when strong men were not afraid to cry (or weep, as they would say), a time when Harriet Beecher Stowe's great novel and Stephen Foster's songs could stir genuine emotions. What seems like bathos or platitudes to us were real pathos and convictions to them. Perhaps readers will take another look at the expressions by soldiers quoted two paragraphs above when they learn that all four of them were subsequently killed in action. They were not posturing for public show. They were not looking back from years later through a haze of memory and myth about the Civil War. They were writing during the immediacy of their experiences to explain and justify their beliefs to family members and friends who shared—or in some cases questioned—those beliefs. And how smugly can we sneer at their expressions of a willingness to die for those beliefs when we know that they did precisely that?

An important question remains. How representative were these assertions of patriotic motivations for fighting? Of the 429 Confederate soldiers and sailors whose letters or diaries form the basis for this book, 283, or 66 percent, affirmed such motivations at one time or another after enlisting. For the 647 Union fighting men, the proportion was virtually the same: 441, or 68 percent. These percentages need some interpretation and qualification, however. On the one hand, the absence of references to patriotic convictions in a soldier's letters or diary does not necessarily mean that he was unmoved by such convictions. By their nature, most personal letters and diaries were descriptive rather than reflective, concerned with day-to-day events in the army and at home— weather, food, sickness, gossip, and other mundane matters. Many soldiers who were motivated by patriotism probably found it unnecessary to mention the fact in such writings. On the other hand, the samples of both Confederate and Union soldiers are biased toward the groups most likely to be moved by patriotic and ideological motives: officers, slaveholders, professional men, the middle class, and 1861–62 volunteers rather than post-1862 conscripts, substitutes, and bounty men. Officers comprised 47 percent of the Confederate sample but only about 10 percent of all soldiers. And the proportion of officers who expressed patriotic motives was 82 percent, compared with 52 percent of Confederate enlisted men. Some 35 percent of the Union sample were officers, and 79 percent of them, compared with 62 percent of the enlisted men, expressed patriotic convictions.

Using army rank as a surrogate for class, patriotic motivations appear to have been shared more evenly across class lines in the Union army than among Confederate troops. This finding is borne out by other data from the samples. In the Confederate army the highest-status groups— members of planter families and of slaveholding professional families— voiced patriotic sentiments at almost twice the rate of nonslaveholding soldiers. A similar though less marked pattern occurred between the deep South, with its higher percentage of slaves and slaveholders, and the upper South. The contrast between South Carolina and North Carolina soldiers was particularly notable: 84 percent from South Carolina avowed patriotic convictions, compared with 46 percent from North Carolina. In the Union army there was no such regional variation, and the disparity between higher-status and lower-status groups was much less marked than between Confederates of slaveholding and nonslave-holding status. Thus there was a greater democratization of patriotic motivations across class and regional lines in the Union sample. It is impossible to know whether the same contrast held true for all three million Civil War soldiers. If so, it might help to explain the dogged determination that sustained Union volunteers through four long years of fighting in enemy territory against a foe sustained by the more con-crete motive of defending that territory.

In both the Confederate and Union samples the draftees, substitutes, and men who enlisted after conscription went into effect are underrepre-sented. To the extent that they *are* represented, the percentages express-ing patriotic convictions were much smaller than among the volunteers of 1861–62. Among yeomen farmers in the Confederate army, for ex-ample, 57 percent of those who enlisted in the first year of the war asserted such sentiments, compared with only 14 percent who enlisted or were drafted after conscription went into effect. Among farmers and blue-collar workers in the Union army the disparity was less: 61 percent of those who enlisted before the conscription act of March 1863 avowed patriotic convictions, compared with 43 percent of those who went into the army after this date.[31]

The prototypical unwilling soldier who expressed no patriotic senti-ments and would have preferred to be at home was a nonslaveholding

Southern married farmer with small children who was drafted in 1862 or enlisted only to avoid being drafted. This is not meant to suggest that only those men who fell into this category were unwilling soldiers— there were many such, from all walks of life and every state, North and South, and they included a substantial number of 1861 volunteers who later regretted their impulsive act. But Southern nonslaveholding married farmers seemed particularly bitter on this matter. They gave substance to the theme of a "rich man's war and a poor man's fight" that is prevalent in modern scholarship on class tensions in both North and South during the Civil War.[32]

There is less emphasis on these tensions in soldiers' letters than in recent scholarship. But there is some. A dirt farmer in the 60th North Carolina complained to his wife in 1863 that "this is a Rich mans Woar But the poor man has to do the fiting." Another farmer drafted into the 57th North Carolina lamented that "I could be at home if it warent for a fiew big rulers who I cannot help but blame for it. . . . These big fighting men cant be got out to fight as easy as to make speaches. . . . They lay at home feesting on the good things of the land . . . while we poor soldiers are foursed away from home." Similar sentiments came from a German-born bricklayer in the 8th New Jersey, who exclaimed in 1862: "By God, I don't know for what I should fight. For the rich man so he can make more money the poor man should risk his life and I should get slaughtered."[33]

The soldiers who felt this way furnished a disproportionate number of deserters and skulkers—according to the letters of highly motivated volunteers. They may have been right. If the sample is biased toward those who expressed patriotic convictions, it is also biased toward those who did most of the fighting. The startling fact noted in the preface is relevant here. While 7 percent of all Civil War soldiers were killed or mortally wounded in action, 21 percent of the soldiers in the samples lost their lives in this way. In the Civil War patriotism was not the last refuge of the scoundrel: it was the credo of the fighting soldier.

NOTES

From James M. McPherson, *For Cause and Comrades: Why Men Fought in the Civil War* (New York: Oxford University Press, 1997), 90–103. Reprinted by permission.

Abbreviations in Notes

CWH	Civil War History
FLPU	Firestone Library, Princeton University
GHQ	Georgia Historical Quarterly
GLC PML	Gilder Lehrman Collection, Pierpont Morgan Library, New York
HEH	Henry E. Huntington Library, San Marino, California
HML LSU	Hill Memorial Library; Louisiana State University
MHI	U.S. Army Military History Institute, Carlisle, Pennsylvania
MO HS	Missouri Historical Society, St. Louis
PLDU	Perkins Library, Duke University
PMHB	Pennsylvania Magazine of History and Biography
SHC UNC	Southern Historical Collection, University of North Carolina, Chapel Hill
SHQ	Southwestern Historical Quarterly
SHS MO	State Historical Society of Missouri, Columbia
TSL	Tennessee State Library, Nashville
VMHB	Virginia Magazine of History and Biography
WLEU	Woodruff Library, Emory University, Atlanta

1. Samuel A. Stouffer et al., *The American Soldier*, 2 vols. (Princeton, 1949), vol. II: *Combat and Its Aftermath*, 169; Elmar Dinter, *Hero or Coward: Pressures Facing the Soldier in Battle*, trans. from German by Tricia Hughes (London, 1985), 177.

2. John Ellis, *The Sharp End: The Fighting Man in World War II* (New York, 1980), 322; Stouffer et al., *The American Soldier*, II: 107–8, 150.

3. Charles C. Moskos, *The American Enlisted Man* (New York, 1970), 148; Ronald Spector, *After Tet: The Bloodiest Year in Vietnam* (New York, 1992), 71.

4. Moskos, *The American Enlisted Man*, 135–36, 147; Frank M. Richardson, *Fighting Spirit: A Study of Psychological Factors in War* (London, 1978), 12.

5. Bell Irvin Wiley, *The Life of Billy Yank* (Indianapolis, 1952), 39–40. See also Wiley, *The Life of Johnny Reb* (Indianapolis, 1943), 309.

6. Pete Maslowski, "A Study of Morale in Civil War Soldiers," *Military Affairs* 34 (1970): 123; Fred A. Bailey, *Class and Tennessee's Confederate Generation* (Chapel Hill, 1987), 78; *The New Yorker*, May 18, 1992, p. 31.

7. James G. Theaker to brother, Aug. 10, 1863, *Through One Man's Eyes: The Civil War Experiences of a Belmont County Volunteer*, ed. Paul E. Rieger (Mount Vernon, Ohio, 1974), 49; Robert A. Moore, diary entry of Jan. 28, 1862, in "Robert A. Moore: The Diary of a Confederate Private," ed. James W. Silver, *Louisiana Historical Quarterly* 39 (1956): 312.

8. Gustave Paul Cluseret, *Armée et democratie* (Paris, 1869), 101–2. 20, Quote translated by Philip Katz. See also a statement by the Comte de Paris, who served for a time on General George B. McClellan's staff, quoted in Belle Becker Sideman and Lillian Friedman, eds., *Europe Looks at the Civil War* (New York, 1960), 52–53.

9. *The Civil War Diary of Allen Morgan Geer*, ed. Mary Ann Anderson (Denver, 1977), 142, 145, 147, 149.

10. N. Thomas W. Stephens Diary, entry of Nov. 25, 1863, SHS MO; Henry Orendorff to William Parlin, Feb. 4, 1864, in *We Are Sherman's Men: The Civil War Letters of Henry Orendorff*, ed. William M. Anderson (Macomb, Ill., 1986), 73; Henry H. Howell to Emily Howell (sister), Dec. 7, 1864, in *This Regiment of Heroes: A Compilation of Primary Materials Pertaining to the 124th New York State Volunteers*, ed. Charles J. LaRocca (Montgomery, N.Y., 1991), 230.

11. Thomas Kilby Smith to Eliza Smith, Feb. 4, 1863, Smith Papers, HEH.

12. *Personal Memoirs of U.S. Grant*, 2 vols. (New York, 1885–86), II: 531; John Keegan, *The Mask of Command* (New York, 1987), 191.

13. See in particular Avery Craven, *The Growth of Southern Nationalism, 1848–1861* (Baton Rouge, 1953), and John McCardell, *The Idea of a Southern Nation . . . 1830–1860* (New York, 1979).

14. William B. Coleman to parents, Jan. 19, 1862, Coleman Letters, Civil War Collection, TSL; William Preston Johnston to wife, Aug. 24, 1862, in "A War Letter from William Johnston," ed. Arthur Marvin Shaw, *Journal of Mississippi History* 4 (1942): 44; H. Christopher Kendrick to father and sister, June 2, 1863, Kendrick Papers, SHC UNC.

15. George W. Dawson to wife, April 26, 1862, in "One Year at War: Letters of Capt. Geo. W. Dawson, C.S.A.," ed. H. Riley Bock, *Missouri Historical Review* 73 (1979): 194; John N. Shealy to Eugenia Shealy, June 27, 1862, Shealy Papers, HML LSU.

16. William C. Porter, diary entries of Feb. 8, 1863, Aug. 2, 1862, in "War Diary of W. C. Porter," *Arkansas Historical Quarterly* 11 (1952): 309, 299.

17. John W. Cotton to Mariah Cotton, Aug. 3, 1862, in *Yours Till Death: Civil War Letters of John W. Cotton* (University, Ala., 1951), 14.

18. John Collins to Mary Collins, April 28, 1862, Collins Papers, VHS.

19. James J. Womack, Diary, entry of Feb. 18, 1862, privately printed copy in the Museum of the Confederacy; Richmond; Richard Pugh to Mary Pugh, May 4, 1862. Pugh-Williams Papers, HML LSU.

20. James West Smith, diary entries of June 2 and 15, 1863, "A Confederate Soldier's Diary: Vicksburg in 1863," *Southwest Review* 28 (1943): 304–312.

21. Paul A. Oliver to mother, Sept. 27, 1862, Oliver Papers, FLPU.

22. Edwin E. Harris to Margaret Harris, June 16, 1862, Harris Papers, GLC PML.

23. T. C. Du Pree to wife, Jan. 31, 1864, in *The War-Time Letters of Captain T. C. Du Pree, C.S.A. 1864–1865* (Fayetteville, Ark., 1953), unpaged; Joseph Branch O'Bryan to sister, July 9, 1863, O'Bryan Papers, TSL.

24. Edward M. Burrus to mother, June 14, 1862, Burrus Family Papers, HML LSU: Harry Lewis to mother, Aug. 9, 1862, Harry Lewis Papers, SHC UNC. Emphasis added.

25. William H. Davis to mother, June 23, 1862, Davis Papers, WLEU (emphasis added); Samuel F. Tenney to Alice Toomer, Jan. 18, 1862, in "War Letters of S. F. Tenney, A Soldier of the Third Georgia Regiment," GHQ (1973): 280.

26. Alexander Swift Pendleton to William N. Pendleton, Feb. 25, 1862, in "The Valley Campaign of 1862 as Revealed in Letters of Sandie Pendleton," ed. W. G. Bean, VMHB 78 (1970): 332.

27. John B. Jones, diary entry of March 29, 1863, in *A Rebel War Clerk's Diary*, ed. Earl Schenck Miers (New York, 1958), 181; H. C. Medford, diary entries of April 4, 8, 1864, in "The Diary of H. C. Medford, Confederate Soldier, 1864," ed. Rebecca W. Smith and Marion Mullins, SHQ 34 (1930): 211, 220; Frederick Bartleson to Kate Bartleson, Feb. 26, 1864, in *The Brothers' War*, ed. Annette Tapert (New York, 1988), 187.

28. Paul A. Oliver to Sam Oliver, Jan. 2, 1863, Oliver Papers, FLPU; Richard S. Thompson to sister & brother, Jan. 14, 1863, in *While My Country Is in Danger: The Life and Letters of Lieutenant Colonel Richard S. Thompson*, ed. Gerry Harder Poriss and Ralph G. Poriss (Hamilton, N.Y., 1994), 40–41.

29. Joseph H. Griner to Sophia Griner, Jan. 3. 1863, in Daniel H. Woodward, "The Civil War of a Pennsylvania Trooper," PMHB 87 (1963): 51; William Henry Wykoff to Richard R. Parry. May 27, 1862, Wykoff Letters, in private possession: George Lowe to Elizabeth Lowe, Sept. 18, 1862. Lowe Papers. HEH; Nelson Chapin to wife, Oct. 19, 1863, Chapin Papers, MHI.

30. Ernest Hemingway, *A Farewell to Arms* (New York, 1929), 191; Paul Fussell. *The Great War and Modern Memory* (New York, 1975), 21–22.

31. These figures for both Confederate and Union soldiers are based on enlisted men only; the number of post-conscription men in the sample who became officers is too small for meaningful comparisons.

32. For a sampling of this scholarship, see Bailey, *Class and Tennessee's Confederate Generation*; Stephen E. Ambrose, "Yeoman Discontent in the Confederacy," CWH 8 (1962): 259–68; Paul D. Escott, "Southern Yeomen and the Confederacy," *South Atlantic Quarterly* 77 (1978); Steven Hahn, *The Roots of Southern Populism: Yeoman Farmers and the Transformation of the Georgia Upcountry, 1850–1890* (New York, 1983); Wayne K. Durrill, *War of Another Kind: A Southern Community in the Great Rebellion* (New York, 1990); Armstead Robinson, "Bitter Fruits of Bondage: Slavery's Demise and the Collapse of the Confederacy" (unpublished manuscript); Frank L. Klement. *The Copper-*

heads in the Middle West (Chicago, 1960); Iver Bernstein, *The New York City Draft Riots: Their Significance for American Society and Politics in the Age of the Civil War* (New York, 1990); Grace Palladino, *Another Civil War: Labor, Capital, and the State in the Anthracite Regions of Pennsylvania* Urbana, Ill., 1990); William F. Hanna, "The Boston Draft Riot," *CWH* 36 (1990): 262–73; and Robert E. Sterling, "Civil War Draft Resistance in the Middle West" (Ph.D. dissertation, Northern Illinois University, 1974).

33. John W. Reese to wife, May 26, 1863, Reese Papers, PLDU; James C. Zimmerman to Adeline Zimmerman, April 13, Aug. 5, 1863, Zimmerman Papers, PLDU; Valentin Bechler to wife, Sept. 17, 1862, in "A German Immigrant in the Union Army: Selected Letters of Valentin Bechler," *Journal of American Studies* 4 (1971): 160.

Chapter 26

—————————

Holding On

Earl J. Hess

Earl Hess's study of Union soldiers also includes a discussion of the "will to combat." In this selection from The Union Soldier in Battle *(1997) he assesses the importance of courage, honor, and other ideals, and explores the ambiguous relationship between religious beliefs and combat.*

Most Northern soldiers stayed well within the acceptable definition of courage. They stayed in line of battle, followed orders, and contributed their small part to winning the war. They did not always perform their duties with enthusiasm and conviction, but they generally avoided the appearance of disobedience. If not for this stoic attitude, the Union war effort would have collapsed at its leading edge, the battlefield.

What held these men to their work? There are as many answers to that question as there were soldiers, for each individual had his own set of reasons for carrying on even after he learned that the reality of combat did not match his romantic conceptions of it. The factors that kept men in line of battle were more complicated, multifaceted, and diverse than the factors that impelled them to support the war effort as civilians and then to join the army. It is impossible to demonstrate with "scientific" accuracy whether one factor was dominant. There are surviving letters, diaries, and memoirs from only a minority of Northern veterans. All one can do is identify the recurrent themes in these personal accounts and construct a multilayered view of the varied ways in which their authors came to grips with the emotional challenges of battle.

Courage, Honor, and Self-Control

Courage itself, enshrined by American culture as a supremely valuable ideal of action and thought, was an immensely potent factor in keeping Northern soldiers on the battlefield. They had been nurtured in a cultural environment that encouraged allegiance to a standard of public conduct few could have guessed would be applied in a conflict against fellow Americans, and they tried hard to live up to that standard. The ideal of courage, which meant to the Northern soldier "heroic action undertaken without fear," was intertwined with a range of other values such as manliness, religion, duty, and honor. Although courage was an ideal oriented toward creating useful citizens, many soldiers consciously asserted it as a factor in their willingness to fight, and large numbers of them died trying to demonstrate it in their personal conduct.[1]

Few soldiers tied together the varied meanings of courage better than Joshua Lawrence Chamberlain of the 20th Maine. College professor, self-made officer, and reflective commentator on the war experience, Chamberlain pondered the meaning of "elementary manhood, the antique virtues that made up valor: courage, fortitude, self-command." He believed that Northern men joined the army because of these things and that they were determined to safeguard what they were accustomed to viewing as a national birthright. "Individual happiness must be subordinated to the general well-being," wrote Chamberlain, "duty to country must outweigh all the narrower demands of self-interest."[2] . . .

Self-control was recognized as an indispensable aspect of courage. One of the greatest fears any soldier harbored before his first battle was the fear of losing control. William A. Ketcham of the 13th Indiana was particularly worried going into his first engagement because he was a seventeen-year-old recruit in a veteran regiment. After receiving his first fire, he felt "quite triumphant—I had. . . . experienced no nervousness and no sense of fear or trepidation, and up to that time I had not known what the experience would mean to me, and I only recall the feeling of relief that my first experience under fire had not been detrimental to me or my standing with the boys." Other soldiers were bombarded with admonitions to "keep cool . . . dont shake in your boots, in fact think of nothing, but how you may but do your duty."[3]

Personal and public honor were so deeply involved that many men felt cheated and shamed if they were wounded in the "wrong" way or suffered an illness. Future president Rutherford B. Hayes noted that one of his men in the 23d Ohio took it hard when he was accidentally shot in the foot by a careless comrade. " 'Oh, if it had only been a secession ball I wouldn't have cared," lamented the wounded soldier when he realized that this injury was not a badge of courage. Another soldier, Stephen Rogers of the 36th Massachusetts, became irritated with his enforced confinement to a hospital at the height of the fierce fighting of May 1864. "I tell you there is no *honor* in a mans *sickness*, but there is about a *wound* in the minds of most men." Like love, great ideals could produce frustration and peckishness when unrealized. This was the extent to which many Northern soldiers embraced the authority of courage, honor, and self-control.[4]

The Cause

Courage and ideals of proper behavior were part of American culture and therefore transcended the particular issues involved in the Civil War. The secession crisis and the armed conflict that followed summoned a different set of cultural values and ideas more closely associated with the political history of the nation. The republican heritage of the United States, with its emphasis on the need to protect representative government, democratic practices, and public virtue, was still strong some eighty years after the American Revolution. The Northern cause, which tried to preserve this unique heritage, was a potent force in mobilizing the Northern population. It explained the Southern rebellion as a perverse revolutionary attempt to create an empire for slavery. By 1861, a widespread belief existed among Northerners that the institution of slavery had degraded white society and destroyed democracy in the South by creating an elite class of wealthy slave owners that had engineered secession for its selfish gain. In the minds of many Northerners, the Confederacy represented values and ideas that were antithetical to the national heritage. Such a dangerous entity and all that it represented had to be destroyed, not only to save the political union of the states but also to preserve the cultural foundations of national unity.

Although ideology played a huge role in motivating Northerners to support the war and to join the army, the extent to which it was a factor in helping them deal with the dangers of the battlefield is controversial. Many historians have discounted its role. Ironically, historians of combat morale in other wars have tended to give patriotism and ideology more credit than do the few historians of the Civil War who have addressed the issue. Ideology certainly played an important role in helping men endure battle. Union soldiers lived only two or three generations removed from their nearly legendary forebears who had triumphed against difficult odds in the War of Independence. They were receptive to simple patriotism, morally charged values, and inspired ideas. Ideology was taken seriously by the generation that fought the Civil War, and belief in it intensified in the wake of the unprovoked attack on Fort Sumter. Defenders of the faith readily embraced an ideologically charged interpretation of all the turmoil that fractured the nation.[5] . . .

Ideology was so strongly embraced by so many soldiers because it ennobled the struggle, draped it in a mantle of transcendent significance not only for the people of the United States but also for the millions who would eventually benefit from the expansion of republican ideals throughout the Western world. Not all Northern soldiers took to this message, but its wide appeal cannot be denied, for it linked the military struggle to fundamentally important goals that justified suffering and sacrifice. John Stahl Peterson of the 20th Ohio Battery authored an essay titled "The Issues of the War" in 1864. He wrote, "If there are real issues of right and wrong involved in the contest, and we are in the right, we may rest assured that the results of a successful prosecution of the war will be worthy of all our sacrifices, and honorable to us as a people and nation."[6]

Admittedly, it was easier for the ideologically committed soldier to pen high-minded phrases of self-sacrifice before he experienced battle, but there were many such men who continued to assert their faith even after witnessing all that combat had to offer. There were men who saw, suffered, and still believed, who consciously used their principles as a shield against the horrors of the battlefield. Using ideology as a tool to maintain their sense of purpose was their way of holding on.

Joshua Lawrence Chamberlain saw this as a confrontation between the physical senses and the intellect. He knew that the instinct to survive was strong. "But men are made of mind and soul as well as body. We deal not only with exercises of the senses, but with deeper consciousness; affection, beliefs, ideals, conceptions of causes and effects, relations and analogies, and even conjectures of a possible order and organization different from what we experience in the present world of sense." Chamberlain believed in his men's ability to subordinate fear to higher ideals, a conscious assertion of ideology as a major force in the Northern soldier's ability to survive combat and triumph over it. "Their life was not merely in their own experiences," the former college professor contended, "but in larger sympathies."[7] . . .

For many Northern soldiers, the cause was the supreme motivation, impervious to setbacks and depression. Their minds and emotions were resilient enough to deal with physical pain, trauma, and the mixture of factors that resulted in victory or defeat on the battlefield. Ideology, therefore, became the most lasting justification for continuing the conflict despite the apparent lack of success. . . .

The authority of ideology was so strong that it inspired comparisons between the Northern cause and Confederate motives for leaving the Union. Northern soldiers naturally concluded that there was no basis for comparison. They viewed the Southern cause as no cause at all and found it difficult to believe that anyone could willingly fight for the Confederacy. Many Northern soldiers believed that Southerners were cruelly misinformed about the nature of the conflict, having been forced into military service by a despotic government and a selfish planter class. They often viewed Rebel soldiers as poorly educated, disadvantaged victims of a social and economic structure that denied them opportunity for individual improvement. Of course, this picture of the Confederate soldier was not only ungenerous but also greatly skewed by the passions aroused by the war; it was powerful and widespread, however. The ideology of the cause added a sharp, bitter edge to the war, in addition to providing a solid foundation for motivation.[8] . . .

Patriotism became so important, passionate, and consuming to some Northern soldiers that it assumed a religious aspect. As such, it compelled even more intense devotion and self-sacrifice than a mere political ideology could command. The ideology of the Northern war effort was deeply concerned with morality and thus had a natural affinity with religion. Men such as Lieutenant William Wheeler, a Yale graduate and New York artillerist, called the war "the religion of very many of our lives." He believed that those soldiers who thought long and hard about the issues of the conflict came to "identify this cause for which we are fighting, with all of good and religion in our previous lives, and so it must be if we are to win the victory. We must have an impulse, made of patriotic fire and a deeper feeling, which takes its rise in the thinking soul." Wheeler combined intellectualism with a passion for prosecuting the conflict. The mind and the heart came together in his conception of the war and its meaning.[9]

Of God and Men

Traditional religion also was a potent force in keeping soldiers to their work. When the war came, churches all over the North answered the call to support the cause and encourage men to join the army. In Sterling, a small town in northwestern Illinois, Will C. Robinson was swept up in the excitement following the attack on Fort Sumter. He listened to a sermon in his Congregational church and found it "running over with patriotism and love to the old Union. It was quite warlike, and proved that every man who fell sustaining the government, fell in a just cause." Robinson soon joined the 34th Illinois, where he undoubtedly heard more sermons from the regimental chaplain that fortified his patriotism. Chaplains struggled to ensure that their charges—often young and im-pressionable men away from home for the first time—remembered their religious upbringing and behaved accordingly. Their sermons were often filled with patriotic fervor, reminding soldiers of the righteousness of the Union cause and urging them to keep the faith until the final victory.[10]

Those men who felt the tug of emotion in these sermons advanced religion to the first rank of justification for killing rebellious countrymen. "*Every man that feels that he is accountable to a just God for the deeds done in the body* should give *himself* as a willing sacrifice to his country in this, her hour of need," proclaimed Benjamin Stevens, an Iowan serving as an officer in a black regiment. Stevens used religion with a mixture of confidence and fatalism. His belief that God was on the side of the Union ennobled the conflict, invested it with a heady sense of righteousness, and endowed the suffering with meaning. If he or his compatriots fell, they were assured that God would take them in. Dying in the nation's cause, which was the Lord's cause as well, would make them martyrs. As an Illinois soldier named Jacob Behm put it, "There will be thousands inflamed with my spirit, and impatient to tread in our steps." The religiously committed soldier could take comfort in the knowledge that his death would not be unrewarded.[11]

It was one thing to be moved by thoughts of martyrdom before a battle, but quite another to maintain that belief during or after a bloody engagement. Many soldiers clung desperately to thoughts of God while bullets flew over their heads and dimly seen lines of Confederates began to appear in their front. This was the elemental role that religion played in the soldier's ability to hold on. It steadied his emotions at a critical time and provided a rock on which he based his courage. . . .

The sword of God had two edges. Whereas the first one provided incentives to pursue the war, the second one offered a serious obstacle to killing. The Sixth Commandment posed a problem for devout Christians who took up arms to suppress the Southern rebellion. The result was ambivalence in the minds of many Northern soldiers about the deed that all tacitly agreed was necessary to save the Union.

The most troublesome aspect of war for some was the impact of deliberate killing on the conscience. To Nelson Chapin, it seemed a "strange phase of the human mind" that men "who would not willingly wound the feeling of the most sensitive" rejoiced over the death of a Confederate "as much and more than if he were a wolf in the woods." Chapin might have been referring to an Illinois infantryman who described the "not unpleasant" sight of enemy wounded "kicking like a flock of dead partridges."[12]

Vigorous supporters of the cause considered any ambivalent attitude toward killing the enemy to be unacceptable. Nathan Webb of the 1st Maine Cavalry tried hard to convince himself that a soldier should have no "squeamishness and tenderness at heart for open-handed Rebels. They must be treated as personal enemies, seeking his individual life. . . . No gloved hands must be used in this war." Many men tried but failed to live up to Webb's standard. Chauncey Cooke was a young Wisconsin abolitionist who found it impossible to hate the Confederates or glory in their deaths. At Resaca, he fired so much that he emptied his cartridge box several times. "I saw men often drop after shooting, but didn't know that it was my bullet that did the work and really hope it was not. But you know that I am a good shot."[13]

Cooke and Webb were wrestling with the same issue that soldiers of all wars have to deal with: reconciling peacetime norms of behavior with the often contradictory demands of war. Bishops and ministers had little difficulty making exceptions to the Sixth Commandment to suit political needs, but they did not have to do the killing; those men who pulled the trigger, crouched in the trench, or walked across an open field into the face of massed musketry often found it more troublesome to come to grips with their consciences than to brave the physical dangers of the battlefield. They often had to conclude that war itself was a hateful phenomenon precisely because it forced moral dilemmas on good Christians. "The spirit of war originates in sin," believed Lieutenant Francis Riddle of the 93d U.S. Colored Infantry. The only way a good man could engage in war was if his "spirit and motive" were strong enough to "give character to his calling, dignify his manhood, exalt his deeds, and make him a factor for good or evil in society."[14]

Those soldiers who joined religious leaders in justifying killing did so by embracing the political cause. John Russell of the 21st Illinois was fully aware of the dangers attending combat but was not afraid. "I firmly believe that every Rebel deserves death yet I have no desire to kill them if it was possible to avoid it consistent with the just demand of our country." But the "present deplorable state of affairs" made him willing to shoot and kill in order to save the country. Other men, such as New Hampshireman Charles Paige, combined God's will with the patriotic demands of the nation to justify killing. A devout Christian, Paige reminded himself of "His Eternal truths and principles of justice" so that he could hold on to a God-ordained reason for shooting Rebels[15]

Even such a man as Walter Stone Poor, a twenty-six-year-old New York infantryman who admitted to being "naturally tenderhearted, almost to being womanish" about the thought of killing another man, was able to bring himself to do it for the cause. "I confess . . . it seems impossible for me to kill, or even wound any one even in self-defense. It seems that I would rather die than do it." Yet Poor believed that a good goal had to be attained by paying a price, and the loss of his innocence was a fitting sacrifice for the Union. For deeply conscientious men like Poor, coming to such a decision could be more painful than losing a limb.[16]

When soldiers accepted killing and the possibility of being killed, they also accepted certain unwritten but widely known conventions of military conduct. Those conventions centered on the business of death as an impersonal process of chance. The battle line delivered fire en masse into often dimly seen enemy lines, with relatively little opportunity to aim at individual targets. Thus, one of these conventions was the understanding that a soldier was not personally responsible for the effect of his fire.

Behavior that violated this or other conventions was considered unfair and was often deeply resented as an atrocious act. Deliberately shooting Rebels who were on picket duty, unless there was some overpowering reason to do so, seemed "too like murder" to Major Rutherford B. Hayes of the 23d Ohio. Pickets were isolated and vulnerable sentinels, and killing them seemed more personal than firing on a battle line. Even in the middle of a battle, instances of individual killing were condemned by worried survivors. At the battle of Wauhatchie, as the enemy retired into the darkness following a failed assault, a single Confederate hid behind a tree for several minutes, then took a potshot at a Union soldier who stood up in the belief that the danger had passed. An outraged Federal called this man an "assasin," expressing the moral revulsion he felt at so personal an act.[17]

Sharpshooters generally were viewed in negative terms. Late in the war, when armies tended to be in continuous contact for months at a time, men were chosen to move from one concealed position to another, taking life on a routine basis. A skilled and determined sharpshooter could compile a long list of victims, taking as much pride in his work "as a hunter does in the chase." One observer of the Atlanta campaign noted that sharpshooters kept track of the killed by placing them in categories such as "certainly," "probably," and "possibly" dead. It seemed to be a dehumanizing way of saving the Union.[18]

Although some soldiers took to sharpshooting with diligence, even fulfillment, most detested the role of the sniper. New Englander John William DeForest noticed that some of his fellow officers tried sharpshooting while their units were on duty in the trenches outside Port Hudson, but he refused to do so. "I could never bring myself to what seemed like taking human life in pure gayety." As much as most soldiers disliked being snipers, they hated being targets even more. When a Rebel sharpshooter targeted Theodore Lyman, a member of George Meade's staff, he hated the experience; "it is so personal," he stated. Imagine how personal it felt when soldiers were shot at while relieving themselves. Most soldiers obeyed what one man called "an unwritten code of honor" that forbade killing a man who was answering nature's call, but sharpshooters did not let this code interfere with their tallies. They often took advantage of a man when he was in this vulnerable position.[19]

Skirmishing was a different form of combat than sharpshooting, and it elicited varied reactions from soldiers. Skirmish lines were commonly used to develop enemy positions, harass opposing infantry lines and artillery units, probe for weaknesses, and scout terrain. Skirmishing was a military necessity, and most Union soldiers spent some time performing this duty. Skirmishing demanded different qualities of the warrior than did the battle line. Men had to be able to work in loose-order formations, taking advantage of natural cover, sniping at the enemy, and generally becoming the gnat that hounds the elephant. This type of warfare did not suit everyone.

Benjamin Thompson of New York thought that fighting on battle lines was "barbarous," but skirmishing was nothing less than "savage—

nay, devilish. To juke and hide and skulk for men and deliberately aim at and murder them one by one is far too bloodthirsty business for Christian men." Those who took to the business did so precisely because the juking, hiding, and skulking tested their personal abilities. They enjoyed the "individuality in the effort," the opportunity to display their acute vision, their wits, their agility, and their marksmanship. Some units that were regularly sent out to skirmish came to like it much better than serving in the battle line. The men of the 190th Pennsylvania grew to enjoy skirmishing so much that they became irritated when other regiments were given the job.[20]

These attitudes toward killing and being killed mirrored an ambivalence in American attitudes toward the soldier and his craft. The warrior hero embodied all that was good in the nation, but he was engaged in a business that inspired violent passion. Deliberate killing, although done in the name of the nation, posed a threat to social order. Was the warrior a patriot, or only an executioner? At what point did his killing cross the line between culturally acceptable violence and outrageous barbarism? Northern society had a responsibility for these men, and it fulfilled that charge by convincing most of them that they fought a morally justifiable war. Only then could soldiers hope to reconcile their religious teachings with the call to arms.[21]

Furthermore, many Northerners came to see the killing of their young men as strengthening the cause. It became something of a ritual purification, a symbol of the regeneration of American society. The war was widely viewed as clearing away political issues that had clouded the country's vision for decades, and the emancipation policy of Lincoln's administration added a revolutionary aspect to the Northern war effort. To view the soldier's sacrifice in the conflict as symbolic of a new life tapped into a deep cultural phenomenon that has been common to all societies from ancient history to the present. It may well have been even stronger in America because of the country's experience at carving Western civilization out of a hostile wilderness and its birth in the midst of a bloody war with England. The regenerative potential of the warrior hero's death soothed the loss of brave young men and ennobled even the most painful and sordid form of death.[22]

Howard Stevens of Illinois lost a brother at the battle of Raymond, Mississippi, during Grant's Vicksburg campaign. More than two months later, he wrestled with his loss in a consolatory letter to an uncle back home. It bothered Stevens that his brother's body still lay buried in what he considered "a traitorous land," but he wondered whether that might not be the most appropriate place after all. Perhaps "the blood of our fallen heroes will purify and place an indellible stamp of true patriotism upon this cursed soil and every hero that falls will be as a nail driven in a sure place rendering the Union one and inseparable forever hereafter." The image of a dead soldier physically bonding the Union together again was striking. It represented a deep willingness to believe that the violent death of a soldier could regenerate the nation.[23]

Northern soldiers had to craft a meaning for their war. With a variety of cultural tools at their disposal—ranging from the ideals of courage, honor, and self-control to the ideology of the cause and to religion— many men became convinced of the transcendent significance of the Civil War. Other soldiers resorted to other ideas or themes to deal with combat. In a costly and seemingly endless conflict, the variety of supports for morale was impressive. The supports discussed here were external to the soldier. He drew them from the cultural life that surrounded him and incorporated them as a meaningful part of his philosophy, his thoughts, and his dreams. These supports connected the fate of the individual soldier to that of thousands of other soldiers in Union service and to the fate of the nation itself. The Northern soldier believed that he was fighting for a universal cause, and this enabled him to hold on.

NOTES

From Earl J. Hess, *The Union Soldier in Battle: Enduring the Ordeal of Combat* (Lawrence: University Press of Kansas, 1997), 95–109. Reprinted by permission.

1. Gerald F. Linderman, *Embattled Courage: The Experience of Combat in the American Civil War* (New York, 1987), 8–17; Michael Barton, *Goodmen: The Character of Civil War Soldiers* (University Park, 1981), 5, 21, 33; E. Anthony Rotundo, "Body and Soul: Changing Ideals of American Middle-Class Manhood, 1770–1920," *Journal of Social History* 16 (Summer 1983): 23–38.

2. Joshua Lawrence Chamberlain, *The Passing of the Armies* (New York, 1915), 11, 15–16.

3. William A. Ketcham Reminiscences, Indiana Historical Society; H. L. Brush to Charles H. Brush, January 23, 1863, Brush Family Papers, Illinois State Historical Library; Lysander Wheeler to parents and sister, November 7, 1862, Lysander Wheeler Papers, Illinois State Historical Library.

4. Charles Richard Williams, ed., *Diary & Letters of Rutherford Birchard Hayes*, vol 2 (Columbus, 1922), 50; Stephen S. Rogers to parents, May 19, 1864, Stephen S. Rogers Papers, Illinois State Historical Library.

5. John A. Lynn, *Bayonets of the Republic: Motivation and Tactics in the Army of Revolutionary France, 1791–94* (Urbana, 1984), 34, and John Baynes, *Morale: A Study of Men and Courage* (Garden City Park, 1967), 224–25, 228–30, 235, 253–54, discuss patriotism and ideology in the French revolutionary wars and World War I. For studies that downplay the role of ideology in the Civil War, see Bell Irvin Wiley, *The Life of Billy Yank: The Common Soldier of the Union* (Baton Rouge, 1952), 44, and Pete Maslowski, "A Study of Morale in Civil War Soldiers," *Military Affairs* 34 (December 1970): 123–24.

6. John Stahl Peterson, "The Issues of the War," *Continental Monthly* 5 (1864): 274.

7. Chamberlain, *The Passing of the Armies*, 18.

8. Earl J. Hess, *Liberty, Virtue, and Progress: Northerners and Their War for the Union* (New York, 1988), 78–80; Reid Mitchell, *Civil War Soldiers: Their Expectations and Their Experiences* (New York, 1988), 109–17.

9. William Wheeler, *Letters of William Wheeler of the Class of 1855* (Cambridge, 1875), 417.

10. Will C. Robinson to Charlie, April 28, 1861, Will C. Robinson Papers, Illinois State Historical Library; Rollin W. Quimby, "Recurrent Themes and Purposes in the Sermons of the Union Army Chaplain," *Speech Monographs* 31 (November 1964): 433.

11. Richard N. Ellis, ed., "The Civil War Letters of an Iowa Family," *Annals of Iowa* 39 (Spring 1969): 585; Jacob Behm to sister and brother, February 1, 1864, Jacob Behm Papers, *Civil War Times Illustrated* Collection, U.S. Army Military History Institute.

12. Ferdinand Davis to brother, April 20, 1862, Raymond Cazallis Davis Papers, Michigan History Collection; Nelson Chapin to wife, April 26, 1862, Nelson Chapin Papers, *Civil War Times Illustrated* Collection, U.S. Army Military History Institute; Arthur Lee Bailhache to brother, October 22, 1861, Bailhache-Brayman Collection, Illinois State Historical Library.

13. Nathan B. Webb Diary, April 15, 1863, Illinois State Historical Library; Chauncey H. Cooke, "A Badger Boy in Blue: The Letters of Chauncey H. Cooke," *Wisconsin Magazine of History* 5 (September 1921): 73.

14. Eric J. Leed, *No Man's Land: Combat and Identity in World War I* (New York, 1979), 6–12; Francis A. Riddle, "The Soldier's Place in Civilization," in *Military Essays and Recollections*, vol. 2 (Chicago, 1894), 515–17.

15. John Russell to sister, December 8, 1862, John Russell Papers, *Civil War Times Illustrated* Collection, U.S. Army Military History Institute; Charles C. Paige Memoir, 4, Wendell W. Lang, Jr., Collection, U.S. Army Military History Institute.

16. James J. Heslin, ed., "A Yankee Soldier in a New York Regiment," *New York Historical Quarterly* 50 (April 1966): 116.

17. Williams, ed., *Diary & Letters*, 104; George P. Metcalf Reminiscences, 129, Harrisburg Civil War Round Table—Gregory Coco Collection, U.S. Army Military History Institute.

18. Henry Otis Dwight, "How We Fight at Atlanta," *Harper's New Monthly Magazine* 29 (October 1864): 666.

19. James H. Croushore, ed., *A Volunteer's Adventures: A Union Captain's Record of the Civil War* (New Haven, 1946), 144; George R. Agassiz, ed., *Meade's Headquarters, 1863–1865: Letters of Colonel Theodore Lyman from the Wilderness to Appomattox* (Boston, 1922), 109; Frank Wilkeson, *Recollections of a Private Soldier in the Army of the Potomac* (New York, 1887), 121.

20. Benjamin W. Thompson Memoir, 40, *Civil War Times Illustrated* Collection, U.S. Army Military History Institute; William A. Ketcham Reminiscences, 81, Indiana Historical Society; R. E. McBride, *In the Ranks from the Wilderness to Appomattox Court House* (Cincinnati, 1881), 97–98.

21. Edward Tabor Linenthal, *Changing Images of the Warrior Hero in America: A History of Popular Symbolism* (New York, 1982), xvi–xvii, 4–5.

22. Ibid., ix–xvii, 69–90; Richard Slotkin, *Regeneration Through Violence: The Mythology of the American Frontier, 1600–1860* (Middletown, 1973), 5.

23. Howard Stevens to uncle, July 21, 1863, Howard Stevens Papers, Harrisburg Civil War Round Table—Gregory A. Coco Collection, U.S. Army Military History Institute.

Chapter 27

The Civil War Soldier and the Art of Dying

Drew Gilpin Faust

Drew Faust began her distinguished career as a prizewinning analyst of southern intellectual life; lately she has made distinctive contributions to our understanding of the inner life of Civil War soldiers. Here, in her 2000 presidential address to the Southern Historical Association, she examines the soldier's art of dying, or Ars Moriendi. Faust shows how the ideal of the Good Death was developed and became a popularly imagined scenario among nineteenth-century Americans, regardless of their section or religion. Particularly instructive is her analysis of letters of condolence, where the details of the Good Death were dutifully and artfully inscribed.

Mortality defines the human condition. "We all have our Dead—we all have our Graves," Stephen Elliott, a Confederate Episcopal bishop, observed in an 1862 sermon. Every age, he explained, must confront "like miseries"; every age must search for "like consolation." Yet in spite of the continuities that Elliott identified in human history, death has its discontinuities as well. Men and women fashion the way they approach the end of life out of their understandings of who they are and what matters to them. And inevitably these understandings are shaped by historical and cultural circumstances, by how others around them regard death, by conditions that vary over time and place. Even though "we all have our Dead" and even though we all die, we are likely to do so quite differently from century to century or even generation to generation, from continent to continent and from nation to nation.[1]

In the middle of the nineteenth century the United States embarked on a new relationship with death, entering into a civil war that proved bloodier than any other conflict in American history, a war that would presage the slaughter of World War I's Western Front and the global carnage of the twentieth century. The number of soldiers who died between 1861 and 1865 is approximately equal to American fatalities in the Revolution, the War of 1812, the Mexican War, the Spanish American War, World War I, World War II, and the Korean War combined. The Civil War's rate of death, its incidence in comparison with the size of the American population, was six times that of World War II; a similar rate of death, about 2 percent, in the United States today would mean almost five million fatalities. Although mortality rates differed North and South, with the percentage of Confederate men who died in the war three times greater than the proportion of Yankees, death seemed omnipresent throughout Civil War America. As the *Daily South Carolinian* observed in 1864, "Carnage floods our once happy land."[2]

But the impact and meaning of the war's casualties were not simply a consequence of scale, of the sheer numbers of Union and Confederate soldiers who died. Death's significance for the Civil War generation derived as well from the way it violated prevailing assumptions about life's proper end—about who should die, when and where and under what circumstances. As a newly appointed chaplain explained to his Connecticut regiment in the middle of the war, "neither he nor they had ever lived and faced death in such a time, with its peculiar conditions and necessities. . . ." Civil War soldiers and civilians alike distinguished what many referred to as "ordinary death," as it had occurred in prewar years, from the way in which so many men were now dying in Civil War battlefields and camps.[3] Historians have only recently begun to consider the social and cultural meanings of Civil War death, perhaps because the war was so long seen as the all-but-exclusive province of military historians, who regarded casualties chiefly as an index to an army's continuing strength and effectiveness. Burgeoning recent interest in the war by social historians, however, has begun to raise questions about the wider impact of battlefield slaughter and to suggest that such mortality, even in a society far more accustomed to death than our own, must have exerted a profound influence on Americans' perceptions of the world around them as well as their hopes for a world to come. Like the Connecticut chaplain, these scholars see Civil War death as representing a new departure—in its scale, in its brutality, in its seeming endlessness as the war continued on and on. The Mexican War had yielded a total of 1,800 American military deaths over a period of two years; the Revolution killed approximately 4,000. More than 4,800 soldiers died on a single day at Antietam in September 1862, and 7,000 more would die from wounds received there. Death was no longer just encountered individually; mortality rates were so high that nearly every American family was touched. Death's threat, its proximity, its actuality became the most widely shared of war's experiences. As Emily Dickinson wrote from western Massachusetts during the conflict, "Sorrow seems to me more general [than] it did, and not the estate of a few persons, since the war began; and if the anguish of others helped one with one's own, now would be many medicines." At war's end, this shared suffering would override persisting differences about the meanings of race, citizenship, and nationhood to establish sacrifice and its memorialization as the common ground on which North and South would ultimately reunite. Even in our own time, this fundamentally elegiac understanding of the Civil War retains its powerful hold.[4]

Our understanding of the impact and influence of Civil War mortality must necessarily begin with an exploration of the deaths themselves, with how they were managed emotionally, spiritually, and ideologically by soldiers and their families. Americans North and South would be compelled to confront—and resist—the war's assault on their conceptions of how life should end, an assault that challenged their most fundamental assumptions about life's value and meaning. As they faced horrors that forced them to question their ability to cope, their commitment to the war, even their faith in a righteous God, soldiers and civilians alike struggled to retain their most cherished beliefs, to make them work in the dramatically altered world that war had introduced. Civil War death would transform America and Americans in ways that new scholarship is just beginning to explore. But this change would emerge only slowly and only out of the often desperate efforts of Yankees and Confederates to mobilize traditional religious and intellectual resources to operate in the dramatically changed circumstances of what has often been called the first modern and the last old-fashioned war. In the experiences of soldiers and their families, we can see this conflict between old and new cast into sharp relief as Americans endeavored to reconstruct conventional consolations to serve new times and a new kind of slaughter. Civil War death must thus be understood as at once old and new, for the effort of Americans to hold on to cherished beliefs and assumptions indelibly shaped the necessarily transformed world that war made.

Mid-nineteenth-century American culture treated dying as an art and the "Good Death" as a goal that all men and women should struggle to achieve. From the fifteenth century onward, texts describing the *Ars Moriendi* ["art of dying"] had provided readers with rules of conduct for the moribund and their attendants: how to give up one's soul "glad-lye and wilfully"; how to meet the devil's temptations of unbelief, despair, impatience, and worldly attachment; how to pattern one's dying on that of Christ; how to pray. With the spread of vernacular printing, such texts multiplied in number, culminating in the mid-seventeenth century with Jeremy Taylor's *The Rule and Exercise of Holy Dying* (1651). . . . [5]

By the nineteenth century Taylor's books had become classics, and the tradition of the *Ars Moriendi* spread both through reprints of earlier texts and through more contemporary considerations of the Good Death. Often these more modern renditions appeared in new contexts and genres: in sermons that focused on one or two aspects of the larger subject; in American Sunday School Union tracts distributed to youth across the nation; in popular health books that combined the expanding insights of medical science with older religious conventions about dying well; or in popular literature, with the exemplary deaths of Dickens's Little Nell, Thackeray's Colonel Newcome, or Harriet Beecher Stowe's Eva. So diverse and numerous were these representations of the Good Death that they reached a wide spectrum of the American population at mid-century, and they would become a central aspect of the popular culture, the songs, stories, and poetry of the Civil War itself. By the 1860s many elements of the Good Death had been to a considerable degree separated from their explicitly theological roots and had become as much a part of respectable middle-class behavior and expectation in both North and South as they were the product or emblem of any particular religious affiliation. Assumptions about the way to die remained central within both Catholic and Protestant faiths but had spread beyond formal religion to become a part of more general systems of belief held across the nation about life's meaning and life's appropriate end. [6]

In the context of the Civil War, the Good Death proved to be a concern shared by almost all Americans of every religious background. An overwhelming majority of Civil War soldiers, like Americans generally in the 1860s, were Protestant, and Protestant assumptions dominated discourse about death. But war's imperatives for unity and solidarity produced an unprecedented degree of religious interaction and cooperation that not only brought Protestant denominations together but to a considerable extent incorporated Catholics and Jews as well. The war encouraged a Protestant ecumenism that yielded interdenominational publication societies, common evangelical gatherings, and shared charitable efforts like the Christian Commission. But Civil War ecumenism extended beyond Protestantism. Catholic chaplains in both Union and Confederate armies remarked on the effective cooperation among pastors and soldiers of differing religious affiliations. . . .

Even Jewish soldiers, who comprised less than 0.3 percent of Civil War armies, partook of this common religiosity. Michael Allen, Jewish chaplain of a Pennsylvania regiment, held nondenominational Sunday services for his men, preaching on a variety of topics, including proper preparation for death. Although we today tend to assume sharp differences between Jewish and Christian views of death, and particularly the afterlife, these contrasts appeared far less dramatic to mid-nineteenth-century Americans. . . . [7]

At the heart of this common understanding lay the assumption of death's transcendent importance. A tract distributed to Confederate soldiers by the Presbyterian Church warned that "Death is not to be regarded as a mere event in our history. It is not like a birth, or a marriage, or a painful accident, or a lingering sickness." It has an "importance that cannot be estimated by men." Death's significance arose from its absolute and unique permanence. . . . How one died thus epitomized a life already led and predicted the quality of the life everlasting. The *hors mori*, the hour of death, had, therefore, to be witnessed, scrutinized, interpreted, narrated—not to mention carefully prepared for by any sinner seeking to demonstrate worthiness for salvation. The sudden and all-but-unnoticed end of the soldier slain charging amidst the chaos of battle, the unattended deaths of unidentified wounded men too ill to reveal their last thoughts, denied these long-cherished consolations. Civil War battlefields could have provided the material for an exemplary text on how *not* to die. [8]

Soldiers and their families struggled in a variety of ways to mitigate such cruel realities, to construct a Good Death even amidst chaos, to substitute for missing elements or compensate for unsatisfied expectations. Their successes or failures influenced not only the last moments of thousands of dying soldiers but also the attitudes and outlook of survivors who contended with the impact of these experiences for the rest of their lives. . . .

One of the most "peculiar" of the "conditions" surrounding Civil War death, one of the most significant ways in which it departed from "ordinary" death, was that it took young, healthy men and rapidly, often instantly, destroyed them with disease or injury. This represented a sharp and alarming departure from prevailing assumptions about who should die. As Francis W. Palfrey of Massachusetts wrote in an 1864 memorial for Union soldier Henry L. Abbott, "the blow seems heaviest when it strikes down those who are in the morning of life."[9]

But perhaps the most distressing aspect of death for many Civil War–era Americans was that thousands of young men were dying away from home. As one group of Confederate prisoners of war observed in a resolution commemorating a comrade's death in 1865, "we . . . deplore that he should die . . . in an enemys land far from home and friends." Most soldiers would have shared the wishes of the Georgia man whose brother sadly wrote after his death in Virginia in 1864, "he always did desire . . . to die at home." As a South Carolina woman observed in 1863, it was "much more painful" to give up a "loved one [who] is a stranger in a strange land."[10]

Civil War soldiers experienced an isolation from relatives uncommon among the free white population. Civil War armies, moreover, segregated men from women, who in the nineteenth century bore such a significant part of the responsibility for care of both the living and the dead. As a Sanitary Commission observer remarked of the Army of the Potomac. "Of this hundred thousand men, I suppose not ten thousand were ever entirely without a mother's, a sister's, or a wife's domestic care before."[11]

Family was central to the *Ars Moriendi* tradition, for kin performed its essential rituals. Victorian ideals of domesticity further reinforced these assumptions about death's appropriate familial setting. As a British social historian has explained in an observation that would apply equally well to nineteenth-century America, "the family was the primary Victorian and Edwardian social institution in which the meaning of individual deaths was constructed and transmitted across the generations."[12] One should die amidst family assembled around the deathbed. Relatives would of course be most likely to show concern about the comfort and needs of their dying loved one, but this was ultimately a secondary consideration. Far more important, family members needed to witness a death in order to assess the state of the dying person's soul, for these critical last moments of life would epitomize his or her spiritual condition. Kin would use their observations of the deathbed to evaluate the family's chances for a reunion in heaven. A life was a narrative that could only be incomplete without this final chapter, without the life-defining last words.

Last words had always held a place of prominence in the *Ars Moriendi* tradition. By the eighteenth century, "dying declarations" had assumed—and still retain—explicit secular importance: a special evidentiary status excepting them from legal rules excluding hearsay. Final words were regarded as possessing an especially high truth status, both because it was believed that a dying person could no longer have any earthly motivation to lie and because those about to meet their Maker would not wish to expire bearing false witness. As Civil War sermonizers North and South reminded their congregations, "A death-bed's a detector of the heart." Not only were last words important because of their assumed honesty, they also imposed a meaning on the life narrative they would conclude. At the same time that they exemplified a life, moreover, they communicated invaluable lessons or insights to those gathered around the deathbed. This educational function provided a critical means through which the deceased could continue to exist in the lives of the survivors. The teachings that last words imparted served as a lingering exhortation and a persisting tie between the living and the dead. To be deprived of these lessons and thus this connection seemed unbearable to many nineteenth-century Americans left at home while their sons, husbands, and brothers died with their last words unrecorded or even unheard.[13]

The effort to overcome separation from kin and to provide a surrogate for the traditional stylized deathbed performance lay at the heart of Civil War–era efforts to manage battlefield death. Soldiers, chaplains, military nurses, and doctors conspired to provide the dying man and his family with as many of the elements of the conventional Good Death as possible, struggling even amidst the chaos of war to make it possible for men—and their loved ones—to believe they had died well. Spiritual wounds demanded attention as powerfully as did those of the flesh.[14]

Determined not to die alone, soldiers worked to provide themselves with replacements, proxies for those who might have surrounded their deathbeds at home. Battlefield descriptions often remark on the photo-

492   DREW GILPIN FAUST

graphs found alongside soldiers' corpses. In March 1864, for example, *Godey's Ladies' Book* reported the death of a soldier discovered with pictures of his three children "tightly clasped in his hands." Denied the presence of actual kin, dying men removed pictures from pockets or knapsacks and spent their last moments communicating with these representations of absent loved ones. In military hospitals, nurses frequently cooperated in this search for substitutes, permitting delirious soldiers to think their mothers, wives, or sisters stood nearby. In a famous lecture with which she toured the country in the years after the war, Clara Barton described her crisis of conscience when a young man on the verge of death mistook her for his sister Mary. Unable to bring herself actually to address him as "brother," she nevertheless kissed his forehead so that, as she explained, "the act had done the falsehood the lips refused to speak."[15] . . .

No effective system of reporting casualties operated on either side during the war. Families most often learned of the deaths of loved ones by scrutinizing unreliable newspaper lists of killed and wounded, lists that were often inaccurate as well as painfully incomplete in their mere enumeration of names with no attempt to explain attendant circumstances. To compensate for the inadequacy of such arrangements, it became customary for a slain soldier's closest companions at the time of his death to write a letter to his next of kin, not just offering sympathy and discussing the disposition of clothes and back pay but providing the kind of information a relative would have looked for in a conventional peacetime deathbed scene. These were condolence letters intended to offer the comfort implicit in the narratives of the *Ars Moriendi* that most of them contained. News of a Good Death represented the ultimate solace—the consoling promise of life everlasting.[16] . . .

Remarkably similar North and South, condolence letters constitute a genre that emerged from the combination of the assumption of *Ars Moriendi* with the "peculiar conditions and necessities" of the Civil War. These letters sought to make absent loved ones virtual witnesses to the dying moments they had been denied, to mend the fissures war had introduced into the fabric of the Good Death. In camp hospitals, nurses and doctors often took on this responsibility, sending the bereaved detailed descriptions not just of illnesses and wounds, but of last moments and last words. Clara Barton kept a notebook filled with such declarations to be forwarded to kin. Some hospital personnel even assumed the role of instructors in the art of dying, eliciting final statements and cueing their patients through the enactment of the Good Death. When Jerry Luther lay wounded after the Battle of Yorktown in 1862, a physician urged him to send a message to his mother. Another soldier, asked by a doctor for his last words to send home, responded by requesting the doctor to provide them. "I do not know what to say. You ought to know what I want to say. Well, tell them only just such a message as you would like to send if you were dying." The expiring soldier obviously regarded the doctor as an expert in the art of dying as well as in medicine. The soldier comprehended that this was a ritual the physician understood far better than he. The Civil War provided a context not just for the performance of the traditions of *Ars Moriendi*, but for their dissemination. Chaplains North and South in fact saw this instruction as perhaps their most important duty toward the soldiers in their spiritual charge, a duty Catholic father William Corby of a New York regiment described as "the sad consolation of helping them . . . to die well."[17]

Sometimes soldiers would attempt to eliminate the need for intermediaries in order to narrate their deaths directly. Many carried letters to be forwarded to loved ones if they were killed, but these did not, of course, provide descriptions of final moments or hours. Some men, however, managed to write home as they lay dying, speaking through their pens instead of from the domestic deathbeds that war had denied them. These letters are particularly wrenching, in part because the last words of more than a century ago appear seemingly unmediated on the page, speaking across the years, serving as a startling representation of immortality for a twenty-first-century reader. Jeremiah Gage of the Eleventh Mississippi wrote his mother after Gettysburg. "This is the last you may ever hear from me. I have time to tell you I died like a man." James R. Montgomery's 1864 letter to his father in Mississippi is rendered all the more immediate by the bloodstains that cover the page. But if the reality of his wounds seems almost present and even tangible, his assumptions about death emphasize the years that distance him from our own time. "This is my last letter to you," he explains. "I write to you because I know you would be delighted to read a word from your dying son." His choice of the word "delight" here—a term that seems strikingly inappropriate within the context of our modern understanding—underlines the importance accorded the words of the dying. Even as his father faced the terrible news of his son's death, Montgomery expected him to have the capacity to be delighted by the delivery of his son's last thoughts.

And even *in extremis*, Montgomery followed the generic form of the Civil War death letter. By the middle of the 1864 Wilderness campaign, Montgomery may well have had a good deal of practice at writing such letters to other families. Now he could use this proficiency in composing his own.[18]

Letters describing soldiers' last moments on earth are so similar, it seems almost as if their authors had a checklist in mind, enumerating the necessary details. In fact, cultural prescriptions about the art of dying specified the elements of a Good Death so explicitly that a letter writer could in large measure anticipate the information that the bereaved would have looked for had they been present at the hour of death: the deceased had been conscious of his fate, had demonstrated his willingness to accept it, had showed signs of belief in God and in his own salvation, and had invoked the idealized domestic deathbed scene by leaving messages and instructive exhortations for those who should have been at his side. But each of these details was in effect a kind of shorthand, conveying to the reader at home a broader set of implications about the dying man's spiritual state and embodying the assumptions that nineteenth-century Americans shared about life and death.[19]

Condolence letters invariably addressed the deceased's awareness of his fate. It was, of course, desirable for the dying man to be conscious and able to confront his impending demise, for only then would he be able to face death's inevitability and thus clearly reveal the state of his soul through his last utterances. One of the Civil War's greatest horrors was that it denied so many soldiers this opportunity by killing them suddenly, obliterating them on the battlefield and depriving them of the chance for the life-defining deathbed experience. Letter writers were honest in reporting such unsatisfactory deaths, explaining to loved ones at home that they were not alone in being deprived of the last words of the departed.

Sudden death represented a profound threat to the most fundamental assumptions about the correct way to die, and its frequency on the battlefield comprised one of the most important ways that Civil War death departed from the "ordinary death" of the prewar period, as well as one of the most significant challenges the "peculiar conditions" of the Civil War posed to prevailing cultural understandings. When two soldiers calmly eating dinner in a tent were instantly and unexpectedly killed by a shell lobbed from nearby Sullivan's Island, Samuel A. Valentine of the legendary Massachusetts Fifty-Fourth wrote that, although he had seen many comrades die, this incident was especially upsetting, and he declared that he had "never had anything to rest on me so much in my life." The suddenness, the lack of preparation made this death a particularly "awful sight."[20] . . .

Such understandings of fate no doubt encouraged one means that soldiers frequently used to defend themselves—spiritually, emotionally, ideologically—against sudden death. Many letters announcing the deaths of comrades commented on the deceased's premonitions that a particular encounter would indeed prove fatal. Even if these men were denied the few poignant and life-defining minutes or hours of knowing that their wound or illness would be their last, they had nevertheless seized their destiny through the mechanism of foresight. They had provided themselves with time for the all-important spiritual preparation one could use effectively only when face to face with unavoidable death. Sure knowledge—even of death—seemed preferable to persisting uncertainty, for it restored both a sense of control and the feeling of readiness so important to the Good Death. Willie Bacon, for example, had told his comrades of his conviction that he would die the night before he entered his last battle in Virginia in 1862. "Strange and mysterious," remarked the preacher who delivered his funeral sermon, "is the fact that God so often permits the shadow of death to be thrown upon us, that we may prepare ourselves for his coming." Early in the war, W. D. Rutherford of South Carolina remarked to his fiancée upon "[h]ow we find ourselves involuntarily longing for the worst," so as simply not to be caught unaware. Rutherford would confront three more years of such uncertainty and "longing" before his death in Virginia in October 1864.[21]

Wounded or sick soldiers who knew they had not long to live made their sense of preparedness explicit by indicating their acceptance of their fate, and letters offered such remarks as important vehicles of condolence to bereaved family members. J. C. Curtwright wrote with sadness to inform Mr. and Mrs. L. B. Lovelace of Georgia that their son had died in April 1862 in Tennessee. But, he reassured them, "[h]e was conscious all the time and expressed a willingness to die." T. Fitzhugh wrote Mrs. Diggs to report the death of her beloved husband in June 1863. He lived "but a short while" after being shot by the Yankees, but "he was in his right mind at the time of his death" and "was perfectly resigned." A nurse in a Virginia military hospital informed the mother of a deceased patient that he had been "conscious of his death and . . .

not afraid but willing to die," which she reassuringly interpreted as "reason to believe that he is better off" now than in this world of woe.[22]

Witnesses eagerly reported soldiers' own professions of faith and Christian conviction, for these were perhaps the most reassuring evidences that could be provided of future salvation. As T. J. Hodnett exclaimed to his family at home after his brother John's 1863 death from smallpox, "Oh how could I of Stud it if it had not of bin for the bright evidence that he left that he was going to a better world." Hodnett was deeply grateful that John's "Sole seme to be . . . happy" as he passed his last moments singing of a heaven with "no more triels and trubble nor pane nor death." Captain A. K. Simonton of North Carolina and Isaac Tucker of New Jersey fought on different sides of the conflict, but both died with the words "My God! My God!" on their lips. Tucker was not a "professed and decided follower of Jesus," but his regular attendance at church, his calm in the face of death, and his invocation of the Divinity at the end suggested grounds for fervent hope about his eternal future. Simonton's presentiment of his end, his attention in the weeks before his death to "arranging his business for both worlds," indicated that he too was ready to greet his Maker, as he did explicitly with his last words.[23]

When soldiers expired unwitnessed and unattended, those reporting on their deaths often tried to read their bodies for signs that would reveal the nature of their last moments—to make their silence somehow speak. Their physical appearance would communicate what they had not had the opportunity to put into words. Many observers believed, as one war correspondent put it, that the "last life-expression of the countenance" was somehow "stereotyped by the death blow," preserved for later scrutiny and analysis. As a witness to the death of Maxcy Gregg wrote the general's sisters, "the calm repose of his countenance indicated the departure of one, at peace with God." In words meant to offer similar reassurance to grieving relatives, a Confederate soldier reporting the death of a cousin in 1863 described the body as he had found it: "His brow was perfectly calm. No scowl disfigured his happy face, which signifies he died an easy death, no sins of this world to harrow his soul as it gently passed away to distant and far happier realms." Clearly such a peaceful countenance could not be on its way to hell. A Michigan soldier, however, discovered just such evidence in the appearance of some "rebells" already many hours dead. "Even in death," he wrote, "their traits show how desperate they are and in what situation their conscience was. Our dead look much more peaceful." Letter writers eagerly reported any evidence of painless death, not just to relieve the minds of loved ones about the suffering a soldier might have had to endure, but, more importantly, because an easy death suggested the calmness, resignation, and quick passage to heaven the bereaved so eagerly hoped for as they contemplated the fate of their lost kin.[24]

Peaceful acceptance of God's will, even when it brought death, was an important sign of one's spiritual condition. But if resignation was necessary for salvation, it could not be sufficient. Condolence letters detailed evidences of sanctified practice that absent relatives had not been able to witness. When Henry Bobo, a Mississippi private, died of wounds received near Richmond in the summer of 1862, his cousin wrote from the field to assure Henry's parents that their son had a better chance of getting to heaven than they might think. There had been, he reported, a "great change" in Henry's "way of living" in the months just before his death. Although he had never actually become a professed Christian, Henry had quit swearing and had began to lead a Christian life. I. B. Cadenhead's sergeant sought to offer similar reassurance to the soldier's widow after her husband's death outside Atlanta in the summer of 1864. "I have had several conversations with him upon the subject of death he sayed to me their was one thing that he was sorry for & and that he had not united himself with the church before he left home." When Asahel Nash was killed in the fall of 1862, his parents wrote their nephews, who had served in the First Ohio with their son, to secure information about his life as well as his death. "[We]e want you to write all you can about Asahel. . . . How were his morals?" The army, they feared, was "a poor place to improve good habits."[25] . . .

Just as the bereaved looked for persuasive evidence of salvation, so too were they eager for last messages from dying kin. Reports of parting communications to loved ones appeared in almost every condolence letter. Sanford Branch wrote his mother in Georgia after First Manassas to say his brother John's last words were "about you. . . ." After Private Alfred G. Gardner of Rhode Island was shot at Gettysburg, the last thing he said was for his sergeant to tell his wife he died happy. T. J. Spurr of Massachusetts expired uttering the word "Mother"; Wiley Dorman "asked for his Mother the last word he spoke." Fathers often exhorted children to complete their education, help their mothers, and say their prayers. With these words, dying soldiers brought at least the names and spirit of absent loved ones to their deathbeds and left their survivors with wishes and instructions that outlived their source. For those at home, news of these final messages reinforced the sense of connectedness to lost kin. Neither family nor soldier was left entirely alone, for these deathbed invocations of absent loved ones worked in some measure to overcome separations.[26]

Soldiers seemed often to invoke names of kin in messages of reassurance—about their certainty of salvation and of meeting them once again in "a better world than this." "Write to mother," implored a dying soldier, "and tell her she must meet me in heaven. I know I am going there." But this soldier, like many others, went beyond the traditional elements of the *Ars Moriendi* in his efforts to provide his mother with consolation. "Tell my mother," he was reported to have said, "I have stood before the enemy fighting in a great and glorious cause. . . ." When Civil War condolence letters enumerated evidence of the deceased's Christian achievements, designed to show his eligibility for salvation, the writer often included details of the soldier's military performance, his patriotism, and his manliness. In a letter to the widow of a comrade who had died the preceding day, T. Fitzhugh reported all the customary information: her husband had been resigned to death, was conscious of his fate, and sent his love to wife and children. But he also added that the soldier had "died a glorious death in defence of his Country."[27]

The image of the Christian soldier encompassed patriotic duty within the realm of religious obligation. But in some instances, patriotism and courage seemed to serve as a replacement for evidence of deep religious faith. Oliver Wendell Holmes lay severely wounded after Ball's Bluff, wondering if his religious scepticism was going to put him "en route for Hell." But he urged his physician to write home in case of his death to say he had done his duty. "I was very anxious they should know that." Some nonbelievers hoped that patriotism would substitute for religious conviction in ensuring eternal life. A dying Confederate asked his friend, "Johnnie if a boy dies for his country the glory is his forever isn't it?" He would have found the views of David Cornwell of the Eighth Illinois reassuring. "I couldn't imagine," he mused, "the soul of a soldier who had died in the defense of his country being consigned to an orthodox hell, whatever his opinion might be of the plan of salvation."[28]

But Cornwell's views, widely held in both armies, seemed to many Protestant clergy an unwarranted theological innovation, generated by earthly necessities rather than transcendent truths. As the *Army and*

Navy Messenger, published in Virginia by the interdenominational Evangelical Tract Society, warned in 1864, patriotism was not piety. "It is not the blood of man but *'the blood of Jesus Christ that cleanseth from all sin.'* "[29]

Yet despite clerical efforts, the boundary between duty to God and duty to country grew increasingly blurred, and dying bravely and manfully came to comprise a significant part of dying well. For some soldiers it almost served to take the place of the more sacred obligations of holy living that had traditionally prepared the way for the Good Death. Letters comforting Wade Hampton after his son Preston was killed in the fall of 1864 emphasized this juxtaposition of military and Christian duty and sacrifice. William Preston Johnston urged Hampton to remember that his son's "heroism has culminated in martyrdom," which should serve as a "consolation for the years he might have lived." James Connor's letter to Hampton merged the imperatives of Christianity, military courage, and masculinity into a hierarchy of condolence. "Your best consolation will I know my dear Genl," he wrote, "be drawn from higher than earthly sources[;] still some alleviation of the sorrow is to be drawn from the reflection that Preston died as he had lived, in the path of duty and honor. Young as he was he had played a man's part in the war." Although Christian principles remained paramount, considerations of courage and honor could also offer "some alleviation of the sorrow" and thus played a significant role in the Civil War condolence letter as well as in more general conceptions of holy living and holy dying. A letter written from North Carolina in 1863 to inform William K. Rash that "your son R. A. Rash is no more" is striking in its deviation from the conventional model. It includes no mention of God or religion, simply reporting the ravages of "the Grim monster Death." All the more significant, then, is its invocation of the only solace available in the absence of appeal to the sacred: "But one consolation he died in the full discharge of his duty in the defence of his home & Country."[30] . . .

Military executions made a powerful statement about the need to be prepared to die. As the condemned prisoner scrambled to change his eternal fate with a last-minute conversion or repentance, he reinforced the centrality of readiness to the Good Death. Spiritual preparedness was of course the essence of the art of dying well, but preparation was often also manifested in more temporal ways. Many popular renditions of the *Ars Moriendi* emphasized the importance of settling one's worldly affairs, and these considerations found their way into soldiers' letters and soldiers' lives. A soldier who arranged for a burial plot on a furlough home was clearly contemplating his mortality in the manner necessary for dying well. But he was also disposing of earthly preoccupations so that his death might bring a satisfactory conclusion to life's narrative. Condolence letters almost inevitably addressed these concerns, usually in their closing sentences or paragraphs. Correspondents often elevated an accounting of soldiers' property and back pay into more transcendent realms by including descriptions of relics or *memento mori* they were forwarding to bereaved kin. Burns Newman of the Seventh Wisconsin Volunteers undertook the "painful duty" of informing Michael Shortell's father of his son's death near Petersburg the preceding evening. "Enclosed," he continued, "send you some trinkets taken from his person by my hand. Think you will prize them as keepsakes." A Bible, a watch, a diary, a lock of hair, even the bullet with which a son or brother had been killed could serve to fill the void left by the loved one's departure, could help to make tangible a loss known only through the abstractions of language. Henry I. Bowditch of Massachusetts described an "amulet" he fashioned out of a ring given his dead son Nathaniel by his fiancée and a "cavalry button cut from his blood-stained vest." Bowditch attached them to his watch. "There I trust they will remain until I die." John S. Palmer of South Carolina carried the ball that had killed his son James with him until he died in 1881, when he took it with him to his grave.[31]

Condolence letters often provided kin with an opportunity for the most important lingering connection with the dead: information about burial, news of a gravesite that could be visited, or the location of a body that might someday be retrieved. Letter writes did their best to provide the consolation of a "decent" burial—mentioning when they could that a coffin had been provided, that a grave had been marked to preserve the identity of the deceased from oblivion. When James Vance of the Thirty-sixth Wisconsin Volunteers wrote Mr. and Mrs. Patton of the death of their son Wesley in Virginia in June 1864, he reassured them that "we buried him decently placed a board with his name, day of death, age and regiment, to his grave that he may be found at any time should you care to move him. I tried all I could to send his body home and the Sargant tried but could not do it." A letter might include directions to a grave, sometimes with descriptions of landmarks—an oddly shaped rock, for example, or a particular species of trees.[32]

All too often, however, a body could not be located, much less returned. When W. N. Pendleton, an Episcopal minister as well as a Confederate general, wrote William Garnett of the death of his son General Richard B. Garnett in Pickett's Charge, he felt pained to report that "his body, in common with those of many officers there, was not recovered." This was rarely the case for a general, but it was all too common among the rank and file, for hundreds of thousands of men remained missing or unidentified at war's end. Knowing where a loved one had been "decently interred" was a precious consolation indeed. The effort to identify and rebury the Union and Confederate dead after Appomattox was in many senses a continuation of the imperatives of the *Ars Moriendi* into the postwar years. Long after the dying was over, Americans North and South sought to add epilogues to their wartime death narratives.[33]

Even before war's end, Americans had begun to revise and elaborate the accounts of death focused on the *hors mori*. The condolence letter came in many cases to represent a rough draft of a story of holy living and holy dying that was rewritten and perfected in a range of printed genres dedicated to constructing the Good Death amid the chaos of wartime destruction. Obituaries often replicated the structure and content of condolence letters, frequently even quoting them directly, describing last moments and last words and assessing the likelihood of a deceased soldier's salvation. William James Dixon of the Sixth Regiment of South Carolina Volunteers, his obituary reported, had not entered the army as a believer, though he had always "maintained a strictly moral character." Several battles, however, impressed him with "the mercy of God in his preservation," so that before his death at Chancellorsville he had "resolved to lead a new life." His loved ones could, the *Daily South Carolinian* assured them, safely "mourn not as those who have no hope" and could be certain "that their loss is his eternal gain."[34]

Funeral sermons and biographies of the deceased, ranging in size from a pamphlet of a few pages to full-sized octavoes, appeared in print both North and South, further elaborating the narratives of the Good Death. Usually financed by grieving kin, the writings were designed to serve as memorials to the dead and as exhortations to the living. Almost without exception, they drew explicitly on details within condolence letters to fashion a more formalized and self-conscious story of a life and its meaning. In his funeral sermon for John W. Griffin, a young Confederate chaplain who died in 1864, L. H. Blanton referred to descriptions of the deceased's last words and judged that Griffin's "dying testimony was all that Christian friends or the Church of God could desire." Printed sermons or memorials often included the full text of the battlefront letter within an appendix. But the particular circumstances of death served as the foundation for broader consideration of an entire life. Here the presentation of a life turned to the narrative of death as a kind of touchstone, a basis for assessing the meaning and value of the larger whole. More polished than condolence letters written from the front, these published genres were intended for distribution to a wider audience than simply next of kin. But they nevertheless reveal a persisting concern with the Good Death, with the transcendent symbolic and substantive importance of life's last moments. Designed more to extol than to console, these writings endeavored to capture the essence of a life in a form that would ensure it would be remembered, to place the life within a cultural narrative of holy living and holy dying that would make it intelligible and thus both meaningful and memorable. The funeral sermon and the published biography were memorials, not in granite, but in words, memorials that sought, like the Good Death itself, to ensure that dying was not an end but a foundation for immortality—of eternal life, of lasting memory.[35] . . .

The construction of the Good Death became a persisting imperative in the aftermath of Civil War slaughter, for it had not been fully accomplished even at war's end. It seems useful to suggest that we attend to the way the *Ars Moriendi* continued to exert power after the war—and served as a determining force in efforts to identify and rebury missing soldiers, to memorialize Union and Confederate dead. For example, when William Cox delivered an address on the "Life and Character" of Stephen Ramseur to the Ladies Memorial Association of Raleigh, North Carolina, in May 1891, nearly thirty years after the Confederate general's death at Cedar Creek, the orator included with "no apology" the text of the 1864 condolence letter sent by Major R. R. Hutchinson to announce the Confederate officer's death to his wife. The assumptions of the *Ars Moriendi* would retain their hold and ultimately contribute to a sectional reconciliation grounded not so much in the genuine resolution of political differences as in national acknowledgment of the shared experience of death and loss.[36]

NOTES

From Drew Gilpin Faust, "The Civil War Soldier and the Art of Dying," *Journal of Southern History* 67, no. 1 (February 2001): 3–35. Reprinted by permission.

1. [Stephen Eliott], *Obsequies of the Rev. Edward E. Ford. D.D., and Sermon by the Bishop of the Diocese.* . . . (Augusta, Ga., 1863), 8. For a thoughtful consideration of the art of dying in contemporary culture see Anne Hunsaker Hawkins, "Constructing Death Myths about Dying," in *Reconstructing Illness: Studies in Pathography* (West Lafayette, Ind., 1993). 91–124. I would like to thank Charles Rosenberg, Barbara Savage, Steven Stowe, David Nord, Reid Mitchell, and Tony Horwitz for comments on this essay. I am also grateful for the helpful responses of groups to whom earlier versions of this paper were presented: Peter Stallybrass's Seminar on the History of Material Texts, the Philadelphia Old Baldy Civil War Roundtable, and audiences at Penn State, the University of Texas, and the Missouri Historical Society.

2. *Daily South Carolinian*, February 26, 1864; see also June 22, 1864. James David Hacker, The Human Cost of War: White Population in the United States, 1850–1880" (Ph.D. diss., University of Minnesota, 1999), 1, 14. Hacker believes that Civil War death totals may be significantly understated because of inadequate estimates of the number of Confederate deaths from disease. Almost twice as many Civil War soldiers died from disease as from battlefield wounds. See also Maris A. Vinovskis, "Have Social Historians Lost the Civil War?" in Vinovskis, ed., *Toward a Social History of the American Civil War: Exploratory Essays* (Cambridge, Eng., and other cities, 1990), 3–7; Drew Gilpin Faust, *"A Riddle of Death"*: Mortality and Meaning in the American Civil War (Gettysburg, Pa., 1995); and Faust, "Christian Soldiers: The Meaning of Revivalism in the Confederate Army," *Journal of Southern History*, LIII (February 1987), 63–90. On the melodramatic rendering of the meaning of the war and death's centrality to this understanding, see Alice Fahs, *The Imagined Civil War: Popular Literature of the North and South, 1861–1865* (Chapel Hill and London, 2001), 93–119, 300.

3. H[enry] Clay Trumbull, *War Memories of an Army Chaplain* (New York, 1898), 67; Earl J. Hess, *The Union Soldier in Battle: Enduring the Ordeal of Combat* (Lawrence, Kans., 1997), 38.

4. Emily Dickinson quoted in Shirn Wolosky, *Emily Dickinson: A Voice of War* (New Haven and London, 1984), 36. In his influential 1980 study, *Inventing the American Way of Death*, James J. Farrell almost managed not to mention the war at all in its overview of the changing place of death in nineteenth-century society; see Farrell, *Inventing the American Way of Death, 1830–1920* (Philadelphia, 1980). See also Karen Halttunen, *Confidence Men and Painted Women: A Study of Middle Class Culture in America, 1830–1870* (New Haven and London, 1982), whose chapter on "Mourning the Dead" (Chap. 5) does not refer to the Civil War; Faust, *"A Riddle of Death"*: Gerald F. Linderman, *Embattled Courage: The Experience of Combat in the American Civil War* (New York, 1987); Phillip Shaw Paludan, *"A People's Contest"*: The Union and Civil War, 1861–1865 (New York, 1988); Gary Laderman, *The Sacred Remains:*

American Attitudes Toward Death, 1799–1883 (New Haven and London, 1996), 124; Hess, *The Union Soldier in Battle*; and Reid Mitchell, *The Vacant Chair: The Northern Soldier Leaves Home* (New York, 1993), 135–50. Probably the most influential contemporary example of such an elegiac rendering of the Civil War is Ken Burns's popular television series (*The Civil War*, Ken Burns, prod. [PBS Video, 1990]).

   5. Jeremy Taylor, *The Rule and Exercises of Holy Dying* (London, 1651). Jeremy Taylor, *The Rule and Exercises of Holy Living* (London, 1650); Mary Catherine O'Connor, *The Art of Dying Well: The Development of the Ars Mariendi* (New York, 1942), 7 (First quotation), 208 (second quotation, from Samuel Coleridge). See also L. M. Beier, "The Good Death in Seventeenth Century England," in Ralph Houlbrooke, ed., *Death, Ritual, and Bereavement* (New York, 1989); Ralph Houlbrooke, *Death, Religion, and the Family in England, 1480–1750* (Oxford, 1998); Houlbrooke, "The Puritan Death-bed, c. 1560-c. 1600," in Christopher Durston and Jacqueline Eales, eds., *The Culture of English Puritanism, 1560–1700* (New York, 1996) 122–44; M. Claire Cross, "*The Third Earl of Huntingdon's Death-Bed*: A Calvinist Example of the *Ars Moriendi*," *Northern History*, XXI (1985), 80–107; Richard Wunderli and Gerald Bose. "The Final Moment Before Death in Early Modern England," *Sixteenth Century Journal*, XX (Summer 1989), 259–75: David Cressy, *Birth, Marriage, and Death: Ritual, Religion, and the Life-Cycle in Tudor and Stuart England* (New York and Oxford, 1997).

   6. Frances M. M. Comper, ed., *The Book of the Craft of Dying and Other Early English Tracts Concerning Death* (London and other cities, 1917); Nancy Lee Beaty, *The Craft of Dying: A Study in the Literary Tradition of the Ars Moriendi in England* (New Haven and London, 1970); Taylor, *Rule and Exercises of Holy Dying*. At least eight editions of *Holy Dying* appeared in London in the first half of the nineteenth century; editions were printed in Boston in 1864 and 1865; in Philadelphia in 1835, 1859, and 1869; and New York in 1864. On conception of *Ars Moriendi* included in advice and conduct books, see Margaret Spufford, *Small Books and Pleasant Histories: Popular Fiction and Its Readership in Seventeenth-Century England* (Athens, Ga., 1981), 200–208. For an example of a sermon see Eleazer Mather Porter Wells, *Preparation for Death . . . Trinity Church, Boston* (1852, n.p.). On popular health see the many American editions of John Willison, *The Afflicted Man's Companion* (Pittsburgh, 1830), which was reprinted again by the American Tract Society of New York in 1851. So popular was Dickens's serialized *The Old Curiosity Shop* that New Yorkers lined the quay for the arrival of the installment that would reveal Little Nell's fate. Harriet Beecher Stowe's *Uncle Tom's Cabin* was among the best-selling American books of the nineteenth century. Charles Dickens, *The Old Curiosity Shop* (London, 1841); William Makepeace Thackeray, *The New-*

comes: *Memoirs of a Most Respectable Family* (London, 1854–55); Harriet Beecher Stowe, *Uncle Tom's Cabin, or Life Among the Lowly* (Boston, 1852). On Stowe see Mary Kelley, *Private Woman, Public Stage: Literary Domesticity in Nineteenth-Century America* (New York and Oxford, 1984), 14, 26; on Dickens, see James D. Hart, *The Popular Book: A History of America's Literary Taste* (New York, 1950), 102. Cf. the rendition of death in Samuel Richardson's *Clarissa, or, the History of a Young Lady* (London, 1748).

7. Bertram W. Korn, *American Jewry and the Civil War* (Philadelphia, 1951), 59; D[avid] de Sola Pool, "The Diary of Chaplain Michael M. Allen, September 1861." *Publications of the American Jewish Historical Society*, XXXIX (September, 1949), 177–82.

8. *Once to Die*, Presbyterian Committee of Publication, No. 45 (Richmond, Va., n.d. [1861–1865]; microfilm, *Confederate Imprints* [New Haven, 1974], reel 135), 3. See also Karl S. Guthke, *Last Words: Variations on a Theme in Cultural History* (Princeton, 1992), 36.

9. [Francis W. Palfrey], *In Memoriam: H[enry]. L. A[bbott].* (Boston, 1864; microfiche, *Selected Americana from Sabin's* Dictionary . . . [Woodbridge, Conn., 1998]). 5. Vital statistics for this period are very scarce, and the most complete cover only Massachusetts. My thanks to historical demographer Gretchen Condran of Temple University for discussing these matters with me. See U.S. Bureau of the Census, *Historical Statistics of the United States, Part I* (Washington, 1975), 62–63. On the "untimely death of an adult child" as "particularly painful" in mid-nineteenth-century England, see Patricia Jalland, *Death in the Victorian Family* (Oxford and New York, 1996), 39. On the expectation that one would die at home, see Robert V. Wells, *Facing the "King of Terrors": Death and Society in an American Community, 1750–1990* (Cambridge, Eng., and other cities, 2000), 195.

10. Minutes, March 31, 1865, Confederate States Christian Association for the Relief of Prisoners (Fort Delaware), Francis Atherton Boyle Books, Southern Historical Collection (University of North Carolina at Chapel Hill) (first quotation); James Gray to Sister, June 12, 1864, in Mills Lane, ed., *Dear Mother: Don't Grieve About Me. If I Get Killed, I'll Only Be Dead: Letters from Georgia Soldiers in the Civil War* (Savannah, Ga., 1990), 300 (second quotation); and unsigned letter to Mattie J. McGaw, May 5, 1863, McGaw Family Papers, South Caroliniana Library, University of South Carolina, Columbia (third quotation). See also William Stilwell to wife [Molly], September 18, 1862, in Lane, ed., *Dear Mother*, 185.

11. Frederick Law Olmsted, comp., *Hospital Transports: A Memoir of the Embarkation of the Sick and Wounded from the Peninsula of Virginia in the Summer of 1862* (Boston, 1863), 80. Disruptions of African American family ties through the slave trade to the southwestern states was, of course, another

matter—both in its coerciveness and its permanence; see Michael Tadman, *Speculators and Slaves: Masters, Traders, and Slaves in the Old South* (Madison, Wis., 1989).

12. Jalland, *Death in the Victorian Family*, 2. The English queen's own lengthy bereavement after Albert's death in 1861 focused additional attention on death as a defining element in Anglo-American family and cultural life.

13. *The Dying Officer* (Richmond, Va., n.d. [1860s]; microfilm, *Confederate Imprints*, reel 134), 6; Hiram Mattison quoted in Michael Sappol, *"A Traffic in Dead Bodies": Anatomical Dissection and Embodied Social Identity in Nineteenth-Century America* (Princeton, forthcoming), Chap. 2, p. 28 (citation is to manuscript page). I am grateful to Professor Sappol for letting me see his unpublished manuscript. On dying declarations see Guthke, *Last Words*, 27–28; on the evidentiary status of last words see John Henry Wigmore, *Evidence in Trials at Common Law* (Boston, 1904; rev. ed., 1974), Vol. V, 289 ("The utterances of the dying person are to be taken as free from all ordinary motives to misstate."). See also John William Strong, ed., *McCormick on Evidence* (4th ed., St. Paul, Minn., 1992), 523–27. My thanks to Albert J. Beveridge III, Sarah Gordon, and Kim Schepple for their advice on legal history. There is evidence of dying declarations granted hearsay exception from at least the early eighteenth century, always in cases of murder victims naming their killers; see Wigmore, *Evidence at Trials*, Vol. V, Chap. 49. See also the statement on the meaning of last words in Susie C. Appell to Mrs. E. H. Ogden, October 20, 1862, Ogden Papers, Gilder-Lehrman Collection, Morgan Library, New York City, as well as the discussion of the significance of last words in *Frank Leslie's Illustrated Weekly*, December 7, 1861, p. 44.

14. See Gregory A. Coco, *Killed in Action: Eyewitness accounts of the Last Moments of 100 Union Soldiers Who Died at Gettysburg* (Gettysburg, Pa., 1992); Coco, *Wasted Valor: The Confederate Dead at Gettysburg* (Gettysburg, Pa., 1990); Warren B. Armstrong, *For Courageous Fighting and Confident Dying: Union Chaplains in the Civil War* (Lawrence, Kans., 1998).

15. "Reminiscence of Gettysburg," *Frank Leslie's Illustrated Newspaper*, January 2, 1864, p. 235; on photographs see Steven R. Stotelmyer, *The Bivouacs of the Dead: The Story of Those Who Died at Antietam and South Mountain* (Baltimore, 1992), 6; *Godey's Ladies Book*, March 1864, p. 311; Clara Barton, Lecture Notes [1866], Clara Barton Papers, Library of Congress.

16. On condolence letters see Michael Barlon, "Painful Duties: Art, Character, and Culture in Confederate Letters of Condolence," *Southern Quarterly*, XVII (Winter 1979), 123–34; and Barton, *Goodmen: The Character of Civil War Soldiers* (University Park, Pa., and London, 1981), 57–62. See also William Merrill Decker, *Epistolary Practices: Letter Writing in America before Telecommunications* (Chapel Hill and London, 1998); and Janet Gurlin Altman, *Epistolarity: Approaches to a Form* (Columbus, Ohio, 1982). Contemporary guide-

books for letter writers include *The American Letter-Writer and Mirror of Polite Behavior* . . . (Philadelphia, 1851); and *A New Letter-Writer, for the Use of Gentlemen* (Philadelphia, 1860). For an acknowledgement of the ritual of the condolence letter in Civil War popular culture, see the song by E. Bowers. *Write a Letter to My Mother!*, broadside (Philadelphia, n.d. [1860s]).

17. William Fields to Mrs. Fitzpatrick, June 8, 1865, Clopton Hospital Papers, Eleanor S. Brockenbrough Library, Museum of the Confederacy (Richmond, Virginia); Clara Barton, Manuscript Journal, 1863, Barton Papers; see also Elizabeth Brown Pryor, *Clara Barton: Professional Angel* (Philadelphia, 1987), 94, 148; "Our Army Hospitals," clipping, Madeira Scrapbook, Vol. A. Library Company of Philadelphia: William Corby, *Memoirs of Chaplain Life* (Notre Dame, Ind., 1894), 93. For an example of a nurse cueing a soldier to leave a message for his wife, see William H. Davidson, ed., *War Was the Place: A Centennial Collection of Confederate Soldier Letters*, Chattahoochic Valley Historical Society Bulletin No. 5 (November 1961), 117. On the important role of hospital personnel in good death, see Laderman, *Sacred Remains*, 131; and the Linderman, *Embattled Courage*, 29. See also Jestin Hampton to Thomas B. Hampton, January 25, 1863, Thomas B. Hampton Papers; and S. G. Sneed to Susan Piper, September 17, 1864. Benjamin Piper Papers, both in the Center for American History, University of Texas, Austin.

18. Richard Rollins, ed., *Pickett's Charge: Eyewitness Accounts* (Redondo Beach, Calif., 1994), 96; James R. Montgomery to A. R. Montgomery, May 18, 1864, File M-634E, Brockenbrough Library.

19. Contrast this "check list" with the "stock messages" Jay Winter describes from British officers in World War I informing relatives of a soldier's death: "[He] was loved by his comrades; he was a good soldier; and he died painlessly." This is a remarkably secular formula in comparison to the Civil War's embrace of the *Ars Moriendi* tradition. Jay Winter, *Sites of Memory, Sites of Mourning: The Great War in European Cultural History* (Cambridge, Eng., and New York, 1995), 35. For a Civil War condolence letter written almost in the form of a checklist—indentations and all—see John G. Barrett and Robert K. Turner, Jr., eds., *Letters of a New Market Cadet: Beverly Stannard* (Chapel Hill, 1961), 67–68. For a Catholic example see Thomas McEvoy, ed., "The War Letters of Father Peter Paul Cooney of the Congregation of the Holy Cross," in *Records of the American Catholic Historical Society*, LXIV (1933), 153–54. Much of the "checklist" had its origins in deathbed observers' search for reassurance that a dying person was successfully resisting the Devil's characteristic temptations: to abandon his faith, to submit to desperation or impatience, to demonstrate spiritual pride or complacence, to show too much preoccupation with temporal matters; see Comper, *Book of the Craft of Dying*, 9–21. For a brief discussion of consolation letters see Mitchell, *Vacant Chair*, 83–86.

20. Edwin S. Redkey, ed., *A Grand Army of Black Men: Letters from African*

American Soldiers in the Union Army, 1861–1865 (Cambridge, Eng., and New York, 1992), 67. Preparation comprised a significant dimension of the Good Death for Jewish soldiers as well; for example, note the emphasis that Albert Moses Luria's family placed on preparedness in his epitaph: "He went into the field prepared to meet his God." Raphael Jacob Moses, *Last Order of the Last Cause: The True Memoirs of a Jewish Family from the "Old South,"* compiled and edited by Mel Young (Lanham, Md., and London, 1995), 147. On sudden death see also W. D. Rutherford to Sallie F. Rutherford, June 23, 1864, William Drayton Rutherford Papers, South Caroliniana Library; and Houlbrooke, *Death, Religion, and the Family*, 208.

21. William J. Bacon, *Memorial of William Kirkland Bacon, Late Adjutant of the Twenty-Sixth Regiment of New York State Volunteers* (Utica, N.Y., 1863), 57; W. D. Rutherford to Sallie Fair. July 26, 1861. Rutherford Papers. On premonitions of death see also Corby, *Memoirs*, 238–39; Alonzo Abernethy, "Incidents of an Iowa Soldier's Life, or Four Years in Dixie," *Annals of Iowa*, 3d ser., XII (October 1920), 408–9. For a Jewish example see the report on the death of Gustave Poznanski in "The Fight at Secessionville," Charleston *Daily Courier*, June 18, 1862, p. 1; Mel Young, *Where They Lie: The Story of the Jewish Soldiers . . .* (Lanham, Md., New York, and London, 1991), 39–40. On presentiment and on soldiers' deaths more generally, see James M. McPherson, *For Cause and Comrades: Why Men Fought in the Civil War* (New York and Oxford, 1997), 63–71. See also E. S. Nash to Hattie Jones, August 19, 1861, Herbert S. Hadley Papers, Missouri Historical Society, St. Louis; and Wells, *Facing the "King of Terrors,"* 162–63.

22. J. C. Curtwright to Mr. and Mrs. L. B. Lovelace, April 24, 1862, in Lane, ed., *Dear Mother* 116; T. Fitzhugh to Mrs. Diggs, June 23, 1863. File D-291A; and Sallie Winfree to Mrs. Bobo, October 9, 1862, Henry Bobo Papers, both in the Brockenbrough Library.

23. T. J. Hodnett, quoted in Davidson, ed., *War Was the Place*, 80, 77; Elijah Richardson Craven, *In Memoriam, Sermon and Oration . . . on the Occasion of the Death of Col. I. M. Tucker . . .* (Newark, N.J., 1862), 5–6; Walter W. Pharr, *Funeral Sermon on the Death of Capt. A. K. Simonton of Statesville, N.C.* (Salisbury, N.C., 1862), 11.

24. J[ames]. B. Rogers, *War Pictures: Experiences and Observations of a Chaplain in the U.S. Army, in the War of the Southern Rebellion* (Chicago, 1863), 182; J. Monroe Anderson to the Sisters of Gen. Gregg, January 9, 1863, Maxcy Gregg Papers, South Caroliniana Library; Guy R. Everson and Edward W. Simpson, Jr., eds., *"Far, Far From Home": The Wartime Letters of Dick and Talley Simpson, Third South Carolina Volunteers* (New York and Oxford, 1994), 287; John Weissart to Dearest Wife and Children, October 17, 1862, Bentley Historical Library, University of Michigan, Ann Arbor. My thanks to Elana Harris for this citation. For a Catholic example of reading the body for

signs of the state of the soul, see Sister Catherine to Father Patrick Reilly, December 5, 1862, Patrick Reilly Papers, Archives of the Archdiocese of Philadelphia, which described the death of Sister Bonaventure "with sweet peace and joy" and reported that "the peace and calm of her soul was evident on her countenance."

25. L. S. Bobo to Dear Uncle, July 7, 1862, August 14, 1862, Bobo Papers; James T. Moore to [Leusa F.] Cadenhead, July 23, 1864, in "Some Confederate Letters of I. B. Cadenhead," *Alabama Historical Quarterly*, XVII (Winter 1956), 568; E. and E. Nash to Respected Nephews in Camp, November 11, 1862, Alpheus S. Bloomfield Papers, Library of Congress.

26. Sanford Branch to his mother, July 26, 1861, in Lane, ed., *Dear Mother*, 36 (first quotation); Coco, *Killed in Action*, 91; Alonzo Hill, *In Memoriam. A Discourse . . . on Lieut. Thomas Jefferson Spurr* (Boston, 1862) (second quotation); Davidson, ed., *War Was the Place*, 119 (third quotation). Chaplain Corby observed that nearly all men called to their mothers as they lay dying (Corby, *Memoirs*, 95), and this was enshrined in Civil War popular songs; see, for example, Thomas MacKellar, *The Dying Soldier to His Mother*, broadside (New York, n.d. [1860s]), and C. A. Vosburgh, *Tell Mother, I Die Happy*, broadside. (New York, 1863). For an example of a song popular in the South see Charles Carroll Sawyer, *Mother Would Comfort Me!*, broadside (Augusta, Ga., n.d. [1860s]). There were so many songs written as messages to mother from the battlefield that they began to generate parodies and satirical responses. See John C. Cross, *Mother on the Brain*, broadside (New York, n.d. [1860s]); and Cross, *Mother Would Wallop Me*, broadside (New York, n.d. [1860s]).

27. William W. Bennett, *A Narrative of the Great Revival Which Prevailed in the Southern Armies During the Late Civil War Between the States of the Federal Union* (Philadelphia, 1877), 243–44; T. Fitzhugh to Mrs. Diggs, June 23, 1863. For a letter in almost identical language see E. W. Rowe to J. W. Goss, December 16, 1863, Capt. William W. Goss File, Nineteenth Virginia Infantry, CSA Collection, Brockenbrough Library.

28. Mark DeWolfe Howe, ed., *Touched With Fire: Civil War Letters and Diary of Oliver Wendell Holmes, Jr., 1861–1864* (1947; repr., New York, 1969), 27; A. D. Kirwan, ed., *Johnny Green of the Orphan Brigade: The Journal of a Confederate Soldier* (Lexington, Ky., 1956), 37; David Cornwell, quoted in Hess, *The Union Soldier in Battle*, 143.

29. *Army and Navy Messenger*, April 1, 1864, quoted in Kurt O. Berends, " 'Wholesome Reading Purifies and Elevates the Man': The Religious Military Press in the Confederacy," in Randall M. Miller, Harry S. Stout, and Charles Reagan Wilson, eds., *Religion and the American Civil War* (New York and Oxford, 1998), 132–33, 154 (quotation on p. 154). See also Fales Henry Newhall, *National Exaltation: The Duties of Christian Patriotism . . .* (Boston, 1861); William Adams, *Christian Patriotism* (New York, 1863); Joseph Fransi-

oli, *Patriotism: A Christian Virtue. A Sermon Preached . . . at St. Peter's Church, Brooklyn, July 26th, 1863* (New York, 1863). Also note Sister Matilda Coskey's disapproval of a father who refuses to permit his wounded son to be baptized, arguing "he has served his country, fought her battles & that is enough—he has nothing to fear for his soul." Sister Matilda Coskey to Father Patrick Reilly, October 18, 1864, Reilly Papers.

30. William Preston Johnston to Wade Hampton, November 3, 1864; James Connor to Wade Hampton, November 6, 1864, Wade Hampton Papers; and N. A. Foster to William K. Rash, Fifty-second North Carolina Papers, both in the Brockenbrough Library. For another discussion of gallantry see Eleanor Damon Pace, ed., "The Diary and Letters of William P. Rogers, 1846–1862," *Southwestern Historical Quarterly*, XXXII (April 1929), 298–99.

31. Burns Newman to Mr. Shortell, May 24, 1864, Michael Shortell Letters, State Historical Society of Wisconsin, Madison; Henry I. Bowditch, *Memorial Volume for Nathaniel Bowditch*, 1036, Nathaniel Bowditch Memorial Collection, Massachusetts Historical Society; Louis P. Towles, ed., *A World Turned Upside Down: The Palmers of South Santee, 1818–1881* (Columbia, S.C., 1996), 650, 761, 871. See also Disposition of Personal Effects of Dead Wisconsin Soldiers, 1863, Governor's Papers, State Historical Society of Wisconsin.

32. James Vance to Mr. and Mrs. Patton, June 6, 1864, Wesley W. Patton Papers, State Historical Society of Wisconsin. See the extraordinary description of the condition of the corpse in M. D. Locke's letter of August 14, 1861, informing Dr. James D. Rumph of the death of his son Langdon, in Henry Eugene Sterkx and Brooks Thompson, eds., "Letters of a Teenage Confederate," *Florida Historical Quarterly*, XXXVIII (April 1960), 344–45.

33. W. N. Pendleton to William Garnett, July 9, 1863, File G-392, Brockenbrough Library.

34. *Daily South Carolinian*, May 29, 1864. For other examples see the obituaries of William James Dixon, May 29, 1864; W. W. Watts, August 23, 1864; H. L. Garlington, August 13, 1864; Milton Cox, August 9, 1862; Joseph Friedenberg, September 15, 1862, all in the *Daily South Carolinian*; George Nichols in the Richmond *Daily Whig*, December 24, 1862; Walter Matthews in the Richmond *Daily Dispatch*, December 25, 1862; the account of Isaac Valentine's death in "The Fight at Secessionville," Charleston *Daily Courier*, June 18, 1862; and the obituary for Thomas B. Hampton, unidentified newspaper clipping, n.d. [March 1865], in the Hampton Papers, Center for American History.

35. L. H. Blanton, "*Well Done thou good and faithful servant," Funeral Sermon on the death of Rev. John W. Griffin, chaplain of the 19th Va. Regt.* (Lynchburg, Va., 1865), 8. On funeral sermons see Larissa Juliet Taylor, "Funeral Sermons and Orations as Religious Propaganda in Sixteenth-Century France," in Bruce Gordon and Peter Marshall, eds., *The Place of the Dead: Death and Remembrance in Late Medieval and Early Modern Europe* (Cam-

bridge, Eng., and New York, 2000), 224–39; and Houlbrooke, *Death, Religion, and the Family.* Chap. 10.

36. William R. Cox, *Address on the Life and Character of Maj. Gen. Stephen D. Ramseur Before the Ladies' Memorial Association of Raleigh, N.C., May 10th, 1891* (Raleigh, 1891), 45–47, 50–51 (quotation on p. 50). Thanks to Gary Gallagher for bringing this to my attention.

Index

Arms, 98–100, 105 n, 199; ammunition, 156; bayonet, 203, 391, 403, 412; firepower, 202; musketry, 207–12, 267
Artillery, 18, 159, 389, 409–11
Atrocities, 239–43, 406–8; barbarism, 191–98; brutes, 25, 149; cruelty, 191, 406; plunder, 221–22; savagery, 359, 367

Barton, Michael, 1, 425
Battle, nature of, 155–75, 199–227, 267, 404
Battlefield: chaos, 261–62, 266, 406; command and control, 270; fortifications, 273–77; horror, 234, 405, 414, 475; scene, 161, 411–13; terrain, 262–63, 268, 278 n; vegetation, 262–63, 272, 278n
Black(s): soldiers, 14–15, 143–54, 228–59; body servant, 13–14; laborers, 14
Bravery. See Courage

Camp life, 72, 85–91, 92–107, 122–40, 297, 367; bugle calls, 126–27; bull sessions, 129; drill, 71–72, 147, 224; fistfights, 128; food, 101–2, 155, 402; games, 128; humor, 130–31; letter-writing, 123; music, 89, 124–26; quarters, 101, 106 n; reading habits, 124, 458; sports, 127; tobacco, 133–34; training, 269
Cavalry, 18–19, 22, 31n
Chaplains, 330, 332, 334, 491
Civilians, 361–63, 374, 377, 379; disloyalty, 378
Colors, 157, 236, 166–67, 444. See also Flag
Combat, 199–227, 230, 260–80, 318, 323, 368–70, 386–95, 396–422; accelerating attack, 219–24; charge, 159–60, 205, 219–24, 234; continuous campaigning, 272–74; firefights, 199–227; formations,199–227, 261; friendly fire, 263; frontal assaults, 234–35, 271, 405; hand-to-hand, 264–65; infantry tactics, 199–227; night fighting, 265; pickets, 158; range of fire, 207–12, 225 n, 233, 267–68, 279 n, 405; rate of fire, 269; rebel yell, 158–59, 165, 172 n, 233; "shock action," 203–7; skirmishing, 158, 480–81; surrender, 242; trench fighting, 164, 217, 276; varieties of attack, 212–19; will to combat, 472
Combat stress, 247–48, 260–80, 338–39, 341, 351 n, 372, 391, 396–422; baptism of fire, 388; fear, 402; gore, 161–62, 239; post-traumatic stress disorder, 396; terror, 402
Conscription, 22–23, 57–68, 289, 307 n, 375–76; conscientious objectors, 61; deferments, 67 n; draft evasion and resistance, 62–65, 285, 293; substitutes, 60, 286–87, 307n
Content analysis, 3, 312, 386, 425, 434
Courage, 144–46, 155–75, 195, 304, 369, 387, 391, 436–55, 472–74, 477, 482, 498; self-control, 387, 473–74, 482. See also Cowardice; Heroism
Cowardice, 155–75, 237–38, 301, 377, 439, 449–51; panic, 168–70. See also Courage

Dean, Eric T., Jr., 396
Death, 76, 103, 244; Ars Moriendi (art of dying), 485–511; burial, 161, 359; condolences, 485, 492, 494, 497, 499–502, 506 n, 507 n; corpses, 76, 161, 360, 370, 413; deathbed, 490

Dehumanization, 356, 364, 368, 480
Desertion, 94, 258, 294, 301, 306, 310 n, 337, 436, 467; absent without leave, 299–301; execution, 414, 499–500
Discipline, 95, 102, 153, 177–78, 182, 332, 334, 337, 347 n, 355, 375; disrespect for authority, 179; punishments, 336
Disease, 39, 103, 154, 357–58, 400–401, 415 n. *See also* Medical Care
Donald, David, 176, 354
Draft. *See* Conscription

Emotions, 147, 220, 283–311, 340, 354–85, 386–95, 396–422; depression, 288; sentimentality, 125, 464, 477
Esprit de corps. *See* morale

Family, 363, 371, 374, 376, 430, 460. *See also* Home
Faust, Drew Gilpin, 327, 485
Female soldiers, 69–82; cross-gender "passing," 70; imposture (women posing as men), 69–78
Flag, 166. *See also* Colors
Frank, Joseph Allan, 386
Furloughs, 295–96, 299, 361–62

Geary, James W., 57
Glatthaar, Joseph T., 228
Griffith, Paddy, 199

Heroism, 155–75, 231, 367. *See also* Courage
Hess, Earl J., 260, 472
Higginson, Thomas Wentworth, 143, 228
Historiography, 2–4, 4 n, 343 n, 470 n; moonlight-and-magnolia school, 19
Home, 364, 430, 461, 490. *See also* Family

Ideology, 314, 316–17, 323, 427, 435, 456, 459–60, 474–76, 482, 483 n. *See also* Values
Infantry, 22, 199

Jamieson, Perry D., 190

Keegan, John, 260
Killed, 38–39, 493; killing, 371, 373, 478–79, 481; dying, 485–511

Leonard, Elizabeth D., 69
Linderman, Gerald F., 436, 456
Logue, Larry M., 1, 44

March, 85–91, 157, 397–98
Maslowski, Pete, 312
McCarthy, Carlton, 85
McPherson, James M., 4, 456
McWhiney, Grady, 190
Medical care, 245–47, 358, 400; hospitals, 75. *See also* Disease
Methodology, 3, 46–47, 55 n, 66 n, 313, 425; Multiple Classification Analysis (MCA), 42 n; sampling, 36, 46, 54 n, 465–67
Military administration and organization, 93–94, 295, 322; and Confederate social structure, 184–85; election of officers, 180–82; pay, 293–94, 401; promotions, 322
Mitchell, Reid, 354
Morale, 27, 170, 283–311, 312–26, 338, 389; disillusionment, 210; pessimism, 290
Morality: braggarts, 24–25; chastity, 151; drunkenness, 102, 134–36, 367; gambling, 132–33; laziness, 364; loafers, 27; pranksters, 26; profanity, 131–32, 149–50, 336, 349 n; shirkers, 306, 388–89; slackers, 298, 367; stragglers, 90
Motivations. *See* Values

Patriotism, 27–28, 284, 292, 297, 302–4, 367, 374, 377, 426, 435, 436, 467, 476, 482, 498; nationalism, 392, 460, 462–63, 465, 474, 476
"Poor man's" fight, 33, 36, 287, 467. *See also* Social class
Prejudices, 20–24, 234, 251

Racism, 46, 48, 51–52, 228, 406–7
Reaves, George A., 386
Recruitment, 57–68; enlistment rates, 47; re-enlistment, 291, 296; soldier enlistments in Mississippi, 44–56
Religion, 150, 327–53, 371, 438–39, 445, 472, 476–79, 482, 485–511; conversions, 327–28, 333, 338, 340; evangelicalism, 327, 335, 342, 489; revivalism, 327–53

Robertson, James I., Jr., 122
Romanticism, 103, 368, 465, 472

Shannon, Fred A., 92
Shiloh, 386–95
Slavery, effects of, 146, 152–53, 229, 239, 315, 355–56
Social class, 20, 38, 43 n, 182–85, 285, 302, 333, 335, 341, 355, 357, 442, 466, 488; snobs, 25; southern aristocracy, 29 n, 182–84, 188n
Soldiers: ages, 15–16, 36, 48, 60, 188 n; appearance, 26–27; "average Rebel," 28; black, 14–15, 143–54, 228–59; black, and white officers, 228–52; boy, 16–18, 73; Celtic heritage, 192–98; common, in Union Army, 92–107; comparison of black and white, 248–52; comparison of Union and Confederate, 61, 176–77, 191–94, 248–50, 312–26, 329, 380, 425–35; comradeship, 391; Confederate traits, 9–28, 171, 176–89, 190–98; demographics, 9–32, 33–43, 40 n, 44–56; education, 18–20, 37, 43 n, 430–32; enlisted-officer relations, 180–82; fighting qualities, 155–75, 176–89, 190–98; foreign-born, 10–11, 36, 42 n, 60, 197 n; guerrillas, 241; identity, 333, 342, 354, 365, 368; illiterate, 19; Indian, 11–13; Mississippi, 44–56; of Newburyport, Massachusetts, 34–43, 46; number of, 53 n; occupations of, 15, 30 n, 48, 58–60, 66 n; planters, 49;

prisoners of war, 243; student, 17–18; Union traits, 92–107, 191–92
Stouffer, Samuel A., 312–14, 317–19, 321–23
Suffering, 87; drudgery, 103; fatigue, 160, 390; hunger, 161; mud, 399; thirst, 160; trauma, 396, 402, 413

Uniforms, 72–73, 95–97, 108–21; shoes, 88, 97, 117–19, 397

Values, 192, 333, 342, 357, 391, 425–35, 436–37, 456–71, 473–74; chivalric ideal, 443; duty, 440; honor, 440–43, 472, 482; motivations, 44, 53, 57, 66 n, 148, 436; Victorian ethos, 387, 490
Vietnam War, comparisons, 61, 343, 396–421, 457; post-traumatic stress disorder, 396
Vinovskis, Maris A., 33

Wiley, Bell Irvin, 2–4, 9, 71, 92, 108, 122, 155, 176, 193, 283, 313, 317, 322–23, 460
Williams, Robin, 425–26, 435
World War I, comparisons, 261, 408, 410–11
World War II, comparisons, 176–89, 313–14, 316, 319, 321–23, 341, 390, 456–57, 486
Wounded, 38–39, 245–47, 298, 388, 404, 495; disabled, 38. *See also* Medical Care